OTTOMAN TRANSLATIONS

Edinburgh Studies on the Ottoman Empire
Series Editor: Kent F. Schull

Published and forthcoming titles

Migrating Texts: Circulating Translations around the Ottoman Mediterranean
Edited by Marilyn Booth

Ottoman Translations: Circulating Texts from Bombay to Paris
Edited by Marilyn Booth and Claire Savina

Death and Life in the Ottoman Palace: Revelations of the Sultan Abdülhamid I Tomb
Douglas Scott Brookes

Ottoman Sunnism: New Perspectives
Edited by Vefa Erginbaş

Jews and Palestinians in the Late Ottoman Era, 1908–1914: Claiming the Homeland
Louis A. Fishman

Spiritual Vernacular of the Early Ottoman Frontier: The Yazıcıoğlu Family
Carlos Grenier

Armenians in the Late Ottoman Empire: Migration, Mobility Control and Sovereignty, 1885–1915
David Gutman

The Kizilbash-Alevis in Ottoman Anatolia: Sufism, Politics and Community
Ayfer Karakaya-Stump

Çemberlitaş Hamamı in Istanbul: The Biographical Memoir of a Turkish Bath
Nina Macaraig

The Kurdish Nobility in the Ottoman Empire: Loyalty, Autonomy and Privilege
Nilay Özok-Gündoğan

Nineteenth-Century Local Governance in Ottoman Bulgaria: Politics in Provincial Councils
Safa Saraçoğlu

Prisons in the Late Ottoman Empire: Microcosms of Modernity
Kent F. Schull

Ruler Visibility and Popular Belonging in the Ottoman Empire
Darin Stephanov

The North Caucasus Borderland: Between Muscovy and the Ottoman Empire, 1555–1605
Murat Yasar

Children and Childhood in the Ottoman Empire: From the 15th to the 20th Century
Edited by Gülay Yılmaz and Fruma Zachs

euppublishing.com/series/esoe

OTTOMAN TRANSLATIONS

CIRCULATING TEXTS FROM BOMBAY TO PARIS

Edited by Marilyn Booth and Claire Savina

EDINBURGH
University Press

Edinburgh University Press is one of the leading university presses in the UK. We publish academic books and journals in our selected subject areas across the humanities and social sciences, combining cutting-edge scholarship with high editorial and production values to produce academic works of lasting importance. For more information visit our website: edinburghuniversitypress.com

© editorial matter and organisation Marilyn Booth and Claire Savina, 2023
© the chapters their several authors, 2023

Edinburgh University Press Ltd
The Tun – Holyrood Road
12 (2f) Jackson's Entry
Edinburgh EH8 8PJ

First published in hardback by Edinburgh University Press 2023

Typeset in Jaghbuni by
Cheshire Typesetting Ltd, Cuddington, Cheshire

A CIP record for this book is available from the British Library

ISBN 978 1 3995 0257 3 (hardback)
ISBN 978 1 3995 0258 0 (paperback)
ISBN 978 1 3995 0259 7 (webready PDF)
ISBN 978 1 3995 0260 3 (epub)

The right of Marilyn Booth and Claire Savina to be identified as editors of this work has been asserted in accordance with the Copyright, Designs and Patents Act 1988 and the Copyright and Related Rights Regulations 2003 (SI No. 2498).

Contents

Note on Translation, Transliteration and Form   vii
Acknowledgements   viii
Notes on Contributors   x

Introduction – Ottoman Central: Circulating Translations from the Indian Ocean to the Eastern Mediterranean and on to the Far West of Europe   1
Marilyn Booth

PART I PROLIFERATING CLASSICS

1. A Pilgrim Progressively Translated: John Bunyan in Arabic, Urdu, Hindi and Bengali   29
   Richard David Williams and Jack Clift

2. 'Pour Our Treasures into Foreign Laps': The Translation of *Othello* into Arabic and Ottoman Turkish   69
   Hannah Scott Deuchar and Bridget Gill

3. Shared Secrets: (Re)writing Urban Mysteries in Nineteenth-century Istanbul   99
   Şehnaz Şişmanoğlu Şimşek and Etienne Charrière

PART II MEDITERRANEAN MULTIPLES

4. Khayr al-Din al-Tunisi's *Muqaddima* to *Aqwam al-masalik fi ma'rifat ahwal al-mamalik* (*The Surest Path to Knowing the Condition of Kingdoms*), in Arabic, French and Ottoman Turkish   121

Contents

Part I Khayr al-Din al-Tunisī's *Aqwam al-masalik/Réformes nécessaires*: A Dual Intervention in Arabic and French Political Discourses 121
Peter Hill

Part II The *Muqaddima* of Khayr al-Dīn Pasha's *Aqwam al-masālik fī maʿrifat aḥwāl al-mamālik* and its Ottoman Turkish Translation 140
Johann Strauss

5. Finding the Lost Andalusia: Reading Abdülhak Hamid Tarhan's *Tarık or the Conquest of al-Andalus* in its Multiple Renderings 190
Usman Ahmedani and Dženita Karić

PART III WOMEN IN TRANSLATION

6. Translating Qasim Amin's Arabic *Tahrir al-marʾa* (1899) into Ottoman Turkish 227
Ilham Khuri-Makdisi and Yorgos Dedes

7. *Muslim Woman*: The Translation of a Patriarchal Order in Flux 286
Maha AbdelMegeed and A. Ebru Akcasu

8. Fatma Aliye's *Nisvan-ı İslam*: Istanbul, Beirut, Cairo, Paris, 1891–6 327
Marilyn Booth and A. Holly Shissler

Index 389

Acknowledgements

We are grateful for the enthusiasm, tenacity and dedication of our contributors to this volume, who have worked together, and with the two of us, through a difficult period. The stresses of the pandemic perhaps led all of us to recall with special fondness the series of workshops that we have collectively held, and we want to thank all of the colleagues who have participated in the five workshops that this project has entailed to date, and that have led to our informal constitution of this shifting group as the Ottoman Translation Study Group. Even when we could not meet physically, the camaraderie and mutual support that have characterised this network remained visible and reassuring. Both in person and remotely, this has been the kind of intellectual collegial exchange that scholarship ought to always embrace, and that amidst otherwise stressful schedules and duties, is an ongoing reminder of the joys and rewards of scholarly research. For the first time, in this volume and the two workshops that preceded it, we have researched and written in pairs, and through many conversations – a learning experience for most of us. Everyone has shown cheer and patience, and some lasting intellectual partnerships have been formed.

The two workshops that gave rise to this volume in an immediate sense were held in the beautiful and very different surroundings of St-Erme-Outre-et-Ramecourt, France, and Prague, the Czech Republic. We are grateful to the Performing Arts Forum (PAF) and its astounding home, an ancient convent in St-Erme, for the enchanting garden surroundings and accommodations that allowed a magic week of working together in June 2018. Claire Savina imagined this possibility and then made it happen, and we are all indebted to her vision and work. Amy Pennington provided amazing catering and taught some of us temporary sous-chefs new dishes. We are grateful for having been able to draw on funding from the Higher

Acknowledgements

Studies Fund, University of Oxford, and we thank Stephanie Yoxall for her help with the finances. For making our stay and our work at PAF possible, we want to particularly thank Stéphanie Barbier, Jean-Félix Macéraux and Daniel Lucas. The fifth workshop took place at Charles University, Prague, in July 2019, and we are enormously grateful to the Department of Middle Eastern Studies of the University, and more particularly, to the KREAS (Creativity & Adaptability as Conditions of Success in Europe in an International World) project, for providing generous meeting spaces and for funding our accommodations. This venue and possibility were proposed by our colleague and contributor A. Ebru Akcasu, who then worked tirelessly to make it happen, institutionally and financially. For her work and her patience, we are more grateful than we can say.

We are equally thankful for our generous funders and hosts of the earlier workshops (2015–17) in which the Ottoman Translation Study Group (*avant la lettre*) first came together and where – in the third workshop – we began to formulate the concept behind the present volume. Marilyn Booth convened the first two workshops, at the Abu Dhabi Institute Humanities Research Fellowship Program, New York University Abu Dhabi, and through the Centre for the Advanced Study of the Arab World, University of Edinburgh. The third one, convened by Marilyn Booth and Claire Savina, was indebted to the Higher Studies Fund and TORCH, University of Oxford.

Finally, we want to thank Kent Schull and Nicola Ramsey for so warmly welcoming this book (and its predecessor), and the Press Committee of EUP and anonymous readers for their insightful and useful suggestions. We thank Eddie Clark and his colleagues at EUP for their help and patience in the production process, and Lel Gillingwater for painstakingly copyediting a text incorporating many languages.

Marilyn Booth and Claire Savina
October 2021

Notes on Contributors

Maha AbdelMegeed is Assistant Professor of Arabic Literature at the American University in Beirut. Her current research focuses on imploding the Arab Enlightenment as the projected point of origin of modern Arabic narrative ideology. She is also tracing the changing conceptions of language and time in the Arab Enlightenment and earlier, in the late Mamluk period.

Usman Ahmedani is a doctoral candidate at the University of Amsterdam, working within the Study Platform on Interlocking Nationalisms. Their research project looks at the development of Turkish cultural nationalism in the late Ottoman Empire. They hold an MPhil in Modern Middle Eastern Studies from Oxford University, where they worked on the transnational history of pan-Islamist activism in the interwar period.

A. Ebru Akcasu is an Ottomanist whose research focuses on the history of the Empire's engagement with modernity from the nineteenth to the early twentieth century. Her publications include 'Nation and Migration in Late Ottoman Spheres of (Legal) Belonging: A Comparative Look at Laws on Nationality', *Nationalities Papers* (2021) and 'Migrants to Citizens: An Evaluation of the Expansionist Features of Hamidian Ottomanism, 1876–1909', *Die Welt des Islams* (2016). Her translations include 'Letters to the Author: Late-Ottoman Debates about the Equality between the Sexes, an Extract from Halil Hamid's *Müsavat-ı Tamme*', *SOAS Journal of Postgraduate Research* (2015/16). She teaches at the Anglo-American University in Prague and is currently a visiting researcher at the Orient-Institut in Istanbul.

Marilyn Booth is Khalid bin Abdallah Al Saud Professor of the Study of the Contemporary Arab World at Oxford University. She was Senior

Notes on Contributors

Humanities Research Fellow, New York University Abu Dhabi (2014–15) and, before that, Iraq Professor in Arabic and Islamic Studies at the University of Edinburgh. Her recent monographs are *The Career and Communities of Zaynab Fawwaz: Feminist Thinking in Fin-de-siècle Egypt* (2021) and *Classes of Ladies of Cloistered Spaces: Writing Feminist History in Fin-de-siècle Egypt* (Edinburgh University Press, 2015). Her edited volumes include *Migrating Texts: Circulating Translations around the Ottoman Mediterranean* (Edinburgh University Press, 2019) and *Harem Histories: Envisioning Places and Living Spaces* (2010). She has translated many novels, short story collections and memoirs from the Arabic and was the co-winner of the 2019 Man Booker International Prize, for her translation of Jokha Alharthi, *Celestial Bodies*.

Etienne Charrière was Postdoctoral Fellow in the Koç University Research Center for Anatolian Civilizations in Istanbul, 2016–17, and Assistant Professor, Department of Turkish Literature, Bilkent University, Ankara, 2017–21. He has recently joined the Directorate for Innovation, Research and Knowledge at the French Agency for Development in Paris. His research has focused on the emergence of novel writing in literary communities of the late Ottoman Empire, primarily Greeks, Armenians and Sefardi Jews. He recently co-edited *Ottoman Culture and the Project of Modernity: Reform and Translation in the Tanzimat Novel* (2020).

Jack Clift completed his doctoral thesis at SOAS, University of London, in 2020, where his research explored the relation of the 'historical' and the 'fictional' in Hindi and Urdu historical novels from the mid-twentieth century. He was part of the European Research Council-funded *Multilingual Locals, Significant Geographies* (MULOSIGE) project, which brought together literary texts and genres from North India, North Africa and the Horn of Africa to develop a grounded approach to comparative and world literature. Jack's research has previously focused on expressions of Spanish and Egyptian nationalism in Spanish and Arabic literary fiction and the use of Arabic by Islamic reformist groups in North India in the twentieth century.

Yorgos Dedes is Senior Lecturer in Turkish at SOAS and has also taught regularly for the Intensive Ottoman and Turkish Summer School in Cunda. His research focuses on Ottoman literature and Turkish culture with special reference to frontier epic traditions and relations with Byzantium and Greece. Another area of interest is the *aljamiado* literature of Greek-speaking Muslims in the Ottoman Empire. Recent publications include a chapter on Bursa in David Wallace (ed.), *Europe: A Literary History* (2015); an edition of the Greek *aljamiado* translation of Süleymân Çelebî's *Mevlid-i nebî* (*Journal of Turkish Studies*, 2013); and an article on Ottoman poetry with Stefan Sperl ('"In the rose-bower every leaf is a page of delicate meaning": An Arabic perspective on three Ottoman kasides', *Eski Edebiyat Çalışmaları*, 2013).

Hannah Scott Deuchar is Lecturer in Arabic and Comparative Literature at Queen Mary, University of London. She received her PhD from New York University in 2021, where her research focused on modern Arabic and Ottoman literature, translation and intellectual history. She has published in, among others, *Alif: Journal of Comparative Poetics* and *Comparative Literature Studies*, and her first book project addresses intersections of translation, policing and law in the nineteenth- and twentieth-century Middle East.

Bridget Gill is an independent scholar based in Washington, DC, USA. She has a BA (Hons) in Arabic and Islamic Studies from Oxford University, and a dual MA/MSc in International and World History from Columbia University and the London School of Economics, for which her dissertation focused on constructions of race in the nineteenth-century Arabic press. Her research interests include representations of Arab-ness and otherness in Nahda-era public discourse, transnational south–south solidarities in the postcolonial world, and the reception of premodern Arab-Islamic literature and intellectual heritage in the modern Arab world.

Peter Hill is a historian of the modern Middle East, specialising in the Arab world during the long nineteenth century. He is currently a Vice-Chancellor's Research Fellow in History at Northumbria University. His first book, *Utopia and Civilisation in the Arab Nahda*, appeared in 2020. He has also published articles in journals including *Past & Present*, the *Journal of Arabic Literature* and the *Journal of Global History*.

Dženita Karić is a research fellow at the Berlin Institute for Islamic Theology, Humboldt University. Her current research deals with Ottoman devotional piety, and looks at the transformations of religious discourses over the early modern and modern periods. She contributed to the *Oxford Encyclopaedia of Islam and Women*, and has published articles in the *British Journal of Middle Eastern Studies*, *Archiv Orientalni* and *Prilozi za orijentalnu filologiju*.

Note on Translation, Transliteration and Form

Due to considerations of space and complexity, texts are not provided in their original languages in these chapters. Unless otherwise noted, translations are by chapter contributors.

We have allowed the authors of each chapter to determine their own transliteration preferences. Ottoman Turkish is rendered according to conventions used in modern Turkish to represent the Ottoman language. In most chapters, transliterations of Arabic preserve only the ʿayn and internal *hamza*, but some have chosen a fuller transliteration. We have also permitted flexibility on the spelling of Arabic/Ottoman terminology according to each chapter's linguistic environment. Because this is a book about translators and translations, sometimes works are referenced by the translator's name as in effect author of the text. This decision, too, has been left up to individual chapter authors.

Notes on Contributors

Ilham Khuri-Makdisi is Associate Professor in Middle East and World History, Northeastern University, Boston. She is the author of *The Eastern Mediterranean and the Making of Global Radicalism, 1860–1914* (2010). Book chapters and articles include 'The Conceptualization of *the Social* in Late Nineteenth- and early Twentieth-century Arabic Thought and Language', in M. Pernau and D. Sachsenmaier (eds), *Global Conceptual History: A Reader* (2016), and, co-authored with Asli Niyazioğlu, 'Conjuring Emotions in Nineteenth-century Istanbul through the Journalistic Writings of Ahmad Faris al-Shidyaq (1805–87) and Basiretçi Ali (1845?–1910)', in Goshgarian, Khuri-Makdisi and Yaycioğlu (eds), *Crafting Ottoman History: Essays in Honor of Cemal Kafadar* (forthcoming; 2022). Current projects include a study of translations between Arabic and Ottoman Turkish in the late-nineteenth and early-twentieth centuries.

Claire Savina is an independent author, translator and researcher. She pursued Arabic Studies and Comparative Literature at the Sorbonne and was research associate at the University of Oxford, working with Marilyn Booth on the 'Translation in the Nahda' project. Her research focuses on the history of literary translations from and into Arabic, French and English in the long nineteenth century, with an approach that aims to resynchronise Orientalist and Nahdist histories, engages with gender problematics, and invites a post-Eurocentric approach to Comparative Literature and Translatology. She has collaborated on several collective translation projects in English, including Selma Dabbagh (ed.), *We Wrote in Symbols* (2020), and in French, and edited *Words of Desire, Translation of Arabic Erotica* (2020).

A. Holly Shissler studied Ottoman history and received her PhD in History from UCLA. Her research interests focus on the intellectual history of the late Ottoman Empire and early Turkish republic, including questions of nationalism, identity formation, gender and the history of the press. Her publications include *Between Two Empires: Ahmet Ağaoğlu and the New Turkey* (2002), and an edited special issue on 'Sex, Gender and Family Structure' in *Comparative Studies on South Asia, Africa, and the Middle East*, including her article 'Beauty is Nothing to Be Ashamed of: Beauty Contests as Tools of Women's Liberation in Early Republican Turkey'. She has published articles on the fiction of Ahmet Midhat Efendi and on the journalistic activities of Sabiha Sertel. She is Associate Professor of Middle Eastern History, Department of Near Eastern Languages and Civilizations, University of Chicago.

Notes on Contributors

Şehnaz Şişmanoğlu Şimşek is Assistant Professor at Kadir Has University, Istanbul, where she coordinates the Turkish courses. She earned her PhD from Boğaziçi University, Department of Turkish Language and Literature, with a thesis on nineteenth-century Karamanlidika literature (Turkish in Greek script). Her research interests also include nineteenth-century Ottoman-Greek culture and literature, Ottoman minority literatures, the serial novel, rewriting, intertextuality and gender studies. She has recently contributed to the forthcoming *Routledge Handbook for Turkish Literature* about Karamanlidika literary production in the nineteenth century. Her latest article is about *The Count of Monte-Cristo* in Karamanlidika. In 2021–2 she was a postdoctoral fellow in the European Research Council's (ERC) Starting Grants Programme, 'Staging National Abjection: Theatre and Politics in Turkey and Its Diasporas'.

Johann Strauss studied German, Romance languages and Turcology at the University of Munich, and his PhD (1987) focused on a seventeenth-century Ottoman chronicler. He has taught at the *Institut für Geschichte und Kultur des Nahen Orients sowie für Turkologie*, Munich; the *Centre for Byzantine, Ottoman & Modern Greek Studies*, Birmingham University; and the *Orientalisches Seminar*, Freiburg University; and was Referent at the *Orient Institut* of the *Deutsche Morgenländische Gesellschaft* in Istanbul. From 1997 until his retirement in 2018 he taught at the Turkish Department, Strasbourg University. He has published numerous articles in English, French and German on topics including translations from Western languages, the history of printing and publishing, and linguistic and cultural contacts between communities in the Ottoman Empire.

Richard David Williams is Senior Lecturer in Music and South Asian Studies at SOAS, University of London. His research brings music and sound studies into conversation with the study of religion and Indian cultural history. He received his PhD from King's College London, with a doctoral thesis on the impact of colonialism on Hindustani music in the nineteenth century. From 2015 to 2017, he was a Leverhulme Early Career Fellow at the University of Oxford, where he worked on vernacular literature and aesthetics in early-modern north India. He is currently finalising a book on the circulation of musicians, genres and musicologists between upper India and Bengal, c. 1750–1900. He has also written on Bengali-language musicology, the performance repertoires of courtesans, and sound arts in Shi'i Islam.

Introduction

Ottoman Central: Circulating Translations from the Indian Ocean to the Eastern Mediterranean and on to the Far West of Europe

Marilyn Booth

On 25 August 1905, at al-Jumhur Printing House 'next to the Khedival Library and [Museum of] Arabic Antiquities' on al-Khalij Street in Cairo, printing was completed of a translation by Salim Qub'ayn (1870–1951). This book was an Arabic rendering of Azerbaijani scholar Ahmad Aghayev's (1869–1939) Russian-language treatise on the relationship between 'Islam' and 'women' (1901). A journalist, public intellectual and political activist, Aghayev supported Azerbaijani nationalism; moved between the Russian and Ottoman Empires and Iran; and thought in five languages. Also known as Ahmet Ağaoğlu, he would relocate to the Ottoman capital in 1909 due to political pressures in Azerbaijan.[1]

By 1905, the relationship between 'Islam', 'women' and the modern era had been a topic of intense debate and publication across the Ottoman Empire for two decades, and – as the volume before you attests – was at the thematic core of much translation energy. *The Rights of Women in Islam* was one of Aghayev's earlier works. It was one of Qub'ayn's earliest books, too, but not his first. He had published translation-adaptations of works by Tolstoy and, having relocated to Cairo from Palestine in 1897, founded periodicals in which translations from the Russian appeared.[2]

In translation, Aghayev's treatise cited a linguistically and generically eclectic range of sources: an Indian periodical, French orientalist Ernest Renan (whom Aghayev had known in Paris), Voltaire (with verses in French, carried over untranslated into the Arabic) and German orientalist Max Müller. Aghayev referenced the first Russian translation of the Qur'an to be made directly from Arabic into Russian;[3] the *Ruba'iyyat* of Omar al-Khayyam; the *Shahnameh*; works by Anglophone and Russophone scholars (such as George Rawlinson's on ancient 'eastern' monarchies); and an essay on 'women's influence in Islam' by the Bengali lawyer and writer Syed Ameer Ali, who wrote in English and sought to influence public opinion in Britain. The famous Persian Shi'i *tafsir* of Mulla Fathallah Kashani made an appearance, as did 'the book *Ashhar al-nisa'* ('The most famous women') by the late Mu'tamad al-Saltana, Minister of Education in the government of Iran'.[4] Aghayev drew on premodern Arabophone scholar-compilers (al-Tabari, al-Suyuti, Ibn Khaldun, al-Mas'udi), too, as well as the ancient Persian *Zendavesta*. The book, made available by Qub'ayn for an Arabophone readership, was a polyphonic work manifesting the multilingual breadth of the author's knowledge and the complex political-cultural milieu in which he moved, along with the global reach of the issue under discussion.

In Arabic translation, the text's polyphony was intensified. In a final chapter penned by himself, the translator explained that he had written to the author seeking permission to 'expand discussion of famous women who are mentioned in the book, as I indicate at the appropriate moments'.[5] His differently numbered footnotes, interspersed with Aghayev's own, cited classical Arabic sources that offered vignettes and poetry of Muslim women: the Prophet's biography by Ibn Hisham; al-Isbahani's *Kitab al-Aghani*; historians, travellers and compilers Ibn Khallikan, Ibn al-Jawzi, Ibn al-Athir, Ibn Jubayr, al-Mas'udi, Ibn Iyas, Ibn Battuta; and one or two others. Most often, Qub'ayn cited a contemporary also living in Egypt: Zaynab Fawwaz (c. 1850–1914), who had produced a massive biographical dictionary of women across the world in Arabic a decade before. But even this expansion of the source text did not seem sufficient to him. In his finale, he admitted that

> I neglected to mention the biographies of some [women], and so I decided, in order to round out [this work's] usefulness, to end the book in this way, by adding biographies of some famous contemporary women, among them the renowned Turkish writer Fatma Aliye, who is often mentioned.[6]

Qub'ayn's biography of Fatma Aliye (1862–1936) was nearly identical to that included in Fawwaz's *al-Durr al-manthur*; both mentioned Aliye's own translations and the translation of her work *Nisvan-ı İslam* into Arabic, French and (it was said) English. Qub'ayn followed with a short sketch of Egyptian-Turkish writer 'A'isha Taymur (1840–1902), who composed poetry in Arabic, Ottoman and Persian; and finally, a brief sketch of Fawwaz, the writer from whose work he drew these and other biographies. In translation, then, the work was expanded by bringing to it Arabic sources – including one compiled by a contemporary female writer – that themselves highlighted textual movement between Arabic, Turkish, Persian and French. Conscientiously explaining his translation strategy, the translator and the material he added – both in his own paratexts and by embellishing the text with additional historical detail – gave further, and explicit, play to the work as a multilingual, geographically and historically capacious space that stretched from Russia through the Ottoman Empire and on to Egypt, Iran and India. His brief introduction heralded this translation as a bridge between geographically and confessionally linked populations. It was

> a gift to my brethren, the Muslims of the East . . . that they may know, after reading it, that the rising generation of Muslims in Russia have the same complaints as Muslim youth in Egypt have, in terms of the bad state of the Muslim woman and her restricted, difficult position in human society; may the book be akin to a connecting link between the Muslims of the North and the Muslims of the East.[7]

These paratexts highlighted the work of translation as research and compilation in its own right. In his afterword, the translator remarked, 'Before embarking on this translation I did not imagine the toil and troubles I would face, due to its many Qur'anic verses, prophetic hadith, and historical points, absolutely inappropriate to translate. Rather, these must be sought in the original [language], and just as they came down in Arabic.'[8]

Qub'ayn dedicated his translation-expansion to the celebrated – and often reviled – Egyptian judge and reformer, Qasim Amin (1849–1908), in a fulsome dedicatory address.[9] Amin's books on women in Muslim society, published half a decade earlier, had unleashed a firestorm of criticism and counter-criticism.[10]

Qub'ayn clearly placed himself amongst young male reformers eager to ameliorate the gender regimes of their societies. In the dedication, he aligned himself with Amin in language he would echo in his afterword, as 'the link bringing together the reformers of North and East'.[11] Qub'ayn would go on to produce further works of Russian literature in translation (Tolstoy, Gorky); a graduate of the Imperial Orthodox Palestine Society's flagship Russian school in Nazareth, he was amongst the first Arabophones to translate directly from Russian into Arabic. His books on Baha'ism, the Ottoman–Italian hostilities of 1912, and the Romanovs, likely combined a range of rewriting and compilation practices. He translated a work by French writer Marcel Prévost, and a book on health from the Russian.[12] This energetic contributor to the Arabic cultural scene also founded a later periodical, *al-Ikha'* (1924–33), with a roster of contributors from Egypt, Palestine, and elsewhere.

Salim Qub'ayn and his work exemplify this volume's focus and aims. His rendering of Aghayev's work shows translation as both appropriation and transformation, as an echo rather than a copy, and as an original in its own right, with its particular agenda for a new readership explicitly named. Names of individuals that he introduces into the volume – complete with short biographies of them – suggest a particular interest in contemporary women who are contributing to the debate 'on women' (and these are individuals who show up elsewhere in our volume: Fatma Aliye, Zaynab Fawwaz, Qasim Amin). His self-presentation as a translator-compiler who decided on his own agenda, and his embeddedness in Arabophone heritage, Egyptian culture, and a larger, polyphonic Muslim-defined community, exemplify the multiple personae that many translators constructed through their presentations of the works they chose to render. His evident anxiety about gender politics, and his gender-reformist aims, were ones voiced by many intellectuals. (That we include three chapters on the turn-of-the-century gender debate(s) on changing gender relations and identities speaks for itself, while Ahmedani's and Karić's chapter also suggests the relevance of gender debates to translation choices.[13]) That Qub'ayn was a self-motivated maker of culture, but one whose works are difficult to access and whose biography and outlook remain somewhat obscure even as his name appears across myriad publication venues in his time, is rather typical of translation activists, through history and across the globe.[14]

Translation and adaptation were vital to the dynamic cultural life and intellectual ferment of the nineteenth-century Eastern Mediterranean region, as they were in the cities of South Asia and across Europe, including the Ottoman Empire's European territories. Translations contributed heavily to key debates (such as that on gender) about the shape of local yet globally connected modernities. In the process, translators became commentators, shaping or paratextually framing their chosen source texts to emphasise the agendas they sought to further. The region's publishing hubs were the stage for translations and circulations of texts from Western European languages; works produced in Europe might be translated near-simultaneously into myriad Ottoman languages, or spawn new versions that proliferated sequentially from one Ottoman language to another. But this was no unidirectional west-to-east route. Within the Mediterranean region itself (and further to the east), works were translated from and among the region's languages, notably Arabic, Persian, Turkish, Urdu, Greek, Hebrew, Armenian, Ladino and Karamanlidika. Thus, many texts translated in the Empire were also originally produced in the Empire. Texts in one Ottoman language became models for works in others. Texts published first in Arabic were quickly translated into Turkish and Persian; and we must not forget that French *was* an Ottoman language. Its appearance untranslated in so many Ottoman texts – across languages – reminds us of how many Ottomans used it in their daily lives.

The abundance of such textual transmissions has drawn increasing scholarly interest. Such work – drawn upon and cited throughout this volume – has made it possible to think beyond aggregate spatial-historical description of the field of translation and beyond commonly accepted geographical and linguistic frameworks, and to elucidate practices of translation and adaptation by working microcosmically on specific texts, across languages. Still, and with some exceptions, the emphasis has tended to fall more on translations into Ottoman languages from European languages, thereby minimising alternative sites of translation and thus, alternative intellectual preoccupations. This has tended to reinforce – or at least, to not contribute to dismantling – the now-outdated Westernisation paradigm vis-à-vis our understandings of Ottoman modernity. This volume, to the contrary, focuses on the un-bordered intellectual spaces and multiple languages that were simultaneously engaged by Ottoman thinkers. While Europe was present in the minds of late-Ottoman intellectuals, it was one of many frames of reference. Relatedly, translation in the historical context of the nineteenth-century globalising – and imperialised – world has often been imagined as either acts of decolonial resistance or as means of imperial seduction or, put differently, 'assimilation' to a Eurocentric worldview. But studying translations in a granular fashion shows these acts to be more complex, ambiguous and heterogeneous than these categories would suggest.

Furthermore, such an approach offers a decentred perspective on Ottoman literary production itself, de-emphasising exclusivist, monolingual or national paradigms in favour of how translation acts as a commentary on Ottoman modernity as a multilingual project. Our focus questions the status of Ottoman Turkish as 'the' lingua franca of the Empire, seeing it instead (in the company of much current research) as one among many. At the same time, we explore cultural transactions among actors within and beyond the Empire, a larger movement of Ottoman texts with and through translation. Studying translation into and among the Ottoman Empire's many languages – and those of constituencies elsewhere looking to the Empire – enriches our understanding of late nineteenth-century intellectual debates in and beyond the Empire. Our case studies of translation as intellectual history gaze east and west of Istanbul, across languages and geographies, from and into Arabic, Bengali, Bosnian, English, French, Greek, Hindi, Ottoman Turkish, Persian and Urdu.

To displace the epicentre of Translation Studies eastward, by focusing on discrete textual transactions, examining Ottoman-centred cultural activity, and emphasising translation or adaptation *into* more than *from* European languages, is to challenge assumptions about text dissemination that centre 'the West' as privileged source of knowledge and imply other regions as belated, derivative or passive recipients. Moreover, translation activities in the Indian subcontinent saw translators looking towards both Ottoman and European-language sources and comparing audiences. At the same time, our work shows also how European works continued to be strongly salient; studied herein are translations and adaptations of three renowned Western European works: Bunyan's *Pilgrim's Progress*, Shakespeare's *Othello*, and Eugène Sue's phenomenal bestseller *Mystères de Paris*. These texts have had vast, complex histories – or afterlives – as translated texts, and our studies demonstrate their vitality within the polyglot Ottoman publishing scene.

Ottoman Translations is the outcome of an ongoing research network, the Ottoman Translation Study Group, which has emerged from a series of workshops beginning with one that I convened at New York University Abu Dhabi in 2015. Three workshops yielded an earlier volume, *Migrating Texts: Circulating Translations around the Ottoman Mediterranean*.[15] It brought together scholars of translation, comparative literature and intellectual history working in a range of languages and genres, to consider not just the *what* but also the *how*, *for whom* and *where* of translations and linguistic contexts in the late Ottoman era. The present volume – and two further workshops – represent a further stage in this project, studying translation across languages through paired work. Co-authors with expertise in different (often overlapping) languages, and with complementary disciplinary foci, worked together throughout, resulting in studies that examine discrete texts closely yet are able to do so across two, three or four languages. And in the workshops, we found further opportunities for thinking across categories and languages, as we located converging themes and parallel concerns, which no doubt readers of this volume will notice. Through studying texts and concepts in translation, and various translation-adaptation practices across languages, the resulting chapters elucidate shared and circulating aspects of knowledge production, public conversation and cultural transfer in an era of enormous political, social and economic flux characterised by new communications technologies, emerging collective resistance to colonialisms, and new political solidarities across linguistic and political borders. The Empire had been multilingual long before the nineteenth century, of course, but new technologies of production and circulation, as well as expanding and changing perceptions of how human societies and individuals were interconnected – recognitions and debates which were partly made possible by those new technologies – meant that nineteenth-century translation was qualitatively different. This enormously complex cultural scene, and the different if related institutional histories of translation in Istanbul and Cairo, are mapped in the introduction to *Migrating Texts*,[16] which serves as a historically focused introduction to this volume as well, for the studies in this volume continue the explorations and analyses we launched there.

Creating works out of a continuum of rewriting practices – works including novels, plays, conduct books, social science treatises and other kinds of commentary – were at the heart of the Nahda.[17] Reading translations, we can ask: what readerships did these culture workers believe they had, or aspire to have, or try to shape? What sorts of political imagination can we envision from studying these translators' work, in the specific ways they appropriated and reworked their chosen sources? This is intellectual history from the ground up, thinking about the production and reception of texts, their languages and their conditions of appropriation, and reading meaning from the shifts between source text, rewriting and new paratexts. Centring translation in (or as) the Nahda – in both its reformist 'managerial' varieties, anxious to preserve some kind of (elite) 'authenticity', and its more subaltern, exuberant, non-canonical presence (although I think these distinctions can be overdone) – and taking Ottoman urbanity as a hub of such culture production, intervenes in our understanding of 'the global', of literary histories, of 'the novel' as a world form.[18] Such work has the ambition of altering perspectives; it participates in the decolonisation of the academic disciplines of Comparative Literature and Translation Studies. This is not just a turn away from Eurocentric perspectives but a multiply located critique of those perspectives, now occurring at many sites of scholarly production, to which we hope this volume contributes.

As in the previous collection, we attend closely here to translations' internal fabrics and the variety of possible translation-adaptation agendas that specific practices of translation expose. Again, we emphasise 'adaptation' as much as 'translation' to characterise the range of practices we find. But just what does 'adaptation' mean, and what are the consequences for the possible modes of reception of the text in its new linguistic and social space? Our collaborative work in this second volume has yielded a comparative and experimental practice, imagining ourselves into the historically, contextually specific task of the translator(s) and considering proliferating translations, multiple versions across languages that become lenses through which to scrutinise the original. We are thus aligned with an approach to translation that has recently been labelled 'prismatic translation', the various ways in which translation is constituted by a sort of 'multiplier effect', each text as a prism that contains and can generate numerous facets and colours, through the translator's pen and also in the eyes of the translation's readers.[19]

Our approach builds on the recent scholarly energies devoted to 'global', transnational and transregional intellectual histories, especially work that highlights 'intermediating agents or modes of circulation . . . that allow for new conceptual movement or networking practices'.[20] Practices – and people. In a 2014 article, Translation Studies scholar Jeremy Munday called for 'microhistories' of translators and their work, 'reclaiming the details of the everyday lives and working processes of sometimes little-known or forgotten translators and contextualising them to construct a social and cultural history of translation and translators'.[21] A paucity of sources on individuals such as Salim Qub'ayn leaves the sort of archival archaeology that Munday has in mind impossible for most of our subjects – and he notes that '[w]hen it comes to the study of translation, until recently exclusion seems to have been the norm. Traces of the translator are generally hard to find' in archives.[22] But we welcome this attention to the work of translation as both creative and workaday, and to the subjectivities of translators in their overlapping identities as political beings, earnest reformers, institutional professionals, eager amateurs. People like Qub'ayn were instrumental to the Nahda, as it is called in Arabic – the knowledge and institution-building movement of the nineteenth century – and they need to be studied alongside the intellectual labours of more famous individuals who came to prominence in their own time. Often, translators propagated the work of those – like Aghayev – who were important to the political ideas and work of their time yet who did not become intellectually 'pivotal' figures with lasting renown.[23] Lesser-known writers and non-canonical writing (including many translations) perhaps appealed more to emerging readerships than did their more famous correlates.

We recognise the importance of institutions – the role of state patronage and its other side, surveillance and regulation – but we also try to think about translators as individual agents, as intellectuals with agendas that emerge through their translational choices, both what to translate and how to translate it. We try to think about the labour of translation, and the resulting product as a new original with complicated points of linkage to the text that birthed it. Thus, with Munday, we argue for the study of translation in context as microhistory.[24]

Indeed, one achievement of the now lively academic field of Translation Studies has been to highlight translators as creative cultural mediators. We have tried to peer over the shoulders of working translators to ask how they creatively transported texts between as well as beyond Ottoman languages, our studies stretching linguistically and geographically from Bengal to London, Istanbul to Paris, Andalusia to Bosnia. Our historical focus in this volume, as in the previous one, puts the spotlight on figures who have more often remained behind the scenes in historical study if not in the cultural movements of their own era.

As in the previous volume, we eschew a centre-periphery model of cultural diffusion, instead focusing on 'local' initiatives and circles of text transmission, some rather direct in their literary transactions and others more indirect, creative rewritings. We highlight what Francesca Orsini has called 'the multi-lingual local',[25] and we consider how cultures of translation do not so much subtend monolingual identities in the sites we study as they highlight the rarity of monolingualism. Or perhaps, another way to describe our work is to suggest that we are shifting, pluralising and complicating the notion of 'centre'. While translation-adaptation from French and English remains salient, this is in a sense on the peripheries of the cultural circuits adumbrated here, which are more concerned with intra-Ottoman and 'East–East' transactions, and with generating Western European texts *from* Ottoman texts than vice versa. We thus continue to focus on what the previous volume's introduction labelled 'lateral cosmopolitanism': transits of texts and text-makers across adjacent languages, geographically and culturally. And we continue to ask how translation redefines 'original'. What can the 'insides' of these texts across languages tell us about local preoccupations? For instance, when a text published first in the 1890s is reworked into other languages a decade later, how does the weight of various themes shift? Or, when a text published serially in Istanbul in 1891 is almost immediately translated and published serially in Beirut, and then included soon after in Fawwaz's biographical compilation in Cairo, which is already mentioning a French translation, what does that tell us about conversations across languages? We have found that studying translations through bringing our varied scholarly backgrounds together often allows us to see the source texts themselves in new and different ways. Translations, studied in concert with each other and with the texts that engendered them, highlight thematic features of texts, shifting and overlapping audiences, and the longevity and extent of particular debates, in ways that the originals, on their own, rarely do.

That the period addressed here was one of emerging nationalist ferment in the region is significant, given the tendency (by patriots then, and by scholars later) to associate 'nations' with languages. Studying the field of inter-Ottoman translation-adaptation requires us to rethink the question of what an Ottoman nation was, at the end of empire. It challenges the notion that there was a distance between those who belonged to different language groups (and presumed proto nations) and posits interconnectivity through translations as a mode of communication and an effort to sustain meaningful conversation on common topics as an alternative perspective: an endeavour that could signal or foster kinds of unity, sympathy, connection.

Among languages familiar to Ottomans, how might knowledge transmission facilitate possibilities for cross-lingual community in the multi-ethnic and multiconfessional Eastern Mediterranean region and areas to its east? How did text re/production articulate, rework, disseminate and/or erase resilient and emerging notions of what participating in a Muslim-majority, 'worldly' networking community meant? Did translations possibly solidify minority-community identities? But equally, did they create common points of reference? To study translation within a multilingual empire is to interrogate the very definition of a community, as one must always ask: for whom? Class and interest groups may have more in common across linguistic communities than members of those communities have with others within them. Moreover, a translated work does not address a whole linguistic community but addresses those who share an intellectual/class profile with counterparts within the linguistic group of the original's intended audience. These are questions that we can only begin to answer. And, in tandem (or in tension) with questions of multiple identities is the realisation, particularly evident in some of these chapters, that – as Ilham Khuri-Makdisi and Yorgos Dedes declare in their chapter on Ottoman Turkish translations of Qasim Amin's Arabic work – the translations they probe

> were part of an integrated, cohesive ecology for intellectual production ... that formed a joint Ottoman textual canon, and that the study of translations between these two languages [Arabic and Ottoman Turkish] ought to be a central preoccupation in the study of late Ottoman intellectual and cultural history.

And – others would chime in – translations between them and other Ottoman languages, too. Concerning the gender debates, for instance, while many works pertinent to these debates were translated from French and English (including anti-feminist works), and also from Russian, there was vigorous translation on this subject between Arabic and Ottoman, and related debates in the presses of both, where writers were reading each other across languages.[26]

More individually, can we discern the agendas and senses of hoped-for audience of the intermediaries enacting this work? Chapters consider questions of how translation study can help us understand reading practices, material textual forms, and the important role of periodicals in fostering and disseminating translations. Some address the issue of secondary translation (for instance, when an English original is translated, but via a French translation, as happened frequently in the contexts on which we work). But such situations remind us that the 'cultures of translation' – the norms, conceivable strategies, favoured languages, and so forth – in a given time or place may differ enormously from those in our own context, becoming part of a microhistory of translation.[27] As in some other nineteenth-century venues, that one could openly announce having translated a text from an intermediary language suggests this was not seen as a negative or even possibly questionable practice.[28] And the multiplicity of translational strategies, again, encourages us to think in terms of adaptation: of 'translation' as a wide range of prismatic practices, sometimes of apparent incommensurability that may produce unexpected meanings.[29] As we see in the chapter by Şehnaz Şişmanoğlu Şimşek and Etienne Charrière on urban *mystères*, adaptation can also entail translating genre: adopting a model and adapting it to one's own 'culture of translation'. All in all, one cannot make assumptions about 'translatability' or 'reproduction', a point that becomes more starkly obvious when considering renderings into multiple languages.

Much remains to be done on how this rich multilingual field of text circulation might affect – or shape – reading practices and local pedagogies, social identities and economic fortunes, notions of collective being and of 'nation', agendas for language reform and resistances to them. While it is difficult to assess histories of reception among readers of translations, we can glimpse how translators were reading, and how they were telling their envisioned audiences to read. This entails keeping in mind the difference, as Anne Middleton has put it, between 'audience' and 'public' – the historical readership of a work versus a 'readership imagined and posited by the composer as a necessary postulate in the practical process of bringing the work into being'. This public, notes Sif Rickardsdottir, 'can be discerned in the rhetorical and formal characteristics of a text'.[30] This gesture to publics is evident in the two French translations of Fatma Aliye's *Nisvan-ı İslam* studied by Marilyn Booth and Holly Shissler in this volume, and less so in the first Arabic translation of that work, though its serial publication in a major Beirut newspaper that hailed a particularly Muslim audience suggests the editor (who was possibly the translator) had a well-defined sense of the public he envisioned for this work.

And of course, the translator is also a reader, perhaps melding 'audience' and 'public'. One of the benefits and joys of reading translations along the grain of the works they are rewriting – and closely within their historical context of emergence as translations – is that one can witness reading in practice, reading as ongoing interpretation of the 'forms of life' that, the reader-translator believes, grounded the original and those that must ground the translation.[31] Thinking 'prismatically' – in terms of how the translation can release or explore or imagine multiple possibilities latent in the original – may also help us to disentangle deliberate strategies from possible effects on envisioned or historical readers.[32] What is often called 'domestication' in Translation Studies may occur not in the translator's mind but in the minds of readers, and close-grained attention to translations' historical moments of emergence means thinking about the conditions of possibility for diverse kinds of reading.

One can also witness ideas and perhaps even readerships shifting. When Qasim Amin's 1899 *Emancipation of Women* was translated from Arabic into Ottoman twice after the Young Turk Revolution of 1908, both translators rendered what had been 'pleasure' in the Arabic – and a Qur'anic term – into 'benefits', which Khuri-Makdisi and Dedes argue was a more secular, and perhaps cautious, usage. 'Benefits' was also a usage in Arabic (*manafi'*) for similar purposes. I wonder whether perhaps this translation alerts us not only to how reformists were increasingly articulating marriage in socially functional terms, but also to an increased reticence around sexuality. My work on gender discourses in this era has led me to speculate that male writers were increasingly aware in this period of a growing female readership. Girls' schools were a relatively new institution, spurring translation-adaptation because new curricula were needed but also perhaps (re)shaping writing practices, reflected in modes of translation.[33]

After all, as Matthew Reynolds reminds us, translation 'is always done, not just into a language, but into a moment of that language',[34] and also into a set of perceived social needs. The geographically broad historical context(s) in which we work was one in which translators actively appropriated texts they saw as locally useful. As Yvonne Howell remarks for the history of translation in Russia,

> [t]here was no place in the Russian cultural context for extolling the merits of 'fidelity' or 'equivalence' between two texts, when the historical task at hand was to imitate, adapt, and augment foreign material so as to grow new varieties out of borrowed soil.[35]

Yet, thinking about the turn-of-the-century translation scene we surveil, we must recall that anything-goes translation was subjected to critique, and this was not always or simply 'elite' anxiety over controlling literary production, nor necessarily an early instance of what became a later critique of Nahda translation as almost by definition corrupt and corrupting. Sometimes, observers made valid points about translation quality. In November 1899, the Cairo magazine *al-A'ila* ('The family', est. 1899 by

Esther Azhari [Moyal]) published an article on 'Translation', replete with double meanings metaphorising translation as a ride across difficult terrain on a rough, spirited mount – or in a flimsy vessel through a choppy sea:

> Some people fancy that translation is easier than original composition and so they flock to it like butterflies to a brightly lit lamp; usually, they embark on this rough mount/vessel unprovisioned by anything more than a superficial knowledge of the source language and sometimes even of the language into which they are translating. And so they must follow a rocky route, whereon they stamp on/knock against the thoughts of adroit writers with haphazard and noisy frequency. They make Voltaire into a pallid stylist, Shakespeare into a foolish creator, and Corneille into a poet of dull imagery. Anyone who has attended plays in our Arabic theatres can vouch for the truth of what I say.[36]

The article was scathing: bad translation was much worse than none:

> So leave it alone, O ignorant translator. Leave the ink to dry up, the paper to rot, the pen to be eaten by worms ... corrupt translation is an unforgivable sin, a reprehensible crime heavier than that of murder. A writer would prefer their heart be torn to shreds by killers' daggers than for their ideas to be torn to shreds by the quills of your likes among translators. You can be certain that the author of *Hamlet* would turn in his grave if he heard the kind of language used to transmit his thoughts into the Arabic language – that poetic language of delicate meanings and ample figures of speech.[37]

Such commentary was part of the scene, too; it was not just about policing boundaries, but about how one opened new territories to view. At the same time, 'a sense of distrust' tended to greet Nahda translators (then and later), an ambivalence about what their abilities and their contributions truly were.[38]

The 'borrowed soil' for translation could be far away, or very nearby; it could be that of Arabic texts, or that of European classics. Such active transposition is evident in our first section, 'Proliferating Classics'. Three chapters take up the uses to which celebrated works by John Bunyan, William Shakespeare and Eugène Sue were put by translators in the Ottoman Empire and to its east. If this section does focus on the travels of European works, the multiple circulations and linguistic configurations that greeted these European visitors in their 'host' languages attest to the local, polylinguistic but interconnected cultural field that fostered translation. In 'A Pilgrim Progressively Translated: John Bunyan's *Pilgrim's Progress* in Arabic, Urdu, Hindi and Bengali', Richard David Williams and Jack Clift trace this didactic favourite of Christian missionaries from Malta (Arabic) to Calcutta (Bengali) and on into versions in Hindi and Urdu across the nineteenth century. Reading across and between these translations, they examine different approaches brought to bear on the text, and the different settings and rationales behind its translation, to excavate the history of the South Asian *Bunyan*. What was the role of this text in missionary practice, and how did local contexts of reading and performance influence adaptations of the English text? For instance, how were fictionalised Christian allegories incorporated into the imaginaries of Hindus and Muslims, in the Middle East, the Punjab and Bengal? Different translations spoke to different confessional and proselytising agendas; they were produced in separate, local contexts, yet were connected by global networks, especially those stemming from North American and British churches. South Asian genres and literary tropes were redeployed in the translations, as when prose forms transitioned into metrical versions. This sheds light on the invisible labour inherent in the translation process, the 'native' informants who were not always credited in the final works. The different material forms of the translation – including various scripts, bilingual and parallel texts, and commentarial traditions – suggest the reading practices imagined and prescribed for these works in their different social settings. Bringing these different texts into conversation, examining them at diverse scales – regional, subcontinental, transnational – underscores commonalities and disjunctures in how the *Pilgrim* was navigated by translators.

'"Pour Our Treasures into Foreign Laps": The Translation of *Othello* into Arabic and Ottoman Turkish' compares the earliest translations of *Othello* into Ottoman Turkish (1878) and Arabic (performed 1884, published 1898), alongside the English (1602) and French (1770) *Othello*s from which they were themselves adapted. Hannah Scott Deuchar and Bridget Gill ask: how is Othello recast in each text as an Arab tragic hero? These translations were made as European racial discourses were circulating alongside new literary genres and production venues in Istanbul and Cairo, and as relationships between the Ottoman Empire and its Arab provinces were being reconfigured by British colonial activity. *Othello*, with its contested status as an English 'vulgar' tragedy and its narrative of imperial war, race and revenge, crystallised concerns about newly shifting cultural and political categories. What reimaginings of tragedy as a form, and of 'Arab' as an emergent identity, spoke to the transformations people perceived in their societies? How did *Othello*'s long history of translation in Europe make itself known in these new texts, challenging notions of national ownership and origin? Different presentations in each language of Othello as an 'Arab' or Moor fighting the Ottomans on behalf of Europe shaped attendant shifts in the semantic field pertaining to his characterisation. How did these concepts of 'Arabness' interact with understandings of the function of a stage play and modulate the tragedy's narrative structure? Paratextual materials also conditioned readings and possibly performances. How might the Ottoman translators' description of *Othello* as 'an Italian opera that Ducis made into a tragedy' – displacing the text's English heritage, speaking to its contested 'tragic' form, and opening the possibility of musical performance – explain certain transformations? How does the humanist gloss of the Arabic subtitle, *Hiyal al-rijal* ('The wiles of men') condition the play's racial discourses? For these translations intervened in, and perhaps contributed to reconfiguring, racial and literary hierarchies that were in flux.

In 'Shared Secrets: Rewriting Urban Mysteries in Nineteenth-century Istanbul', Etienne Charrière and Şehnaz Şişmanoğlu Şimşek draw on scholarly reappraisals of French novelist Eugène Sue and the significance of the so-called *roman de mystères*, the type of urban fiction inaugurated by Sue's bestselling novel *Les Mystères de Paris* (1842–3), to the internationalisation of the modern novel. The transnational spread of Sue's narrative template through adaptation and imitation shortly after the original's serialisation was a factor in the emergence of globalised literary communities, including members of the various linguistic groups living side by side in the Ottoman Empire's imperial capital. Their appropriations of this template highlight literary translation as a vector of transcommunal contact. The chapter focuses on a Greek novel published in Istanbul and inspired by Sue's *Mystères de Paris*, and a translation of that novel into Karamanlidika (Greek-scripted Ottoman Turkish) published almost simultaneously in the same city. Serialised in the newspaper owned by its author, Epaminondas Kyriakides' *The Mysteries of Pera* (Πέραν Απόκρυφα) was one of many novels inspired by Sue to appear in Istanbul. An 'original' novel, it domesticated the narrative features of Sue's urban fiction, investing them with new meanings reflecting cultural expectations and social anxieties in their Ottoman context of reception. The novel incorporated recent historical events into its convoluted and melodramatic plot, notably the 1870 Great Fire of Pera, which precipitated massive change in Istanbul's urban fabric; it is read here as a commentary on cultural mutation and a subtly self-reflexive interrogation on the poetics of translation, adaptation and mimicry. Soon after, Evangelinos Misailidis 'translated' and serialised Kyriakides' novel in Greek-scripted Ottoman Turkish in his own newspaper, as *The Secrets of Beyoğlu* (*Beyoğlu Sırları*), abridging and deleting major sections. Practices of condensation, expansion and paratextual commentary show both works' creative engagements with the archetypes of the *roman de mystères*. Modalities of text circulation through translation-adaptation open a window on relations among linguistic and ethno-religious communities in and around the late Ottoman Empire.

Part Two, 'Mediterranean Multiples', features two instances of 'Mediterranean'-Ottoman circulation of political imaginaries through the genres of treatise and playscript. Peter Hill and Johann Strauss study the work of Tunisian statesman and intellectual Khayr al-Din al-Tunisi in a two-part contribution that focuses on questions of origin, circulation and language use. Khayr al-Din Pasha's work of political theory *Aqwam al-masalik* – above all, its *Muqaddima* or lengthy 'Introduction' – was a key text of nineteenth-century Islamic and political reformism. It is best known in its Arabic version, presented to the ruler of Tunis in 1867 and printed in Tunis soon thereafter. But versions of the *Muqaddima* also appeared in other languages: a French version shortly after the Arabic one, in 1868, and an Ottoman translation in 1878 after Khayr al-Din was appointed Grand Vizier in Istanbul. A Circassian-born, Ottoman-raised Mamluk who lived for several years in Europe, Khayr al-Din was familiar with all three languages. In the first part, 'Khayr al-Din al-Tunisi's *Aqwam al-masalik/ Réformes nécessaires*: A Dual Intervention in Arabic and French Political Discourses', Peter Hill considers these issues of timing and cosmopolitan, multilingual biographical experience in the relationship between the work's different versions. If Khayr al-Din Pasha was in some measure responsible for all of them, then what is the translational significance of the connections and crossings between Arabic, Ottoman and French political vocabularies which they employ? Were these versions shaped by a consciousness of speaking to different – or overlapping – audiences? Comparing these three versions which appeared during Khayr al-Din's lifetime, Hill focuses on questions of how thematic density and conceptual transfer vary between the French and Arabic texts. In the second part, 'The *Muqaddima* of Khayr al-Dīn Pasha's *Aqwam al-masālik fī ma'rifat aḥwāl al-mamālik* and its Ottoman Turkish Translation', Johann Strauss scrutinises specific translation mechanics and in particular how they modulate the Ottoman text. What kinds of changing usages, variant spellings and geographically distinct language patterns does the translation exhibit, and what does this tell us about linguistic change in the era? Do these practices imply a particular sense of audience?

Modern Turkish literary critics have often cast Abdülhak Hamit Tarhan's play *Tarık yahut Endülüs'ün Fethi* (1879) as a proto-nationalist work. But the play's early popularity outside of the Ottoman Empire and in other Ottoman languages (Arabic, Bosnian) suggest the resonance of the Andalusia trope across Mediterranean literatures, in its representation of the spread of Islamicate culture and rule to the southern Iberian

Peninsula, and the period of its flourishing. Examining Bosnian, Persian and Arabic adaptations of Abdülhak Hamit's work, Usman Ahmedani and Dženita Karić elaborate on several major points in 'Finding the Lost Andalusia: Reading Abdülhak Hamid Tarhan's *Tarık or the Conquest of al-Andalus* in its Multiple Renderings'. First, paratextual elements imply that the translators were motivated by the desire to preserve affective ties between their respective nations and (post-)Ottoman Turkey, even as each society embarked on their own nation-building processes. Why was the Andalusia trope – and Abdülhak Hamit's treatment of it – so useful in these multiple settings? Second, these adaptations show awareness of evolving conceptions of Islam as a reified entity, an awareness that was less overt in the original Ottoman play. Third, the time lag between the original publication of the play and its translations – appearing in a cluster from 1910 onwards – invites attention to the thematic weight of these later renderings. Commonplace earlier nineteenth-century tropes such as the importance of women's education and appropriate 'modern' gender relations took on a novel valence in the context of the 1910s. The lack of consistency even within certain translations (let alone between them) with regard to the terminology of political sovereignty and military nomenclature used for the play's Muslim and Christian sides is indicative of the flux of the period. In sum, to explore these translations is to foreground cross-cultural exchanges within the Middle East and South Asia (and recent scholarship on these), rather than notions of a binary encounter between European Romanticism and its reception in the 'Islamic world', another context in which the trope of 'Andalusia' is sometimes placed.

The chapter's attention to how gender was translated links it to our final Part, 'Women in Translation'. In 'Translating Qasim Amin's Arabic *Tahrir al-mar'a* (1899) into Ottoman Turkish', Ilham Khuri-Makdisi and Yorgos Dedes compare two translations of Amin's work. Despite the fact, noted earlier in this introduction, that the 'status of women' had been a focus of intent debate for some time, Amin's book was enormously controversial and spurred many responses. The first translation, which appeared in 1908 (the year of Amin's death), was penned by Yusef al-Asma'i, an intellectual and journalist based in Cairo who was particularly active in translations between the two languages. The second translation (1913) was that of Zaki Mugamiz,[39] a Christian Arab from Aleppo, a writer and employee in the state translation bureau in Istanbul. The translation of key concepts and terms in Arabic into both Ottoman versions and the degree of stability these linguistic choices manifest, as well as interventions in the texts through additions or omissions and occasional reordering of arguments, suggests each translator was partly governed by a set of commitments within a shifting social-political scene. Mugamiz's translation was more inflected with notions that became more prevalent and hegemonic after the 1908 Young Turk Revolution. The two translations must be viewed within the larger body of writings and translations that al-Asma'i and Mugamiz penned.

One of the best-known Arabic Egyptian responses to Amin (in this case, to his response to critics, *The New Woman*, 1901) was Muhammad Farid Wajdi's *al-Mar'a al-muslima* ('The Muslim woman', 1902), whose translation into Ottoman by the Istanbul-based poet Mehmet Akif is the focus of '*Muslim Woman*: The Translation of a Patriarchal Order in Flux' by Maha AbdelMegeed and A. Ebru Akcasu. Following the 1908 Constitutional Revolution and the resulting relaxed censorship laws in the Ottoman dominions, a new audience was exposed to Wajdi's book-length refutation of Amin's work in serialised, Ottoman Turkish form on the pages of the freshly established newspaper *Sırat-ı Müstakim*. Scrutinising Wajdi's Arabic text against Akif's Ottoman Turkish translation provides fresh insight into sociopolitical and linguistic features of the original *Muslim Woman*, a work that has remained mostly a footnote in accounts of author and translator both. The chapter analyses excerpts representative of the work's dominant features, notably its reliance on a scientific ideology of 'observation and experience' to make an argument for naturally ordained and divinely confirmed limits on 'men' and 'women'. Translation of the debates surrounding 'the woman question' elucidates one way the relationship between rapid material transformations in social reality and interventionist social thought was seen. Through processes of translation, 'the woman question' becomes the crux of a complex process of paradigm (re)formation, enabling the very act of *seeing* modernity from within specific social positionalities. The assumption of a labour-free domestic sphere coupled with a society organised around waged labour is a key element in such arguments: it is the translation of Wajdi's work that highlights this conceptual move. Key terms, such as those that connote the veil, also indicate assumptions about the projected readers of the book in its Ottoman rewriting.

Our final chapter turns to the translational travels of a celebrated 1890s Ottoman text. In 'Fatma Aliye's *Nisvan-ı İslam:* Istanbul, Beirut, Cairo, Paris, 1891–6', Marilyn Booth and A. Holly Shissler argue that this work by an elite Ottoman woman – who produced fiction translations from French – was 'translational' even before it was translated. *Nisvan-ı İslam* ('Women of Islam', published serially, 1891; in book form, 1892) circulated internationally almost immediately. A series of three 'dialogues' with European women, it was said to be based on exchanges

Aliye had with European women who visited her at home, in that popular tourist stop for European and American elite female visitors, 'the harem visit'. Ostensibly an explication for these foreign interlocutors of Muslim women's experiences and outlooks, this canny work turned the tables on European Orientalist representations of 'Eastern women' as it self-represented articulate and knowledgeable Istanbul women, likely for purposes of self-modelling to Ottoman female peers. Written in Ottoman Turkish, the text calls attention to its own 'oral' original as conversations conducted in French through on-the-spot interpreting, which the work's narrator repeatedly mentions. *Nisvan* was translated twice into French, in 1893 by Ol'ga Lebedeva ('Gülnar Hanim'), a transnational figure in her own right who translated Russian literature into Ottoman; and in 1894 by 'Nazimé-Roukié', probably two Ottoman women. It had already appeared in Arabic in a Beirut newspaper; it would be fully reprinted in Lebanese-Egyptian Zaynab Fawwaz's biographical dictionary of world women, taking up sixty large-folio pages. Later, different editions in Arabic were produced. The chapter compares the Ottoman original with the Arabic and French, taking into account paratextual apparatuses. How was *Nisvan* reframed for each new audience? How did it intervene in debates on women's rights, gender and space, and 'civilisational hierarchy' in different venues? Why were sartorial practices so central to the acts of translation that made this text an international one? We consider moments of heightened emphasis in the French translations, speculating about the difference it might have made to translatorial practice that the translators into French were women who were clearly concerned about reductionist, Orientalist views in Western Europe of 'the Muslim woman' or 'the Turkish woman' – but from their own standpoints, which were not exactly those of the male reformers who wrote and translated on 'the woman question' across the Ottoman Empire.

In conclusion, common themes thread throughout these chapters. Perhaps most central is the multidirectionality of translation, and how this may reposition literary production and revisionist polemics across languages. This includes the translational traffic between Ottoman and Arabic on the one hand, and Urdu, Hindi and Persian on the other: a long history of relationship subtending the vigour of printed translations in the era we study. As one of our anonymous readers so nicely put it, this offers 'a new geography', wherein Ottoman texts and Ottoman translation circulate outside the Empire's physical borders. Second, we consider the historicity of translations, how they were shaped by local circumstances and literary-linguistic conventions, as well as by specific temporalities that undergirded shifting political grounds. This is particularly evident in the chapters by

AbdelMegeed and Akcasu on translations of responses to Qasim Amin, and by Khuri-Makdisi and Dedes on translations of Amin: read together, these chapters demonstrate the impact of political sensitivities on what could be translated, and how audiences therefore sometimes had access to 'responses' before they did to the 'responded-to' text. Third, the focus on the details of how works were rewritten is related to our emphasis on the labour of translation and the translator as intellectual, often active in a number of related culture-productive activities – and as composer of paratexts that may shape reader reception or at least set out desired agendas. Fourth, the impact of language reform on translation, and possibly of translation on language reform, with the related emergence of new ideas about writing for communication, is evident in our close analyses, especially in Strauss' and Hill's examinations of Khayr al-Din Pasha's treatise between Ottoman, French and Arabic, and Khuri-Makdisi's and Dedes' chapter on translations of Qasim Amin. Fifth, within the intellectual productivity and political ferment of the time, we place the politics of gender as a key area of translation in multiple directions, while issues of race, blackness and slavery surface in the chapter on *Othello* by Gill and Scott Deuchar, and to a lesser extent in that on Fatma Aliye. Sixth, the theme of 'journey' emerges, in the chapters by Williams and Clift, Ahmedani and Karić, Booth and Shissler, and Charrière and Şişmanoğlu Şimşek, as both a concern of works chosen for translation and as a metaphor for translation itself. The project that this volume represents has been a journey for all of us, too, into fascinating texts with their many trajectories, and into multilingual collaborative work that has blessed us with many, and ongoing, conversations about how we understand the work of translation in – and on – the world.

Notes

1. On this fascinating figure, A. Holly Shissler, *Between Two Empires: Ahmet Ağaoğlu and the New Turkey* (London: I. B. Tauris, 2003). On this work, 136–51.
2. Ayida Ibrahim Nusayr, *al-Kutub al-'arabiyya alati nushirat fi Misr bayna 'amay 1900–1925* (Cairo: Qism al-nashr li-l-Jami'a al-amrikiyya bi-l-Qahira, 1983), 11, 266, with thanks to Ken Cuno. I am grateful to Margaret Litvin for sharing her ongoing research on Qub'ayn and other translators from the Russian.
3. The translator was Gordii Semionovich Sablukov (1803–80), professor at the Kazan Theological Academy; the translation came out in 1873. I thank Carina Hamilton for this information. In the Arabic version, the name is transliterated as Sāblūjūf. Ahmad Bek Ajayif [Aghayev], *Huquq al-mar'a fi*

al-Islam, trans. Salim Qub'ayn (Cairo: Matba'at al-jumhur, 1905), 20 n. 9. Aghayev objected to the view of many clerics that the Qur'an could not be translated from Arabic (Shissler, *Between Two Empires*, 136).
4. Aghayev was a Shi'i, and in his early career and writings, he identified strongly with Iran and Persian culture and history; he saw Shi'ism as a forward-looking belief system more capable than Sunnism of formulating a suitable modern polity – although as Shissler argues, this may have had more to do with the influence of certain European thinkers who highlighted 'Aryan' superiority than with Iranian sympathies. Shissler, *Between Two Empires*, chap. 3. Back from France and in Azerbaijan, he was more focused on commonalities within Muslim communities (134).
5. Salim Qub'ayn, 'Khatimat al-kitab, li-l-mu'arrib', in Ahmad Bek Ajayif [Aghayev], *Huquq al-mar'a fi al-Islam*, trans. Salim Qub'ayn (Cairo: Matba'at al-jumhur, 1905), 152–63; 152. All translations from Arabic in this Introduction are my own.
6. Qub'ayn, 'Khatimat al-kitab', 152. It is not clear whether he is referring to mentions in the book or in public discourse generally. Aliye was quite well known by then. See the chapter by Booth and Shissler herein.
7. Salim Qub'ayn, 'Kalima li-l-mu'arrib', in Ahmad Bek Ajayif [Aghayev], *Huquq al-mar'a fi al-Islam*, trans. Salim Qub'ayn (Cairo: Matba'at al-jumhur, 1905), 4–5; 4.
8. Qub'ayn, 'Khatimat al-kitab', 152. He uses the verb *nazila*, connoting the Divine communication of texts.
9. Salim Qub'ayn, 'Taqdimat al-kitab', in Ahmad Bek Ajayif [Aghayev], *Huquq al-mar'a fi al-Islam*, trans. Salim Qub'ayn (Cairo: Matba'at al-jumhur, 1905), 3.
10. On Amin's works in translation, see the chapter by Khuri-Makdisi and Dedes. For recent studies on these works that revise earlier scholarship, see Hussein Omar, 'Arabic Thought in the Liberal Cage', in Faisal Devji and Zaheer Kazmi (eds), *Islam after Liberalism* (London: Hurst, 2017), 17–45; Marilyn Booth, 'Before Qasim Amin: Writing Histories of Gender Politics in 1890s Egypt', in Marilyn Booth and Anthony Gorman (eds), *The Long 1890s in Egypt: Colonial Quiescence, Subterranean Resistance* (Edinburgh: Edinburgh University Press, 2014), 365–98; Murad Idris, 'Colonial Hesitation, Appropriation and Citation: Qāsim Amīn, Empire, and Saying "No"', in Burke A. Hendrix and Deborah Baumgold (eds), *Colonial Exchanges: Political Theory and the Agency of the Colonized* (Manchester: Manchester University Press, 2017), 180–216.
11. Qub'ayn, 'Taqdimat al-kitab', 3.
12. On WorldCat, we find: *Hukm al-nabi Muhammad lil-filsuf Tolstoy wa-shay'un 'an al-Islam wa-Urubba*, trans from the Russian by Salim Qub'ayn (Cairo: Matba'at al-taqaddum, 1912); Tulistuwi, *Mamlakat Jahannam wa-al-hamr* (Cairo: al-Matba'a al-tijariyya al-kubra, 2d pr., 1926); Salim Qub'ayn, *'Abd al-Baha' wa-al-baha'iyya* (Cairo: Matba'at al-'umran, 1922). Nusayr,

al-Kutub, gives somewhat different titles as well as the additional works mentioned here. Neither Nusayr nor WorldCat mentions the Aghayev translation.

13. This was also a major theme in our 2019 volume (see below), not simply because of the editor's interest in it but because it was so prominent at the time, and in translation; see chapters by Dimitrioula and Kazamias, Shissler, and Booth.
14. Nahda translators of Russian are receiving more attention. In addition to Litvin's work, see, e.g., Spencer Scoville, 'Reconsidering Nahdawi Translation: Bringing Pushkin to Palestine', *The Translator* 21: 2 (2015): 223–36, on the better-known Khalil Baydas.
15. Marilyn Booth (ed.), *Migrating Texts: Circulating Translations around the Ottoman Mediterranean* (Edinburgh: Edinburgh University Press, 2019).
16. Marilyn Booth, 'Introduction: Translation as Lateral Cosmopolitanism in the Ottoman Universe', in Marilyn Booth (ed.), *Migrating Texts: Circulating Translations around the Ottoman Mediterranean* (Edinburgh: Edinburgh University Press, 2019), 1–54.
17. There is much work on this by now. Recent works that focus strongly on translation include: Samah Selim, *Popular Fiction, Translation and the Nahda in Egypt* (Cham: Palgrave Macmillan, 2019); Peter Hill, *Utopia and Civilisation in the Arab Nahda* (Cambridge: Cambridge University Press, 2020); Rebecca Johnson, *Stranger Fictions: A History of the Novel in Arabic Translation, 1835–1913* (Ithaca, NY: Cornell University Press, 2021). A decade earlier, and with a distinct focus, Shaden Tageldin, *Disarming Words: Empire and the Seductions of Translation in Egypt* (Berkeley: University of California Press, 2011). Abdulrazzak Patel also emphasises translation as 'a key role among nearly all Nahda intellectuals'; those 'conservatives' most cautious about European imports did also participate. Abdulrazzak Patel, *The Arab Nahḍah: The Making of the Intellectual and Humanist Movement* (Edinburgh: Edinburgh University Press, 2013). Scoville also places translation at the centre of the Nahda ('Reconsidering *Nahdawi* Translation'). Even the earlier scholarship that criticised and bemoaned the translation work of the Nahda saw it as central – a challenge, in the later terms of (for instance) Egyptian national canonicity, to instituting a 'true' national literature. This earlier literature tended to focus nationally and monolingually; thus, it ignored the inter-Ottoman translation scene, also partly because, in nationalist narratives, the 'Ottoman Turks' were seen as the forces mitigating against 'enlightened' nationalism.
18. Johnson, *Stranger Fictions*; Selim, *Popular Fiction*.
19. Matthew Reynolds (ed.), *Prismatic Translation* (Cambridge: Modern Humanities Research Association/Legenda, 2019).
20. Samuel Moyn and Andrew Sartori, 'Approaches to Global Intellectual History', in Samuel Moyn and Andrew Sartori (eds), *Global Intellectual History* (New York: Columbia University Press, 2013), 3–30; 5.
21. Jeremy Munday, 'Using Primary Sources to Produce a Microhistory of

Translation and Translators: Theoretical and Methodological Concerns', *The Translator* 20: 1 (2014): 64–80; 64.
22. Munday, 'Using Primary Sources', 71.
23. On Aghayev in this regard, Shissler, *Between Two Empires*, 1 and throughout.
24. For Arabic, issues of labour and the 'modest' provenance of translators are also emphasised by Yves-Gonzalez Quijano, 'La renaissance arabe au XIXe siècle: Médiums, médiations et médiateurs', in Boutros Hallaq and Heidi Toelle (eds), *Histoire de la littérature arabe moderne*, vol I: 1800–1945 (Paris: Sindbad/Actes sud, 2007), 71–104. Increasing attention within 'Nahda Studies' to material forces and political economy is significant as well.
25. Francesca Orsini, 'The Multilingual Local in World Literature', *Comparative Literature* 67: 4 (2015): 345–74.
26. In addition to relevant chapters in this volume, see, for another example, an exchange between Hasan Husni al-Tuwayrani and Ahmed Midhat, in *al-Mu'ayyad* and *Tercüman-ı Hakikat*, discussed in Marilyn Booth, *The Career and Communities of Zaynab Fawwaz: Feminist Thinking in Fin-de-siècle Egypt* (Oxford: Oxford University Press, 2021), chap. 2.
27. On 'cultures of translation', Peter Burke, 'Cultures of Translation in Early Modern Europe', in Peter Burke and R. Po-Chia Hsia (eds), *Cultural Translation in Early Modern Europe* (Cambridge: Cambridge University Press, 2007), 7–38. Speaking of European venues, Burke notes the relative freedom before the nineteenth century with which translators 'improved' texts and would sometimes 'declare changes with pride' (31). This is a consistent theme throughout that collection. See also a fascinating study of how gender-themed texts at the inception of mass publishing were reformulated from French into English: Anne E. B. Coldiron, *English Printing, Verse Translation, and the Battle of the Sexes, 1476–1557* (Farnham: Ashgate, 2009). Equally engrossing on this subject is Sif Rikhardsdottir, *Medieval Translations and Cultural Discourse: The Movement of Texts in England, France and Scandinavia* (Cambridge: D. S. Brewer, 2012).
28. Burke, 'Cultures of Translation', 27.
29. On incommensurability, see Lydia H. Liu (ed.), *Tokens of Exchange: The Problem of Translation in Global Circulation* (Durham, NC: Duke University Press, 1995).
30. Anne Middleton, 'The Audience and Public of *Piers Plowman*', in David Lawton (ed.), *Middle English Alliterative Poetry and Its Literary Background* (Cambridge: D. S. Brewer, 1982), 101–23; 102, quoted in Rickardsdottir, *Medieval Translations*, 12. The second quote is from Rickardsdottir, *Medieval Translations*, 12.
31. The inspiration here is scholarship that has drawn on Wittgenstein as a thinker on translation. See Philip Wilson, *Translation after Wittgenstein* (London: Routledge, 2016); Silvia Panizza, 'Wittgenstein', in Piers Rawling and Philip Wilson (eds), *The Routledge Handbook of Translation and Philosophy* (London and New York: Routledge, 2019), 63–75.

32. For a particularly cogent observation on this, see Manal Al-Natour, 'Translating Images of the 2011 Syrian Revolution: A Contratextual Approach', in Sameh Hanna, Hanem El-Farahaty and Abdel-Wahab Khalifa (eds), *The Routledge Handbook of Arabic Translation* (Abingdon: Routledge, 2020), 189–204; 190–2. This emerges from a critique of the foreignisation/domesticising dichotomy famously advanced by Lawrence Venuti, a focus of critique in a number of the cited collection's chapters.
33. See for instance – and at a slightly earlier period – Butrus al-Bustani's comments in his preface to his translation of *Robinson Crusoe*, on translating for a female audience, translated in Booth, 'Introduction', 34. The impact of reading on girls was a fraught topic of debate, as it was elsewhere.
34. Matthew Reynolds, 'Introduction', in Matthew Reynolds (ed.), *Prismatic Translation* (Cambridge: Modern Humanities Research Association/Legenda, 2019), 1–18; 6. Reynolds' focus here is on how translations, like 'originals', can become 'dated' but also can themselves become canonised as works that continue to marshal 'extraordinary cultural resources' (5) that foster continued appreciation amongst readers. But I find his succinct phrasing useful in thinking about the immediate and 'political' historicity of translations in the times of their emergence. This sensitivity to the moment of emergence is highlighted by the sources listed in note 26 above.
35. Yvonne Howell, 'Through a Prism, Translated: Culture and Change in Russia', in Matthew Reynolds (ed.), *Prismatic Translation* (Cambridge: Modern Humanities Research Association/Legenda, 2019), 121–39; 123. Another very good study of this is Doris Jedamski, 'Translation in the Malay World: Different Communities, Different Agendas', in Eva Hung and Judy Wakabayashi (eds), *Asian Translation Traditions* (Manchester: St Jerome, 2005), 209–43. Many scholars working in venues across the world have noted that the idea of an 'original' to which 'fidelity' was owed is relatively recent, though it predates the nineteenth century, even if the notion of 'fidelity' can be found in much earlier texts.
36. [Istir Azhari?], 'al-Tarjama', *al-'A'ila* 1: 14 (15 November 1899): 217–19; 217.
37. 'Al-Tarjama', 219. The essay ends with brief praise of Fathi Bek Zaghlul's recent translation into Arabic of Edmond Demolins' *A quoi tient la supériorité des Anglo-Saxons?*, understandably controversial in the context of the British Occupation of Egypt, where the translation was published.
38. Scoville, 'Reconsidering *Nahdawi* Translation', 224. This theme is prominent in Samah Selim's *Popular Literature* and her other writings on translation.
39. The proper Arabic transliteration of this individual's name is Zakī Mughāmiz. However, we have chosen to use Zaki (Arabic)/Zeki (Turkish) Mugamiz, because this is generally how he chose to represent himself and how he appears in biographical dictionaries and other sources. One finds multiple spellings and transliterations of his name.

Bibliography

Ajayif [Aghayev], Ahmad Bek, *Huquq al-mar'a fi al-Islam*, trans. Salim Qub'ayn (Cairo: Matba'at al-jumhur, 1905).

Al-Natour, Manal, 'Translating Images of the 2011 Syrian Revolution: A Contratextual Approach', in Sameh Hanna, Hanem El-Farahaty and Abdel-Wahab Khalifa (eds), *The Routledge Handbook of Arabic Translation* (Abingdon: Routledge, 2020), 189–204.

Booth, Marilyn, 'Before Qasim Amin: Writing Histories of Gender Politics in 1890s Egypt', in Marilyn Booth and Anthony Gorman (eds), *The Long 1890s in Egypt: Colonial Quiescence, Subterranean Resistance* (Edinburgh: Edinburgh University Press, 2014), 365–98.

Booth, Marilyn, *The Career and Communities of Zaynab Fawwaz: Feminist Thinking in Fin-de-siècle Egypt* (Oxford: Oxford University Press, 2021).

Booth, Marilyn, 'Introduction: Translation as Lateral Cosmopolitanism in the Ottoman Universe', in Marilyn Booth (ed.), *Migrating Texts: Circulating Translations around the Ottoman Mediterranean* (Edinburgh: Edinburgh University Press, 2019), 1–54.

Booth, Marilyn (ed.), *Migrating Texts: Circulating Translations around the Ottoman Mediterranean* (Edinburgh: Edinburgh University Press, 2019).

Burke, Peter, 'Cultures of Translation in Early Modern Europe', in Peter Burke and R. Po-Chia Hsia (eds), *Cultural Translation in Early Modern Europe* (Cambridge: Cambridge University Press, 2007), 7–38.

Coldiron, Anne E. B., *English Printing, Verse Translation, and the Battle of the Sexes, 1476–1557* (Farnham: Ashgate, 2009).

Hill, Peter, *Utopia and Civilisation in the Arab Nahda* (Cambridge: Cambridge University Press, 2020).

Howell, Yvonne, 'Through a Prism, Translated: Culture and Change in Russia', in Matthew Reynolds (ed.), *Prismatic Translation* (Cambridge: Modern Humanities Research Association/Legenda, 2019), 121–39.

Idris, Murad, 'Colonial Hesitation, Appropriation and Citation: Qāsim Amīn, Empire, and Saying "No"', in Burke A. Hendrix and Deborah Baumgold (eds), *Colonial Exchanges: Political Theory and the Agency of the Colonized* (Manchester: Manchester University Press, 2017), 180–216.

Jedamski, Doris, 'Translation in the Malay World: Different Communities, Different Agendas', in Eva Hung and Judy Wakabayashi (eds), *Asian Translation Traditions* (Manchester: St Jerome, 2005), 209–43.

Johnson, Rebecca, *Stranger Fictions: A History of the Novel in Arabic Translation, 1835–1913* (Ithaca, NY: Cornell University Press, 2021).

Liu, Lydia H. (ed.), *Tokens of Exchange: The Problem of Translation in Global Circulation* (Durham, NC: Duke University Press, 1995).

Moyn, Samuel and Andrew Sartori, 'Approaches to Global Intellectual History', in Samuel Moyn and Andrew Sartori (eds), *Global Intellectual History* (New York: Columbia University Press, 2013), 3–30.

Munday, Jeremy, 'Using Primary Sources to Produce a Microhistory of Translation and Translators: Theoretical and Methodological Concerns', *The Translator* 20: 1 (2014): 64–80.

Nusayr, Ayida Ibrahim, *al-Kutub al-'arabiyya alati nushirat fi Misr bayna 'amay 1900–1925* (Cairo: Qism al-nashr li-l-Jami'a al-amrikiyya bi-l-Qahira, 1983).

Omar, Hussein, 'Arabic Thought in the Liberal Cage', in Faisal Devji and Zaheer Kazmi (eds), *Islam after Liberalism* (London: Hurst, 2017), 17–45.

Orsini, Francesca, 'The Multilingual Local in World Literature', *Comparative Literature* 67: 4 (2015): 345–74.

Panizza, Silvia, 'Wittgenstein', in Piers Rawling and Philip Wilson (eds), *The Routledge Handbook of Translation and Philosophy* (London and New York: Routledge, 2019), 63–75.

Patel, Abdulrazzak, *The Arab Nahḍah: The Making of the Intellectual and Humanist Movement* (Edinburgh: Edinburgh University Press, 2013).

Qub'ayn, Salim, 'Kalima li-l-mu'arrib', in Ahmad Bek Ajayif [Aghayev], *Huquq al-mar'a fi al-Islam*, trans. Salim Qub'ayn (Cairo: Matba'at al-jumhur, 1905), 4–5.

Qub'ayn, Salim, 'Khatimat al-kitab, li-l-mu'arrib', in Ahmad Bek Ajayif [Aghayev], *Huquq al-mar'a fi al-Islam*, trans. Salim Qub'ayn (Cairo: Matba'at al-jumhur, 1905), 152–63.

Qub'ayn, Salim, 'Taqdimat al-kitab', in Ahmad Bek Ajayif [Aghayev], *Huquq al-mar'a fi al-Islam*, trans. Salim Qub'ayn (Cairo: Matba'at al-jumhur, 1905), 3.

Quijano, Yves-Gonzalez, 'La renaissance arabe au XIXe siècle: Médiums, médiations et médiateurs', in Boutros Hallaq and Heidi Toelle (eds), *Histoire de la littérature arabe moderne*, vol I: 1800–1945 (Paris: Sindbad/Actes sud, 2007), 71–104.

Reynolds, Matthew, 'Introduction', in Matthew Reynolds (ed.), *Prismatic Translation* (Cambridge: Modern Humanities Research Association/Legenda, 2019), 1–18.

Reynolds, Matthew (ed.), *Prismatic Translation* (Cambridge: Modern Humanities Research Association/Legenda, 2019).

Rikhardsdottir, Sif, *Medieval Translations and Cultural Discourse: The Movement of Texts in England, France and Scandinavia* (Cambridge: D. S. Brewer, 2012).

Scoville, Spencer, 'Reconsidering *Nahdawi* Translation: Bringing Pushkin to Palestine', *The Translator* 21: 2 (2015): 223–36.

Selim, Samah, *Popular Fiction, Translation and the Nahda in Egypt* (Cham: Palgrave Macmillan, 2019).

Shissler, A. Holly, *Between Two Empires: Ahmet Ağaoğlu and the New Turkey* (London: I. B. Tauris, 2003).

Tageldin, Shaden, *Disarming Words: Empire and the Seductions of Translation in Egypt* (Berkeley: University of California Press, 2011).

Wilson, Philip, *Translation after Wittgenstein* (London: Routledge, 2016).

PART I
PROLIFERATING CLASSICS

Chapter 1

A Pilgrim Progressively Translated: John Bunyan in Arabic, Urdu, Hindi and Bengali

Richard David Williams and Jack Clift*

Over the long nineteenth century, John Bunyan's *The Pilgrim's Progress* (1678 and 1684)[1] was extensively translated into Asian languages, from Tamil in 1793 to Korean in 1895.[2] While Isabel Hofmeyr has traced how Bunyan's book circulated in African languages and through the 'broader space of the mission empire',[3] the circuits that *The Pilgrim's Progress* followed across the Middle East and Asia have only partially been examined.[4] This chapter reconstructs how Bunyan's work was progressively translated into South Asian languages – especially Bengali, Hindi and Urdu – and reads these re-workings alongside versions in Arabic, Tamil and Oriya.[5]

When we began reading the same text in multiple languages and from different contexts, we hoped to interrogate a South Asian portion of a global history of Bunyan's circulation. Reality has proven to be more complicated. First, there was no single Ur-text for Bunyan: English versions appeared in many forms even in their circulation in the British Isles;[6] moreover, certain translators working in Arabic and Urdu did not need to refer to Bunyan's English at all, as they already had earlier translations (in Greek or Hindi) at hand. Furthermore, as we began to historicise the immediate conditions of translation work, and the forms of cultural 'domestication'[7] involved in rendering this Christian allegory into local contexts, it became increasingly apparent that the different translators had extremely different audiences, priorities and literary approaches. Some translations were the work of small teams of missionaries and local consultants:[8] they appeared to operate in relative isolation but were closely engaged with how their peers were working, and several were trying to make sense of how their Indian audiences might receive Bunyan's mediated message. However, we found that by the end of the nineteenth century, Indian translators were developing work for highly specific missionary programmes, yet simultaneously departing from earlier translations to present their own interpretations of Bunyan's narrative. This variety gestures to the challenges of thinking in terms of a global Bunyan, and drove us to move away from a uniform history of *The Pilgrim's Progress* in north India.

This chapter introduces the multilingual context of nineteenth-century north India, and considers how missionaries and translators navigated languages, colonial agendas and genres in their projects. We consider the connections between a series of translated versions of *The Pilgrim's Progress*, moving in a loosely chronological order from Bengali, to Hindi, and finally to Urdu. In particular, we examine how certain missionary projects appropriated local intellectual genealogies, embedding a transplanted Bunyan into precolonial literary imaginaries. We argue that Indian authors creatively interpreted Bunyan through styles and conventions with longer histories, but also by learning from earlier translation efforts. Missionaries and indigenous Christians navigated overlapping considerations in their translations, including changes in colonial language policies and expanding print industries, as well as evolving policies towards missionary work. While there was a missionary context to all these versions of *The Pilgrim's Progress*, examining translations produced in the Mediterranean, on the Gangetic plains and around the Bay of Bengal suggests quite different priorities, reading practices and intended readerships, rather than a homogenous and universal proselytising project. On the one hand, *The Pilgrim's Progress* testifies to a global network of missionaries, translators, poets, readers, illustrators, book makers and publishers. At the same time, reframing *The Pilgrim's Progress* as a South Asian text provides significant insights into a specifically regional history of literary consumption, performance practices, oratory and cultural exchange.

Many Missionaries, Many Languages

Across the nineteenth century, South Asian literatures circulated across a highly multilingual landscape, and both European colonial administrators and Indian intellectuals endeavoured to chart, categorise and distinguish the diversity of oral and written language cultures.[9] Pandits, Mughal connoisseurs and Orientalists invested themselves in the 'classical' scholarly literatures – especially in Sanskrit, Persian and Arabic – at a time when the public life of these languages was changing. This was partly a reflection of colonial language policies – such as the British decision to strip Persian of its administrative functions in 1837 – but also of longer cultural sea changes that favoured 'vernacular' languages. For missionaries, writing in the vernacular (let alone in a form that would be unfamiliar to their converts, like a prose novel) posed many challenges, not least intelligibility. Although the entrenched multilingualism of north India lent itself to oral and aural exchanges, at the level of writing, a combination of script and register could close off a text to key audiences. 'Hindustani' alone could refer to a linguistic spectrum, which, over time, became polarised as Urdu (written in Persianate *nasta'līq* script) and Hindi (in Sanskritic *devanāgarī*).[10] Hindustani writers also used the Roman alphabet in certain contexts.

From the point of view of missionary literature, this multilingualism could shape the individual's journey to Christ.[11] For example, Avril Powell has discussed the case of Talib Masih Khan, a physician based in Bharatpur who was baptised in 1813: Khan had been given an Arabic Old Testament by a Catholic priest, and then read the Gospels through a Persian translation from a Baptist missionary, but only became convinced by Christianity after conversing – presumably in Hindustani – with 'Abdul Masih (c. 1769–1827).[12]

What were the implications of introducing Bunyan's English prose into this highly multilingual landscape? Translating *The Pilgrim's Progress* had a proselytising propulsion, allied to simultaneous projects of circulating the Word of God in South Asian languages: though not scripture, Bunyan's text was seen as a transformative vessel of sound Christian values. Missionaries also reflected on how translation could be transformative in other senses too: it was thought that linguistic training offered converts possibilities for social mobility. In Agra, Daniel Corrie (1777–1837) and 'Abdul Masih had planned to train boys in Persian, Hindustani and English to give them greater opportunities in life, though it is unclear whether this worked out in reality.[13] Postcolonial scholars have since viewed this combination of Christian *and* English values as a strategy of colonialism, inculcating Western ideals and eradicating local epistemologies: while Jeffrey Cox has cautioned against reductionist approaches to the colonial mission,[14] our readings of *The Pilgrim's Progress* underline how translation was embedded in processes of transforming minds and literary tastes, as well as listening and musical practices.[15] Certainly, missionary historiographies have traditionally championed the injection of English literary sensibilities and modes of composition into Asian languages, underlining the contribution of the translators even to the extent of brazenly dismissing the condition of literature before their efforts:

> These languages had no prose literature and only a few of them a poetic literature, and nearly all, save perhaps Tamil, Telugu, and Hindi, were in a condition of the greatest literary destitution. For one ignorant of the languages of India and of their very involved history it is quite impossible to gain any adequate idea of the services rendered by missionaries in the renaissance of

individual Indian tongues; we would only call to mind [William] Carey and his work for Bengali, the creation of a modern literature in Hindi, and kindred performances.[16]

Generalisations of this variety had a highly damaging influence on South Asian literary historiography. However, it is also possible to examine certain missionary projects in terms of local intellectual genealogies, reading the transplanted Bunyan for its entanglements with precolonial literatures. We are especially interested in how translators connected Bunyan to long-standing local literary styles and conventions, the agency and creativity of Indian authors in the history of *The Pilgrim's Progress*, and the relationships between the different translations.

It is worth noting that many translators were working through their predecessors' efforts, rather than directly from Bunyan's English original. The 'fortuitous discovery of the English book'[17] was a highly mediated, un-spontaneous event. Parallels might be drawn to the situation around the Arabic Bunyan. *The Pilgrim's Progress* was translated into Arabic (as *Siyāḥat al-masīḥī*) around 1828 by a priest of the Greek rite based in Jerusalem, 'Isa Petro (d. 1834). It was published in 1834 by Church of England missionaries operating out of the Church Missionary Society base at Malta. Peter Hill points out that 'Isa Petro did not know English, so most likely worked from a Greek version, printed in Malta in 1824.[18] By 1844, American missionaries in Beirut had published a second Arabic version,[19] by the Protestant convert Butrus al-Bustani (1819–83), which was designed to be a more refined reworking that would appeal to the literary sensibilities of a learned Arabic readership. Reading these versions together, Hill has considered the different ideologies of translation – from Evangelical universality to a more tailored, *adab*-oriented approach – at work in the missionary Mediterranean.[20]

It appears that these Arabic versions did not influence the South Asian translations, although it is possible that examining a larger set of languages (such as Persian and Pashto) would shed light on unexplored connections.[21] Rather than presenting a connected history, then, this chapter considers the network of texts in north India on its own terms, in order to provide a more nuanced context for the simultaneous work in Arabic, and to excavate the larger landscape of mobilised literature.

Although there was a comprehensive missionary architecture that framed all these translations, missionary cultures varied enormously according to both local contexts and transnational shifts in policy. While these different renditions of Bunyan might be read collectively as a global reception history, that history was neither continuous nor monotone. Examining these nineteenth-century translations, it is worth remembering how, in 1813, the East India Company's new charter included a 'pious clause', which created new possibilities for Protestant missionary activity in north India.[22] However, Company officials had a mixed relationship with missionaries: a Baptist preacher, John Chamberlain (1777–1821), was sanctioned for proselytising in religious fairs at Haridwar, which was considered incendiary and potentially damaging to the Company's influence. Missionary activity was sternly discouraged within the Company's military personnel: famously, when one Brahman orderly sergeant named Naick Prabhu Din was baptised in Meerut in 1819, he was expelled from the army.[23] As we will see, by the time of the later translations in the 1870s, this context had changed again, with colonial officials developing new policies towards missionary activities that had a direct impact on approaches to translation.

The intersections between colonialism – from shifting language policies to an explosive print industry – and missionary activities had significant implications for how missionaries and indigenous Christians translated. Reading these translations of *The Pilgrim's Progress* together presents points of comparison and contrast: our four primary languages have complex interconnected histories, especially in the nineteenth century, when expectations about their definitive features and relationships to one another were refashioned under European colonialism.[24]

Early South Asian Pilgrims

The earliest Indian-language translation of Part One of *The Pilgrim's Progress* appears to be the 1793 Tamil *Paradēsiyin Payanam* ('The traveller's, or foreigner's, journey', alternatively translated as, 'A traveller, having left this world, makes a journey to the next'). Scholars of Tamil literature, such as Stuart Blackburn, regard the *Paradēsiyin Payanam* as an extremely accomplished work, which 'achieved a storytelling technique unprecedented in Tamil. It soon proved to be a favourite among Tamils, and not only Christians; according to one missionary's report in the nineteenth century, it was often read aloud to large groups of people.'[25] The year 1853 saw a Tamil version of the entire work, the *Iraṭcaṇiya yāttirikam* of Henry Albert Krishna Pillai (1827–1900), and another followed in 1882.[26]

Despite the success of the Tamil Bunyan, missionaries in Calcutta were unsure whether other translations would be worthwhile. In 1810, a plan to prepare a Hindustani version was scuppered by negative responses from the target readership: 'Upon making the attempt, the style of that celebrated work and the manners therein displayed were found so entirely repugnant to the Oriental taste, as to render the prosecution of such design no longer desirable.'[27] Instead, Mary Martha Sherwood (1775–1851) was asked to prepare an English retelling of Bunyan, with Indian characters and cultural details, from peepal trees to Brahmins.[28] This plan also went awry, and Sherwood's book was published in 1818 in Shropshire and sold in London instead.

Bunyan was first translated into Bengali, instead of Hindustani, by Felix Carey (1786–1822) at the Baptists' centre in Serampore. Felix was the eldest son of the celebrated missionary scholar, William Carey (1761–1834),[29] and having grown up in Serampore relocated to Burma where he published portions of the New Testament in Burmese (1815). He returned to Bengal in 1815 and his Bengali translation, *Yātrirder Agresaraṇ Bibaraṇ arthāt Ihlokahaite paraloke gamanbibaraṇ* ('Description of a pilgrim's progress, or description of a journey from this world to another world'), was published in 1821.[30]

Over the following fifty years, *The Pilgrim's Progress* was reimagined in several north Indian languages. In summary (see Figure 1.1), Carey's Bengali translation (1821) inspired an anonymous Bengali version in 1854. This provided the basis for a Hindi translation by John Parsons (1817–69) in 1867. However, this was not the first Hindi *Pilgrim*. Between these translations, the Reverend William Buyers (1804–65) had composed another Hindi version in 1835, which provided the basis for an 1840 Urdu translation by the Reverend William Bowley (1785–1843), which also appeared in the Roman alphabet in 1845. From Bowley, the transmission forked into three directions. First, John Hari and Yunis Singh (*fl.* c. 1850–80) reworked the text in 1853 and then in 1869, and this work continued to circulate into the late 1880s, with the addition of footnotes. Bowley's

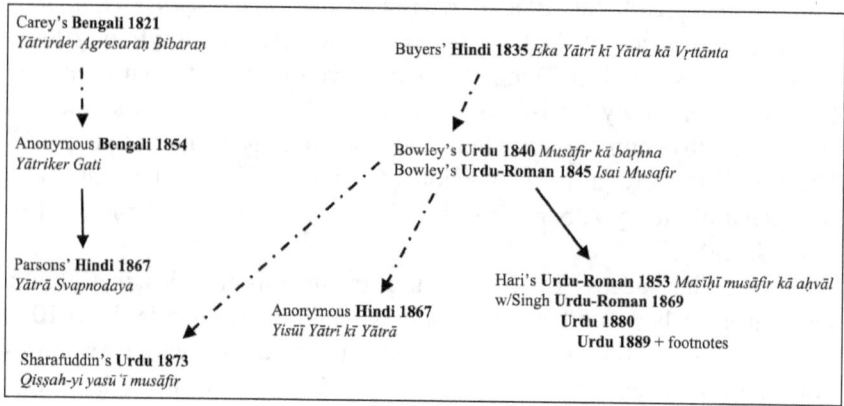

Figure 1.1

text was also loosely followed as the basis for another anonymous Hindi version in 1867. Finally, Bowley also inspired a more radical retelling in Urdu by one Sharafuddin (*fl.* c. 1870–80) in 1873.

Why was *The Pilgrim's Progress* so heavily translated? In her research on the African case studies, Isabel Hofmeyr challenges several assumptions that have hindered perceptions of the reception of *The Pilgrim's Progress*: that *The Pilgrim's Progress* was considered translatable due to both its *internal* features – its evangelical message, or (following Christopher Hill) its political radicalism – and *external* factors, that is, the 'relentless imperialism' which provided the infrastructure for the book's dissemination.[31] Hofmeyr argues that such assumptions ignore the specifically African trajectory of the text, and the particular ways in which it appealed to local literary tastes and became embedded in a precolonial cosmology; she also emphasises the distinctions between how colonialism, white settlers and missionaries operated, warning against conflating their histories.

Looking across these South Asian examples, several further reasons emerge for why *The Pilgrim's Progress* was so avidly translated in north India. First, the narrative was entertaining, with a linear plot that was easy to follow and did not require the same kind of explanatory contextualisation as more complicated works, especially the Bible. More than this, *The Pilgrim's Progress* could also be read as an allegory of conversion: one man's journey from destruction to paradise. Over the nineteenth century, certain missionaries involved with these translation projects were also producing fictive autobiographies, allegedly written by Indian converts, which emulated the didactic thread of *The Pilgrim's Progress*.[32]

Second, we should also remember that many of the translators were simultaneously involved in translating the New Testament. Being a work of fiction rather than scripture, far less was at stake in translating *The Pilgrim's Progress*. John Parsons, who translated both *The Pilgrim's Progress* and the New Testament into Hindi over the 1860s, wrote about his anxieties and concerns over biblical translation:

> To my own mind, it is more satisfactory to touch a work of such magnitude and importance with a cautious and deliberate hand. The effect of so many editions of the Scriptures speedily following one another, each differing from its predecessor, on the minds of thinking natives, is not good.[33]

In a similar vein, as a non-scriptural text, *The Pilgrim's Progress* was a 'safer' option to distribute to the unconverted masses, who might do all kinds of inappropriate things with a cheap book. This was a serious concern among missionaries, and noted by the assistant secretary of the British and Foreign Bible Society in 1879:

Ask any Missionary from India or China what he thinks of flooding those empires with Scriptures, regardless of the power of the people to read and understand, and he will reply that the Bible distributed after this fashion will be sure to be dishonoured, will be collected for waste paper, or at best be valued as a charm, and a true thirst for God's Word be postponed.[34]

Missionaries from Allahabad to Madras discovered that cheap Bibles were used as waste paper in bazaars, while more expensive copies were kept as curious objects and then sold on. Were this to happen to Bunyan's novel, the disappointment would not be so devastating.

Finally, Bunyan's original text was versatile and varied in form, comprising a combination of prose, dialogues and songs, which allowed for a variety of translation strategies, and entertaining reading and performance practices. The majority of our translators incorporated the dialogues into the prose by inserting short narrations – 'Christian replied . . .' and so forth[35] – and retained the direct speech of the conversations, making the narrative a lively tale. The recurrent songs in the English provided opportunities for the translators to shift gear and present those passages in verse: in the case of Hindi, several versions contain the *caupaī* and *dohā* metres, which were established choices for narrative poems, as discussed below.

Translating Carey

How did translators build upon each other's efforts in order to refine an Indian literary style for Bunyan? A second Bengali version of *The Pilgrim's Progress* was published in 1854, *Yātriker Gati* ('Pilgrim's way') from the Baptist Mission Press for the Calcutta Christian Tract and Book Society. Superficially, this version seems different from Carey's translation, but on closer inspection, the anonymous author(s) of *Yātriker Gati* were clearly using Carey as a model. For example, the opening paragraph:

Bunyan's original:
As I walked through the wilderness of this world, I lighted on a certain place where was a Den, and I laid me down in that place to sleep: and, as I slept, I dreamed a dream. I dreamed, and behold, I saw a man clothed with rags, standing in a certain place, with his face from his own house, a book in his hand, and a great burden upon his back. I looked, and saw him open the book, and read therein: and, as he read, he wept, and trembled; and, not being able longer to contain, he brake out with a lamentable cry, saying, 'What shall I do?'

Felix Carey's Bengali version (1821):
kāntār rūp ei jagate bhraman karata yekhāne ek guhā [?] chila emata ek sthāne āmi upasthita haiyā śayan karata nidrāy parilām. pare dekha svapne darśan karata chinnabastra parihita āpana grher dige bimukha ek pustaka haste ebaṅg

pṛṣṭhe ek bhāri bojhā emata ek lokake svapne dekhilām. pare dṛṣṭi karata sei lokake sei pustak khuliyā pāṭha karate dekhilām ebaṅg pāṭh karata se byakti krandamān o kampamān haite lāgila. pare adhik dhairyya karaṇe asamartha haiýā se byakti ek mahābilāp śabda kariýā <u>āmi ki kariba ei kathā kahiýā</u> ceṅcāite lāgila.

Journeying through this world, a dense wood in form, I came to one place where there was a cave, I <u>lay down and</u> fell <u>asleep</u>. Then, behold, in a dream I saw dressed-in-rags, <u>turned against his own house</u>, a book in his hand and a heavy burden on his back, in the dream I saw a person like that. Then as I looked, I saw that person open that book and read it, and reading it that individual began to weep and tremble. Then, being incapable of forbearance, this individual uttered a great wail, <u>'What shall I do?', saying this</u>, he began to yell.

(Anonymous) *Yātriker Gati (1854)*:
ye samaýe āmi ei durgam araṇýasvarūp jagater madhýe bhramaṇ karite2 ek parbbater guhāte <u>upasthita haiýā śaýan kariýā nidrita</u> chilām, **tatkāle** ei svapna dekhiýāchilām, yeno khaṇḍa2 jīrṇa bastra parihita ek byakti <u>nija gṛher prati bimukh</u> haiýā ebaṅg pṛṣṭadeśe bṛhat bhārākrānta haiýā ek khāni pustak pāṭh karate lāgila. ār ai pustak pāṭh karite2 se bhīt byaktir nyāý romāñchita haiýā kāṅpite2 rodan karite lāgila. pare manoduḥkher adhik beg sambaraṇ karite nā pāriýā, <u>āmi ki kariba? e kathā kahiýā</u> uccaiḥsvare kāṅdiýā uṭhila.

At the time [when] I was *travelling and travelling* through this impenetrable forest-like world, I came to a mountain cave, <u>I lay down and</u> was <u>sleep</u>ing, **in that moment** I beheld a dream, a person dressed in *tattered-tattered*, ragged clothes, he was <u>turned against his own house</u>, and he was hugely weighed down upon his back, he began to read a book. And *reading and reading*, he shuddered like a frightened person, *trembling and trembling* he began to cry. Then, being incapable of containing excessive toil of the pain of his heart, <u>'What shall I do?' saying this</u> in a loud voice, he cried out.

Yātriker Gati is a re-phrasing of Carey's translation, in the sense that while the majority of words have been replaced with synonyms and portions of the syntax have been altered, some phrases (underlined here) have been retained and the overall structure of the narrative and approach to tackling Bunyan's phrasing is recognisably the same. Carey attempted to follow Bunyan clause by clause, while following the conventions of Bengali speech, especially in his use of participles, and also providing extra details where Bunyan was spare.

For example, in Bunyan's phrase 'not being able longer to contain, he brake out with a lamentable cry, saying, "What shall I do?"' – 'contain' is missing an identified object (himself? his emotions? his torment?), and Carey reconstructed the phrase as 'being incapable of forbearance'. Bunyan ends with the provocative question, 'What shall I do?', whereas

Carey and the 1854 translator ended with a colloquial participle phrase, followed by a dramatic pairing of a participle with the (simple) past: 'saying this, he began to yell.' The 1854 author revisited the question of *what* the man in the dream was unable to 'contain': he amplified the text with 'being incapable of containing the excessive toil of the pain of his heart' (*manodukher adhik beg sambaraṇ karite nā pāriyā*).

The other changes in the second version bring the substance of Carey's translation closer to Bengali speech patterns: the translator combined phrases into a longer opening sentence; used typical time-phrase pairings (marked above in bold) ('At the time [when] ... in that moment', *ye samaye ... tatkāle*); and added four doublings (marked above in italics), marked in print by the numeral 2. Some phrases are also arguably more refined: Carey's 'a heavy burden on his back' (*pṛṣṭhe ek bhāri bojhā*) has been adapted to 'he was hugely weighed down upon his back' (*pṛṣṭadeśe bṛhat bhārākrānta haiyā*).

Both Carey and the 1854 editor developed poetic flourishes, as seen in their treatment of Bunyan's 'he wept, and trembled': Carey opted for alliteration and internal rhyme – '*krandamān o kampamān haite lāgila*' – while the editor amplified the text with a simile: '*bhīt byaktir nyāý romāñchita haiyā kāṅpite2 rodan karite lāgila*' ('he shuddered like a frightened person, trembling and trembling he began to cry'). The word for 'shuddered', *romāñchita*, is a particularly evocative word in north Indian poetry: literally 'horripilating', it refers to an overpowering emotional response, when the entire body breaks out in gooseflesh. In Sanskrit aesthetic theory, this is a typical sign of the 'embodied response' (*anubhāva-vibhāva*), and is often used in love and devotional poetry. This perhaps explains why the editor clarified that the ragged dream-man was not aroused or inspired, but was 'like a frightened person'. Although these colloquial shadings and literary flourishes might suggest that the editor was Indian, this was not necessarily the case. While *romāñchita* is elegant in its connotations, the text does not aspire to 'high literature' per se. This elegance, along with other Sanskritic words like *bṛhat* (instead of Carey's more everyday *bhāri*) might also gesture to a European student of Sanskrit and literature, rather than a native speaker. Were the many colloquial doublings read by contemporary Indians as artificial, 'trying too hard' to sound authentic?

The translated (*anubādita*) work of 1854 contains a preface that elaborated Bunyan's biography in some detail. Rather than underlining Bunyan's identity as a Christian, the language is open-ended and non-sectarian: the irreligious (*dharmahīn*) contrasting with the 'service of the Supreme God' (*parameśvarer sebā*), and 'faith in the Lord' (*prabhu āśīrbbād*). These terms would not have been out of place in a Hindu devotional work. In the body of the translation, allegorical names are translated into Bengali but marked with an asterisk to identify them as proper names (for example, Prudence as *pariṇāmdarśinī (fem.)[36]), while names like Christian, Zion and Apollyon have been transliterated and also asterisked. The combination of these difficult transliterations, asterisks and unusual combinations of personified abstract nouns marked the text as a translation of a foreign text, despite the work of the translator to keep the vocabulary familiarly Bengali and not overtly Christian.

The Hindi Pilgrim

This Bengali *Yātriker Gati* of 1854 was the basis for a Hindi version, the *Yātra Svapnodaya* ('Dreaming of a pilgrimage', 1867) by Reverend John Parsons. This was a substantial work of 380 pages with illustrations borrowed from *Yātriker Gati*, but now annotated with additional Hindi labels. An English Baptist missionary, John Parsons was in India from 1840, where he preached across the major northern cities, including Agra, Allahabad and Benares, and was latterly based at a school in Monghyr. His work in Hindi included biblical translations, children's books, hymnals and anthologies of poetic verses designed to stimulate spiritual reflection.[37]

Parsons was deeply interested in north Indian music as a tool in conversion. One of his projects was to print Indian songs in European staff notation:

> The predilection of the natives for their national style of music is very strong, and not weakened, so far as I see, by a sincere attachment to Christ and Christianity; and though our own more solemn and majestic psalmody is, to our taste, vastly superior, it has little charms for them; and those, at least, who have been brought to the Saviour in adult life, never learn to sing our tunes properly. It seems to me, therefore, a very desirable step towards naturalising Christianity in the land, to supply our native brethren with hymns in their own metres, and to the tunes they admire, and when they know them, sing with zest and enjoyment, especially as the Hindoos are a people intensely fond of poetry and music.[38]

Parsons may well have been inspired by the extensive proliferation of songbooks in Hindi and Bengali from the 1850s onwards:[39] the enormous popularity of these books made song lyrics a convenient way into the ears and minds of possible converts. His comments echo those of 'Abdul Masih, the aforementioned missionary and translator operating out of Agra forty years earlier, who had come to the same conclusion and had composed new hymns and devotional Christian poetry in Hindustani, as a preferred alternative to translating English verses.[40] Nonetheless, many missionaries were hesitant about composing songs in Hindustani, and most late nineteenth-century collections were translations (often published in Roman script) of Moody and Sankey's influential hymnal, *Sacred Songs and Solos* (1877). Rather than writing their own lyrics, other missionaries collected hymns composed by Indian Christians, determining a stable notation for the tunes, and harmonising them for congregational singing.[41] These hymns were based on the sounds and structures of *bhajan* (Hindu devotional songs, primarily in Hindi) and *ghazal* (Urdu or Persian).

While the Bengali translators had treated 'songs' in Bunyan's narrative as 'poems' (often in simple rhyming couplets), Parsons' musical interests motivated him to compose in the style of a *bhajan*.

[Bunyan:]
Then Christian gave three leaps for joy, and went on singing.
   Thus far I did come loaden with my sin,
   Nor could ought ease the grief that I was in,
   Till I came hither: What a place is this!
   Must here be the beginning of my bliss?
   Must here the burden fall from off my back?
   Must here the strings that bound it to me, crack?
   Blest cross! blest Sepulcher! blest rather be
   The Man that there was put to shame for me.[42]

[Parsons:]
us samay Krīṣṭiyān harṣase tīn biriyāṅ kūd yah bhajan gātā 2 calā.
   bhajan

dhanya dhanya te puruṣa dayālū	mama hita lajjā pāī
jhuki jhuki meṅ nija pīṭhahi lādyau	agha bojhā dukhadāī
kāhu na mero bojha utāsyau	kaṣṭī jīva churāī
āyo bhāgi yahāṅ lagi meṅ jaba	aginita sukha taba pāī
krūśahi dekhi bhāra nija khoyau	yā sukhadāyaka ṭhāṅī
ṭuṭe bandha gisyo agha merau	kavarahi gayau samāī
krūśa kavara dou dhanya kahata hauṅ	dhanya yīśu adhikāī

At that time, Christian leapt with glee three times and went on, singing this *bhajan*:
   Bhajan:

Blessed, blessed is that compassionate man,	my love is humbled
Dropping down, laden on my back	with a burden of tormenting sin
Nothing can take away my burden	and liberate this afflicted soul
I began to be fortunate when I came here	when I obtained countless joys
Beholding the cross, my load is lost,	the place of that bestower of bliss

| The broken bonds of my sin fall away | and I am absorbed in (his) grave |
| I bless them both, the cross, the grave | and blessings more on Jesus.⁴³ |

Parsons changed his dialect for this song verse, composing in a poetic register of classical Hindi, most closely associated with music and devotional poetry. Keywords like *dayālū* (compassionate) and *sukhadāyaka* (bestower of bliss) in particular echo the language of Hindu *bhajan*s. That said, the hymn also has a markedly Christian vocabulary: the cross (*krūśa*); the sepulchre, translated with an Islamicate term for grave (*kabara*, that is, *qabr*); and, in a departure from Bunyan, the name of Jesus (*yīśu*).

Although Parsons retained several phrases and images from Bunyan's song, his priority was to render the text into a performable 'native Christian' hymn: four couplets have become three couplets and a repeated refrain, based on the model of a Hindi *pad*. The *bhajan* also complies with the metrical model for a *pad* (*sār* metre, 16+12 and 16+11), which would allow it to be performed very easily in *tīntāl* (the standard tempo for singing *bhajan*).

Performance was a significant concern to the missionaries. They had entered a religious marketplace that was especially musical. Hindu vernacular homiletics combined a lesson with recited verses, singing, musical interludes and congregational participation, and Europeans had to be ear-catching and entertaining in order to compete. Amos Sutton (1802–54), who translated *The Pilgrim's Progress* into Oriya in 1838 (*Svargīya Yatrīr Vrittānta*), was very conscious of this, and over the 1830s prepared an Oriya hymnal, adopting 'as many plain metres as possible'.⁴⁴

Sutton was invested in refining his practices, and published a letter from a colleague, one Mr Bampton, on his own experience in Oriya translation and sermonising:

> I have been long employed, and am still employed in preparing myself to say just what the Scriptures say on the great topics of the gospel ministry. I have already written eight or nine sheets in English, very carefully, and have made preparation for a great deal more, which will not take much finishing; a part of what I have finished is translated into Oriya, and I am going on with that work. I tried to read some of my translations to the people, but it does not seem to do. Numbers will hear me speak, who would not stop to hear me read, so I must read them in private, till I get, (if such it should be,) a good system of sound doctrine well wrought into memory, and then I shall be prepared to do all my health and strength will admit. Opposite every page of my translations, I leave a blank page for the reception of emendations as to language, which I hope to make first, with the help, of a pundit, and then with the common people, till it becomes as good and intelligible Oriya as I can make it. Work of this sort employs my time and pen a good deal.⁴⁵

Bampton's process was thus to prepare notes in English, translate these into Oriya, then review the language with both a native scholar and 'the common people' (which gestures to the larger question in the missionaries' minds about the difference between literary 'high' Oriya and the Oriya of the street). His attempts at reading his notes aloud were not rewarded, so his aim was to become an orator in the language.[46] Bampton had also translated hymns from Bengali into Oriya, and on one occasion bumped into the convert Gunga Dhor singing one of his compositions. Gunga related to Bampton that Indians who had received Christian books approached him to ask him to explain them.[47] This brief exchange indicates how the literary dimension of missionary work was a complex combination of text, songs, oratory and spoken commentary, engaging English missionaries, Oriya pundits and villagers, operating between English, Bengali and Oriya.

John Parsons appears to have considered a similar set of issues in his own translation practice over the late 1850s and early 1860s. In the pursuit of linguistic accuracy and aesthetic appeal, he collaborated with local intellectuals – including the head Hindi pandit of Benares College – recalling what Isabel Hofmeyr has called systems of 'brokerage' between missionary agents and local auxiliaries.[48] That said, while missionaries in Bengal, north India and Punjab would have been familiar with Sutton and Bampton's efforts, the Bengali and Urdu translations in particular gesture to regional differences in how missionaries imagined their audiences engaging with their translations: some were pleasurable books to read as novels, or as adventurous tales, rather than as tools for street tellings. In the case of Urdu translations of *The Pilgrim's Progress*, we see another set of local concerns intersected with broader changes in missionary practice and the colonial administration.

Becoming a 'True' Christian: Urdu Translations of The Pilgrim's Progress

The earliest translations of *The Pilgrim's Progress* into Urdu appear at the hand of the Reverend William Bowley in the 1840s. Bowley's *Musāfir kā baṛhnā* ('The progress of the pilgrim', 1840), written in the Perso-Arabic script, was followed by his *'Īsā'ī musāfir* ('The Christian pilgrim', 1845), a rendering of the earlier work in the Roman script.[49] Bowley's two texts draw on an earlier Hindi translation published at the Baptist Mission Press in Calcutta, *Ek Yātrī kī Yātrā kā Vṛttānt* ('The story of a pilgrim's pilgrimage', 1835), by the Reverend William Buyers.[50] These, in turn, fed into the certain Urdu versions from the 1850s onwards.

John Bunyan in Arabic, Urdu, Hindi and Bengali

Most prominent among these later recensions are the multiple editions of *Masīḥī musāfir kā aḥvāl* ('The story of the Christian pilgrim'), first published in Roman Urdu in 1853 at the Presbyterian Mission Press in Allahabad, where Bowley's second translation had been published. This work was reprinted in Ludhiana in 1869, before being rewritten in the Perso-Arabic script for editions in 1880 and 1889, the latter with a print run of 1000 copies.[51]

The first edition of *Masīḥī musāfir kā aḥvāl* is credited to a translator and 'native catechist' called John Hari, who in 1850 had been 'licensed to preach the gospel by the Presbytery of Allahabad'.[52] The subsequent three editions were made in collaboration with another translator called Yunis Singh, details of whom are comparatively scarce.[53] It is unclear how Hari and Singh worked together: intriguingly, Singh is listed as the sole author of the second part of *Masīḥī musāfir kā aḥvāl*. Their shifting collaboration is indicative of a larger transition in the latter half of the nineteenth century, when translation efforts led by Western missionaries were supplemented – or in some cases replaced – by the endeavours of local Christians.

Hari and Singh's *Masīḥī musāfir kā aḥvāl* is indicative of other changes, too. In a preface to the first part of the 1889 edition, an anonymous contributor – cryptically referred to as '*sī—ḍabalyiū—if*' (C-W-F) – sets out the purpose of, and audience for, Bunyan's original work and, by extension, Hari and Singh's translation:

> This book, the name of which is *The Christian Pilgrim* ('*Īsā'ī musāfir*), was written in English for the kind of people who are nominally Christian; it was not written for those who are born in countries where other religions are prevalent. As such, in this book, the intention of the author is not to make the kinds of arguments that might convince the elders of another religion of the veracity of the holy book of the Christians, and which would affirm the need for baptism. This and many other necessary matters have come to be thought of and widely understood as being obligatory. What the author asserts here is that even if a person is born in a Christian country in the house of Christian parents, [even if] they have understood the Truth in the Christian books, and [even if] they submit to the Christian rites, even completely aside from all these matters, there is still much to do in order to become a 'true' Christian (*ḥaqīqī 'īsā'ī hone ke lī'e*). So much so that the author, by way of a model example, makes clear that every one of us human beings, whether we deny Christ or whether we sin by our own actions, should be aware of the burden of our sin (*gunāh ke bhārī bojh*) by virtue of the spreading of the Word of God and His grace in cleansing our souls; and the author wishes that those who are aware of their sin, and of the impending calamity [that is, the Day of Judgement], should be saved; meanwhile, those who remain apostates continue to afflict him.[54]

This preface complicates assumptions about the rationale behind these translation projects. According to this author, Bunyan's intention had not been to convert non-Christians – the so-called 'elders of another religion' – but to shore up the belief of his co-religionists. The genealogy connecting this 1889 edition to the works of earlier Western Christians in India would suggest a shared emphasis on the production of texts that would be useful for effecting conversion. Yet, by the time of Hari and Singh, it seems that the translated Bunyan was read less as a tool of proselytisation, and more as a means to cultivate Christian morality. The audience is not so much the 'apostates' to which the author of the preface refers, nor those who need convincing of the necessity of baptism into the Church, but rather local Christians, converts or otherwise, whose adherence to the moral and social aspects of Christian faith needed buttressing. The implication here is that Hari and Singh aligned their translation to Bunyan's original purposes in very different temporal, geographic and cultural contexts.

The discussion that follows illustrates these changing attitudes through a focus on a slightly earlier text, published in 1873 and penned by a *munshī* known only as Sharafuddin 'Isa'i (literally, Sharafuddin 'The Christian'). Like Hari and Singh's translation, both the contexts for and content of Sharafuddin's work reflect a move away from the production of texts purely as a method of proselytising Christianity, emphasising instead the proliferation of models for right praxis within a Christian evangelical framework. At the same time, Sharafuddin's work reveals a set of changing dynamics between missionary groups and colonial administrators that impacted the ways in which local translator-authors went about their work.

Patrons and Prizes

Departing from all the other translations, Sharafuddin's *Qiṣṣah-yi yasū'ī musāfir* ('The tale of the Christian pilgrim', 1873) is a verse composition written in an Urdu heavily inflected with Persian vocabulary and imagery. Bunyan's prose is rendered into rhymed verses (*bait*), two of which occupy a single line on the pages of Sharafuddin's text, with each hemistich afforded its own column. The two hemistichs of each verse rhyme, and each hemistich consists of ten syllables, bringing the text broadly into line with the conventions of the *masnavi* poetic form. The work – which runs to fifty-three tightly packed pages – is divided into twenty chapters (*bāb*), each of which is preceded by a short description of its content.[55]

The provenance of this text reveals the changing dynamics that informed translations in this period. This 1873 edition was produced at the behest of – and seemingly not in collaboration with – the American Presbyterian missionary Augustus Brodhead (*fl.* c. 1850–80).⁵⁶ Brodhead was stationed in Allahabad from 1872, and was one of the principal organisers of a conference on mission translations into Hindi and Urdu held in the city in 1875, though the conference proceedings note that by this time he had moved to the Presbyterian station at Farrukhabad.⁵⁷

Though the frontispiece of Sharafuddin's translation credits Brodhead with '[having] the work printed (*ṭabaʿ karāyā*) for the general benefit of all (*wāsṭe fawā'īd-i ʿām ke*)', no further mention of Brodhead is made by Sharafuddin.⁵⁸ He instead uses the introduction of his text to praise another, more prominent figure: Sir William Muir (1819–1905), the British Lieutenant-Governor of the North-Western Provinces between 1868 and 1874. As we demonstrate below, in his eulogy, Sharafuddin employs tropes that position the Lieutenant-Governor as an exemplary statesperson who straddles both Western Christian and Indo-Persianate Islamicate literary and cultural traditions. The central position that Sharafuddin affords Muir is more generally indicative of the milieu within which this work operated. Muir's position as a fulcrum between colonial-administrative and missionary interests at this time helps to position Sharafuddin's work less as a translation of Bunyan's work and more as an original work responding to changing cultural and literary sensibilities.

Avril Powell has provided extensive details of Muir's life, along with that of his older brother John Muir (1810–82), a colonial administrator and scholar of Sanskrit.⁵⁹ William Muir's direct support for 'Low Church' missionary societies while based in and around Agra between 1847 and 1857 emulated the close links fostered between the colonial administration and evangelical Protestant groups by James Thomason (1804–53), former Lieutenant-Governor of the North-Western Provinces. Muir was navigating East India Company-era rules that precluded the overt expression of religious affinity by civil servants based in India, a so-called 'neutrality policy' first introduced in the 1790s. Administrators like Muir circumvented such proscriptions 'by the conviction that what Indians needed for reassurance on "government neutrality" was more open witness to their Christian identity by Company servants': that is, a more transparent acknowledgement from officials of the Christianity that undergirded their actions. Powell situates Muir and those like him as mediating the two extremes of imperial and missionary interaction.⁶⁰

Although it is commonly assumed that colonists and mission actors in India were closely connected, sharing a sense of 'civilisation' at the core of their endeavours, this has, as already mentioned, been challenged.⁶¹ What has been overlooked, Powell suggests, is 'the role of such civilians as the Muirs in their capacities as scholarly aides to the missionary society enterprises', intermediaries between the civil administration and the religious institutions of north India.[62] Muir's connection with Sharafuddin's work, through the conduit of Augustus Brodhead, adds a further complication.

During his tenure as Lieutenant-Governor, Muir actively encouraged missionary societies to reconsider the kinds of material they were publishing. At the level of language, Muir advocated for the use of north Indian vernacular languages in both publishing and education – that is, he supported the use of Hindi and Urdu, instead of Sanskrit and Persian.[63] He was equally concerned with literary form. For Muir, the 'bare transfer of European ideas into an Urdu dress, without attempt at adaptation' by translators and scholars had previously produced work that was effectively meaningless 'to young Indian students knowing no English, and more importantly, whose cultural background was entirely different from readers in Europe'.[64]

Muir was not alone in these ruminations. The proceedings of the conference on Hindi and Urdu Christian literature in 1875 in Allahabad are replete with quotes from mission representatives calling on their peers to engage more proactively with the requirements of potential Indian audiences: 'Writers proposing to introduce foreign books into the languages of this country should not confine themselves to a closely literal translation, but rather endeavour to transfuse and adapt such works to the special necessities of the people of this country.'[65] The proceedings urge that 'tracts and books should be made to look as much as possible like native publications' as unless they are 'very skilfully orientalised, they will meet with very small success'. The Reverend Thomas Valpy French (1825–91), the founder of St John's College in Agra, was more specific in his recommendations: 'None of the works, I would suggest, should be translated word for word; but with free rendering, and even paraphrasing, into Oriental idioms, points of view, figures of speech, and modes of thought.'[66]

To this same end, Muir had introduced prizes for 'the production of useful works in the vernacular, of approved design and style, in any branch or literature', a development that shaped not only the language but also the context for later works.[67] The offer of rewards for works of literature met with retroactive support from the delegates of the 1875 conference.[68] The competitions ran for a number of years, starting in Muir's first year as Lieutenant-Governor and subsequently awarded in 1869, 1872 and 1873.[69] The scope for works submitted to the prizes was expansive; the announcement of the first competition, which ran in the Allahabad Government Gazette in August 1868, noted that

John Bunyan in Arabic, Urdu, Hindi and Bengali

the only condition is that the book shall serve some useful purpose, either of instruction, entertainment, or mental discipline; that it shall be written in one or other of the current dialects, Oordoo or Hindee; and that there shall be excellence both in the style and treatment.[70]

One important caveat to Muir's prizes was that 'theological treatises will not be received, nor treatises containing anything obnoxious to morality.' Key, here, is the desire for works to be moral and didactic without appearing overtly confessional. Muir's interest was less in commissioning texts aimed at conversion, which had been the earlier focus of missionary tract societies. By the mid-1870s, the emphasis was on works that had a moral value to them and could be used in government-sponsored educational institutions. At the 1875 conference, Reverend French observed that

> the books needed ... are 'works of a less controversial and more devotional and spiritual cast ... almost the whole range of our [existing] religious literature, with the exception of a few hymns and commentaries, being dwarfed and shrunken into polemical discussion, truth in its offensive and defensive attitude, not that which is hortatory and authoritative and most effective to bring hearts into captivity to the obedience of Christ'.[71]

The Reverend Thomas P. Hughes (1838–1911), a missionary based in Peshawar and affiliated with the CMS, agreed, noting that 'our great want is *suitable devotional books*, especially for *converts* from Islam.'[72] Erstwhile Muslims, Hughes suggested, were particularly susceptible to alienation from life within the Church, given the relative infrequency of devotional acts in Christianity in comparison to Islam:

> In the event of a religious Muhammadan being brought to Christ, the necessity of some systematic provision for his spiritual wants is increased tenfold ... The Muhammadan [convert] of modern times will have to join a Christian Church the most striking features of which, *to his mind*, will be the absence of devotional life.[73]

Rather than polemics aimed at discrediting local religious traditions, Muir and his peers were calling for more discursive works that could be used to affirm the devotions and ethics of those who had already converted, in a style and form that was familiar to them.[74] *Qiṣṣah-yi yasū'ī musāfir* should be read in light of these developments. Sharafuddin's translation met Muir's criteria and was more concerned with promoting adherence to the principles of Christianity than attracting would-be converts. Sharafuddin's emphasis on facets of civil society indicates a concern not merely for the Christian as a believer, but also as a citizen within society at large. This resonates with Sylvia Brown's comments on how Bunyan became a useful tool in the agenda of evangelical pedagogy: *The Pilgrim's Progress* 'became a primer not only of the gospel message but also of the basics of Western subjectivity as constituted by literacy, numeracy, and the clock'.[75]

However, *Qiṣṣah-yi yasū'ī musāfir* is not simply a derivative text aimed at satisfying an administrative requirement or the passive object of Western influence. With great originality, Sharafuddin melded together features of existing Indo-Persianate literary genres with a narrative lifted from a seventeenth-century English allegory. By foregrounding his autonomy and creativity, it is possible to highlight the agency of local actors in the production of religious tracts and devotional texts.[76]

From Vanity Fair to **Baṭlān kā melā**

Despite Brodhead's role in bringing Sharafuddin's work to print, it is Muir who is the focus of the author's attention in the opening of the *Qiṣṣah*. Sharafuddin's laudatory comments not only acknowledge Muir's backing for the work, but also the shifting priorities of writers in this period. The emphasis on Muir's leadership qualities – and the precedents to which Sharafuddin compares him – are but one part of the changing appetite for suitable literature spurred on by missionary interests, and, in this case, supported by colonial officials. The images used by Sharafuddin fold the text into a longer historical tradition of Indo-Persianate treatises on the morality of kingship. At the same time, Sharafuddin's praise sets the scene for a longer excursus on the nature of the state and the individual's position within it. Sharafuddin here centres the appeal of Christianity not in the 'theological' details, which Muir had cautioned against, but rather in the practical relevance of this belief system to more 'temporal' concerns.

Sharafuddin's *Qiṣṣah* is prefaced first by a *ḥamd*, a generic praise poem in the name of God, and a subsequently by a *madḥ*, a panegyric dedicated to Muir. The *ḥamd* initially engages in formulaic thanksgiving to God – 'There is not one who compares to Him / No-one but Him so revered'[77] – before moving on to thank the Lord specifically for His role in helping Sharafuddin compose this work:

> The story that I write is so incomparable
>   That each line is the envy of the crescent moon.
> The light of His support shines so brightly
>   That on the dots of the letters dances the mirage of the sun.
> This translation of *The Pilgrim's Progress* (*Yasū'ī musāfir*)
>   Reveals reality just like a mirror:
> From prose I have versified this tale
>   Revealing what is hidden in a clear way;

Reading it, the people of this country will find joy and happiness
So much so that its purpose will be remembered long after I am gone.⁷⁸

Sharafuddin alludes explicitly here to a purposeful balancing of entertainment and didacticism, a characteristic of the text that would undoubtedly have endeared it to the Lieutenant-Governor. Muir himself receives a panegyric stretching to almost a page:

> I will describe the praiseworthy man who occupies this position
> The minister of the provinces, the greatest of princes
> Whose honourable name is William Muir
> At a time in our country that is plagued by weaknesses
> A statement on his justice and equity I make
> That would put the era of Anushirvan to shame ...
> ... The dignity of the humble has now so much increased
> That on this earth none are now heavily burdened
> Those customs of oppression are with the stroke of a pen abandoned
> Thus bringing together the paths of the wolves and the sheep.⁷⁹

Anushirvan is the epithet given to the Sasanian king Khusrau I (r. 531–78/9), a monarch famed for his justice, fairness and political reforms.⁸⁰ Sharafuddin's comparison stylises Muir as a strong ruler supported by the rule of law. The eulogy incorporates specific examples of Muir's leadership, crediting him with countering a famine that had afflicted the region:

> It was a year of camelthorn, and famine befell us
> But then rain like silver and gold began to fall
> Such that there was not a single place
> Where the clouds of generosity did not provide rain ...
> ... If there had not been this age of strong government
> Then the situation of our times would have been much worse
> Of the poor, there is now no mention whatsoever
> And the rich are no longer reduced to barley bread.⁸¹

Camelthorn (*javās*) is an invasive species of prickly, thorny plant that thrives in dry and arid soils, causing and perpetuating famine, an image that is featured in early Hindi and Rajasthani poetry. Barley bread (*nān-i javvīn*) was considered inferior to bread made of wheat, a trope that appears in Sa'adi's *Gulistān* (1258), among other texts. Sharafuddin here alludes to Muir's role in developing relief measures in the aftermath of the inadequate British response to the devastating famine in Orissa in 1866. In 1868, the year he took power as Lieutenant-Governor, Muir stated that 'every district officer would be held personally responsible that no deaths occurred from starvation', an announcement that prompted concerted relief mobilisation during the widespread famine of 1869.⁸² (It is worth noting that, despite Muir's announcement, upwards of 1.5 million people are thought to have died in this famine alone.)

Elsewhere, provocatively, Sharafuddin suggests that Indian prosperity under Muir's rule meant that 'each Portia tree (*kavac*) became the envy of the rose garden (*rashk-i gulshan*).'[83] The images here pit a type of flowering hibiscus common in India, also known as the 'Indian tulip', against the garden rose, the archetypal symbol of English beauty, positioning India as a paragon of civilisation and sophistication surpassing even the colonial centre. Sharafuddin's message is clear: Muir's tenure as Lieutenant-Governor has in his opinion heralded a time of unequalled prosperity in the North-Western Provinces, a prosperity encouraged by Muir's purportedly judicious hand and strong leadership. That this message is underpinned by numerous images and tropes from South Asian and, particularly, Indo-Persianate literary antecedents reveals Sharafuddin's attempt to localise Muir's governorship and make his achievements recognisable in literary terms to an educated north Indian audience.

Muir is not the only authority figure to which Sharafuddin refers. In his translation of one of the more famous episodes of Bunyan's *The Pilgrim's Progress* – the persecution of Christian and Faithful at Vanity Fair – Sharafuddin utilises the interactions between his pilgrims and representatives of government to reflect on the central tenets of Christian faith. These are, he demonstrates, not confined to a belief in God, but extend to the practice of good citizenship within society more broadly. Where other translators of *The Pilgrim's Progress* might position the Vanity Fair episode as an affective – and thus effective – instigation for conversion, Sharafuddin's version is oriented towards promoting righteous behaviour and Christian morality.

In Bunyan's *The Pilgrim's Progress*, the incidents at Vanity Fair occur about halfway through the first volume, after the protagonist Christian and his fellow pilgrim Faithful have emerged from the Valley of the Shadow of Death. The two pilgrims are directed to the town of Vanity by Evangelist, who has previously sent both men on their way from the City of Destruction to the Celestial City. Evangelist tells them about Vanity, where, he says, the pilgrims 'will be hard beset with enemies, who will strain hard but that they will kill you'.[84] On their approach to Vanity, the narrator intercedes to introduce the reader to the fair held year-round in the town:

> Almost five thousand years ago, there were pilgrims walking to the Celestial City, as these two honest persons are; and Beelzebub, Apollyon, and Legion, with their companions, perceiving by the path that the pilgrims made that their

way to the city lay through this town of Vanity, they contrived here to set up a fair; a fair, where should be sold *all sorts of vanity*, and that it should last all the year long.[85]

Walking through Vanity Fair, the pilgrims are challenged to purchase 'merchandizes', entailing a range of worldly pleasures. When they refuse, the pilgrims are attacked by the residents of Vanity and dragged before the local Judge. Faithful attracts the disdain of the Judge, and faces trial alone. Three witnesses are called and a jury of twelve men returns a guilty verdict, calling for the execution of the pilgrim. Faithful is 'put to the most cruel death that could be invented' but then Christian and all those around him witness Faithful's soul ascending to heaven on a chariot, to a fanfare of trumpets. Christian himself somehow escapes and continues his journey to the Celestial City.

Sharafuddin's version of this episode follows Bunyan's closely in some respects. The advice the pilgrims receive from Evangelist is, for example, rendered fully, while Sharafuddin's description of the wares of Vanity Fair mirrors Bunyan's, albeit with some more abstract items included. While Sharafuddin removes the reference to 'whores' and 'bawds', for example, he places more emphasis on conceptual entities such as 'pride' and 'affluence'.[86]

The criminal proceedings against Imandar (Faithful) in Sharafuddin's work, by contrast, exhibit more obvious differences from Bunyan's text.[87] The Hakim (the Judge), when concluding the trial, defers not to a jury of twelve men, but instead 'turned his gaze to the people of the gathering (*ahl-i majlis*)', appealing to a more informal arrangement of representatives.[88] Similarly, Imandar's execution – a lengthy affair ending in Bunyan's Faithful being burnt at the stake – takes on a different form in Sharafuddin's text, with the Hakim's appeal to an appointed executioner being overruled by the townspeople:

> And the Hakim said, 'What is your view, all of you?
>   Is his error certain and beyond doubt?'
> All those present then told the judge,
>   'Certainly, he should be killed.'
> The judge gave the executioner his order
>   To come quickly and kill him,
> But hearing this everyone at once
>   Fell to stoning him to death.[89]

More substantial differences between these two episodes point to the rationale undergirding Sharafuddin's translation. Sharafuddin's decision not to include a particular section of the Judge's concluding speech is one of a number of absences or elisions that shift the underlying moral of the Vanity Fair section away from Bunyan's version.

After testimonies from Envy, Superstition and Pickthank, Bunyan's Judge turns to the jury and tells them that 'it lieth now in your breasts to hang him, or save his life: but yet I think meet to instruct you in our law.'[90] What follows is a description of selected historical rulers – Pharaoh, Nebuchadnezzar, Darius – who have cast themselves as both temporal leaders and divine beings. All three, the Judge says, punished with death those 'of a contrary religion' – that is, those who committed idolatry or apostasy by worshipping anyone other than themselves. The Judge here equates these rulers with Beelzebub, and suggests that Faithful has committed a 'treason' worthy of execution by insulting the founder and ruling 'prince' of Vanity, and, by extension, worshipping false gods (that is, the Christian God).

Sharafuddin completely ignores this section in his translation, segueing instead from Imandar's final defence speech to the Hakim's appeal for a verdict from the *majlis*. The absence of the Judge's comments points to Sharafuddin's disinterest in the issue of idolatry or apostasy as it is discussed by Bunyan – that is, of the conflation of temporal and divine leadership and the punishment of those who disobey. His focus, instead, is on matters decidedly more temporal, particularly the corruption of the leadership of the town and the constitution of its legal structure. The connection that Bunyan makes between Beelzebub's temporal and transcendent power, as both 'prince' of Vanity and 'enemy of our Lord', is absent here, with Sharafuddin focused instead on the tangible institutions of civil government that exist without the specific support of the town's 'prince'.

A number of details from the *Baṭlān kā melā* (Vanity Fair) episode speak to this point. Notable among them is Sharafuddin's silence on the constitution of the ruling classes of *Baṭlān kā shahar* (the town of Vanity). Like Bunyan, Sharafuddin notes the role that Balzabul (Beelzebub), Hilako (Apollyon) and Laja'un (Legion) had in erecting Vanity Fair as a way to tempt pilgrims en route to the *Shahar-i āsmānī* (the Heavenly City).[91] Yet this is, in Sharafuddin's work, the only reference made to Balzabul, in contrast to the multiple references that Bunyan makes to Beelzebub as 'prince' or 'lord' of Vanity. In his testimony against Imandar, for instance, Dunya-Saz (Pickthank, literally 'world-deceiver') condemns the abuse Imandar has purportedly directed at the government of *Baṭlān kā shahar*, but at no point mentions Beelzebub:

> The third [witness] was Dunya-Saz
> Who said, 'It's true, your honour!

He said that he doubted our *sulṭān*
  And I heard with my own ears
The abuse that he levelled at you.
  How could he speak in such a way!'
Hearing what these three witnesses had to say,
  The *bādshāh* became enraged.⁹²

The *sulṭān* in this extract is the – unnamed – ruler of Vanity, while the *bādshāh* is an epithet for the Hakim, both of whom, Dunya-Saz claims, Imandar has insulted. In contrast to Bunyan's Faithful, whose criticism is directed both at Beelzebub's rule over the worldly town of Vanity and his attempts to usurp God, Sharafuddin's Imandar – it is claimed – homes in on the terrestrial representatives of the corrupt regime. The testimony of Kinah (Envy, literally 'malice' or 'spite'), meanwhile, critiques Imandar's disrespect not for representatives of government but for the order of civil society in *Baṭlān kā shahar*:

I know that this is that Imandar
  Who is so corrupt and wicked
He is against the rule of our law (*hamārī sharī'at*)
  He is faithless, and he is wayward.⁹³

The idea of the 'law' (*sharī'at*) to which Kinah alludes becomes a central plank of the defence speech that Imandar subsequently makes in response to his detractors. In both cases, the men do not refer to the specifically Islamic concept of *sharī'at*, which denotes the divine law ordained by God and contained in the Qur'an and the Hadith. Instead, *sharī'at* here takes on a broad meaning, alluding to a more general set of principles that define the moral and legal structure of society. While the accusations against him focus on his opposition to the societal status quo of *Baṭlan kā shahar*'s *sharī'at*, Imandar utilises his speech to advocate for another *sharī'at*, pointing to the imbrication of personal belief and the effective functioning of civil society:

I want to respond to these two witnesses
  As in my heart there is intense distress . . .
 . . . Anyone who denies the word of God (*kalām-i khudā*)
  Is undoubtedly an enemy of the Lord (*khudāvand*)
Anyone who does not follow the law (*sharī'at kī taqlīd*)
  Is not a follower of God (*allāh*)
The word of God (*khudā kā kalām*) is the basis of belief
  And opposing this is the work of an infidel (*kāfir*) . . .
 . . . The light of sincere belief in one's heart
  Is the word of God the Merciful (*kalām-i khudā-yi ghufūr*)

> If one works against the word of God (*kalām-i khudā*)
> Then one's belief is defective and incomplete
> Drawing benefit from this is not possible
> And no good can ever come of it.[94]

Bunyan's Faithful also makes a speech in his own defence, but this has a tripartite structure that responds to each of his accusers' criticisms in turn. Sharafuddin's Imandar, by contrast, flattens these finer points of contention into one easily digestible message that consolidates the three lines of Faithful's argument: belief in the word of God is the abiding prerequisite for Christian belief. The accusation of irreligiousness that Imandar levels against the townspeople is couched in their rejection of this central message.

Yet in making this assertion, Imandar binds tightly together the observance of the word of God (*kalām-i khudā* or *khudā kā kalām*) and compliance with the rule of law (*sharī'at kī taqlīd*) in society more generally. It is here that we see a subtle yet fundamental shift in Sharafuddin's work away from Bunyan's text. Bunyan uses this section to assert his opposition to the temporal and transcendental power of Beelzebub as it is exerted in Vanity Fair. Beelzebub is positioned both as an emblematic opponent of the Lord and as a custodian of a town in which the depravities of the mortal world are gathered. Sharafuddin, meanwhile, turns his attention away from the ethereal Balzabul to those officials – the Hakim, the unnamed *sultān* of the town – who represent the rottenness of the ruling classes, who persecute and execute Imandar in part because of his outspoken criticism of them, and who follow a rule of law that suits their own interests – 'our law' (*hamārī sharī'at*), as Kinah succinctly puts it. The *Batlān kā shahar* scene does not elaborate the logic of Christian belief, as in Bunyan, but rather asserts the propriety of certain behaviours, both in one's belief system and in one's participation in civil society. Sharafuddin's concern is with creating not only good Christian believers, but also, by extension, good Christian citizens. It is here that the didacticism for which Muir and others had begun to push can be seen in Sharafuddin's work: his call for compliance with the law still, necessarily, couched in Christianity yet not contained in overly complex theological contexts.

The allusion to different forms of *sharī'at* in Sharafuddin's *Batlān kā melā* has broader ramifications, too. On one level, the dichotomisation of the *sharī'at* to which Kinah refers and that which Imandar mentions in his defence speech suggests that there are 'bad' and 'good' legal codes, the latter of which – if Imandar is to be believed – is that preferred by the Christian God. While Sharafuddin does not imply that this *sharī'at* is mandated directly by God, he hints at the increasingly overt Christian quality of civic institutions, including the law, which echoes the shifts that Muir and others advocated in distancing themselves from the East India Company's 'neutrality policy' in the aftermath of the Indian Rebellion of 1857.

At the same time, the use of the term *sharī'at* reveals one of the principal methods through which Sharafuddin and other translator-authors like him were able to create texts that would resonate with their readership. Terms like *sharī'at* – as well as *taqlīd, allāh* and *kāfir* – all appear in Imandar's defence speech, and all have particular significance within Islam.[95] Similarly, Sharafuddin's references to particular institutions – the *sulṭān*, the *bādshāh*, the *ḥākim*, the *ahl-i majlis* – also allude to specifically Islamicate social structures and histories. These examples suggest that Sharafuddin composed *Qiṣṣah-yi yasū 'ī musāfir* with a specifically Muslim or Muslim-convert audience in mind, drawing, as he does, on linguistic, cultural and religious particularities to render Bunyan's narrative in a way that is more familiar to a local readership. In addition to re-orientating the narrative to better reflect the dominant ideology within circles of missionary publishing, Sharafuddin also used his own familiarity with the north Indian milieu to create a text that would resonate with his local audience. The translator here essentially caters for two readerships simultaneously: a colonial administrator-missionary collective that is pushing for new publications that speak to the devotional needs of Muslim Indian converts, and a local audience who brought with them into their new religious affiliation a particular set of cultural and religious markers.

Conclusion

The survey of translations offered in this article is merely a small cross-section of the dozens of editions produced in the Indian subcontinent across the long nineteenth century; as well as the languages referenced here (Arabic, Bengali, Burmese, Hindi, Oriya, Pashto, Persian and Tamil), we have also found *The Pilgrim's Progress* translated into Kannada, Khasi, Marathi, Panjabi and Sinhala. Despite the linguistic and attendant cultural breadth of these texts, what emerge from the in-depth case studies on Bengali, Hindi and Urdu translations are sets of translation strategies and translation rationales through which particular commonalities can be traced.

These translations strategies are, for the most part, forms of domestication, through which *The Pilgrim's Progress* is rendered according to local literary tastes and conventions. The use of Sanskrit tropes, and terminology evocative of Hindu devotional works, by the anonymous Bengali translator of *Yātriker Gati* (1854), for example, positions *The Pilgrim's Progress* within an existent Bengali literary milieu; in much the same way, Sharafuddin's appeals to Indo-Persianate poetic ideals of kingship in *Qiṣṣah-yi yasūʿī musāfir* (1873) echo not only literary precedents but also expectations of societal praxis in the 'real' world. The incorporation of *bhajan*s by the likes of Parsons in his *Yātra Svapnodaya* (1867), meanwhile, speaks to a set of intersecting priorities: while these *bhajan*s are intended to recreate local Indian practices of recitation and performance that broach the written text and the oral and aural spheres, they also play into broader Christian preoccupations with 'best practice' in the dissemination and affirmation of belief, which made frequent use of the affective power of hymns. The strategies of these translators differ, but they are united in their efforts to produce a *Pilgrim* that is recognisable to its readers and are, as such, not dissimilar from the endeavours of Mary Sherwood in her *Indian Pilgrim* (1818).

Underlying these commonalities of strategy are a set of shifting rationales or aims embedded in these translation projects. As noted previously, early editions of *The Pilgrim's Progress* were produced as an alternative to the Bible, through which missionaries could encourage conversion without the labours – and risks – inherent to the translation of scripture. The works of Parsons, Carey and the anonymous Bengali editor stand out in this regard, emphasising the linear trajectory of the narrative's protagonist from doubter to believer that, it was hoped, readers and listeners would themselves recreate. By contrast, some of the later translations included here break away from this emphasis on proselytisation to stress the place of Christian morality within wider society. Hari and Singh's *Masīhī musāfir kā aḥvāl* (1889) makes explicit mention of its desire to make its readers 'true' Christians, even – and especially – those who have been born and raised as Christians. Sharafuddin, in the same vein, stresses not the theological details of the Vanity Fair episode but its resonance in conceptualisations of statecraft and good governance, and how these should be imbued with Christian norms. This pivot away from proselytisation to practice is reflected in contemporaneous debates within mission circles, which overlapped with the interests of officials within the colonial government.

In this chapter, we have stressed the importance of an emphasis on embedded practices of translation, acculturation, and consumption when discussing a text like *The Pilgrim's Progress*, which has moved – and continues to move – across broad temporal and geographic spaces. The concerns to which these translators responded were often local and, by extension, located in the communities to which these texts were addressed.

John Bunyan in Arabic, Urdu, Hindi and Bengali

But the strategies and rationales that inform these translations echo reworkings of Bunyan's text on a global scale. The annotated English edition (1786) prepared by George Burder offers a clear example: his chapterisation of *The Pilgrim's Progress* to create a 'user-friendly' volume echoes the structures of many of the texts under discussion here, including Sharafuddin's *Qiṣṣah-yi yasū'ī musāfir*; and his interest in hymns, and his inclusion of them in his commentary on Bunyan's text, mirrors the work of Parsons in embedding the text within broader structures of oral and aural affect.[96] This is not to say that these translators were merely engaged in a derivative exercise, emulating precedents set by earlier authors, translators and editors; as we have indicated above, these actors produced innovative and exciting texts that were grounded in their own literary, cultural and religious milieu. Yet it does point to the complex, interwoven histories and genealogies of texts like *The Pilgrim's Progress*, and the potential for further fruitful investigations in the future.

Notes

* We are especially grateful to Marilyn Booth, Claire Savina and Peter Hill for their advice on this chapter. All translations in this chapter are our own, unless otherwise stated.
1. *The Pilgrim's Progress* of John Bunyan (1628–88) was published in two parts, Part 1 in 1678 and Part 2 in 1684.
2. Mr and Mrs James Scarth Gale (trans.), *T'yŏllo Ryŏktyŏng* (Seoul: Trilingual Press, 1895).
3. Isabel Hofmeyr, *The Portable Bunyan: A Transnational History of The Pilgrim's Progress* (Princeton: Princeton University Press, 2004), 25.
4. See Peter Hill, 'Early Translations of English Fiction into Arabic: *The Pilgrim's Progress* and *Robinson Crusoe*', *Journal of Semitic Studies* 60: 1 (2015), 177–212; Laurent Mignon, 'A Pilgrim's Progress: Armenian and Kurdish Literatures in Turkish and the Rewriting of Literary History', *Patterns of Prejudice* 48: 2 (2014), 182–200; Shef Rogers, 'Crusoe Among the Maori: Translation and Colonial Acculturation in Victorian New Zealand', *Book History* 1 (1998), 181–91; and Xiaobai Chu, 'Memories of the Gate: On the Rhetoric in *The Pilgrim's Progress* and Its Chinese Versions', *Religions* 10: 6 (2019), 357.
5. European translation and preaching had an extensive history in south Indian languages, which extends beyond the scope of this work. See, for example, Ines G. Županov, *Missionary Tropics: The Catholic Frontier in India (16th–17th Centuries)* (Ann Arbor: The University of Michigan Press, 2005), 232–58; Ângela Barreto Xavier and Ines G. Županov, *Catholic Orientalism: Portuguese Empire, Indian Knowledge (16th–18th Centuries)* (New Delhi: Oxford University Press, 2015), 202–41; and James Elisha Taneti, *Caste,*

Gender, and Christianity in Colonial India: Telugu Women in Mission (New York: Palgrave Macmillan, 2013).
6. Isabel Rivers, 'The Pilgrim's Progress in the Evangelical Revival', in Michael Davies and W. R. Owens (eds), The Oxford Handbook of John Bunyan (Oxford: Oxford University Press, 2018), 537–54.
7. Lawrence Venuti, The Translator's Invisibility: A History of Translation (Abingdon: Routledge, 2008).
8. Compare Hofmeyr, The Portable Bunyan, 14.
9. See, for example, Javed Majeed, Colonialism and Knowledge in Grierson's Linguistic Survey of India (Abingdon: Routledge, 2019).
10. Christopher R. King, One Language, Two Scripts: The Hindi Movement in Nineteenth Century North India (Bombay: Oxford University Press, 1994); Walter N. Hakala, Negotiating Languages: Urdu, Hindi, and the Definition of Modern South Asia (New York: Columbia University Press, 2016).
11. Barbara D. Metcalf, Islamic Revival in British India: Deoband, 1860–1900 (Princeton: Princeton University Press, 1982), 206–34.
12. Avril A. Powell, 'Creating Christian Community in Early-nineteenth-century Agra', in R. F. Young (ed.), India and the Indianness of Christianity: Essays on Understanding – Historical, Theological, and Bibliographical – in Honour of Robert Eric Frykenberg (Cambridge: William B. Eerdmans, 2009), 82–107; 91–2.
13. Powell, 'Creating Christian Community', 95, 104.
14. Jeffrey Cox, Imperial Fault Lines: Christianity and Colonial Power in India, 1818–1940 (Stanford: Stanford University Press, 2002), 10–16.
15. On the place of The Pilgrim's Progress in relationship to empire, see Hofmeyr, The Portable Bunyan; Sylvia Brown, 'Bunyan and Empire', in Michael Davies and W. R. Owens (eds), The Oxford Handbook of John Bunyan (Oxford: Oxford University Press, 2018), 665–82; Tamsin Spargo, The Writing of John Bunyan (Aldershot: Ashgate, 1997), 22–7; and Isabel Hofmeyr, 'Bunyan: Colonial, Postcolonial', in A. Dunan-Page (ed.), The Cambridge Companion to Bunyan (Cambridge: Cambridge University Press, 2010), 162–76.
16. Julius Richter, A History of Missions in India, trans. Sydney H. Moore (Edinburgh and London: Oliphant Anderson and Ferrier, 1908), 301–2. For an overview of missionary translation projects and publishing societies in this period, see 287–306.
17. Homi Bhabha, The Location of Culture (London: Routledge, 1994), 144.
18. This was S. Sheridan Wilson's Êproodos tou Hristianou apodêmêtou ek tou parontos kosmou mehri tou mellontos. See Hill, 'Early Translations of English Fiction into Arabic', 184.
19. The non-denominational American Board of Commissioners for Foreign Missions.
20. That is, oriented towards the shared principles of appropriate comportment for nobles and gentlemen in the Islamic world.

21. For example, the Persian *Sīyāḥat-i masīḥī az īn jihān bi-jihān-i āyandah* (1883/4) and the Pashto *Sair al-Salikin* (1877).
22. Avril A. Powell, *Muslims and Missionaries in Pre-Mutiny India* (Abingdon: Routledge, 1993); Bhabha, *The Location of Culture*, 148.
23. Richter, *A History of Missions in India*, 131–2. See also Penelope Carson, *The East India Company and Religion, 1698–1858* (Woodbridge: The Boydell Press, 2012).
24. The literature on these issues is vast. For Hindi and Hindustani, see, for example, Vasudha Dalmia, *The Nationalisation of Hindu Traditions: Bharatendu Harischandra and Nineteenth-century Banaras* (Ranikhet: Permanent Black, 2010); on Bengali, see Sudiptu Kaviraj, 'The Two Histories of Literary Culture in Bengal', in S. Pollock (ed.), *Literary Cultures in History: Reconstructions from South Asia* (Berkeley and Los Angeles: University of California Press, 2003), 503–66. Far less work has been conducted on Arabic in South Asia; see Tahera Qutbuddin, 'Arabic in India: A Survey and Classification of Its Uses, Compared with Persian', *Journal of the American Oriental Society* 127: 3 (2007), 315–38.
25. See Stuart H. Blackburn, *Print, Folklore, and Nationalism in Colonial South India* (Delhi: Permanent Black, 2003), 65.
26. For notes on the 1853 translation, see Kamil Zvelebil, *Tamil Literature* (Weisbaden: Otto Harrassowitz, 1974), 161.
27. Mary Martha Sherwood, *The Indian Pilgrim; or, the Progress of the Pilgrim Nazareenee* (Wellington: F. Houlston and Son, 1818), v–vi.
28. Ashok Malhotra, 'Attempting to Transform the Mental Landscape of the Indian "Heathen" in Mary Sherwood's The Indian Pilgrim (1818)', *Literature and Theology* 32: 3 (2018), 270–89.
29. Richter, *A History of Missions in India*, 132–43.
30. The Burmese translation of *The Pilgrim's Progress*, *Kharac'yān' e* vatthu*, was composed by Sarah Boardman Judson (1803–45) and published in 1840 (re-print 1855) by the American Baptist Mission Press.
31. Hofmeyr, *The Portable Bunyan*, 15–16.
32. For example, Augustus Brodhead's *Keśav Rām kī Kathā* (Allahabad: Allahabad Mission Press, 1875).
33. *Annual Report of the Committee of the Baptist Missionary Society for the Year Ending 31 March 1861* (London: The Mission House, 1861), 40.
34. Cited in Leah Price, *How to Do Things with Books in Victorian Britain* (Princeton: Princeton University Press, 2012), 157.
35. As in *Yātriker Gati* (1854) and *Masíhí Musáfir ká Ahwál* (1869).
36. Felix Carey, *Yātrirder Agresaraṇ Bibaraṇ arthāt Ihlokahaite paraloke gamanbibaraṇ* ('Description of a pilgrim's progress, or description of a journey from this world to another world') (Serampore: The Mission Press, 1821), 15.
37. For example, *Markus racīt maṅgal samācār – Gospel of Mark in Hindi-Kaithi* (1851); *Bhaktibodhaka* (1863); *Chand-Saṅgrah* (second edition 1875). See

Timothy Whelan, *Baptist Autographs in the John Rylands University Library of Manchester, 1741–1845* (Macon, GA: Mercer University Press, 2009), 428.
38. *Annual Report of the Committee of the Baptist Missionary Society*, 39–41. See, for example, John Parsons, *Hindustani Choral Book, or, Swar sangrah: Containing the Tunes to those Hymns in the Gīt sangrah which Are in Native Metres* (Benares: Medical Hall Press, 1861).
39. Francesca Orsini, *Print and Pleasure: Popular Literature and Entertaining Fictions in Colonial North India* (Ranikhet: Permanent Black, 2017). For Bengali songbooks in this period, see Richard David Williams, 'Music, Lyrics, and the Bengali Book: Hindustani Musicology in Calcutta, 1818–1905', *Music and Letters* 97: 3 (2016), 465–95.
40. Powell, 'Creating Christian Community', 98.
41. For instance, Mrs J. D. Bate's *North India Tune-Book* (1886) and Mrs Emma More Scott's *Hindustani Tune Book* (1888). See Jeffrey Cox, *Imperial Fault Lines*, 112–13.
42. John Bunyan and N. H. Keele (eds), *The Pilgrim's Progress* (Oxford: Oxford University Press, 1984), 32.
43. John Parsons, *Yātra Svapnodaya* ('Dreaming of a pilgrimage') (Banaras: Medical Hall Press, 1867), 40.
44. Andrew Sterling, *Orissa: Its Geography, Statistics, History, Religion and Antiquities to which is Added History of the Baptist Mission Established in the Province by James Peggs* (London: John Snow, 1846), 222.
45. Cited in Amos Sutton, *A Narrative of the Mission to Orissa (The Site of the Temple of Jugurnath)* (Boston, MA: David Marks, 1833), 103.
46. There was already a long history of public sermonising and homiletics in India – see, for example, Monika Horstmann, 'The Example in Dadupanthi Homiletics', in Francesca Orsini and Katherine Butler Schofield (eds), *Tellings and Texts: Music, Literature and Performance in North India* (Cambridge: Open Book Publishers, 2015), 31–60.
47. Sutton, *Narrative*, 278.
48. *The Baptist Magazine for 1859, Volume LI* (London: Pewtress and Co., 1859), 460; *Annual Report of the Committee of the Baptist Missionary Society*, 39–41.
49. The latter edition was published posthumously; Bowley died in 1843 after nearly thirty years as an Anglican missionary in the town of Chunar. He was born in 1785 to a European soldier and an Indian mother, and attended an orphan school in a village outside Calcutta where the Church Missionary Society (CMS) had set up a 'missionary training school for native Christians'; see P. Gottschalk, *Religion, Science and Empire: Classifying Hinduism and Islam in British India* (New York: Oxford University Press, 2013), 113. For more on Bowley, see also Powell, *Muslims and Missionaries*, 123–31, 146.
50. Buyers's correspondence features frequently in missionary publications – see, for example, *The Evangelical Magazine, and Missionary Chronicle* 15

(London: Thomas Ward and Co., 1837), 95–6 – and a selection of his letters was later collated in a single volume – see William Buyers, *Letters on India: With Special Reference to the Spread of Christianity* (London: John Snow, 1840). For more on Buyers, see Joseph Belcher, *William Carey: A Biography* (Philadelphia: American Baptist Publication Society, 1853), 193.

51. John Hari and Yunis Singh, *Masīhī musāfir kā ahvāl* ('The story of the Christian pilgrim') (Allahabad: Punjab Religious Book Society, 1889), frontispiece.
52. John C. Lowrie, *A Manual of Missions: or, Sketches of the Foreign Missions of the Presbyterian Church* (New York: Anson D. F. Randolph, 1855), 82. For further details on Hari's background see Elwood Morris Wherry, *Our Missions in India, 1834–1924* (Boston, MA: Stratford, 1926), 73. He translated while working with Joseph Warren, the founder of the Presbyterian Mission Press at Allahabad. In 1866, Hari also published a translation of Bunyan's *The Holy War* entitled *Jang-i Muqaddas* that stretched to nearly 350 pages, also at the Allahabad Press; see Augustus Brodhead and John Murdoch (eds), *Conference on Urdu and Hindi Christian Literature, Held at Allahabad, 24th and 25th February, 1875* (Chennai: Christian Vernacular Education Society, 1875), 67, 98.
53. Noting a diminishing quota of missionaries affiliated with the station in Allahabad in the late 1850s, the Reverend E. M. Wherry comments that 'fortunately there were a number of well qualified Indian assistants', including 'Messrs. John Hari [and] Yunas Singh [sic]', who, as 'licentiates, conducted the church services' (Wherry, *Our Missions*, 152). Little else is known about Singh's background.
54. Hari and Singh, *Masīhī*, 1–2.
55. In England, George Burder's 1786 annotated edition was the first to be subdivided into chapters. See Rivers, '*The Pilgrim's Progress* in the Evangelical Revival', 543–4.
56. Brodhead arrived in India in 1858; see 'This Day in Presbyterian History – April 4: Augustus Brodhead'. Available at <http://www.thisday.pcahistory.org /2018/04/april-5-5/> (last accessed 10 September 2018). Brodhead and his wife Emily feature repeatedly in the letters of Rachel Kerr Johnson, who accompanied her husband William Johnson to the North-Western Provinces in 1860. See Barbara Mitchell Tull (ed.), *Affectionately, Rachel: Letters from India, 1860–1884* (Kent, OH; London: Kent State University Press, 1992); this collection of Johnson's letters also contains a photograph taken in Allahabad in 1868 that features the Johnsons, the Brodheads, and other Presbyterian mission families at their annual meeting (242).
57. Brodhead and Murdoch, *Conference*.
58. Sharafuddin 'Isa'i, *Qissah-yi yasū'ī musāfir* ('The tale of the Christian pilgrim') (Allahabad: Presbyterian Mission Press, 1873), frontispiece.
59. Avril A. Powell, *Scottish Orientalists and India: The Muir Brothers, Religion, Education and Empire* (Woodbridge: Boydell and Brewer, 2010).

60. Powell, *Scottish Orientalists*, 93.
61. See Andrew Porter, *Religion Versus Empire? British Protestant Missionaries and Overseas Expansion, 1700–1914* (Manchester: Manchester University Press, 2004); Cox, *Imperial Fault Lines*.
62. Powell, *Scottish Orientalists*, 14–15
63. Powell, *Scottish Orientalists*, 114–16.
64. Powell, *Scottish Orientalists*, 115–16.
65. Brodhead and Murdoch, *Conference*, 12.
66. Brodhead and Murdoch, *Conference*, 30, 15, 7. For more on Valpy, see Vivienne Stacey, 'The Legacy of Thomas Valpy French', *International Bulletin of Missionary Research* (January 1989).
67. C. M. Naim, 'Prize-Winning Adab: A Study of Five Urdu Books Written in Response to the Allahabad Government Gazette Notification', in B. D. Metcalf (ed.), *Moral Conduct and Authority: The Place of Adab in South Asian Islam* (Berkeley: University of California Press, 1984), 290–314; 292–3.
68. Brodhead and Murdoch, *Conference*, 18.
69. Powell, *Scottish Orientalists*, 230.
70. Naim, 'Prize-Winning Adab', 292–3.
71. Brodhead and Murdoch, *Conference*, 7.
72. Brodhead and Murdoch, *Conference*, 8, emphasis in original.
73. Brodhead and Murdoch, *Conference*, 7–8, emphasis in original.
74. Muir had himself engaged with the genre of religious polemics in preceding decades, particularly with the publication of his *Life of Mahomet* (1861).
75. Brown, 'Bunyan and Empire'.
76. See Daniel Jeyaraj, 'Indian Participation in Enabling, Sustaining, and Promoting Christian Mission in India', in R. F. Young (ed.), *India and the Indianness of Christianity: Essays on Understanding – Historical, Theological, and Bibliographical – in Honour of Robert Eric Frykenberg* (Cambridge: William B. Eerdmans, 2009), 26–40; 27; Powell, 'Creating Christian Community'.
77. Sharafuddin, *Qiṣṣah*, 1.
78. Sharafuddin, *Qiṣṣah*, 1.
79. Sharafuddin, *Qiṣṣah*, 1–2.
80. Anushirvan features prominently in Firdausi's epic *Shāhnāmah*, in which his relationship with his vizier, Bozorgmehr, is cited as an example of the necessary balance between king and counsellor. See Fitzwilliam Museum, 'Structure and Themes of the Shahnameh: Myth, Legend and History'. Available at <https://www.fitzmuseum.cam.ac.uk/gallery/shahnameh/structure.html> (last accessed 12 September 2018).
81. Sharafuddin, *Qiṣṣah*, 2.
82. Naresh Chandra Sourabh and Timo Myllyntaus, 'Famines in Late Nineteenth-century India: Politics, Culture and Environmental Justice', Environment and Society Portal Virtual Exhibition 2 (2015). Available at <http://www.envi

ronmentandsociety.org/exhibitions/famines-india> (last accessed 25 March 2018).
83. Sharafuddin, *Qiṣṣah*, 2.
84. Bunyan, *The Pilgrim's Progress*, 111.
85. Bunyan, *The Pilgrim's Progress*, 112, emphasis in original.
86. Sharafuddin, *Qiṣṣah*, 36.
87. Sharafuddin offers a range of terms that are used in Urdu to refer to Jesus, most commonly drawn from Arabic origins: *Yasū'* (as in the title) is the term most commonly used by Arabic-speaking Christians to refer to Jesus; *'Īsā* (as in Sharafuddiin's full name), meanwhile, is the Arabic word used in the Qur'an to refer to Jesus as a prophet in Islam; and, finally, *Masīḥ* (as in the name of Sharafuddin's protagonist), is an epithet meaning 'the anointed one', a cognate of the English word 'Messiah'.
88. The Hakim's full name is Bhala'i ka Dushman (literally, 'enemy of goodness'), reminiscent of Bunyan's Lord Hate-Good.
89. Sharafuddin, *Qiṣṣah*, 38.
90. Bunyan, *The Pilgrim's Progress*, 122.
91. Sharafuddin, *Qiṣṣah*, 36.
92. Sharafuddin, *Qiṣṣah*, 37–8.
93. Sharafuddin, *Qiṣṣah*, 37.
94. Sharafuddin, *Qiṣṣah*, 38.
95. *Sharī'at*, as noted previously, is widely used to refer to the divine law that forms part of the Islamic juridical tradition (alongside *fiqh*, jurisprudence constituted by human scholastic endeavour). *Taqlīd*, literally 'imitation', denotes the adherence to Islamic legal precepts; in Islamic reformist trends in the eighteenth and nineteenth centuries, this came to be contrasted with *ijtihād*, the exercise of independent reason in the development of law. *Allāh* is the word used in Islamic tradition for 'God', although it is also used in the Arabic Christian tradition with the same meaning. *Kāfir* is a term for an 'unbeliever' or an 'infidel'.
96. Rivers, *'The Pilgrim's Progress* in the Evangelical Revival', 550.

Bibliography

Primary Resources

ROMAN SCRIPT

Bowley, William, *'Īsā'ī musāfir* ('The Christian pilgrim') (Allahabad: Presbyterian Mission Press, 1845).
Hari, John, *Masīḥī musāfir kā aḥvāl* ('The story of the Christian pilgrim') (Allahabad: Presbyterian Mission Press, 1853).
Hari, John and Yunis Singh, *Masīḥī musāfir kā aḥvāl* ('The story of the Christian pilgrim') (Ludhiana: Punjab Religious Book Society, 1869).

PERSO-ARABIC SCRIPT

Bowley, William, *Musāfir ka barhnā* ('The progress of the pilgrim') (Ludhiana: American Mission Press, 1840).
Hari, John and Yunis Singh, *Masīhī musāfir kā ahvāl* ('The story of the Christian pilgrim') (Ludhiana: Punjab Religious Book Society, 1880).
Hari, John and Yunis Singh, *Masīhī musāfir kā ahvāl* ('The story of the Christian pilgrim') (Allahabad: Punjab Religious Book Society, 1889).
Sharafuddin 'Isa'i, *Qissah-yi yasū'ī musāfir* ('The tale of the Christian pilgrim') (Allahabad: Presbyterian Mission Press, 1873).

DEVANĀGARĪ SCRIPT

Buyers, William, *Ek Yātrī kī Yātrā kā Vrttānt* ('The story of a pilgrim's pilgrimage') (Calcutta: Baptist Mission Press, 1835).
Parsons, John, *Yātra Svapnodaya* ('Dreaming of a pilgrimage') (Banaras: Medical Hall Press, 1867).

BENGALI SCRIPT

[Anonymous], *Yātriker Gati* ('Pilgrim's way') (Calcutta: Baptist Mission Press, 1854).
Carey, Felix, *Yātrirder Agresaran Bibaran arthāt Ihlokahaite paraloke gamanbibaran* ('Description of a pilgrim's progress, or description of a journey from this world to another world') (Serampore: The Mission Press, 1821).

Secondary Resources

Annual Report of the Committee of the Baptist Missionary Society for the Year Ending 31 March 1861 (London: The Mission House, 1861).
Belcher, Joseph, *William Carey: A Biography* (Philadelphia: American Baptist Publication Society, 1853).
Bhabha, Homi, *The Location of Culture* (London: Routledge, 1994).
Blackburn, Stuart H., *Print, Folklore, and Nationalism in Colonial South India* (Delhi: Permanent Black, 2003).
Brodhead, Augustus, *Keśav Rām kī Kathā* (Allahabad: Allahabad Mission Press, 1875).
Brodhead, Augustus and John Murdoch (eds), *Conference on Urdu and Hindi Christian Literature, Held at Allahabad, 24th and 25th February, 1875* (Chennai: Christian Vernacular Education Society, 1875).
Brown, Sylvia, 'Bunyan and Empire', in Michael Davies and W. R. Owens (eds), *The Oxford Handbook of John Bunyan* (Oxford: Oxford University Press, 2018), 665–82, <https://www.oxfordhandbooks.com/view/10.1093/oxfordhb

/9780199581306.001.0001/oxfordhb-9780199581306-e-39> (last accessed 12 July 2018).

Bunyan, John and N. H. Keele (eds), *The Pilgrim's Progress* (Oxford: Oxford University Press, 1984).

Buyers, William, *Letters on India: With Special Reference to the Spread of Christianity* (London: John Snow, 1840).

Carson, Penelope, *The East India Company and Religion, 1698–1858* (Woodbrige: The Boydell Press, 2012).

Chu, Xiaobai, 'Memories of the Gate: On the Rhetoric in *The Pilgrim's Progress* and Its Chinese Versions', *Religions* 10: 6 (2019): 357.

Cox, Jeffrey, *Imperial Fault Lines: Christianity and Colonial Power in India, 1818–1940* (Stanford: Stanford University Press, 2002).

Dalmia, Vasudha, *The Nationalisation of Hindu Traditions: Bharatendu Harischandra and Nineteenth-century Banaras* (Ranikhet: Permanent Black, 2010).

Fitzwilliam Museum, 'Structure and Themes of the Shahnameh: Myth, Legend and History', <https://www.fitzmuseum.cam.ac.uk/gallery/shahnameh/structure.html> (last accessed 12 September 2018).

'French, Thomas Valpy (1825–1891): Missionary Evangelist, Educator, and Islamicist in India', <http://www.bu.edu/missiology/missionary-biography/e-f/french-thomas-valpy-1825-1891/> (last accessed 11 September 2018).

Gale and Gale, Mr and Mrs James Scarth (trans.), *T'yŏllo Ryŏktyŏng* (Seoul: Trilingual Press, 1895).

Gottschalk, P., *Religion, Science and Empire: Classifying Hinduism and Islam in British India* (New York: Oxford University Press, 2013).

Hakala, Walter N., *Negotiating Languages: Urdu, Hindi, and the Definition of Modern South Asia* (New York: Columbia University Press, 2016).

Hill, Peter, 'Early Translations of English Fiction into Arabic: *The Pilgrim's Progress* and *Robinson Crusoe*', *Journal of Semitic Studies* 60: 1 (2015): 177–212.

Hofmeyr, Isabel, *The Portable Bunyan: A Transnational History of The Pilgrim's Progress* (Princeton: Princeton University Press, 2004).

Hofmeyr, Isabel, 'Bunyan: Colonial, Postcolonial', in A. Dunan-Page (ed.), *The Cambridge Companion to Bunyan* (Cambridge: Cambridge University Press, 2010), 162–76.

Horstmann, Monika, 'The Example in Dadupanthi Homiletics', in Francesca Orsini and Katherine Butler Schofield (eds), *Tellings and Texts: Music, Literature and Performance in North India* (Cambridge: Open Book Publishers, 2015), 31–60.

Jeyaraj, Daniel, 'Indian Participation in Enabling, Sustaining, and Promoting Christian Mission in India', in R. F. Young (ed.), *India and the Indianness of Christianity: Essays on Understanding – Historical, Theological, and Bibliographical – in Honor of Robert Eric Frykenberg* (Cambridge: William B. Eerdmans, 2009), 26–40.

Kaviraj, Sudiptu 'The Two Histories of Literary Culture in Bengal', in S. Pollock (ed.), *Literary Cultures in History: Reconstructions from South Asia* (Berkeley and Los Angeles: University of California Press, 2003), 503–66.

King, Christopher R., *One Language, Two Scripts: The Hindi Movement in Nineteenth Century North India* (Bombay: Oxford University Press, 1994).

Lowrie, John C., *A Manual of Missions: or, Sketches of the Foreign Missions of the Presbyterian Church* (New York: Anson D. F. Randolph, 1855).

Majeed, Javed, *Colonialism and Knowledge in Grierson's Linguistic Survey of India* (Abingdon: Routledge, 2019).

Malhotra, Ashok, 'Attempting to Transform the Mental Landscape of the Indian "Heathen" in Mary Sherwood's The Indian Pilgrim (1818)', *Literature and Theology* 32: 3 (2018): 270–89.

Metcalf, Barbara D., *Islamic Revival in British India: Deoband, 1860–1900* (Princeton, NJ: Princeton University Press, 1982).

Mignon, Laurent, 'A Pilgrim's Progress: Armenian and Kurdish Literatures in Turkish and the Rewriting of Literary History', *Patterns of Prejudice* 48: 2 (2014): 182–200.

Mitchell Tull, Barbara (ed.), *Affectionately, Rachel: Letters from India, 1860–1884* (Kent, OH; London: Kent State University Press, 1992).

Naim, C. M., 'Prize-Winning Adab: A Study of Five Urdu Books Written in Response to the Allahabad Government Gazette Notification', in B. D. Metcalf (ed.), *Moral Conduct and Authority: The Place of Adab in South Asian Islam* (Berkeley: University of California Press, 1984), 290–314.

Orsini, Francesca, *Print and Pleasure: Popular Literature and Entertaining Fictions in Colonial North India* (Ranikhet: Permanent Black, 2017).

Parsons, John, *Hindustani Choral Book, or, Swar sangrah: Containing the Tunes to those Hymns in the Gít sangrah which Are in Native Metres* (Benares: Medical Hall Press, 1861).

Porter, Andrew, *Religion Versus Empire? British Protestant Missionaries and Overseas Expansion, 1700–1914* (Manchester: Manchester University Press, 2004).

Powell, Avril A., *Muslims and Missionaries in Pre-Mutiny India* (Abingdon: Routledge, 1993).

Powell, Avril A., '"Pillar of a New Faith": Christianity in Late-nineteenth-nentury Punjab from the Perspective of a Convert from Islam', in R. E. Frykenberg (ed.), *Christians and Missionaries in India: Cross-cultural Communication since 1500* (London: RoutledgeCurzon, 2003).

Powell, Avril A., 'Creating Christian Community in Early-nineteenth-century Agra', in R. F. Young (ed.), *India and the Indianness of Christianity: Essays on Understanding – Historical, Theological, and Bibliographical – in Honor of Robert Eric Frykenberg* (Cambridge: William B. Eerdmans, 2009), 82–107.

Powell, Avril A., *Scottish Orientalists and India: The Muir Brothers, Religion, Education and Empire* (Woodbridge: Boydell and Brewer, 2010).

Price, Leah, *How to Do Things with Books in Victorian Britain* (Princeton: Princeton University Press, 2012).

Qutbuddin, Tahera, 'Arabic in India: A Survey and Classification of Its Uses, Compared with Persian', *Journal of the American Oriental Society* 127: 3 (2007): 315–38.
Richter, Julius, *A History of Missions in India*, trans. Sydney H. Moore (Edinburgh and London: Oliphant Anderson and Ferrier, 1908).
Rivers, Isabel, *'The Pilgrim's Progress* in the Evangelical Revival', in Michael Davies and W. R. Owens (eds), *The Oxford Handbook of John Bunyan* (Oxford: Oxford University Press, 2018), 537–54.
Rogers, Shef, 'Crusoe Among the Maori: Translation and Colonial Acculturation in Victorian New Zealand', *Book History* 1 (1998): 181–91.
Sherwood, Mary Martha, *The Indian Pilgrim; or, the Progress of the Pilgrim Nazareenee* (Wellington: F. Houlston and Son, 1818).
Sourabh, Naresh Chandra and Timo Myllyntaus, 'Famines in Late Nineteenth-century India: Politics, Culture and Environmental Justice', Environment and Society Portal Virtual Exhibition 2 (2015), <http://www.environmentandsociety.org/exhibitions/famines-india> (last accessed 25 March 2018).
Spargo, Tamsin, *The Writing of John Bunyan* (Aldershot: Ashgate, 1997).
Stacey, Vivienne, 'The Legacy of Thomas Valpy French', *International Bulletin of Missionary Research* (January 1989): 22–7.
Sterling, Andrew, *Orissa: Its Geography, Statistics, History, Religion and Antiquities to which is Added History of the Baptist Mission Established in the Province by James Peggs* (London: John Snow, 1846).
Sutton, Amos, *A Narrative of the Mission to Orissa (The Site of the Temple of Jugurnath)* (Boston, MA: David Marks, 1833).
Taneti, James Elisha, *Caste, Gender, and Christianity in Colonial India: Telugu Women in Mission* (New York: Palgrave Macmillan, 2013).
The Baptist Magazine for 1859, Volume LI (London: Pewtress and Co., 1859)
The Evangelical Magazine, and Missionary Chronicle 15 (London: Thomas Ward and Co., 1837).
'This Day in Presbyterian History – April 4: Augustus Brodhead', <http://www.thisday.pcahistory.org /2018/04/april-5-5/> (last accessed 10 September 2018).
Venuti, Lawrence, *The Translator's Invisibility: A History of Translation* (Abingdon: Routledge, 2008).
Whelan, Timothy, *Baptist Autographs in the John Rylands University Library of Manchester, 1741–1845* (Macon, GA: Mercer University Press, 2009).
Wherry, Elwood Morris, *Our Missions in India, 1834–1924* (Boston, MA: Stratford, 1926).
Williams, Richard David, 'Music, Lyrics, and the Bengali Book: Hindustani Musicology in Calcutta, 1818–1905', *Music and Letters* 97: 3 (2016): 465–95.
Xavier, Ângela Barreto and Ines G. Županov, *Catholic Orientalism: Portuguese Empire, Indian Knowledge (16th–18th Centuries)* (New Delhi: Oxford University Press, 2015).
Young, R. F., 'Holy Orders: Nehemiah Goreh's Ordination Ordeal and the Problem

of "Social Distance" in Nineteenth-century North Indian Anglicanism', *Church History and Religious Culture* 90: 1 (2010): 69–88.

Županov, Ines G., *Missionary Tropics: The Catholic Frontier in India (16th–17th Centuries)* (Ann Arbor: The University of Michigan Press, 2005).

Zvelebil, Kamil, *Tamil Literature* (Weisbaden: Otto Harrassowitz, 1974).

Chapter 2

'Pour Our Treasures into Foreign Laps': The Translation of *Othello* into Arabic and Ottoman Turkish

Hannah Scott Deuchar and Bridget Gill

In the more than 400 years since it was first performed in 1604, Shakespeare's *Othello* has been translated into French over thirteen times and into German over thirty, as well as into dozens of other languages. This Shakespeare success story seems part of a familiar narrative of English language and literature's rise to global dominance, beginning in the colonial period and reaching new heights in an Anglo-centric world literary market.[1] Yet a closer look at *Othello*'s translation history also recalls the historic limits of English's cultural power. The tragedy of the 'jealous Moor' was itself, after all, based on an existing Italian text by Giovanni Batistia Giraldi Cinthio, *Un Capitano Moro* (1565). And while Shakespeare's new title would endure through future translations, many aspects of his narrative would not. In fact, by the time *Othello* arrived in Istanbul and Cairo in the late nineteenth century, some aspects of the play were almost unrecognisable. Seemingly the first Shakespeare play translated into both languages, *Othello* was rewritten as the tragedy not of a Moorish but of an Arab hero – the first of several ways in which the English text was recast to serve new political agendas, religious norms and aesthetic tastes.[2] Written in a period during which the relationship between the Empire and its Arab provinces was reconfigured, partly in response to British and French colonial activity, the new *Othello*s provide a case study through which to examine the interconnected imperial, racial and literary hierarchies of the period, and the ways in which literary translations worked to reproduce or to complicate them.

The Ottoman Turkish translation, titled *Otâlo*, was published in Istanbul in 1876. This was the beginning of the short-lived First Constitutional Era following the dethroning of Sultan Abdülaziz, and the run-up to the 1877–8 Russo-Ottoman War. The deposing of the sultan had followed a period of power struggles between the powerful bureaucracy of the Sublime Porte and the royal court; the former ruler was replaced by his nephew Murad V, who was succeeded almost immediately by his brother, Abdülhamid II (r. 1876–1909). The latter had promised to promulgate the constitution proposed by the group of reformists known as the Young Ottomans, but in fact, the first parliament was discontinued by late 1877, after less than a year.[3] The first Arabic translation of *Othello*, meanwhile, would not appear until 1899, and it was published in Cairo, which was then largely out of the Ottoman Empire's hands. The Anglo-Egyptian occupation of Sudan had begun the same year, and Egypt itself, largely autonomous from the Ottomans for most of the nineteenth century, was effectively under British rule. By the time the Arabic *Othello* was published, discontent with the British was on the rise, and a nascent pan-Arab and Egyptian nationalist movement was emerging.[4]

The Turkish and Arabic versions of *Othello* were produced therefore at highly significant junctures in Ottoman and Egyptian political history. Their translators were interpreting a text written in the language of an aggressive imperial power, and a narrative driven by questions of ethnicity and imperial war. Historians of translation, from Lawrence Venuti onwards, emphasise that even the closest and most 'accurate' translations of literary texts are interpretative works whose semantic choices can reveal as much about the cultural and political milieu of the translator as they do about the original text itself.[5] As such, one might expect a comparative reading of these *Othello* translations to produce insights into Ottoman versus Egyptian perspectives on, for instance, past Ottoman–European relations; on ethnicity and skin colour; on tragedy as a genre, or on England as a cultural power. However, the ad hoc nature of nineteenth-century translation, in which translations were frequently pseudo- or relay translations, and in which scant respect for authorial ownership led to misattribution and what would now be considered plagiarism, complicates such expectations.[6]

In fact, the similarities and differences between the final translations and their respective translation histories point to a larger story, that of the still-entangled cultural spheres of Istanbul and Cairo in the late nineteenth century, and of a shared literary marketplace deeply structured by both older imperial, and newer colonial, cultural hierarchies. To read the translations together is thus necessarily to offer alternatives to the binaries of (indigenous) originality versus (European) influence that have in the past dominated in Middle Eastern literary and translation studies.[7] In recent years we have witnessed repeated calls for comparative historical studies of colonies and empires. Such appeals emphasise the ways in which parallels and divergences between the histories of colonised territories or colonial powers serve to complicate traditional narratives of, for instance, metropole and colony, and point to the comparatist inclinations of imperialism and colonialism themselves.[8] Historians of the Middle East have particularly stressed the importance of resisting nationalist historiographic trends in Arab and Turkish history to produce work that takes into consideration the Ottoman history of Arab nations, and the place of the Ottoman Empire with regards to other imperial powers.[9] As a result, historical studies of the late Ottoman period use both Ottoman Turkish and Arabic sources, and ask how the entangled histories of what are today separate national territories complicate understandings of, among other things, imperialism and nationhood.

However, there remains as yet remarkably little work comparing Arabic and Ottoman Turkish literatures, and indeed Middle Eastern literatures in general. This is partly because of a Eurocentrism that privileges comparing Middle Eastern 'peripheral' texts with the European literature of the metropole.[10] The comparative history of Middle Eastern literary translations offers a useful point of departure, providing a way to place non-European texts and the relationships between them at the centre of the study, while also acknowledging the context of global imperialism in which they have operated. A recent, collectively written article by Margaret Litvin, Abraham Oz and Parvaz Partovi, 'Middle Eastern Shakespeares', does in fact begin this process, providing a useful overview of the many translations of Shakespeare into Persian, Armenian, Arabic and Turkish, and highlighting the importance of relay, indirect and pseudo-translation in the reception of Shakespearean texts.[11] However, it does not engage in close or comparative readings of the texts.

In this chapter, we also address our texts firstly as artefacts, asking how their respective translation histories can illuminate the material aspects of translation in the Middle East in this period. However, we also read closely within and across the texts themselves, attending particularly to their respective alterations to the linguistic style and form of their source texts. Perhaps unsurprisingly, the changes made in each text are of different kinds, each responding to different literary pressures and tastes. However, certain similarities also point to common anxieties about the connections between language, nation and empire in the era of European colonial conquest. We focus in particular on the ways in which both texts choose to present their titular character, Othello, as an 'Arab hero'. Their contrasting interpretations of this shared notion indicate the divergent conversations about 'heritage' and – or versus – 'modernity' unfolding in literary and theatrical spheres in British Egypt and Ottoman Turkey.

Both translations prove to be deeply shaped firstly by the language politics of each city, where early Arabic and Turkish language reform unfolded against a cultural and educational context in which English, French and Italian also vied for superiority: choices regarding authorial attribution, linguistic style, and even the naming of characters can be read as interventions into the language debates of the day. The texts also respond to, and participate in, emergent discussions about national and imperial identity, exploiting and transforming the notions of race and personhood found in their source texts to produce distinct understandings of terms like 'citizen', 'subject' and 'nation'. A comparative reading of both texts produces insights about the connections and divergences of the Arabic and Ottoman Turkish cultural spheres, but it also reveals that the translators were themselves working comparatively, to a certain extent. Rather than re-enacting the politics and perspectives of the European source texts, these translations provide stages on which to perform the categories of, and relationships between, 'Ottomans', 'Arabs' and 'Europeans'.

Relay Translation: Shakespeare in Europe

A closer look at the paratextual material of these translations offers an immediate reminder of the complex networks of textual production in this period, and the tenuous authority of authorship within these networks. The Ottoman text, for instance, is a relay translation, based on a French rather than an English 'original'. Produced by prolific translators Manastırlı Mehmet Rifat Paşa (1850–1907) and Hasan Bedreddin (1851–1912), it was published as part of the *Temaşa* (*Spectacle*) series, which published an extensive number of translations of, primarily, French, eighteenth- and nineteenth-century plays. Among other things, Rifat Paşa and Bedreddin also translated Alexandre Dumas' *Antony* in 1875, as part of the same series.[12] On the title page of their *Otâlo*, a short translators' introduction explains that the play was originally by the French author Ducis, who translated it from an Italian opera to turn it into a tragedy. Shakespeare, and the English language, have been completely erased from the play's provenance.[13] By contrast, the front page of the Arabic bears no reference to translation, presenting the author directly as 'Shakespeare, the English writer', as if he had produced the play in Arabic himself, and positively insisting that the provenance of its original is English.[14] Within the Arabic play, somewhat confusingly, the Italian names of the characters have either been Arabised or Gallicised.[15]

Simply as artefacts, therefore, these texts are a reminder that translation's intervention into the circulation of ideas, so far from being simple transmission, entailed relay, delay and sometimes complete transformation. The status of the Ottoman and Arabic *Othellos*, as a relay translation

Translation of Othello into Arabic and Ottoman Turkish

and a translation of uncertain origin respectively, indicates the complicated process by which a 'European' text might make its way into 'Middle Eastern' languages. In the late nineteenth century, France and England competed for cultural and political dominance in the Middle East as much as they aligned in their attempts to control it, and the struggle leaves traces here, in the ways in which the translators seek to mobilise the cultural capital accruing to different European languages.

The Ottoman text arguably bears witness to the relative unimportance of English in 1870s Ottoman Turkey, before it came to usurp French as a global hegemonic language. As noted above, the play is described as the translation of a tragedy by Ducis, itself based on an Italian opera. This might, of course, be an honest mistake: *Othello* had by this time been made into two operas, one by Rossini and one by Verdi, and French author Jean-Francois Ducis' 1794 translation of *Othello* was the text on which Rossini's libretto was based. Since the history of opera in Istanbul dates back to the seventeenth century, and the city by this time had more than one opera house, one might speculate that translators had heard, or heard of, the opera first, been inspired by the opera to seek out the play, and as such never encountered Shakespeare as part of the chain of transmission.[16] However, even the earliest editions of Ducis' text include their own preface, which clearly identifies the original author as Shakespeare; it seems unlikely that the Ottoman translators could not know.[17]

Their representation of the play as French tragedy and Italian opera therefore reads rather as an affirmation of the comparatively greater cultural capital of Italian and French in the Ottoman Empire in this period. 'Donizetti Paşa' had been adopted by Ottoman Istanbul, while French literature was translated into Ottoman far more than English literature was: Johann Strauss notes that ever since the Tanzimat era, changes to elite education (among many other things) had meant that 'in a way reminiscent of English in the contemporary world, French was almost omnipresent in the Ottoman lands'.[18] France had been working for some measure of control over Ottoman North African provinces since 1830, and also maintained a strong French presence beyond the borders of the Ottoman Empire. In Egypt, for instance, which in the 1870s was yet to come under British control, French had for some time been a second language among the elites; in fact, it would remain so for several decades following the 1882 British occupation, even as English also became increasingly prominent.[19]

It is worth noting, however, that Ducis' text, so far as it can be considered an emissary of French language and literature, is an idiosyncratic one. The author himself was strongly associated with the burgeoning Romantic

73

movement and in particular with Orientalists such as Chateaubriand, a personal friend; his own work, however, was considered somewhat popular and lowbrow.[20] He completed his prolific translations of Shakespeare without ever learning English, and Byron famously derided the Rossini libretto based on his *Othello* as mere drama, guilty of '*crucifying* "Othello" into an opera'.[21] On another level, the translation's publication date, 1794, and its dedication to Ducis' brother, a slave-owner in St Domingue, are reminders that the French text was embroiled in a very particular history, that of the reorganisation of French society after the 1789 revolution. When the text reached Ottoman translators the story of Othello had already been refracted through Ducis' own concerns with revolutionary republicanism and the so-called 'Mulatto' question in post-revolutionary France.[22] The ways in which Ducis' text's lowbrow status and political leanings are transformed in its Ottoman translation are elaborated below, but the very fact of their significant departure from the Shakespearean *Othello* points to the fragility of concepts like 'originality' and 'authorship' in the context of global eighteenth- and nineteenth-century translation.

The Arabic *Othello*, meanwhile, is testament to the slightly different set of cultural and linguistic hierarchies in place in British-ruled Egypt twenty years later, at the end of the nineteenth century. Although in Istanbul literary translation, now under heavier censorship, was still largely from French texts, in Egypt an interest in, and increase in translation from, English works had emerged since the British occupation of 1882.[23] The Arabic translation of *Othello*, subtitled *Ḥiyal al-rijāl* ('The wiles of men') was first printed and published anonymously in 1899, but was translated a few years before to be performed in Arabic: reports exist of several performances of the play in Cairo from 1884 onwards, making *Othello* also the first Shakespeare play to be translated and performed in Arabic.[24] Although earlier translations may have been different, this appears to be the earliest printed and published version, or at least the earliest surviving one. As noted, the translator's name is elided from the edition, but Litvin, Oz and Partovi cite it as Ṭānyūs 'Abdū (1869–1926), who translated *Hamlet* from Alexandre Dumas' version.[25]

Lack of certainty regarding the translator makes the source text difficult to identify. The significant Arabising changes carried out in the Arabic text, discussed further below, include the truncation of speeches and scenes, the Arabisation of names, and the addition of songs and classical poetry, and further obscure the 'original' source. The Arabic play is still structurally quite close to the English, and in some cases lines are similar enough to the English original to concur with the title page's implication that it is, if not written directly by Shakespeare, at least a direct translation from the English.[26] At the same time, if the translator were Ṭānyūs ʿAbdū, it seems not unlikely that he might use a French source, as he had done for his *Hamlet*. By 1899 there existed several French translations of *Othello*, including a prose translation by Victor Hugo produced in 1868 that is close enough to the English to make it an equally likely source text; Victor Hugo was also particularly widely translated into Arabic in this period.

In any case, the Arabic translator apparently chose to elide the presence not only of a possible French source text but of any translator, in order to claim *Othello* decisively as the work of an English author. Almost twenty years after the British began their effective rule in Egypt – and twenty years before the 1919 Egyptian revolution against the British – there was, then, some cultural capital accruing to English literature; but French's hold as the primary European language of the educated had not necessarily been lost. The question of the Arabic *Othello*'s origins becomes complicated further, for instance, when one turns attention to the character names in the Arabic text. Within the text, the name of Othello is Arabised further to ʿUṭayl, and the same is true for other key characters: Desdemona becomes Damūna, Iago Yaʿqūb (in this period commonly, but by no means always, a Jewish name), Cassio Quṣayy and Bianca Suʿda. Such Arabisation was a fairly common practice at the time, but combined with the failure to mention explicitly that the text was translated it serves to present the final text as a strange Arabic–English hybrid, of unclear origins. Additionally, the remaining names are Gallicised – despite the fact that in the possible French source text by Hugo, they are left in their original Italian form. The decision to introduce French into the text here, having erased it elsewhere, must therefore be that of the Arabic translator. There were in this period large communities of Italians living in Cairo, so Italian names would not be particularly unfamiliar to the audience; to retain Italian names would also serve to explain why the action of the play takes place in Venice. As such, the choice to Gallicise could be read as evidence of the enduring cultural power of French as the signifier of European literature writ large. It ultimately serves to strengthen an impression of confused origins in the text – preserving, in fact, the convoluted circumstances of its translation.

The points of difference and similarity in these two translation histories are intriguing. Both texts are relay translations, produced from French source texts of different periods. The cultural importance of opera in Istanbul, as already suggested, potentially explains the Ottoman translators' choice of Ducis' text as a source. Opera had by this time, Adam Mestyan argues, taken root in Cairo, mostly famously with the commission of Verdi's *Aida*, set in Egypt and performed there at the Khedivial Opera House in 1871. It was, according to Mestyan, key to 'the return of Egypt's Ottoman attachment in public texts', and provided a platform for, effectively, the public petitioning of the Khedive.[27] The extent to which the Arabic *Othello* can be seen as demonstrative of 'Egypt's Ottoman attachment' is discussed later in this chapter, but it is worth noting that Mestyan's own definition of 'attachment' is rather expansive, as is his definition of 'opera', the latter apparently encompassing all the musical theatre performed in the Opera House. Much of this theatre in fact consisted of original Arabic plays, but there were also dramatisations of French texts such as, in 1882, *Télémaque*.[28] Prolifically translated and popular across the board, meanwhile, were texts by nineteenth-century French Romantics like Dumas and Vigny – hence, perhaps, the Arabic translator's choice of a source text.

The differing status of opera and theatre as art forms in Istanbul and Cairo seemingly led to the translators of *Othello* in each city working, quite by chance, from French source texts of different periods, with entirely different politics. These translators' choices stand as a reminder of the stilted and even haphazard way in which 'European' cultural concepts and forms actually circulated in this period. The different linguistic and literary hierarchies in place in each context also, we have suggested, led the Ottoman and Arab translators to obfuscate the origins of their text, in the first case mobilising the play's translation history in Italian and French to obscure its humble English origins, and in the second claiming a greater proximity to the English source than was the case, while Arabising much of the content and retaining a French connection.

Style and Substance: Language Politics in Translation

Kamran Rastegar, in one of the few existing studies to compare modern Arabic and Persian literary production, uses Bourdieusian notions of capital and the literary field to argue that Arabic and Persian writers of this period, far from being 'influenced' by or 'imitating' European literatures, engaged in 'textual transactions', skilfully manipulating the perceived value of their intertexts to accrue cultural capital to their own work.[29] Rastegar does not address dramatic texts, and focuses primarily on 'original' rather than translated material; he also tends to flatten the notion of the 'European' intertext, not discussing the ways in which author-translators might play off the value of differently European intertexts or source texts against one another, or how this might map onto their respective imperial contexts. However, the evidence of the texts above certainly suggests that Ottoman and Arabic translators were navigating a complex cultural and linguistic economy, connected but not reducible to broader political questions; and turning to the form and content of the translations themselves, this impression only increases.

Both sets of translators make significant changes to the style and form of their respective source texts, but along different, even opposite, lines. The Ottoman text, though constructed as a script, was not during this period performed on stage. According to Litvin, Oz and Partovi, a version of *Othello* was performed within the Empire in Armenian by an Armenian theatre troupe in the 1840s, but there is no record of another performance of the play prior to the twentieth century.[30] Like other texts from the *Temaşa* series of which it was a part, the script's linguistic style recalls the new norms of Turkish journalistic and literary prose – namely, of texts designed for an emergent and expanding reading public. By contrast, the Arabic script is imbued with the conventions of contemporaneous popular theatre, such as the addition of poetry and songs; as such it is structurally as well as linguistically very different from both Shakespeare's original text and Hugo's translation. In both cases, the texts attest to translators' attempts to navigate the shifting literary norms of their respective multilingual environments. Read together, they shed light on the ways in which notions of national language and culture manifested in Istanbul, at the centre of the Ottoman Empire, and in Cairo, capital of a post-Ottoman province and recent British colonial acquisition.

In the case of the Ottoman play, it is important first to disentangle which of the text's non-Shakespearean formal features appear to be the work of the French translator Ducis, whose alterations to Shakespeare's text were, as has been noted already, extensive. Ducis sought to render *Othello* a tragedy in the strict, neoclassical French sense of the word. In his translation, the plot is constricted in obedience to the 'three unities' of time, place and action that structured French classical drama. Cyprus is erased from the play's setting, which is restricted to Venice, while a number of events are cut so that the action might conceivably take place in a single day.[31] Seemingly for the sake of simplification, all mention of Ottomans or Turks (the enemy vanquished by Othello in the war between Venice and Constantinople that provides the background action of the play) is erased. Ducis even changed the ending of the play. Ducis' *Othello* was published in Paris in the second year of the French Republic, 1794, but as its title page attests, it had in fact been performed for the first time just over a year beforehand, in November 1792.[32] Since that first performance, Ducis had altered his own text for publication and for future performances, a decision he explains at some length in a three-page *Avertissement*. In 1892, he says, he had produced a play that followed Shakespeare's structure and tragic ending, in which both Othello and Desdemona are killed. However, the English tragedy proved too much for Paris: the sensibilities of his French audiences were, the playwright claims, so offended by the vulgarity of the original ending that he was forced to rewrite it with a happier conclusion.[33]

In the Ottoman text, too, therefore, the protagonists' lives are spared – and in general, in terms of content, the Ottoman translators prove far more faithful to Ducis than he was to Shakespeare. The major change they make is to his style. Shakespeare plays in English were rendered mainly in iambic pentameter, largely unrhymed save for occasional rhyming couplets; in *Othello*, however, there also appear speeches in plain prose.[34] The possibility of multiple variations to pentameter's rhythm meant that texts could be rendered both recognisably 'poetic' and seemingly 'natural'.[35] Ducis transformed Shakespeare's prose into its less malleable French 'equivalent', the alexandrine or *tétramètre*: twelve-syllable lines in rhyming couplets, with a strict two-hemistich rhythmic structure.[36] No attempt is made in the Ottoman text to transform it into a classical Ottoman poetic equivalent; instead, the alexandrine vanishes, and the French dialogues are transformed into a prose that, even more than in the English, seems designed to recall natural conversation.

For instance, when Othello describes to Odalbert (Brabantio) his first encounter with Hédelmone (Desdemona), the French text reads: 'Un jour, jour trop fatal! (souffrez que je poursuive) / Dans un long entretien, à sa pitié naïve / J'offris tout le tableau des maux que j'ai soufferts.' Or: 'One day, one fatal day! (Let me go on) / We talked long, and to her simple compassion / I offered up [all] the evils I'd endured.'[37] The Ottoman, however, reads: '... Ah bir gün ... bir dehşetli gün idi ki Hedelmon ile yalnız olarak uzunca musahebe ettik. Rugerdan gördüğüm eza ve cefalari bir bir hikaye ettim.' Or: '... Ah, one day ... one astonishing day, when Hedélmone and I, [finding ourselves] alone, talked for a long time. Seeing [her] turning face, I told a story of torture and punishment.'[38] This translation is characteristic of the text in that, as can be seen, it is distinctly oral in style. Not only are the strict rhythm and rhyme of the French entirely erased, but the sentences are shortened, and their import stripped of figurative language ('tout le tableau') and literalised. The ellipses, used to express the pauses produced by emotion on the part of the speaker, are the first of seven introduced into a speech where the French contains only one. All these features recall the new, purportedly 'simple' Ottoman prose called for in the reformist journals of the period; and which they themselves often failed to produce, certainly to the extent achieved here and indeed in the other plays rendered by this pair of translators.[39]

Translation of Othello into Arabic and Ottoman Turkish

It is well known that Shakespeare's writings played a significant role in the rise of vernacular English literature both nationally and internationally.[40] Here, the transformation of poetic French Shakespeare into a more 'oral' style than the English original reads as part of the process of vernacularisation and, specifically, phoneticisation of Turkish that Nergis Ertürk has argued took place throughout the nineteenth and early twentieth centuries.[41] According to Ertürk, this alienating process should be read in terms of an emergent Turkish ethno-nationalism, and a modernity '[h]aunted doubly by the external difference of an encroaching Europe and by the internal difference of atrophied and mortified Ottoman imperial multilingualism'.[42] Certainly, arguments that read Ottoman Turkish literary and linguistic change in terms of European 'influence' or 'imitation' seem inadequate in the face of an Ottoman Turkish translation whose proto-nationalist commitment to a more spoken style leads it to shatter the weighty stylistic conventions of the French play it translates. At the same time, its focus on an Arab hero might also betray an enduring commitment to a multi-ethnic, multilingual Ottoman Empire. Ertürk's work engages the novel as a literary mode that, against and within phonocentric language reform, might 'harbour the possibility of another order of things'. To judge by the Ottoman *Othello*, a study of linguistic style in late Ottoman theatre might add valuable insight to understandings of Ottoman linguistic and literary change.

Ziad Fahmy and, differently, Adam Mestyan have emphasised the importance of Arab theatre and opera to changes to the Arabic language in the nineteenth and early twentieth centuries, and in particular to the manifestation of Egyptian nationalism.[43] The notion that classical written Arabic, known as *fuṣḥā* and differing considerably from the many oral dialects of the Arabic-speaking world, required an active process of reform had been posited since at least the 1830s.[44] By 1899, the 'simplification' and 'modernisation' of Arabic via various strategies – from the incorporation of European terms into Arabic to the abandonment of classical stylistic processes such as rhymed prose or *sajʿ* – was a process debated, advocated and increasingly carried out in the literary press.[45] Mestyan, indeed, goes so far as to suggest that *fuṣḥā* as an object was created in the nineteenth century as simultaneously a bearer of history and a herald of modernity. He sees this as contributing primarily to the 'Egyptian Ottoman patriotism' he considers a feature of the period, but the capacity of *fuṣḥā* to forge a shared history for Arabic speakers across older and emerging imperial borders surely made it an equally key motor in the nascent pan-Arabism of the late nineteenth century.[46] The 1890s also saw the emergence of a second linguistic debate in Egypt: the question of adopting Egyptian dialect as a written and even literary language, or of incorporating it into the existing literary language, was newly on the table. Mestyan has argued that *fuṣḥā* was by the 1870s established as the language of the theatre, and certainly in the 1890s the vernacular had been by no means embraced by the literary establishment.[47] However, Fahmy offers compelling evidence of the presence of a strong tradition of vernacular comedic and vaudeville theatre throughout the late nineteenth century, and the importance of these (often Syrian) theatre troupes to the emergent Egyptian nationalism of the period.[48]

It is this complex linguistic environment that the Arabic *Othello* would have to navigate; that it succeeded well enough for multiple performances makes it an interesting case study of the language politics of the time. Although the plot remains in broad terms similar to that of the English text, the Arabic is considerably shortened and condensed, with minor characters such as attendants and clowns eliminated. Long scenes are also broken up into shorter ones, though the breaks between acts tend to fall in roughly the same place. The elimination of characters and scenes deemed extraneous causes some of the dialogue and speeches by two different characters to be spliced together, or if originally spoken by one character, to occur together rather than several lines apart, so the pacing is somewhat altered.[49]

The text is largely produced in prose *fuṣḥā*, but the orthography is not strict. Colloquial variations are added to some verb conjunctions, for instance with the addition of a *yā* to the end of a past second-person feminine singular past-tense verb, instead of just a *kasra* (short vowel), so that the word is written in accordance with the norms of colloquial pronunciation rather than the formal rules of grammar. Beyond the use of prose, the phrasing also tends towards the conversational, much like the Ottoman: for instance, in the first encounter between Brabantio and Othello, the English runs as follows:

Brabantio: O foul thief, where hast thou stowed my daughter?
Damned as thou art, thou hast enchanted her:
For I'll refer to me all things of sense
If she in chains of magic were not bound,
Whether a maiden so tender, fair, and happy,
So opposite to marriage that she shunned
The wealthy curled darlings of our nation
Would ever have, t'incur a general mock,
Run from her guardage to the sooty bosom
Of such a thing as thou.[50]

The Arabic, however, significantly truncates the speech, producing the snappier: 'Ikhsa' ya nadhl al-rijāl ya sābī rabāt al-ḥajāl ayna ibnatī allatī ikhtaṭafatahā kayfa aqbal an takūna ibnatī ḥalīlat li-wajhak al-shanī'' ('Away, vilest of men, enchanter of women; where is my daughter whom you have kidnapped? How can I accept that my daughter be wed to your hideous face?')[51] Here and throughout the text, sentence structures are thus significantly simplified, and the pentameter transformed into prose.[52]

Unlike in the Ottoman text, however, verse and rhythm have not been abandoned, but are replaced with an alternative pattern. The internal rhyme of the phrase above, *ya nadhl al-rijāl ya sābī rabāt al-hajāl*, recalls the *saj'* that characterised much pre-nineteenth-century Arabic prose, and such short partially rhymed sections re-occur throughout the play, often as here in particularly emotive or dramatic passages.[53] Further, and as noted already, an important aspect of the Egyptian theatre scene at the time was the inclusion of frequent songs, poetry and music, most often written as rhyming *abyāt* in a classical *qaṣīda* metre. Several of these are included in the Arabic play, typically occurring at the end of scenes and between acts, as well as at momentous occasions.[54] While the rest of the translation stays fairly close in to the French or English source, these additions are typically entirely original, and tend like the *saj'* to adhere to the standards of classical Arabic poetry and song rather than to the 'new' and occasionally colloquial *fuṣḥā* characterising the rest of the play.[55]

Also added is a chorus, named in the script *al-jamī'*, which performs the aforementioned songs and musical interludes as well as fulfilling the function of a crowd, voicing interjections such as 'God forbid!' at key moments.[56] Such an addition was a commonplace in the Arabic popular theatre developed in the nineteenth century largely by Syrian theatrical troupes; local translators, playwrights, impresarios and commentators believed this would make plays more 'Eastern' and as such more palatable to Egyptian audiences.[57] They also served to render the place of theatre in existing literary hierarchies ambiguous. On the one hand, the inclusion of songs and musical interludes would seemingly act to lower a tragedy like *Othello* to the status of popular entertainment; on the other, and as noted already, the same songs and verses recalled Arabic's venerable classical literary heritage through their recourse to the attributes of both Arabic classical poetry and classical prose, such as the metre of the *qaṣīda* or ode and the rhymed prose of Arabic *adab* or belles-lettres.

The key stylistic similarity between the Ottoman and Arabic translations of *Othello* is that both make concerted effort to adapt the play to the theatrical conventions of their own languages and environments. In both cases, this means rejecting the particularities of French and English theatrical style, and in both cases, the translators appear to be responding to contemporaneous positions on language that tend to advocate a 'modernised' style à la European literature. However, the Ottoman *Othello* adopts a prose style that recalls the increasing orality of Ottoman journalistic writing and new literary prose, while the Arabic employs a *fuṣḥā* that makes claims on a range of Arabic linguistic practices and a shared Arab heritage. For the most part, scholars have tended to treat Arabic and Turkish linguistic reform as separate processes, but the points of similarity and divergence between these translators' linguistic strategies, particularly in terms of how they relate to the shifting imperial loyalties and emergent nationalisms of the time, certainly suggest a need for further comparative work in this area, too.[58]

Othello: *Arab, Hero, Citizen*

While there is no verifiable historical link between the Arabic and Turkish texts, there is also a sense in which the translations offer a point of connection *through* comparison.[59] It may not be coincidence that *Othello* was the first Shakespeare play to be translated into both Ottoman Turkish and Arabic: it is a play about relations between Venice and the Ottoman Empire, and both sets of translators interpret the main character as an Arab hero. Of course, 'Arab' would mean something quite different to Ottoman Turkish translators in 1876, as debates about citizenship and sovereignty in the Ottoman Empire circulated, and to Arab translators in 1899, when British colonisers in Egypt were imposing quite a new kind of imperial rule in the former province. Yet in both languages, the translated text becomes a space in which 'Arabs' and 'Ottomans' – two uncertain and overlapping categories – may look at one another. To compare these translations' characterisation of an Arab Othello is to attend to the cultural dynamics of what Laura Doyle, advocating attention to the relationship between European colonialism and the empires that predated and competed with it, has termed 'inter-imperiality'.[60] It is also, arguably, to find traces of what Stoler has called the 'comparative nature' of empire itself.[61]

The translators' introduction to the Ottoman *Othello* begins by explicitly presenting the Arab hero as a selling point of the play. The translators chose the text, they write, because of its depiction of the 'valour' (*mertlik*) of the Arabs; the worthiness of such a depiction is apparently self-evident.[62] Importantly, the terms 'Ottoman' and 'Turk' make no appearance in the French text, where Othello's enemy is largely erased from the plot; thus, for the readers of *Otâlo*, 'Arab' may be associated with, rather than opposed to, Ottoman. Equally important, 'Arab' is never used in either the French or the English *Othello* to refer to Othello, and in fact, Ducis frequently describes him not as *Maure* ('Moor', Shakespeare's preferred epithet), which might support a translation as 'Arab', but as *Africain*.[63] The French racial depiction of Othello, in fact, differs quite sharply from the English. Shakespeare's *Othello*, for instance, consistently expresses an anxiety about the supposed sexual prowess of black men; in the French text, perhaps for propriety's sake, the number of explicit references to this (particularly by Iago) are erased, as indeed are most references to skin colour. That is not to say that Othello's ethnicity is not remarked on; there remains an anxiety about the mixing of 'blood', and characters refer to Othello's person as *sauvage* (once) or *barbare* (eight times) as a *tigre africain* (once), and so on.[64] However, such epithets tend to be found in the mouths of characters like Pezare (Iago) and Odalbert (Brabantio), who are clearly the villains of Ducis' piece. Racial discrimination is castigated in the French play rather more clearly than in Shakespeare's version.

Ducis was by no means an anti-racist: there is plenty of the 'noble savage' trope in his depiction of Othello, while the play's introduction contains remarks about the shock of French ladies upon sighting the 'yellow' complexion of the actor playing Othello.[65] Ducis was, however, deeply involved in the eighteenth-century French humanist project, and his abolitionist inclinations are evidenced in a pointed notice dedicating the play to his brother, a slave-owner in Saint-Domingue.[66] As Ducis' *Othello* attests, in fact, the humanist and abolitionist movements of the time were both quite capable of encompassing racism and Orientalism.

What is interesting about the Ottoman translation of Ducis' text is that its strategy for presenting an 'Arab hero' entails not minimising but rather embellishing the racialised descriptions of Othello in the French text. For instance, in an early speech by the character Odalbert (Brabantio), extra references to the fact that Othello is from 'Africa' are added to the original one in the French;[67] while Odalbert's description of Othello as a *tigre africain* is erased, it is replaced by additional mentions of his being '*barbar*' (barbarian).[68] The French text mentions Othello's having spent time in the desert, and additional, frequent mention of this, as well as to the sun producing his dark skin, is made in the Ottoman *Othello*, including in speeches by the hero himself.[69] The Ottoman text does not, however, emphasise the French text's condemnation of racial discrimination. The 'Arab' portrayed here is a stereotype of a Bedouin tribesman, a reminder on the one hand of the fact that the term 'Arab' (*'arab/arap* in Arabic and Ottoman) originally referred to inhabitants of the Arabian Peninsula, a usage which persisted into the nineteenth century. On the other hand, the deserts in which this play's 'Arab' grew up were not in Arabia, but in Africa: the stereotype is a composite one, and slightly confused.

Selim Derengil and Ussama Makdisi have drawn attention to what Makdisi terms a form of 'Ottoman Orientalism', which drew strongly on European Orientalism.[70] According to Makdisi, Ottoman self-definition against the West in the late nineteenth century rested on the production of an ethnic opposition between modern (reformed and reformist) Muslim, Turkish Ottoman subjects, and premodern ones, encompassing Arabs, Armenians, Kurds and so on.[71] Derengil emphasises that Arabs, in particular, were conceived as noble desert savages, residing on an undefined 'periphery' of the Empire towards which the Empire adopted a 'colonial attitude'.[72] Further, Mustafa Minawi has argued that in the 1880s the Ottoman Empire was hoping to expand its imperial ambitions in Africa, in competition with the European empires encroaching on its holdings there.[73] If Ottoman Orientalism existed, it was arguably not simply a received discourse, but directly connected to the drive to European-style, competitive colonialism.

Although the acting profession was actually dominated by minorities, particularly Armenians, the Ottoman literary scene of which these translators were a part included an important group of Ottoman officials and intelligentsia, all associated with precisely the 'modernising' Muslim reformism discussed by Makdisi. On one level, therefore, it is possible to read the Ottoman *Othello*'s stereotyping of the title character as a dark-skinned desert tribesman, characterised by qualities such as 'valour', 'bravery' and 'loyalty', as part of this larger trend of reformist Ottoman Orientalism.[74] However, Ottoman Orientalism is not the only discourse to which the depiction of the Arab Othello responds. It also enters urgent contemporaneous debates around nationality and citizenship.

The French text, produced in the direct aftermath of the French Revolution, is invested in proclaiming its revolutionary spirit. As a result, in Ducis' script, the author himself is referred to as '*le citoyen*', while the term is used as a form of address between characters throughout the play; the term 'citizen', by contrast, occurs only once in the English play.[75] *Citoyen* as a form of address was of course popularised by the revolution. However, Ducis was also an advocate of the right of freed slaves to French citizenship, a matter of debate at the time. In this light, references to Othello's 'citizenship' of Venice are pointed. As historian Will Hanley has argued, at the time of the French text's translation into Ottoman Turkish, the conditions of membership in the Ottoman Empire were also being redefined; in particular, Hanley suggests that the 1869

Translation of Othello into Arabic and Ottoman Turkish

Ottoman Nationality Law (*tabiiyet-i osmaniye kanunamesi*) played a role in defining the growing distinctions between nationality and citizenship, and specifically clarified the limits of citizenship, as opposed to nationality.[76] The Ottoman translators, too, were writing at a time when 'citizen' (*vatandaş*) was newly coming into popular use, derived from the term *vatan*, homeland or fatherland.

Vatan itself was strongly associated with the new reformist nationalism of the Young Ottomans who had campaigned to reconceive the relationship between people and government along the lines of European nations, but it had a particular resonance within the theatre. Eigar Wigen describes *vatan* as Young Ottoman playwright Namık Kemal's reinterpretation of the Arabic *watan* via the French term *patrie*,[77] and Kemal was in fact exiled in 1873 for his controversial play, *Vatan Yahut Silistre*, which championed the loyalty of an Ottoman (Turkish) soldier to his 'fatherland' as demonstrated by the hero's decision to defend the Bulgarian town of Silistra against the Russians.[78] However, in the Ottoman *Othello*, *vatan* is used to translate both the territorial entity '*patrie*' (country or home country); and the political one, '*état*' (state); it describes a Venetian city-state whose inhabitants have French names, and which is defended by an Arab general. Here at least, *vatan* is not nearly so simple as a French *calque*.

The term *citoyen* also causes problems. A couple of times, it is rendered as *vatandaş*, but far more common in the Ottoman text is simply to erase it: for example, '*citoyens et soldats*', a phrase which occurs in the French, is rendered simply *herkes* (everyone).[79] Elsewhere, *teba* is used for *citoyens* in the plural: the term is much closer in meaning to 'subject', a more common, less reformist term in the period for describing the relationship between Ottomans and the state. Othello is at no point addressed as *vatandaş*, so Ducis' abolitionist stake in the term is lost. Indeed, at one point when the Ottoman text translates a reference in the French text to Othello's status as a former slave, the word slave actually appears in neither version, only a reference to chains, *zincirler*. Further, although in the Ottoman text Hedélmone bemoans the fact that Othello was a slave, she does so not because slavery is wrong, but because he was ill-suited to it, being a man 'unmatched in bravery' (*emsalsiz bir cesur*). This is, once more, a quality associated with a stereotypical 'desert Arab'.[80] In the continuing narrative, Othello's bravery earns him his freedom, and he is now firmly considered a loyal subject – if not *vatandaş* – of the Venetian *vatan*. In the Ottoman *Othello*, the hero's Arab status is one of partially redeemed marginality: he is rewarded with full membership in the *vatan*, but his passion (and, it is half-implied, 'barbaric' nature) leads him, in the end, to death. Relying as this narrative does on a decidedly flexible definition of the term 'Arab' to indicate internal Ottoman others, it evinces a sometimes-unhappy marriage between nascent Ottoman Turkish nationalist discourses and Ottoman Orientalism.

The Arabic translation, perhaps unsurprisingly, offers a different interpretation of the Arab hero – but it has similar recourse to a highly flexible definition of the term 'Arab', and it too seems invested in elaborating a non-hostile relationship between 'Arabs' and 'Ottomans'. In both Shakespeare's and Hugo's *Othellos*, as noted already, the enemy against whom Othello showed his valour in battle were the 'Turks', and the contested territory was Cyprus. As such, the absence of Ottomans and Turks in the Arabic text, and the erasure of Cyprus as a setting (although it is briefly mentioned in the play) are clearly choices made by the Arabic translator.[81] The decision to champion the main character as an Arab, but to erase all other references to the Ottoman context, might simply be a strategy for avoiding potentially controversial or incendiary topics. Certainly, a drama featuring, effectively, an Arab–Ottoman conflict would be risky in an Ottoman province in this period of heavy censorship and might even prove so in British-ruled Cairo. It could also, of course, be a positive decision: Mestyan, as noted, has argued for the presence of an Ottoman Arab patriotism in Egypt that by no means conflicted with, and indeed was a precursor to, subsequent Arab and pan-Arab nationalism, and the theatre and performance culture more generally is for him deeply implicated in this.[82] However, the play hardly reads as an outright assertion of Ottoman loyalty; rather, the erasure of a clearly defined enemy or setting, exacerbated by the combination of French and Arabic names, serves to take the play out of contemporary contexts, lending it instead a slightly timeless, placeless feel.

Ottomans are not the only ones to be erased from the translation: so too are the mentions of Christians and Christianity present in the French and English texts.[83] These are replaced by a far greater number of Muslim religious expressions, mentions of God, and so on, so that the characters are clearly identified as (Sunni) Muslim, and it is God – and not, for instance, Fate – who becomes the arbiter of the tragedy.[84] Like the Arabisation of names, this was quite common practice in translations earlier in the nineteenth century, and especially in theatrical translations designed for a popular audience: it reproduced the common religiosity of everyday speech.[85] However, like the ahistoricity described above, and the stylistic decisions noted earlier, it also has the effect of situating the play very firmly within an extensive imagined Arab/ic heritage.

The capaciousness and flexibility of this shared heritage is further demonstrated by the text's treatment of race and skin colour, as they relate to 'Arabness'. By the 1890s, notions such as race and ethnicity were newly under discussion in Egypt: historically fluid and malleable ethnic and racial identifiers were becoming crystallised along European lines of pseudo-scientific or biologised colour classification and racial hierarchies.[86] Cairene intellectuals translated and consumed European and American texts on race hierarchies, eugenics, phrenology and other such topics with increasing frequency, often in order to establish Arabs' and Egyptians' good racial standing in the world, as well as their capacity for 'progress and civilisation' – as compared, for instance, with black Africans like the inhabitants of the Sudan, which Egypt, under the British, colonised in 1899.[87] This process was arguably part of a larger epistemological shift, with a focus on scientific objectivity and rationalism, natural laws, and a teleological and ordered conception of time and history: the production of the human as a biological individual.[88]

However, the Arabic *Othello*'s relationship to race is distinctly ambiguous, and seems to call on quite different notions of history and community. Unlike in the Ottoman text, the use of 'black' (*aswad*) as a descriptor for Othello's character is retained: Othello is referred to as 'black' five times in the Arabic text, two more than in the English, and the instances occur at different points in the English. On two occasions, 'black' is used where 'Moor' is employed in the English.[89] That the term is considered perjorative seems likely, in that it is used exclusively by relative villains of the piece (three times by Ya'qub/Iago, once by Rodrigue/Rodrigo, and once by Brabante/Brabantio).[90] However, the explicit English descriptions of sex and sexual prowess are absent from the text, presumably for reasons of propriety; since these are often linked to racial slurs and epithets, the quantity of the latter is also much smaller.

Furthermore, the repeated contrast in the French and English texts between Othello's 'blackness' and Desdemona's 'whiteness' is absent from the Arabic texts. Instead, Desdemona is described in terms of the attributes whiteness is used to imply (chastity, duty, submission, purity) but never using any reference to colour or ethnicity, except in the single, aforementioned reference to the black ram and white ewe, which the Arabic translates directly. Given that so-called 'miscegenation' was a major concern of some of the pseudo-scientific texts circulating in Arabic in this period, it is significant that anything touching on it is erased from this text. Rather, the distinction between Damūna and 'Uṭayl is one of class: it is mentioned that Damūna is from 'an honourable house', unlike, presumably, Othello.

In the Arabic text, after all, both Damūna and 'Uṭayl have Arabic names: they are both Arab and, as such, the notion of ethnic difference between them is not what drives the play. The colour prejudice against Othello, so far as it is present, occurs within the category 'Arab', which is one term used to describe him. He is identified as North African, but it is presented more as factual information than as a slight, and the references to this are in general far fewer than in the English. 'Uṭayl is identified as 'al-maghribī'(the North African) several times, but this occurs more sparsely than does the term 'More' in French, and he is introduced by name, rather than referred to as 'the Moor' as in the French.[91] When Iago tells Roderigo that Othello is taking Desdemona to Mauritania in the English (4:2:257), this becomes 'bilādihi al-jazā'ir' (his land, Algeria) in the Arabic, proposing a closer North African home for Othello.[92] A notable exception occurs in a speech by Emilia in the Arabic text after the death of Damūna, in which it is specifically 'Uṭayl's North African status that is made an insult. Here, she calls him 'savage beast, annihilating barbarian wolf, spiller of blood' (*inta waḥsh dārī wa dhi'b kāsir barbarī saffāk al-dimā'*); later in the lengthy speech, she adds that 'the Moor has killed my lady' (*al-maghribī qatala mawlātī*).[93] But this description contains no colour markers.

Aside from this instance, it is on positive associations that the play's presentation of Othello as a dark-skinned Arab seems to draw. 'Uṭayl is referred to using the epithet *baṭal* (hero) and his prowess in battle, noted in the English, is emphasised in the Arabic. In one particular instance, the storm that destroyed the enemy fleet in the original text is replaced by Othello in the Arabic: 'As for the fleet, they perished in the depths of the seas; some of them drowned, and some of them returned to their country in defeat, because of the determination of our exceptional hero, 'Uṭayl.'[94] The theme of the noble Arab *baṭal* was after all a common one in Cairene theatre in the 1880s and 1890s. As Mestyan has noted, some of the most popular plays, in both the Arab Opera and in the private theatres throughout both cities, were those about the pre-Islamic warrior 'Antara ibn Shaddād or 'Antar, previously the hero of his own long *sīra* and, notably, a black Arab. For the 1882 season at the Arab Opera, as Colonel Ahmad 'Urābī and his associates briefly took control of the government in a time of considerable political turmoil in Egypt, two out of the six plays performed were 'Antar plays, *Zifāf 'Antar* and *Fursān al-'Arab* (*'Antar's Wedding* and the *Knights of the Arabs*).[95]

It is on this image of the black Arab, rather than European racialised scientific notions, that the Arabic *Othello* seems to call when it emphasises the skin colour of its hero: the play draws connections between North Africa and ancient Arabia through the theatres of Cairo. As such, it transforms an English play set during Europe's war with the Ottomans into a tale of a pan-Arab, Muslim hero brought low by the machinations of French characters (Brabante, Rodrigue) and their Arab collaborators. The ambiguity, in fact, of 'Uṭayl's ethnicity – black, North African, Arab – is exploited in the play to make him not a catch-all internal Other, as is arguably the case in the Ottoman text, but a composite Arab self, closely mapped onto the mytho-historical trope of the brave *fāris* of the Arabian desert.

Conclusions

Through comparative close reading of the earliest Ottoman and Arabic translations of Shakespeare's *Othello* we have explored the ways in which nineteenth-century Middle Eastern literary translations were shaped not only by the content of their source texts, but also by their own cultural and political contexts. The Arabic and Ottoman Turkish *Othello*s, we have suggested, are situated at the confluence of competing and sometimes contradictory discourses about literature, language, nation, empire and ethnicity. The English *Othello* turns on the tragic undoing of a Moorish general navigating white Venice, and is set against a backdrop of inter-imperial war. In the two translated texts read here, those conflicts are mediated through a new, but not unrelated, set of struggles: the jockeying for position between different imperial languages, as well as between imperial and local ones, that shaped the nineteenth-century Ottoman and Egyptian literary scenes; the emergence of new identity categories in a period of nascent nationalisms; and the global rise of 'race science' as a discourse. Though they may give the play itself a cheerier ending, the translations cannot resolve these conflicts: they read rather as palimpsests, layered records of the successive political, literary and linguistic discourses that combined to produce the curious final text.

Setting out to investigate, for instance, how these translations' source texts were manipulated to better serve reformist or nationalist ends, we found in fact that the translations sometimes come to betray such ends, bearing witness as they do to the flexibility and uncertainty of concepts such as nation and, indeed, reform in this period. The Ottoman Turkish *Othello* covered up its English origins to claim a grander Franco-Italian heritage; but its translators' reverence for French convention did not extend to preserving the play's poetic form, and instead the play was rendered in an Ottoman prose whose orality was as foreign to the French on which it was ostensibly modelled as it might be to some Ottoman readers. The nationalist-reformist leanings of the translators appeared once more in the text's liberal use of *vatan*; but their limitations were revealed in a distinct avoidance of the term *vatandaş*. The Arab *Othello*, too, chose to obscure its origins, this time in order to proclaim its own Englishness; yet it, too, nevertheless abandoned the poetic form retained by both its likely source texts. In fact, the Arabised and content made for an odd hybrid, an obfuscation of origins that might be read as a parallel to the nature of British rule in Egypt at the time, which maintained an Egyptian monarch and nominally Egyptian judiciary alongside the British High Commissioner and each Ministry's British 'Advisor'.

In both cases, 'Arab' proved an expansive concept; it was even at times able to function as a stand-in for the absent 'Ottoman'. In the Arabic play, the character Othello was used to imagine a composite Arab hero, and to draw on a pan-Arab heritage that seemed to ignore the distinctions racial science was introducing into Arabic scientific discourse at the time. In the Ottoman play, by contrast, the multi-ethnic Ottomanism implied by the translators' celebration of an Arab hero sat awkwardly throughout with the racialised descriptions of the protagonist.

In choosing to compare these translations we have sought to approach the wider question of how the 'Arab' and 'Ottoman' literary worlds related to one another in a period when these categories were in flux, and to ask what might be learned from studying them in conjunction. Such a comparison has the potential to shed interesting light on the complex connections between nationalisms and language reform; by attending to literatures and languages produced at the intersection of different imperialisms, it has the potential also to complicate our understanding of literature and imperialism.

Notes

1. See, for instance, Aamir Mufti, *Forget English! Orientalisms and World Literatures* (Cambridge, MA: Harvard University Press, 2016), xi.
2. See Margaret Litvin, Avraham Oz and Parviz Partovi, 'Middle Eastern Shakespeares', in Jill Levinson (ed.), *The Shakespearean World* (London: Routledge, 2017), 97–115; 99.
3. For further details on the First Constitutional Era and subsequent Hamidian regime, see Selim Deringil, *The Well-protected Domains: Ideology and the Legitimation of Power in the Ottoman Empire, 1876–1909* (London and New York: I. B. Tauris, 2011).
4. See Zachary Lockman, 'The Social Roots of Nationalism: Workers and the National Movement in Egypt, 1908–19', *Middle Eastern Studies* 24: 4 (1988): 445–59.
5. See Lawrence Venuti, *The Translator's Invisibility: A History of Translation*,

third edn (New York: Routledge, 2018); Susan Bassnett, *Translation Studies* (London: Routledge, 2014).

6. See Şehnaz Tahir Gurçağlar, 'Scouting the Borders of Translation: Pseudotranslation, Concealed Translations and Authorship in Twentieth-century Turkey', *Translation Studies* 3: 2 (2010): 172–87; 172–3; Samah Selim, 'Translations and Adaptations from the European Novel, 1835–1925', in Wail Hassan (ed.), *The Oxford Handbook of Arab Novelistic Traditions* (Oxford: Oxford University Press, 2017), 119–34; 121.

7. Kamran Rastegar, *Literary Modernity between the Middle East and Europe: Textual Transactions in Nineteenth-century Arabic, English and Persian Literatures* (London: Routledge, 2010), 4.

8. Ann Laura Stoler, 'Tense and Tender Ties: The Politics of Comparison in North American History and (Post) Colonial Studies', *The Journal of American History* 88: 3 (2001): 829–65; 862–3.

9. Adam Mestyan, *Arab Patriotism: The Ideology and Culture of Power in Late Ottoman Egypt* (Princeton: Princeton University Press, 2017), 1–17; Khaled Fahmy, *All the Pasha's Men: Mehmed Ali, His Army and the Making of Modern Egypt* (Cairo: The American University in Cairo Press, 2010), 17–38; Will Hanley, *Identifying with Nationality: Europeans, Ottomans, and Egyptians in Alexandria* (New York: Columbia University Press, 2017), 27–52.

10. Exceptions include comparisons between Arabic and Persian texts such as Rastegar's *Literary Modernity* (2007) and Amir Moosavi, 'How to Write Death: Resignifying Marytrdom in Two Novels of the Iran-Iraq War', *Alif: Journal of Comparative Poetics*, no. 35 (2015): 9–31. Ceyhun Arslan has also recently written on connected Ottoman and Arabic literary modernities in C. Ceyhun Arslan, 'Entanglements between *the Tanzimat* and *al-Nahḍah*: Jurjī Zaydān between *Tārīkh ādāb al-lughah al-turkiyyah* and *Tārīkh ādāb al-lughah al-'arabiyyah*', *Journal of Arabic Literature* 50: 3–4 (2019): 298–324.

11. Litvin, Oz and Partovi, 'Middle Eastern Shakespeares', 97–8.

12. Mehmet Rifat Paşa and Hasan Bedreddin, *Antony*, Temaşa (Istanbul: Kırk Anbar Matbaasi, 1876), 291–354.

13. Mehmet Rifat Paşa and Hasan Bedreddin, *Otâlo*, vol. 3, Temaşa (Istanbul: Kırk Anbar Matbaasi, 1876), 121.

14. William Shakespeare, *Riwāyat Ūṭillū, aw, Ḥiyal al-rijāl* (Cairo: Maṭba'at al-Tawfīq, 1899), 1.

15. For example, Iago becomes Ya'qūb, Rodrigo Rodrigue. Shakespeare, *Riwāyat Ūṭillū*, 2.

16. Nermin Menemencioglu, 'The Ottoman Theatre 1839–1923', *Bulletin (British Society for Middle Eastern Studies)* 10: 1 (1983): 48–58; 49.

17. Jean-François Ducis, *Othello ou le More de Venise: Tragédie* (Paris: Maradan, 1792), 3.

18. Johann Strauss, 'Language and Power in the Late Ottoman Empire',

in Rhoads Murphy (ed.), *Imperial Lineages and Legacies in the Eastern Mediterranean: Recording the Imprint of Roman, Byzantine and Ottoman Rule* (London: Routledge, 2016), 115–42; 121.

19. Algeria was invaded by the French in 1830 and declared a French province in 1848, while the French Protectorate of Tunisia would be established in 1881.
20. E. Preston Dargan, 'Shakespeare and Ducis', *Modern Philology* 10: 2 (1912): 137–78; 1.
21. John W. Klein, 'Verdi's "Otello" and Rossini's' in *Music & Letters* 45: 2 (1964): 130–40; 130; emphasis in original.
22. The 'Mulatto question' concerned the granting of French citizenship to freed slaves.
23. Aside, that is, from translations of English and American detective fiction, of which Sultan Abdülhamid himself was reportedly particularly fond. See Şehnaz Tahir Gürçaglar, 'Sherlock Holmes in the Interculture: Pseudotranslation and Anonymity in Turkish Literature', in Anthony Pym, Mariam Schlesinger and David Simeoni (eds), *Beyond Descriptive Translation Studies: Investigations in Homage to Gideon Toury* (Amsterdam: John Betjemans Publishing Company, 2008): 133–52. On the shift to English, see Shaden M. Tageldin, *Disarming Words: Empire and the Seductions of Translation in Egypt* (Berkeley: University of California Press, 2011), 29. Of course, this was not a perfect shift: translation from French texts continued, as did adaptations of Russian and classical texts.
24. M. M. Badawi, *Coleridge: Critic of Shakespeare* (Cambridge: Cambridge University Press, 1973), 183.
25. Litvin, Oz and Partovi, 'Middle Eastern Shakespeares', 99. Of course, without another source this is difficult to confirm.
26. For instance, the line 'An old black ram / is tupping your white ewe', erased from all French translations in this period save for Victor Hugo's, is present in the Arabic (*kabsh aswad ikhtaṭafa na'jatak al-baydā*). Shakespeare, *Riwāyat Ūṭillū*, 4.
27. Mestyan, *Arab Patriotism*, 164.
28. Mestyan, *Arab Patriotism*, 193.
29. Rastegar, *Literary Modernity*, 29.
30. Litvin, Oz and Partovi, 'Middle Eastern Shakespeares', 98.
31. The long sea journey of the English play is, for instance, conspicuously absent.
32. Ducis, *Othello*, 2.
33. Ducis, *Othello*, 6.
34. William Shakespeare and John Dover Wilson, *Othello* (Cambridge: Cambridge University Press, 2010), 6–7. A particularly vulgar speech by Iago.
35. David Keppel-Jones, *The Strict Metrical Tradition: Variations in the Literary Iambic Pentameter from Sidney and Spenser to Matthew Arnold by David Keppel-Jones* (Montreal: McGill-Queen's University Press, 2001), 16.

36. J. A. Cuddon and M. A. R. Habib, *The Penguin Dictionary of Literary Terms and Literary Theory: Fifth Edition*, 5th revised edn (London: Penguin Books, 2015), 19–20.
37. Ducis, *Othello*, 13.
38. Mehmet Rifat Paşa and Hasan Badreddin, *Otâlo*, 127. We are at a loss to explain the phrase about wind!
39. For further discussion of nineteenth-century journalistic writing, see Geoffrey Lewis, *The Turkish Language Reform: A Catastrophic Success* (Oxford and New York: Oxford University Press, 2002), 14–18.
40. See Neil Rhodes, *Shakespeare and the Origins of English*, new edition (Oxford and New York: Oxford University Press, 2004), 118–20.
41. Nergis Ertürk, *Grammatology and Literary Modernity in Turkey* (Oxford and New York: Oxford University Press, 2013), 13.
42. Erturk, *Grammatology*, xiv.
43. Ziad Fahmy, *Ordinary Egyptians: Creating the Modern Nation through Popular Culture* (Stanford: Stanford University Press, 2011), 10–19, 61–95; Mestyan, *Arab Patriotism*, 2–17, 126–98.
44. For instance, with the publication of Rifāʻa Rāfiʻ al-Ṭahṭāwi's *Takhlīṣ al-ibrīz* in Cairo in 1835.
45. Abdulrazzak Patel, *The Arab Nahḍah: The Making of the Intellectual and Humanist Movement* (Edinburgh: Edinburgh University Press, 2015), 102–22.
46. See Youssef M. Choueiri, *Arab Nationalism: A History: Nation and State in the Arab World* (Oxford: Blackwell Publishers, 2000), 56–100.
47. See Mestyan, *Arab Patriotism*, 170.
48. Fahmy, *Ordinary Egyptians*, 64. Fahmy takes care not to overstate the importance of theatre, emphasising other dialect literary forms such as *zagal* and the spread of a popular Egyptian vernacular press.
49. Scenes 1–3 of Act I, for instance, are entirely combined, and all the senators from Scene 3 erased; the first scene note comes on page 7, and announces Scene 4.
50. Shakespeare, *Othello*, 12.
51. Shakespeare, *Riwāyat Ūṭillū*, 8. The elision of the racial connotations in the English speech is addressed below.
52. If the translation is from the Hugo, this is still a shift: Hugo retains the rhythm of the English by inserting dashes where iambic pentameter would dictate the end of a line. See William Shakespeare et al., *Macbeth Othello* (Paris; Dijon: Impr. de Darantière, 1949), 252.
53. For instance, much of the Arabic version of Othello's description of his first encounter with Damūna (Desdemona) is in a loose *sajʻ*, perhaps to emphasise and explain the effect of his stories on her. See Shakespeare, *Riwāyat Ūṭillū*, 14.
54. Margaret Litvin notes that 'Italian and French styles shaped Egyptian acting: dialogue was de-emphasized; soliloquies and other climactic speeches were

declaimed like arias, facing the audience, often *fortissimo*.' Margaret Litvin, 'The French Source of the Earliest Surviving Arabic Hamlet', *Shakespeare Studies* (2011): 133–51; 142.

55. Examples may be found at the end of Act I, Scene 8 in the Arabic play (Act I, Scene 3 in the English), where Rodrigo's rhyming couplet in the English is expanded into several rhymed lines, organised as *bayt*s; and 48–9 where Othello's lengthy, despairing speech is rendered entirely in verse.
56. It appears first in the Arabic Act I, Scene 8, where Othello and Desdemona speak before the Senators.
57. Consequently, some of the biggest acting stars in Egypt were the primary singers, such as the Alexandrine Sheikh Salāma Ḥigāzī (1852–1917).
58. Yasir Suleiman is perhaps an exception in that he insists on the influence of Ottoman Turkish language reform on Arabic language debates. See Yasir Suleiman, *The Arabic Language and National Identity: A Study in Ideology* (Edinburgh: Edinburgh University Press, 2003), 82–95.
59. Though many translations exist between Ottoman and Arabic in this period, there is no evidence that Ṭānyūs 'Abdū, if he was in fact the Arabic translator, read Ottoman Turkish.
60. Laura Doyle, 'Inter-imperiality', *Interventions* 16: 2 (March 2014): 159–96; 160.
61. Ann Stoler, 'Tense and Tender Ties', 862–3.
62. Mehmet Rifat Paşa and Hasan Bedreddin, *Otâlo*, 121.
63. See, for example, Ducis, *Othello*, 11, 15, 37, etc.
64. Ducis, *Othello*, 10, 11, 13, 16, 19, 28, 35, 39, 50, 63; and 37.
65. Ducis, *Othello*, 5.
66. Ducis, *Othello*, 2.
67. Mehmet Rifat Paşa and Hasan Bedreddin, *Otâlo*, 125.
68. Mehmet Rifat Paşa and Hasan Bedreddin, *Otâlo*, 125, 126, etc.
69. See, for instance, Mehmet Rifat Paşa and Hasan Bedreddin, *Otâlo*, 127.
70. Selim Deringil, '"They Live in a State of Nomadism and Savagery": The Late Ottoman Empire and the Post-colonial Debate', *Comparative Studies in Society and History* 45: 2 (2003): 311–42; 312; Ussama Makdisi, 'Ottoman Orientalism', *The American Historical Review* 107: 3 (June 2002): 768–96; 769.
71. Makdisi, 'Ottoman Orientalism', 770.
72. Derengil, 'They Live in a State of Nomadism and Savagery', 313.
73. Mostafa Minawi, *The Ottoman Scramble for Africa: Empire and Diplomacy in the Sahara and the Hijaz* (Stanford: Stanford University Press, 2016), 3–4.
74. See, for instance, in Hedélmone's speech about her love for Othello. Mehmet Rifat Paşa and Hasan Bedreddin, *Otâlo*, 128.
75. Ducis, *Othello*, 10, 38, 69, etc.
76. Will Hanley, 'What Ottoman Nationality Was and Was Not', *Journal of the Ottoman and Turkish Studies Association* 3: 2 (2016): 277–98; 277–8. The

former, he notes, was a far less protected category than the latter, and included 'children and wives of foreigners, orphans, emigrants, and immigrants'.
77. Einar Wigen, 'Ottoman Concepts of Empire', *Contributions to the History of Concepts* 8: 1 (June 2013): 44–66; 62.
78. Menemencioğlu, 'The Ottoman Theatre', 53.
79. Mehmet Rifat Paşa and Hasan Bedreddin, *Otâlo*, 124. Interestingly the term *vatandaş* is included in a different context, later on the same page.
80. Mehmet Rifat Paşa and Hasan Bedreddin, *Otâlo*, 127.
81. Mentioned on page 2 in the translation of the phrase 'Cyprus and Rhodes', glossed in Arabic as 'famous cities', *al-mudun al-shahīra*.
82. Mestyan, *Arab Patriotism*, 10–17.
83. See Shakespeare, *Othello*, 4. Erased in Shakespeare, *Riwāyat Ūṭillū*, 2.
84. Shakespeare, *Riwāyat Ūṭillū*: Othello says of his marriage to Desdemona, 'bal tazawajtuhā bi-sunnati lillāhī wa sharī'hi al-sharīf', 12. Ya'qūb/Iago says in response to Rodrigue's death, 'lā ḥawla wa lā quwwa illā bi-llāh', 73.
85. However, the process was not always so complete. For further detail on the complex ways in which non-Muslim theologies, such as Greek polytheism, were 'domesticated' (but also, sometimes, 'foreignised' in Arabic translations of theatrical works, see Raphael Cormack, 'Lords or Idols? Translating the Greek Gods into Arabic in Nineteenth-century Egypt', in Marilyn Booth (ed.), *Migrating Texts: Circulating Translations around the Ottoman Mediterranean* (Edinburgh: Edinburgh University Press, 2019), 215–35; 222–5.
86. Bridget Gill, 'Egypt and Her Inhabitants: Translation of the Science of Race in *al-Muqtaṭaf*, 1885–1907', unpublished MA thesis, Columbia University, New York, 2015), 2.
87. Samah Selim, 'Languages of Civilization: Nation, Translation and the Politics of Race in Colonial Egypt', *The Translator* 15: 1 (April 2009): 139–56.
88. Gill, 'Egypt and Her Inhabitants', 3–5.
89. Shakespeare, *Riwāyat Ūṭillū*, 19, 22.
90. On only one occasion is an explicit racial signifier added, with a reference to Othello's being '*shanī' al-wajh*' (8) – which is dubious anyway.
91. See, for instance, Shakespeare, *Riwāyat Ūṭillū*, 35, 46.
92. Shakespeare, *Riwāyat Ūṭillū*, 70.
93. Shakespeare, *Riwāyat Ūṭillū*, 78–9.
94. Shakespeare, *Riwāyat Ūṭillū*, 21.
95. Mestyan, *Arab Patriotism*, 191.

Bibliography

Arslan, C. Ceyhun, 'Entanglements between *the Tanzimat* and *al-Nahḍah*: Jurjī Zaydān between *Tārīkh ādāb al-lughah al-turkiyyah* and *Tārīkh ādāb al-lughah al-'arabiyyah*', *Journal of Arabic Literature* 50: 3–4 (November 2019): 298–324.

Badawi, M. M., *Coleridge: Critic of Shakespeare* (Cambridge: Cambridge University Press, 1973).
Bassnett, Susan, *Translation Studies* (London: Routledge, 2014).
Choueiri, Youssef M., *Arab Nationalism: A History: Nation and State in the Arab World* (Oxford: Blackwell Publishers, 2000).
Cormack, Raphael, 'Lords or Idols? Translating the Greek Gods into Arabic in Nineteenth-century Egypt', in Marilyn Booth (ed.), *Migrating Texts: Circulating Translations around the Ottoman Mediterranean* (Edinburgh: Edinburgh University Press, 2019), 215–35.
Cuddon, J. A., and M. A. R. Habib, *The Penguin Dictionary of Literary Terms and Literary Theory: Fifth Edition* (London: Penguin Books, 2015).
Dargan, E. Preston, 'Shakespeare and Ducis', *Modern Philology* 10: 2 (1912): 137–78.
Deringil, Selim, '"They Live in a State of Nomadism and Savagery": The Late Ottoman Empire and the Post-Colonial Debate', *Comparative Studies in Society and History* 45: 2 (2003): 311–42.
Deringil, Selim, *The Well-protected Domains: Ideology and the Legitimation of Power in the Ottoman Empire, 1876–1909* (London and New York: I. B. Tauris, 2011).
Doyle, Laura, 'Inter-imperiality', *Interventions* 16: 2 (March 2014): 159–96.
Ducis, Jean-François, *Othello ou le More de Venise: Tragédie* (Paris: Maradan, 1792).
Ertürk, Nergis, *Grammatology and Literary Modernity in Turkey* (Oxford and New York: Oxford University Press, 2013).
Fahmy, Khaled, *All the Pasha's Men: Mehmed Ali, His Army and the Making of Modern Egypt* (Cairo: The American University in Cairo Press, 2010).
Fahmy, Ziad, *Ordinary Egyptians: Creating the Modern Nation through Popular Culture* (Stanford: Stanford University Press, 2011).
Gill, Bridget, 'Egypt and Her Inhabitants: Translation of the Science of Race in *al-Muqtaṭaf*, 1885–1907', unpublished MA thesis, Columbia University, New York, 2015.
Hanley, Will, 'What Ottoman Nationality Was and Was Not', *Journal of the Ottoman and Turkish Studies Association* 3: 2 (2016): 277–98.
Hanley, Will, *Identifying with Nationality: Europeans, Ottomans, and Egyptians in Alexandria* (New York: Columbia University Press, 2017).
Keppel-Jones, David, *The Strict Metrical Tradition: Variations in the Literary Iambic Pentameter from Sidney and Spenser to Matthew Arnold by David Keppel-Jones* (Montreal: McGill-Queen's University Press, 2001).
Klein, John W., 'Verdi's "Otello" and Rossini's', *Music & Letters* 45: 2 (1964): 130–40.
Lewis, Geoffrey, *The Turkish Language Reform: A Catastrophic Success* (Oxford and New York: Oxford University Press, 2002).
Litvin, Margaret, 'The French Source of the Earliest Surviving Arabic Hamlet', *Shakespeare Studies* (2011): 133–51.

Litvin, Margaret, Avraham Oz and Parviz Partovi, 'Middle Eastern Shakespeares', in Jill Levinson (ed.), *The Shakespearean World* (London: Routledge, 2017): 97–115.

Lockman, Zachary, 'The Social Roots of Nationalism: Workers and the National Movement in Egypt, 1908–19', *Middle Eastern Studies* 24: 4 (October 1988): 445–59.

Makdisi, Ussama, 'Ottoman Orientalism', *The American Historical Review* 107: 3 (June 2002): 768–96.

Menemencioglu, Nermin, 'The Ottoman Theatre 1839–1923', *Bulletin (British Society for Middle Eastern Studies)* 10: 1 (1983): 48–58.

Mestyan, Adam, *Arab Patriotism: The Ideology and Culture of Power in Late Ottoman Egypt* (Princeton: Princeton University Press, 2017).

Minawi, Mostafa, *The Ottoman Scramble for Africa: Empire and Diplomacy in the Sahara and the Hijaz* (Stanford: Stanford University Press, 2016).

Moosavi, Amir, 'How to Write Death: Resignifying Marytrdom in Two Novels of the Iran-Iraq War', *Alif: Journal of Comparative Poetics* 35 (2015): 9–31.

Mufti, Aamir, *Forget English! Orientalisms and World Literatures* (Cambridge, MA: Harvard University Press, 2016).

Paşa, Mehmet Rifat and Hasan Bedreddin, *Antony*, Temaşa (Istanbul: Kırk Anbar Matbaasi, 1876).

Paşa, Mehmet Rifat and Hasan Bedreddin, *Otâlo*, Temaşa (Istanbul: Kırk Anbar Matbaasi, 1876).

Patel, Abdulrazzak, *The Arab Nahḍah: The Making of the Intellectual and Humanist Movement* (Edinburgh: Edinburgh University Press, 2015).

Rastegar, Kamran, *Literary Modernity between the Middle East and Europe: Textual Transactions in Nineteenth-century Arabic, English and Persian Literatures* (London: Routledge, 2010).

Rhodes, Neil, *Shakespeare and the Origins of English*, new edition (Oxford and New York: Oxford University Press, 2004).

Selim, Samah, 'Languages of Civilization: Nation, Translation and the Politics of Race in Colonial Egypt', *The Translator* 15: 1 (April 2009): 139–56.

Selim, Samah, 'Translations and Adaptations from the European Novel, 1835–1925', in Wail Hassan (ed.), *The Oxford Handbook of Arab Novelistic Traditions* (Oxford: Oxford University Press, 2017): 119–34.

Shakespeare, William, *Riwāyat Uṭillū, aw, Ḥiyal al-rijāl* (Cairo: Maṭbaʻat al-Tawfīq, 1899).

Shakespeare, William, François-Victor Hugo, Christine Lalou and René Lalou, *Macbeth Othello* (Paris; Dijon: Impr. de Darantière, 1949).

Shakespeare, William and John Dover Wilson, *Othello* (Cambridge: Cambridge University Press, 2010).

Stoler, Ann Laura, 'Tense and Tender Ties: The Politics of Comparison in North American History and (Post) Colonial Studies', *The Journal of American History* 88: 3 (2001): 829–65.

Strauss, Johann, 'Language and Power in the Late Ottoman Empire', in Rhoads

Murphey (ed.), *Imperial Lineages and Legacies in the Eastern Mediterranean: Recording the Imprint of Roman, Byzantine and Ottoman Rule* (London: Routledge, 2016): 115–42.

Suleiman, Yasir, *The Arabic Language and National Identity: A Study in Ideology* (Edinburgh: Edinburgh University Press, 2003).

Tageldin, Shaden M., *Disarming Words: Empire and the Seductions of Translation in Egypt* (Berkeley: University of California Press, 2011).

Tahir Gürçağlar, Şehnaz, 'Sherlock Holmes in the Interculture: Pseudotranslation and Anonymity in Turkish Literature', in Anthony Pym, Mariam Schlesinger and David Simeoni (eds), *Beyond Descriptive Translation Studies: Investigations in Homage to Gideon Toury* (Amsterdam: John Betjemans Publishing Company, 2008): 133–52.

Tahir Gürçağlar, Şehnaz, 'Scouting the Borders of Translation: Pseudotranslation, Concealed Translations and Authorship in Twentieth-century Turkey', *Translation Studies* 3: 2 (2010): 172–87.

Venuti, Lawrence, *The Translator's Invisibility: A History of Translation*, third edn (New York: Routledge, 2018).

Wigen, Einar, 'Ottoman Concepts of Empire', *Contributions to the History of Concepts* 8: 1 (June 2013): 44–66.

Chapter 3

Shared Secrets: (Re)writing Urban Mysteries in Nineteenth-century Istanbul

Şehnaz Şişmanoğlu Şimşek and Etienne Charrière

The cultural and literary interconnectedness of the communities that inhabited the nineteenth-century Ottoman imperial capital – Muslim Turks, Greek Christians, Armenian Christians, Sephardic Jews and others[1] – was partly effected by literary translation as a vector of 'trans-communal' contact. Juxtaposing a Greek novel published in Istanbul and inspired by the model of Eugène Sue's (1804–57) *Les Mystères de Paris* (1842–3) with a translation of the same text into Greek-scripted Ottoman Turkish (Karamanlidika) published almost simultaneously in the same city, this chapter engages with translation, adaptation and circulation as both a cross-border phenomenon and a cross-community one. Setting two versions of a single, translated text – separated by language, but sharing the same script – side by side reveals nuances in cultural and intellectual relations between linguistic and ethno-religious communities. Moreover, by highlighting intra-lingual transliteration as an alternative form of translation, this case study challenges entrenched conceptual categories in the field of translation studies.

First serialised in Athens in 1888–9 in *Ephimeris*, the newspaper owned by its author, and later reprinted in book form in 1890,[2] Epaminondas Kyriakidis' (1861–1939) *Πέραν Απόκρυφα* ('The mysteries of Pera') was one of many novels directly inspired by the works of French novelist Eugène Sue to appear in Istanbul, and in several local literary idioms, in the second half of the nineteenth century.[3] Although Kyriakidis' work was technically an 'original' novel, it was evidently an attempt to domesticate the narrative templates and conventions of urban popular fiction developed by Sue, investing them with new meanings shaped by cultural expectations and social anxieties specific to late-imperial Istanbul.

'Urban Mysteries' in Greece and in the Ottoman Empire

It is useful first to situate Kyriakidis' *The Mysteries of Pera*, and its Greek-scripted Ottoman Turkish (Karamanlidika) translation, *The Mysteries of Beyoğlu*, by Evangelinos Misailidis (1820–90), within the larger context of Greek reception of Western popular fiction – the French *roman de mystères* in particular – in the Ottoman environment. It would be incorrect to describe Eugène Sue as the sole inventor of the popular novel, a category that emerged gradually, integrating existing features of Western European prose fiction into new forms that reflected emerging social realities especially in evolving urban settings. But the importance of Sue's work in redefining the genre and fuelling its expansion in the mid-nineteenth century cannot be overstated. With 131 book-length translations (including reprints) between 1845 and 1900, Eugène Sue was the second most popular foreign author in the Greek world during the nineteenth century after Alexandre Dumas. Almost one in every twenty translated books published in Greek during the period, regardless of genre, was one of his novels.[4] Sue's massive presence in Greek in the Ottoman Empire started with the translation of his two most famous works, *Les Mystères de Paris* (*The Mysteries of Paris*, 1842–3) and *Le Juif errant* (*The Wandering Jew*, 1844), both in 1845–6 and both in Izmir, translated by Isidoros Skylissis (1819–90) and Giorgos Rodokanakis (dates unknown) respectively. These first two Greek translations were reprinted several times before the end of the century and were followed, in the Ottoman Empire, by the translation into Greek of several of Sue's other novels, including the entire series of novels titled *Les Sept Péchés capitaux* (*The Seven Deadly Sins*, 1847–52), as well as some isolated *romans de moeurs* such as *Mathilde: Mémoires d'une jeune fille* ('Mathilde: a young girl's memoirs', 1841) and a few of his early works of maritime fiction such as *Atar-Gull* (1831).

In the wake of Sue's success on the Greek and Greek-Ottoman literary markets, a number of his followers and imitators in the genre of popular urban fiction also attained a level of fame that sharply contrasts with their position in the canon of the nineteenth-century French novel – at least as we conceive of it today. For instance, although his work has since fallen into relative obscurity, Xavier de Montépin (1829–1902) was, throughout Europe and beyond, one of the most-read authors of French popular literature in the late nineteenth century. His fame was particularly great in the Ottoman Empire, as evidenced by the fact that some of his most famous novels were translated into virtually all of the major literary languages in use in the Ottoman Empire in the 1880s and 1890s.[5] With over thirty translations, Montépin came third, after Dumas and Sue, in terms of the number of Greek translations published during the nineteenth century. Most of these Greek translations appeared in the Ottoman Empire rather than in the independent Greek state.

Equally forgotten today, but extremely popular both in France and abroad in the late nineteenth century, Emile Richebourg (1833–98) and Jules Mary (1851–1922) belonged to the same category of highly melodramatic fiction represented by Montépin. Richebourg's works achieved considerable success under the Third Republic, when they were serialised in the conservative daily *Le Petit Journal*, the newspaper with the largest readership in France until the First World War.[6] His novels were very quickly translated into Greek, first in Athens in the late 1870s, but after that primarily in the Ottoman Empire, starting with a translation of his most famous novel, *L'Enfant du faubourg* ('The child of the faubourg', 1876)[7] followed by numerous others in Istanbul and Izmir. These Greek translations were often reprinted in Cairo and Alexandria until the beginning of the twentieth century. The innumerable novels published by Jules Mary in the French popular press from the late 1870s until the early 1920s granted him the title of *roi des feuilletonistes* (king of serial writers). Mary's exploitative treatment of the topic of urban poverty through a form of bastardised naturalism made him immensely popular both in France and abroad, including in the Ottoman Empire where the first translations of his work started to appear in the early 1880s, with *La Faute du Docteur Madelor* ('Doctor Madelor's sin', 1878) and continued well into the twentieth century with over thirty volumes. Full of improbable plot twists and outrageous cliffhangers, the popular crime novels of Pierre-Alexis Ponson du Terrail (1829–71) started to be translated into Greek in the mid-1860s with the novel *Les Gandins* ('The dandies', 1860). But it is with the long series of novels dedicated to his recurring hero Rocambole, a criminal turned masked avenger, that the author became a household name both in France and in the Ottoman Empire. The success of his novels in Greek translation was such that, in the second half of the nineteenth century, no fewer than four editions (and at least three different translations) of the Rocambole cycle were published in Istanbul (starting in 1869), Izmir (starting in 1887) and Athens (with a first version starting in 1868 and a second one starting in 1883).

Finally, with more than twenty Greek translations, the novels of Paul Féval (1816–87) belonged to two distinct categories of popular fiction. A first group included imitations or unauthorised sequels of works by Eugène Sue, such as *Les Mystères de Londres* (*The Mysteries of London*, 1844[8]) or *La Fille du Juif errant* (*The Wandering Jew's Daughter*, 1863). A second group was composed of numerous swashbuckling historical novels modelled on Alexandre Dumas' fictions. Greek translations of his novels published in the Ottoman Empire included several examples from both categories.

This intense movement of translation of French popular fiction into Greek had a direct effect on the development of the domestic novel. The works of Eugène Sue – in particular *Les Mystères de Paris* – were rapidly imitated by Greek novelists active either in the Greek Kingdom, in the Ottoman Empire or in other parts of the Greek-speaking world,[9] as was the case throughout Europe and beyond during the same period.[10] At an unknown date, but presumably almost concurrently with the first Greek translation of *The Mysteries of Paris*, itself published very shortly after the original serialisation of the novel in French, a first Greek adaptation titled *Αθηνών Απόκρυφα* ('The mysteries of Athens') and penned by Giorgos Aspridis (dates unknown) was published in instalments, most of which are now lost. This first Greek adaptation of Sue was soon followed by similar novels also set in Athens or in Istanbul, as well as on the islands of Syros and Zakynthos or in Egypt: Petros Ioannidis (dates unknown), *Η Επτάλοφος ή Ήθη και Έθιμα Κωνσταντινουπόλεως* ('The city of seven hills, or Customs of Constantinople', 1855); Demosthenes Lymberiou (dates unknown), *Απόκρυφα Σύρου* ('The mysteries of Syros', 1866); Christophoros Samartzidis (1843–1900), *Απόκρυφα Κωνσταντινουπόλεως* ('The mysteries of Constantinople', 1868); Sokrates Zervos (dates unknown), *Έν ζακύνθιον απόκρυφον* ('A Zakynthos mystery', 1875); Maria Michanidou (c. 1855–after 1891), *Τα φάσματα της Αιγύπτου* ('The spectres of Egypt', 1875); Konstantinos Goussopoulos (dates unknown), *Τα δράματα της Κωνσταντινουπόλεως* ('The dramas of Constantinople', 1888); Epaminondas Kyriakidis (1861–1939), *Πέραν απόκρυφα* ('The mysteries of Pera, 1888–9); Ioannis Zervos, *Απόκρυφα της Αιγύπτου* ('The mysteries of Egypt', 1894).

How can we make sense of the extraordinarily rich reception of the genre of the *roman de mystères* in the Greek market for fiction – and, by extension, across the Ottoman world and the Eastern Mediterranean region at large – during the second half of the nineteenth century? One particular trait of the genre may partially account for the genre's immense popularity, both in its original context of publication in Western Europe and in the Ottoman Empire: its capacity to create forms of popular identification. Although the claim made by some that the French *roman de mystères* of the nineteenth century was a genre 'written by the people for the people'[11] seems somewhat exaggerated, it is certain that the emergence of this particular category of fiction set in motion new and complex mechanisms of identification for its diverse audiences. One of the defining characteristics of the genre was that, perhaps more than any other type of novel before it, it was populated by characters belonging at once to the lowest and highest strata of society – and to virtually every echelon in between. At a time when multiple political and social ruptures allowed for the consolidation of new social groups (an economically dominant bourgeoisie, an increasingly literate working class, and so forth), the particular interest of the popular novel in representing the coexistence and frequent intermingling of characters from various social backgrounds provided, in unprecedented ways, the various components of a socially diverse reading public with the opportunity to look at one another, often with a mixture of repulsion and fascination.[12]

However, nothing seems to indicate that, when these works of popular literature started to migrate from Western Europe to the Greek-speaking world and the Eastern Mediterranean at large in the 1840s, the overall structure of their social use as it had crystallised at the source remained intact. In France and elsewhere in Western Europe, part of the original appeal of the *roman de mystères* lay in the fact that it mobilised mechanisms of social identification while articulating at the same time a discourse of multidirectional othering. It is precisely the nature of this double movement of identification and distanciation that would become radically altered once put to the test of translation far away from the place of the novels' original composition. In the original French and Western European contexts, middle-class readers of urban mysteries could find an echo of their political and moral anxieties in the often rather conservative ideology that permeated these works (Sue's late conversion to 'socialism' notwithstanding).[13] At the same time, the exoticising gaze that these same texts cast upon both the lower and upper classes served as a gratifying confirmation of their audience's intermediary social status. For all their artificiality, the topographies in which urban mysteries unfolded largely overlapped, at least in name, with the ones that the large Parisian segment of their French audience inhabited. At the same time, for the subgenre's many readers in the provinces, the spaces that served as a backdrop for the novels' often convoluted plots belonged, due to their relative geographic proximity, to the realm of the familiar.

On the contrary, for the first Greek and Ottoman readers of French *romans de mystères*, such points of reference were to a large extent inoperative. In other words, the class-based exoticism that was a defining characteristic of the genre in its original context of composition partially survived the translation process but was subsumed by a more generalised form of exoticism *tout court*. For readers of translated *romans de mystères* in the Eastern Mediterranean region, the appeal of the foreign in these types of novels was not limited, as it was for their Western European audiences, to characters and situations located at opposite extremes of the social ladder. Indeed, foreignness seeped through the texts and encompassed locales, customs and entire articulations of the social fabric depicted in the novels. Therefore, it became the task of translators to negotiate this added layer of distance between texts and readers, one that went beyond the mere suspension of disbelief that the implausible plots so characteristic of urban mysteries demanded.[14]

From Paris to Pera: Epaminondas Kyriakidis' Πέραν Απόκρυφα ('The mysteries of Pera')

The narrative of Kyriakidis' *Πέραν Απόκρυφα* begins *in medias res*, with an elegant young woman walking down Feridiye Street in the Istanbul district of Pera on a Sunday in May 1870. Unbeknownst to her, she is being watched by an equally elegant man who follows her into a shabby-looking house in the vicinity of Tarlabaşı Boulevard, near modern-day Taksim Square. We quickly come to understand that the two characters are husband and wife, and that the young woman is suspected of adultery. As she is claiming her innocence, a handsome young man – her alleged lover – enters the scene, but is immediately shot and killed by the angry husband who then pushes his wife into an underground well, sets fire to the house to hide the double murder and is about to jump into the well himself when he is rescued *in extremis* by another – unknown – man, who helps him out of the burning house as the fire spreads to the entire neighbourhood. The long and convoluted plot that follows this inaugural scene is, like that of Eugène Sue's *Mysteries of Paris*, largely structured around the melodramatic story of a child lost and found. The main character of the novel – the unknown man who rescues the murderer in the first chapters – is Georgios Kallimahis, scion of an aristocratic family of Greek dragomans from the Danubian Principalities exiled to Anatolia after the start of the Greek Revolution in 1821. Educated by private tutors who teach him Turkish, Arabic and Persian, the young Georgios moves to Istanbul under an assumed identity after the death of his parents and falls in love with Ivi, the daughter of his lodger, whom he quickly marries. Dissatisfied with her husband's lack of wealth, the evil young bride runs away with their daughter Ermioni – who is later revealed to be none other than the woman thrown down the well by her jealous husband at the beginning of the novel. The paths of the three main characters (Georgios Kallimahis, Ivi and Ermioni) intersect with those of a host of minor figures, many of them belonging to the underworld of the imperial capital.

(Re)writing Urban Mysteries in Nineteenth-century Istanbul

In many respects, however, the main character of the novel is the city of Istanbul itself. More specifically, Kyriakidis is particularly interested in highlighting the constant intermingling of different social groups that a rapidly modernising urban landscape seems to facilitate, following here a template set by Sue and his followers. As Stephen Knight emphasises:

> From Sue on the writers' purpose was to tell the story of the cities themselves through the people – and all the people – who lived in them. . . . it is the interrelation of the rich and the very poor, and also the people awkwardly in the middle, for the good and ill of all parties, that is the recurring dynamic of these stories and the succession of their interweaving narrative threads.[15]

Indeed, Kyriakidis' *Mysteries of Pera* offers perhaps one of the most detailed accounts of the urban spaces of Istanbul found in any novel published in the city during the nineteenth century. The attention given to a realist topographical mapping of the city is particularly evident at the beginning of the novel, in the numerous chapters dedicated to a detailed account of the Great Fire of Pera (*Beyoğlu harik-i kebir*), a real event that took place in 1870 and which, in the novel, is accidentally started by Ermioni's jealous husband. In these passages, Kyriakidis describes with journalistic precision the progression of the fire through the neighbourhood of Pera and the massive destruction that it causes. A journalist himself, the author seems to have consulted newspaper articles on the event, which had received considerable coverage in the Istanbul press of the time and remained very much alive in the local collective memory at the time of the novel's publication, almost two decades later. In fact, many details of his narrative correspond to the historical reality of the event, in particular the precise location of the house where the fire was thought to have originally started, situated indeed on Feridiye Street.[16] The description of the 1870 Great Fire of Pera also provided Kyriakidis with the opportunity to insert, in the form of long interpolated digressions, purely documentary passages into the fictional core of his work, devoting for instance more than thirty pages to a detailed discussion of Istanbul's fire patrol (*tulumbacılar*) among other digressions on brothels, hospitals and other civic buildings in which the author writes as a sort of social historian of the city *avant la lettre*.

However, as is almost always the case in nineteenth-century *romans de mystères*, Kyriakidis' Istanbul simultaneously exists on two intersecting planes: the visible, legible city, apprehended through the means of documentary realism, and its invisible double, the hidden domain of the uncanny, marked by dark symbolic tones, echoing the opposition identified by Michel de Certeau between what he identifies as 'geometrical' or 'geographical' practices on the one hand and a 'mythic experience of space' on the other.[17] Thus, in *The Mysteries of Pera*, the various urban spaces where the plot of the novel unfolds all lend themselves to a potential unveiling that deterritorialises them, as ordinary looking houses can hide illegal brothels and familiar city landmarks conceal the activities of gangs of criminals.

Finally, Kyriakidis' novel, composed and published in Istanbul, is notable for the almost complete absence of any reference to the majority Muslim community of the Ottoman capital – or to any minority group outside of the Greek community, to which virtually all of the novel's characters belong. The reasons for this absence which disrupts the novel's realistic ambitions are unclear and it is hard to determine whether it should be interpreted as a form of wishful thinking on the part of Kyriakidis who imagines an entirely 'de-Islamicised' and 're-Hellenised' city or as evidence of the segmented nature of the late Ottoman reading public, largely segregated along communal lines. In any case, it stands in stark contrast to an important portion of the novelistic production published in Istanbul in the last decades of the nineteenth century, notably with the Ottoman Turkish novels of Ahmet Midhat Efendi, in which non-Muslim characters are numerous. However, as Henri Tonnet has emphasised, this characteristic is also present in other Greek novels of the period set in Istanbul and inspired by the work of Eugène Sue, notably in Christophoros Samartzidis' *Mysteries of Constantinople* (1868), where the mentions of Turks are scarce.[18] Interestingly the complete absence of any reference to Muslims or non-Greeks in Kyriakidis' *Mysteries of Pera* was preserved in its Greek-scripted Ottoman Turkish version, Evangelinos Misailidis' *Mysteries of Beyoğlu*, despite the fact that *Temaşa-i Dünya ve Cefakâr u Cefakeş* ('Theatrum Mundi, or tormentor and tormented', 1871–2), his earlier adaptation of a Greek novel and a rewriting of Grigorios Palaiologos' *Ο Πολυπαθής* ('Man of many adventures', 1839) paid particular attention to the complex and diverse ethno-linguistic landscape of Istanbul.

From Pera to Beyoğlu: Evangelinos Misailidis' The Mysteries of Beyoğlu

A prominent writer, translator and journalist, and one of the key figures in the world of Greek-scripted Ottoman Turkish letters (Karamanlidika), Evangelinos Misailidis serialised his translation of Kyriakidis' novel in his own newspaper *Anatoli* (est. 1850) under the title *Beyoğlu Sırları* ('The mysteries of Beyoğlu') almost immediately after the publication of the Greek novel in instalments and before its reprinting in book form. The serialisation of the Karamanlidika version began on 28 June 1888 and continued with an additional 164 instalments ending on 26 August 1889.[19]

In addition to this and other Karamanlidika translations of French and Greek novels, Misailidis is primarily remembered as the author of the aforementioned *Temaşa-i Dünya*, one of the first novels written in Ottoman Turkish, albeit in the Greek script. He was also the founder and principal editor until his death of *Anatoli*, the most important Karamanlidika newspaper of the nineteenth century,[20] primarily read by Karamanlis, that is, Turcophone Orthodox Christians of the Ottoman Empire, either in their ancestral home region of broader Cappadocia or in Istanbul, where large Karamanli communities also resided. *Anatoli* was one of the first Turkish-language newspapers to serialise translated novels, which included, among others, Heliodorus' *Aethiopica* in 1851, Defoe's *Robinson Crusoe* in 1852 and Christoph von Schmid's *Genevieve* in 1853.[21] Later on – and, in fact, only *after* the serialisation of Kyriakidis' novel which was largely inspired by these texts – Misailidis would translate and publish in *Anatoli* the two most famous works in the corpus of nineteenth-century *romans de mystères*, Eugène Sue's *The Mysteries of Paris*[22] and *The Wandering Jew*.[23]

As mentioned earlier, Misailidis retained in his translation of Πέραν Απόκρυφα Kyriakidis' exclusive focus on Greek characters and complete erasure of the city's Muslim and non-Greek population. However, the title of the work bears the trace of a degree of 'Turkification', the toponym of Pera (associated with ideas of cosmopolitanism since at least the mid-nineteenth century) being replaced by that of Beyoğlu, the Turkish name that would ultimately prevail in the twentieth century. This substitution reflects the general conventions of nineteenth-century Karamanlidika literature, which had a tendency to prefer the 'Ottoman' (that is, Turkish) versions of places names.[24] Beyond this difference in the title of the novel, the text of Misailidis' *Mysteries of Beyoğlu* mostly corresponds to that of Kyriakidis' *Mysteries of Pera*, with the notable exception of the final five chapters of the latter, which appear in a much-abridged version in the former. In addition, Misailidis opted to introduce a small – yet crucial – modification to the plot as a way to conform to the political stances shared by most of the Turkish-speaking Greek community of the Empire. In Kyriakidis' version, the main character Kallimahis and his daughter Ermioni leave Istanbul at the end of the novel and settle in Athens where, some years later, the young woman is ultimately reunited with her lover Iakovos upon his return from serving as a volunteer in the 1879–84 War of the Pacific. On the contrary, in Misailidis' Karamanlidika version,

Kallimahis and his family decide to remain in the Ottoman capital. Far from trivial, this difference in the plot of the two texts sheds light on the wide political chasm between the Greek bourgeoisie in the independent Greek state (which presumably constituted the largest portion of the readership of Kyriakidis' novel) and the Turkish-speaking Greek minority in the Ottoman Empire to which Misailidis and his readers belonged. While the former increasingly framed the Greek Kingdom as the natural homeland of Hellenism, the hope of better prospects for non-Muslim minorities in the wake of the Tanzimat reforms led the latter to remain durably committed to the idea of Ottoman subjecthood, as echoed by the two alternative outcomes of Kallimahis and Ermioni's trajectory.[25]

The very rapid translation of Kyriakidis' novel into Karamanlidika, which began to be serialised even before the publication of the original work in book form in Greek, was undoubtedly due to the broad popularity of the *romans de mystères* as a genre across the various communities of the Ottoman Empire, as well as to Misailidis' desire to provide the subscribers of *Anatoli* with content both contemporary and enjoyable. In parallel, however, it is possible to hypothesise that a dominant motif of the novel and of the genre at large, that of disguise, might also have had a particular resonance with the Turcophone Orthodox Christian readers of Misailidis' newspaper. Indeed – as it was already the case in Sue's novels – cases of hidden, disguised or mistaken identity abound in the plot, as do broken family relations whose rupture is almost always ultimately resolved in highly melodramatic moments of recognition and reunion. It is quite possible that this particular theme might have found an echo in the anxieties of the community to which Misailidis and his Turkish-speaking Greek readers belonged.

From the second half of the nineteenth century onwards, public discourses in both Greek and Turkish increasingly framed this group respectively as either 'lost kin' (that is, inner-Anatolia Greeks who had 'forgotten' their native tongue and adopted that of their Muslim neighbours) or as a case of 'disguised identity' (that is, Turks who had converted to Orthodox Christianity during the Byzantine era but retained their language while adopting the 'Christian' script[26]). In fact, these discussions were still prominently featured in the pages of *Anatoli* at the time of the serialisation of Misailidis' translation. The newspaper devoted ample space to a refutation of the idea, especially common among Greek speakers, that the Karamanlis of inner Anatolia constituted a cultural anomaly that needed to be corrected and that they lagged behind other Greeks in terms of their educational and 'civilisational' level[27] due to the fact that their linguistic alterity prevented them from fully participating in the *genos*, a conception of national identity relying upon both religion and language.²⁸

In addition, a particular plot point in Kyriakidis' novel might have provided an additional point of identification to the Karamanli readers of Misailidis' Karamanlidika translation: Georgios Kallimahis, the central character of the story, is presented as a migrant from inner Anatolia (specifically the city of Ankara, then little more than an isolated provincial centre) to Istanbul, a characteristic shared by many of *Anatoli*'s readers themselves, either because they belonged to the Karamanli communities who had migrated to the imperial capital but retained strong connections with their Anatolian homeland, or because they still resided in Anatolia, as many of the subscribers of the newspaper did, but had family ties with recent migrants who relocated to Istanbul in search of better economic prospects.

To an extent, it is possible that Kallimahis' difficulties in Istanbul and his feeling of estrangement might have also functioned as a sort of cautionary tale warning Anatolian Greeks against the ills of the 'debauched' imperial capital. This implicit opposition between the 'lascivious' capital and its 'modest' hinterland is notably visible in the text in passages that underline sartorial differences between the Christian women of Istanbul and those of Anatolia, the former being represented in the novel by the evil, Europeanised femme fatale Ivi, while the narrator notes that Anatolian Christian women commonly wear the *ferace* and the *yaşmak*, respectively a long coat and a veil, traditionally associated with Muslim women.

In parallel, another of the elements of Giorgos Kallimahis' biography might have served Misailidis' ideological agenda: in addition to having spent his formative years in Anatolia before coming to Istanbul, the central character of the novel also has family roots in aristocratic circles of the Danubian Principalities of Moldavia and Wallachia, ruled in the name of the Ottoman sultan by dynasties of Phanariot Greeks, for more than a century from the beginning of the eighteenth century to the Greek Revolution of 1821. Thus the novel establishes a symbolic – and entirely fictional – link between the isolated Orthodox Christian communities of inner Anatolia and Danubian Phanariots, a community that not only constituted the closest thing that Greece had to a nobility in the Western sense in recent memory, but was also perceived at once as a beacon of civilisation due to its familiarity with the ideas of the Enlightenment that had penetrated the Phanariot courts in the eighteenth century and as directly connected to the national awakening due the role it had played in the Greek uprising of the 1820s.

Coming back to Kyriakidis' *The Mysteries of Pera*, we would like to end by suggesting two possible venues for further theoretical inquiry opened up by a study of that particular text, both in its own right and in articulation with its Karamanlidika version, *The Mysteries of Beyoğlu*. First, the particular position of this Greek-Ottoman novel vis-à-vis its obvious French source compels us to rethink the very terminology that we use in order to define it. With respect to the model of which it constitutes a variation (Sue's *Mysteries of Paris* and other works inspired by it), Kyriakidis' work is neither fully 'original', nor is it a direct 'translation' in the sense of textual correspondence. Concurrently, it is also not *sensu stricto* an adaptation of Sue, in the sense that none of the episodes of the French work's convoluted narrative make their way into the Greek text. Yet, at the same time, every single element of the Greek text, from the melodramatic twists of its plot to the hordes of stock characters that populate it, gives the impression of having been lifted from the work of Sue or of one of his epigones. In that regard, a case like that of *The Mysteries of Pera* allows us, when we study its relationship with its Western source of inspiration, to think of translation as a phenomenon of *transposition*, not only because it makes ample use of the topoi associated with the specific genre of the *roman de mystères*, but also, quite literally, because it stages the 'displacement' and 'migration' of these same narrative tropes from one urban space to another. As has often been noted, Sue's text in *The Mysteries of Paris* ultimately came to overlap with the *tissu urbain*, the urban fabric of the French capital in the mid-nineteenth century. In Kyriakidis' novel, the (symptomatically alliterative) transfer of generic stereotypes from *Paris* to *Pera* is highlighted in the ways in which a specifically Parisian blueprint is projected upon – and ultimately becomes blended with – the topography of Istanbul, where the 'Grand Rue de Péra' becomes a symbolic extension of the Parisian boulevards and where the Prince Islands, where part of the Kyriakides' work is set, function as a counterpart to the non-central locales (the Bois de Boulogne, the various points of the peri-urban *zone*, to use a slightly anachronistic term) that the characters of Sue's work frequently visit.

Finally, when studied in articulation with its Karamanlidika translation by Misailidis, Kyriakidis' *Mysteries of Pera* allows us to think of translation in articulation with yet another notion, that of *transcription*. As an example of literary exchange not between ethno-religious communities but within one of them, a study of the pair formed by *The Mysteries of Pera* and *The Mysteries of Beyoğlu* provides us with tools to counter the diffusionist narratives that have approached late-Ottoman literary translation as a largely unidirectional phenomenon of transfer between

(Re)writing Urban Mysteries in Nineteenth-century Istanbul

Western Europe and the Ottoman world. In mobilising the notion of 'script', we can expand our exploration of the practice of translation in the late Ottoman Empire, where the existence of shared alphabets and the complexity of the social uses of competing writing systems often interfered with the theoretical compartmentalisation imposed by the so-called millet system. Examples of these tensions around scripts during the period included, among others, the coexistence of at least three writing systems used for the printing of Ottoman Turkish (the Arabo-Persian script, as well as the Greek and Armenian alphabets), the debates around the choice of a 'national' script among the Albanian intellectual circles of Istanbul, or the particular situation of Judeo-Spanish, commonly printed in the semi-cursive *rashi* script interspersed with Hebrew block characters).

In framing late-Ottoman translation as *transcription*, it is possible to read the rapid and massive increase in the number of translations of foreign prose fiction in the various literary idioms of the Ottoman Empire during the second half of the nineteenth century in articulation with the proliferation of scripts employed for the printing of these translated texts. Additionally, by making use of the various connotations carried by the idea of script, a recourse to the concept and to its dual meaning of 'typeface' and 'template' or 'convention' (as it is used, for instance, in the notion of 'cultural scripts') can lay the ground for an analysis of late Ottoman translation going beyond the exclusive study of textuality and encompassing both typographic traces and cultural practices.[29]

Notes

1. See notably Johann Strauss, 'Who Read What in the Ottoman Empire (19th–20th Centuries)?', *Middle Eastern Literatures* 6: 1 (2003): 35–76; Mehmet Fatih Uslu and Fatih Altuğ (eds), *Tanzimat ve Edebiyat: Osmanlı İstanbulu'nda Modern Edebi Kültür* (Istanbul: Türkiye İş Bankası, 2014); Etienne Charrière, '"We Must Ourselves Write About Ourselves": The Transcommunal Rise of the Novel in the Late Ottoman Empire', PhD dissertation, University of Michigan, 2016; Monica Ringer and Etienne Charrière (eds), *Ottoman Culture and the Project of Modernity: Reform and the Tanzimat Novel* (London: I. B. Tauris, 2020).
2. The novel was concurrently serialised in *Epitheorisis*, a Greek-language newspaper published in Istanbul. We thank Prof. Georgia Gotsi (University of Patras) for providing us with this information.
3. Interestingly, the work shares a title with an unrelated novel, *Les Mystères de Péra*, published in French in Istanbul by Sephardic author Jacques Loria less than a decade later in 1896. See Johann Strauss, 'Le roman d'Istanbul',

Revue des mondes musulmans et de la Méditerranée 87–8 (1999): 19–38; 29.
4. Data used in this overview of Sue's Greek-Ottoman reception come from the bibliography of Greek translations compiled in Konstantinos G. Kasinis, Βιβλιογραφία των ελληνικών μεταφράσεων της ξένης λογοτεχνίας, ΙΘ'–Κ'αι. Αυτοτελείς Εκδόσεις, vol. 1: 1801–1900 (Athens: Syllogos pros Diadosin Ophelimon Vivlion, 2006). See also Etienne Charrière, 'Borrowed Texts: Translation and the Rise of the Ottoman-Greek Novel in the Nineteenth Century', Syn-Thèses 6 (2013):12–26; Charrière, 'We Must Ourselves Write About Ourselves'; Ringer and Charrière, Ottoman Culture, 12–18. Unsurprisingly, considering Sue's truly global fame in the second half of the nineteenth century, translations of his works appeared in large numbers in other languages of the Ottoman Empire during the same period – although slightly later than the first Greek translations: the first translation of Sue into Ottoman-Turkish, an Armenian-scripted translation of *The Mysteries of Paris*, attributed to Garabed Panosyan (1826–1905), seems to have appeared as early as 1858, while *The Wandering Jew* appears to have been translated for the first time into Ottoman-Turkish by Mehmet Tevfik (1860–1910). The same two novels were translated into Armenian in 1863 (by Matteos Mamurian, 1830–1901) and 1867 (by Garabed Utudjian, 1823–1904) respectively, while they appeared in Ladino translation in 1876 (by Eliau Moshe ben Nahmias and David Yosef Saporta, dates unknown) and 1896 (by Victor Levy, dates unknown).
5. Aude Aylin de Tapia 'De *La Porteuse de pain* (1884) à *l'Etmekçi Hatun* (1885). Un roman populaire français chez les *Karamanli*s', in Evangelia Balta and M. Ölmez (eds), *Cultural Encounters in the Turkish-speaking Communities of the Late Ottoman Empire* (Istanbul: The Isis Press, 2014), 223–56.
6. Ivan Chupin, Nicolas Hubé and Nicolas Kaciaf, *Histoire politique et économique des médias en France* (Paris: La Découverte, 2009).
7. Faubourg, originally 'suburb', is not easily translated. Many of these neighbourhoods were absorbed by the city in the second half of the nineteenth century. The term, however, was still used, and in this title has working-class implications.
8. Féval's novel was published the same year as George W. M. Reynolds' similarly titled but entirely unrelated English-language novel.
9. For more on the Greek tradition of the *romans de mystères* see, among others, Pantelis Voutouris, Ως εις καθρέπτην... Προτάσεις και υποθέσεις για την ελληνική πεζογραφία του $19^{ου}$ αιώνα (Athens: Nefeli, 1995); Sophia Denisi, 'Μυθιστόρημα των Αποκρύφων: μια μορφή κοινωνικού μυθιστορήματος του 19ου αιώνα', *Periplous* 43 (1997): 38–63; Georgia Gotsi, 'Η μυθιστορία των "Αποκρύφων". Συμβολή στην περιγραφή του είδους', in Nasos Vagenas (ed.), *Από τον Λέανδρο στον Λουκή Λάρα. Μελέτες για την πεζογραφία της περιόδου 1830–1880* (Heraklion: Crete University Press, 1997), 149–68;

Georgia Gotsi, 'Υποθέσεις για το εικονογραφημένο μυθιστόρημα του 19ου αιώνα. Η περίπτωση των Αποκρύφων', *Anti* 641 (1997): 42–7; Henri Tonnet, Ο χώρος και η σημασία του στα "Απόκρυφα Κωνσταντινουπόλεως" (1868) του Χριστόφορου Σαμαρτσίδη', *Anti* 641 (1997): 26–31; Henri Tonnet, '"Les Mystères de Constantinople" (1868) de Christophoros Samartsidis, un roman populaire grec à la française', in Henri Tonnet, *Etudes sur la nouvelle et le roman grecs modernes* (Athens: Daedalus, 2002), 165–70; Effie Amilitou, 'Apocryphes urbains, ou la construction d'un mystérieux genre romanesque en Grèce', *Médias 19*, online, updated 7 December 2013. Available at <http://www.medias19.org/index.php?id=14891> (last accessed 29 May 2022); Filippos Katsanos, 'Réceptions croisées: les enjeux de la traduction des *Mystères de Paris* en Grande-Bretagne et en Grèce', *Médias 19*, online, updated 21 March 2015. Available at <http://www.medias19.org/index.php?id=17191> (last accessed 29 May 2022).

10. On the global 'mysterymania' that followed the publication of Sue's novel, see notably Berry Palmer Chevasco, *Mysterymania: The Reception of Eugène Sue in Britain, 1838–1860* (Oxford and Bern: Peter Lang, 2005). This focuses on the British reception of the work. See also the online proceedings of a series of conferences organised by the Médias 19 platform. The platform also maintains a database referencing a very large number of nineteenth-century urban mystery texts. Available at <http://mysteres.medias19.org> (last accessed 1 June 2019).

11. See, for instance, Christopher Prendergast's reading of Sue's *Mysteries of Paris* as a collectively produced work: Christopher Prendergast, *For the People, by the People?: Eugene Sue's 'Les Mystères De Paris' – A Hypothesis in the Sociology of Literature* (Leeds: Legenda, 2004).

12. On the position of the *roman de mystère* in nineteenth-century French popular literature, see notably Michel Ragon, *Histoire de la littérature prolétarienne de langue française: littérature ouvrière, littérature paysanne, littérature d'expression populaire* (Paris: Librairie générale française, 1974); Marc Angenot, *Le Roman populaire, recherches en paralittérature* (Montréal: Presses de l'Université du Québec, 1975); Francis Lacassin, *A la recherche de l'empire caché: mythologie du roman populaire* (Paris: Julliard, 1991); Dominique Kalifa, *L'Encre et le Sang: récits de crimes et société à la Belle Époque* (Paris: Fayard, 1995); Vittorio Frigerio, *Les Fils de Monte Cristo: idéologie du héros de roman populaire* (Limoges: Presses de l'Université de Limoges, 2002); Dominique Kalifa, *Crime et culture au XIXe siècle* (Paris: Perrin, 2005); Daniel Compère, *Les romans populaires* (Paris: Presses de la Sorbonne Nouvelle, 2012).

13. On Sue's readers and their politics, see notably Jean-Pierre Galvan, *Les Mystères de Paris: Eugène Sue et ses lecteurs* (Paris: L'Harmattan, 1998).

14. For a detailed analysis and examples of the challenges involved in rendering Sue into Ottoman languages, see Charrière, 'We Must Ourselves Write About Ourselves', 130–60.

15. Stephen Knight, *The Mysteries of the Cities: Urban Crime Fiction in the Nineteenth Century* (Jefferson, NC and London: McFarland & Company, 2012), 11.
16. Zeynep Çelik, *The Remaking of İstanbul: Portrait of an Ottoman City in the Nineteenth Century* (Seattle: University of Washington Press, 1993), 64. The fire described in the novel took place, in fact, in the Pera area in the spring of 1870 and destroyed more than 3,000 buildings, rendering hundreds of people homeless and significantly impacting the social and cultural life of the European side of Istanbul. The exact location where the fire started was identified by Ottoman newspapers of the time (such as, for instance, *Takvim-i Vekayi*, the first Turkish newspaper published under Mahmud II) as a private house rented by a Hungarian citizen named Rechini (Macar Reçini) or Richini (Riçini). The fire started around noon on 5 June 1870 around noon and spread quickly around the neighbourhood due to the strong winds that were blowing that day. With the exception of its initial starting point, the details match Kyriakidis' description of the event in his novel. At a later point in the novel, Kyriakidis stages a conversation between his main character Kallimahis and Greek banker Georgios Zafiris who organised rescue efforts in the wake of the fire. This minor character is probably inspired by the figure of Georgios Zarifis, a well-known Greek-Ottoman banker and philanthropist – and a possible patron of the author. On this figure and his role in Ottoman banking, see Murat Hulkiander, *Bir Galata Bankerinin Portresi George Zarifi 1806–1884* (Istanbul: Osmanlı Bankası, 2003).
17. Michel de Certeau, *The Practice of Everyday Life*, trans. Steven F. Rendall (Berkeley and Los Angeles: University of California Press, 1984).
18. Tonnet, 'Ο χώρος και η σημασία', 29. It is not, however, the case in Stephanos Xenos' *The Devil in Turkey* (1851), an earlier novel probably partially inspired by Sue, originally published in English translation and which includes Muslim Turks, Jews and Armenians among its characters.
19. Epaminondas Kyriakidis, *Beyoğlu Sırları*, trans. Evangelinos Misailidis, *Anatoli*, 28 June 1888 (No. 3926) – 26 August 1889 (No. 4091). The text has recently been reprinted in book form and in the Latin alphabet: Epaminondas Kyriakidis, *Beyoğlu Sırları*, edited by E. Balta and S. Payır (Istanbul: Istos, 2020).
20. Şehnaz Şişmanoğlu Şimşek, 'The *Anatoli* Newspaper and the Heyday of the Karamanli Press', in Evangelia Balta and Matthias Kappler (eds), *Cries and Whispers in Karamanlidika Books – Proceedings of the First International Conference on Karamanlidika Studies (Nicosia 11th–13th September 2008)* (Wiesbaden: Harrassowitz, 2010), 429–48; Foti and Stefo Benlisoy, 'Reading the Identity of Karamanli Through the Pages of Anatoli', in Evangelia Balta and Matthias Kappler (eds), *Cries and Whispers in Karamanlidika Books – Proceedings of the First International Conference on Karamanlidika Studies (Nicosia 11th–13th September 2008)* (Wiesbaden: Harrassowitz, 2010), 93–108.

21. For a general overview of fiction published in Karamanlidika, see Ioanna Petropoulou, 'From West to East: The Translation Bridge: An Approach from a Western Perspective', in Anna Frangoudaki and Çaglar Keyder (eds), *Ways to Modernity in Greece and Turkey: Encounters with Europe, 1850–1950* (London and New York: I. B. Tauris, 2007), 91–112; for a list of the novels and short stories serialised in *Anatoli*, see Şehnaz Şişmanoğlu Şimşek, 'Karamanlidika Literary Production at the End of the 19th Century as Reflected in the Pages of *Anatoli*', in Evangelia Balta and Mehmet Ölmez (eds), *Cultural Encounters in the Turkish-speaking Communities of the Late Ottoman Empire* (Istanbul: The Isis Press, 2014), 109–24; and Şehnaz Şişmanoğlu Şimşek, 'Osmanlı Tefrika Çalışmalarında Göz Ardı Edilen Bir Kaynak: Karamanlıca Anatoli Gazetesi', *Kebikeç* 44 (2017): 145–88.
22. Eugène Sue, *Paris Sırları (The Mysteries of Paris)*, trans. Evangelinos Misailidis, *Anatoli*, 25 February 1897 (No. 5471) [unfinished].
23. Eugène Sue, *Serseri Yahudi (The Wandering Jew)*, trans. Evangelinos Misailidis, *Anatoli*, 17 July 1897 (No. 5587) [unfinished].
24. This convention was also reflected in the choice of the names used to identify Istanbul as the place of publication on the cover of *Karamanlidika* books: *Der-i Saadet, Der Aliye, Konstantiniye*, or *Istanbol* were usually used in lieu of the Greek *Konstantinoupolis*.
25. Interestingly, Misailidis had already adopted the same trope in his earlier rewriting of a Greek novel, the aforementioned *Temaşa-i Dünya*, where the main character also opts to remain in Istanbul at the end of the plot instead of moving to Athens as in the original text.
26. For a detailed account of these debates, see notably Evangelia Balta, 'Gerci Rum Isek de Rumca bilmez Türkçe Söyleriz: The Adventure of an Identity of the Triptych: Vatan, Religion and Language', *Türk Kültürü İncelemeleri Dergisi* 8 (2003): 25–44.
27. Foti and Stefo Benlisoy, 'Türkdilli Anadolu Ortodoksların Kimlik Algısı', *Tarih ve Toplum Yeni Yaklaşımlar* 11: 251 (2010): 7–22;
28. Peter Mackridge, *Language and National Identity in Greece, 1766–1976* (Oxford and New York: Oxford University Press, 2009).
29. On the intersections of transcription and translation in late Ottoman literature, see Etienne Charrière, 'Translation, Transcription, and the Making of World Literature: On Late Ottoman and Modern Turkish Scriptworlds', in Burcu Alkan and Çimen Günay-Erkol (eds), *Turkish Literature as World Literature* (London: Bloomsbury, 2020), 36–54.

Bibliography

Amilitou, Effie, 'Apocryphes urbains, ou la construction d'un mystérieux genre romanesque en Grèce', *Médias 19*, online, updated 7 December 2013, <http://www.medias19.org/index.php?id=14891> (last accessed 29 May 2022).

Angenot, Marc, *Le Roman populaire, recherches en paralittérature* (Montréal: Presses de l'Université du Québec, 1975).

Balta, Evangelia, 'Gerci Rum Isek de Rumca bilmez Türkçe Söyleriz: The Adventure of an Identity of the Triptych: Vatan, Religion and Language', *Türk Kültürü İncelemeleri Dergisi* 8 (2013): 25–44.

Balta, Evangelia, 'Ottoman Evidence about the Greek and Karamanlı Editions of Evangelinos Misailidis', *Osmanlı Araştırmaları* 34 (2017): 49–71.

Benlisoy, Foti and Stefo Benlisoy, 'Türkdilli Anadolu Ortodoksların Kimlik Algısı', *Tarih ve Toplum Yeni Yaklaşımlar* 11: 251 (2010): 7–22.

Benlisoy, Foti and Stefo Benlisoy, 'Reading the Identity of Karamanli Through the Pages of Anatoli', in Evalngelia Balta and Matthias Kappler (eds), *Cries and Whispers in Karamanlidika Books – Proceedings of the First International Conference on Karamanlidika Studies (Nicosia 11th–13th September 2008)* (Wiesbaden: Harrassowitz, 2010), 93–108.

Çelik, Zeynep, *The Remaking of İstanbul: Portrait of an Ottoman City in the Nineteenth Century* (Seattle: University of Washington Press, 1993).

de Certeau, Michel, *The Practice of Everyday Life*, trans. Steven F. Rendall (Berkeley and Los Angeles: University of California Press, 1984).

Charrière, Etienne, 'Borrowed Texts: Translation and the Rise of the Ottoman-Greek Novel in the Nineteenth Century', *Syn-Thèses* 6 (2013): 12–26.

Charrière, Etienne, '"We Must Ourselves Write About Ourselves": The Trans-communal Rise of the Novel in the Late Ottoman Empire', PhD dissertation, University of Michigan, 2016.

Charrière, Etienne, 'Translating Communities: Reading Foreign Fiction across Communal Boundaries in the Tanzimat Period', in Monica Ringer and Etienne Charrière (eds), *Ottoman Culture and the Project of Modernity: Reform and the Tanzimat Novel* (London: I. B. Tauris, 2020), 177–92.

Charrière, Etienne, 'Translation, Transcription, and the Making of World Literature: On Late Ottoman and Modern Turkish Scriptworlds', in Burcu Alkan and Çimen Günay-Erkol (eds), *Turkish Literature as World Literature* (London: Bloomsbury, 2020), 36–54.

Chupin, Ivan, Nicolas Hubé and Nicolas Kaciaf, *Histoire politique et économique des médias en France* (Paris: La Découverte, 2009).

Compère, Daniel, *Les romans populaires* (Paris: Presses de la Sorbonne Nouvelle, 2012).

Denisi, Sophia, 'Μυθιστόρημα των Αποκρύφων: μια μορφή κοινωνικού μυθιστορήματος του 19ου αιώνα', *Periplous* 43 (1997): 38–63.

Frigerio, Vittorio, *Les Fils de Monte Cristo: idéologie du héros de roman populaire* (Limoges: Presses de l'Université de Limoges, 2002).

Galvan, Jean-Pierre, *Les Mystères de Paris: Eugène Sue et ses lecteurs* (Paris: L'Harmattan, 1998).

Gotsi, Georgia, 'Η μυθιστορία των "Αποκρύφων". Συμβολή στην περιγραφή του είδους', in Nasos Vagenas (ed.), *Από τον Λέανδρο στον Λουκή Λάρα. Μελέτες*

για την πεζογραφία της περιόδου *1830–1880* (Heraklion: Crete University Press, 1997).
Gotsi, Georgia, 'Υποθέσεις για το εικονογραφημένο μυθιστόρημα του 19ου αιώνα. Η περίπτωση των Αποκρύφων', *Anti* 641 (1997): 42–7.
Hulkiender, Murat, *Bir Galata Bankerinin Portresi George Zarifi 1806–1880* (Istanbul: Osmanlı Bankası, 2006).
Kalifa, Dominique, *L'Encre et le Sang: récits de crimes et société à la Belle Époque* (Paris: Fayard, 1995).
Kalifa, Dominique, *Crime et culture au XIXe siècle* (Paris: Perrin, 2005).
Kasinis, Konstantinos G., Βιβλιογραφία των ελληνικών μεταφράσεων της ξένης λογοτεχνίας, ΙΘ'–Κ'αι. Αυτοτελείς Εκδόσεις, vol. 1: 1801–1900 (Athens: Syllogos pros Diadosin Ophelimon Vivlion, 2006).
Katsanos, Filippos, 'Réceptions croisées: les enjeux de la traduction des Mystères de Paris en Grande-Bretagne et en Grèce', *Médias 19*, online, updated 21 March 2015, <http://www.medias19.org/index.php?id=17191> (29 May 2022).
Knight, Stephen, *The Mysteries of the Cities: Urban Crime Fiction in the Nineteenth Century* (Jefferson, NC; London: McFarland & Company, 2012).
Kyriakidis, Epaminondas, *Beyoğlu Sırları*, trans. Evangelinos Misailidis, *Anatoli*, 28 June 1888 (No. 3926) – 26 August 1889 (No. 4091).
Kyriakidis, Epaminondas, *Πέραν απόκρυφα Κωνσταντινουπόλεως: πρωτότυπον κοινωνικόν μυθιστόρημα* (Istanbul: N. G. Kephalidis, 1890).
Kyriakidis, Epaminondas, *Beyoğlu Sırları*, edited by E. Balta and S. Payır (Istanbul: Istos, 2020).
Lacassin, Francis, *A la recherche de l'empire caché: mythologie du roman populaire* (Paris: Julliard, 1990).
Mackridge, Peter, *Language and National Identity in Greece, 1766–1976* (Oxford and New York: Oxford University Press, 2009).
Palmer Chevasco, Berry, *Mysterymania: The Reception of Eugène Sue in Britain, 1838–1860* (Oxford and Bern: Peter Lang, 2005).
Petropoulou, Ioanna, 'From West to East: The Translation Bridge: An Approach from a Western Perspective', in Anna Frangoudaki and Çaglar Keyder (eds), *Ways to Modernity in Greece and Turkey: Encounters with Europe, 1850–1950* (London and New York: I. B. Tauris, 2007), 91–112.
Prendergast, Christopher, *For the People, by the People?: Eugene Sue's 'Les Mystères De Paris'* – *A Hypothesis in the Sociology of Literature* (Leeds: Legenda, 2004).
Ragon, Michel, *Histoire de la littérature prolétarienne de langue française: littérature ouvrière, littérature paysanne, littérature d'expression populaire* (Paris: Librairie générale française, 1974).
Ringer, Monica and Etienne Charrière (eds), *Ottoman Culture and the Project of Modernity: Reform and the Tanzimat Novel* (London: I. B. Tauris, 2020).
Şişmanoğlu Şimşek, Şehnaz, 'Karamanlidika Literary Production at the End of the 19th Century as Reflected in the Pages of Anatoli', in Evangelia Balta and Mehmet Ölmez (eds), *Cultural Encounters in the Turkish-speaking*

Communities of the Late Ottoman Empire (Istanbul: The Isis Press, 2014), 109–24.

Şişmanoğlu Şimşek, Şehnaz, 'Osmanlı Tefrika Çalışmalarında Göz Ardı Edilen Bir Kaynak: Karamanlıca Anatoli Gazetesi', *Kebikeç* 44 (2017): 145–88.

Şişmanoğlu Şimşek, Şehnaz, 'The Anatoli Newspaper and the Heyday of the Karamanli Press', in Evangelia Balta and Matthias Kappler (eds), *Cries and Whispers in Karamanlidika Books – Proceedings of the First International Conference on Karamanlidika Studies (Nicosia 11th–13th September 2008)* (Wiesbaden: Harrassowitz, 2017), 429–48.

Strauss, Johann, 'Le roman d'Istanbul', *Revue des mondes musulmans et de la Méditerranée* 87–8 (1999): 19–38.

Strauss, Johann, 'Who Read What in the Ottoman Empire (19th–20th Centuries)?', *Middle Eastern Literatures* 6: 1 (2003): 35–76.

de Tapia, Aude Aylin, 'De *La Porteuse de pain* (1884) à *l'Etmekçi Hatun* (1885). Un roman populaire français chez les Karamanlis', in Evangelia Balta and Mehmet Ölmez (eds), *Cultural Encounters in the Turkish-speaking Communities of the Late Ottoman Empire* (Istanbul: The Isis Press, 2014), 223–56.

Tonnet, Henri, 'Ο χώρος και η σημασία του στα "Απόκρυφα Κωνσταντινουπόλεως" (1868) του Χριστόφορου Σαμαρτσίδη', *Anti* 641 (1997): 26–31.

Tonnet, Henri, '"Les Mystères de Constantinople" (1868) de Christophoros Samartsidis, un roman populaire grec à la française', in Henri Tonnet, *Etudes sur la nouvelle et le roman grecs modernes* (Athens: Daedalus, 2002), 165–70.

Uslu, Mehmet Fatih and Fatih Altuğ (eds), *Tanzimat ve Edebiyat: Osmanlı İstanbulu'nda Modern Edebi Kültür* (Istanbul: Türkiye İş Bankası, 2014).

Voutouris, Pantelis, *Ως εις καθρέπτην ... Προτάσεις και υποθέσεις για την ελληνική πεζογραφία του 19^{ου} αιώνα* (Athens: Nefeli, 1995).

PART II
MEDITERRANEAN MULTIPLES

Chapter 4

Khayr al-Din al-Tunisi's *Muqaddima* to *Aqwam al-masalik fi ma'rifat ahwal al-mamalik* (*The Surest Path to Knowing the Condition of Kingdoms*), in Arabic, French and Ottoman Turkish

PART I

Khayr al-Din al-Tunisi's *Aqwam al-masalik/Réformes nécessaires*: A Dual Intervention in Arabic and French Political Discourses

Peter Hill

Is the Muslim world now merely a set of dead nations, which ought to be, following a harsh but memorable saying, 'quickly buried before they infect the living' – or does it still contain elements of life, of regeneration, of futurity? Does it preserve enough latent forces that, in finally manifesting themselves through reforms, they can one day give it the right to claim its place and its role in the progressive movement of humanity?

Thus opened a long book review in the French *Revue de l'instruction publique* of 2 April 1868.[1] For readers concerned with the fate of 'the Muslim world', the question so sonorously posed here might well have seemed a pressing one. The great Eurasian Muslim dynasties of the Mughals and the Qajars had fallen or dwindled, while the Ottoman Empire, Christendom's historically formidable adversary, was derided in European capitals as 'the sick man of Europe'. Several of its provinces, most dramatically perhaps Algeria from 1830, had succumbed to varying degrees of European control.

The author of the work under review, 'M. le général Khérédine', approached the issue somewhat more guardedly. '[E]very sensible Muslim' must accept, his preface noted, that 'the rapidity of communications' was making the world resemble 'a single country inhabited by different races, in ever more frequent contact with each other, having identical interests to satisfy, and contributing, albeit separately, to the common good'.[2] He accepts realistically this initial fact of a world shrinking under the impetus of 'the progressive movement of humanity', or what we might call the global expansion of a Europe-centred capitalist system. His problem is not how to avoid integration into this new reality, but how best to manage its terms: he seeks to control the manner in which the spheres of Muslim world and outside world would be conjoined, where there would be compatibility and equivalence ('identical interests', 'common good'), and where distinctiveness and separation. In this way, he sets out to argue that the Muslim world could indeed regenerate itself via reforms, and so join the nineteenth-century march of progress – and to suggest exactly what sort of reforms would be required.

At the same time as Francophone reviewers were grappling with the eighty-page French text entitled *Réformes nécessaires aux états musulmans*, scholars in the author's home country of Tunisia, and elsewhere, were reading its Arabic incarnation. This was entitled *Aqwam al-masalik fi ma'rifat ahwal al-mamalik* (*The Surest Path to Knowing the Conditions of Kingdoms*), by 'the prince of princes, *al-sayyid* Khayr al-Din al-Tunisi' and comprised, in addition to the ninety-page introduction (*Muqaddima*) which was the basis of the French text, a further 377 pages of analytical description of the Ottoman Empire and nineteen European countries. One of these Arabophone scholars would praise its project as one of 'acquainting both ourselves and the foreigner (*al-ajnabi*) with the other's condition':

> If we don't know his condition, we can't prepare to encounter him in battle (*law-la ma'rifat-na bi-hali-hi * ma amkana al-isti'dad li-nizali-hi*) or weave on his loom so as to achieve the means of resistance (*wa-l-nasj fi tahsil asbab al-muqawama 'ala minwali-hi*)

The book would equip Muslims – this author combatively suggests – with the practical means to resist being 'buried'. But, he continues, it would teach 'the foreigner' a correct appreciation of 'our *shari'a*': not merely (as foreigners had tended to assume) 'a foolish dream of ours', but instead 'suitable for all our ages'.[3] In particular, this implies, the quintessentially Muslim *shari'a* is suited to *this* age – no dead letter but, in the parlance of the French reviewer, a source of 'life, regeneration, futurity'. As another Tunisian contemporary put it, Khayr al-Din shows a way for Muslim states to 'grasp the means of prosperity (*'umran*) . . . in a way that the mighty Law (*shar'*) does not reject, but instead requires . . . and urges'.[4] His book has a dual project: to give 'us' the 'means of resistance' and prosperity, but also to convince 'the foreigner' that we can be part of this modern, 'progressive' world, by means of rather than despite our religio-legal distinctiveness.

Khayr al-Din al-Tunisi's Muqaddima *to* Aqwam al-masalik

For such a dual project – as many of his readers were aware – it was necessary to address two audiences, Muslims and Europeans, representatives of the two spheres whose relationship was in question. The simultaneous publication of the long Arabic treatise and of the French version of its introduction was an integral part of the author's project. This has been overlooked in many subsequent accounts of Khayr al-Din: the French *Réformes nécessaires* has generally been overshadowed by its Arabic counterpart, and the two have rarely been read in tandem. Outlining the composition and simultaneous publication of both versions, as well as the overlapping audiences they were intended for, suggests an interpretation of Khayr al-Din's project. It allows us to see what kind of juncture of spheres Khayr al-Din was aiming for: where he sought to affirm equivalences, and where to maintain separations.[5]

Khayr al-Din

The period when *Aqwam al-masalik/Réformes nécessaires* was written was one of relative retirement from politics for 'the pride of critical ministers' (*fakhr al-wuzara' al-nuqqad*), as one of his Tunisian allies called him.[6] Khayr al-Din (c. 1820–90) belonged to the last generation of Circassian mamluks to be bought as elite military slaves by the Husaynid Beys of Tunis, who held this 'Regency' of the Ottoman Empire as vassals of the sultan in Istanbul. In their service he rose in the military and then politics, taking part in several diplomatic missions to Europe and Istanbul in the 1840s and 1850s. He was Minister of the Navy in the administration which introduced the 'Ahd al-Aman or Fundamental Pact of 1857 – the Tunisian version of the Ottoman Empire's Tanzimat decree – and its successor, the 'law of state' (*qanun al-dawla*) of 1861, which became famous as the Arab world's first constitution. In 1861 he became head of the Supreme Council, the parliament-like assembly of notables created by these reforms – but resigned the following year; he would later blame the obstruction and corruption of other courtiers, especially his great rival Mustafa Khaznadar (1817–78). Two years later, in 1864, a major popular rebellion against increased taxation and what were seen as the European-dominated, un-Islamic reforms, led to the constitution's abrogation. In the 1860s he lived in semi-retirement in his palace at Manuba outside Tunis, travelling frequently to Europe and Istanbul and keeping considerable influence in Tunisian politics. He would return in 1873–7 to head a centralising, reformist ministry in Tunis; and then serve for six brief months as grand vizier of the Ottoman Empire itself, in 1878–9, in the political ferment following the deposition of Sultan Abdülaziz (r. 1861–76), the granting of the first Ottoman Constitution and the convoking of its first parliament in 1876.[7]

His career has often been presented by sympathetic biographers as a gifted statesman's heroic struggle for reform and good government against enormous odds. He resigned from high office three times, in each case – as he and his defenders have presented it – blocked in his reforms by the malice or incompetence of others: in 1862 corrupt courtiers such as Mustafa Khaznadar, whose plunder of the state treasury he sought to end; in 1877 the European powers and their diplomats, on whose interests his reforms threatened to encroach; in 1879 reactionary Ottoman ulama and Sultan Abdülhamid II (r. 1876–1909), who would soon end the parliamentary government Khayr al-Din had upheld in favour of a thirty-year 'despotism' of personal rule.[8]

Complexities can, though, be discerned. For all his attacks on Khaznadar's profiteering, Khayr al-Din himself amassed considerable wealth in the bey's service;[9] despite his insistence on strict ministerial accountability, he took care, while out of office, to maintain his own influence among Tunisian officials.[10] While subsequent generations would claim him as a proto-nationalist, he owed his ascent to power in 1873, as well as his fall in 1877, to European pressure, and worked closely for much of his career with European financiers and consuls.[11] He was also a firm defender of the Ottoman role in Tunisia, and in his foray into Ottoman high politics sought to play the part of a pan-Ottoman rather than simply a Tunisian statesman.[12] Despite his protests that Tanzimat-style reforms should not require a heavier tax burden on the populace,[13] those of 1857–64 evidently did, while paying a large part of the proceeds to European creditors – as the nomads and peasants who rose in rebellion and forced the abrogation of the *qanun al-dawla* were well aware.[14] He was a controversial figure during his lifetime, accused of being a French and an Ottoman agent, as well as a pretender to the beylicate; his friends punned on his name, Khayr al-Din (meaning 'the good of religion') to dub him 'Khayr al-din wa-l-dunya' ('the good of religion and the present world'), but his enemies turned this into 'Kharab al-din' ('the ruin of religion'), and 'Sharr al-din wa-l-dunya' ('the evil of religion and this world').[15] Finally, his posthumous reputation was built above all on his political treatise and its arguments for constitutionalism and limits on arbitrary power, but he was himself attacked sharply by former allies for betraying these principles during his 1873–7 ministry.[16]

The crucial point for us about his career is its trans-Mediterranean nature, spanning Tunis, a number of European cities – especially Paris – and Istanbul. Between these nodes Khayr al-Din and his allies sought to weave together a network of connections reaching into European and

Khayr al-Din al-Tunisi's Muqaddima *to* Aqwam al-masalik

Ottoman ministries, circles of learning, public opinion and finance; at the same time, they sought to pull apart the parallel networks of their rivals, like Mustafa Khaznadar and his allies. As Julia Clancy-Smith suggests, he can be seen as a 'borderland intellectual', 'operat[ing] at multiple points of intersection'.[17] But he did not only cross borders: he sought to shape and direct the traffic between them. His project was a bid to control the way in which particular components of the Islamic world and the outside world – meaning principally Europe – would be connected together. His treatise, *Aqwam al-masalik/Réformes nécessaires*, was both a contribution to and a reflection upon this enterprise.

Aqwam al-masalik fi ma'rifat ahwal al-mamalik/Réformes nécessaires

Aqwam al-masalik contributed greatly to Khayr al-Din's reputation as a sagacious statesman in his lifetime; since his death it has been the main foundation of his claim to be one of the leading figures of Ottoman reform, Islamic modernism and the Arab Nahda. In establishing this reputation, it is the Arabic version of *Aqwam al-masalik* which has drawn most attention, and above all its introduction, the *Muqaddima*, which sets out his positive proposals for state reform. It puts in clear and concise terms the rationale for the Ottoman Tanzimat and analogous reforms: the power and prosperity of Europe, the need to learn from its political institutions and enact comparable reforms, the belief that such reforms would not contradict but would in fact strengthen the Islamic *shari'a*, and the benefits that could be expected to flow from them. The French incarnation of this *Muqaddima, Réformes necessaires*, has by contrast often been overlooked as a simple derivative translation. The chief exception is a thorough study by Magali Morsy which served as introduction to her re-edition of the French text in 1975.[18] A comparative study of the two versions has never to my knowledge been attempted.

The neglect of the French version, and an oddity in the dating of the Arabic text, have also obscured the fact that the two appeared simultaneously. The date usually given for the publication of the Arabic text is 1867, and for the French the following year, 1868. In fact, while the Arabic manuscript was completed in September 1867, it only received approval for printing on the bey's press in Tunis in January 1868, and was then printed in fascicules. By the time all of these were complete, in August 1868, the French version had already been published by the well-known firm of Paul Dupont in Paris, and had been reviewed several times. Over this same period, April to August 1868, the fascicules of the Arabic text that had been printed so far were being circulated among Tunisian and other Arab literati, who composed the twenty-four *taqariz* (endorsements or blurbs) which were appended to the printed Arabic version.[19] These two simultaneous versions were followed by a second edition of the French (1874), an English translation published in Athens (1874), a serialisation of the Arabic text in the *al-Jawa'ib* newspaper in Istanbul and then a separate book edition from that newspaper's press (1876), and an Ottoman translation printed, again at the *al-Jawa'ib* press, during Khayr al-Din's stint as grand vizier (1879).[20] There was talk of a Persian translation as early as 1868, but this does not seem to have made it into print.[21]

The Arabic, nonetheless, seems to have been the prior text chronologically. The French edition bears on the title page the words 'traduit de l'arabe sous la direction de l'auteur' ('translated from the Arabic under the author's direction'); it contains several passages in italics, in the voice of the translator-editor, referring to abbreviations made from the Arabic original, as well as a 'note du traducteur' listing the contents of the rest of the Arabic *Aqwam al-masalik*. Yet these very divergences from the Arabic strengthen the argument that the French version was a work in its own right rather than a 'mere translation' – as scholars such as Morsy and Daniel Newman have claimed.[22]

But how much of either version was the work of Khayr al-Din himself, and how much of other collaborators? It seems likely that he retained overall direction of the line taken in both texts – but also that for each one he relied considerably on the participation of others.[23] This participation could have taken place at numerous levels. As many scholars have suggested, the fine literary style of the Arabic text and its many references to Islamic scholarship suggest some collaboration by ulama: it was not usual for a mamluk, even one so well educated as Khayr al-Din, to have this level of erudition. The Arabic version contains a note stating it was 'corrected' for the press by Muhammad al-Bashir al-Twati – and in the publishing practices of the time the corrector's role could be quite an interventionist one.[24] Khayr al-Din himself thanks for help in 'refining its language' (*tahdhib alfazi-hi*) one, or more, of the 'sons of the homeland' (*ba'd abna' al-watan*),[25] that is of Tunis: this perhaps refers again to al-Twati, but other ulama close to Khayr al-Din have also been suggested as participants. Names often cited are the ulama Salim Buhajib (d. 1924) and Muhammad Bayram V (1840–89); Ibn Abi Diyaf's (1804–74) influence is also seen as important. Others in the circle of like-minded ulama and statesmen who gathered around Khayr al-Din in the 1860s – Generals Husayn (d. 1887) and Rustum (d. 1886), Larbi Zarruq, Muhammad al-Sanusi – might also have played a role.[26]

Khayr al-Din al-Tunisi's Muqaddima *to* Aqwam al-masalik

Another level at which others may have participated is in the translation of the French sources used in the main body of *Aqwam al-masalik*, and in parts of the introduction. The bulk of the sections on nineteen European states were – as Daniel Newman has shown – compiled from translated French sources, Larousse's *Grand dictionnaire universel* being a favourite.[27] The Arabic *Muqaddima* also contains long passages translated from French works, which are omitted in the French *Réformes nécessaires* (and replaced by notes in the voice of the translator-editor). Newman suggests that this translation was the work of several hands, a major role being played by Conti (d. 1893), a secretary-dragoman in the bey's service who was a close confidante of Khayr al-Din.[28] Khayr al-Din's French secretary at the time, Rey, would be another likely candidate.[29]

It is Conti, too, who has often been held to be the translator of the French version, though working as the title-page states 'under the direction of the author'.[30] Van Krieken asserts that 'many persons' worked on it, while Khayr al-Din corrected the proofs – he cites a letter from Khayr al-Din's colleague, the Tunisian statesman Husayn, who he says was one of these collaborators.[31] As Morsy argues, Khayr al-Din's French was adequate to his playing a significant role, since he composed many letters, memoirs and political documents in French.[32] His practices in this composition give a clue to the likely relationship between himself and others in the composition of the French – and perhaps of the Arabic also. His French letters and memoirs were almost all dictated to a secretary rather than penned with his own hand: this secretary could no doubt make suggestions and emend the style of the text, but Khayr al-Din would likely retain oversight by having the final result read back to him.

Audiences

Many scholars have noted that the Arabic *Aqwam al-masalik* was intended chiefly to convert two groups to the necessity of 'political *tanzimat*': the ulama, and bureaucrat-statesmen of Khayr al-Din's own stamp.[33] Several have also noted that the French *Réformes nécessaires* was designed to convince European statesmen and perhaps a broader public of the capacity of Muslim countries to carry out such reforms.[34] This would suggest that the two versions had two distinct audiences – which is not entirely false. But there was more overlap between the intended and actual readers of the Arabic and French versions than this neat division suggests.

On the one hand, many of the most receptive readers of the Arabic text were themselves already familiar with Europe and European writings. Those writing the *taqariz* for the Arabic edition include ulama such as

Ibn Abi Diyaf (1804–74), who along with Khayr al-Din had accompanied Ahmad Bey to France in 1846;[35] Mahmud Qabadu (1812–72), author of an 1850 essay arguing for the study of European sciences;[36] and Khalil al-Khuri (1836–1907), a Beiruti newspaper editor who played an important role as a transmitter of French and English texts and culture.[37] Another appreciative reader was Rifa'a al-Tahtawi (1801–73), whose narrative of his own trip to Paris in 1826–31 is warmly praised in Khayr al-Din's *Muqaddima*.[38] Salim Faris (1826–1906), meanwhile, who undertook to serialise the Arabic version in *al-Jawa'ib* in Istanbul, was the son of Ahmad Faris al-Shidyaq (1805/6–87) and had grown up leading a peripatetic life with his father around Europe and the Ottoman Empire.[39] Many statesmen close to Khayr al-Din, meanwhile, had almost as much experience of Europe as he had: this goes for his close ally General Husayn, said to have taken a hand in preparing the French edition, who was for several years Tunisian plenipotentiary in Florence;[40] for General Rustum;[41] and for the Young Ottoman statesman Midhat Pasha (1822–83), who is known to have read one or other of its versions by 1877.[42]

As for the French text, it is striking that several of the substantial and mostly very positive reviews published in the French press on its appearance were by writers with strong links to the Mediterranean-Ottoman world. The first to appear was by Nonce Rocca (1837–81), a French citizen (probably of Corsican extraction, like Conti) who spent many years living at Tunis; others were by the Paris-based Greek writer Marino Vréto (1828–71) and the French Orientalist Léon Cahun (1841–1900), who spent many years travelling in the Ottoman lands, which he used as the setting for a historical novel which would inspire the Young Turks.[43] Khayr al-Din's allies and collaborators, meanwhile, who played a substantial behind-the-scenes role in gaining a favourable reception for the work, had of course Tunisian connections: they included Victor Villet (1821–89), the French inspector on the Tunisian Financial Commission, and Jules de Lesseps (1809–87), brother to Ferdinand of Suez Canal fame, who had been French consul at Tunis and was then the bey's diplomatic representative in Paris.[44] Meanwhile, reviews sometimes recommended the book principally to 'those interested in eastern questions'.[45]

Then there were the Young Ottomans. In 1867, as Khayr al-Din was preparing the Arabic manuscript of *Aqwam al-masalik*, Mustafa Fazil Pasha (1830–75), the brother of the Khedive of Egypt, published an open letter to Sultan Abdülaziz demanding an Ottoman constitution. It was the first overt act of what would become the Young Ottoman opposition, which crystallised over the summer of 1867 in Parisian exile.[46] As

Khayr al-Din al-Tunisi's Muqaddima *to* Aqwam al-masalik

G. S. van Krieken and Albert Hourani suggest, it is undoubtedly to them that Khayr al-Din refers in a long passage of *Aqwam al-masalik*, where he refutes the arguments of 'a party of Muslims, along with other [non-Muslim] subjects' for an elected Ottoman parliament.[47] Fazil's letter, like other early texts of the movement, was published at Paris in French, although it also circulated in Ottoman in Istanbul – and as van Krieken notes, Arabic newspapers including *al-Ra'id al-Tunisi* commented on it.[48] As with the polemics Khayr al-Din conducted with rivals and enemies, the Young Ottomans' debates took place in Arabic and Ottoman and French, on both sides of the Mediterranean, and principally between people familiar with contacts between the Ottoman Empire and Europe.[49] It was to a similar nexus of contacts, conversations and controversies that *Aqwam al-masalik/Réformes nécessaires* spoke most immediately.

In short, there was considerable overlap in experience and knowledge between those who might be expected to be the most engaged readers of the Arabic and of the French versions of Khayr al-Din's text. Beyond these groups, the readership presumably spread out into both French-speaking and Arabic-speaking circles who were less engaged with cross-Mediterranean links: French statesmen and intellectuals without special links to the Ottoman world, like Francis Aubert (d. 1875) and Frédéric Baille (1848–1910), authors of two more detailed and laudatory reviews;[50] the reviewer of the second French edition in the 'official, confidential sheet of the Prince of Bismarck';[51] and perhaps also Tunisian and Arab ulama or officials without much prior interest in Europe or reformism.

The publication of his political treatise in both Arabic and French was necessary to Khayr al-Din's project, to his intervention in the trans-Mediterranean field of force in which these two distinct audiences overlapped. With his increasing involvement in Ottoman politics in the later 1870s, an Ottoman Turkish version would also become necessary (see Johann Strauss's contribution to this volume). Khayr al-Din sought in his political career to affirm certain trans-Mediterranean networks (his own with Tunisian reformist ulama and statesmen, journalists like Baille, Salim Faris and Khalil al-Khuri, French politicians and bureaucrats like Villet) and to disaggregate others (those linking enemies like Khaznadar, Lebanese journalist Rushayd al-Dahdah (1813–89), members of the Tunisian Financial Commission, publicists like Edouard Desfossés (1848–1923)).[52]

His intellectual work was directed in a similar way towards affirming the connection, commensurability or equivalence of certain European and Islamic spheres or concepts, while maintaining boundaries between others, insisting on their non-equivalence. To summarise, his central argument is that Islamic and Ottoman legal-political traditions – *siyasa, qanun* and *shari'a* – offer equivalents to European notions of constitutional liberalism and ministerial responsibility. This allowed him to argue that *tanzimat* – modern political institutions or reforms – were not only compatible with but actually enjoined by both *shari'a* and Ottoman statecraft.[53] Such institutions would empower people like himself and his collaborators, reform-minded statesmen and ulama, against the 'despotic' inclinations of rulers – in a similar fashion to the empowerment of the propertied and respectable classes by bourgeois liberalism in Europe.[54] On this basis, he was able to argue that there was no major 'gap' between the civilisational status of Europe and the Islamic world, and therefore no justification for any form of imperial 'tutelage' of European over Muslim states.[55] On the other hand, certain spheres of European and Muslim life he regarded as incommensurable, to be kept distinct – notably, the *shari'a*, 'notre loi théocratique' as he called it in French, was a domain with no real equivalent in Europe. Nonetheless it offered, in political terms, an additional, divine, justification for constitutional reforms, which Europeans did not possess.[56]

Conclusion

Taken together, *Aqwam al-masalik/Réformes nécessaires* thus amounts to an outline for how Muslim states might hope to control their own mode of juncture with the European-dominated capitalist world which was expanding so palpably around and within them. As in his political career, he sought to gain control of intellectual 'points of intersection' and to regulate just how particular spheres would be joined together, or kept apart. European states and the Islamic *umma*, constitutional liberalism and Ottoman-Islamic political thought, the *shari'a* and Western-patterned civilisation, had to be joined together or kept distinct, in particular and complex ways. This necessarily meant preventing their being related together in other ways. One such way was Algeria's subsumption under French sovereignty and the subordination of its Muslim population to the separate legal regime of the *indigénat*.[57] But others included the rejection of *tanzimat* or constitutional reforms by ulama or Tunisian rebels, the unwillingness of autocratic rulers and bureaucrats to accept restraints on their power, and even the too-hasty demands of the Young Ottomans for immediate parliamentary democracy.

Rather than simply moving around a multipolar trans-Mediterranean network, Khayr al-Din thus aimed to control and direct traffic through it. In practical terms, this required him to affirm his own connections while undoing those of his rivals. He also attempted to affirm his own way of managing the relations between Tunis and its finances and European governments and capitalists – by the standards of bourgeois probity rather than Khaznadar's extravagant corruption – as well as between different sets of Tunisian residents, in his attempted abolition of the Capitulations regime which gave extra-legal status to European protégés in favour of a 'mixed courts' system. Khayr al-Din's was a skilful realist's attempt to negotiate the conditions with which he was presented. The pressures to which it ultimately succumbed were already clear in his writings and career: his reformist project was exposed on both sides of the intersection, to domestic rebellion and rivalries and to the withdrawal of goodwill by Britain, France and the bondholders of Tunis's debt.[58]

It might be argued that such a project was always doomed to failure, even on its own terms – that the juncture of spheres he sought was impossible, whether because of the incompatibility some French reviewers suggested between Islamic laws and norms and Europeans, or because of the overwhelming conditions of European capitalist ascendancy.[59] But similarly unfeasible, we might argue, was the project of bourgeois liberals like Guizot or Mill, for constitutionalism without democracy – like the projects of Tanzimat reformers or Khayr al-Din, it was based on small elite classes which could not summon major popular or military force in their support. Its own 'juncture of spheres' proved vulnerable both to authoritarian states and to the renewed onslaught of democratic forces.[60] The modes of juncture between Europe and the Islamic world, between the two sides of the Mediterranean, which actually followed on Khayr al-Din's attempt, also carried with them their contradictions. Colonial regimes like the Algerian *indigénat* or the Tunisian protectorate provoked nationalist agitation and violent struggle before giving way to formally independent nation-states which themselves became the terrain of contestations over just how 'national' and 'foreign', 'secular' and 'Muslim', authoritarian and popular, spheres should be conjoined – while control of the 'points of intersection' between the two sides of the Mediterranean has remained a major concern of European states. Khayr al-Din's specific solutions, which one of his Tunisian supporters thought would cause even 'the deaf and dumb [to] submit to the truth',[61] may have receded into the past; but many of the problems he posed are still with us.

Notes

1. Nonce Rocca (1837–81), *Revue de l'instruction publique, de la literature et de sciences, en France et dans les pays étrangers: recueil hebdomadaire*

politique, 2 April 1868, 166. The 'harsh but memorable saying' seems to be a misquotation from Destutt de Tracy (in a letter to Maine de Biran, 20 April 1810): *Oeuvres de Maine de Biran: Tome VI, Correspondance philosophique* (Paris: Félix Alcan, 1930), 354. All English translations are the author's.

2. Le Général Khérédine [Khayr al-Dīn al-Tūnisī], *Réformes nécessaires aux états musulmans: essai formant la première partie de l'ouvrage politique et statistique intitulé: La plus sure direction pour connaître l'état des nations* (Paris: Imprimerie administrative de Paul Dupont, 1868), 3–4. The Arabic is rather different: Khayr al-Dīn al-Tūnisī, *Aqwam al-masālik fī ma'rifat aḥwāl al-mamālik* (Tunis: Maṭbaʿat al-Dawla, 1867), 3; Khayr al-Dīn al-Tūnisī, *The Surest Path: The Political Treatise of a Nineteenth-century Muslim Statesman*, trans. L. Carl Brown (Cambridge, MA: Harvard University Press, 1967), 71–2.

3. Sālim Būḥājib's *taqrīẓ*: Tūnisī, *Aqwam al-masālik*, *taqārīẓ* (separate pagination), 9. The passage alludes to Khayr al-Dīn's citations in the text of Muḥammad's borrowing of military devices from his enemies: Tūnisī, *Aqwam al-masālik*, 6, 8; Tūnisī, *Surest Path*, 75–6, 78–9; Tūnisī, *Réformes nécessaires*, 11–12 (the first instance is omitted from the French). For biographical information on the writers of *taqārīẓ*, see Tūnisī, *Aqwam al-masālik fī ma'rifat aḥwāl al-mamālik: al-Muqaddima wa-taqārīẓ al-muʿāṣirūn*, edited by Munṣif Shannūfī (Tūnis: al-Dār al-Tūnisiyya li-l-Nashr, 1972), notes to 231–90.

4. Muḥammad al-ʿArabī Zarrūq's *taqrīẓ*: Tūnisī, *Aqwam al-masālik*, *taqārīẓ*, 14.

5. For a more extended analysis of the French and Arabic texts, see Peter Hill, 'Khayr al-Din al-Tunisi and Arab Constitutionalism', unpublished manuscript (to appear in a volume on Ottoman and Qajar Constitutionalism, ed. Erdal Kaynar and Denis Hermann).

6. Zarrūq's *taqrīẓ*: Tūnisī, *Aqwam al-masālik*, *taqārīẓ*, 14.

7. Julia Ann Clancy-Smith, *Mediterraneans: North Africa and Europe in an Age of Migration, c. 1800–1900* (Berkeley and London: University of California Press, 2011), 294–313; Brown, introduction, *Surest Path*, 11–36; G. S. van Krieken, *Khayr al-Dîn et la Tunisie, 1850–1881* (Leiden: Brill, 1976); *Khayr al-Dîn et la Tunisie*, passim.

8. See Khayr al-Din's own apologetic account, in Mohamed-Salah Mzali and Jean Pignon (eds), 'Documents sur Khérédine. – *A mes enfants. Mémoires de ma vie privée et politique*', *Revue Tunisienne*, nouvelle série 18 (2e trimestre 1934): 177–225; Mzali and Pignon, 'Documents sur Khérédine. – *A mes enfants. Mémoires de ma vie privée et politique* (suite)', *Revue Tunisienne*, nouvelle série 19–20 (3e et 4e trimestres 1934): 347–96; and Clancy-Smith, *Mediterraneans*, 312; G. S. van Krieken, 'K̲h̲ayr al-Dīn Pas̲h̲a', in *Encyclopaedia of Islam, Second Edition*, edited by P. Bearman, Th. Bianquis, C. E. Bosworth, E. van Donzel, W. P. Heinrichs. Available at <http://dx.doi.org/10.1163/1573-3912_islam_SIM_4257> (last accessed 28 October 2019).

Khayr al-Din al-Tunisi's Muqaddima *to* Aqwam al-masalik

9. Van Krieken, *Khayr al-Dîn*, 15, 166–7; Clancy-Smith, *Mediterraneans*, 303–4.
10. His correspondence makes this clear: see Mohamed-Salah Mzali (ed), *La situation en Tunisie à la veille du protectorat: d'aprés [sic] les lettres de Conti à Khéreddine et d'autres documents inédits* (Tunis: Maison tunisienne de l'édition, 1969); Mzali and Pignon, 'Documents sur Khérédine. – VII. *Réponse à la calomnie* (suite et fin)', *Revue Tunisienne*, nouvelle série 33–4 (1er et 2e trimestres 1938): 79–153; Mzali and Pignon, 'Documents sur Khérédine. – VIII. *Correspondance* (suite)', *Revue Tunisienne*, nouvelle série 41–2 (1er et 2e trimestres 1940): 71–108; Mzali and Pignon, 'Documents sur Khérédine. – IX. *Correspondance* (suite)', *Revue Tunisienne*, nouvelle série 43–44 (1er et 2e trimestres 1940): 251–302.
11. Clancy-Smith, *Mediterraneans*, 299–301, 304–8; Magali Morsy, introduction to Khayr al-Dīn al-Tūnisī, *Essai sur les réformes nécessaires aux Etats musulmans* (La Calade, Aix-en-Provence: Edisud, 1987), 53–5; van Krieken, *Khayr al-Dîn*, 69–72, 74–7, 89–90, 151–3, 161–4, 237–41, 248–52, 263–7; and 213–14 on his working with French Algerian authorities against refractory tribes in the south.
12. See Mzali and Pignon, 'Documents sur Khérédine. – *A mes enfants*'; Mzali and Pignon, 'Documents sur Khérédine. – *A mes enfants . . . (suite)*'; Mzali and Pignon, 'Documents sur Khérédine. – *Mon programme*', *Revue tunisienne*, nouvelle série 21 (1er trimestre 1935): 51–80; Mzali and Pignon, 'Documents sur Kheredine. – IV. *Le Problème tunisien vu à travers la question d'Orient* (suite)', *Revue Tunisienne*, nouvelle série 26 (2e trimestre 1936): 223–54; Mzali and Pignon, 'Documents sur Khérédine. – VI. *Réponse à la calomnie* (suite)', *Revue Tunisienne*, nouvelle série 31–2 (3e et 4e trimestres 1937): 409–32.
13. Tūnisī, *Aqwam al-masālik*, 48–9; Tūnisī, *Surest Path*, 133–4; Tūnisī, *Réformes nécessaires*, 61–2; and 'À mes enfants', where he notes the measures he took to lower taxes after the rebellion: Mzali and Pignon, 'Documents sur Khérédine. – *A mes enfants*', 191–7.
14. Kenneth J. Perkins, *A History of Modern Tunisia*, 2nd edition (Cambridge: Cambridge University Press, 2014), 32–3.
15. A. Demeersman, 'Un grand témoin des premières idées modernistes en Tunisie', *Revue de l'Institut des Belles-Lettres Arabes* 76 (1956): 349–73; 367; Tūnisī, ed. Shannūfī, *Aqwam al-masālik*, 235, n. 6.
16. Van Krieken, *Khayr al-Dîn*, 260–1.
17. Clancy-Smith, *Mediterraneans*, 312.
18. Morsy, *Essai*.
19. Van Krieken, *Khayr al-Dîn*, 106, 133; Tūnisī, *Aqwam al-masālik*, 20–1. For the fact fascicules were circulated, see note of director of the press and *taqārīẓ* of Sālim Būḥājib, Yūnis al-ʿArūsī Ibn ʿAyyād and Muṣṭafā Riḍwan (Tūnisī, *Aqwam al-masālik*, *taqārīẓ*, 2, 8, 17, 19). The manuscript was completed on Monday 10 Jumada 1, 1284 (9 September 1867) and printing complete on 28 Rabīʿ 2, 1285 (18 August 1868): Tūnisī, *Aqwam al-masālik*, 462, 464. The

first French press mention I found was 26 March 1868; they continued to appear till December 1868; the first *taqrīẓ*, Ibn Abī Ḍiyāf's, is dated 20 April 1868 (Tūnisī, *Aqwam al-masālik, taqārīẓ*, 4), and they continued to appear through to August 1868.
20. *Necessary Reforms of the Mussulman States. Essay which Forms the First of the Political and Statistical Work Entitled: 'The Surest Way to Know the State of Nations' by General Khérédine* (Athens: Printing Office of the *Indépendance Hellénique*, 1874); the only locatable copy is in the National Library, Tunis. On the *Indépendance Hellénique*, see Despina Provata, 'La presse francophone grecque. Revendications nationales et ouverture vers l'Europe', in *Presses allophones de Méditerrannée*, 281–96; 287. For the *al-Jawā'ib* versions, see van Krieken, *Khayr al-Dîn*, 135–6; they were followed by a further Arabic edition published at Alexandria in 1881–2. For the Ottoman versions, see Johann Strauss in the present volume.
21. Clancy-Smith, *Mediterraneans*, 305.
22. Morsy, *Essai*, 7, 32–3; Daniel Newman, 'The European Sources of the *Aqwam al-Masalik fi Ma'rifat al-Mamalik*', *Revue de l'IBLA* 198 (2007): 209–28; 211.
23. See Newman, 'European Sources', 211–15; Morsy, *Essai*, 31–2.
24. Tūnisī, *Aqwam al-masālik*, 464. On correctors, see Peter Hill, *Utopia and Civilisation in the Arab Nahda* (Cambridge: Cambridge University Press, 2020), 54–5.
25. Tūnisī, *Aqwam al-masālik*, 461.
26. Newman, 'European Sources', 214–15; van Krieken, *Khayr al-Dîn*, 132; Morsy, *Essai*, 30–1.
27. Newman, 'European Sources', 213.
28. Newman, 'European Sources', 213.
29. Conti: see Mzali, *La situation en Tunisie*, 14–18. Rey: Mzali and Pignon, 'Documents sur Khérédine. – A mes enfants', 181 n. 2.
30. Newman, 'European Sources', 211.
31. Van Krieken, *Khayr al-Dîn*, 133, 134: letter dated 25 Shawwāl 1284 (19 February 1868).
32. Morsy, *Essai*, 7–8.
33. Brown, *Surest Path*, 38, 60–4 (ulama); van Krieken, *Khayr al-Dîn*, 129–30; Albert Hourani, *Arabic Thought in the Liberal Age, 1798–1939* (London: Oxford University Press, 1962), 88–9. Khayr al-Din himself says his book is aimed at (1) statesmen and men of religion and (2) all Muslims. Tūnisī, *Aqwam al-masālik*, 5; Tūnisī, *Réformes nécessaires*, 7–8.
34. Brown, *Surest Path*, 37–8 (French statesmen), Newman, 'European Sources', 211–12; van Krieken, *Khayr al-Dîn*, 133; Morsy, *Essai*, 8.
35. See his account: Daniel Newman (trans.), 'Ahmad Bey's journey to the land of the *Fransîs* (1846)', *Revue de l'IBLA* 201 (2008): 43–102.
36. Van Krieken, *Khayr al-Dîn*, 13.
37. Basiliyus Bawardi, 'First Steps in Writing Arabic Narrative Fiction: The Case

Khayr al-Din al-Tunisi's Muqaddima *to* Aqwam al-masalik

of *Hadīqat al-Akhbār'*, *Die Welt des Islams* 48: 2 (2008): 170–95; Fruma Zachs, 'Building a Cultural Identity: The Case of Khalil al-Khuri', in Thomas Philipp and Christoph Schumann (eds), *From the Syrian Land to the States of Syria and Lebanon* (Beirut: Ergon in Kommission, 2004), 27–39; Peter Hill, 'Arguing with Europe: Eastern Civilisation versus Orientalist Exoticism', *PMLA* 132: 2 (2017): 405–12. Another *taqrīẓ*-writer, Muḥammad Bayram V, would visit Europe three times by the 1890s, at least: Arnold H. Green, 'Political Attitudes and Activities of the Ulama in the Liberal Age: Tunisia as an Exceptional Case', *International Journal of Middle East Studies* 7: 2 (1976): 209–41; 231 n. 2.

38. Tūnisī, *Aqwam al-masālik*, 69; Tūnisī, *Surest Path*, 155–6; Khaldun Sati Husry, *Three Reformers: A Study in Modern Arab Political Thought* (Beirut: Khayats, 1966), 37; van Krieken, *Khayr al-Dîn*, 135.
39. See Nadia Al-Bagdadi, Fawwaz Traboulsi and Barbara Winckler (eds), *A Life in Praise of Words: Ahmad Faris al-Shidyaq and the Nineteenth Century* (Wiesbaden: Reichert, 2015).
40. M'hamed Oualdi, 'Slave to Modernity? General Ḥusayn's Journey from Tunis to Tuscany (1830s–1880s)', *Journal of the Economic and Social History of the Orient* 60: 1–2 (2017): 50–82.
41. Who was out of Tunisia in 1868–70: Mzali and Pignon, 'Documents sur Kheredine. – IV . . . (suite)', 245. See also the biographical note on Rustum in Mzali and Pignon, 'Documents sur Khérédine. – VII', 99 n. 21.
42. Ḥusayn to Khayr al-Dīn, 25 Sha'bān 1294, cited in van Krieken, *Khayr al-Dîn*, 135.
43. Rocca, 'Réformes nécessaires' (review). Marino P. Vréto, review of *Réformes nécessaires*, *Revue moderne* 49: 5 (25 December 1868): 957–8. Léon Cahun, 'Les bédouins aussi' (review of *Réformes nécessaires*), *La Liberté*, 3 April 1868. On Vréto, see Barbara Dimopoulou, 'Autour de Marino Papadopoulo-Vreto. Circonstances et documents peu connus', *Cahiers Mérimée* 6 (2014): 63–91. Cahun's novel was *La Bannière Bleue* (1877). *Réformes nécessaires* is also cited approvingly the following year in an article on Islam and art by Florian Pharaon, scion of a famous Syrian-Levantine family and an interpreter to the French forces in Algeria turned littérateur: Pharaon, 'La peinture et la sculpture chez les musulmans', *Gazette des beaux-arts: courrier européen de l'art et de la curiosité*, 1 January 1869, 442–6; 442–3. On Pharaon, see Alain Messaoudi, 'Orientaux orientalistes: Les Pharaon, interprètes du Sud au service du Nord', in Colette Zytnicki and Chantal Bordes-Benayoun (eds), *Sud-Nord. Cultures coloniales en France (XIXe–XXe siècles), actes du colloque organisé en mars 2001 par l'Université de Toulouse Le Mirail* (Toulouse: Privat, 2004), 243–55.
44. Their efforts around the second edition of the French work are clear from Khayr al-Din's correspondence: see Mzali and Pignon, 'Documents sur Khérédine. – IX'. This lists several further reviews and mentions in the French, German and Italian press, which I have not examined.

45. For instance. Vréto, '*Réformes nécessaires*' (review), 957.
46. Andrew Arsan, 'The Strange Lives of Ottoman Liberalism: Exile, Patriotism and Constitutionalism in the Thought of Mustafa Fazıl Paşa', in Maurizio Isabella and Konstantina Zanou (eds), *Mediterranean Diasporas: Politics and Ideas in the Long Nineteenth Century* (London: Bloomsbury, 2016), 153–70; 156–7.
47. Van Krieken, *Khayr al-Dîn*, 135; Hourani, *Arabic Thought*, 93; Tūnisī, *Aqwam al-masālik*, 35–6; Tūnisī, *Surest Path*, 116–17; Tūnisī, *Réformes nécessaires*, 38–41.
48. Van Krieken, *Khayr al-Dîn*, 135.
49. As is abundantly clear from the correspondence and polemics published by Mzali and Pignon: 'Documents sur Kheredine. – IV . . . (suite)'; 'Documents sur Khérédine. – V. *Réponse à la calomnie*', *Revue Tunisienne*, nouvelle série 30 (2e trimestre 1937): 209–52; 'Documents sur Khérédine. – VI'; 'Documents sur Khérédine. – VII'; 'Documents sur Khérédine. – VIII'; 'Documents sur Khérédine. – IX'.
50. Francis Aubert, *Le Constitutionnel: journal politique, littéraire, universel*, 9 August 1868. Aubert co-authored, the same year, a dystopian critique of Second Empire France, *La cité nouvelle: quo?* Frédéric Baille, *Revue de France* 16 (1875): 730–3. Khayr al-Dīn mentions this review appreciatively in his correspondence: Khayr al-Dīn to G. Robert, 15 December 1875, in Mzali and Pignon, 'Documents sur Khérédine. – IX', 300. Baille would go on to become a prominent French colonial administrator in Indochina.
51. Khayr al-Dīn to G. Robert, 15 December 1875, in Mzali and Pignon, 'Documents sur Khérédine. – IX', 300.
52. Mzali and Pignon, 'Documents sur Khérédine. – VIII', 83–4; van Krieken, *Khayr al-Dîn*, 163–4.
53. Tūnisī, *Aqwam al-masālik*, 4; Tūnisī, *Surest Path*, 73; Tūnisī, *Réformes nécessaires*, 6.
54. See, for instance, Tūnisī, *Aqwam al-masālik*, 12, 15; Tūnisī, *Surest Path*, 85, 88–9; Tūnisī, *Réformes nécessaires*, 19, 24–6. My analysis on these points is indebted to Magali Morsy's introduction to the French text: Morsy, *Essai*, esp. 11, 32–3, 49–52.
55. Tūnisī, *Aqwam al-masālik*, 37–8, 44; Tūnisī, *Surest Path*, 119–20, 130; Tūnisī, *Réformes nécessaires*, 43, 54.
56. For instance, Tūnisī, *Aqwam al-masālik*, 3, 5, 6; Tūnisī, *Surest Path*, 72, 74, 76 and n. 11; Tūnisī, *Réformes nécessaires*, 4, 6.
57. For this, see James McDougall, *A History of Algeria* (Cambridge: Cambridge University Press, 2017), 122–5. Khayr al-Dīn does not refer to Algeria explicitly in his treatise, but was of course constantly aware of the nearness of the French imperial presence: see Mzali (ed.), *La situation en Tunisie*, 50.
58. Perkins, *A History of Modern Tunisia*, 22–44.
59. Morsy suggests this interpretation: *North Africa 1800–1900: A Survey from the Nile to the Atlantic* (London and New York: Longman, 1984), 300–2.

Khayr al-Din al-Tunisi's Muqaddima *to* Aqwam al-masalik

60. Eric Hobsbawm, *The Age of Capital* (London: Abacus, 1995), 132–3, makes this argument for European bourgeois liberalism.
61. Muḥammad al-Bājī al-Masʿūdī's *taqrīẓ*: Tūnisī, *Aqwam al-masālik, taqārīẓ,* 5.

Bibliography

Al-Bagdadi, Nadia, Fawwaz Traboulsi and Barbara Winckler (eds), *A Life in Praise of Words: Ahmad Faris al-Shidyaq and the Nineteenth Century* (Wiesbaden: Reichert, 2015).
Arsan, Andrew, 'The Strange Lives of Ottoman Liberalism: Exile, Patriotism and Constitutionalism in the Thought of Mustafa Fazıl Paşa', in Maurizio Isabella and Konstantina Zanou (eds), *Mediterranean Diasporas: Politics and Ideas in the Long Nineteenth Century* (London: Bloomsbury, 2016), 153–70.
Aubert, Francis, review of *Réformes nécessaires, Le Constitutionnel: journal politique, littéraire, universel*, 9 August 1868.
Baille, Frédéric, review of *Réformes nécessaires, Revue de France* 16 (1875): 730–3.
Bawardi, Basiliyus, 'First Steps in Writing Arabic Narrative Fiction: The Case of *Hadīqat al-Akhbār*', *Die Welt Des Islams* 48: 2 (2008): 170–95.
Biran, Maine de, *Oeuvres de Maine de Biran: Tome VI, Correspondance philosophique* (Paris: Félix Alcan, 1930).
Brown, L. Carl, introduction to Khayr al-Dīn al-Tūnisī, *The Surest Path: The Political Treatise of a Nineteenth-century Muslim Statesman* (Cambridge, MA: Harvard University Press, 1967).
Cahun, Léon, 'Les bédouins aussi' (review of *Réformes nécessaires*), *La Liberté*, 3 April 1868.
Clancy-Smith, Julia Ann, *Mediterraneans: North Africa and Europe in an Age of Migration, c. 1800–1900* (Berkeley and London: University of California Press, 2011).
Demeersman, A., 'Un grand témoin des premières idées modernistes en Tunisie', *Revue de l'Institut des Belles-Lettres Arabes* 76 (1956): 349–73.
Dimopoulou, Barbara, 'Autour de Marino Papadopoulo-Vreto. Circonstances et documents peu connus', *Cahiers Mérimée* 6 (2014): 63–91.
Green, Arnold H., 'Political Attitudes and Activities of the Ulama in the Liberal Age: Tunisia as an Exceptional Case', *International Journal of Middle East Studies* 7: 2 (1976): 209–241.
Hill, Peter, 'Arguing with Europe: Eastern Civilisation versus Orientalist Exoticism', *PMLA* 132: 2 (2017): 405–12.
Hill, Peter, *Utopia and Civilisation in the Arab Nahda* (Cambridge: Cambridge University Press, 2020).
Hill, Peter, 'Khayr al-Din al-Tunisi and Arab Constitutionalism', unpublished manuscript (to appear in a volume on Ottoman and Qajar Constitutionalism, edited by Erdal Kaynar and Denis Hermann).

Hobsbawm, Eric, *The Age of Capital* (London: Abacus, 1995).
Hourani, Albert, *Arabic Thought in the Liberal Age, 1798–1939* (London: Oxford University Press, 1962).
McDougall, James, *A History of Algeria* (Cambridge: Cambridge University Press, 2017).
Messaoudi, Alain, 'Orientaux orientalistes: Les Pharaon, interprètes du Sud au service du Nord', in Colette Zytnicki and Chantal Bordes-Benayoun (eds), *Sud-Nord. Cultures coloniales en France (XIXe–XXe siècles), actes du colloque organisé en mars 2001 par l'Université de Toulouse Le Mirail* (Toulouse: Privat, 2004), 243–55.
Morsy, Magali, *North Africa 1800–1900: A Survey from the Nile to the Atlantic* (London and New York: Longman, 1984).
Morsy, Magali, introduction to Khayr al-Dīn al-Tūnisī, *Essai sur les réformes nécessaires aux Etats musulmans* (La Calade, Aix-en-Provence: Edisud, 1987).
Mzali, Mohamed-Salah (ed.), *La situation en Tunisie à la veille du protectorat: d'aprés [sic] les lettres de Conti à Khéreddine et d'autres documents inédits* (Tunis: Maison tunisienne de l'édition, 1969).
Mzali, Mohamed-Salah and Jean Pignon (eds), 'Documents sur Khérédine. – *A mes enfants. Mémoires de ma vie privée et politique*', *Revue Tunisienne*, nouvelle série 18 (2e trimestre 1934): 177–225.
Mzali, Mohamed-Salah and Jean Pignon (eds), 'Documents sur Khérédine. – *A mes enfants. Mémoires de ma vie privée et politique* (suite)', *Revue Tunisienne*, nouvelle série 19–20 (3e et 4e trimestres 1934): 347–96.
Mzali, Mohamed-Salah and Jean Pignon (eds), Mzali and Pignon, 'Documents sur Khérédine. – *Mon programme*', *Revue tunisienne*, nouvelle série 21 (1er trimestre 1935): 51–80.
Mzali, Mohamed-Salah and Jean Pignon (eds), 'Documents sur Kheredine. – IV. *Le Problème tunisien vu à travers la question d'Orient* (suite)', *Revue Tunisienne*, nouvelle série 26 (2e trimestre 1936): 223–54.
Mzali, Mohamed-Salah and Jean Pignon (eds), 'Documents sur Khérédine. – V. *Réponse à la calomnie*', *Revue Tunisienne*, nouvelle série 30 (2e trimestre 1937): 209–52.
Mzali, Mohamed-Salah and Jean Pignon (eds), 'Documents sur Khérédine. – VI. *Réponse à la calomnie* (suite)', *Revue Tunisienne*, nouvelle série 31–2 (3e et 4e trimestres 1937): 409–32.
Mzali, Mohamed-Salah and Jean Pignon (eds), 'Documents sur Khérédine. – VII. *Réponse à la calomnie* (suite et fin)', *Revue Tunisienne*, nouvelle série 33–4 (1er et 2e trimestres 1938): 79–153.
Mzali, Mohamed-Salah and Jean Pignon (eds), 'Documents sur Khérédine. – VIII. *Correspondance* (suite)', *Revue Tunisienne*, nouvelle série 41–2 (1er et 2e trimestres 1940): 71–108.
Mzali, Mohamed-Salah and Jean Pignon (eds), 'Documents sur Khérédine. – IX. *Correspondance* (suite)', *Revue Tunisienne*, nouvelle série 43–44 (1er et 2e trimestres 1940): 251–302.

Khayr al-Din al-Tunisi's Muqaddima *to* Aqwam al-masalik

Newman, Daniel, 'The European Sources of the *Aqwam al-Masalik fī Ma'rifat al-Mamalik*', *Revue de l'IBLA* 198 (2007): 209–28.
Newman, Daniel (trans.), 'Ahmad Bey's journey to the land of the *Fransîs* (1846)', *Revue de l'IBLA* 201 (2008): 43–102.
Oualdi, M'hamed, 'Slave to Modernity? General Ḥusayn's Journey from Tunis to Tuscany (1830s–1880s)', *Journal of the Economic and Social History of the Orient* 60: 1–2 (2017): 50–82.
Perkins, Kenneth J., *A History of Modern Tunisia*, 2nd edition (Cambridge: Cambridge University Press, 2014).
Pharaon, Florian, 'La peinture et la sculpture chez les musulmans', *Gazette des beaux-arts: courrier européen de l'art et de la curiosité*, 1 January 1869, 442–6.
Provata, Despina, 'La presse francophone grecque. Revendications nationales et ouverture vers l'Europe', in *Presses allophones de Méditerrannée*, 281–96.
Rocca, Nonce, '*Réformes nécessaires aux États musulmans*' (review), *Revue de l'instruction publique, de la literature et de sciences, en France et dans les pays étrangers: receuil hebdomadaire politique*, 2 April 1868, 166–8.
Sati Husry, Khaldun, *Three Reformers: A Study in Modern Arab Political Thought* (Beirut: Khayats, 1966).
Tūnisī, Khayr al-Dīn al-, *Aqwam al-masālik fī ma'rifat aḥwāl al-mamālik* (Tunis: Maṭba'at al-Dawla, 1867).
Tūnisī, Khayr al-Dīn al-, *The Surest Path: The Political Treatise of a Nineteenth-century Muslim Statesman*, trans. L. Carl Brown (Cambridge, MA: Harvard University Press, 1967).
Tūnisī, Khayr al-Dīn al-, *Aqwam al-masālik fī ma'rifat aḥwāl al-mamālik: al-Muqaddima wa-taqārīẓ al-mu'āṣirūn*, edited by Munṣif Shannūfī (Tūnis: al-Dār al-Tūnisiyya li-l-Nashr, 1972).
Tūnisī, Khayr al-Dīn al-, *Essai sur les réformes nécessaires aux Etats musulmans*, edited by Magali Morsy (La Calade, Aix-en-Provence: Edisud, 1987).
[Tūnisī, Khayr al-Dīn al-] le Général Khérédine, *Réformes nécessaires aux états musulmans: essai formant la première partie de l'ouvrage politique et statistique intitulé: La plus sure direction pour connaître l'état des nations* (Paris: Imprimerie administrative de Paul Dupont, 1868).
[Tūnisī, Khayr al-Dīn al-], *Necessary Reforms of the Mussulman States. Essay which Forms the First of the Political and Statistical Work Entitled: 'The Surest Way to Know the State of Nations' by General Khérédine* (Athens: Printing Office of the *Indépendance Hellénique*, 1874).
[Tūnisī, Khayr al-Dīn al-], Hayreddin Paşa, *Mukaddime-yi Akvem ül-mesâlik fi ma'rifet-i ahval il-memâlik tercümesi*, trans. Abdurrahman Efendi Süreyya (Istanbul: El-Cevaib Matbaası, 1879).
Van Krieken, G. S., *Khayr al-Dîn et la Tunisie, 1850–1881* (Leiden: Brill, 1976).
Van Krieken, G. S., 'Khayr al-Dīn Pasha', in *Encyclopaedia of Islam, Second Edition*, edited by P. Bearman, Th. Bianquis, C. E. Bosworth, E. van Donzel, W. P. Heinrichs, <http://dx.doi.org/10.1163/1573-3912_islam_SIM_4257> (last accessed 28 October 2019).

Vréto, Marino P., review of *Réformes nécessaires*, *Revue moderne* 49: 5 (25 December 1868): 957–8.

Zachs, Fruma, 'Building a Cultural Identity: The Case of Khalil al-Khuri', in Thomas Philipp and Christoph Schumann (eds), *From the Syrian Land to the States of Syria and Lebanon* (Beirut: Ergon in Kommission, 2004), 27–39.

Part II

The *Muqaddima* of Khayr al-Dīn Pasha's *Aqwam al-masālik fī maʿrifat aḥwāl al-mamālik* and its Ottoman Turkish Translation

Johann Strauss

Introduction: Ottoman Translation(s) of the Muqaddima

The Ottoman translation of the *Muqaddima* of Khayr al-Dīn Pasha's *Aqwam al-masālik fī maʿrifat aḥwāl al-mamālik*[1] analysed in this chapter was the last of several Ottoman translations to be published, and it appeared more than a decade after the French version, in 1296/1879. But it was made directly from the Arabic text and includes chapters omitted in the French version.[2] Despite minor omissions[3] (usually shorter than in the French version) and additions of a few phrases, this Ottoman version can be considered as a translation (and not as an adaptation) of Khayr al-Dīn's *Muqaddima*.

The late appearance of this translation is perhaps not surprising. Many educated Ottoman readers were able to read the original Arabic. Others may have read the French version. Some *hoca*s are said to have used the Arabic original of Khayr al-Dīn's work in their teaching. But in his preface, written in an extremely flowery style,[4] our Ottoman translator says that because it was written in Arabic, this work was not accessible to potential admirers (*arz-ı meftuniyet edenler*), and that it did not suit patriotism and generosity (*hamiyet ü fütüvvet*) to deprive compatriots of such a 'guide to happiness' (*eser-i saadet-rehber*).[5] He also mentions that he had taught himself the *Muqaddima* in institutions of higher education.[6]

This Ottoman version of the *Muqaddima* or introduction to Khayr al-Dīn Pasha's *Aqwam al-masālik fī maʿrifat aḥwāl al-mamālik* represents one of the most interesting translations in the nineteenth century. In particular, it provides us with clues to a deeper understanding of Islamic

Khayr al-Din al-Tunisi's Muqaddima to Aqwam al-masalik

languages and their relationship during a period of intense reforming and reworking in the domain of language. The comparison of the two texts can show the relationship between the Westernised varieties of Ottoman Turkish and Arabic in the second half of the nineteenth century in an exemplary way. This chapter focuses on the linguistic choices made by the translator, highlighting the transitions that were going on in both Arabic and Ottoman Turkish at the time, and how parallel needs in both languages often generated diverse strategies.

The Ottoman Translator(s)

The first attempt to translate Khayr al-Dīn Pasha's *Muqaddima* had been made by İsmail Hakkı (Bereketzade; 1851–1918), who published his translation in the newspapers *İstikbal* and *Basiret*, under the title *Rehber-i Saadet* ('The guide to happiness'). This modernist thinker had made the translation during his exile in Acre in 1873, on the suggestion of (Hacı) Ibrahim Efendi (1826–88),[7] a specialist in the Arabic language and reform of its teaching method.[8] İsmail Hakkı's exile ended with the ascension to the throne of Sultan Murad V (30 May 1876). An attempt to publish the translation in book form never transpired.

A new translation of the *Muqaddima* was initiated when Khayr al-Dīn Pasha was invited by the new sultan, Abdülhamid II, to come to Istanbul. It appeared serially in *Ceride-i askeriyye* and *Hakikat*. The printed version eventually came out from the press of the Arabic newspaper *al-Jawā'ib* in Istanbul which had published the Arabic original.[9] The translator appears on the title page as Abdurrahman Efendi, editor (*muharrir*) at the *Ceride-i askeriyye*.

Abdurrahman (Süreyya; Mirduhizade; 1841–1904),[10] a journalist and writer known for his works and articles on rhetoric (*belâgat*),[11] was a native of Baghdad.[12] His father's name was Abū Ḥāmid Muḥammad.[13] In his writings, especially his critique of Cevdet Pasha's treatise on rhetoric, *Belâgat-i osmaniyye* (1298–9/1881–2), published under the title *Tâlikaat-i Belâgat-ı osmaniyye* (1299/1882), he deals especially with the correct use of Arabic words in Turkish. After first training in his native city, he continued his studies in Istanbul. Apart from Arabic and Persian, which he knew so well that he was able to understand and to comment on the classical texts in all their subtleties, he also learnt French.

He was afterwards employed in government service in the provinces of Adana and Konya. Then he taught Persian at the *rüşdiye* of the Beylerbeyi neighbourhood in Istanbul (1867), and at the Teachers' Training College (1870). At the *Mahrec-i aklâm* training college he taught Arabic (1876), at the Law School (1884) Ottoman literature. He was also the editor of the papers *Ceride-i askeriyye* (1872) and *Hakikat* (1876). It is said in most Turkish sources that he participated in the Orientalist Congress in Lisbon in 1890. But this congress, scheduled for 1892, never took place.[14] Abdurrahman Süreyya died in 1904 and was buried in Istanbul near the Eyüb Sultan Mosque.

Reception of the Translation

In his preface, Abdurrahman Süreyya is very outspoken against despotism (*istibdad*). He had encountered problems when publishing the translation serially, he notes. More serious problems were to come. Unfortunately, this translation was produced on the eve of a period known in Turkish history as *İstibdad dönemi* (period of despotism). This likely explains why it was withdrawn rapidly from the market, and its reprinting forbidden. On 1 April 1879 (8 Rabī' al-ākhir 1296), during Khayr al-Dīn's vizierate (4 December 1878–29 July 1879), the following notice (*tezkere*) was sent to the author:

> Since the publication of such writings is not wise or useful given conditions of the moment, in order to avoid any sort of distortions,[15] and because it has been established by experience that some people in our country lack understanding of such publications and usually give them meanings outside of their essence and truth, so, even if it is obvious that they are based on good ideas and purposes, it is necessary, according to the above-mentioned objections, to prevent for the moment their publication, since there appears prejudice [in them] considering the needs of the time.[16]

Following a denunciation, publication of the *Muqaddima* was again banned in 1880 and its copies confiscated.[17]

A sort of *damnatio memoriae* concerning Khayr al-Dīn's work continued until recent times in Turkey: both the original and the translation were usually omitted in biographical sketches or quoted incorrectly.[18] One should also mention that the modern Turkish version of the *Muqaddima* was not adapted from the Ottoman version but translated from Brown's English translation![19]

Ottoman Translation Activity in the Nineteenth Century: Translating from Arabic

Like Latin in the West, Arabic had been the language of science par excellence in the Ottoman Empire before the nineteenth century. Thus,

Khayr al-Dīn al-Tūnisī's Muqaddima *to* Aqwam al-masalik

Ottoman scholars (ulama) usually wrote their scientific and philosophical works in Arabic and therefore did not feel the need for translations from this language. However, a relatively small number of Arabic works were translated by the Ottomans into Turkish, in particular some major historical works during the Tulip Era (*Lâle Devri*, early eighteenth century). Among the most important was a (partial) translation of Ibn Khaldūn's (1332–1406) *Muqaddima* or 'Introduction' to his massive *Kitāb al-'ibar*.[20]

After the Tanzimat reforms, the number of translations began to increase considerably. The Turkish scholar Hilmi Ziya Ülken (1901–74), a translation specialist, explains that

> [d]uring this period, people started, as a reaction to the inevitable interest in Western technology, to turn their regard especially concerning fundamental issues, towards the East, and to translate more works. For this reason, the nineteenth century, when Western influences gradually were enforced and grew, was the period when the greatest number of translations were made from the East, and of its most important works.[21]

It is fair to say that in some cases, these translations also seem to have been motivated by the interest shown in Arab authors in the West (for example, in the case of Ibn Baṭṭūṭa (d. 1377) and his travelogue).

Nearly all philosophical translations from Eastern authors in the nineteenth century were made from Arabic, including works by Avicenna and al-Ghazzāli. Ibn Khaldūn's *Muqaddima* continued to attract Ottoman translators.[22] This may explain what one Muhiddin Mahvî wrote in his *Mazbatat'ül-Fünûn* (1289/1873), asserting that Ottoman society could not attain a sound basis by imitating European regulations and laws.

> The people will not be able to progress by learning French and translating works from this language into Ottoman Turkish. For the elevation of a people, it is necessary to rely on its own knowledge and culture (*maarif*). Therefore, it is necessary to take the precious works of the forefathers and to work on them.[23]

Many of these Ottoman translations of classical authors remained in manuscript. It is also sometimes difficult to distinguish between translation and the traditional commentary (*şerh*). In Pirizade's eighteenth-century translation of Ibn Khaldūn's *Muqaddima*, translation and commentary are often interwoven,[24] whereas Khayr al-Dīn's contemporary Cevdet Pasha (1822–95), who translated the remaining (sixth) part of the *Muqaddima* (dealing with science, philosophy, education, language and literature) added so many commentaries ('by the translator', *lilmütercim*) that they comprise almost one third of the text.[25]

Under these circumstances, the Ottoman translation of Khayr al-Dīn Pasha's *Muqaddima* to his *Aqwam al-masālik* is exceptional. First, it is the translation of a contemporary Arabic work. Second, its content is modern; and third, it deals substantively with modernity, in the sense of institutions of the West that were viewed as a model. There is one comparable case: the Turkish translation of Rifā'a al-Ṭahṭāwī's famous travelogue published under the title *Takhlīṣ al-ibrīz fī talkhīṣ Bārīz* (1834) ('The extraction of gold or an overview of Paris'), which is mentioned in the *Muqaddima* as recommended reading.[26] This translation was accomplished in Egypt (published in the government press at Būlāq, Cairo in 1839),[27] in order to facilitate its reading by Egypt's de facto ruler, Mehmed Ali Pasha, whose knowledge of Arabic was limited, and who had strongly encouraged translations from European languages, into both Turkish and Arabic.[28]

Ottoman Turkish and Arabic

Turkish and Arabic are unrelated, since they belong to two different language families, Altaic and Semitic. They have very few features in common. Word structure, word order and sentence structure are completely different. On the other hand, Ottoman Turkish had adopted so many foreign (Arabic and Persian) elements (*vide infra*) that translation from Arabic into Ottoman Turkish posed far fewer problems than one might expect. In Ottoman Turkish, especially in the written language, Arabic (and Persian) influence was truly extraordinary; there is no equivalent in any modern European language.[29] Not only simple words, but (as in Persian) even Arabic plurals, especially 'broken' plurals (Ottoman *cem'-i mükesser*) of nouns and adjectives, and even whole phrases or constructions known as *terkib*, were used without modification.[30] Any Arabic verb could be integrated into Ottoman thanks to what are called 'phraseological verbs', formed by the Arabic verbal noun (*maṣdar*) combined with a Turkish verb meaning 'to do' (*etmek, eylemek*, and so on).[31] This method was first used by the Iranians, whose language served as a model for the Ottoman Turks.[32]

Given this impact, even Arabic syntax could be imitated: the Persian *izafet* (or *terkîb-i izafî*)[33] corresponds to the Arabic *iḍāfa* (genitive of possession), for instance. This device allows one to render almost literally the Arabic constructions, even though the rules of Turkish syntax would require another construction. In such cases, even endings were adapted according to the rules of Arabic grammar. Consider these examples from our translation:

Khayr al-Din al-Tunisi's Muqaddima *to* Aqwam al-masalik

Arabic (*Muqaddima*, 65/193)	Ottoman (*Mukaddime*, 117)
'ilm al-akhlāq	*ilm-i ahlâk*
uṣūl al-diyāna	*usul-i diyanet*
al-funūn al-awwaliyya	*fünun-ı evveliyye*
al-mufradāt al-lughawiyya	*müfredat-ı lügaviyye*

The Turkish constructions would have been: *ahlâk ilmi, diyanet usulü, evvelî fenler, lügavî müfredler.*[34]

The linguistic proximity that resulted from this situation can be illustrated by the following typical example, an extract from Cevdet Pasha's translation of Ibn Khaldūn's *Muqaddima* (1861).[35]

'Ilmu l-adab	The science of literature[38]	İlmü 'l-Edeb
Hadha al-'ilm lā mawḍū' lahu yunẓar fī ithbāt 'awāriḍihi aw nafyihā	This science has no object the accidents of which may be studied and thus be affirmed or denied.	Bu ilmin isbât ü nefy ile *avârız*ından *bahs olunur* bir mevzû'u olmayıp
wa innamā al-maqṣūd minhu 'inda ahl al-lisān[36] *thamaratuhu wa hiya al-ijāda fī fannay al-manẓūm wa al-manthūr 'alā asālīb al-'Arab wa manāhīhim*	Philologists consider its purpose identical with its fruit, which is (the acquisition of) a good ability to handle prose and poetry according to the methods and ways of the Arabs. Therefore, they collect and memorize (documents) of Arabic speech that are likely to aid in acquiring the (proper linguistic) habit. (Such documents include) high-class poetry, rhymed prose of an even quality, and (certain) problems of lexicography and grammar, found scattered among (documents of Arabic poetry and prose) and from which the student is, as a rule, able to derive inductively most of the rules of Arabic.	bundan maksud, ancak gerek fenn-i nazımda ve gerek fenn-i nesirde esâlîb ü *usul*-i Arab üzre icâde *ve hüsn-i ifade*den ibaret olan *gayet* ve semeresi olduğuna mebnî, kelâm-ı Arab'da tabakası âli olan şi'r ü seci'den *medar-ı husul-i meleke* olabilecek sözleri cem' ve *ara*larına kavanin-i arabiyye'nin *ekseri*sine *mûcib-i ıttıla'* olacak vechile ilm-i lügat ile ilm-i nahivden dahi *bir takım* mesaili müteferrik olarak *bast u îrâd ederler*[39]
fa-yajma'ūn lidhālika min kalām al-'Arab mā 'asāhu taḥṣul bihi al-kalima min shi'r 'ālī al-ṭabaqa wa saj' mutasāwin fī al-ijāda wa masā'il min al-lugha wa al-naḥw mabthūtha athnā'a dhalika mutafarriqa yastaqrī minhā al-nāẓir fī al-ghālib mu'ẓam qawānīn al-'arabiyya . . .[37]		

Most of the words, including Arabic 'broken' plurals *('awāriḍ, masā'il, qawānīn)* are identical from the Arabic to the Turkish. One of the rare words that does not occur in the Ottoman translation is *manḥan* ('form, sphere', and so forth, replaced by *usul*). There are just two Turkish nouns (*söz, takım*). In two cases, a single Arabic expression becomes a *atf-ı tefsir* (*vide infra*): icade ve hüsn-i ifade (and note the use of *seci*, or rhymed prose!) for Arabic *ijāda*; gayet ve semere for Arabic *thamara*.

Ottoman Turkish of the Tanzimat period was paradoxical. On the one hand, tremendous efforts were made at adaptation, to catch up with inventions and new concepts from the West. On the other hand, the literary language remained strongly attached to traditions long embedded in Islamicate *adab*, in particular the composite lexicon, where Arabic and Persian elements dominated; and the style known as *inşa* (*vide infra*), characterised by the abundant use of metaphors, rhetorical figures, pleonasms, and even rhymed prose (*seci*). The creation of a more 'natural', simplified language was a constantly debated topic among writers and intellectuals in the nineteenth century. But simplification of the language, especially in the sense it is understood today, did not actually take place.[40] Even if our translator asserts that he is producing a translation in a style comprehensible for everybody (*herkesin anlayabileceği siyakda*),[41] this seems rather doubtful.

Both (Arabic and Persian) plurals and *terkib*s played an important role in the development of a modern terminology capable of rendering intelligible new institutions and concepts from the West: consider *encümen-i dâniş* for 'academy', *matbuat* for 'press' or *efkâr-ı umumiyye* for 'public opinion'. For lexical innovation, Arabic and to a much lesser extent Persian[42] continued to remain the unique source. Although some Western terms entered the language,[43] the general attitude remained 'purist', focused on using terms from this shared or adjacent lexicon.

One of the most conspicuous devices of Ottoman style (*inşa*) was the *atf-ı tefsir(î)* – a sort of hendiadys, that is, the use of two (or even three) words of the same meaning.[44] It was considered amongst the beauties of the language.[45] The synonymous words were united by a و (*vâv*), generally pronounced /u/ or /vu/, not /ve/ as in the ordinary language. This stylistic device is also known in Arabic[46] and in Persian (from which the Ottomans adopted it). Whereas Redhouse defines *atf-ı tefsir* as 'the addition of a word to a preceding one by means of a copulative conjunction, in order to fix more precisely the meaning',[47] others have described it more appropriately as 'to use two and even three words of the same meaning (*Kélimatî mûteradîfé*) in the same sentence to express one idea'.[48]

The two elements have to be Persian or Arabic; Turkish or Western words are not admitted. That this device permits combining Arabic and

Persian words makes it particularly attractive and offers more possibilities to Ottoman writers than it does for those writing in Arabic. In classical Ottoman *inşa*, *atf-ı tefsir* is used excessively; its use remained very popular in the nineteenth century. Even in this late nineteenth-century translation of Khayr al-Dīn's *Muqaddima*, these pairs of synonyms are infinitely more frequent than in the Arabic original and are supposed to contribute to a more elegant or rhetorically 'high' style.

We find numerous examples of a simple Arabic term translated by an Ottoman *atf-ı tefsir*. Cf.:

al-'ulamā' alladhīna namat bihum *al-ma'ārif* (56/177) ('scholars thanks to whom knowledge increased')	*maarif* ve *fünunun* terakkisine medar-ı âzam olan *ulema* ve *fuzela* (102) ('knowledge and sciences ... the scholars and the learned')

Here, Arabic *al-ma'ārif* is rendered in Ottoman Turkish by the hendiadys *maarif ü fünun*, and *al-'ulamā'* by *ulema vu fuzela*. They are accompanied by other embellishments: the translator speaks of 'the scholars and learned men who had the *greatest share* in the progress of the sciences'.

The creative variations made possible by introducing Persian are evident when an Arabic term is rendered by an *atf-ı tefsir* containing a Persian element. Cf.:

kaff aydī al-ma'mūrīn 'an al-ta'addī 'alā al-ra'iyya (85/222)	'the restraining of the hands of the officials from aggression against the subjects'	*tebaa*[49] *vü* zirdestân*dan memurînin zulm ü taaddisini men'* (140)

Or, a Persian term may replace an Arabic term, as *serbestlik*[50] for *hürriyet*, or *sermaye* instead of *re'sülmal*. Cf.:

shay' yusammā ḥurriyyat al-maṭba'a (75/208)	'something called freedom of the press'	*bir serbestlik vardırki ana 'hürriyet-i matbuat ıtlak olunur* (127)
ra's māluhu thalāthūn milyūn frank (78/213)	'his capital of 30 million francs'	*otuz milyon frank sermaye* (133)

Another feature appropriated from Arabic, mentioned above, was *seci'*, rhymed prose, common in classical Arabic[51] and Persian literature, nicely conveyed by Hagopian's term, 'symphonious terminations'.[52] It is particularly frequent with honorific epithets, also in this translation. Cf.:

Al-marḥūm sulṭān Maḥmūd wa walidayhi 'the late Sultan Mahmud and his two sons' (33/139–40)	Cennet-mekân sultan Mahmud Han hazretleriyle encal-ı kiram-ı mâdelet-ittisamları (61) 'His Majesty Sultan Mahmud Khan whose abode is the paradise, and his noble descendants characterized by justice'

We also find elaborate uses of metaphor in the Ottoman translation, compared to the Arabic text which may themselves reflect Arabic usages. Compared with the rather sober and laconic Arabic text, the Ottoman translation therefore is often much more flowery. As a result, the Ottoman phrases are often longer than in the Arabic original. Cf.:

Arabic	Ottoman
al-'udwān 'alā l-amwāl yaqṭa' al-āmāl[53] (76/210)	Ahalinin emval u emlâkine itale-i dest-i taaddi keyfiyeti kat'-ı rişte-i ümid ü âmâla vesile olub... (129)
'hostile action against property cuts off hopes'	'The matter of stretching out the hand of aggression against the property and the belongings of the people is a means of cutting the thread of hope and aspirations.'

'Ottoman Arabic' and Modern Arabic

We have noted that the two languages had much vocabulary in common. It could even be said that in principle, any Arabic lexical item had the right to be admitted into Ottoman Turkish. But it is also clear that, even in the composite literary language, only a relatively small selection was in actual use.[54] Ottoman writers were aware of this. Cevdet Pasha, in his treatise on Ottoman rhetoric, gave an example: 'Even if in the Arabic language, *ijtināb* and *tajannub* have the same meaning [avoidance], only the word *ictinab* is familiar [in Ottoman Turkish] whereas *tecennüb* is not commonly used.'[55]

An example from our texts: 'agriculture' is usually *filāḥa* in the Arabic text. Although this Arabic term is not unknown in Ottoman Turkish, it is almost always rendered by a more familiar term, *ziraat*,[56] occasionally also together with *filahat*. Cf.:

al-filāḥa wa sā'ir al-ṣanāyi' (68/198)	'agriculture and the other arts'	ziraat ve sanayi (120)
wa ammā al-filāḥa fa-lā yu'lam lahum naẓīr fīhā (26/127)	'They have no peer in agriculture.'	ziraat ve filahat hususunda ise Arabların ru-yi arzda misl ü naziri olmayub... (49)

Khayr al-Dīn al-Tūnisī's Muqaddima *to* Aqwam al-masalik

In some cases, the Ottoman translation has different Arabic terms formed from the same root. Cf.:

| talkhīṣ al-muktashafāt wa al-mukhtara'āt (61/186) | 'summary of discoveries and inventions' | keşfiyat ve ihtiraatın hulâsası (110) |

The Ottoman translator also uses here exclusively Arabic terms. But since the Arabic *muktashafāt* and *mukhtara'āt* were not commonly used in Ottoman Turkish, he chose different forms – that, as in the case of *kashfiyyāt*[57] (discoveries), are not used in modern Arabic. *Ikhtirā'* exists in Arabic as a synonym for *mukhtara'*, but denotes the action rather than the invented thing, whereas in the translation, it is used for the thing, the outcome of the action.

This 'Ottoman Arabic' seems to have puzzled educated Arabs, as the following example shows. The German Orientalist scholar Martin Hartmann (1851–1918), dragoman at the German Consulate General in Beirut (1876–87), mentions a conversation with the Beirut representative in the Ottoman Parliament, 'Abdurrahīm Badrān, whom he met in Beirut when the latter had returned from Istanbul in 1877. The Arab deputy was amazed, Hartmann said, at how the Arabic language was treated by the Turks. To ease his understanding, they had used many Arabic terms in conversation. But most of them Badrān found incomprehensible, since the Turks gave their own meanings to Arabic words.[58] Hartmann, perfectly familiar with Ottoman Turkish, added: 'Das gilt im höchsten Maße für die arabischen Gegenwerte moderner Begriffe' ('This is particularly true for the Arabic equivalents of modern concepts').

Indeed, numerous – both old and new – 'Arabic' terms in Ottoman Turkish make no sense in Arabic. For some reason, the suffix *-iyet* (< Arabic *-iyya*) had become extremely popular among the Ottomans.[59] A great number of words using this ending existed in Ottoman Turkish but were uncommon in Arabic, where only the simple form was used. In our text, for example, *emniyet* is used for Arabic *amn* (security); *harabiyet* for *kharāb* (ruin), *istiklâliyet* for *istiqlāl* (independence), *islâmiyet* for *islâm*, and there are others. Occasionally, we do not even find an equivalent for such terms as *milliyet* (nationality) in the Arabic text. Cf.:

| wa lā yatabaddal ṭab'u-hum bi-kathrat al-mukhālaṭa wa lā yansūna aṣla-hum alladhī kharajū minhu (31/135) | 'and their [i.e. the Arabs'] nature does not change as a result of frequent mixing and they do not forget their origins from which they sprang' | tabiat-i asliyyeleri zerrece kabil-i tebeddül olmadığı gibi kavmiyet[60] ve milliyet*lerini dahi kat'an unutmazlar* (56-7) ('they do not forget at all their nationality')[61] |

Perhaps the most famous such example is *meşrutiyet* (constitutionalism, constitutional (period)), about whose origin various theories exist.[62] It had become popular among the Ottomans in the 1870s (and was also adopted by the Iranians). The expression *hükûmet-i meşruta* (constitutional government), that also occurs in the Ottoman version of the *Muqaddima*, had already been used by Ottoman travellers in early nineteenth-century Europe, where they encountered this relatively new type of government.[63] Cf.:

'adam qābiliyyat al-umma li-tamaddunāti-hā (43/157)	'the incapability of the *umma* to (accept) its civilizations'	*millet-i islâmiyyenin hükûmet-i meşruta ve medeniyete adem-i kabiliyet* (79) 'to accept constitutional government and civilization'
Innahā tastad'ī mazīd al-ḍarā'ib 'alā al-mamlaka bimā tastalzimuhu min kathrat al-waẓā'if li-idārātihā al-mutanawwi'a (43/157)	'It [i.e. the Tanzimat] requires an increase in taxation for the country due to the high number of various administrative functions.'	*Tanzimatın vaz'ı üzerine hükûmet-i meşrutanın teessüsiyle* ('and with the foundation of constitutional government') *ümur-ı idarenin fevkalâde tenevvu vu taaddüd etmesi ve bunların hüsn-i cereyanı içün masraf haneleri açdırılub memlekete iktidarından aşırı vergünün tahmiline lüzum görünmesi* (79)

The examples found in our translation for *hükûmet-i meşruta* and *meşrutiyet* are particularly interesting. As has been seen, they are often additions made by the translator who seems to have been keen to introduce these rather novel terms. *Meşrutiyet* occurs several times in the Ottoman *Muqaddima* without a direct Arabic equivalent, for example, *usul-i meşrutiyet* (the principles of constitutionalism) (146) is meant to render the Arabic *al-taṣarrufāt al-siyāsiyya al-maḍbūṭa bi-al-tanẓīmāt* (the political activities regulated by *tanzimat*) (88/228). It is sometimes used together with *tanzimat*: *Tanzimat ve meşrutiyet aleyhinde bulunanlar* (those against *tanzimat* and constitutionalism); *Hükûmetin meşrutiyetile tanzimatın tesisi* (85) (the foundation of a government of constitutionalism and *tanzimat*).

To what extent did this terminology exert influence on modern Arabic? Did the Arabs adopt these Ottoman inventions[64] or did they prefer to develop their own terminology? The answer, across the nineteenth century, must await further research. Some official texts seem to have been translated into Arabic using these inventions.[65] The Arabic version of the Ottoman Constitution (Ottoman *Kanun-ı esasî*), published in *al-Jawā'ib*, follows almost slavishly the Ottoman Arabic terminology. Cf.:[66]

| Bilcümle mektebler devletin taht-ı nezaretindedir. Tebaa-i osmaniyyenin terbiyesi bir siyak-ı ittihad üzere olmak içün iktiza eden esbaba teşebbüs olunacak ve milel-i muhtelifenin umur-ı i'tikadiyyelerine müteallik usul-i ta'limiyyeye halel getirilmiyecedir | 'All schools are under the supervision of the state. Necessary steps will be undertaken for a unified education for the Ottoman subjects and no harm shall be done to the teaching methods related to the religious affairs of the different communities.' | *Tūḍa' jamī' al-makātib taḥta naẓārat al-dawla wa yajib al-tashabbuth fī al-asbāb allatī taj'al al-tarbiya al-'uthmāniyya 'alā nasaq wāḥid fī al-ittiḥād wa al-intiẓām wa lā yaqa' khalal fī uṣūl al-ta'līm al-muta'alliq bi-umūr mu'taqadāt al-milal al-mukhtalifa* |

Today, the Ottoman (Arabic) terminology that we find in these translations has become largely obsolete, including the term for 'constitution' itself, *al-qānūn al-asāsī* (fundamental law). Used in the first Arabic translation, it was later replaced by *al-dustūr*, a term (of Persian origin) which Khayr al-Dīn did not use (*vide infra*).[67] But this usage of *al-dustūr* as 'constitution' in Arabic yielded a *faux-ami*; Ottoman-Turkish *düstur* was used to designate the printed collection of laws and rulings introduced after the Tanzimat reforms (first published 1863), of which there is even an Arabic translation,[68] but never the Constitution.

Examples of the New Political Terminology of Ottoman Turkish Popularised through the Constitution

Khayr al-Dīn's *Aqwam al-masālik* appeared nine years *before* the proclamation of the Ottoman Constitution of 1876 whereas the Ottoman translation of the *Muqaddima* was published three years *after* that event. It therefore made use of many terms introduced with the Constitution. The term *Kanun-ı esasî* (basic law), for example, is used consistently in the Ottoman translation, whereas the Arabic text of 1867 had used the French term.[69] Cf.:

| *mukhālifa uṣūl al*-kūnstitūsyūn (85/222) | 'contrary to the principles of the Constitution' | Kanun-ı esasîye mugayir (139) |

The Ottoman translator, like Khayr al-Dīn a staunch defender of constitutionalism, seemed keen to employ this term, which he used also at points where there was no Arabic equivalent in the text (recall the case of *meşrutiyet*). Cf.:

Fa-kullu mā wāfaqū 'alayhi mimmā lā yukhālif tilk al-uṣūl al-lāzim fīhā mushārakat al-'āmma (83/219)	'Everything they agree to, provided it does not contradict those principles where the participation of the common people is necessary.'	Umumun müdahale vü iştirakı lazım ve kanun-ı esasînin ahkâmına mutabık olan her hangi maddede ittifak-ı arâ hâsıl olursa ... (136–7)
ḥimāyat sharī'at al-waṭan li-nafsihi, wa 'irḍihi wa mālihi (33/139)	'the protection of the Law of the fatherland for his life, honour and property'	vatanın kanun-ı esasîsi ırz, can, mal ve namusun muhafazası[70] (60–1)

Other political terms in the text of the Constitution itself, which had become familiar during the First Constitutional Period (Ottoman (*Birinci*) *Meşrutiyet*), occur in the Ottoman text.[71] In these examples, the Arabic *Muqaddima* again used a different, sometimes less stringent, terminology.

'National Assembly':

Ottoman Turkish	**Arabic**
millet meclisi (126)	*majlis nuwwāb*[72] *al-'āmma, majlis al-nuwwāb* (75/208)
millet meclis*leri* ... *bilcümle Avrupa devletlerinde mevcud olub* (127), 'national assemblies exist in all European states'	*majlis al-nuwwāb ... mawjūd fī sā'ir al-mamālik al-ūrubbāwiyya* (75/208)

These terms have lasted: modern Arabic uses *majlis nuwwāb al-umma* whereas Turkish retains *millet meclisi*.[73]

'chamber of deputies'

Meclis-i meb'usân[74] (136)	Majlis al-wukalā'[75] (83/219)

But there is also confusion:

meb'usân meclisi âzasından (35), 'a member of the chamber of deputies'	aḥad a'ḍā' majlis al-nuwwāb (18/112)

'majority'

meclis-i meb'usânın ekseriyet*i* (137)	'the majority of the members of the chamber of deputies'	ghālib[76] a'ḍā' majlis al-wukalā' (83/229)

Khayr al-Din al-Tunisi's Muqaddima to Aqwam al-masalik

'senate'[77]

meclis-i âyan (136)	al-majlis al-a'lā (83/219)
	majlis al-sinātū (87/225)

'to vote'

yiğirmi beş yaşına varmadıkca rey vermek[78] salahiyetini haiz olamaz (123)	'does not have the competence to vote until he has become 25 years old'	wa lā yakūn lahu kalām fīhi ('has no word in . . .') illā idha balagh min al-'umr khamsan wa 'ishrīn sana (72/204)

'(governmental) minister'

vekil, vükelâ[79]	wazīr[80]
mes'ūliyet-i vükelâ (137) 'the ministers' responsibility'	mas'ūliyyat al-wuzarā' (83/220)

Wazīr has remained the common term in Arabic for 'minister', whereas in Ottoman Turkish *vezir* was only used for the grand vizier (*vezir-i a'zam* or *sadr-ı a'zam*) or to designate a rank (*rütbe*).[81] In our text, *wazīr* is sometimes also translated by *reisülvükelâ* (= Turkish *başvekil*) 'prime minister' (27–9) or *vekil-i mutlak* (actually a designation for the grand vizier). The term *al-wazīr al-mubāshir* is also identified with the grand vizier (26). Apart from *vekil* for 'minister', *nazır*[82] also occurs: Victor Duruy is referred to as the French *maarif-i umumiyye* nazırı (42; Arabic *wazīr al-ma'ārif al-'umūmiyya*, 22/120), that is 'ministre de l'instruction publique'.[83]

'(political) party'

Even a new term for political party (Arabic *ḥizb*;[84] Ottoman *fırka*[85]) already occurs although political parties did not formally exist yet in the Middle East.

ahali fırka fırka ayrılub (128)	'The subjects are divided into parties.'	taftariqu al-ra'āyā aḥzāban (75/209)
fırka-i mezkûre (60)	'the aforesaid party'	al-ḥizb al-madhkūr (35/144)

Although they often diverge in vocabulary, Ottoman Turkish and Arabic use the same term for 'republic', a term that has remained in use.

ister cümhuriyet ister veraset üzere (135)	'the state, whether republican or hereditary monarchy'	al-dawla jumhūriyya[86] aw warāthiyya (82/218)

Unlike the Arabic version of the *Kanun-ı esasî*, the Arabic of *Aqwam al-masālik* makes few concessions to 'Ottoman' Arabic.[87] Even the Ottoman terminology concerning taxation is not echoed in the Arabic text. The most frequent terms used there (*majban, ḍarība*) are unknown in Ottoman Turkish. They are translated by *vergü, tekâlif-i miriyye* and others. For *nāzila* (pl. *nawāzil*) (legal action) (a term proper to Tunisia according to Wehr), the standard term *dâva* (pl. *deâvi*) is used.

However, one term coined by the Ottoman Turks occurs regularly in the Arabic text: *tanzimat*.[88] It denotes 'political reform' in general[89] (for which the Ottomans also used the Arabic term *ıslâhat*), and even reforms in Europe (cf. *al-tanẓīmāt bi-Urūbbā*, 81/217).

uṣūl tanẓīmātihim al-siyāsiyya, allatī hiyya asās al-tamaddun wa al-tharwa (81–2/217)	'the bases of their political tanzimat which are also the foundation of their civilization and wealth'	servet ve medeniyetin esası olan Avrupanın tanzimat-ı siyasiyyesi (135) ('Europe's political Tanzimat ...')

Unsurprisingly, purely Turkish elements are almost non-existent in the Arabic text of the *Muqaddima*.[90] (They are also exceedingly few in the Ottoman version.)

Thus, despite the possibility of a unified modern terminology for both Arabic and Ottoman Turkish, modern Arabic eventually emancipated itself from the impact of Ottoman Turkish (Arabic) terminology and introduced and popularised its own terms.[91] This is a process we see occurring in the Arabic *Muqaddima*, where such new terms are already quite visible. Not all of them have stood the test of time. Whereas in the Arabic *Muqaddima*, the 'senate' is referred to as *al-majlis al-a'lā* ('the Upper Assembly'), modern Arabic has *majlis al-shuyūkh* ('Assembly of the Elders'). Other terms are used with a different meaning today, such as *majma'*, which translates the French *collège*[92] in the *Muqaddima*, whereas it has come to be used, among other terms, for 'academy' (a term still conveyed as *akadimiyya* in the *Muqaddima*).[93] Paradoxically, for 'Middle Ages', the Arabic text uses *al-qurūn al-mutawassiṭa* (passim) whereas the modern language seems to have adopted the Ottoman term *al-qurūn al-wusṭā* (Ottoman *kurun-ı vusta*)!

Even if, in some cases, the Arabic of the original text is already close to contemporary usage, gaps are still visible: *'āṣima* as 'capital city' (origi-

Khayr al-Din al-Tunisi's Muqaddima to Aqwam al-masalik

nally one of the names of Medinah, 'the preserving city')[94] was not yet used; this meaning was rendered as *takht* (pl. *tukhūt*), another loanword from Persian.[95] Nor do we find the modern term for 'newspaper', *jarīda*,[96] although *ceride* had been familiar to the Ottoman Turks for some decades already[97] (and was used as a more literary synonym for the usual *gazete*). Various terms are used in the Arabic *Muqaddima*, such *ṣuḥuf al-akhbār* (80/215f.), rendered by *evrak-ı havadis* (134) in the Ottoman Turkish version.[98] Otherwise, *jūrnāl* (*vide infra*) seems to have been particularly popular.[99] It has also been observed that Khayr al-Dīn's work seems to ignore more or less *shaʻb* 'people' (a key word that has become immensely popular), and uses *ahāli*, *ʻāmma*, or – imitating French usage – *umma* 'nation' instead.[100]

On the other hand, *Aqwam al-masālik* already included *thawra* (revolution).[101] The latter term had not been adopted in Ottoman Turkish, which employed *inkılâb*[102] or *ihtilâl* (Ar. اختلال;[103] especially for the French Revolution). Cf. the following examples from the *Muqaddima*:

thawrat ahl Firānsa[104] (59/182)	'the French Revolution'	Fransa ihtilâli (107)
irjāʻ Frānsa ilā al-ḥāla ... qabl al-thawra (19/114)	'returning France to the pre-revolutionary situation'	Fransayı ihtilâldan evvelki haline ircâ (39)
al-thuwwār (31/136)	'the revolutionaries'	ihtilâlcılar (57)

This modern Arabic terminology seems to have had little influence on Ottoman terminology. Essential new terms or even 'key words'[105] (such as *thawra*) were not transmitted.[106] However, at a few points in the Ottoman translation, the choice of terms does seem to have been influenced by the Arabic original's use of recent coinages. Cf.:

al-talghrāf al-kahrubāʼī (65/192)	'the electric telegraph'	telgraf-ı kehrübaî (115)

The Arabic term *kahrubāʼ* (electricity (lit. 'amber')), is said to have been coined by Rifāʻa al-Ṭahṭāwī.[107] The respective adjective (Ottoman *kehrübaî*) was eventually replaced in Ottoman Turkish by *elektrikî* which was treated like an Arabic word, used in *izafet* constructions like *cereyan-ı elektrikî* (electrical current).[108]

Another identical usage is *müstaʻmere* (Arabic *mustaʻmara*) for 'colony'. Cf.:

mustaʻmarāt al-Injilīz bi al-Hind (78/213)	'the British colonies in India'	Hindustan müstaʻmeratı (133)

Müsta'mere is the current term in the Ottoman translation but it is not listed in Ottoman dictionaries of the period.[109] In Ottoman Turkish, *müstemleke* became the common term[110] which is unfamiliar to modern Arabic.

In some cases, this influence generates errors.

| al-lughāt al-qadīma wa l-ḥāditha (66/194) | 'ancient and modern languages' | *eski ve yeni lûgatler* (117) |

This is an improper usage since '*lugha*' in Arabic means 'language' whereas in Ottoman Turkish the meaning of *lûgat* (لغت) is 'word' or – mainly – 'dictionary' (for 'language', Ottoman Turkish uses Arabic *lisan*[111]).

Modern Ottoman Coinages in the Translation

As noted, in the wake of the Tanzimat, Ottoman Turkish had developed its own modern terminology and discourse, independently from Arabic. This terminology was modern in the sense that it was *new*, displaying the need to create equivalents for hitherto unknown (or unfamiliar) Western terms and concepts. Thousands of terms were introduced to meet these needs.[112] But whereas in the West new terms were usually coined from Latin or Greek (or both), this was not envisaged as an option by Ottoman intellectuals, although they were perfectly aware of this as a potential vehicle. Nevertheless, they considered Arabic (and Persian) as the basic source for coining new terms.[113] This conception prevailed even with Ziya Gökalp (1876–1924), a Turkish nationalist thinker who declared that *all* Islamic languages had to coin their technical terms from Arabic or Persian roots, as an obligation towards the *umma*, just as the Christian *umma* had created its terms from Latin and Greek.[114] Gökalp himself coined new words from Arabic roots, such as *hars* (حرث) (culture), *mefkûre* (مفكوره) (ideal), or *şe'niyet* (< شأنية) (reality), all of them completely alien to modern Arabic.

Ottoman writers and intellectuals were well aware of these divergences in meaning. Even Gökalp, who once had dreamt of a unified terminology for all Muslim peoples,[115] observed, 'when we adopt words from the Arabs and the Persians, we will have only adopted their phonetic form. The "national" meanings which we shall give them are no longer understood by their former owners.'[116] Said Bey Kemalpaşazade (1848–1921), a specialist in translation, had written in 1893: 'All these expressions are required by the style (*şive*) of *our* language. Even if they contradict the style of the Arabic language, or indeed the rules of all languages of the world, we shall nevertheless use them.'[117]

When the Ottoman translation of Khayr al-Dīn's *Muqaddima* appeared, many of these new coinages were already well established in their usage, and not all of them were derived from Arabic.[118] In Arabic, though translators such as al-Ṭahṭāwī had come up with new usages, there was still much hesitation in this regard. In some cases, no such terms existed, or loanwords and different terms were used. Thus, we see different strategies in the Arabic *Muqaddima* as compared to the Ottoman translation.

A few examples:

'university': Ottoman *darülfünun*. A name used to designate various institutions in Islamic history, was used by the Ottomans for 'university' from the time of their first such projects in the 1840s,[119] whereas the Arabs translated the concept as *madrasa jāmiʿa* (later reduced to *jāmiʿa*).[120]

wa assas bi-Bārīs madrasa jāmiʿa (51/167)	'And he (i.e. Charlemagne) founded a university in Paris.'	*ve Paris'de bir darülfünunun tesisine dahi muvaffak olmuş'* (93) (lit. 'he managed to found')

'academy': *Encümen-i daniş* (Persian: 'Council of knowledge'[121]) was introduced to designate the 'Ottoman Academy' founded in 1851. (This is one of the rare Ottoman terms based exclusively on Iranian roots.) In the Arabic *Muqaddima*, the Latin/Italian/Greek (?) term is used.

jamʿiyyāt min kibār ʿulamāʾihim, yusammā kullu minhā Akadimiyya (68/197)	'societies of their great scholars, all of them called Academy'	*Fuzela-yı ulemadan mürekkeb bir kaç* 'Encümen-i daniş' (119)

Among the academies mentioned (Ar. 68/197 – Ottoman 119) are the Académie française (Akadimiyyat Frānsa – Fransa encümen-i danişi), the Académie des Beaux-Arts (Akadimiyyat al-būzār – Sanayi-i nefise encümen-i danişi) and the Académie des Sciences (Akadimiyyat al-ʿulūm – Fünun[122] encümen-i danişi).

'nobility'

Ottoman Turkish uses the plural of the Persian *-zāde* (born of, son of) (which, used as a suffix, has the same meaning as Turkish *-oğlu*).[123] In the Arabic *Muqaddima*, the French term, 'noblesse' appears, with various Arabic explanations. Cf.:

al-wajāha al-musammāt ʿindahum bi-al-nūblīs[124] (82/219)	'the nobility, called by them "*noblesse*"'	*zadegân* (136)
kubarāʾ al-umam ... al-musammīn bi-al-nūblīs (9/96)	'grandees of the nations called '*noblesse*'	*zadegân* (16)

Western Terms, from Arabic to Ottoman Turkish

The use of Western terms, which occur both in the Arabic text and in the Ottoman translation, is a complex matter. In some cases, both Arabic and Ottoman Turkish use loanwords of identical origin (for example, *madālyā/ medalya, dīktātūr/diktatör, fabrīka/fabrika,*[125] as 'factory'; *fābūr*[126]/*vapur,* 'steamship'). Cf. also:

Kūmbāniyyat al-Hind[127] (78/214)	'the East India Company'	Hind kumpanyası (132)
al-janarāl Krūnwāl (88/226)	General Cromwell	Ceneral[128] Kronvel (145)

In other cases, the Arabic text has older loanwords than the Ottoman. In the following case, the Arabic term for 'knight' comes from Italian, whereas the Ottoman text uses the more modern French form. Cf.:

ḥizb al-fursān alladhīna ishtaharū bi-ism al-kawalyīr (< Italian cavaliere) (51/168)	'the group of horsemen which became famous under the name of knights'	(şövalye) ismiyle . . . bir fırka-i mümtaze ('a distinguished group named chevalier')

After the Tanzimat reforms, Italian, until then the best-known Western language in the Ottoman Empire, lost its status and many words were Gallicised (for example, *Fransa* replaced *França*). Also, an older Ottoman Turkish *kavalir, kavalyer*[129] was replaced by the French term *chevalier.*[130]

Sometimes different Western loanwords are used. Cf.:

jūrnālāt (75/208)	'newspapers'	gazeteler ve risaleler (127) 'newspapers and journals'
karūsa (< Italian carozza) (65/192)	'coach'	vagon (116)

In Ottoman Turkish, certain words of Western origin could alternatively be used instead of Arabic terms, for example, *politika*[131] instead of *siyaset, kumpanya* instead of *şirket* (< Arabic *sharika*). Cf.:

siyāsat al-duwal al-ūrubbāwiyya (39/150)	'the policy of the European states'	Avrupa devletlerinin . . . politikaları (71)
al-jam'iyyāt (77/211)	'the companies'	kumpanyalar (131)

In the Arabic text of Khayr al-Dīn's treatise, Western terms are usually followed by an explanation introduced with *ayy* (that is, i.e.). The same need is not always felt by the Ottoman translator, perhaps suggesting a sense that the terms are already familiar to Ottoman readers. Cf.:

Khayr al-Din al-Tunisi's Muqaddima to Aqwam al-masalik

al-futūghrāfī ayy irtisām al-ṣūra bi-wāsiṭat al-mir'āt wa baqā'uhā (65/193)	'photography, i.e. the drawing of pictures by mirrors and their preservation' (151)	fotoğrafi san'ati (116) 'the art of photography'

There are cases where the Western term appears only in Arabic[132] and no loanword is used in the Ottoman version. Cf.:

ālat al-dhanb al-musammāt ālīs (64/191)	'the back machine called hélice'	yandan olan çarha bedel kuyrukdan vida (115) ('instead of the wheel on the side, the use of a screw on the back')
al-ikūnūmī būlītīk ayy al-iqtiṣād al-siyāsī (68/198)	'économie politique, i.e. political economy'	fenn-i iktisad-i siyasî (120)
al-krītīk (25/125)	'criticism'	muhakemât u tenkidât (47)
'ulūm al-fīzīk (30/134)	'physics'	hikmet-i tabiiyye (55)

Occasionally, the opposite occurs. Cf.:

fī . . . al-iqtiṣād al-siyāsī (59/184)	'in political economy'	ekonomi politik yâni fenn-i iktisad-ı siyasî[133]de (108)

In the following examples, only French loanwords are used in the Ottoman translation, whereas the Arabic text uses a paraphrase:

kayfiyyat taqwiyat al-a'ṣāb bi-al-ḥarakāt al-riyāḍiyya (66/194)	'the matter of strengthening of the sinews by exercise'	cimnastik[134] fenleri (117)
abnā' al-'ā'ila al-malakiyya (72/204)	'the sons of the royal family'	prensler (122)
isti'māl al-āthār al-ṭabī'iyya ka-al-taṣwīr bi-al-mir'āt (67/196)	'the use of physical means such as the representation by mirror'	fotoğrafya[135] (118)
midfa' al-shashakhān[136] wa mukhulat[137] al-ibra wa al-safīna al-mudarra'a (8/95)	'the rifled cannon, the ignition needle rifle, the armoured ship' (79, n. 22)	mitrayöz toplarına, iğneli tüfenklerine, zırhlı sefinelerine (14f.)

| allaf kitāban sammāhu ... Makātīb[138] ahl al-qurā (56/178) | 'he [i.e. Pascal] wrote a book called 'Letters by people from villages' | 'Letr de Provens'[139] nâm kitabı telif etmiş (103) |

A French loanword with a much shorter Ottoman paraphrase (adopted from the Arabic original) also appears in the following examples:

| ikhtara' Franklin jawādhib al-sā'iqa allatī tajdhab al-quwwa al-kahrubā'iyya min al-siḥāb wa tadkhul bihā fī al-arḍ (61/187) | 'Franklin invented lightning rods which attract the electrical power from the clouds and causes it enter the earth.' | Franklen 'paratoner'[140] yâni cazibe-i saikayı ihtira etmişdir (111) 'Franklin invented the lightning rod, i.e. the attraction of the lightning.' |

Sometimes, new Ottoman terms are used to render an Arabic paraphrase.

| ālat al-billawr allatī tukabbir al-ashyā' (55/174) | 'the glass instrument that magnifies things' | rasad durbini (100) 'the astronomical telescope' |
| al-mir'āt allatī tukabbir al-ashyā' (61/186) | 'the mirror that magnifies things' | rasad durbini (111) |

Some of these examples suggest that, in some respects, Western influences were already more firmly implanted in Ottoman Turkish than they were in modern Arabic. Ottoman Turkish also appeared closer to Western languages in another sense. One advantage of Ottoman Turkish was its larger inventory of consonants represented by the letters p, ž (j), ç and so forth, all unknown in Arabic. They allowed a more precise rendering of Western (French) names and terms: Ottoman *Paris* versus Arabic *Bārīs*. But the Ottoman translation of the *Muqaddima* could not take advantage of this, since unfortunately most of the proper names in the Ottoman translation are misprinted to the point of being unrecognisable. Surely readers could not identify them.

Keywords of Modernity

In both Arabic and Ottoman Turkish, words took on new meanings according to the leading debates of the day. Although these debates were common to Arabophone and Turcophone intellectuals, they did not always choose the same terms. The Ottoman term *medeniyet*[141] was a keyword during the Modernisation period, used as the equivalent of French *civilisation*.[142] But *madaniyya* did not enjoy the same popularity among Arabs (and Persians). In Khayr al-Dīn's work, another term (although one derived from the same root), *tamaddun*,[143] is employed instead. This term was not unfamiliar to the Ottoman Turks (Ottoman *temeddün*).[144] But Jurjī Zaydān's 'History of Islamic civilisation' (*Ta'rīkh al-tamaddun al-islāmī*) – still popular among the Turks! – was translated into Turkish by Zeki Megamiz (Zakī Mughāmiz; a key figure in Khuri-Makdisi's and Dedes' chapter, as translator of Qāsim Amīn) as *Medeniyet-i islâmiyye târihi* (1913). *Tamaddun*, signifying the process of 'becoming-civilised', was the more common usage in Arabic.[145]

A synonym, *ḥaḍāra*,[146] had been used much earlier, by Ibn Khaldūn (with the sense of 'sedentary culture'), together with *tamaddun* and *'umrān*.[147] The latter term also occurs in our *Muqaddima*, often with the meaning of 'prosperity'. Not unknown in Ottoman Turkish, it was usually translated as *mâmuriyet*,[148] from the same root.

a'lā darajāt al-'umrān (77/210)	'the highest degrees of prosperity'	*derece-i aksa-yı servet ü mâmuriyet* (130) 'wealth and prosperity'

The use of the word *hadaret* (*hazaret*)[149] was extremely rare in Ottoman Turkish. If ever, it was used in the sense of 'presence (opposite of *giybet* 'absence, invisibility')'.[150] But there are exceptional cases, as in the following *atf-ı tefsir* imitating partly the Arabic:

fa-bi-al-sabab al-madhkūr – wa huwa mukhālaṭat al-ūrubbāwiyīn li-al-umma al-islāmiyya al-mutaqaddima 'alayhim fī al-tamaddun wa al-ḥaḍāra kān ibtidā' al-tamaddun 'indahum (52/169)	'for this reason, i.e. the association of the Europeans with the Islamic *umma*, more advanced than they in civilization and culture, there was the beginning of civilization with them'	*Avrupa medeniyetin başlangıcı medeniyet ü hadaret hususunda Avrupalıları fersah fersah geçmiş olan millet-i islamiyye ile ihtilâta başladığı tarihden itibar olunmakda* (95)

This demonstrates a point made earlier: in Ottoman Turkish, in principle, *all* Arabic words had the right to citizenship. But the Ottoman translation also shows us what was common usage: *hadaret* was here only a sort of embellishment whereas the common term was *medeniyet*. This also appears in the following examples:

ladhdhat al-saṭwa wa al-ḥaḍāra (85/223)	'the pleasure of authority and civilization'	*lezzet-i medeniyet*[151] (140) 'the pleasure of civilization'
akhlāq al-ḥaḍar[152] (52/169)	'the morals of settled civilization'	*akvam-ı medeniyye ahlâkı* (95) 'the morals of civilized peoples'

One of the preceding quotations also hints at another difference of usage, indeed a striking case of it: *millet* and *umma*. Both terms acquired new meanings during the era of modernisation in the Middle East: equivalent to French *nation*. Although there was a fierce debate among Ottoman intellectuals over which term to use for that purpose (*millet* or *ümmet*),[153] *millet* became the common term in (Ottoman) Turkish whereas Arabic adopted *umma*.

In the *Muqaddima*, Arabic *milla* only occurs in the sense of religious community. Cf.:

min ghayr ahl millatihim (6/91)	'from outside their religious community' (76)	milel-i saireden (10)

Otherwise, Ottoman *millet* regularly corresponds to *umma* in the Arabic text. Moreover, it is used for any nation, both past and present.

idhā i'tabarnā tasābuq al-umam fī mayādīn al-tamaddun (3/82)	'if we consider the competition of nations in the field of civilization ...'	meydan-ı medeniyete milletlerin yekdiğerleriyle yarışa çıkub ... nasb-ı ayn-ı i'tibar eylediğimizde... (2–3)
al-umam al-māḍiya (82/218)	'the nations of the past'	milel-i sâlife (135)
al-umma al-frānsāwiyya (19/114)	'the French nation'	Fransız milleti (37)
al-umma al-ifranjiyya (6/90)	'the Frankish nation'[154]	Avrupalılar (9)

Occasionally, *umma* is translated by other terms, such as *kavim* (people, tribe) (< Arabic *qawm*) – or not at all.

balda muttaḥida, taskunhā umam muta'addida (3/82)	'a united country inhabited by various nations'	bir takım akvam-ı muhtelife ile meskûn bir belde[155] ('peoples') (3)
al-umma al-rūmāniyya (73/206)	'the Roman nation'	Roma cümhuru[156] (124)
kāfiya li-ḥifẓ ḥuqūq al-umma (74/207)	'sufficient for the preservation of the rights of the nation'	tebaanın muhafaza-i hukukuna kâfi (126) ('subjects')

Sometimes, *millet* is used in the Ottoman translation, where the Arabic text uses a term other than *umma*.

Khayr al-Din al-Tunisi's Muqaddima *to* Aqwam al-masalik

al-mamālik *allatī tanālū al-ḥurriyya* (76/209)	'the kingdoms that have attained freedom'	*hürriyete nail olan* millet (129)
al-dawla wa al-mamlaka (84/221)	'the state and the kingdom'	*devlet ü* millet (138) 'the state and the nation'
ḥifẓ *al-dīn wa al-waṭan* (73/205)	'protection of religion and fatherland'	mülk ü millet*in muhafaza vu müdafaası* (124) 'the country and the nation (?)'[157]

Even in cases where the Islamic *umma* is referred to, the Ottoman translator prefers *millet* (to *ümmet*), sometimes accompanied by honorific epithets.[158]

tawārīkh al-umam al-mushār ilayhā wa tawārīkh al-umma al-islāmiyya (87/225)	'the history of the nations referred to and of the Islamic *umma*'	*akvam-ı mezkûre ile* millet-i islamiyye*nin tevarihi* (143)
fīmā kānat 'alayhi wa ālat ilayhi al-umma al-islāmiyya (2/82)	'the Islamic *umma*, its attributes and its future ...' (71)	millet-i muazzame-i islamiyye ... *ne hal-i şanda olub mürur-ı zaman ile ne hale girdiği* ...

The Arabic plural (*milel* in Ottoman spelling) is also frequently used:

aḥwāl *al-umam* (69/198)	'the conditions of nations'	*fenn-i* milel ve nihal[159] (121)
*al-ḥuqūq al-mu'tabara bayn al-*umam *fī khulaṭihā al-siyasiyya wa al-matjariyya* (58/181)	'the laws respected between nations in their political and commercial relations'	hukuk-ı beynelmilel[160] ki *münasebat-ı siyasiyye ve ticariyyece beynel*ahali *mu'teber olan hukukdu*r (106) 'International Law which are the laws respected among the peoples in political and commercial relations'

Another keyword of the Tanzimat era was 'progress'. The Ottoman Turks eventually adopted *terakki* (< *taraqqin*),[161] whereas *taqaddum* has become the most common term in Arabic (Arabic *taraqqin* was used in the related sense of 'becoming refined' or 'elevating oneself'). The divergence between the languages becomes clear in our text. Cf.:

taqaddum *ahl Ūrubbā fī maydān al-tamaddun* (65/193)	'the progress of the Europeans in the field of civilization'	*Avrupa' nın meydan-ı medeniyetde* terakki*si* (116)

But *taraqqi* also occurs in the Arabic text of the *Muqaddima*. Cf.:

thumma akhadh al-tamaddun fī al-taraqqī bi-madārij al-'ulūm wa al-a'māl (53/171).	'Then civilization began to elevate itself in paths of the sciences and the crafts.'	Bundan sonra ulûm ve sanayiin terakkisi nisbetince medeniyet dahi ilerülemeğe başlamış . . . (97)
taraqqū fī sā'ir al-ma'ārif (56/177)	'they advanced in the other sciences'	maarif-i sairede terakki ederek (103)

In Ottoman Turkish, *takaddüm* is mainly used with the sense of 'priority, precedence'. It occurs also in our translation, occasionally in a *atf-ı tefsir* together with *terakki*, echoing the case of *ḥaḍāra/hadaret*:

al-'ulūm allatī lahum al-faḍl fīhā (25/125)	'the sciences in which they attained superiority'	Arabların fazl u takaddüm ihraz eyledikleri fenler (46)
sābiqiyyat al-taqaddum fī miḍmāray al-'irfān wa al-'umrān (4/85)	'the superiority in the two fields of knowledge and prosperity'	medeniyet ve maarifce hakk-ı takaddüm (5)
taqaddum al-Ifranj fī al-ma'ārif (8/ 94)	'the Europeans' progress in the field of knowledge'	maarif ve fünunda Avrupalıların terakki ve takaddümü (13)

An exceptional case is the occurrence of a purely Turkish term (*ilerülemek*[162]), a calque of the Arabic verb (*taqaddama*):

taqaddumuhum fī al-'ulūm wa al-ṣinā'āt (86/223)	'their progress in the sciences and the arts'	sanayi ve maarifde ilerülemek (141) 'to advance in the arts and in knowledge'
bidūn taqaddum fī . . . asbāb al-'umrān (8/95)	'without progress in the means of prosperity'	esbab-ı mâmuriyetde ilerülemeksizin (15)
al-taqaddum fī al-'ulūm wa al-ṣinā'āt (9/98)	'progress in the sciences and industries'	fünun ve sanayide ilerüleyişleri (17)
sabab taqaddumihim fīhā (25/125)	'the reason for their progress'	ilerülemelerinin sebebi (46)

Sometimes, Ottoman *terakki* corresponds to Arabic *numūw* (growth, progress):

akhadh 'ilm al-falsafa fī al-numūw (51/168)	'The science of philosophy began to grow.'	fenn-i felsefe dahi terakki bulmağa başladı (94)
numūw 'umrān mamālikihā (35/144)	'the growth of prosperity of their kingdoms'	Memleketin terakki-i mâmuriyeti (64)

The opposite, 'decline', and so forth, was frequently expressed in Ottoman Turkish by *tedenni* (< *tadannin*),[163] whereas in Arabic *ta'akhkhur* (backwardness) has been more common. This is also demonstrated by our texts.

ba'd an ta'ammalt ta'ammulan ṭawīlan, fī asbāb taqaddum al-umam wa ta'akhkhuri*hā* (2/82)	'after I had long contemplated the causes of the progress and backwardness of nations ...' (71)	*bir milletin esbab-ı* tedenni *ve terakkisi uzun uzadıya nazar-ı im'ân u tedkikden geçirdikden sonra* (2)
*asbāb al-taqaddum wa al-*ta'akhkhur *fī al-umma al-islāmiyya* (49/165)	'the causes of progress and backwardness of the Islamic *umma*'	*millet-i islâmiyyenin terakki ve* tedenni*si* (90)

The same as with *ilerülemek*, exceptionally also a Turkish phrase occurs. Cf.:

ta'akhhur al-umma fī al-ma'ārif (7/93)	'the backwardness of the *umma* in terms of knowledge'	*maarif ü fünunda milletin gerü kaldığı*[164] (12) 'lagging behind'

Other, similar terms were *inhitat, inkıraz, ızmıhlal*, the latter two also frequently used in the Arabic text.

Al-sabab alladhī kaburat bihi al-dawla al-rūmāniyya wa ta'āẓamat, wa alladhī saqaṭat bihi wa inqaraḍat. (58/181)	'*Considérations sur les causes de la grandeur des Romains et de leur décadence*' (Montesquieu)	*Roma devletinin büyüyüb tevessu etmesi ve müteâkıben* inhita*ta yüz tutub münkarız olması esbabı* (105)
*al-*idmihlāl *wa al-duthūr* (74/206)	'disappearance and extinction'	*mahv u* ızmıhlal (125)

Occasionally, somewhat ambiguous French terms that were picked up as key words were interpreted differently in Arabic and Ottoman Turkish. *Liberté de la presse* was rendered in Ottoman Turkish as 'freedom of the [periodical] press' whereas in Arabic, it was understood as 'freedom of the [printing] press'.[165]

wa baqiya warā'a dhālik li- al-'āmma shay' ākhar yusammā ḥurriyyat al-maṭba'a (75/208)	'In addition to this there remains to the public something else which is called freedom of the press ...'	*Şu iki hürriyetden başka umum-ı ahali içün dahi bir serbestlik vardır ki ana* 'hürriyet-i matbuat[166] *'ıtlak olunur*

Part of the process of modernity was a re-evaluation of social categories, and this, too, shows up in the translation of key terms – another way in which translation gives us a window into the thought processes of some intellectuals who were contemplating the conditions of their societies. During the classical period, the (tax-paying) subjects of the Ottoman Empire were referred to as the *reaya* (pl. of *raiyet*) also in official documents (firmans, berats and so forth). After the Tanzimat reforms, this term, also meaning 'herd' or 'flock',[167] was considered too patronising or condescending and was officially replaced by the new term *tebaa* (pl. of *tâbi'* 'follower'),[168] meant to be an equivalent for French *sujet* (subject).[169] The Arabic *Muqaddima* continued the traditional usage,[170] while the Ottoman translation drew on the new understanding.

ḥuqūq al-duwal 'alā ra'āyāhā wa bi-al-'aks (58/181)	'the rights of states on their subjects and vice versa'	*devletin* tebaası *ve* tebaa*nın devleti üzere olan hukuku* (106)
ḥifẓ huqūq ra'āyāhum (40/151)	'the protection of the rights of their subjects'	tebaa*larının hıfz-y hukuku* (72)
tafaqqud aḥwāl al-ra'āyā (75/205)	'inspection of the conditions of the subjects'	tebaa *vü zirdestānın ahvalini taharri* (124)
*al-qawānīn tuqayyid al-ru'āt kamā tuqayyid al-*ra'iyya (74/207)	'laws bind the rulers the same as the subjects'	*kavanîn-i mevzua* tebaayı *kayd altına alacağı gibi kâffe-i harekât u sekenatında evliya-yı ümur dahi mukayyed edecekdir* (126)

In rare instances, the same terminology is used in both Arabic and Turkish:

al-rā'ī wa al-ra'iyya (85/223)	'the ruler and the ruled'	*râî ile raiyet* (141)
*tasāwī al-*ra'āya (36/145)	'the equality of the subjects'	reaya*nın müsavatı* (65)
al-ḥuqūq al-mar'iyya bayn al-dawla wa al-ra'iyya (82/218)	'laws observed between the state and the subjects'	*devlet ve raiyet miyanelerinde mer'î olan hukuk* (135)

Another classical term for non-Muslims, *dhimmī*, for the same reasons as quoted above, also had to be avoided in Ottoman Turkish. It was no longer seen as politically or socially appropriate to refer to non-Muslims with a term that suggested 'protected' subjects. Cf.:

al-kathīr min ahl al-dhimma (33/139) 'many dhimmīs'	*ahali-i gayr-ı müslime*den *bir çok kimesneler* (60) 'many of the non-Muslim population'

Khayr al-Din al-Tunisi's Muqaddima *to* Aqwam al-masalik

Literature and Art

While keywords central to the era's political vocabulary showed marked tendencies in each language, the terminology of (Western) art and literature seems to have posed particular problems in both languages, for we find hesitation in the lexicon, between loanwords (*tiyātrāt* 'plays') and attempts at translation, not always successful. Inconsistencies and different strategies within each language also found their way into acts of translation.[171]

The rendering of 'literature' itself was problematic, due to the polysemy of the Arabic term *adab*, classically, 'refinement, good manners' including moral refinement, which an individual would both acquire and demonstrate through learning and practicing literary composition as well as other branches of learning. At the time, the term was in transition, between its broader sense and the contemporary referent, 'literature'. In the Arabic *Muqaddima*, the plural *ādāb* seems to be privileged, perhaps under the influence of French *lettres*.[172] But it is not always clear what is meant; the Ottoman translation is of no help.[173]

ādāb *al-Yūnān, al-shi'r al-lātīnī wa l-fränsāwī wa ādāb al-ajānib* (67/196)	'the literature [culture?] of Greece, Latin and French poetry and foreign literature [culture?]'	*Yunan ve ecnebî* âdâb*ıyla lâtin ve Fransız eş'ârı* 'Greek and foreign *âdâb* and Latin and French poems'
*ahl ītālyā ightanamū... shuhra bi-al-*ādāb (55/175)	'The Italians captured fame in literature.' [174]	*İtalyalılar* âdâb*-ı şi'riyye*[de] *kesb-i iştihar edüb*... 'in poetic *âdâb*' (101)

Cf. also:

al-inshā' wa sā'ir al-'ulūm al-adabiyya (67/196)	'Composition and the other literary (?) sciences'	*Fenn-i inşa ve sair* ulûm-ı *edebiyye* (118)

Another term is *kitāba*, which corresponds to *kātib* (writer):

*Wultīr wa huwa mimman akhadh rāyat al-*kitāba *bi-al-yamīn wa al-shimāl* (59/182)	'Voltaire who was one of those who grasped the banner of literature with the right and the left (hand)'	'Volter' dirki ki sahra-yı vesî'ul-enha-yı *şi'r ü inşa*[175]*da alem-efraz-ı fesahat* [...] *ederek*...' 'Voltaire raising the banner of eloquence in the vast field of poetry and prose'

The Ottomans had coined *edebiyat*[176] (which is less familiar in Arabic). In the Ottoman translation this term occurred several times. It is introduced once without an equivalent in the Arabic text (*edebiyat-ı tehzibiyye* 'their [that is, the Arabs'] refining literature'; *Mukaddime*, 57)[177] another time (*Mukaddime*, 108), referring to Goethe's works, *edebiyat* is a translation of *ādāb* (*Muqaddima*, 59/183).

More specific literary terms were problematic, too. For 'theatre', a loanword was used both in the Arabic and Ottoman text.[178]

al-majāmi' al-mu'adda li-tahdhīb al-akhlāq al-musammāt 'indahum bi-al-tiyaṭrāt (54/173)	'the meeting places intended for the polishing of manners, called "theatres" by them'	tehzib-i ahlâk içün tehiye vü ihzar olunmuş olan tiyatrolar (98) 'theatres prepared for the polishing of manners'

But in Ottoman Turkish, *tiyatro*[179] was also used for 'play' (= *tiyatro oyunu*), as becomes clear from the following example:

istaḥaqq ism al-mujaddid li-tiyaṭrāt al-almān (59/183)	(Schiller) 'he deserved the name of restorer of German theatre'	Almanyaca oynanılan tiyatroların müceddid-i sânisi unvanı dibace-i şeref ü şanıdır (108) 'of the plays staged in Germany'

In Arabic, the terms *kūmīdiyā* and *trājīdiyā* came into use, *kūmīdiyā* initially with the meaning of '(theatre) play' in general.[180] The Ottoman Turks had coined their own terms for 'comedy' and 'tragedy', *mudhike* and *haile* (or *facia*) respectively, but they were also familiar with the Greek and French terms.

al-trājīdiyā ... (wa hiyya muḥakāt al-ḥurūb wa al-waqā'i') wa al-kūmīdiyā (wa hiyya muḥākāt umūr fī qālib al-hazl) (57/179)	'tragedy (which is the representation of wars and battles)' and 'comedy (which is the representation of events in a humorous framework)'	trajedya[181] ve komedya (104)

'Fable' was another puzzle. For this apparently unknown genre, Şemseddin Sami (1886) proposed *hikâye, mesel, kıssa* and *masal*,[182] all terms drawn from Arabic.[183]

Lāfūntīn fī al-amthāl (57/179)	'La Fontaine in fables'	durūb-ı emsal*da* '*Lafonten*'

Khayr al-Din al-Tunisi's Muqaddima *to* Aqwam al-masalik

The term was not really appropriate: Arabic *amthāl* are 'examples', including parables and proverbs,[184] whereas Ottoman *durub-ı emsal* (sing. *darb-ı mesel*) means 'proverbs'.[185]

Whereas the category of 'poet' (*shā'ir/şair*) was well established in both languages, various terms were used for 'writer', in the Arabic text, mostly *kātib* (pl. *kataba*) or *kātib al-inshā'*. The essayist Addison, for example, is presented as *min katabat al-inshā'* (58/180); the Ottoman translator renders it closely with the term *münşilerden* (105).[186]

For beaux-arts or Fine Arts, whereas modern Arabic uses a calque from the French, *al-funūn al-jamīla*, Khayr al-Dīn's text gives us the impression that such an equivalent did not exist yet in Arabic. Instead, we find the French word transcribed as *al-būzār*.

şinā'āt al-būzār (56/177)	*Beaux-arts*	*sanayi-i nefise* (103)
Maktab al-būzār (67/196)	*Ecole des Beaux-Arts*	*Sanayi-i nefise mektebi* (120)
Akādīmiyyat al-būzār (68/197)	*Académie des Beaux-Arts*	*Sanayi-i nefise encümen-i danişi* (119)

In Ottoman Turkish, the term *sanayi-i nefise* (*nefis* 'excellent, exquisite, fine, precious, beautiful') was about to become common. The Arts School founded in Istanbul in 1882 was to be known as Sanayi-i nefise Mektebi.[187] This term remained in use until the language revolution of the 1930s. But in the translation of the *Muqaddima*, there was still hesitation: other adjectives occurred. Cf.:

ahl Itālyā ightanamū fī dhālik al-waqt shuhrat bi- ... al-şinā'āt al-mustazrafa[188] *al-musammāt 'indahum* 'būzār' (55/175)	'The Italians in this time captured fame in the elegant crafts called "beaux-arts" by them.'	*İtalyalılar ... sanayi-i bediada*[189] *kesb-i iştihar edüb ...* (101)

In the following example, the translator seems to have identified the term with handicraft:

fa-bihim wa bi-talāmidhati-him tajaddad al-būzār (56/177)	'Through them and their disciples, the fine arts were renewed.'	*bunlar ve bunlardan tilmiz eden zevat vasıtasıyla Avrupa'nın nevahi-i sairesinde elle işlenen sanayi-i zarife taze revnak bulmuşdur* 'handmade fine arts' (!) (103)

There was also no clear term for 'artists'.[190]

arbāb al-ṣinā'āt ... (56/177)	'the artists (Raphael and Michelangelo)'	ashab-ı sanayi ... (102)

The polysemy of other terms apparently posed problems to the Ottoman translator. In the following example, he did not grasp the meaning of Arabic *naqsh* (also 'engraving, drawing, painting'), meaning 'sculpture' in the Arabic text, for which the Ottoman Turks used *(fenn-i) nakr* or – more frequently – *heykeltıraşlık*. The Ottoman translator gave *naqsh* the meaning it had in Ottoman Turkish: 'decoration, painting':

ṣinā'at al-dahn, wa al-naqsh, wa al-binā' (56/177)	'the art of oil painting, sculpture and architecture'	yağlı boya ve fenn-i mimarî ve ressamî (102) 'oil painting, architecture and painting' (!)
al-ṣinā'āt al-mustaẓrafa al-musammāt 'inda-hum 'būzār', wa hiya al-dahn wa al-naqsh, wa handasat al-binā', wa al -musīqā. (55/175)	'the fine arts, called by them "beaux-arts", i.e. painting, sculpture, architecture and music'	sanayi-i bediada ..., alelhusus yağlı boya ve nakkaşlık[191] ve hendese-i mimariyye ve fünun-i musikiyye (101)

Strangely enough, the author(s) of the Arabic text even seem, at a first glance, to be unable to find an equivalent for 'architecture' and only transcribe French *'architecture'* (*aršitaktūr*). But the text also speaks of *'handasat al-binā'* whereas in Ottoman Turkish *(fenn-i) mimarî* or *mimarlık (fenni)*, both (47) based on Arabic, was well established.[192]

ṣinā'at al-aršitaktūr ayy handasat al-binā' (25/126)	hendese-i mimariyye sanatı (47)
handasa fī al-abniya (51/168)	fenn-i mimarî (94)

Conclusion

The Ottoman rendering of Khayr al-Din's *Muqaddima* offers a window into the intellectual history of the era of transition in which it was composed and published. It displays the many ways in which intellectuals working between Arabic, Ottoman Turkish, and perhaps French, were grappling with how to communicate key debates and questions about social formation and political organisation, as well as other aspects of human society and creativity. Language use allows us to see some of the ways they were thinking about these processes, and about audiences to

Khayr al-Din al-Tunisi's Muqaddima to Aqwam al-masalik

whom they wanted to speak. During this transition period, the impact of the West became visible in both languages on different levels. As far as the lexicon is concerned, both remained purist, and relatively few Western (French) terms were adopted. In Arabic, most of them were later replaced by Arabic neologisms. The Turks, too, coined hundreds of new terms from Arabic roots as equivalents of modern (or hitherto unknown) Western terms and concepts.[193]

Since Khayr al-Dīn's work dealt mainly with history and politics, the comparison is particularly interesting for the study of the political language of Arabic and Ottoman Turkish that developed in the wake of the Tanzimat reforms. But also for the *Zivilisationswortschatz* in general it contains valuable material. The Ottoman version of the *Muqaddima* shows that standardisation had already been achieved to a certain extent in Ottoman Turkish, suggesting that many new terms were already well established (for example, *encümen-i daniş* for 'academy'). Arabic, on the other hand, had to use the Western terms themselves and/or to paraphrase them.

Ottoman Turkish was, in principle, prepared to accept any Arabic lexical item. This is also demonstrated by the translation. The Ottoman translator cannot avoid being influenced by the Arabic original. Occasionally, we see the influence of Arabic on the choice of terms by the Ottoman translator, who could have chosen to benefit from new terminology in Ottoman Turkish (for instance, *edebiyat* for 'literature', instead of *âdâb* or other terms). But it becomes clear that the Ottoman Turks, in most cases, stuck to their own terminology, terms coined from Arabic roots, in particular in the nineteenth century. The Ottoman translation appeared during a crucial period of both European and Ottoman history[194] and the translator seems to be keen to introduce and to employ the new terminology engendered by constitutionalism (*meşrutiyet!*) in his Ottoman version.

The translation alerts us to the distinctive practices of Ottoman Arabic as compared to modern Arabic. The comparison allows us to recognise what was actually in use and to distinguish more clearly between 'Ottoman' and Modern Arabic (for example, as we have seen, *umma* versus *millet*). It thereby contributes to ongoing research into the nature of Ottoman Turkish. There is, compared with other texts (such as in the Arabic version of the Ottoman Constitution or other administrative texts), little if any influence of 'Ottoman Arabic' that one can detect in the Arabic text. It should also be noted that even the sections on the Ottoman Empire in the main text are mainly based on 'Frankish' sources[195] and use terms unfamiliar to the Ottomans.[196]

This may lead to the conclusion that the Arabic *Muqaddima* was the work of people who were more or less unfamiliar with Ottoman Turkish usage, most probably, Tunisian *'ulamā*, while it could be argued that Khayr al-Dīn, the future grand vizier, had some knowledge of the language. It raises the question to what extent this work, in Arabic, was written by Khayr al-Dīn Pasha himself. But in order to clarify this, more research, in particular on the position of the Turkish language during the last decades of Ottoman rule in Tunisia, is necessary.[197]

Postscriptum: A Note on the Modern Turkish Version of the Muqaddima

The Modern Turkish version of Khayr al-Dīn's *Muqaddima* is, surprisingly enough, a translation from the English version! This method has both its advantages and inconveniences: had it been based on the Ottoman version and 'simplified',[198] it would have had to reproduce not only occasional mistakes and the shortenings and omissions but also the translator's additions, the embellishments through *atf-ı tefsîr*, parallelisms, metaphorical expressions, and so forth, which characterise this translation (and even translations from Arabic in general, in the period). But there are also inconveniences to making the translation from the English version: the Arabic terms denoting modern subjects seem to have been at times clearer to the Ottoman translator than to the American one. Whereas C. Brown is speculating about the meaning of *istidlāl bil-mawjūdāt al-arḍiyya*[199] (natural history? zoology and biology combined?), Abdurrahman Efendi identifies it, probably correctly, as 'geology', for which the term he uses, *fenn-i tabakātu l-arz*, had already been introduced into Ottoman Turkish. While the text suggests that Abdurrahman Efendi was perhaps not a meticulous translator in terms of consistency, his work also suggests that he was intent upon producing a readable, meaningful text for Ottoman readers of his time. But one mark of consistency does suggest a particular agenda: his zealous care to extol the virtues of constitutionalism which, at the time he was translating, was about to collapse in the Empire.

Notes

1. Quoted as *Muqaddima* in this chapter. Page numbers indicated are those of the original edition of 1867, followed by those of al-Shanūfī's edition (1972). The Ottoman translation, *Mukaddime-i Akvemü l-mesalik fî mârifeti ahvali l-memalik tercemesi*, is quoted henceforth as *Mukaddime*. The main text of the treatise, of which there is no Ottoman translation, shall be quoted as *Aqwam*. Page numbers given from this part follow the original edition. For full citations of the various versions and editions, see the Bibliography.

Khayr al-Din al-Tunisi's Muqaddima *to* Aqwam al-masalik

2. Notably, the chapters on 'European Civilisation' (*Muqaddima*, 51–60/167–87) and the 'Summary of Discoveries and Inventions' (*Muqaddima*, 61–5/186–93; see *Réformes nécessaires*, 66). These sections are particularly interesting for our purpose.
3. Some of them may have been due to fear of censorship. The translator sometimes refers to these omissions. In the section on exhibitions (*sergi*), for instance, he resumes: 'Müellif hazretleri Sergi-i umumînin feth ü küşadına dair daha ba'z-ı mâlumat-ı mufassale verdiği sırada Avrupa'nın tanzimat-ı siyasiyyesine intikal ederek derki . . .', *Mukaddime*, 134–5). The section on European libraries (*Muqaddima*, 69–72/200–3) is omitted the same way as in the French version (cf. *Réformes nécessaires*, 66).
4. See the text in Mehmed Zeki Pâkalın, *Son Sadrâzamlar ve Başvekiller*, vol. IV (Istanbul: Ahmet Sait Matbaası, 1944), 348–51. Pâkalın calls it '*çok muğlak*' (348).
5. *Mukaddime*, 3f.
6. 'memur olduğu mekâtib-i âliyede Mukaddime-yi mezkûrenin tâlim ü tedrisine ibtidar . . .' (*Mukaddime*, 4). Publication of the Arabic *Muqaddima* in instalments began in *al-Jawā'ib* in June 1876. In his correspondence with Aḥmad Fāris al-Shidyāq, publisher of *al-Jawā'ib*, Khayr al-Dīn Pasha suggested explaining that this publication was due to 'the request of the *'ulamā'* in Istanbul'. See Leon Carl Brown (trans.), *The Surest Path: The Political Treatise of a Nineteenth-century Muslim Statesman: A Translation of the Introduction to The Surest Path to Knowledge Concerning the Condition of Countries by Khayr al-Din al-Tunisi* (Cambridge, MA: Harvard University Press, 1967), 8.
7. See İsmail Hakkı, Bereketzade, *Yad-ı mazi* (Istanbul: Tevsi-i Tıbaat, 1332), 144: 'Merhum [İbrahim Efendi] bana Tunuslu Hayreddin Paşa'nın Akvemü l-mesaliğini göndermiş olduğundan mukaddime-i kitabı Akkâ'da iken terceme ve Dersaadet'e avdetimizde, Rehber-i saadet' unvanile İstikbal ve bir mikdarını da Basiret gazetelerinde neşr eylemişdim.'
8. He founded the Darüttâlim in Istanbul in 1882, as a special school for training in Arabic where students were expected to learn this language within two years.
9. See note 1. This is the text used for this paper. Another printing by the Office of the General Staff in the Ottoman Ministry of War is mentioned by Atillâ Çetin, *Tunuslu Hayreddin Paşa* (Ankara: Kültür ve Turizm Bakanlığı, 1988), 95.
10. On Abdurrahman Süreyyâ, see Kâzım Yetiş, 'Abdurrahman Süreyyâ (Mîrdûhîzâde)', *TDVİA*, vol. 1 (Istanbul: TDV İslâm Araştırmaları Merkezi, 1988), 173–4.
11. *Mizan'ül-Belaga* (Istanbul 1303), *Sefine-i Belâgat* (Istanbul 1305).
12. One may speculate about his origins (Kurdish?).
13. In the preface (*Mukaddime*, 4), the translator presents himself as 'Abdurrahman bin Abi Hâmid'.

14. See Alexandra Nepomuceno, 'Les brumes de l'orientalisme: brève histoire d'une rencontre fantomatique', in *Bérose – Encyclopédie internationale des histoires de l'anthropologie* (Paris: IIAC-LAHIC, UMR 8177, 2017).
15. '*ta'rifâta bâdî olmamak* ...': probably a misprint for *tahrifât* (distortions).
16. Document from the Başbakanlık Arşivi, quoted by Çetin, *Tunuslu Hayreddin Paşa*, 94.
17. See the text of the *tezkire* of 11 Ramadan 1297 (18 August 1880) sent to the Ministry of Education in İbnülkemal Mahmut İnal, *Son sadrazamlar*, vol. II (Istanbul: Dergâh Yayınları, 1982), 934. İnal adds the following comment: 'On the one hand to have the Pasha write memoranda, wishing to benefit from his ideas, on the other hand to confiscate as harmful *(muzır)* his work, this is one of the strange things proper to the late Abdülhamid.'
18. Çetin, *Tunuslu Hayreddin Paşa*, 95.
19. Brown, *The Surest Path*.
20. The translation by the *şeyhülislâm* Pirizade Mehmed Sahib (1674–1749) contains the first five parts of Ibn Khaldūn's *Muqaddima*. It was finished in 1730, when the new sultan Mahmud I ascended to the throne. Two volumes were printed in Istanbul, 1858–9. See the new edition in Latin script by Yıldırım et al. Also see note 22 below.
21. 'Bu devirde garp tekniğine karşı gösterilen mecburî alâkanın aksülâmeli olmak üzere, esasa ait mevzularda şarka daha fazla dönülmüş ve daha çok tercümeler yapılmağa başlamıştır. Bunun için olacak ki şarktan en çok tercüme yapılan ve en mühim eserlerin nakledildiği devir, garp tesirlerin gittikçe kuvvetlendiği ve büyüdüğü bu on üçüncü asır [miladî ondokuzuncu] dır.' Hilmi Ziya Ülken, *Millî uyanış devrinde tercümeni rolü* (Istanbul: Vakit, 1935), 352.
22. Ahmed Cevdet Pasha (1822–95) translated the remaining, sixth part of the *Muqaddima*. See the new edition of this translation (first published in 1861): Ahmed Cevdet Paşa, *Tercüme-i Mukaddime-i İbn Haldun* (= *Tercüme-i Mukaddime-i İbn Haldun*, vol. III), edited by Yavuz Yıldırım et al. (Istanbul: Türkiye Yazma Eserler Kurumu Başkanlığı, 2015).
23. Cited by Mustafa Ülger, '19. yüzyılda Osmanlı'da felsefî tercüme faaliyetlerine bir bakış', *Fırat Üniversitesi İlahiyat Fakültesi Dergisi* 13: 2 (2008): 297–306; 304.
24. 'tercüme ile şerhin iç içe geçtiği bir metindir'. Yavuz Yıldırım et al. (eds), Pîrîzâde Mehmed Sâhib, *Tercüme-i Mukaddime-i İbn Haldun. Mukaddime tercümesi*, 2 vols (Istanbul: Türkiye Yazma Eserler Kurumu Başkanlığı, 2015), I: 42.
25. 'Bu yorumların hacmi yaklaşık olarak çevirdiği kısmın üçte birine ulaşmaktadır', in Yıldırım et al. (eds), Pîrîzâde Mehmed Sâhib, *Tercüme-i Mukaddime-i İbn Haldun*, I: 45.
26. *Muqaddima*, 69/199. Cf. Brown, *The Surest Path*, 155–6.
27. Translated by Rüstem Besim, one of Muhammad 'Alī's *arzuhalci*s, and published at Bulaq 1839. See Johann Strauss, *The Egyptian Connection*

Khayr al-Din al-Tunisi's Muqaddima *to* Aqwam al-masalik

in *Nineteenth-century Ottoman Literary and Intellectual History* (Beirut, 2000) (ser. Beirut Zokak El Blat(t) no. 20), 41, 439.
28. In the preface, it is said: 'derununda münderic olan mevadd Hıdiv-i ekrem efendimizin icmalen mâlum-i âlileri ise de tafsiline vukuf içün terceme olunmasına irade-i seniyyeleri taâlluk edüb . . .'. Rifāʻa al-Ṭahṭāwī, *Seyahatname*, trans. Rüstem Besim (Cairo: Maṭbaʻat Būlāq, 1255), 3. The impact of this work among Ottomans needs further study. Rifāʻa al-Ṭahṭāwī enjoyed a certain reputation. Known as 'Rifaa(-i) Bedevî', he was even elected corresponding member of the Ottoman Academy (Encümen-i dâniş) in 1851.
29. Perhaps with the exception of Yiddish with its Hebrew elements. On Arabic and Persian influences on Ottoman Turkish, the best study remains Maximilian Bittner, 'Der Einfluss des Arabischen und Persischen auf das Türkische. Eine philologische Studie', *Sitzungsberichte der philosophisch-historischen Classe der kaiserlichen Akademie der Wissenschaften in Wien* 142, Abh. II, 1–116 (Vienna 1900).
30. In modern Persian, they have not disappeared from the language and continue to be used even today: *fāregho t-tahsil* (graduate'); *lavāzemo t-tahrir* (stationary shop).
31. Cf. Korkut Buğday, *The Routledge Introduction to Literary Ottoman*, trans. Gerald C. Frakes (London: Routledge, 2009), 19.
32. See Bert G. Fragner, *Die 'Persophonie': Regionalität, Identität und Sprachkontakt in der Geschichte Asiens* (Berlin: Das Arabische Buch, 1999), 29.
33. On *izafet*, see Jean Deny, *Grammaire de la langue turque (Dialecte osmanli)* (Paris: Editions Ernest Leroux, 1921), 773–85.
34. The use of such *terkib*s in Turkish was first challenged by the partisans of the 'New Language' (*Yeni lisan*) in the early twentieth century. Its principles were first developed by the collaborators of the journal *Genç Kalemler*, published in Salonika 1911–12.
35. See note 22 above. This extract is part of chap. 44: 'The sciences concerned with the Arabic language'.
36. Lacking in the Ottoman translation.
37. Ibn Khaldūn, *Muqaddimat al-ʻallāma Ibn Khaldūn*, 5th edn (Beirut: Dār al-Kitāb al-ʻarabī, n.d.), 553.
38. The *Muqaddimah* translated by Franz Rosenthal. Available at <http://www.muslimphilosophy.com/ik/Muqaddimah/Chapter6/Ch_6_44.htm> (last accessed 1 September 2021). Franz Rosenthal (trans.), *The Muqaddimah: An Introduction to History, by Ibn Khaldun*, 3 vols (New York: Pantheon Books, 1958).
39. Ahmed Cevdet Paşa, *Tercüme-i Mukaddime-i İbn Haldun*, 337.
40. 'The *Tanzimat* writers did make important contributions to Turkish literature and culture, but these do not include creating or even simplifying Turkish prose'. Fahir İz, 'Ottoman and Turkish', in Donald P. Little (ed.),

Essays on Islamic Civilization, presented to Niyazi Berkes (Leiden: Brill, 1976), 118–39; 121. It started, on a rather modest scale, only after the Young Turkish Revolution (1908) with the movement *Yeni Lisan* ('New Language'; *vide supra* note 33). It is only in the 1930s, with what has been rightfully called in Turkish the 'Language Revolution' (*Dil Devrimi*) that the language regained its Turkish character by systematically eliminating Arabic and Persian elements and replacing them with Turkish terms (neologisms in the first place). 'Simplification' (*sadeleştirme*) for modern Turks has been reduced basically to replacement of 'foreign', that is, Arabic and Persian, elements with Turkish terms.

41. This was a most common formula used by Ottoman writers of the Tanzimat period even if it hardly ever corresponded to reality.
42. That is, genuine Iranian elements. It has to be stressed that Arabic elements had also become an integral part of the Persian lexicon.
43. On the sorts of terms that had entered Ottoman Turkish prior to the twentieth century, see 'Mots étrangers introduits et conservés tels quels dans la langue turque', in Bedros Kérestédjian, *Quelques matériaux pour un dictionnaire étymologique de la langue turque* (London: Luzac, 1912), 340–55.
44. Deny, *Grammaire*, 668–9.
45. V. H. Hagopian, *Ottoman-Turkish Conversation Grammar* (Heidelberg: Julius Groos, 1907), 400.
46. Specialists speak of 'the use of two words with different but overlapping semantic spectra'. A. F. L. Beeston, *The Arabic Language Today* (London: Hutchinson University Library, 1970), 112. But it is certainly true that 'they represent a single concept and should be so rendered in English' (112).
47. James Redhouse, *A Turkish and English Lexicon, Shewing in English the Signification of the Turkish Terms* (Constantinople: A. H. Boyajian, 1890), 1306.
48. Hagopian, *Ottoman-Turkish Conversation Grammar*, 400.
49. *Vide infra*, p. 166.
50. On *serbest*, see Heidemarie Doganalp-Votzi and Claudia Römer, *Herrschaft und Staat: Politische Terminologie des Osmanischen Reiches der Tanzimatzeit* (Vienna: Verlag der Österreichischen Akademie der Wissenschaften, 2008), 101–3.
51. On *saj'* in Arabic prose, cf. Beeston, *The Arabic Language Today*, 112–13.
52. Hagopian, *Ottoman-Turkish Conversation Grammar*, 402.
53. Note the *saj'*.
54. Most of the Arabic elements entered the Turkic languages via Persian, not as a result of direct language contact. Thus, in general, Arabic words used in Ottoman Turkish are also common in Persian, and usually with the same meaning.
55. 'lisan-ı arabîde "ijtināb" wa "tajannub" bir mânaya gelür ise de lisanımızda "ictinab" lafzı me'nusü l-isti'mal olub "tajannub" lafzı zebanzed değildir'.

Khayr al-Din al-Tunisi's Muqaddima *to* Aqwam al-masalik

Ahmed Cevdet, *Belâgat-i osmaniyye*, 4th edn (Istanbul: Nişan Berberyan Matbaası, 1310), 13.
56. *zirā'a* has also become the more common usage in Arabic. It is occasionally also used in the Arabic text of the *Muqaddima*. In Modern Turkish, *ziraat* tends to be replaced by the neologism *tarım*.
57. Technical terms with this ending (*-iyat*) were extremely popular in Ottoman Turkish. They are often unfamiliar to Arabic usage, such as *felekiyat* (astronomy), for *'ilm al-falak* (which also occurs in our text). Ziya Gökalp later propagated such terms instead of the clumsier Arabic *terkib*s (for instance, *ictimaiyat* for *'ilm-i ictima* (sociology)).
58. 'man habe, um ihm verständlicher zu sein, recht viel Arabisches in der Unterhaltung mit ihm angebracht; das meiste habe er aber nicht verstanden, weil eben die Türken den arabischen Wörtern einen anderen Sinn unterlegen'. Martin Hartmann, 'Die Osmanische "Zeitschrift der nationalen Forschungen" (Milli Tetebbüler)', *Der Islam* VIII (1918), 304–26; 319–20.
59. See on this suffix also Bittner, 'Der Einfluss des Arabischen und Persischen auf das Türkische', 85–7.
60. On Ottoman *kavmiyet* and Arabic *qawmiyya* (today, 'nationalism'), cf. Helga Rebhan, *Geschichte und Funktion einiger politischer Termini im Arabischen des 19. Jahrhunderts (1798–1882)* (Wiesbaden: Harrassowitz, 1986), 17–19.
61. Curiously enough, this resembles to some extent the French original, an extract from Sédillot's *Histoire des Arabes* (omitted in the *Réformes nécessaires*, cf. 31f.), where it is said: 'sans abjurer toutefois, en dépit de ce perpétuel échange de contrées, leur caractère **national** et les souvenirs traditionnels de leur patrie originaire'. L. A. Sédillot, *Histoire des Arabes* (Paris: L. Hachette et Cie, 1854), 334. Brown, *The Surest Path*, 111 n. 120, deplores 'that Khayr al-Dīn did not feel compelled to attempt a literal translation when faced with his sentence'. The Ottoman translator, however, seems to have been sensitive enough to introduce terms reflecting the idea of 'nation' or 'nationality'.
62. According to some, it was influenced by French *charte*. Also see Doganalp-Votzi and Römer, *Herrschaft und Staat*, 124–6.
63. Mustafa Sami, in his *Avrupa Risalesi* (1840), mentions Belgium as *devlet-i meşruta*. M. Fatih Andı (ed.), *Bir Osmanlı bürokratının Avrupa izlenimleri: Mustafa Sâmi Efendi ve Avrupa Risalesi* (Istanbul: Kitabevi, 2002), 44.
64. Cf. those 'Chinese' terms coined by Japanese writers and adopted by the Chinese themselves later on.
65. See Johann Strauss, 'Mouvements de convergence et de divergence dans le développement d'un vocabulaire de civilisatio n des langues islamiques (turc-arabe-persan)', in Michel Bozdémir and Sonel Bosnalı (eds), *Contact des langues II: les mots voyageurs et l'Orient* (Istanbul: Presses universitaires de Boğaziçi, 2006), 87–127; 103–7.
66. Cf. Strauss, 'Mouvements', 108.

67. It became central to Tunisian political life later on (cf. the 'Néo-Destour'); also see Brown, *The Surest Path*, 164 n. 302. On *dustūr*, see also Ami Ayalon, *Language and Change in the Arab Middle East: The Evolution of Modern Political Discourse* (New York and Oxford: Oxford University Press, 1987), 94–6.
68. A first volume of an Arabic translation of this code of laws by two Christian Arabs, Niʻmatullāh Nawfal (1812–87) in collaboration with Khalīl al-Khūrī (1836–1907), was published in Beirut in 1301/1883–4 under the title *al-Dustūr, tarjamahu min al-lugha al-turkiyya ilā al-ʻarabiyya Nawfal Afandī Niʻmat Allāh Nawfal bāshkātib kamārik ʻArabistān sābiqan, bi-murājaʻa wa tadqīq Khalīl Afandī al-Khūrī, mudīr maṭbūʻāt wilāyat Sūriya*. Not only the title of this work is 'Ottoman Arabic'!
69. The term occurs in almost every part of *Aqwam al-masālik* concerning various countries in Europe. On *kūnstitūsyūn*, also see Rebhan, *Geschichte*, 39.
70. The choice of terms and addition of *namus* clearly refer to the text of the *Hatt-ı şerif* of Gülhane (1839), also known as the *Tanzimat fermanı*, which speaks of 'emniyet-i can ve mahfuziyet-i ırz ne namus ve mal'.
71. Most of these are also noted by Doganalp-Votzi and Römer, *Herrschaft und Staat*.
72. On *nāʼib, nuwwāb*, cf. Ayalon, *Language and Change*, 76–8.
73. The Turkish National Assembly is called the Türkiye Büyük Millet Meclisi (TBMM).
74. Plural of *mebʻus* (< Arabic *mabʻūth*) with the Persian plural ending *-ān*.
75. On this term cf. Ayalon, *Language and Change*, 75.
76. Modern Arabic *ghālibiyya* (majority), corresponds to Ottoman Turkish *ekseriyet* (< *akthariyya*). For *ekseriyet*, the neologism *çoğunluk* has been introduced in Modern Turkish.
77. Rebhan, *Geschichte*, 81, 91.
78. *rey* (< Arabic *raʼy*) also means 'opinion'. It has been replaced in Modern Turkish by *oy* (a new word, perhaps adopted from Turkmen) also having both meanings.
79. See on *vekil* and *vezir*, Doganalp-Votzi and Römer, *Herrschaft und Staat*, 131–8.
80. Cf. Brown, *The Surest Path*, 88–9 n. 42.
81. It was used to denote the highest civil grade corresponding to the military grade of *müşir*. Cf. Hagopian, *Ottoman-Turkish Conversation Grammar*, 458.
82. This is the term from which Modern Turkish *bakan* (minister, lit. 'the one who watches') was calque-d.
83. Cf. *Réformes nécessaires*, 31.
84. Cf. Bernard Lewis, *The Political Language of Islam* (Chicago: University of Chicago Press, 1988), 123 n. 25; Rebhan, *Geschichte*, 97–8; Ayalon, *Language and Change*, 124–6. Also, the order of the Jesuits is called a

Khayr al-Din al-Tunisi's Muqaddima *to* Aqwam al-masalik

ḥizb: *al-jizwīt* (*ḥizb yu'raf bi al-yasū'iyya* (56/178, in the Ottoman version simply *Cezvitler* (103)). Ottoman *hizib* also occurs, with various meanings, in the translation. In modern Turkish *hizip* is rather a sect (*hizipçilik* 'sectarianism').

85. This was the common term in Turkish for political party until its replacement by *parti* (< French).
86. In the main text, occasionally also *ribūblīk* occurs, referring to the French Republic: *'uwwidat al-mulk bi-al-ribūblīk* (*ayy al-jumhūriyya*) (*Aqwam*, 121); *qunṣul awwal li-al-ribūblīk* ('Premier Consul') (124); *ra'īs al-ribūblīk* ('Président de la République') (137), and so forth.
87. Exceptions are rare; for instance, in the *Muqaddima*, *maktūb* for 'letter' (today *risala*), *maktab* for 'school' (today *madrasa*), *ḥiṣṣa* for 'share' (*ḥiṣaṣ*, 212, 219), usually replaced in modern Arabic by *sahm*.
88. Originally '*Tanzimat-ı hayriyye*'; its starting point was the reform edict known as the *Hatt-ı şerif* of Gülhane (1839).
89. This term was also successful in Persian for a while, and was used for instance by the reformist Mirza Malkum Khan. See Johann Strauss, 'Turco-iranica: échanges linguistiques et littéraires irano-ottomans à l'époque des Tanzimat', in Taghi Azadarmaki et al. (eds), *Contact des langues dans l'espace arabo-turco-persan I: actes du colloque organisé par l'INALCO (ERISM), l'Université de Téhéran et l'IFRI* (Tehran: Institut français de recherche en Iran, 2005), 59–87; 71.
90. There is one single Turkish term in the Arabic *Muqaddima*: *dārabay* < *derebey* 'feudal lord, local potentate' ('*umarā' al-iyālāt al-musammāt 'indahum bi-al-dārabay*'; 33/140). There are, however, a number of Turkish terms used for the military (*yūzbāshī*, *ūnbāshī*, *ālāy amīnī*, *ṭūbjiyya*, etc.) that occur in the main text of *Aqwam al-masālik*.
91. For modern readers, the Arabic elements in Ottoman Turkish resemble at times French terms used in English: having preserved their ancient meanings, they have become 'faux amis'.
92. modern Arabic: *ma'had*. In some cases, it rather corresponds to French *faculté*.
93. Cf. al-Majma' al-'ilmī al-'arabī (Damascus; founded in 1919); or Majma' al-lugha al-'arabiyya (Cairo; founded in 1932). In the Arabic *Muqaddima*, *majāmi' al-'ulūm* (77/211) stands for 'learned society', *cemiyet-i ilmiyye* in Ottoman Turkish (131).
94. Vincent Monteil, *L'Arabe moderne* (Paris: Librairie C. Klincksieck, 1960), 169.
95. < Persian: *taxt* (throne). Ottoman Turkish uses *payi*taht.
96. It occurs in the main text with the meaning 'list, register' (for instance, in *Aqwam*, 140).
97. Cf. the name of the Ottoman newspaper *Ceride-i havadis*, founded in 1840.
98. Sing. *varaka-yı havadis*. This is a good example showing how Arabic terms were literally translated by using other Arabic terms!

99. In the main text, even the Istanbul papers are referred to as '*al-jūrnālāt allatī tutba' bi-Dār al-khilāfa*' (Aqwam, 106).
100. 'Population growth' is translated by *takāthur al-khalq* (Aqwam, 169).
101. On *thawra*, see Ayalon, 'From Fitna to Thawra', *Studia Islamica* LXVI (1987): 155–74; 160–5, who does not quote Khayr al-Dīn's work. It can be said that *Aqwam al-masālik* has hardly ever been used for studies on the chronology of lexical innovations.
102. In modern Arabic, *inqilāb* is '*coup d'état*'. In the main text, it is also used as a synonym for *thawra*. Cf. '*al-inqilāb al-frānsāwī mabda' ta'rīkh jadīd li al-ijtimā' al-insānī*" (Aqwam, 121).
103. On Arabic *ikhtilāl*, cf. *Muqaddima*, 76/210: *al-ikhtilāl al-mufḍī ilā al-iḍmiḥlāl*, 'destitution (disrepair? confusion?) that leads to annihilation' which is translated into Ottoman Turkish by '*ızmıhlâl intac eden ihtilâl-i umumî*' (130).
104. Also, *al-thawra al-frānsāwiyya* (Aqwam, 121). Many other *thawra*s are mentioned there including the Greek Revolution (referred to as '*thawrat al-Ighrīq*').
105. On such 'mots-clés', cf. Monteil, *L'Arabe moderne*, 36, 214–17.
106. Other Islamic languages have been more receptive in this respect, for example, Urdu which uses *vafd* (delegation), *thiqāfat* (culture) or *sahāfat* (press).
107. Atia Abul Naga, *Recherches sur les termes de théâtre et leur traduction en arabe moderne* (published thesis) (Algiers: SNED, 1973), 123.
108. Şemseddin Sami gives for *kehrübaî* only the meaning 'ambré' whereas *kehrübüiyet* (sic), whose meaning is also given as 'electricity' (with a reference to *elektrikıyet*), is termed a 'mot barbare'. [Şemseddin Sami], Ch. Samy Bey Frachery, *Dictionnaire turc–français – Kamus-ı fransevî. Türkceden fransızcaya lugat* (Istanbul: Mihran, 1885), 925.
109. For instance, in Redhouse, *A Turkish and English Lexicon*, 1890.
110. Replaced by the Turkish neologism *sömürge* since then. Şemseddin Sami, *Dictionnaire turc-français*, in 1885, only gives *müstemlekât*.
111. Cf.: *devletin lisan-ı resmîsi olan Türkce* (Mukaddime, 66; for Arabic *al-lugha al-turkiyya allatī hiyya lughat al-dawla*; *Muqaddima*, 36/145).
112. To get an idea of the situation in the second half of the nineteenth century, one can consult the bilingual dictionaries by Şemseddin Sami or the more specialised work by A. Tinghir and K. Sinapian, listed in the Bibliography.
113. The anonymous compilers of a medical dictionary published in 1873 wrote: 'bizce de bu tarîk muhtar olmuş ise de fakat latince ve yunanca yerine şive-i lisanımıza muvafik olan arabî ve farisî kelimeler ihtiyar ve istimal olundu'. *Lugat-ı tıbbiyye* (Istanbul: Ottoman Medical Society, 1290), 5.
114. Johann Strauss, 'Modernisation, nationalisation, désislamisation: la transformation du turc aux XIXe – XXe siècles', *Revue des Mondes musulmans et de la Méditerranée* 124 (2008): 141–59; 146.

Khayr al-Din al-Tunisi's Muqaddima *to* Aqwam al-masalik

115. In his *Türkleşmek, İslâmlaşmak, Muasırlaşmak* (1918), a collection of articles originally published in the journal *Türk Yurdu* in 1913.
116. 'Biz de Arap ve Acemlerden kelimeler aldığımız zaman, bu kelimelerin yalnız lafızlarını almışız. Bunlara vereceğimiz millî manaları bu kelimelerin eski sahibleri artık anlamıyorlar.' This is quoted from an article published by Gökalp in the *İctimaiyat Mecmuası* in May 1917; see Ferit Rağıp Tuncor (ed.), *Ziya Gökalp, Makaleler VIII* (Ankara: Kültür Bakanlığı Yayınları, 1981), 142f.
117. 'Bu terkibatın cümlesi lisanımızın şivesi muktaziyatından olub, değil yalnız şive-i lisan-ı arabîye hattâ elsine-i umum-i âlemiyanın doğrudan doğruya kavaidine muhalif olsa, biz yine anları böyle istimal ederiz.' Said Bey wrote this in the preface of his famous translation (first published in 1311/1882) of Rousseau's treatise 'Si le progrès des sciences et des arts a contribué à corrompre ou à épurer les mœurs'. See Kemalpaşazade Said Bey (trans.), Rousseau, *Fezail-i ahlâkiyye ve kemalât-ı ilmiyye*, 2nd edn (Istanbul: Matbaa-i Ebuzzıya, 1311), 57.
118. The Persian terms are usually unknown with their respective meanings in the modern Persian language.
119. The new attempt at a foundation in 1863 is also mentioned in the main text: 'wa qad futiḥat fī al 'ām al-fāriṭ madrasa tu'raf bi-Dār al funūn' (*Aqwam*, 107). The Istanbul Darülfünunu became İstanbul Üniversitesi in 1934.
120. In the main text, a variety of terms is used, for instance, *madrasa 'āmma li al-'ulūm* (referring to the University of Coimbra; *Aqwam*, 738); *maktab a'lā li-kulliyyāt al-'ulūm* (University of Athens; *Aqwam*, 775); there are other examples.
121. Unknown in modern Persian which uses, besides *ākādemi*, the neologism *farhangestān*.
122. The terms *fen* and *ilim* are often interchangeable in Ottoman Turkish. But *fen* also means 'technique'. Even in modern Turkish, the ambiguity of *fen* remains.
123. *zadegân* as 'nobility' occurs in the earliest translations from Western languages in the late eighteenth century. It is unknown in this sense in Persian.
124. In the main text, also other Arabic synonyms occur, cf.: '*jamā'at al-nūblīs ayy* al-a'yān' (referring to the Russian nobility; *Aqwam*, 273).
125. Today usually *maṣna'*, a neologism.
126. Still popular in North African Arabic, it is in standard Arabic now *bākhira*.
127. Today *Sharikat al-Hind (al-sharqiyya)*.
128. In modern Turkish, *general* (< German?).
129. 'a European knight; especially, a knight of the order of St. John of Jerusalem'. Redhouse, *A Turkish and English Lexicon*, 1478.
130. A similar, interesting case occurs in *Aqwam* (250): *thalāthat a'yān yusammā* shānsilyī *ayy* kanshilyīr ('chancellor': < French *chancelier*; Italian *canceliere*).
131. The term was not unknown in Arabic but does not appear in the *Muqaddima*.

132. Cf. Brown's remark: 'which must have been bewildering to Khayr al-Din's Arabic readers'. (Brown, *The Surest Path*, 154 n. 259).
133. For French 'économie politique', a great variety of terms was used in Ottoman Turkish during the nineteenth century: *ilm-i tedbir-i menzil* a (an old calque of Greek οικονομία), *ilm-i servet, ilm-i servet-i milel, ilm-i maişet*, etc. In the twentieth century, *iktisadiyat* was introduced, but, curiously enough, not *iktisad-ı siyasî*.
134. Today, *jimnastik*.
135. Today, *fotoğraf*.
136. From Persian *shashxāna* (a rifled barrel of a gun, a rifled firearm).
137. Also known in North African Arabic (*mkoḥla*).
138. *maktūb* for 'letter' reflects Ottoman usage (*mektub*).
139. Visibly, the Ottoman translator had some French culture but it did not go very far. He rendered the Arabic title of Pascal's *Provincial Letters* (translated as *Makātīb ahl al-qurā* in the *Muqaddima*), as *Letr de provens* ('Lettres de province') but the original title is in fact *Lettres provinciales*.
140. < French *paratonnerre*.
141. On *medeniyet*, see Doganalp-Votzi and Römer, *Herrschaft und Staat*, 224.
142. The Ottoman diplomat and traveller Sadık Rifat Pasha (1806–58), in his *Avrupa ahvaline dair risale*, written in 1837, speaks of '*Avrupa'nın şimdiki sivilizasyonu, yani usul-i me'nusiyet ve medeniyeti*. Mehmet Kaplan et al. (eds), *Yeni Türk Edebiyatı Antolojisi*, vols 1–2 (Istanbul: Edeboyat Fakültesi Matbassı, 1974–8), I: 27f. Also see on this topic Tuncer Baykara, *Osmanlılarda Medeniyet Kavramı ve Ondokuzuncu Yüzyıla Dair Araştırmalar* (İzmir: Akademi Kitabevi, 1992).
143. 'urbanization' (from *madīna*).
144. For example, *esbab-ı temeddünün tedricen neşv ü neması*' (82) for *numūw asbāb al*-tamaddun (45/158).
145. See, on *tamaddun*, Peter Hill's superb *Utopia and Civilisation in the Arab Nahda* (Cambridge: Cambridge University Press, 2020), esp. chapter 2.
146. Cf. Brown, *The Surest Path*, 138 n. 189.
147. Monteil, *L'arabe moderne*, 215.
148. Also the Arabic form occurs in *Aqwam*: '*ma'mūriyyat mamāliki-hā*" (*Aqwam*, 93).
149. The Arabic character *ḍād* is pronounced as either /z/ or /d/ in Ottoman Turkish, without any precise rule. Devellioğlu has *hazaret* whereas in the new edition of Cevdet Pasha's Ibn Khaldūn translation (cf. n. 22), it is transcribed *hadaret*. Ferit Devellioğlu, *Osmanlıca – Türkçe ansiklopedik lûgat (eski ve yeni harflerle), 28th edn* (Ankara: Aydın Kitabevi, 2011).
150. Cf. Devellioğlu's remark, *Osmanlıca – Türkçe ansiklopedik lûgat*, 402; *hadaret*, however, appears quite frequently in Cevdet Pasha's translation of Ibn Khaldūn's *Muqaddima*. It is usually combined with *medeniyet* (for instance, 158, 203, 320).

Khayr al-Din al-Tunisi's Muqaddima to Aqwam al-masalik

151. One of the extremely rare examples where only the Arabic text has a hendiadys!
152. Arabic: 'a civilized region with towns and villages and a settled population'.
153. See Johann Strauss, 'Ottomanisme et "ottomanité". Le témoignage linguistique', in Hans-Lukas Kieser (ed.), *Aspects of the Political Language in Turkey (19th–20th Centuries)* (Istanbul: Isis, 2002), 15–39; 20–4.
154. Brown, *The Surest Path*, 75, translates as 'the French'.
155. In Ottoman *belde* is usually 'city'.
156. Redhouse, *A Turkish and English Lexicon*, 678, also indicates 'republic' and 'nation' as meanings of *cümhur*.
157. Since *millet* seems to translate as *dīn* here, the religious connotation may be intended. See on *mülk ü millet*, which occurs in the preamble of the *Kanun-ı esasî*, Doganalp and Votzi/Römer, *Herrschaft und Staat*, 217.
158. This expression (*al-milla al-islāmiyya*) was also used by Ibn Khaldūn whose works had been translated into Ottoman Turkish in the nineteenth century. Cf. for example, '*ḥamalat al-'ilm fī al-milla al-islāmiyya aktharuhum al-'Ajam* ('Most of those who promoted science in the Islamic *milla* were Persians') (Ibn Khaldūn, 543).
159. A learned reference to Shahrastānī's *Kitāb al-milal wa al-niḥal* ('The book of sects and creeds') on religious communities.
160. This *terkib* became, in Ottoman Turkish, the term for 'International Law' (Law of Nations). Ottokar von Schlechta-Wssehrd's pioneering work, *Hukuk-ı milel* (1847) was translated into Arabic, under the title *Ḥuqūq al-umam* (1873).
161. In Turkish, *terakki* (pl. *terakkiyat*) survives as a historical term due to the Young Turkish *İttihad ve Terakki* ('Union and Progress') Committee but has otherwise become obsolete. The modern terms for 'progress' are *ilerleyiş, ilerleme*, both words also occurring in the Turkish *Mukaddime*.
162. In modern Turkish, *ilerlemek*.
163. Cf. the famous article, commonly attributed to Namık Kemal, '*Türkistan'ın esbab-ı tedennisi*' ('The reasons for Turkey's decline'), published in the paper *Hürriyet* (London) in 1868.
164. Modern Turkish has *gerileme, gerileyiş* (regression, retardation).
165. In modern Arabic, 'freedom of the press' is clearly 'freedom of the periodical press' (*ḥurriyyat al-ṣiḥāfa*). The term *ṣiḥāfa* does not occur in our text but rather, *ṣuḥuf (al-akhbār)* 'newspapers'.
166. '*matbuat*' (press, lit. 'printed matter') is a particularly successful term coined by the Ottomans in the nineteenth century. It is still used in other Turkic languages and in Persian whereas in modern Turkish it has been replaced by the neologism *basın* (< *basmak*, 'to press').
167. On this usage, see also Rebhan, *Geschichte*, 31–2.
168. In modern Turkish, only the plural form was used; but it was eventually replaced by the neologism *uyruklu*.
169. See, on these regulations, Strauss, 'Ottomanisme et "ottomanité"', 17f.

170. It is also used for subjects of Western states, for example French *ra'āyā*.
171. It has to be stressed that literature and art are hardly ever dealt with in the main text, with the exception, perhaps, of Italy.
172. In the section translated from Duruy's *Histoire du Moyen-Age, depuis la chute de l'empire d'Occident jusqu'au milieu du XVe siècle*, 13me edn (Paris: Hachette, 1890) (*Muqaddima*, 22/120–28/130), the following renderings of French 'littérature' are given: *'ulūm al-adab* (for 'littérature' and 'littérature poétique'); *ādāb* (for 'littérature lyrique').
173. The sentence 'Une vive lumière de littérature, de philosophie, de science, d'arts, d'industrie inondait toutes les capitales de l'islamisme' from Duruy's *Histoire* (122) is translated into Arabic as follows: 'saṭa' nūr qawwī min jānib al-umma al islāmiyya, min 'ulūm al-adab, wa falsafa, wa ṣinā'āt, wa a'māl yad, wa ghayr dhālik' (*Muqaddima*, 22/120). This is translated into Ottoman Turkish as: 'ulûm-ı edebiyyye ve felsefiyye ve sınaiyye ve daha bunlara mümasil elle işlenilen maarif-i garibeyi irae eder barika-i envar-ı medeniyet ufk-ı islamiyetden lemeân ederek . . .' (*Mukaddime*, 42).
174. Brown, *The Surest Path*, 141, translates as 'humanities'.
175. This is also the title of a famous article by Ziya Pasha on Turkish language and literature, published first in the paper *Hürriyet* (London) in 1868. It is commonly understood as 'Poetry and *Prose*' (although there is also *nesir*).
176. The term is said to have been coined by Şinasi (1826–71).
177. In the Arabic original is only *tahdhībāt*.
178. Modern Arabic has coined *masraḥ*.
179. A term adopted from Italian (< *teatro*), akin to numerous other terms referring to theatre and music in the Turkish language.
180. See Abul Naga, *Recherches*, 88f.
181. A somewhat hybrid form (in modern Turkish: *trajedi*).
182. *Masal* is the popular variant of *mesel* (< Arabic *mathal*). Its meaning is 'fairy tale' in modern Turkish.
183. Aesop's fables were known among the Turkish-speaking Christians as *Ezopos'un meselleri* or *masallarï*. See Evangelia Balta (ed.), *19. Yüzyıl Osmanlıca ve Karamanlıca Yayınlarda Ezop'un Hayatı ve Masalları* (Istanbul: Libra, 2019).
184. Modern Arabic has *usṭūra* ('*asaṭīr Lāfūnten*'). In Ottoman Turkish *esatir* is 'mythology'.
185. A famous collection of Turkish proverbs was published by Şinasi in 1863 as *Durub-ı emsal-i osmaniyye*.
186. This seems to be somewhat outdated since in Ottoman Turkish the term *muharrir* (today replaced by *yazar*) had become increasingly popular.
187. The same school is now known as the Güzel Sanatlar Üniversitesi. In modern Turkish, only the singular *sanat* (< *ṣan'a*) is used for 'art'; the plural, *sanayi*, means 'industry' today (synonym: *endüstri*).
188. Arabic *mustaẓraf* (elegant). The same term is also used in the main text of *Aqwam al-masālik*, for example: '*wa baqiyat Iṭāliyā muddatun min*

Khayr al-Din al-Tunisi's Muqaddima *to* Aqwam al-masalik

al-zamān maqarran li-al-ṣanā'i' al-mustaẓrafa *(a'nī al-taṣwīr wa al-naqsh)* ...' *(Aqwam,* 611). The love for the arts of King Louis I of Bavaria is referred to as '*ḥubb* al-funūn al-mustaẓrafa' (704).

189. < Arabic ('ilm al-) *badī'*, 'the science of metaphors and good style'.
190. Both Arabic and Turkish now have standard terms: *fannān* (Arabic), *sanatçı* (*sanatkâr*) (Turkish). However, Şemseddin Sami, in his French–Turkish dictionary (1886), only had to offer the following explanation: 'artiste – *sanayi-i nefisenin biriyle meşgul olan (ressam, mimar, heykeltraş, çalgıcı, tiyatro oyuncusu, muganni, muganniye ve saire)*'.
191. 'drawing, painting', also the art of miniature painting.
192. In 1873, a bilingual treatise on Ottoman architecture was published under the title '*Architecture ottomane – Usul-i mimarî-i osmanî*' for the Vienna World Exhibition. Modern Arabic seems to privilege now for 'architecure' *(fann al-)'imāra*. The architect is *(muhandis) mi'mārī*.
193. These 'Ottoman' neologisms were for the most part replaced by supposedly pure Turkish terms during the 'Language Revolution' starting in the 1930s.
194. Among the most significant changes that occurred in Europe after the publication of the Arabic *Aqwam al-masālik* was the fall of Napoleon III in France, and the German unification in the wake of the Franco-German war (1871). Much of what had been written in some chapters of *Aqwam al-masālik* had therefore become obsolete a few years later.
195. Cf.: 'al-kutub allatī lakhkhaṣnāhā minhā hādhā al-mukhtaṣar aktharuhā ifranjiyya'. However, statistical yearbooks in Ottoman Turkish (*salname*) existed since 1847.
196. Although the authors of *Aqwam al-masālik* were already aware of the new law on provincial reform ('reform of the vilayets') passed in 1864 (cf. *Muqaddima,* 34/141), they still use the old term *iyāla* (Ottoman *eyalet*) for 'province' whereas the Turkish translation speaks, more appropriately, of *idare-i* vilayât (62).
197. It can be said that translations from Ottoman Turkish were rather insignificant in Tunis. Cf. Muḥammad Muwā'ada, *Ḥarakat al-tarjama fī Tūnis wa ibrāz maẓāhirihā fī al-adab, 1840–1955* (Tunis, al-Dār al-'arabiyya li al-kitāb, 1986). Moreover, the official gazette, *al-Rā'id al-Tūnisī* (est. 1860) appeared, unlike other Ottoman provincial papers (*vilayet gazeteleri*) of the Arab provinces in the Ottoman Empire, not in a bilingual edition but only in Arabic.
198. Cf. note 40 above.
199. It is translated somewhat clumsily as 'classification of the earth's creatures'. Brown, *The Surest Path,* 151.

Bibliography

Texts and Translations

Abdurrahman Efendi (trans.), *Akvemü l-mesalik fi ma'rifeti ahvâli l-memâlik tercemesi* (Istanbul: El-Cevaib Matbaası, 1296).

Alatlı, Alev and Şehabettin Yalçın (trans.), *Tunuslu Hayreddin Paşa, En emin yol* (Istanbul: Da Yayıncılık – Ufuk Kitapları, 2004). [Translation of Brown, including preface].

Brown, Leon Carl (trans.), *The Surest Path: The Political Treatise of a Nineteenth-century Muslim Statesman: A Translation of the Introduction to The Surest Path to Knowledge Concerning the Condition of Countries by Khayr al-Din al-Tunisi* (Cambridge, MA: Harvard University Press, 1967).

Khayr al-Dīn al-Tūnisī, *Kitāb Aqwam al-masālik fī ma'rifat aḥwāl al-mamālik* (Tunis: Maṭba'at al-Dawla, 1286).

Khayr al-Dīn al-Tūnisī, *Aqwam al-masālik fī ma'rifat aḥwāl al-mamālik: al-Muqaddima wa-taqārīẓ al-mu'āṣirīn*, edited by al-Munṣif al-Shanūfī (Tunis: al-Dār al-Tūnisiyya li-l-nashr, 1972).

Khérédine, *Réformes nécessaires aux états musulmans: essai formant la première partie de l'ouvrage politique et statistique intitulé: La plus sûre direction pour connaître l'état des nations* (Paris: Imprimerie administrative de Paul Dupont, 1868).

Other Works

Abul Naga, Atia, *Recherches sur les termes de théâtre et leur traduction en arabe moderne* (published thesis) (Algiers: SNED, 1973).

Ahmed Cevdet, *Belâgat-i osmaniyye*, 4th edn (Istanbul: Nişan Berberyan Matbaası, 1310).

Ahmed Cevdet Paşa, *Tercüme-i Mukaddime-i İbn Haldun* (= *Tercüme-i Mukaddime-i İbn Haldun*, vol. III), edited by Yavuz Yıldırım, Sami Erdem, Halit Özkan and M. Cüneyt Kaya (Istanbul: Türkiye Yazma Eserler Kurumu Başkanlığı, 2015).

Andı, M. Fatih (ed.), *Bir Osmanlı bürokratının Avrupa izlenimleri: Mustafa Sâmi Efendi ve Avrupa Risalesi* (Istanbul: Kitabevi, 2002).

Ayalon, Ami, 'From Fitna to Thawra', *Studia Islamica* LXVI (1987): 155–74.

Ayalon, Ami, *Language and Change in the Arab Middle East: The Evolution of Modern Political Discourse* (New York and Oxford: Oxford University Press, 1987).

Ayalon, Ami, 'Sihafa: The Arab Experiment in Journalism', *Middle Eastern Studies* 28: 2 (April 1992): 258–80.

Balta, Evangelia (ed.), *19. Yüzyıl Osmanlıca ve Karamanlıca Yayınlarda Ezop'un Hayatı ve Masalları* (Istanbul: Libra, 2019).

Khayr al-Din al-Tunisi's Muqaddima *to* Aqwam al-masalik

Baykara, Tuncer, *Osmanlılarda Medeniyet Kavramı ve Ondokuzuncu Yüzyıla Dair Araştırmalar* (İzmir: Akademi Kitabevi, 1992).

Beeston, A. F. L., *The Arabic Language Today* (London: Hutchinson University Library, 1970).

Bittner, Maximilian, 'Der Einfluss des Arabischen und Persischen auf das Türkische: Eine philologische Studie', *Sitzungsberichte der philosophisch-historischen Classe der kaiserlichen Akademie der Wissenschaften in Wien* 142, Abh. II, 1–116 (Vienna 1900).

Buğday, Korkut, *The Routledge Introduction to Literary Ottoman*, trans. Gerald C. Frakes (London: Routledge, 2009).

Çetin, Atillâ, *Tunuslu Hayreddin Paşa* (Ankara: Kültür ve Turizm Bakanlığı, 1988).

Deny, Jean, *Grammaire de la langue turque (Dialecte osmanli)* (Paris: Editions Ernest Leroux, 1921).

Devellioğlu, Ferit, *Osmanlıca – Türkçe ansiklopedik lûgat (eski ve yeni harflerle)*, 28th edn (Ankara: Aydın Kitabevi, 2011).

Doganalp-Votzi, Heidemarie and Claudia Römer, *Herrschaft und Staat: Politische Terminologie des Osmanischen Reiches der Tanzimatzeit* (Vienna: Verlag der Österreichischen Akademie der Wissenschaften, 2008).

Duruy, Victor, *Histoire du Moyen-Age, depuis la chute de l'empire d'Occident jusqu'au milieu du XVe siècle*, 13me edn (Paris: Hachette, 1890).

al-Dustūr, vol. I., trans. Ni'mat Allāh Nawfal and Khalīl al-Khūrī (Beirut: al-Maṭba'a al-adabiyya, 1301).

Fragner, Bert G., *Die 'Persophonie': Regionalität, Identität und Sprachkontakt in der Geschichte Asiens* (Berlin: Das Arabische Buch, 1999).

Hagopian, V. H., *Ottoman-Turkish Conversation Grammar* (Heidelberg: Julius Groos, 1907).

Hartmann, Martin, 'Die Osmanische "Zeitschrift der nationalen Forschungen" (Milli Tetebbüler)', *Der Islam* VIII (1918), 304–26.

Hill, Peter, *Utopia and Civilisation in the Arab Nahda* (Cambridge: Cambridge University Press, 2020).

Ibn Khaldūn, *Muqaddimat al-'allāma Ibn Khaldūn*, 5th edn (Beirut: Dār al-Kitāb al-'arabī, n.d.).

İnal, İbnülkemal Mahmut, *Son sadrazamlar*, vol. II (Istanbul: Dergâh Yayınları, 1982).

İsmail Hakkı, Bereketzade, *Yad-ı mazi* (Istanbul: Tevsi-i Tıbaat, 1332).

İz, Fahir, 'Ottoman and Turkish', in Donald P. Little (ed.), *Essays on Islamic Civilization, presented to Niyazi Berkes* (Leiden: Brill, 1976), 118–39.

Kaplan, Mehmet, İnci Enginün and Birol Emil (eds), *Yeni Türk Edebiyatı Antolojisi*, vols 1–2 (Istanbul: Edebiyat Fakültesi Matbaası, 1974–8).

Kérestédjian, Bedros, *Quelques matériaux pour un dictionnaire étymologique de la langue turque* (London: Luzac, 1912).

Lewis, Bernard, *The Political Language of Islam* (Chicago: University of Chicago Press, 1988).

Lugat-ı tıbbiyye (Istanbul: Ottoman Medical Society, 1290).

Mehmed Sadık Rifat Pasha, 'Avrupa ahvaline dair risale', in Mehmet Kaplan, İnci Enginün and Birol Emil (eds), *Yeni Türk Edebiyatı Antolojisi*, vol. I (Istanbul: Edebiyat Fakültesi Matbaası, 1974), 26–34.

Monteil, Vincent, *L'Arabe moderne* (Paris: Librairie C. Klincksieck, 1960).

Muwāʻada, Muhammad, *Ḥarakat al-tarjama fī Tūnis wa ibrāz maẓāhiri-hā fī al-adab, 1840–1955* (Tunis: al-Dār al-ʻarabiyya li-al-kitāb, 1986).

Namık Kemal, 'Türkistan'ın esbab-ı tedennisi', in Mehmet Kaplan, İnci Enginün and Birol Emil (eds), *Yeni Türk Edebiyatı Antolojisi*, vol. II (Istanbul: Edebiyat Fakültesi Matbaası, 1978), 90–4.

Nepomuceno, Alexandra, 'Les brumes de l'orientalisme: brève histoire d'une rencontre fantomatique', in *Bérose – Encyclopédie internationale des histoires de l'anthropologie* (Paris: IIAC-LAHIC, UMR 8177, 2017).

Pâkalın, Mehmed Zeki, *Son Sadrâzamlar ve Başvekiller*, vol. IV (Istanbul: Ahmet Sait Matbaası, 1944).

Rebhan, Helga, *Geschichte und Funktion einiger politischer Termini im Arabischen des 19. Jahrhunderts (1798–1882)* (Wiesbaden: Harrassowitz, 1986).

Redhouse, James, *A Turkish and English Lexicon, Shewing in English the Signification of the Turkish Terms* (Constantinople: A. H. Boyajian, 1890).

Rosenthal, Franz (trans.), *The Muqaddimah: An Introduction to History, by Ibn Khaldun*, 3 vols (New York: Pantheon Books, 1958).

Said Bey, Kemalpaşazade (trans.), Rousseau, *Fezail-i ahlâkiyye ve kemalât-ı ilmiyye*, 2nd edn (Istanbul: Matbaa-i Ebuzzıya, 1311).

Sédillot, L. A., *Histoire des Arabes* (Paris: L. Hachette et Cie, 1854).

[Şemseddin Sami], Ch. Samy Bey Frachery, *Dictionnaire turc-français – Kamus-ı fransevî: Türkceden fransızcaya lugat* (Istanbul: Mihran, 1885).

[Şemseddin Sami], Ch. Samy Bey Frachery, *Petit dictionnaire français-turc – Küçük Kamus-ı fransevî: Fransızcadan Türkceye lugat* (Istanbul: Mihran, 1886).

Strauss, Johann, *The Egyptian Connection in Nineteenth-century Ottoman Literary and Intellectual History* (Beirut, 2000) (ser. Beirut Zokak El Blat(t) no. 20).

Strauss, Johann, 'Ottomanisme et "ottomanité": le témoignage linguistique', in Hans-Lukas Kieser (ed.), *Aspects of the Political Language in Turkey (19th–20th Centuries)* (Istanbul: Isis, 2002), 15–39.

Strauss, Johann, 'Turco-iranica: échanges linguistiques et littéraires irano-ottomans à l'époque des *Tanzimat*', in Taghi Azadarmaki, Christophe Balaÿ and Michel Bozdémir (eds), *Contact des langues dans l'espace arabo-turco-persan I: actes du colloque organisé par l'INALCO (ERISM), l'Université de Téhéran et l'IFRI* (Tehran: Institut français de recherche en Iran, 2005), 59–87.

Strauss, Johann, 'Mouvements de convergence et de divergence dans le développement d'un vocabulaire de civilisation des langues islamiques (turc-arabe-persan)', in Michel Bozdémir and Sonel Bosnalı (eds), *Contact des langues II:*

les mots voyageurs et l'Orient (Istanbul: Presses universitaires de Boğaziçi, 2006), 87–127.

Strauss, Johann, 'Modernisation, nationalisation, désislamisation: la transformation du turc aux XIXe–XXe siècles', *Revue des Mondes musulmans et de la Méditerranée* 124 (2008): 141–59.

Strauss, Johann, 'A Constitution for a Multilingual Empire: Translations of the *Kanun-ı Esasi* and Other Official Texts into Minority Languages', in Christoph Herzog and Malek Sharif (eds), *The First Ottoman Experiment in Democracy* (Würzburg: Ergon, 2010), 21–51.

al-Ṭahṭāwī, Rifāʿa, *Seyahatname*, trans. Rüstem Besim (Cairo: Maṭbaʿat Būlāq, 1255).

Tinghir, A., and K. Sinapian, *Dictionnaire français–turc des termes techniques des sciences, des lettres et des arts*, 2 vols (Constantinople: Bagdadlian, 1891).

Tuncor, Ferit Rağıp (ed.), *Ziya Gökalp, Makaleler VIII* (Ankara: Kültür Bakanlığı Yayınları, 1981).

[*TDVİA*] *Türkiye Diyanet Vakfı İslâm Ansiklopedisi*, 44 vols (Istanbul: TDV İslâm Araştırmaları Merkezi, 1988–2013).

Ülger, Mustafa, '19. yüzyılda Osmanlı'da felsefî tercüme faaliyetlerine bir bakış', *Fırat Üniversitesi İlahiyat Fakültesi Dergisi* 13: 2 (2008): 297–306.

Ülken, Hilmi Ziya, *Millî uyanış devrinde tercümenin rolü* (Istanbul: Vakit, 1935).

Yetiş, Kâzım, 'Abdurrahman Süreyyâ (Mîrdûhîzâde)', *TDVİA*, vol. 1 (Istanbul: TDV İslâm Araştırmaları Merkezi, 1988), 173–4.

Yıldırım, Yavuz, Sami Erdem, Halit Özkan and M. Cüneyt Kaya (eds), *Pîrîzâde Mehmed Sâhib, Tercüme-i Mukaddime-i İbn Haldun. Mukaddime tercümesi*, 2 vols (Istanbul: Türkiye Yazma Eserler Kurumu Başkanlığı, 2015).

Ziya Gökalp, *Türkleşmek, İslâmlaşmak, Muasırlaşmak* (Istanbul: Yeni Mecmua, 1918).

Ziya Pasha, 'Şiir ve inşa', in Mehmet Kaplan, İnci Enginün and Birol Emil (eds), *Yeni Türk Edebiyatı Antolojisi*, vols 1–2 (Istanbul: Edebiyat Fakültesi Matbaası, 1974–8), II: 45–50.

Chapter 5

Finding the Lost Andalusia: Reading Abdülhak Hamid Tarhan's *Tarık or the Conquest of al-Andalus* in its Multiple Renderings

Usman Ahmedani and Dženita Karić

The creation of a 'new woman' was a crucial project for reforming empires and nations in the second half of the nineteenth century.[1] An equally daunting transformation was underway regarding conceptions of masculinity, even if this has been less immediately visible to observers. Across societies and linguistic groups, this development can be seen in different venues of cultural activity, from new depictions of the Prophet Muhammad by Orientalists and Muslims alike,[2] to the introduction of mass education for boys,[3] the standardisation of male attire,[4] and the cultivation of the body through sport and physical culture.[5] These shifts happened transregionally and trans-imperially, with bureaucrats, activists and intellectuals in one locale drawing comparisons with and making reference to developments elsewhere to support their arguments. Literary works and their translation were a key venue for proposing and working through redefined notions of masculinity, just as they were crucial to the 'new woman' discourse.

First published in 1879, the play *Tarık yahut Endülüs Fethi* ('Tarik or the conquest of Andalusia'), by the Ottoman playwright and poet Abdülhak Hamid Tarhan (1852–1937), depicted the Muslim conquest of Andalusia in the eighth century CE through the feats of its main character, Tarik, in matters of both love and war. Translations of the play into Arabic (1910, 1959)[6], Bosnian (1915), Dari Persian (1922) and Urdu (1943) suggested its appeal to readers across imperial and national borders, amplifying ongoing local debates about social decline and renewal. This chapter asks how masculinity was construed in the play through a set of techniques tying together the question of *vatan* and the nation, Islam, and gender relations. Contextual, textual and paratextual elements of the play's translations all contributed to representing a new ideal of masculinity central to these contemporaneous, locally sited conversations about the present and future. If the original play offered rich material for thinking about

Abdülhak Hamid Tarhan's Tarık or the Conquest of al-Andalus

masculinity, its translations illustrated the ongoing and nuanced salience of this concern multilingually.

In *Tarık*, Abdülhak Hamid Tarhan follows the fictionalised historical figure of Tarik ibn Ziyad, the eighth-century conqueror of Andalusia. Set in the 'golden age' of Islamic history, its emphasis on contemporary issues of nationalism, patriotism and women's visibility gave the play popular appeal in different contexts decades after it was first published. While the question of women's participation in society took centre stage in the play,[7] we argue that through his depiction of a patriotic, educated and cultured woman, Abdülhak Hamid was equally engaged in presenting a new, idealised vision of masculinity in service of the state. While discussions of masculinity have received less critical attention than debates about the 'new woman', as Hoda Elsadda reminds us, 'overt discussions of masculinity were well under way and ran parallel to discussions on femininity.'[8] Fruma Zachs also observes of late nineteenth-century Arabic fiction that 'although the discourse regarding women and femininity was carried out openly in both non-fictional and fictional texts, views and reflections concerning men and masculinity were overwhelmingly expressed in fictional texts.'[9] In other words, the construction of a new model of masculinity existed even when there was no specific term for it.

Tarık offers a conglomerate of themes through which we can observe the emerging contours of a new ideal of masculinity. *Tarık* points to monogamous marriage between a man and a woman as the building block of the new nation. Furthermore, it opposes the (Muslim) compatriot to the (Christian) enemy and in doing so presents the reader with the core virtues of an idealised masculinity: heroism, courage, righteousness and sacrifice. This 'hegemonic masculinity' is not static but rather 'situated in power relations vis-à-vis both femininity and alternative models of masculinity'.[10] Both this new femininity (as embodied by women) and subordinate masculinities (in the form of the Christian enemy) are counterposed in the play to Tarik's proper masculine comportment. Tarik's idealised masculinity should also be read in the context of 'the subordination of Ottoman non-Western masculinity vis-à-vis the West's hegemonic masculinity'.[11] Ottoman diplomats in the late nineteenth century sought to '[mirror] the gendered arguments that anti-Ottoman Europeans made about the Ottomans'[12] and show that they too possessed masculine-coded traits such as honour and dignity, and thus shared with European states a moral imperative to rule over lesser peoples while remaining uncolonised themselves.[13] As Müge Özoğlu notes, Ottoman modernisation was 'debated in relation to discourses on masculinity, both metaphorically and literally'.[14] Ottoman hegemonic masculinity referred to Turkish-speaking

Muslim men while excluding those who could not conform to its ideals, and 'provided a blueprint for indigenous-cultural identity in keeping with the Empire's masculine role'.[15]

Rediscovering Andalusia

The Andalusian topic – a composite of motifs and tropes relating to the Umayyad conquest of the Iberian Peninsula and the period of Muslim rule from 711 to 1492 – became one of the dominant spatio-temporal frameworks in Eastern Mediterranean literary production by the end of the nineteenth century. Widespread fascination with the history of Andalusia gave *Tarık*'s translators the flexibility to discuss issues of cultural revival through a narrative whose broad contours were increasingly familiar across linguistic lines.

Tarık was the first of five plays by Abdülhak Hamid that were set in Andalusia. It was published shortly after the Ottoman intellectual Şemseddin Sami's own Andalusian play, *Seydi Yahya* (1876). While *Tarık* dealt with the rise to power of Muslims in Spain, his other Andalusian plays such as *Nazife* (1917) and *Abdullahüssagîr* (1917) dealt with its decline. The history of 'Oriental' Muslim Spain was a favourite topic of Romantic writers, such as Washington Irving, whose 1832 classic *Tales of the Alhambra* is often credited with introducing the Alhambra to an American readership. In Germany, Jewish writers looked back to the intellectual flourishing of Jews under Muslim rule in Spain. Heinrich Heine's play *Almansor* (1821) was set in Granada in 1500, and laments the decline in tolerance that followed the *Reconquista*.[16] The movement of *Andalucismo* among Spanish intellectuals in the late nineteenth century also involved a reassessment of the place of the Muslim past in national history. *Andalucismo*, as Charles Hirschkind proposes, reflects critically on European politics and culture through the prism of 'a cultivated appreciation for the histories and legacies of southern Iberia's Muslim and Jewish societies'.[17]

The romantic fascination with Andalusia in Ottoman literatures can be traced back to the translation of Louis Viardot's *Histoire des Arabes et des Mores d'Espagne* (1851) by Edhem Pasha and Ziya Pasha (*Endülüs Tarihi*, 1859–60). The translators corrected what they saw as misconceptions on Viardot's part and declared their aim to restore the legend of Andalusia among Muslims. In 1887, Abdülhamid II sent two scholars from Mauritania and Tunisia on a mission of historical inquiry to survey Islamic manuscripts in Spanish libraries. While the proliferation of cultural production set in Andalusia may suggest nostalgic memories for a particular place, as Svetlana Boym argues, what appears to be a 'longing for a place . . . is actually a yearning for a different time' and 'a rebellion against the modern idea of time'.[18]

The number of Arab visitors to Spain had climbed considerably in the second half of the nineteenth century, when the Alhambra became akin to a 'site of pilgrimage'[19] for Arabs at a time of European colonial expansion. As Peter Wien observes, there are 'two trajectories of cultural meaning' in the historical memory of Andalusia: the 'glory of conquest' and the 'permanent exile from the lost paradise'. This combination of 'pride and longing . . . were at the heart of an invention of a tradition'.[20] In his introduction to the 1984 edition of Jurji Zaydan's (1861–1914) novel *Fath al-Andalus*, Mahmud 'Ali Makki mentions Ibrahim Ramzi and his drama *Al-Mu'tamad ibn Ibad* (1892), a piece about a king from the period of the *tawa'if*, and al-Shaykh Salama Higazi who presented his opera on Andalusia in 1905. The Egyptian nationalist leader Mustafa Kamil, too, wrote a play on the conquest of Andalusia (*Fath al-Andalus*, 1893), which played a role in 'pioneering Islamic pan-Arab nationality for the whole Arab world'.[21] For William Granara, 'Jurji Zaydan exploited the textual resources of the classical literary heritage to assert an ethnically based and historically uninterrupted Arab identity against the onslaught of western modernity and political and cultural imperialism.'[22] Both Muslim and Christian authors participated in this valorisation of Arabic language and culture during the Nahda. A notable example was Butrus al-Bustani and his fascination with the Abbasids, as well as his appropriation of classical lexicography for nationalist causes. Indeed, narratives structured around the idealisation of a 'golden age' – whether set in Muslim Spain or on the Mongolian steppes – were integral to the historicisation of collective national identities in the Eastern Mediterranean and beyond.

This literary heritage served as a form of cultural capital for Arab intellectuals at the turn of the century to express their superior intellectual standing (vis-à-vis Turks) and reverse the terms of 'Ottoman Orientalism'.[23] However, tracing the importance of the Andalusian theme only through the construction of discrete national literary canons can risk anachronism given that, as Ceyhun Arslan notes, Arab intellectuals referred to Andalusian history 'not only to guide their national communities, but also the multilingual and multicultural Ottoman Empire of which they were a part'.[24] The Ottoman Turkish intellectual Namık Kemal (1840–88), too, regarded Arabic literature as part of a broader historical canon of Islamic heritage.[25] His focus on selected parts of idealised Islamic history as literary inspiration is evident in his biography of Saladin (1872) or his play set in thirteenth-century Central Asia, *Celaleddin Harzemşah* (1876).

Usman Ahmedani and Dženita Karić

While the rise of ethno-linguistic national identities in the Arab world and Turkey raises important questions about the reception of *Tarık* in the twentieth century, these concerns cannot be read back onto the period of *Tarık*'s original publication in 1879. Instead, interest in Arab history and language appeared in varied Muslim contexts, often taking the form of an apologetic discourse on the history of Islam.[26]

In India, for example, authors writing in Urdu drew a parallel between the decline of Islam in India and the forced expulsion of Muslims from Spain. Abdul Halim Sharar's novel *Flora Floranda* (1899) is set at the zenith of Muslim rule in Spain and, much like *Tarık*, pits a heroic Muslim army against their Christian foes.[27] The poet Muhammad Iqbal visited Andalusia and composed his much-celebrated ode to Cordoba in 1933, while Naseem Hijazi's *Shahin* (1948) compared the loss of Andalusia with the events of Partition, when the eastern portion of Punjab became part of India rather than Pakistan. Andalusia also formed the setting for the Crimean Tatar author İsmail Gaspıralı's *Darürrahat Müslümanları* ('Muslims in the land of comfort', 1906), in which the main character Mullah Abbas travels back in time to see Andalusia.[28] Gaspıralı's novel belongs to a tradition of Turkish-language utopian fiction that includes works such as Halide Edip's *Yeni Turan* ('New Turan', 1912) and Ahmet Ağaoğlu's *Serbest İnsanlar Ülkesinde* ('In the land of free people', 1930).[29]

Andalusia thus served as a potent narrative framework for contemporary social critique. It is this quality that unites these varied works, whose authors could make use of a growing popular familiarity with Andalusian history to convey a range of ideological messages. Our emphasis in this chapter is on Abdülhak Hamid's use of the Andalusian setting to discuss appropriate masculine behaviour. Masculinity was often brought up in discussions of the perceived social and political decline of the Muslim world. As Mana Kia has observed, 'progress, order, and systemized law are posed in opposition to idleness, carelessness, and lethargy, and linked to states of masculine honour/dishonour.'[30] In this way, masculinity was closely tied to the perceptions of the state of Muslims as a whole. By referring to the glories of Andalusia, authors could reverse this situation and portray Muslims as progressive and orderly, but the same dichotomy of honour and dishonour was retained. The setting of the drama in early Islamic history served as a visible message to contemporary readers: the roots of Muslim progress need to be sought in the circumstances of past success. In this framework, the (dishonourable) present was not mentioned, but still indirectly referred to through a string of issues.

In this chapter, we bring to light the formation of a new hegemonic masculinity in three crucial dimensions: Islam, the nation, and gender relations. To better understand the appeal of these issues, we take a close look at the Bosnian, Arabic, Urdu and Persian translations, to note potential deviations from the original text, but also to examine the terminology used to address these issues. First, we introduce Abdülhak Hamid Tarhan's career and the plot of the play, before turning to the paratextual and contextual elements of the translations.

Şair-i Azam

Abdülhak Hamid Tarhan was born in 1852 to a prominent family in Istanbul: his grandfather Abdülhak Molla was a court physician, and his father Hayrullah Efendi was a historian and ambassador. Abdülhak Hamid spent part of his childhood in Tehran and, following his education in the Ottoman Empire and France, served as a diplomat in London, Paris, Bombay and Brussels. *Tarık* was published a few years after his return from Paris. His book-length poem *Sahra* (1878) was regarded as the first pastoral poem in Ottoman Turkish. The Scottish Orientalist E. J. W. Gibb praised him as 'the first to introduce the European verse-forms into Turkish'[31] and translated sections of his work into English. Literary historians have debated the extent to which his style was influenced by the work of the French Romantics he had read: the verse drama *Eşber* (1880), for instance, introduced a rhyme called *kavafı-ı mukayyede*, which bears some resemblance to French *rime riche*.[32] While greatly influenced by the Young Ottoman intellectual Namık Kemal (1840–88), Abdülhak Hamid eschewed overt discussion of political matters under the authoritarian rule of Abdülhamid II (1876–1909).

In addition to his poetic output, he wrote eighteen plays. Five of these were set in Andalusia: *Tarık* (1879), *Tezer yahut Melik Abdurrahmani'sâlis* (1880), *Nazife* (1917), *Abdullahüssagîr* (1917), and *İbni Musa yahut Zâtü'l-cemâl* (1917). *Tarık* and *İbni Musa* in particular were acclaimed for their romantic portrayal of a medieval Muslim society. His play *Duhter-i Hindu* ('The Indian daughter', 1876) was a love story set in India that critiqued colonial power relations,[33] while *Sardanapal: Bir Facia-i Tarihiye* (1919), based loosely on Lord Byron's play of the same name, criticised authoritarianism in the Ottoman Empire.[34] The conclusion to *Duhter-i Hindu* contained some of his thoughts on *milli tiyatro* (national theatre): he writes that while audiences prefer national plays, they do not like translated works or works that are unsuitable for national morality, such as works on the morals and customs of Iran or China. (As far as we know, the translated plays were not staged.) He states three criteria that could make for a national play: first, it could be about the tribes that made up the Ottoman state, such as the Laz, Kurds and Albanians, about whom there was no sufficient information. Second, it could describe an important event in the history of Islam. Lastly, it could take its subject from the history of the Ottomans.[35]

As a paragon of an older generation of post-Tanzimat authors, Abdülhak Hamid occupied an ambiguous literary position in the period following the 1908 Revolution. The *Milli Edebiyat* (National Literature) movement broke with both Persianate tradition and French influence to construct an indigenous literary tradition, for instance by using materials from Turkic folk literature. Indeed, Namık Kemal had previously criticised Abdülhak Hamid's fondness for Persian styles and vocabulary, and Abdülhak Hamid himself admitted that 'before I grew familiar with our own poets, I learned of Hafez and Saadi.'[36] He served as a parliamentary deputy in the new Turkish Republic until his death in 1937, by which time a fierce debate had erupted over his literary merits. In 1929 the communist poet Nazım Hikmet denounced the canonisation of famous Ottoman poets. His first target was none other than the *Şair-i Azam*: 'Translate Hamid's best poems into a foreign language, or even contemporary Turkish, and see how his genius bursts like a soap bubble . . .'[37] Conversely, the novelist Halide Edip maintained during a lecture delivered in Delhi in 1935 that he was 'our last great romantic . . . I believe he would be accepted as an international figure if he were translated.'[38]

The Play

Tarık's narrative framework is similar to that of other contemporary works set in Andalusia, sharing with them the idealisation of a historical Muslim society whose morally pristine character could inspire audiences in the present day. The play begins with the speech of Musa bin Nasir (640–716), one of the first Muslim conquerors of Spain, on the eve of his conquest in 711. Conveniently for the audience, Musa's speech includes a brief history of the conquest of North Africa up to that point. The play introduces a set of binary oppositions at this point: Islam and Christianity, Berber and Arab (the whiteness of the Berber clothes counterposed against the darkness of their skin),[39] as well as, crucially, men and women.

This last opposition is introduced through Musa's daughter Zehra, who is at once a warrior and a poet. The play emphasises the importance of both these roles in the formation of an ideal society. Tension arises between Zehra and her brothers, Aziz and Marwan, who reveal to the readers the secret of her love for Tarik, the famed conqueror of Spain. Abdülhak Hamid presents us with two different but complementary sides of Zehra, who not only physically protects Tarik, but also corresponds with him through her poetic verse. Their love is soon challenged by Salha, a young servant girl who appears infatuated with Tarik but is also in awe of Zehra, seeking her friendship and approval. Their somewhat unclear relationship involves jealousy, but also forgiveness and tolerance. This tension is resolved by Salha's abrupt death, leaving the path clear for Zehra to dedicate herself both to Tarik and the nation.

The play vividly depicts the disunity within the Christian camp and shows how the Muslim characters are able to outwit them in the course of their conquest. This part of the plot resembles other plays and stories dealing with the Andalusian theme. As the two armies prepare to clash, their numbers are uneven and the Muslim side confronts the likelihood of defeat. However, a surprising factor contributing to the eventual Muslim victory is the presence of women as brave soldiers on the Muslim side. This is contrasted with the portrayal of women in Christian ranks as sexually objectified companions. The Christian ranks are in disarray, and are exposed to view as indulging in decadent luxury even when the Arabs are about to attack them. This debilitating luxury is shown through the lavish clothing of the king and his entourage as well as by their drinking parties. The king himself is dressed in colourful and flamboyant clothes and rides in an expensive carriage, in contrast to the humble austerity of the Muslim leadership. The Muslims' moral superiority over the Christian camp is represented by the character of the priest who stalks a Christian girl, Lusi, who has fallen in love with a fallen Muslim soldier. The Visigoth king Roderick is eventually killed: the head of this central villain of the play is presented to Zehra's father Musa as Tarik's wedding gift.

Love is central to the play's narrative, both in the context of marriage but also separately from it. Marriage is presented as both a practical goal and a fulfilment of ethical development. Significantly, Zehra and Tarik cannot marry until the death of Salha: in other words, monogamous unions must overcome polygamous ones, even at the cost of death. While Abdülhak Hamid portrays the tension between Zehra and Salha, this does not threaten the status of Tarik, who remains unharmed. This self-conscious attitude towards love reflects contemporary beliefs about the priority of love for the homeland over romantic attachment.

Translations of Tarık

The play's translations into many 'adjacent' languages point to a remarkable interest in the Andalusian theme across a vast geographical region. We pay particular attention to the paratextual material surrounding the translations to explore how and why *Tarık* was reframed for different readerships. A closer analysis of the translators' choice of terminology allows us to discuss how Abdülhak Hamid's engagement with issues of cultural revival and gender relations resonated across linguistic boundaries long after the play's original publication.

Ottoman Turkish (1)	Abdülhak Hamid Tarhan	[unidentified]	1879
Bosnian	Salih Bakamović	Prva muslimanska nakl. knjižara (Muhamed Bekir Kalajdžić) *Mostar*	1915
Ottoman Turkish (2)	Abdülhak Hamid Tarhan	Matbaa-yi Amire *Istanbul*	1916
Dari Persian	Sultan Ahmad Khan	Cihan Birader Matbaası *Istanbul*	1922
Urdu	Sajjad Hyder Yildirim	*Nigar* (43: 4, 43: 5) *Lucknow*	1943
Arabic	Ibrahim Sabri	[unidentified]	1959
Modern Turkish	Sadi Irmak and Behçet Kemal Çağlar	İnkılap Kitabevi *Istanbul*	1960

The play was translated twice into Arabic, as well as into Bosnian, Urdu and Persian. From Vienna, Henri Dunn, a friend of Abdülhak Hamid, also translated *Tarık* into German, although Abdülhak Hamid himself was unsure if the translation had been published. Halide Edip (1884–1964) translated a short portion of the play for a lecture she delivered at Jamia Millia in Delhi.[40] Abdülhak Hamid was aware that his work had been translated into different languages within his lifetime. He commented on foreign interest in his work in the updated preface to the play's second edition in 1916, observing that the play had been published in Egypt and Bosnia with some changes. He added that he was unaware of the details surrounding their publication.

Paratexts: Bosnian

As we learn from the Bosnian preface, this work was not the first translation of Abdülhak Hamid's work into this language.[41] In 1911/12, Abdülhak Hamid Tarhan's play *Duhter-i Hindu* was published in a journalistic series, translated by Šemsudin Sarajlić who claimed that the gentleness of the Turkish language in this play made it all the more inspiring for him.[42] Sarajlić also emphasised the dedication of the author to study of the

Abdülhak Hamid Tarhan's Tarık or the Conquest of al-Andalus

characters, especially in this play which brings to light the life of 'Indian people under the British yoke'.[43] In 1912/13, the Bosnian translator, Salih Bakamović, also translated *Feth, or Conquest of Spain* in a serialised version in the journal *Biser* (Pearl). It was published in its complete form in 1915 by the Muslim Library of Bekir Kalajdžić. This venture had been established with the aim of publishing works translated from Turkish, Arabic and Persian, which had previously been serialised in *Biser* and *Behar*. Its aim was to publish books of religious and cultural relevance for the spiritual uplift of 'our *millet*, and especially our family'.[44]

The Bosnian paratextual material points to an ongoing fascination with contemporary Turkish literature and its authors.[45] Late Ottoman authors were often put in the context of the European writers and critics and judged against their literary peers.[46] As was the case with much of the period's print culture, translations of plays tended to reach their respective audiences with a time lag of a few decades. In the Bosnian context, the translation arrived in the midst of the debates on female visibility, although the fact itself was not stressed. The Bosnian preface starts by acknowledging Abdülhak Hamid as the greatest Ottoman poet, basing this assessment on the judgements of European critics (Fazie, Mister Chipick) who regarded Ottoman poetry and prose as being in decline and saw in Abdülhak Hamid a successful literary reformer. That Salih Bakamović himself was a proponent of the Young Turks can be seen from his quoting Fazie as saying that 'future generations will not say that Abdülhak Hamid Tarhan lived in the age of Sultan Abdülhamid, but that Sultan Abdülhamid lived in the age of Abdülhak Hamid Tarhan.'[47]

Salih Bakamović gives us a biographical sketch of Abdülhak Hamid's life, interweaving it with impressionistic comments about his poetic output. He says that Abdülhak Hamid was influenced by Persian poetry, sometimes emphasising that some of his works 'do not contain any artistic value' but that they were nonetheless noticed for their originality. Bakamović analyses different poetic and dramatic words individually, and parts of poems are translated. Bakamović stresses in his preface that Abdülhak Hamid's intention was not to spread ideas in society, but to create art for arts' sake, unlike the Young Ottoman intellectuals Namık Kemal and Ziya Pasha. The characteristics Bakamović connects with the main protagonists of Abdülhak Hamid's works are all idealised: courage, honesty and pride are all presented as sets of immovable abstractions. This is also how the translator announces the play and its main protagonist, Tarik. Aside from this introduction, the play also includes a translated conclusion by Abdülhak Hamid, which does not exist in the other adaptations we are studying. In this conclusion, Abdülhak Hamid explains the play's origins, and also discusses the relation between historical facts and imagination, connecting information taken from histories to imagining the relations between individual characters. In that context, Abdülhak Hamid emphasises Tarik whose character, he notes, was also recognised by European historians.

Paratexts: Arabic

The focus of the Arabic translation's introduction is remarkably different. Ibrahim Sabri, the translator (and possibly the son of Mustafa Sabri, the last Ottoman şeyhülislam), highlights aspects of the playwright's biography. Through the words of his critics, Sabri is placing the author in the line of other great Ottoman poets, emphasising their geniality. He also shows interest in Abdülhak Hamid's private life: for example, he notes that he married an English woman in London. We also find out who his father and grandfather were. Unlike the Bosnian translator, Ibrahim Sabri's sources were other Turkish writers, such as Ismail Habib Sevuk (1892–1954) and Rıza Tevfik Bölükbaşı (1869–1949). Long passages based on translation of these critics' evaluations show how Abdülhak Hamid is exceptional for the feelings he can provoke and descriptions he can offer. The word *al-'abqari*, genius, is used throughout to stress this. In the translation of their excerpts, Sabri uses Arabic descriptions with French alternatives in the brackets. Most of this passage deals with so-called *al-thunaiyya al-shakhsiyya* (*dualité de la personne*). Throughout the introduction, Abdülhak Hamid's psychological traits are highlighted.[48] He is presented as possessing multiple personalities (*dhu shakhsiyyat 'adida*), of which the most glorious is his personality as a poet.[49]

The overwhelming focus of the introduction is on the personality of Abdülhak Hamid Tarhan, with little interest in the historical circumstances that shaped his intellectual and political career. Instead, Abdülhak Hamid's productivity and unusual life spanning multiple geographies are noted as evidence of his remarkable nature as a poet and thinker. At the end of his introduction, Sabri says that he agrees with the critics, in particular Sevük, but announces his intention to produce his own independent study, which we were unable to find.

Paratexts: Persian

Sultan Ahmad Khan's translation into Dari Persian was published by Cihan Birader Matbaası in 1922. Sultan Ahmad Khan served as the Afghan ambassador to Turkey in the 1920s, after Afghanistan won the right to independent diplomatic contacts in 1919 following its victory in the Third Anglo-Afghan War. His preface dedicates the translation to his fellow countrymen as a token of his time in the Turkish consulate. At a ceremony in 1921 to celebrate his appointment as ambassador, Sultan Ahmad Khan remarked in Mustafa Kemal's presence that 'the Afghan nation's dream of sending an ambassadorial commission to Turkey, whom the Afghan nation has abiding respect for, is guided by, and considers a leader for itself, has finally come true.'[50] The Ottoman press covered Sultan Ahmad Khan's statements, such as his intention to tour the western coast and areas bordering Greece in 1922. The following year Sultan Ahmad Khan lauded the establishment of the Turkish Republic, describing the new state as 'the star of the earth, illuminating all the Islamic countries'.[51]

Sultan Ahmad Khan's translation of *Tarık* in 1922 was thus published at the height of global Muslim support for Mustafa Kemal; this support became sharply divided over Mustafa Kemal's subsequent abolition of the caliphate in 1924. The translation was also a product of intense intellectual exchange between Afghanistan and the Ottoman Empire. The movement of the Young Afghans (Jawanan-i Afghan) was inspired by the example of the Young Turks in their pursuit of constitutional rule and the overthrow of British control over Afghanistan. Most prominently, Mahmud Tarzi (1865–1933) spent several years in Damascus and Istanbul, and served as the minister for foreign affairs under Amanullah Khan, who ruled Afghanistan from 1919 to 1929. Tarzi's Persian-language newspaper *Seraj al-Akhbar* ('The torch of the news'), established in 1911, was an important conduit for the dissemination of social and political ideas from the Ottoman Empire to Afghanistan. Many of the extracts from Western European literatures that appeared in the newspaper had been translated into Persian via Ottoman Turkish. Significantly, Tarzi emphasised the importance of promoting Pashto, referred to by him as 'Afghani'. However, he also believed that only Persian could remain workable as the language of the state in this period, leading him to regard Persian as a *rasmi* (official) language and Pashto/Afghani as *milli* (national).[52]

Wali Ahmadi has discussed the 'purposive aesthetics' of modern Afghan literature that 'was principally engaged with the development of the nation and the state or, more precisely, the political formation of the nation-state'.[53] For in addition to his affection for the themes explored in *Tarık*, Sultan Ahmad Khan also saw his translation as an opportunity to acquaint Afghans with modern drama as part of their own efforts to build a national literature. This was especially urgent given that, he claims, the practice of reading literary works remained relatively uncommon in Afghanistan. He comments that the work has been written in the everyday language of people in Kabul. He also apologises for any shortcomings in the translation, admitting to the difficulties he faced in rendering the work of such a great poet as Abdülhak Hamid in another language. Most notably, Sultan Ahmad Khan provides instructions on how to read a play in three steps. First, the reader should note whatever is mentioned at the top of each page and try to keep it in their mind. Second, they should keep in mind the characters who were mentioned in previous parts of the play. Lastly, they should try to imagine the situation of each person, and to place themselves in their situation, and to speak their words as though that character were speaking them.[54]

Paratexts: Urdu

Sajjad Hyder Yildirim (1880–1943) was born to an *ashraf* family in the *qasba* of Nehtaur in Bijnor district. After graduating from Aligarh Muslim University, he learned Turkish and became assistant editor of the Urdu journal *Maarif*. This journal was modelled on the Ottoman journal *Servet-i Fünun*, whose contributors rejected utilitarian approaches to art and developed a highly ornamental style of writing. He translated and serialised extracts of Turkish literature for the journal under the pseudonym 'Yıldırım' (lightning). In 1902 he published *Salis Bilkhair* ('The best third'), a translation of Ahmet Hikmet Müftüoğlu's novella *Lane Mukaser* ('The broken house', 1901). His preface to the translation explained his motivations in translating Turkish literature into Urdu, stating that he found it 'necessary to present Turkey's social life in Urdu, because they have already faced the kind of change and social revolution in their country which we are encountering today'.[55]

In 1904 Yildirim went to Basra to work as a dragoman for the British consulate. His home there became a secret meeting place for the local branch of the Young Turks, whom he dubbed 'the Indian National Congress of Turkey'.[56] His first short story collection, *Khayalistan* ('The realm of thoughts', 1910) broke with the realism associated with authors such as Premchand (1880–1936). His prose contained a higher number of Persian- and Arabic-derived vocabulary and figures of speech than did that of his Urdu contemporaries, giving his prose a 'more classical feel'.[57] Yildirim's short stories for *Makhzan* included *Azdawaj-i Mohabat* ('Love marriage', 1907), whose main character married a man of her choice, and *Suhbat-i Najins* ('Disparate companions', 1906). Yildirim's wife Nazrul Baqar (1894–1967) was also a prominent author, and campaigned for dowry reform and the abolition of polygamy; they married without a customary dowry payment. Their daughter Qurratulain Hyder (1927–2007) went on to become one of the most acclaimed figures in modern Urdu literature.

The Urdu translation of the play was serialised in two issues of the literary journal *Nigar*, in April and May 1943.[58] The journal's editor Niyaz Fatehpuri (1884–1966) was a prominent literary critic and poet who studied at Farangi Mahal in Lucknow. His writings, including *Man o Yazdan* ('Self and God', 1935), aroused controversy for their advocacy of religious reform. Fatehpuri founded *Nigar* journal in 1922, naming it after the prominent Ottoman poet Nigar Hanım (1856–1918). While the journal featured both Muslim and Hindu contributors, its main readership was the North Indian Muslim intelligentsia. *Nigar* quickly became a major forum for literary and social debate. Each issue featured regular columns by Fatehpuri, such as his *istifsarat* (enquiries) column in which he answered readers' questions on issues ranging from the appropriateness of birth control to the origins of April Fools' Day.[59] Later in life, Fatehpuri would recall how his encounters with Yildirim's translations of Turkish literature had inspired him in his own career as a writer.[60] In 1962, Fatehpuri left Lucknow for Karachi, where he lived until his death in 1966.

The serialisation of Yildirim's translation was cut short at the start of the play's second act owing to the translator's sudden death from a heart attack. Announcing the news in *Nigar*, Fatehpuri stated that he had written to Yildirim's widow to request the complete translation, regretting that without a satisfactory response the play's serialisation would have to stop.[61] Yildirim had laid out some of his thoughts on translation in a lecture on the Urdu–Hindi controversy in 1938, lamenting that many Urdu translations of French and Russian literature were in fact based on English translations of the original. He argued that if even the best translations were 'merely a vague shadow of the original', the practice of translating from a translation would be 'even more vague' and should therefore not be accepted.[62]

Arabism without Arabs

While Arabic-language engagement with Andalusia can in part be explained by the historicisation of modern Arab identities, how did cultural producers writing in other languages relate to the figure of the Arab in *Tarık*? The play's characters, notably Tarik and Zehra, continually relate their virtuous qualities to their Arabness.[63] We can see that Abdülhak Hamid's play presents Arabs not as 'the other' but as 'one of us'. But at times in Sultan Ahmad Khan's translation, references in the original Ottoman Turkish text to the fighters are translated with reference to their

'Muslimness' rather than their 'Arabness': *'Arap mücahit ve mücahideler'* is rendered as *'mucahidin u mujahideha-i musulman'*, for instance. While Tarik in one dialogue refers to the 'Arab army' and the 'Arab government' in the original, the Persian translation refers both to the 'army of Islam' and the 'Arab government'.[64] Tellingly, the preface to a Turkish edition of *Tarık* published in 1960 reminds readers of the Turks' historical role in stopping Christian attacks on Islam. Without dwelling on his Arabness, it states that 'we do not regard Tarik as a stranger to ourselves.'[65]

How can we understand the fascination with Arabness in these translations? The case of post-Ottoman intellectual developments in Bosnia can shed some light. After the Austro-Hungarian occupation in 1878, and annexation in 1908, Bosnian intellectuals cultivated a range of political allegiances. However, the Balkan Wars did not provoke an outpouring of support for the Slavic states (Bulgaria, Serbia, Montenegro). Instead, many Bosnian Muslim intellectuals emphasised a strong link with the 'Islamic community' and called for 'the awakening of an Islamic consciousness'.[66] Moreover, the interest in Arabic language and culture was fostered by the Austro-Hungarian Empire itself, and as Katalin Rac shows, there was a need to provide colonised populations with textbook material on what they perceived as the essential parts of Islamic culture and civilisation, employing the efforts of both Orientalist scholars in their service, and indigenous Bosnian translators who conveyed this material to the local audiences.[67] Bosnian interest in the 'Orient' was mediated in part by translations of the works of German Romantic authors;[68] interest in repositories of Arab/Islamic culture and civilisation was evidenced by Bosnians' own authorship of works on various aspects of Arabic and Islamic culture.[69]

Masculinities of Islam

The usage of religious vocabulary in the play also exemplifies a broader phenomenon: the reification of 'Islam' as an abstract entity in the nineteenth century. Wilfred Cantwell Smith has discussed the shift from the verbal noun *islam* denoting an individual act to describing 'an external, mundane religious system, and finally by shifting still further from that religious system to the civilization that was its historical expression'.[70] While these shifts have shaped the ways in which Islam became seen in this period, it remains unclear how these shifts were connected to emergent discourses on gender relations. This section considers the pairing of Islam with gendered words and expressions, and examines 'Islam' in comparison and contrast to other important concepts at the time, such as nation and marriage.

Abdülhak Hamid Tarhan's Tarık or the Conquest of al-Andalus

The following table contrasts the phrases 'Islamic daughter', 'Islamic sister' and 'Islamic citizen' in *Tarık*'s Ottoman original with the Arabic, Bosnian, Persian and Urdu translations. We can see that this phrasing was faithfully rendered in all languages, despite its relative novelty in all languages concerned:

Ottoman Turkish	Islam kızı, Islam hemşiresi, Islam vatwandaşı
Arabic	bint al-Islam, ukht al-Islam, muwatina muslima
Bosnian	Islamska kći, islamska sestra, islamska zemljakinja
Persian	duhter-e Islam, hemshire-i Islam, vatandar-e Islam
Urdu	mein Islam ki larki, Islam ki hemshire, Islam ki rafiqa

This table shows the consistency of translations of the play across the languages, while at the same time raising questions about the usage of the term 'Islam'. There are abundant references to both 'Islam' and 'Islamic' throughout the play, often used as denominators both for abstract notions of religion and glory ('holy Islamic faith' and 'Islamic glory') and for collective nouns such as 'Islamic army', 'Islamic soldiers', 'Islamic homes' or 'Islamic notables'. Both of these are instances of reification in the sense of the objectification of religion, as well as its essentialisation by ascribing a set of fixed values to humans and inanimate objects. The reification of Islam in the play could also be interpreted as reflective of a broader trend of functional secularisation in the late Ottoman Empire.[71] What this implied was a thorough anthropomorphisation of Islam (especially in terms of gender), its relegation to a realm beyond history, and the role of human agency in its reshaping.

Presenting Islam as a fixed and unchangeable entity allowed authors such as Abdülhak Hamid Tarhan to posit it in a relationship to other analogous notions. In the play, Islam is not juxtaposed with Christianity (although Christians appear as a label and denomination), but rather with the geographical unit of Spain. The tension between the two is gendered: the motif of Tarik and Zehra's relationship and eventual marriage is paralleled by the Muslim conquest of Spain. In this way, a reified Islam is depicted as masculine by contrast to feminine Spain/Andalusia, a *melike* (queen)[72] whose weakness compels her to finally succumb to Islam. This gendered division between the Spaniards and the Muslim conquerors is emphasised throughout the play, with the Spanish king's exaggerated effeminacy contrasted with Tarik's austere appearance and stature. The wedding ceremony of Tarik and Zehra is, in the end, likened to a union between Islam and Spain, which is further depicted as the unification of Islam and humanity. The translations show some differences here: the

Bosnian emphasises the 'unification of all peoples of all faiths'[73] (despite highlighting Islam), and the Arabic translation employs the phrase *umma wahida* without specifying religions.[74] The Persian, like the original, refers to the union of 'humanity and Islam' *(insaniyat va Islamiat)*.[75] This union is also a transaction: for his successful feats in war, Tarik gets Zehra from her father; and if Tarik conquers Spain, it will be given to Islam. An object of this bargain, Zehra is also secondary to Tarik's duties to the state.

Islam is thus presented as a movable abstract unit which exists separately from ordinary humans, but also exists in interaction with them. In this regard, some translations prefer more reified choices: the Bosnian often uses the word 'Islam' in place of 'Muslims', unlike in the Arabic text.[76] Its existence is not bound to time, but at the same time, it receives help from God and humans. Islam enters the relation with other fixed abstractions; thus, human rights and appeals to humanity are brought in connection with it. While Christianity is not juxtaposed with Islam, Christians appear throughout the play, often interchangeably with the designation 'Goth', and they are not labelled as natural enemies, in an effort to promote a vision of religious tolerance. This, however, is undermined by the acts of conversion which turn some Christian characters not only into Muslims, but also into ethnically differentiated subjects them through their renunciation of Spanishness.

What, then, is the human's relation towards Islam? In Abdülhak Hamid's vision, spoken through the words of Zehra's friend and rival Salha, love is the basic motive that proceeds hierarchically and implicates the *shari'a*, conceived as a set of duties to be obeyed; Islamiyet (or Islam), a set of different values such as living in brotherhood with everyone, respect for the scholars, helping the weak, and being just and merciful. The *shari'a* and Islam in these translations have a blurry and shifting relation: either juxtaposed (Bosnian), or with one following the other (Islam after the *shari'a*, in Arabic translation).[77] Furthermore, Islam seems to coexist with the nation in terms of sharing the same goal of cultivating humankind and the homeland. Just as Zehra and Salha await romantic union with Tarik, so too does the geographical territory of Spain succumb to Islam's masculine glory. However, despite the abundance of the denominator 'Islamic', religious symbolism only appears in discussions of war: through the figures of *mujahid/mujahida* or *shahid*, or the comparison of Muslim soldiers to Qur'anic verses descending from the sky. Yet Islam is secondary to God, and in its reified form is depicted as a separate entity from God.

A comparison of the translations reveals some crucial differences that can be attributed to the contextual environment in which they were written.

Despite referring to Islam in its reified sense, the Bosnian translation does not use much Islamic vocabulary, such as the terms 'jihad' and 'caliph'. The omission of Islamic terminology in the Bosnian case can to some extent be attributed to the awareness of widened readerships that included non-Muslims as well as Muslims. In this way, the term Islam stood in a highly essentialised form that allowed the translators to adjust it to notions of the equality of people of all religions.[78]

Vatan *and Nationalism*

The concerns that animate *Tarık* were the product of two connected historical phenomena: the rise of pan-Islamic sentiment and the development of modern nationalism. The popular resonance of a play depicting Muslim military victories against perfidious Christians for audiences in the heyday of European colonialism goes without saying. This is true both for the play's original publication in 1879 and the wave of translations beginning in the 1910s, when the Balkan Wars became a cause célèbre for many Muslims outside the Ottoman Empire, particularly in India.[79] As Cemil Aydın argues, the reconceptualisation of Muslims as a unitary body with shared political priorities was in some respects novel to the late nineteenth century. He identifies the major characteristics of an emerging transnational Muslim discourse, all of which are on display in *Tarık*. The history of Muslims was characterised as one of decline caused by European humiliation, leading to nostalgia for a past golden age: 'The arc of glory, humiliation, and redemption offered a potent political image.'[80] In this narrative of perpetual struggle between Islam and the Christian West, conflict became the principal lens through which to understand history.

Another striking feature of *Tarık* is its imbrication of religious and patriotic vocabulary. *Tarık* is replete with references to *vatan* and *millet*, and emphasises the importance of social cohesion as key to the Muslims' strength over the hopelessly split Christians. Cohesion among Muslims was of primary importance: as Zehra comments, 'is there sedition in the midst of Islam?' ('İslâm beyninde bir fitne mi var?'). Salha proclaims at one point that she 'loves the *vatan*, because it is by means of the *vatan* that I am living' ('vatanı severim; çünkü onun sayesinde ömür sürüyorum'). The term *vatan* had undergone a conceptual rearticulation, from referring to a localised space such as a birthplace or hometown to that of a national homeland, over the course of the nineteenth century.[81] Namık Kemal's play *Vatan Yahut Silistre* ('Homeland or Silistra', 1872) was a major influence on Abdülhak Hamid's writing. While Kemal was by no means unique in his usage of the term *vatan*, *Vatan Yahut Silistre* was the first modern play to introduce the concept to a mass audience. *Vatan Yahut Silistre* was set during the Crimean War (1853–6) and follows the efforts of local volunteers to defend the castle of Silistra (in Bulgaria) from Russian attack. The play's main character, Islam Bey, falls in love with Zekiye, the daughter of an army officer whose whereabouts are unknown. Hearing Zekiye proclaim her love for him, Islam Bey tells her that he must defend the *vatan*. Zekiye decides to wear a man's uniform so she can follow Islam Bey into the battlefield without being recognised. With her help, the Russians are eventually forced to retreat. Returning to report their victory, Islam Bey and Zekiye realise that Sitki Bey, one of the forces' commanders, is actually Zekiye's father. After revealing her identity, Zekiye and Islam Bey can finally marry with her father's blessing, now that the *vatan* has been secured from enemy attack. Alarmed by the popular fervour with which the play was received on its opening night in April 1873, authorities shut down Istanbul's Gedikpaşa theatre. Kemal was exiled to Cyprus and the play was not freely performed again until after the 1908 Revolution.

Both *Vatan Yahut Silistre* and *Tarık* emphasised the importance of prioritising love for the *vatan*, or homeland, over romantic attachment. In a letter to Abdülhak Hamid, whom he addressed as *kardeş* (brother), Kemal argued that writing about the *vatan* had become a duty, and that literature could share the same honour as joining the military in terms of service to one's country.[82] While often translated into English as 'fatherland' by analogy to the German *Vaterland*, *vatan* here could be more appropriately rendered as 'motherland'. As Afsaneh Najmabadi has argued with reference to a similar conceptual shift in Qajar Iran, 'The more the homeland became a protected female category, the more the state became the male protector.'[83] Indeed, ideas about modern citizenship have been 'tied almost inexorably to a gendered language of manhood'.[84]

With the outbreak of the Balkan Wars in the 1910s, the term *vatan* took on increasingly militarised connotations.[85] During the First World War, Abdülhak Hamid was summoned to the War Ministry and urged to write works to encourage the soldiers.[86] His collection of patriotic poetry *Ilham-ı Vatan* (1918), on the importance of defending the motherland, contained an extract from his Andalusian play *İbn-i Musa*. All the translations of *Tarık* under study here continue to use the word *vatan* or *watan*, but these terms had specific connotations for readers in different locations. We regard these translations of *Tarık* as interventions in Egyptian, Bosnian, Afghan and Indian Muslim debates about building a modern nation.

To varying degrees, each of these countries took the Turkish experience of social and political modernisation as a reference point, inspiration, model, or even cautionary tale for their own national projects. For

Abdülhak Hamid Tarhan's Tarık or the Conquest of al-Andalus

instance, the Bosnian translation tends to avoid using terms with overtly Islamic connotations. This is especially clear in the translation of terms of governance: classical Islamic notions of *shura* (consultation) and *al-ta'a lil-khalifa* (obedience to the caliph) are in Bosnian translation rendered such that the first becomes '*megjusobno savjetovanje*' (mutual counselling), while the second one is simply dropped. The Urdu translation, referring to the decision of Culyanus to leave the Christian camp and defect to the Arabs, uses the terms *ghadari* (betrayal) and *wafadari* (loyalty),[87] both terms freighted with nationalistic significance. Yildirim had previously translated Namık Kemal's play *Celaleddin Harzemşah* in 1925. In his translator's note, Yildirim expressed his hopes that Urdu readers could become acquainted with Kemal's concept of *vatan* so as to strengthen their own patriotism.[88] The translations of *Tarık* thus point to the mediating role played by Turkish literature in debates about carving out a modern nation for each of our translators.[89] In the midst of these debates stood new formations of masculinity and femininity.

The New Woman and the New Man

The previous two sections have discussed the implications of the reification of Islam and the national project on the formation of masculinity. Just as Islam Bey cannot marry Zekiye until the Russian enemy is defeated in *Vatan Yahut Silistre*, Tarik and Zehra cannot be united while the greater struggle for the conquest of Andalusia remains unfinished. This reflects a wider trend described by Marilyn Booth in her discussion of women's journals in Egypt at the turn of the century. Booth points to the mutual constitution of gendered behaviour through discussions of proper femininity that were bound up in anxieties over masculine identity and the image of the ideal man.[90]

In this context, marriage represented the ultimate model for shaping a new ideal of masculinity. Men's personal willingness to sacrifice themselves in defence of their nation was linked to their duty to enter into companionate marriages with women. Marriage in turn was subordinated to the higher ideal of service to the nation. The play *Tarık* gives a particular answer to ongoing debates on the desirability of different types of marriage by comparing the polygamous union of Tarik, Zehra and Salha, with the monogamy of Tarik and Zehra. While the play's conclusion appears to advocate monogamy as a marker of the modern age, Zehra's acquiescence to a polygamous union also suggests a certain ambivalence towards polygamy on the part of Abdülhak Hamid.[91] A functional modern marriage needed women to undergo a transformation in their behaviour that heightened their social visibility. This could make them suitable companions for their husbands. The translators' choices regarding the play's gendered vocabulary reflect the shared preoccupations of Muslim intellectuals across borders in this period. Abdülhak Hamid gives us a modernist portrayal of women as complementary to but different from men: men possessed physical strength and honour, and women retained beauty and gentleness even while taking on active roles in society.[92] This clear differentiation between men and women required constant effort to maintain, plagued as it was by the memory of older, more undifferentiated models of beauty.

Throughout the play, two roles which women held in the imagined framework of Andalusia were those of a literate and educated (even artistic) person, and of a soldier, with her physical strength and prowess employed for the *vatan*. The two roles were intertwined, with the strength of the tongue often subdued to that of the sword. Of these two, the second role appeared to be more troublesome for the translators, because it presented them with a vocabulary that ushered in the corporeal visibility of women coupled with the religious rhetoric surrounding warfare. *Tarık* contains long monologues on how women should be educated, visible and active just like men, and drawing a parallel between the advancement of women and the progress of society as a whole. One of the first images in the play is that of Muslim women as *mujahidat*: warriors who participate in the public sphere and spread the message of Islam but who remain subordinated to the leadership of men. In this way, the play touched upon male anxieties around the role of women in society. This focus on women as fighters may be related to the greater participation of women in military campaigns of the period. In a letter he wrote to Abdülhak Hamid in 1879, Namik Kemal emphasised the participation of women as fighters throughout Islamic history, notably in the military units of Tarik ibn Ziyad, as well as during the Crimean War.[93]

We can see a similar process at work outside the Ottoman Empire. In India, Megan Robb has discussed how Urdu press accounts of female warriors during the Balkan Wars served to strengthen existing gender boundaries:

> They had sacrificed traditional femininity for the glory of Islam and the Ottoman Empire. If men responded to the example of women warriors with their own acts of bravery, the women were sources of inspiration; if men failed to rise to the occasion, women warriors became a source of shame.[94]

For Yildirim, the 'New Turkish Woman' provided a potential model for the progress of Indian Muslim women. This continued a debate that had begun much earlier among elite north Indian Muslims, reflecting a dual concern for women to receive a modern education while remain-

Abdülhak Hamid Tarhan's Tarık or the Conquest of al-Andalus

ing within the bounds of *haqiqi nisvaniyat* (real femininity).[95] Niyaz Fatehpuri, for instance, supported women's education while expressing concern that women working outside the home disturbed natural gender roles.[96] Mahmud Tarzi, meanwhile, cited Halide Edip as a role model for women's advancement in Afghanistan. His daughter Soraya was married to King Amanullah Khan and played a prominent, if controversial, role in promoting women's advancement in the 1920s. As Marya Hannun has detailed, for Tarzi, 'Women provided a critical component in connecting Afghanistan's progress to that of its Muslim neighbors.'[97] In Bosnia, the play's translation indicated rising anxieties regarding the public role of women and their visibility: one of the translators, Musa Ćazim Ćatić, also translated Muhammad Wajdi's refutation of Qasim Amin's works in 1915,[98] in a period saturated with fierce debates on the subject.

Ottoman Turkish	Mujahide/ pl. Mujahideler	Musellah (silahli) bir kız	Peri-i masum	Cihat aşığı veya İbn-i Ziyad sevgilisi
Arabic	mujahida/mujahidat (female soldier/s)	al-fata al-musallaha (armed girl)	al-fatina al-tahira (pure seductress)	'ashiqatu jihad aw ma'shuqatu Ibn Ziyad (in love with warfare or Ibn Ziyad's lover)
Bosnian	pl. vojnici sg. – mudžahida/ mudžahide ženski borci/ mudžahidske žene (female soldiers)	vila bajna; anđeo (enchanting fairy/angel)	nevina ona vila, angjeo mileni (innocent fairy, dear angel)	zaljubljena u rat/Ibni zijadova ljubavnica (translation same as above
Persian	mujahide/ mujahideha (female soldiers)	duhter mah-yu-re maghruq-e silah (moon-faced, heavily armed daughter)	gol-e khoshbu (fragrant rose)	ashiqa-i jihad ya hod ma'shuqa-i Ibn Ziyad (translation same as above
Urdu	mujahid khawateen (female soldiers)	n/a	n/a	ashiqa-i jihad, ma'shuqa-i Ibn Ziyad (translation same as above

The table on page 211 displays different choices of translation regarding women as fighters in *Tarık*, as well as a final column with a description of women as 'innocent fairies', which is contrasted with the previous terms. This displays the challenges that translators of *Tarık* grappled with. The Bosnian translation, for example, recognised gender in the case of 'female soldiers' but struggled with translating the 'armed girl', opting instead for standardised depiction of women as angels and fairies. A similar problem arose with the usage of the singular noun depicting female soldiers (*vojnik*) without using the Arabic-Ottoman term *mujahida*. The term seems to be of crucial importance within the play itself, where a discussion of whether a *mujahida* is the one who did not kill and is only using the arms to defend herself comes right in the beginning. The insecurity of the term made the translators reluctant to render it into their respective languages at all times: the Bosnian translation uses *pobjediteljica* (winner)[99] occasionally, thus adding an additional meaning to the role of soldier and warrior.

These problems were not present when it came to the translation of 'heroine' and 'poetess' (*junakinja, pjesnikinja*). These difficulties point to how constructions of femininity were set by perceived differences between acceptable male and female conduct that were not easily adaptable to contemporary circumstances (including, for example, women who bore arms and fought in wars). In that context, the Bosnian translation has excised the most out of all the translations we have examined. It does not offer the bold interpretation of the roles women can assume and – on a linguistic level – it almost purifies the translation of possible Ottoman and Arabic solutions. This is consistent with the general tendency of the Bosnian translation: terms that might have sounded archaic or were not as widely used at the time were replaced with more commonly understood terms even if by doing so, the translation was not as linguistically suitable to the original. In order for men to be fully realised in the new age, women had to become so as well, since their union (in the form of monogamous marriage) was made in service to the nation and yet remained secondary to it. The full participation of women in the public space came through two roles, but one of them caused problems for the translators.

Conclusion

The sentiments evoked by *Tarık* resonated with translators and readers far beyond an Ottoman Turkish readership, and for decades after its original publication in 1879. The play's nostalgic imagination of a morally pristine Muslim community as well as its understanding of progress and reform account for its continued popularity into the second half of the twentieth

Abdülhak Hamid Tarhan's Tarık or the Conquest of al-Andalus

century. In this chapter, we have focused on the theme of masculinity through three elements: the reification of Islam, the pervasiveness of patriotic and nationalist sentiment, and the creation of a 'new woman'. The translators' choice of terminology raises broader questions about translation between languages with similar vocabularies and reference points, but different social and political contexts.

Linguistically, the translations revealed a high degree of fidelity to the original text. However, our comparison between the Ottoman original and the translations also reveals certain instabilities which occurred when the translators met with hitherto unknown or lesser-known concepts. The translations displayed a tension regarding the translation of more militarised terms for women, as well as some instability regarding the terms 'Muslim' and 'Islam', especially as they related to gender. A major point of contestation for all the translators here was how to render into their respective languages the varied roles given to women in the play. Since this period witnessed a reformulation of both masculinity and femininity, it was important to introduce concepts that readers and audiences could readily understand. In some cases those concepts were not easily translatable, leading to the translators reaching for solutions with an adjacent meaning.

That *Tarık* was translated into several languages in the decades after it was published speaks to the relevance of themes such as women's education and national 'progress', as well as the popularity of al-Andalus as an imagined space. We argue that Abdülhak Hamid was primarily responding to a contemporary crisis of Ottoman masculinity, and that resolving this crisis entailed an overhaul not only of hegemonic ideals of masculinity and femininity, but also of dominant understandings of religion and patriotism. The translations' paratexts discuss the idealism and strength of the characters, without questioning the limits of the new constellation of gender relations. This suggests to us that, ultimately, the translators were engaged in portraying a reformulated model of masculinity.

Notes

1. Gürbey Hiz, 'The Making of the 'New Woman': Narratives in the Popular Illustrated Press from the Ottoman Empire to the New Republic (1890–1920s)', *Early Popular Visual Culture* 17: 2 (2019): 156–177.
2. Kecia Ali, *The Lives of Muhammad* (Cambridge, MA: Harvard University Press, 2016); Sherali Tareen, *Defending Muhammad in Modernity* (Notre Dame: Notre Dame University Press, 2020).
3. Afsaneh Najmabadi, *Women with Mustaches and Men without Beards: Gender and Sexual Anxieties of Iranian Modernity* (Berkeley: University of California Press, 2005), 193–206.

4. Katja Jana, 'Changing Heads and Hats: Nationalism and Modern Masculinities in the Ottoman Empire and the Republic of Turkey', in Simon Wendt and Pablo Dominguez Andersen (eds), *Masculinities and the Nation in the Modern World: Between Hegemony and Marginalization* (New York: Palgrave Macmillan, 2015), 217–42.
5. Murat Yıldız, '"What is a Beautiful Body?" Late Ottoman "Sportsman" Photographs and New Notions of Male Corporeal Beauty', *Middle East Journal of Culture and Communication* 8: 2–3 (2015): 192–214; Wilson Chacko Jacob, *Working Out Egypt: Effendi Masculinity and Subject Formation in Colonial Modernity, 1870–1940* (Durham, NC: Duke University Press, 2011).
6. We were not able to locate the first Arabic translation of the play. The second translation does not have an exact year of publication, but according to the library catalogues we consulted, the year of publication is 1959. All translations are our own unless otherwise cited.
7. See Can Eyüp Çekiç, 'On the Front and at Home: Women in the Modern Ottoman Epic', *Middle Eastern Studies* 52: 4 (2016): 623–39, on *Tarık* in the context of women's presence in Ottoman epic literature.
8. Hoda Elsadda, 'Imaging the "New Man": Gender and Nation in Arab Literary Narratives in the Early Twentieth Century', *Journal of Middle East Women's Studies* 3: 2 (2007): 31–55; 35.
9. Fruma Zachs and Sharon Halevi, *Gendering Culture in Greater Syria: Intellectuals and Ideology in the Late Ottoman Period* (London and New York: I. B. Tauris, 2015), 67.
10. Sivan Balslev, *Iranian Masculinities: Gender and Sexuality in Late Qajar and Early Pahlavi Iran* (Cambridge: Cambridge University Press, 2019), 11. See pp. 10–12 for a discussion of Raewyn Connell's concept of 'hegemonic masculinity'.
11. Ali Bilgiç, *Turkey, Power and the West: Gendered International Relations and Foreign Policy* (London and New York: I. B. Tauris, 2016), 64.
12. Kyle Clark, 'Ottoman Diplomacy and Hegemonic Masculinity during the Great Eastern Crisis of 1875–78', *Middle East – Topics & Arguments* 14 (2020): 121–33; 121.
13. See Arif Camoğlu, 'Inter-imperial Dimensions of Turkish Literary Modernity', *Modern Fiction Studies* 64: 3 (2018): 431–57, on Abdülhak Hamid's 'imperial affiliations'.
14. Müge Özoğlu, 'Modernity as an Ottoman Fetish: Representations of Ottoman Masculinity in Kesik Bıyık', *Masculinities: A Journal of Identity and Culture* 6 (2016): 79–101; 87.
15. Özoğlu, 'Modernity', 82.
16. Ned Curthoys, 'Diasporic Visions, Taboo Memories: Al-Andalus in the German Jewish Imaginary', *Arena Journal* 33/34 (2009): 110–38.
17. Charles Hirschkind, *The Feeling of History: Islam, Romanticism, and Andalusia* (Chicago: University of Chicago Press, 2021), 3.

18. Svetlana Boym, 'Nostalgia', *Atlas of Transformation* (blog). Available at <http://monumenttotransformation.org/atlas-of-transformation/html/n/nostalgia/nostalgia-svetlana-boym.html> (last accessed 5 February 2021).
19. Edhem Eldem, 'Ottomans at the Alhambra, 1844–1914: An Investigation into the Perception of al-Andalus by Ottoman Subjects in Times of Modernity', *Turcica* 49 (2018): 239–359; 265.
20. Peter Wien, *Arab Nationalism: The Politics of History and Culture in the Modern Middle East* (London: Routledge, 2017), 50.
21. Dennis Walker, 'Egypt's Arabism: Mustafa Kamil's 1893 Play (Fath al-Andalus) on the Muslim Conquest of Spain', *Islamic Studies* 33: 1 (1994): 49–76; 49.
22. William Granara, 'Nostalgia, Arab Nationalism, and the Andalusian Chronotope in the Evolution of the Modern Arabic Novel', *Journal of Arabic Literature* 36: 1 (2005), 57–73; 63.
23. Ussama Makdisi, 'Ottoman Orientalism', *The American Historical Review* 107: 3 (2002): 768–96.
24. Ceyhun Arslan, 'Translating Ottoman into Classical Arabic: Nahda and the Balkan Wars in Ahmad Shawqi's "The New al-Andalus"', *Middle Eastern Literatures* 19: 3 (2016): 278–97; 279.
25. Fatih Altuğ, 'Modernity and Subjectivity in the Literary Criticism of Namık Kemal', PhD dissertation, Boğaziçi University, 2007, 197–205.
26. See, for instance, the debates between Renan and Afghani, as discussed by Monica Ringer and Holly Shissler, 'The Al-Afghani-Renan Debate, Reconsidered', *Iran Nameh* 30: 3 (2015), XXVIII–XLV. On Indian Muslim discourses on modernity, see Faisal Devji, 'Apologetic Modernity', *Modern Intellectual History* 4: 1 (2007): 61–76.
27. See Maryam Wasif Khan, *Who Is a Muslim? Orientalism and Literary Populisms* (New York: Fordham University Press, 2021), 120–3. C. M. Naim notes that Zaidan's work enjoyed wide circulation in Urdu translation, and suggests that the popularity of Sharar's own historical novels 'must have contributed to the easy acceptance of Zaidan's novels in Urdu'. C. M. Naim, 'Interrogating "The East", "Culture", and "Loss", in Abdul Halim Sharar's Guzashta Lakhna'u', in Alka Patel and Karen Leonard (eds), *Indo-Muslim Cultures in Transition* (Leiden: Brill), 189–204; 198.
28. Nergis Ertürk, 'An Uncanny Turkic: İsmail Gasprinskii's Language Lesson', *Middle Eastern Literatures* 19: 1 (2016): 34–55.
29. Engin Kılıç, 'The Balkan War (1912–1913) and Visions of the Future in Ottoman Turkish Literature', PhD dissertation, Leiden University, 2015.
30. Mana Kia, 'Moral Refinement and Manhood in Persian', in Margrit Pernau (ed.), *Civilizing Emotions: Concepts in Nineteenth-century Asia and Europe* (New York: Oxford University Press, 2015), 146–69; 151.
31. Elias John Wilkinson Gibb, *A History of Ottoman Poetry*, vol. IV (London: Luzac, 1900), vii.

32. See Petra de Bruijn, *The Two Worlds of Eşber: Western Orientated Verse Drama and Ottoman Turkish Poetry by Abdülhak Hamid Tarhan* (Leiden: Research School CNWS, 1997).
33. See Syed Tanvir Wasti, 'The Indian Sojourn of Abdülhak Hamid', *Middle Eastern Studies* 34: 4 (1998): 33–43.
34. See İnci Erginün, 'Byron ve Hamid'in Sardanapal Piyesleri Üzerinde Mukayeseli Bir Araştırma', *Türk Dili ve Edebiyatı Dergisi* 15 (1967): 13–44.
35. Abdülhak Hamid Tarhan, *Duhter-i Hindu* (Istanbul: Tasvir-i Efkâr Matbaası, 1875), 194–8.
36. Abdülhak Hamid Tarhan, as cited in Tanya Elal Lawrence, 'An Age of Trans-Imperial Vernacularisms: The Iranian Dissident Community of the Late Ottoman Empire', PhD dissertation, Yale University, 2018, 143–4.
37. Nazım Hikmet, 'Putları Yıkıyoruz No. 1: Abdülhak Hamid', as cited in Veysel Öztürk, 'The Notion of Originality from Ottoman Classical Literature to Turkish Modern Poetry', *Middle Eastern Literatures* 19: 2 (2016): 135–61; 135–6.
38. Halide Edip, *Conflict of East and West in Turkey* (Delhi: Maktaba Jamia Millia Islamia, 1935), 160.
39. The contrast is emphasised through depiction of the Berbers' clothes as white, but also as funeral shrouds, e.g. Bosnian, *mrtvačko odijelo*; Arabic, *al-akfan al-bayd*; Urdu, *mout ka libaas*.
40. Edip, *Conflict*.
41. Abdülhak Hamid Tarhan, *Tarik (Osvojenje Španjolske): drama u VI. Činova*, trans. Salih Bakamović (Mostar: Prva muslimanska nakladna knjižara i štamparija (Muhamed-Bekir Kalajdžić), 1915), iii.
42. Šemsudin Sarajlić, 'Kći Indije', *Gajret* 4: 12 (15 June 1911), 187–90; 188.
43. Sarajlić, 'Kći Indije', 188.
44. 'Muslimanska biblioteka u Mostaru', *Biser* 12 (1912–13), 277.
45. Abdülhak Hamid's personal life of interest to Bosnian readers deep in the interwar period, where gossip about his liaisons with Belgian women filled the pages of journals. See 'Miss Turska – Miss Universum', *Novi Behar* 4/5 (1932–3), 70–1.
46. Abdülhak Hamid was thus compared to Belgian authors. Abdül-Hak Hamid Tarhan, *Tarik (Osvojenje Španjolske)*, vi.
47. Salih Bakamović, 'Riječ dvije o autoru' (preface), in Abdül-Hak Hamid Tarhan, Tarik (Osvojenje Španjolske): drama u VI. činova (trans. Salih Bakamović) (Mostar: Prva muslimanska nakladna knjižara i štamparija (Muhamed-Bekir Kalajdžić), 1915), iii.
48. This could reflect rising interest in psychology in post-World War II Egypt, as discussed in Omnia El Shakry, *The Arabic Freud: Psychoanalysis and Islam in Modern Egypt* (Princeton: Princeton University Press, 2017).
49. Ibrahim Sabri, ''Abd al-Haqq Hāmid', in Abdulhaq Hāmid Tarhan, *Tāriq aw fath al-Andalus*, trans. Ibrahim Sabri (n.pl.: Ishrāf idārat al-thaqāfa al-'āmma bi-wizāra al-tarbiya wa-al-ta'lim bi-Misr, 1959), 1–20; 14. This is reiterated throughout the translator's introduction.

Abdülhak Hamid Tarhan's Tarık or the Conquest of al-Andalus

50. As cited in Faiz Ahmed, *Afghanistan Rising: Islamic Law and Statecraft between the Ottoman and British Empires* (Cambridge, MA: Harvard University Press, 2017), 178.
51. As cited in Ahmed, *Afghanistan Rising*, 243.
52. Wali Ahmadi, *Modern Persian Literature in Afghanistan: Anomalous Visions of History and Form* (New York: Routledge, 2014), 46–7.
53. Ahmadi, *Modern Persian Literature*, 11.
54. Persian edition: Sultan Ahmad Khan, 'Rija-ye Motarjem', *Tarık ya feth-i Endülüs* (Istanbul: Cihan Biraderler Matbaası, 1922), 3–4.
55. As cited in Suraiya Husain, *Sajjad Hyder Yildirim* (Delhi: Sahitya Akademi, 1992), 18.
56. Husain, *Sajjad Hyder Yildirim*, 22.
57. Christine Everaert, *Tracing the Boundaries Between Hindi and Urdu: Lost and Added in Translation between 20th-century Short Stories* (Leiden: Brill, 2010), 107.
58. Abdülhak Hamid Tarhan, 'Fath-e Andalus', trans. Sajjad Hyder Yildirim, *Nigar* 43: 4 (April 1943), 3–10; and Abdülhak Hamid Tarhan, 'Fath-e Andalus', trans. Sajjad Hyder Yildirim, *Nigar* 43: 5 (May 1943), 3–9.
59. Fay Seen Ejaz, *Niyaz Fatehpuri: Hindustani Adab Ke Memar* (Delhi: Sahitya Akademi, 2011), 67–9.
60. Niyaz Fatehpuri and Syed Ehtisham Husain, 'Yildirim, unke saath aur romani afsana nigari', *Pagdandi* 'Yildirim Number' 9: 5 (1961): 116–21; 118.
61. Niyaz Fatehpuri, 'Mulahazat', *Nigar* 43: 5 (May 1943), 2.
62. As cited in Husain, *Sajjad Hyder Yildirim*, 59.
63. The historical ethnicity of Tarik is disputed. He is believed to have been of Amazigh origin but the adaptations under discussion here consider him to be an Arab.
64. Persian edition: *Tarık ya feth-i Endülüs*, 142–3.
65. Abdülhak Hamit Tarhan, *Tarık*, sadeleştirenler [adaptors to modern Turkish], Sadi Irmak and Behçet Kemal Çağlar (Istanbul: İnkilap Kitabevi, 1960), 7.
66. Sakib Korkut, as cited in Harun Buljina, 'Empire, Nation, and the Islamic World: Bosnian Muslim Reformists between the Habsburg and Ottoman Empires, 1901–1914', PhD dissertation, Columbia University, New York, 2019, 200.
67. Katalin Rac, 'Arabic Literature for the Colonizer and the Colonized: Ignaz Goldziher and Hungary's Eastern Politics (1878–1918)', in Susannah Heschel and Umar Ryad (eds), *The Muslim Reception of European Orientalism: Reversing the Gaze* (New York: Routledge, 2019), 80–103.
68. Rada Stakić, 'Übersetzungsrezeption der deutschen Literatur in der bosnischen Literaturzeitschrift "Bosanska vila"', in Željko Uvanović (ed.), *Nur über die Grenzen hinaus: Deutsche Literaturwissenschaft in Kontakt mit Fremden* (Osijek: Univerzitet u Osijeku, 2010), 361–78.
69. For example, Alija Kadić, *Kakav je narod arapski* (Mostar: Prva muslimanska nakladna knjižara i štamparija (Muhamed-Bekir Kalajdžić), 1915); Alija

Kadić, *Izbor iz arapskog pjesništva* (Sarajevo: Zemaljska vlada za Bosnu i Hercegovinu, 1913).
70. Wilfred C. Smith, *On Understanding Islam: Selected Studies* (The Hague: Mouton Publishers, 1981), 64.
71. Katerina Dalacoura, '"Islamic Civilization" as an Aspect of Secularization in Turkish Islamic Thought', *Historical Social Research* 44: 3 (2019): 127–49.
72. Abdülhak Hamid, *Tarık yahut Endülüs fethi*, Istanbul, 1296, Act IV, scene 1, p. 92.
73. Bosnian: *Tarik (Osvojenje Španjolske)*, 135.
74. Arabic: *Tāriq aw Fath al-Andalus*, 253.
75. Persian: *Tarık ya feth-i Endülüs*, 285–6.
76. For example, after the conquest, a party is thrown by the caliph. In the Bosnian translation, this party is organised for Islam, while in Arabic it is organised for Muslims. The original retains 'Islam' as well, implying that the original intention was to reify Islam.
77. Bosnian: *Tarik (Osvojenje Španjolske)*, 77; Arabic: *Tāriq aw Fath al-Andalus*, 154.
78. Bosnian: *Tarik (Osvojenje Španjolske)*, 135.
79. See Azmi Özcan, *Pan-Islamism: Indian Muslims, the Ottomans and Britain, 1877–1924* (Leiden: Brill, 1997).
80. Cemil Aydın, *The Idea of the Muslim World: A Global Intellectual History* (Cambridge, MA: Harvard University Press, 2019), 76.
81. There is a huge literature on the shifting meanings of the term *vatan* or *watan* in the languages under study here. See Behlul Özkan, *From the Abode of Islam to the Turkish Vatan: The Making of a National Homeland in Turkey* (New Haven, CT: Yale University Press, 2012); Wael Abu-'Uksa, *Freedom in the Arab World: Concepts and Ideologies in Arabic Thought in the Nineteenth Century* (Cambridge: Cambridge University Press, 2018); Afsaneh Najmabadi, 'The Erotic Vatan [Homeland] as Beloved and Mother: To Love, to Possess, and to Protect', *Comparative Studies in Society and History* 39: 3 (1997): 442–67; Edin Hajdarpasic, *Whose Bosnia?: Nationalism and Political Imagination in the Balkans, 1840–1914* (Ithaca, NY: Cornell University Press, 2019); Ali Khan Mahmudabad, *Poetry of Belonging: Muslim Imaginings of India 1850–1950* (Delhi: Oxford University Press, 2020).
82. As cited in Altuğ, 'Modernity and Subjectivity in the Literary Criticism of Namık Kemal', 250.
83. Najmabadi, 'Erotic Vatan', 466.
84. Mrinalini Sinha, 'Unraveling Masculinity and Rethinking Citizenship: A Comment', in Stefan Durdink, Karen Hagemann and Anna Clark (eds), *Representing Masculinity: Male Citizenship in Modern Western Culture* (New York: Palgrave Macmillan, 2007), 261–75; 261.
85. See Yaşar Tolga Cora, 'Asker-Vatandaşlar ve Kahraman Erkekler: Balkan Savaşları ve Birinci Dünya Savaşı Dönemlerinde Beden Terbiyesi Aracılığıyla

Abdülhak Hamid Tarhan's Tarık or the Conquest of al-Andalus

İdeal Erkekliğin Kurgulanması', in Nurseli Yesim Sünbüloglu (ed.), *Erkek Millet Asker Millet / Türkiye'de Militarizm, Milliyetçilik, Erkek(lik)ler* (Istanbul: İletişim Yayınları, 2013), 45–73.
86. Erol Köroğlu, *Ottoman Propaganda and Turkish Identity: Literature in Turkey during World War I* (London and New York: I. B. Tauris, 2007), 89.
87. Urdu: 'Fath-e Andalus', *Nigar* 43: 5 (May 1943), 3.
88. Sajjad Hyder Yildirim, *Jalaluddin Khawarizm Shah* (Aligarh: Muslim University Press, 1925).
89. See Peter Hill's observations about how the 'translational diffusion' of Arabic-language 'works offering a fictionalised account of Islamic civilisation (Zaydan's novels) and a paternalist feminism (Amin's tracts)' helped to incarnate a sense of a 'Muslim world' in this period, in Peter Hill, 'Translation and the Globalisation of the Novel: Relevance and Limits of a Diffusionist Model', in Marilyn Booth (ed.), *Migrating Texts: Circulating Translations around the Ottoman Mediterranean* (Edinburgh: Edinburgh University Press, 2019), 95–121; 117.
90. Marilyn Booth, '*Woman in Islam*: Men and the "Women's Press" in Turn-of-the-20th-century Egypt', *International Journal of Middle East Studies* 33: 2 (2001): 171–201.
91. His other plays such as *Macera-yı Aşk* also included love triangles. As Çekiç observes, he married four times and kept mistresses while married; as such 'it is not clear whether Abdülhak Hamid defended polygamy or simply made use of it through historical distance to create dramatic excitement', in Çekiç, 'On the Front', 631.
92. The Ottoman phrasing of women as *taife-i latife* (the gentle sex) was rendered into different languages as: Bos. *krasni i nježni spol*; Ar. *al-jins al-latif*; Per. *taife-i latife-i zenan*; Ur: n/a.
93. Namık Kemal to Abdülhak Hamid Tarhan (30 March 1879), as cited in Fevziye Abdullah Tansel, *Hususi Mektuplarına Göre: Namık Kemal ve Abdülhak Hamid* (Ankara: Akçağ, 2005), 92.
94. Megan Robb, 'Women's Voices, Men's Lives: Masculinity in a North Indian Urdu Newspaper', *Modern Asian Studies* 50: 5 (2016): 1441–73; 1462.
95. See Faisal Devji, 'Gender and the Politics of Space: The Movement for Women's Reform in Muslim India, 1857–1900', *South Asia* XIV: 1 (1991): 141–53.
96. Juhi Shahin, 'Niyaz Fatehpuri and the Ulama: Criticisms and Debates, 1922–1966', MA thesis, McGill University, 2007, 78–98.
97. Marya Hannun, 'From Kabul to Cairo and Back Again: The Afghan Women's Movement and Early 20th-century Transregional Transformations', *Genre & Histoire* 25 (2020), para. 22. Available at: <https://journals.openedition.org/genrehistoire/5017> (last accessed 4 June 2022).
98. Muhamed Ferid Vedždi, *Muslimanska žena* (Mostar: Prva muslim. nakladna knjižara i štamparija (M. B. Kalajdžić), 1915).
99. Bosnian: *Tarik (Osvojenje Španjolske)*, 9.

Bibliography

Abu-'Uksa, Wael, *Freedom in the Arab World: Concepts and Ideologies in Arabic Thought in the Nineteenth Century* (Cambridge: Cambridge University Press, 2018).

Ahmadi, Wali, *Modern Persian Literature in Afghanistan: Anomalous Visions of History and Form* (New York: Routledge, 2014).

Ahmed, Faiz, *Afghanistan Rising: Islamic Law and Statecraft between the Ottoman and British Empires* (Cambridge, MA: Harvard University Press, 2017).

Ali, Kecia, *The Lives of Muhammad* (Cambridge, MA: Harvard University Press, 2016).

Altuğ, Fatih, 'Modernity and Subjectivity in the Literary Criticism of Namık Kemal', PhD dissertation, Boğazici University, 2007.

Arslan, Ceyhun, 'Translating Ottoman into Classical Arabic: Nahda and the Balkan Wars in Ahmad Shawqi's "The New al-Andalus"', *Middle Eastern Literatures* 19: 3 (2016): 278–97.

Aydın, Cemil, *The Idea of the Muslim World: A Global Intellectual History* (Cambridge, MA: Harvard University Press, 2019).

Bakamović, Salih, 'Riječ dvije o autoru' (preface), in Abdül-Hak Hamid Tarhan, Tarik (Osvojenje Španjolske): drama u VI. činova (trans. Salih Bakamović) (Mostar: Prva muslimanska nakladna knjižara i štamparija (Muhamed-Bekir Kalajdžić), 1915).

Balslev, Sivan, *Iranian Masculinities: Gender and Sexuality in Late Qajar and Early Pahlavi Iran* (Cambridge: Cambridge University Press, 2019).

Bilgiç, Ali, *Turkey, Power and the West: Gendered International Relations and Foreign Policy* (London and New York: I. B. Tauris, 2016).

Booth, Marilyn, 'Woman in Islam: Men and the "Women's Press" in Turn-of-the-20th-century Egypt', *International Journal of Middle East Studies* 33: 2 (2001): 171–201.

Boym, Svetlana, 'Nostalgia', *Atlas of Transformation* (blog), <http://monumenttotransformation.org/atlas-of-transformation/html/n/nostalgia/nostalgia-svetlana-boym.html> (last accessed 5 February 2021).

de Bruijn, Petra, *The Two Worlds of Eşber: Western Orientated Verse Drama and Ottoman Turkish Poetry by Abdülhak Hamid Tarhan* (Leiden: Research School CNWS, 1997).

Buljina, Harun, 'Empire, Nation, and the Islamic World: Bosnian Muslim Reformists between the Habsburg and Ottoman Empires, 1901–1914', PhD dissertation, Columbia University, 2019.

Camoğlu, Arif, 'Inter-imperial Dimensions of Turkish Literary Modernity', *Modern Fiction Studies* 64: 3 (2018): 431–57.

Çekiç, Can Eyüp, 'On the Front and at Home: Women in the Modern Ottoman Epic', *Middle Eastern Studies* 52: 4 (2016): 623–39.

Clark, Kyle, 'Ottoman Diplomacy and Hegemonic Masculinity during the Great

Eastern Crisis of 1875–78', *Middle East – Topics & Arguments* 14 (2020): 121–33.

Cora, Yaşar Tolga, 'Asker-Vatandaşlar ve Kahraman Erkekler: Balkan Savaşları ve Birinci Dünya Savaşı Dönemlerinde Beden Terbiyesi Aracılığıyla İdeal Erkekliğin Kurgulanması', in Nurseli Yesim Sünbüloglu (ed.), *Erkek Millet Asker Millet / Türkiye'de Militarizm, Milliyetçilik, Erkek(lik)ler* (Istanbul: İletişim Yayınları, 2013), 45–73.

Curthoys, Ned, 'Diasporic Visions, Taboo Memories: Al-Andalus in the German Jewish Imaginary', *Arena Journal* 33–4 (2009): 110–38.

Dalacoura, Katerina, '"Islamic Civilization" as an Aspect of Secularization in Turkish Islamic Thought', *Historical Social Research* 44: 3 (2019): 127–49.

Devji, Faisal, 'Gender and the Politics of Space: The Movement for Women's Reform in Muslim India, 1857–1900', *South Asia* XIV: 1 (1991): 141–53.

Devji, Faisal, 'Apologetic Modernity', *Modern Intellectual History* 4: 1 (2007): 61–76.

Edip, Halide, *Conflict of East and West in Turkey* (Delhi: Maktaba Jamia Millia Islamia, 1935).

Ejaz, Fay Seen, *Niyaz Fatehpuri: Hindustani Adab Ke Memar* (Delhi: Sahitya Akademi, 2011).

Elal Lawrence, Tanya, 'An Age of Trans-Imperial Vernacularisms: The Iranian Dissident Community of the Late Ottoman Empire', PhD dissertation, Yale University, 2018.

Eldem, Edhem, 'Ottomans at the Alhambra, 1844–1914: An Investigation into the Perception of al-Andalus by Ottoman Subjects in Times of Modernity', *Turcica* 49 (2018): 239–359.

Elsadda, Hoda, 'Imaging the "New Man": Gender and Nation in Arab Literary Narratives in the Early Twentieth Century', *Journal of Middle East Women's Studies* 3: 2 (2007): 31–55.

El Shakry, Omnia, *The Arabic Freud: Psychoanalysis and Islam in Modern Egypt* (Princeton: Princeton University Press, 2017).

Erginün, İnci, 'Byron ve Hamid'in Sardanapal Piyesleri Üzerinde Mukayeseli Bir Araştırma', *Türk Dili ve Edebiyatı Dergisi* 15 (1967): 13–44.

Ertürk, Nergis, 'An Uncanny Turkic: İsmail Gasprinskii's Language Lesson', *Middle Eastern Literatures* 19: 1 (2016): 34–55.

Everaert, Christine, *Tracing the Boundaries Between Hindi and Urdu: Lost and Added in Translation between 20th-century Short Stories* (Leiden: Brill, 2010).

Fatehpuri, Niyaz, 'Mulahazat', *Nigar* 43: 5 (May 1943): 2.

Fatehpuri, Niyaz and Syed Ehtisham Husain, 'Yildirim, unke saath aur romani afsana nigari', *Pagdandi* 'Yildirim Number' 9: 5 (1961): 116–21.

Gibb, Elias John Wilkinson, *A History of Ottoman Poetry*, vol. IV (London: Luzac, 1900).

Granara, William, 'Nostalgia, Arab Nationalism, and the Andalusian Chronotope in the Evolution of the Modern Arabic Novel', *Journal of Arabic Literature* 36: 1 (2005): 57–73.

Hajdarpašić, Edin, *Whose Bosnia?: Nationalism and Political Imagination in the Balkans, 1840–1914* (Ithaca: Cornell University Press, 2019).

Hannun, Marya, 'From Kabul to Cairo and Back Again: The Afghan Women's Movement and Early 20th Century Transregional Transformations', *Genre & Histoire* 25 (2020), <https://journals.openedition.org/genrehistoire/5017> (last accessed 4 June 2022).

Hill, Peter, 'Translation and the Globalisation of the Novel: Relevance and Limits of a Diffusionist Model', in Marilyn Booth (ed.), *Migrating Texts: Circulating Translations around the Ottoman Mediterranean* (Edinburgh: Edinburgh University Press, 2019), 95–121.

Hirschkind, Charles, *The Feeling of History: Islam, Romanticism, and Andalusia* (Chicago: University of Chicago Press, 2021).

Hiz, Gürbey, 'The Making of the "New Woman": Narratives in the Popular Illustrated Press from the Ottoman Empire to the New Republic (1890–1920s)', *Early Popular Visual Culture* 17: 2 (2019): 156–77.

Husain, Suraiya, *Sajjad Hyder Yildirim* (Delhi: Sahitya Akademi, 1992).

Jacob, Wilson Chacko, *Working Out Egypt: Effendi Masculinity and Subject Formation in Colonial Modernity, 1870–1940* (Durham, NC: Duke University Press, 2011).

Jana, Katja, 'Changing Heads and Hats: Nationalism and Modern Masculinities in the Ottoman Empire and the Republic of Turkey', in Simon Wendt and Pablo Dominguez Andersen (eds), *Masculinities and the Nation in the Modern World: Between Hegemony and Marginalization* (New York: Palgrave Macmillan, 2015), 217–42.

Kadić, Alija, *Izbor iz arapskog pjesništva* (Sarajevo: Zemaljska vlada za Bosnu i Hercegovinu, 1913).

Kadić, Alija, *Kakav je narod arapsk* (Mostar: Prva muslimanska nakladna knjižara i štamparija (Muhamed-Bekir Kalajdžić, 1915).

Khan, Maryam Wasif, *Who Is a Muslim? Orientalism and Literary Populisms* (New York: Fordham University Press, 2021).

Kia, Mana, 'Moral Refinement and Manhood in Persian', in Margrit Pernau (ed.), *Civilizing Emotions: Concepts in Nineteenth-century Asia and Europe* (New York: Oxford University Press, 2015), 146–69.

Kılıç, Engin, 'The Balkan War (1912–1913) and Visions of the Future in Ottoman Turkish Literature', PhD dissertation, Leiden University, 2015.

Köroğlu, Erol, *Ottoman Propaganda and Turkish Identity: Literature in Turkey during World War I* (London and New York: I. B. Tauris, 2007).

Mahmudabad, Ali Khan, *Poetry of Belonging: Muslim Imaginings of India 1850–1950* (Delhi: Oxford University Press, 2020).

Makdisi, Ussama, 'Ottoman Orientalism', *The American Historical Review* 107: 3 (2002): 768–96.

'Miss Turska – Miss universum', *Novi Behar* 4/5 (1932–3): 70–1.

'Muslimanska biblioteka u Mostaru', *Biser* 12 (1913): 277.

Naim, C. M., 'Interrogating "The East", "Culture", and "Loss", in Abdul Halim

Sharar's Guzashta Lakhna'u', in Alka Patel and Karen Leonard (eds), *Indo-Muslim Cultures in Transition* (Leiden: Brill, 2012), 189–204.

Najmabadi, Afsaneh, 'The Erotic Vatan [Homeland] as Beloved and Mother: To Love, to Possess, and to Protect', *Comparative Studies in Society and History* 39: 3 (1997): 442–67.

Najmabadi, Afsaneh, *Women with Mustaches and Men without Beards: Gender and Sexual Anxieties of Iranian Modernity* (Berkeley: University of California Press, 2005).

Özcan, Azmi, *Pan-Islamism: Indian Muslims, the Ottomans and Britain, 1877–1924* (Leiden: Brill, 1997).

Özkan, Behlul, *From the Abode of Islam to the Turkish Vatan: The Making of a National Homeland in Turkey* (New Haven: Yale University Press, 2012).

Özoğlu, Müge, 'Modernity as an Ottoman Fetish: Representations of Ottoman Masculinity', in Kesik Bıyık', *Masculinities: A Journal of Identity and Culture* 6 (2016): 79–101.

Öztürk, Veysel, 'The Notion of Originality from Ottoman Classical Literature to Turkish Modern Poetry', *Middle Eastern Literatures* 19: 2 (2016): 135–61.

Rac, Katalin, 'Arabic Literature for the Colonizer and the Colonized: Ignaz Goldziher and Hungary's Eastern Politics (1878–1918)', in Susannah Heschel and Umar Ryad (eds), *The Muslim Reception of European Orientalism: Reversing the Gaze* (New York: Routledge, 2019), 80–103.

Ringer, Monica and Holly Shissler, 'The Al-Afghani-Renan Debate, Reconsidered', *Iran Nameh* 30: 3 (2015): XXVIII–XLV.

Robb, Megan, 'Women's Voices, Men's Lives: Masculinity in a North Indian Urdu Newspaper', *Modern Asian Studies* 50: 5 (2016): 1441–73.

Sabri, Ibrahim, ''Abd al-Haqq Hāmid', in Abdulhaq Hāmid Tarhan, *Tāriq aw fath al-Andalus*, trans. Ibrahim Sabri (n.pl.: Ishrāf idārat al-thaqāfa al-'āmma bi-wizāra al-tarbiya wa-al-ta'lim bi-Misr, 1959), 1–20.

Sarajlić, Šemsudin, 'Kći Indije', *Gajret* 4: 12 (15 June 1911): 187–90.

Shahin, Juhi, 'Niyaz Fatehpuri and the Ulama: Criticisms and Debates, 1922–1966', MA thesis, McGill University, 2007.

Sinha, Mrinalini, 'Unraveling Masculinity and Rethinking Citizenship: A Comment', in Stefan Durdink, Karen Hagemann and Anna Clark (eds), *Representing Masculinity: Male Citizenship in Modern Western Culture* (New York: Palgrave Macmillan, 2007), 261–75.

Smith, Wilfred C., *On Understanding Islam: Selected Studies* (The Hague: Mouton Publishers, 1981).

Stakić, Rada, 'Übersetzungsrezeption der deutschen Literatur in der bosnischen Literaturzeitschrift "Bosanska vila"', in Željko Uvanović (ed.), *Nur über die Grenzen hinaus: Deutsche Literaturwissenschaft in Kontakt mit Fremden* (Osijek: Univerzitet u Osijeku, 2010), 361–78.

Tansel, Fevziye Abdullah, *Hususi Mektuplarına Göre: Namık Kemal ve Abdülhak Hamid* (Ankara: Akçağ, 2005).

Tareen, Sherali, *Defending Muhammad in Modernity* (Notre Dame: Notre Dame University Press, 2020).

Tarhan, Abdülhak Hamid, *Duhter-i Hindu* (Istanbul: Tasvir-i Efkâr Matbaası, 1875).

Tarhan, Abdülhak Hamid, *Tarik (Osvojenje Španjolske): drama u VI. Činova*, trans. Salih Bakamović (Mostar: Prva muslimanska nakl. knjižara (Muhamed-Bekir Kalajdžić), 1915).

Tarhan, Abdülhak Hamid, *Tarık ya feth-i Endülüs*, trans. Sultan Ahmad Khan (Istanbul: Cihan Biraderler Matbaası, 1922).

Tarhan, Abdülhak Hamid, 'Fath-e Andalus', trans. Sajjad Hyder Yildirim, *Nigar* 43: 4 (April 1943): 3–10; 43: 5 (May 1943): 3–9.

Tarhan, Abdülhak Hamid, *Tāriq aw fath al-Andalus*, trans. Ibrahim Sabri (n.pl.: Ishrāf idārat al-thaqāfa al-'āmma bi-wizāra al-tarbiya wa-al-ta'lim bi-Misr, 1959).

Tarhan, Abdülhak Hamit, *Tarık*, sadeleştirenler [adaptors to modern Turkish], Sadi Irmak and Behçet Kemal Çağlar (Istanbul: İnkilap Kitabevi, 1960).

Vedždi, Muhamed Ferid, *Muslimanska žena* (Mostar: Prva muslim. nakladna knjižara i štamparija (M. B. Kalajdžić), 1915).

Walker, Dennis, 'Egypt's Arabism: Mustafa Kamil's 1893 play (Fath al-Andalus) on the Muslim conquest of Spain', *Islamic Studies*, 33: 1 (1994): 49–76.

Wasti, Syed Tanvir, 'The Indian Sojourn of Abdülhak Hamid', *Middle Eastern Studies* 34: 4 (1998): 33–43.

Wien, Peter, *Arab Nationalism: The Politics of History and Culture in the Modern Middle East* (London: Routledge, 2017).

Yildirim, Sajjad Hyder, *Jalaluddin Khawarizm Shah* (Aligarh: Muslim University Press, 1925).

Yıldız, Murat, '"What is a Beautiful Body?" Late Ottoman "Sportsman" Photographs and New Notions of Male Corporeal Beauty', *Middle East Journal of Culture and Communication* 8: 2–3 (2015): 192–214.

Zachs, Fruma and Sharon Halevi, *Gendering Culture in Greater Syria: Intellectuals and Ideology in the Late Ottoman Period* (London and New York: I. B. Tauris, 2015).

PART III
WOMEN IN TRANSLATION

Chapter 6

Translating Qasim Amin's Arabic *Tahrir al-mar'a* (1899) into Ottoman Turkish

Ilham Khuri-Makdisi and Yorgos Dedes

Introduction: The Context of Qasim Amin's Translation into Ottoman Turkish

To most educated Arabs of the early twentieth century, Qasim Amin (1863–1908) needed no introduction. His work, *Tahrir al-mar'a* ('The emancipation of women', 1899), which was followed by his *al-Mar'a al-jadida* ('The new woman', 1900), had made him famous – as well as notorious – among Arab readers in Egypt as well as the rest of the Ottoman Arab provinces. Even people who hadn't read his work were constantly exposed to articles commenting on it –praising, endorsing, critiquing, and occasionally savagely attacking it.[1] As Ibrahim Ramzi, one of Amin's contemporaries in Cairo, wrote: 'When [the book] appeared, everyone talked about it – on the streets, in public and private social gatherings, among women in seclusion in their quarters, and in their visits [to each other], and between them and their husbands.'[2] *Tahrir al-mar'a* called for women's primary education; deplored their confinement; advocated uncovering the face and hands of women, and thus limiting the covering to the parts of the body mandated by the *shari'a*; and argued for a limited emancipation so as to produce better wives and mothers, both for the family's and the nation's sake. Indeed, Amin's work, as well as subsequent discussions of it, equated Egyptian women's situation with that of the nation. In fact, Lisa Pollard has suggested that

> Amin's agenda in *The Liberation of Women* and *The New Woman* had much less to do with liberating women than it did with exposing the home and its domestic relations as a means of illustrating that Egypt was 'modern' and politically capable, and, therefore, of securing a place for itself among modern, independent nations.[3]

Tahrir al-mar'a was truly epoch-making, precisely because it generated such an intense and long-lasting debate – even if in fact many of its arguments had been made earlier, including by women, without provoking such controversy.[4] As Marilyn Booth has pointed out:

> It was Amin's work that generated a furious and more public debate on gender than had been the case before. It was commentators at the time, not simply historians writing later, who gave his books precedence – including commentators who were knowledgeable about and sympathetic to women's own contributions to the public debate.[5]

Thus, the book generated a trail of articles and books responding to, or countering, Amin's arguments.[6]

And yet, *Tahrir al-mar'a*'s impact and notoriety were not confined to Egyptian or Arab readers, but reached readers throughout the Muslim world who could read the original Arabic or accessed it through translation. Readers in the Ottoman Empire outside of Egypt must have surreptitiously read it in the original until 1908 since the book (like many other Egyptian publications) was banned until then, and the ban itself was lifted only after the Young Turk revolution of 1908.[7] And, suggesting its salience to a wider readership, after the revolution two translations of *Tahrir al-mar'a* appeared in Ottoman Turkish. This chapter analyses these translations and their significance on a number of levels. Adopting a granular approach and through a close reading and comparison of both translations and their paratexts, the chapter seeks to shed light on the broad range of possibilities and translation strategies available to translators from Arabic to Ottoman Turkish during this period. It argues that such choices reflected a combination of overlapping factors, which included the translator's envisioned audience; his own positionality – namely, his ideological stance and his own interpretation of Qasim Amin's text; different interpretations of the translator's role and visibility towards the original text and author; and collective debates taking place in Ottoman Turkish intellectual society regarding the translatability of the Qur'an from Arabic. Through the translation of *Tahrir al-mar'a*, we also analyse the specific and foundational role that translations from Arabic played in expanding the Ottoman Turkish lexicon. While much has been written on the impact of translations from European (and specifically French) texts into Ottoman Turkish, both in terms of content and in their effect on the Ottoman language, there is overall precious little on translations between Arabic and Ottoman Turkish.[8] Our chapter shows that the study of translations from Arabic complicates the standard narrative regarding Ottoman Turkish in the late nineteenth and early twentieth centuries as one organised around the binary of Turkification and simplification on one hand, and a heavily infused, 'conservative' or classical Arabo-Persian highbrow Ottoman language on the other.

Indeed, many historians and literary scholars have read this late Ottoman period as one characterised by the purging of Arabic terms and its replacement by Turkish vernacular ones and as a zero-sum linguistic game, or as Monica Katiboğlu most recently put it, 'the beginnings of the suppression of intimate linguistic others [that is, Arabic and Persian in Ottoman Turkish] as a prerequisite for asserting the Turkish vernacular as the national, unifying language'.[9] Whereas Katiboğlu's own research focuses on the group Edebiyat-i Cedide (New literature, 1896–1901), which 'proposed a vision of linguistic modernisation that embraced Arabic and Persian', she suggests that such a vision went against the grain, and was the exception rather than the norm. Nonetheless, as our chapter shows, such 'mixing and matching' was far from exceptional, and undergirded both translations of *Tahrir al-mar'a*. Finally, moving beyond the evolution of the Ottoman language itself, the chapter argues that the two translations were part of an integrated, cohesive ecology for intellectual production in the late Ottoman period that formed a joint Ottoman textual canon, and that the study of translations between these two languages ought to be a central preoccupation to the study of late Ottoman intellectual and cultural history.

'The Woman Question', Translation and the Making of an Intellectual Ecology

Before delving into Qasim Amin's translations, we should first situate his work within a much larger matrix of works dealing with 'the woman question'. Much has been written by scholars on this topic. Beth Baron has argued that

> the end of slavery, most specifically harem slavery ... generated a series of debates collectively known as the 'woman question' through which questions about the shape of the household, the building-block of the nation, were worked out ... the 'woman question' thus became the fault line along which men and women negotiated ethnic boundaries, cultural identity, and social transformations.[10]

Other scholars such as Marilyn Booth have added to the debate by arguing that at the heart of 'the woman question' lay all kinds of discussions regarding men's own place in society and within the family, and that 'what has been identified as the "woman question" at various historical moments and in a range of societies, including Egypt, needs to be scrutinized equally as the "man question".'[11]

In the late nineteenth and early twentieth centuries, works pertaining to 'the woman question' figured particularly prominently within the large corpus of translated works between Ottoman Turkish and Arabic.[12] And indeed, the numbers of translations of such works reflected the vast body of works published in these languages. According to Irvin Schick, the number of nonfiction books (let alone articles) on 'the woman question' that appeared in Ottoman Turkish in the late nineteenth and early twentieth centuries was around 150 editions published between 1875 and 1907, many of them schoolbooks, and all overwhelmingly printed at private presses especially after 1900. Such a figure witnessed a remarkable increase after 1908, and 'the rate at which books oriented toward women were published more or less doubled after the restoration of the constitution in 1908.'[13] Qasim Amin's book thus fit into an existing and growing body of literature on the topic, including various works written by women, some preceding Amin's.[14]

Nonetheless, a few points are worth underlining. First, and as previously mentioned, the book was translated and published not once, but twice into Ottoman Turkish (and once into Tatar Turkish, in Kazan), within a span of five years (1908 and 1913), by two different translators. The first translation was published in Cairo; the second, in Istanbul. A handful of other contemporary works – on different topics – were translated more than once; but this double-translation was the exception rather than the rule. The multiplicity of translations certainly says something about the book's perceived importance; but as we note further on, this is likely to be only part of the story. Second, many of the works written in Arabic in response to *Tahrir al-mar'a*, and certainly those that seemed to be most critical of it, on religious grounds, were also translated into Ottoman Turkish[15] – or, if penned in Turkish, translated into Arabic. Thus, *Tahrir al-mar'a* spanned a cluster of interconnected, intertexual, interreferential works which formed an intellectual ecology, in the original language as well as in translation.[16] Interestingly, some of the responses to *Tahrir al-mar'a* were translated between the two languages even before the book itself was translated, such as Muhammad Farid Wajdi's response, analysed in Abdelmegeed and Akcasu's chapter.[17] This intellectual ecology encompassing *Tahrir al-mar'a* and 'the woman question' suggests that the intellectual histories of the Arabophone Nahda and the late Ottoman Turkish period were strongly imbricated, and ought to be considered as parts of an interconnected intellectual sphere rather than studied separately. Specific books, authors and periodicals, as well as translators, played a prominent role in producing and circulating texts and creating a shared discursive sphere. Not only did they lead to the formation of an Ottoman Republic of Letters, or an 'Ottoman literary biome' which Ceyhun Arslan has defined as 'the transcultural space of the Ottoman Empire that allowed the circulation of a mutilingual textual repertoire and cultivated a cultural elite',[18] but this intellectual ecology was particularly made and expanded by translators and through the translation of a large corpus of texts in the form of articles and books. Moreover, these translations, which went both ways, helped create a community of readers bound together partly through translation. And by doing so, they 'helped to weave the intellectual fabric' of the Turkish and Arabic speaking worlds 'more closely together'.[19]

A third point is that genre mattered. In other words, certain genres were particularly favoured within the translation movement between Arabic and Ottoman Turkish as well as in translations from European languages. Contemporary social sciences, especially sociological and socio-legal texts written in a certain 'scientific' and objective manner, which showcased their authors' familiarity with European social science works and could also 'talk back' at and refute some of the accusations regarding Eastern societies, seem to have been particularly valued among Ottoman intellectuals, both Turks and Arabs. Such works were present in significant numbers in the corpus of texts translated between Ottoman Turkish and Arabic. This also helps explain *Tahrir al-mar'a*'s galvanising effects in the original and in translation, as the book sought to refute some accusatory claims against Muslim societies made in European and especially French works, while citing from them as well as others. Thus, unlike Arabic literature during this period – which in the words of Ceyhun Arslan, exists in the works on Turkish literature 'only as a source of influence that existed prior to Turkish literature'[20] and was placed in a position of anteriority vis-à-vis Ottoman Turkish literature – non-literary texts, and specifically contemporary socio-legal texts such as *Tahrir al-mar'a* that combined modern legal thought, a sociological approach, a knowledge of European practices and European sociological texts with *shari'a* and Qur'anic studies, were deemed particularly useful and thus worthy of translating and engaging with.

The Two Translators: a Brief Biographical Sketch

Having placed *Tahrir al-mar'a* and its translation into a larger matrix of shared intellectual production, let us turn to the translators themselves. It is no surprise that a work unanimously deemed to be of central importance (albeit controversial) by its contemporaries would get translated by seasoned translators: Yusuf Semih al-Asmaʻi, responsible for *Tahrir al-Mar'a, yahut Hürriyet-i Nisvan* (Cairo: Osmanlı Matbaʻası, 1908), and Zaki Mugamiz, responsible for *Hürriyet-i Nisvan* (İstanbul: Kitaphane-i İslam ve ʻAskeri, 1329 (1913).[21] Unfortunately, not much is known about Asmaʻi (d. 1942?), also known as Yusuf Semih, even though he was a prolific author and translator between Arabic and Ottoman Turkish.[22] In his reference work on Turks in Egypt, Ekmeleddin Ihsanoğlu described him as 'without doubt the most prominent name to have enriched the Turkish language with translations of Arabic works in the fields of religion and politics, most of them written by members of Egypt's religious, political, and intellectual elite'.[23] Various sources indicate that Asmaʻi moved from Istanbul to Egypt and briefly resided in Alexandria before settling in Cairo. He seems to have worked as a correspondent in Egypt for the Istanbul newspaper *Tercüman-ı Hakikat* before subsequently publishing a short-lived Turkish-language newspaper, *Mısır* (1889–90).[24] Among other works, he translated an abridged version of the Egyptian nationalist leader Mustafa Kamil's *al-Mas'ala al-sharqiyya* into Ottoman Turkish in 1902, as well as a book penned in response to Amin's *Tahrir al-mar'a*, entitled *İhticap*. Written by the former Qadi al-Qudat of Egypt, Abdallah Cemaleddin Bereketzade (died 1901), it was first published (posthumously?) in 1901 by Asmaʻi in Ottoman Turkish, in Cairo, and he then translated it into Arabic and subsequently published it under the title *al-Ihtijab* the very same year.[25]

Besides his translation work, Asmaʻi authored a number of works, including works on Ottoman grammar and a travelogue to Sicily. He seems to have also edited a bilingual Arabic–Turkish newspaper, *al-'Arif*, published in Cairo. Evidently, then, he was clearly very much connected to the Cairene intellectual elites and to the world of periodicals, writing both in Arabic and in Ottoman Turkish.[26] In his preface to *Tahrir al-mar'a*'s translation, he described himself as deputy secretary (*vekil*) of the Office of the (British) Commander-in-Chief of the Egyptian Army (Maktab al-Sardar).[27] A few years earlier, in 1906, his name (Yusuf Semih) had appeared as one of the two signatories who certified the translation of the convention between the Ottoman state and the Egyptian state following a disagreement regarding the borders between Egypt and Bilad al-Sham (the Ottoman Syrian territories). He was the secretary at the War Ministry (*katib nazarat al-harbiyya*).[28] Thus, Asmaʻi occupied an important administrative position within the state apparatus, and his translation skills between Ottoman Turkish and Arabic were specifically trusted.

Slightly more is known about Zaki Mugamiz (born in Aleppo 1871, died in Istanbul 1932), the author of the second translation, published in 1913. As Johann Strauss concisely put it,

Translating Qasim Amin's Tahrir al-mar'a *into Ottoman Turkish*

The Arab Christian Zeki Meghamiz . . . is one of the most intriguing figures in late Ottoman intellectual history . . . He was one of the most active writers and journalists of the period and is also famous for having been Pierre Loti's Turkish teacher. He published numerous articles in Turkish papers . . . and played an important role in the transmission of contemporary Arabic literature.[29]

Mugamiz was a Christian Arab from Aleppo who moved to Istanbul where he was employed in the translation department (Tercüme ve Te'lif Dairesi) of the Ottoman Ministry of Education, and also served in the government printing office as redactor and translator.[30] He was a correspondent and contributor to various Egyptian newspapers, and later to important periodicals in Istanbul including *Mekteb* and *Ikdam*. Like Asma'i, he was a seasoned translator who had translated many works from Arabic into Ottoman Turkish, most famously Jirji Zaydan's multivolume *Tarikh al-tamaddun al-islami* ('History of Islamic civilisation'), which was first serialised on the pages of *Ikdam*, then published as a book.[31] He would later also translate some of Zaydan's highly popular historical novels. Rather endearingly, Zaydan consistently referred to him as 'our friend Zaki bey Mugamiz, the famous Arab Turkish author (*al-katib al-'arabi al-turki*)'.[32] In the post-Ottoman period, he became a member of the Damascene Arabic Scientific Society (al-Majma' al-'ilmi al-'arabi) while residing in Istanbul.

In sum, by the time his translation of *Tahrir al-mar'a* appeared in 1913, Mugamiz (who described himself as a 'former member of [Istanbul] City Council (*Şehir emaneti meclisi a'za-yı sabıkasından*)' on the cover of his published translation) had gained visibility – and perhaps notoriety in certain circles – for his many translations. In 1914, a fascicule of his translation of the Qur'an appeared, the first ever to be published under the direct title *Kur'an-i Kerim: Tercüme ve Tefsiri* ('The Noble Qur'an: translation and commentary'), but the publication met with fierce opposition from the Office of Şeyhülislam (Meşihat) and was stopped – due to the tremendous opposition in influential circles to the translation of the Qur'an in the first place, and equally, to the translator's Christian identity. When his complete translation was published in 1926 under the title *Türkçe Kur'an-ı Kerim Tercümesi* ('Turkish translation of the Noble Qur'an') he would become the subject of much greater controversy and vitriol.

By the time their translations of Qasim Amin's work appeared, both translators were thus well-known and well-respected intellectuals and translators, whose works were published by notable publishing houses. Asma'i's translation was published by the Ottoman Press (Osmanlı; Matba'ası) in Cairo, which published thirteen Turkish books between 1907 and 1913, five of them in 1908,³³ and whose distributor in Istanbul was Kana'at Kitaphanesi as indicated on the book's back page.³⁴ Mugamiz's 1913 translation was also published by a well-known publisher, Ibrahim Hilmi (1876?–1963), who had started the Islamic and Military Library (Kitaphane-i Islam ve 'Askeri), which published a number of textbooks, works translated from Western languages, as well as works by Turkish women, specifically the poetess Nigar Hanım (1856–1918).³⁵ According to Strauss, Ibrahim Hilmi was

> an outspoken supporter of Westernization ... [and] considered the lack of Westernization as one of the major causes of what he called 'our catastrophe' (*felaketimiz*). His ideas on language displayed progressive views. Ibrahim Hilmi participated in the linguistic debate that intensified after the Young Turk revolution. In a pamphlet published in 1909 under the title 'Do we need a purification of our language?' (*Tasfiye-i lisana muhtac mıyız?*), he pleaded vehemently for reform and simplification of the language, thus anticipating many of the changes to come.³⁶

More so, he himself was a strong advocate of women's rights. It was also Ibrahim Hilmi who published Mugamiz's translation of the Qu'ran, in 1914 and 1926, both times without mentioning Mugamiz's name but referring to a 'committee' (*heyet*), a subject to which we will return. While we emphasise the work of the translators, we recognise the collaborative work involved in these productions, and the existence of a group of committed intellectuals who played a range of roles we can only allude to here.

Paratexts: The Choice of a Title

The readers first entered the two translations though the cover, title and translators' prefaces, paratextual elements that were all integral components of the text. As Gérard Genette pointed out in *Paratexts*, the paratext – or everything that is added to the text itself: title, preface and footnotes, as well as the cover and the layout – is

> more than a boundary or a sealed border, the paratext is, rather, a threshold, or ... a 'vestibule' that offers the world at large the possibility of either stepping inside or turning back ... or as Philippe Lejeune put it, 'a fringe of the printed text which in reality controls one's whole reading of the text'.³⁷

Before commenting on the titles of the translated works, it bears underlining, following Marilyn Booth's research, that Amin's own title choice in Arabic seems to have been one of the main reasons behind the work's controversy. Indeed, as Ibrahim Ramzi wrote, in the first issue of his

Translating Qasim Amin's Tahrir al-mar'a *into Ottoman Turkish*

periodical *Woman in Islam* (est. 1901), which came out as a response to Amin's *Tahrir al-mar'a* and his *al-Mar'a al-jadida*:

> At first, the uproar people made was not because they disagreed with each other on where the author had erred, or on his analysis, but rather because the title alienated them and they rejected it. . . . 'The Liberation of Woman' rang in their ears like a lion's roar. Their response was just to draw back and hone their skills at casting opprobrium on its author.[38]

And yet, in spite or because of the title's symbolic weight, both of the translators (or their publishers) chose to include the original title 'Tahrir al-Mar'a' in their translations, albeit in slightly different ways. In Asma'i's translation, it appeared in the original Arabic as the main title, followed after a colon by the subtitle 'the freedom of women' in Ottoman Turkish (*Tahrir al-Mar'a: yahut, Hürriyet-i Nisvan*). In Mugamiz's translation, it appeared as a subtitle, after the Ottoman Turkish 'the freedom of women' and the Arabic title in parenthesis followed by an explanation in Ottoman Turkish that this was a translation of the book 'Tahrir al Mar'a' (*Hürriyet-i Nisvan: (Tahrir'ul Mar'a) kitabının tercümesidir*). The Ottoman Turkish equivalent that was given for the title, *Hürriyet-i Nisvan* ('The freedom of women'), loses the potency of the verbal noun's causative meaning (*tahrir*), where somebody is doing the emancipation of women. The word *tahrir* was used in Ottoman Turkish, yet it was clearly avoided in translating Qasim Amin's title, probably because it either carried a connotation of 'freeing from impurity or defect' or 'emancipating a slave' – or, in both Arabic and Ottoman, it could refer to setting down in writing, recording, editing and the like.[39] By the early twentieth century it is likely that it was used mainly in the sense of writing, hence would be unsuitable, while *hürriyet* had great currency, not least because of Namık Kemal's famous *Hürriyet* poem (*kasida*) and more recently, the Young Turk revolution of 1908.

Whether the choice behind the title was left to the translator or engineered by the publisher is not clear. Nonetheless the privileging, in Asma'i's translation, of the original Arabic title (which appears first, and is in bold and larger characters) suggests that the translator's (or his publisher's) intended or envisioned audience might have been one already familiar with Qasim Amin's text and the polemics around it, and who would immediately recognise the title. Most likely, this was an audience with some knowledge of Arabic, and one for whom a text originally written in Arabic carried a certain weight, authority or prestige. On the other hand, the Ottoman Turkish title chosen for Mugamiz's translation (again, appearing first and in bold characters) points to a different envisioned audience, perhaps one who would be more generally interested in the freedom of women rather than in Amin's text per se. Thus, Mugamiz's translation linked Amin's text to a larger corpus of works on the subject of women's freedom or 'the woman question'. In other words, the difference in titles might already suggest different stakes, imagined audiences, and translation choices at hand.

Paratexts: The Translators' Prefaces, or the Translator as Intellectual

After the title, the reader is guided through Amin's translated text first by crossing over the translator's preface. It is there that the translator's motive is articulated. Evidently, the prefaces were public narratives of intent that might have obscured or distorted other, perhaps more genuine, motivations – including individuals or groups that played a central role in commissioning and/or funding these translations, but who preferred to remain invisible. Tellingly, Asma'i and Mugamiz penned radically different prefaces. Asma'i's is striking for its length; around fifteen pages, it is a preface to the preface (four pages), followed by a longer, more conventional preface (eleven pages). Mugamiz's is a mere two pages, and surprisingly, makes no mention of Asma'i's translation (a point to which we will return). Perhaps to bolster his authority as translator-author, Asma'i's preface included his correspondence with Qasim Amin, in which he asked the author's permission to translate his work, as well as referring to responses to and refutations of the book. Specifically, he mentioned Bereketzade's book, *Ihticab*, and his own role in publishing it in Ottoman Turkish, then translating it into Arabic.

Asma'i's preface does not explicitly spell out why the translator had waited until 1908 to publish his translation, which appeared very shortly after Amin's death. While he explicitly praised the freedom of the press (*serbesti-i matbu'at sayesinde*) with reference to Egypt before 1908, which had allowed the publication of various refutations and endorsements of *Tahrir al-mar'a* to be published there, Asma'i made no direct mention of the Young Turk revolution of that year. However, other subsequent references to Asma'i's translations stated that he published his translation after the Young Turk revolution of 1908, which lifted the ban on Qasim Amin's book, and reversed the censorship practices of the Hamidian period (very briefly, it turns out).[40] Asma'i underlined that he had spent eight years closely reading the books written in response to – and mainly in reaction against – Amin's book, weighing the various arguments and criticisms. Using vivid language, Asma'i claimed that along with talk

Translating Qasim Amin's Tahrir al-mar'a *into Ottoman Turkish*

amongst Muslims about obstacles to progress, Amin's book had 'all of a sudden startled Islam (lit. 'struck the eyes of Islam/the Muslims' (*birden bire İslamın gözüne çarpmış*)' – and here, Asma'i's idiomatic turn of phrase reads like a momentary lapse that reveals the translator's own visceral reaction and sense of affront generated by some of Amin's writings. Nonetheless he continued in a more measured, objective style to say that Amin had encouraged Muslim women to give up their habitual lives for more orderly ones, but also to give new currency to their old customs, within the realm of their expertise and in accordance to reason and religious principles/law (*şer'*).[41] This is why it had, in all seriousness, attracted the attention of the public and opened the way to intense debate. In Asma'i's view, because Amin had demonstrated that women (*ta'ife-i nisa*) had been 'the first teachers of the community of Muhammad (*ümmet-i Muhammedin ilk hocaları*)', the contents of his book 'had been subjected to explications and commentaries (*te'vil ve tefsirlere uğratılmış*)' – and here Asma'i uses standard philological terms of Qu'ranic exegesis (*ta'wil wa tafsir*) expressing his sympathy with the criticisms – which claimed that Amin had the temerity to annul the provisions (*hükm*) of the 'explicit divine texts (*nusus-ı sariha-i ilahiyenin*)' and had dared to substitute and change (*tebdil ve tağyir*) 'the laws of family organization (*teşkil-i 'a'ile kanunlarını*)', which are amongst the admirable customs of Islam (*'adat-ı müstahsene-i İslamdan*).[42]

According to Asma'i, many scornful responses had been written attacking Amin's book for 'having the audacity to annul even the provisions (*hukm*) of the explicit divine texts, or having dared to substitute and change the laws of family organization, which are amongst the admirable customs of Islam'.[43] Amin's polarising work triggered radically different reactions among his readers, explained his translator; they could be classified into three categories: the first was that of the extremists (*ifratçılar*), who argued that 'women should study whatever they wanted from the "arts and sciences" (*'ulum ve funun*) . . . and that boys and girls should all study together in one school and in the same class', just as in the American model.[44] Second were the moderate ones (*mu'tedilin*), who 'argued that the education of women should be limited to catechism (*'ilm-i hal*) and domestic matters'; and third were the minimalists (*tefritçiler*), who clamoured that 'one should certainly cover women more and for their uprightness and . . . should stick them in a sack (*'adeta çuvala sokmalıdır*), since the current coverings of Egyptian and Istanbuli women merely serve to 'show off their beauty'.[45] 'This of course is an aberration', Asma'i hastened to add, showing his opposition to such extremist views.[46] Nonetheless, if Asma'i clearly marked his disapproval of this third, intransigent point of

237

view, he also made it clear that an equally problematic consequence of the polemics around women's covering was that it unleashed tensions between Muslims and non-Muslims, and especially that it led to counter-accusations and even smearing regarding Muslim women's honour. As he wrote:

> Non-Muslims took part in the debate. Muslim authors had explained that veiling was a necessity for uprightness and chastity, and that in areas where women went about unveiled, their lineage was broken [that is, they lost their propriety] (*nesli bozuk*) but this only caused the ire of non-Muslims, and made them express views contrary to our national customs. Indeed, they increased their criticisms and argued that there were unchaste ones (*'iffetsizler*) amongst covered women (*nisvan-i mesture*), and that besides adultery the custom of sodomy/lesbianism (*livata*) which went against nature, was prevalent in the provinces of Islam, thus and in many other ways smearing our honour with their pens.[47]

But the much greater problem, for Asma'i, was that 'the Christians, who are convinced that their religion had been an obstacle to progress', made the false assumption that Islam too had been an obstacle:

> [T]hey dared to make the false claim that Islamic teachings were an obstacle. These people (*bu adamlar*) do not know, or do not want to know that the religion of Muhammad (*din-i Muhammedi*) is governed by education and noble morals which are the foundation of every kind of human progress.[48]

Asma'i was categorical: 'The religion of Islam is not an obstacle to progress' and had an answer as to what was:

> Yes, we all know that there has been a strong reason (and others deriving from it) why the various Muhammadan peoples (*akvam-ı muhtelife-i Muhammediye*) have not progressed. The real reason can not be only the veiling and the family composition (*teşkil-i 'a'ile*), but the tyranny and absolutism (*zulm ü istibdad*) of the rulers. The ensuing limitation of freedom has afflicted all the Muslim peoples and thus the lack of education has turned everyone into a victim of the more powerful and a tyrant towards the weaker. And a sluggishness has taken over.[49]

The end result was that, ultimately, 'both ruler and ruled had become a flock of people weak and unworthy of nobility (*na layık–i siyadet*)', and had made the poor Muslims vulnerable to continuous attacks by other people (*ümmetler, kavimler*) who, equipped with an education suitable for their era, 'have taken away our lands and provinces (*dar-u diyarimiz*) and are still busy (*haril haril*) taking what little remains'.[50]

In brief, Asma'i's preface suggested that he approved of Amin's project overall –especially concerning the necessity of female education.

Translating Qasim Amin's Tahrir al-mar'a into Ottoman Turkish

Like Amin, he was primarily concerned with uplifting the family and women, in order to strengthen the nation. And like him, he linked the 'backward' situation of women in Egypt/the Muslim world, to tyranny, which he accused of weakening Muslim societies and peoples and making them vulnerable to European aggression. This, however, did not mean he completely saw eye to eye with the book he was translating, which is why he went to great lengths to summarise the opinion of other influential thinkers about the book; but he deemed it a necessary and important work with which to engage, and this was, according to his preface, his main motivation. In fact, he suggested that one's opinion of the work, as well as of the various arguments for or against it, could (perhaps even should?) change over time:

> I was collecting the serious works among those that were written to refute Qasim Amin's book and subjecting them one by one to a close reading, always noting and retaining to one side the criticisms which I considered to be just (*haklı*). And so in this way, eight years have passed and with time, I found it suitable to revise a great number of criticisms, and to discard a number of others which I had earlier recorded as just (*haklı*). I ascribe this to the changing of my thinking as well, like the changing of judgments with the passing of time.[51]

Such an attitude was in stark contast with the kind of personal attacks and criticisms that had immediately followed publication of Amin's work, and which Asma'i condemned as having 'entirely overstepped their boundaries'. Even worse, 'with time, everybody became silent. Each side, presuming that they had won the argument with words, withdrew victoriously from the field of battle.'[52]

Hence, through penning his fifteen-page preface, Asma'i presented himself not as a 'mere' translator, but as an *intellectual* who had spent eight years reading the heated debates around *Tahrir al-mar'a*, and had developed his own informed, nuanced and authoritative readings of the issues outlined and presented in Amin's work. He thus had the legitimacy, authority and responsibility to translate the text – and as the reader would subsequently see, to explicitly intervene in the debates it raised through his inclusion of lengthy footnotes, attributed explicitly to the translator.

Paratexts: Public Criticism as a Fundamental Need for the Nation's Health

Asma'i's preface laid out the 'state of the field' and the polarisations around the woman's question as unleashed by *Tahrir al-mar'a*, and sought to reignite what he deemed to be a necessary debate on such topics. Mugamiz's extremely brief preface also underlined the need for open debate, but in his case, he emphasised the importance of dignified criticism for the intellectual life of a nation – while also showing the translator's awareness of just how controversial the book was. Like Asma'i, Mugamiz acknowledged that he was well aware that the work would be met with objections 'as far as its principles are concerned' (*esas i'itibarıyle*), 'but there was no cause for worries' (*Fakat ne be's var*), as everyone could voice and make public their criticisms and objections. Critics also deserved respect. In a nation whose intellectual life was devoid of such debates (*münazaralar*), 'the light of truth' would not manifest itself. On the other hand, should criticism take the form of denigration and blasphemy, Mugamiz would feel sorry for 'ourselves and the nation' (*kendimize, millete acırım*), not the deceased author. Just as they reveal our decline in matters of education, Mugamiz argued, 'such criticisms (*intikatlar*) devoid of science and logic simply prove what unworthy followers of our great predecessors we have become, and also gave us a bad name (*bed-nam eyler*).' Mugamiz asserted that Islam was 'the first patron of freedom of thought' (*Serbesti-i efkarin ilk hamisi İslamiyet idi*) on account of which there 'came into being our ancient compositions which can be counted in the millions' (*Milyonlar ile ta'dad edilebilen mü'ellifat-i kadimemiz işte o sayede vucuda gelmiş idi*).[53] Claiming that it would be a disgrace to trample upon such a remarkable legacy, he succinctly concluded his remarks with one of the key mantras of Amin's book: 'The matter of veiling (*tesettür bahsi*) is fundamentally a social problem (*esasen bir mes'ele-i ictima'iyedir*).' Given the brevity of his introduction, this 'truth' acquires particular weight – in the sense that Qasim Amin's assertion was somewhat diluted and buried in the multiple pages and arguments of *Tahrir al-mar'a*, whereas here, Mugamiz extracted it and cast the spotlight on it. However, like Asma'i, Mugamiz argued it would be difficult to withstand the 'flood of occupation and being overwhelmed by the West (*garbın sel-i i'tila ve tağallübü*)' unless one were able to examine such matters in an intellectual and social context. He concluded by stating that he considered himself to have fulfilled an 'abiding obligation' by translating 'this important book'.

The Question of Audience

We've suggested that the titles of the two translations alluded to possibly different anticipated or envisioned reading audiences. The translators' prefaces also gave clues on this matter. Asma'i's preface implicitly suggested that the audience, or reading community he had in mind were (Ottoman) *Muslims*, or more generally, a nebulous Islamic community

Translating Qasim Amin's Tahrir al-mar'a *into Ottoman Turkish*

– as seen by his comments regarding non-Muslims who 'inappropriately' and opportunistically jumped into the conversation and used Amin's book to attack Islam. However, even in a fifteen-page preface, he did not directly address or spell out his audience. Mugamiz, on the other hand, made it clear in his very brief preface that he was writing for the modern, post-1908 Ottoman nation. He began by emphasising that Amin's book was 'one of the important works which needed to be translated for what he called the "national Ottoman library"' (*Osmanlı kütüphane-i milliye*) – a generic reference acknowledging the importance of the work.[54] In fact, Mugamiz had a more explicit and specific audience in mind: the young generation, 'our youths' (*gençlermiz*),[55] on whom fell the duty of according the book the intellectual and social attention it deserved. He also chastised them, 'our inexperienced youth', for believing that nothing worthy had been produced by 'our noble predecessors . . . the scholars of Rum'. Indeed, in order to appreciate the freedom with which our noble predecessors thought and the respect accorded to their writings, he wrote, and especially what sort of works the scholars of Rum composed with a free and learned pen, one should turn to the works which lie abandoned in our libraries and start feeling ashamed of our ignorance. Thus, Mugamiz not only named and interpellated his audience, but also clearly reminded them of who 'our' shared noble predecessors were, namely the scholars of Rum – hence giving a place of prominence to a specific area within the Ottoman world and the 'national Ottoman library', and one which in 1913 was particularly associated with the 'Turkish' element (although Mugamiz did not use that name or adjective). Hence, he also identified one of the main tasks of the post-1908 project as being the recovery and recognition of the works of the ancients, which had been produced in times of great freedom of thought. He thus simultaneously tied Amin's *Tahrir al-mar'a* to the project of recovery and appreciation of the works of the ancients (albeit different ancients, those in Anatolia), as well as slightly decentring it and placing Amin's work within a much larger project of forming the national Ottoman library. Lastly, Mugamiz's preface (and, as we shall see, his translation) was more inflected with concepts and terms that gained grounds with the 1908 Revolution: for instance, the adjective *kudsi* (holy, blessed), which for instance recalls the notion of 'Hukuk-i muqaddese' (holy/blessed rights) that had appeared in the Committee of Union and Progress's decree of April 1327.[56]

Finally, it bears pointing out that neither Asma'i nor Mugamiz's prefaces seemed to include women as potential readers, and even less do they address women directly. While they are not explicitly excluded, it is worth underlining that Amin's *Tahrir al-mar'a* was most definitely not addressed to women or girls. Rather, as Marilyn Booth has pointed out about *Tahrir al-mar'a* and for instance, Ibrahim Ramzi's periodical *al-Mar'a fi'l-Islam*, 'women and girls are the objects of debate, the potential targets of reforms chosen and engineered by men. Men are constructed as "you" and "we", whilst women are almost always "they".'[57]

Caution, Distance and Objectivity: Translator versus Author

Regardless of their different targeted audiences, both prefaces are notable for their authors' caution. In many this way this is not completely surprising. Translation in general represented the safest kind of intellectual production, especially in times of censorship and fear of repression. It afforded the translator distance from the translated text: after all, he wasn't the one who wrote it, so could not be held responsible for its content. In a number of prefaces to translated works, translators claimed that, whilst they did not necessarily agree with the entirety of a work's contents, the benefits of making it accessible to a larger audience outweighed its disadvantages. Nonetheless, it is striking that this strategy was applied by both translators not only during times of censorship but later, during the relatively free period immediately after the Young Turk revolution. More so, it represented a marked departure from their prefaces to other works they translated; in Asma'i's case, the difference is even more striking given that his other prefaces were extremely brief, even laconic,[58] or consisted almost wholly of providing biographical information about the work's author.[59]

Asma'i was judicious and cautious overall, elaborating on a number of points of substance and also detailing various critical responses to Amin's book. He did not openly endorse Amin's views, with the exception of the very generic (and vague) need for female education. Mugamiz also was cautious, with his concern that the translation would draw criticism among Ottoman Turkish readers and his apparent emphasis on the importance of the right to criticise. He refrained from referring to the already published criticisms of Amin's work and in fact strongly hinted that he valued and fully endorsed Amin's call for the abolition of the full veil (the face veil), by referring to the importance of considering veiling in a social context. Interestingly, while both translators tried to mark some distance from Amin's text (Asma'i much more so than Mugamiz), and underlined the importance of open debate, neither one of them made any claims, *as translators*, of faithfulness to the original text. This did not mean that their translations were not faithful. Both were overwhelmingly so, but it is particularly striking, given how expressedly conscious the translators were of translating a polemical and highly controversial text, that in their paratexts framing the work, they would not underline their faithfulness to the original. While such a proclamation of faithfulness seems to have generally been absent in most of the translators' prefaces of works translated between Ottoman Turkish and Arabic before the early twentieth century, a number of prefaces penned in the first decade of the twentieth century suggest a shift had started taking place. But that was not evident in the prefaces to translations of Amin.

An Overview of the Two Translations: Vernacularisation versus Echoing

Overall, both translations were generally faithful to the original. Only very slightly and mostly cosmetically did they modify the book's structure and style, mostly concerning formatting and punctuation. There is the rare occurrence of a minor shift in the order of sentences (at least by Mugamiz), and the occasional few extra words to explain and flesh out an idea expressed in the original, or to introduce a new word by providing the Arabic original, and next to it the term commonly used in Ottoman Turkish.[60]

Generally, Asma'i's translation is competent and faithful in equally remarkable degrees. It is free of serious misunderstandings, indeed even minor ones, except for the occasional slip, including missing a sentence[61] and in one instance a sizeable piece of text, most likely the result of a typographical error rather than a deliberate omission.[62] Asma'i was clearly an experienced translator. He managed to maintain the sentence divisions of the original, the result being faithful renditions in frequently long sentences which are not immediately easy to make sense of.[63] While at times he split long Arabic sentences into shorter ones, on the whole the Ottoman sentences are characteristic of the high-register Ottoman of the time both in terms of vocabulary and structure.[64] In other words, Asma'i was evidently at ease with the proclivity of the Ottoman high register to use Arabo-Persian vocabulary at the expense of more straightforward Turkish synonyms, and to prefer a string of subordinate clauses whose internal divisions are not always clear to detect, and can only be properly understood once one has reached the end of the sentence.[65]

Asma'i frequently takes advantage of Arabic root derivations which allow the terms he chooses in Ottoman to be faithful to the root of the original Arabic wording, in a sort of *figura etimologica*. In that sense the Arabic terms are generally preserved, if sometimes in slightly different forms.[66] In some cases there is a perfect echo of Arabic.[67] Nonetheless, one does land on the occasional vernacularisation or more 'Turkish' rendering of specific sentences and passages. One such example is the insertion of the expression *komşuya gitmekten . . . vazgeçer* (meaning, 'so that the husband doesn't escape to the neighbour'), which really reads like modern Turkish.[68] Once in a while, Asma'i adds superfluous words, based on an overly literal, almost slavish translation of the Arabic original, thus leading the translation to sound a bit contorted in Ottoman Turkish.[69] Rarely, Asma'i also mildly intervenes in the text by fleshing out certain words or terms –as the following pages show.

By contrast, Mugamiz's translation is arguably more skilful. It is simpler and easier to follow as it is a freer, less literal rendition of the Arabic and clearly tries to avoid the highbrow, convoluted style of late Ottoman which is on the whole preferred by Asma'i. Some of Mugamiz's translation strategies and style can be seen as early as the author's preface and introductory remarks. If Asma'i's translation is a more literal translation, Mugamiz's is more flowing, partly as a result of either breaking up longer sentences or being more periphrastic at times, adding short phrases and words not in the original. On the whole it is more Turkish-sounding,[70] with several sentences made more vernacular (in at least one case, almost inappropriately casual in its colloquialness)[71] by adding a word here and there,[72] or employing colloquial expressions (*İslamlar* for *Muslimun*).[73] This is not to say that Mugamiz was not capable of employing the learned register with its flourishes, both on the level of Arabo-Persian vocabulary (for example, his coining an Arabo-Persian phrase, 'worshippers of sluggishness' (*meskenet-perest*) for lazy types without powers of discernment)[74] and of complex syntax with subordinated clauses. He also could deploy fairly recherché hybrid combinations of Persian and Arabic, which Asma'i did not do,[75] and could come up with particularly beautiful translations.[76] Generally, Mugamiz did not shy away from taking some (minor) liberties with the text, occasionally adding emphasis in a slightly interpretative manner,[77] as well as deploying almost poetic license to convey a point.[78] His translation also clarified certain points, managing to overcome the occasional opaqueness of the Arabic original and even in one case rendering it clearer, thus improving on the Arabic original.[79] He turned some of Amin's sentences into rhetorical questions, which simultaneously gave more power to Amin's arguments and also made the text more interactive, drawing the readers into the debate in an engaging and readable style.[80] Overall, then, Mugamiz's translation gives the flair of a friendly narration.

Somebody is telling you a story and is doing it well, whereas with Asma'i, one is at times left wondering about the meaning of some of the sentences, and needs to reread the translation a few times before understanding the gist, as well as the nuances of the text.[81]

What might lie behind these differences in style? Again, this might suggest that the translators had different audiences in mind. Asmaʻi envisioned his readership as consisting of people well versed in a certain kind of Ottoman Turkish that was heavily Arabic-based and more 'elitist' and highbrow, whereas Mugamiz targeted an audience that identified with, and could better understand, a more Turkish-inflected Ottoman Turkish – perhaps a younger audience that he was trying to shape.

A second hypothesis is that Asmaʻi deliberately maintained the 'foreignness' of the text, and did not wish to turn himself into an 'invisible translator',[82] but rather wanted to continuously remind his audience that this was a translated text, and one from a language with a particular prestige and authority when it came to religious and socio-religious matters specifically, but not exclusively. Another possible explanation (to which we will return) is that there were differences between Egyptian Turkish and Istanbuli Turkish. This would raise a very basic question: what was 'Modern Standard Ottoman Turkish', and if there was such a thing, what were the modalities and chronology of its construction and how did translators see this? Yet another explanation might be that Asmaʻi's Turkish was simply not particularly good. This last hypothesis seems the weakest, given that he occupied an important bureaucratic post where his command of Ottoman Turkish would have been crucial, and also in light of the fact that he translated many works from and into Ottoman Turkish authored by important figures such as Bereketzade.

Regardless of the differences between the two translations, one stylistic intervention both translators consistently made is the doubling of words, that is, the translation of one word by two synonyms or near-synonyms – something known in Ottoman as *atf-i tefsir*. For example, Asmaʻi translated the Arabic *fitna* into *fitne ve fesad* (sedition and depravity),[83] and Mugamiz translated the Arabic *ʻazima* as *ʻazm ve sabr* (fortitude and endurance).[84] Some words were almost always translated into the same two words: thus, Mugamiz consistently translated *ʻulum* (knowledge/science) as *ulum ve funun* (arts and sciences),[85] and *tarbiya* (upbringing) as *terbiye ve tehzib* (upbringing and correction/improvement).[86] In some cases, this meant that a very short sentence would be translated into a sentence double its length.[87] The doubling of words did multiple things: first, it displayed the translators' erudition and language skills, and thus magnified their authority as competent translators, but also as authors. Second, it served (intentionally or not) the didactic goal of expanding their readers' lexicon at the same time as it helped hedge their bets, in the case one word was known and the other not, thus expanding the text's reach to a larger audience by offering multiple terms. But the doubling of words as well as other stylistic strategies or choices by the translators also show how language and readership are mutually constitutive categories: having a specific audience in mind most likely informed the lexicographical choice and linguistic strategies adopted by the translators, but simultaneously, the linguistic choices themselves determined or shaped the audience in question.

Translating Concepts, Terms and Clusters

How were certain key words, concepts and clusters of terms in Arabic translated? And how stable were such linguistic choices throughout the translations? As a general rule, both translators tended to translate *al-mar'a* (woman) into a feminine plural (*nisvan* or *kadınlar*).[88] Asma'i usually translated the plural *nisa'* as *nisvan*, whereas Mugamiz favoured *kadınlar* (except in the title where he stuck to *nisvan*).[89] Whereas *nisvan* is derived from Arabic, and *kadınlar* is a Turkish word, both were used interchangeably in Ottoman Turkish during this period, with no seemingly ideological demarcation. More significantly, Asma'i often added the possessive 'ours' to translate a single 'woman' (*imra'a*) into *haremimiz* (our harem),[90] and turned 'women' into 'our women' (*kadınlarımız*), which was in line with much of the writings by men on 'the woman question', and also evidently gestured to a more conservative and patriarchal understanding of gender relations and marriage. Mugamiz occasionally also did the same, but seemingly less frequently. Both translators kept polygyny (*ta'addud al-zawjat*) as such,[91] as well as marriage (*zawaj*), with Mugamiz using a different form (*izdivac*). The Arabic term for family (*'a'ila*) was generally used by both translators; interestingly though, in at least one case, Asma'i translated it as *familia*.[92] This was perhaps to distinguish between nuclear and extended family, but this is not clear from the context. The use of *familia* to occasionally translate *'a'ila* is one of the few differences that Booth and Shissler have found between the Ottoman and Arabic versions of Fatma Aliye's work, both published in the early 1890s (see their chapter in this volume).

Unsurprisingly, the terms pertaining to veiling and seclusion were generally translated into specifically Turkish ones: for instance, the Arabic *tabarqu' wa-satr wujuhihim* becomes in Asma'i *ferace ve çarşaf*, two different kinds of face covers.[93] Hijab, a polyvalent word[94] and the term most commonly used for covering as well as seclusion of women (*hijab al-nisa'*), is avoided in Ottoman, most likely because its primary meaning

Translating Qasim Amin's Tahrir al-mar'a into Ottoman Turkish

in Ottoman Turkish was as a screen or partition or obstacle, and also because the Ottoman Turks had developed their own terms and expressions for such practices and objects over the centuries. Thus, hijab is rendered as (the also Arabic) *tesettür* (from the Arabic root of *satara*, to cover). Asma'i preferred *tesettür-i nisvan* in the Persian *izafet* and Mugamiz *kadınlarda tesettür*, a Turkish construction.[95]

The term for society (*al-hay'a al-ijtima'iyya*) remained the same in both translations (*heyet-i ictima'iye*). The Arabic *umma* (nation, or the Islamic community) presents an interesting case: Mugamiz seemed to consciously avoid using it, fairly consistently translating it as *millet*, unambiguously 'the nation', whereas Asma'i generally translated *umma* as *ümmet*, which in Ottoman Turkish of the period was more ambiguous, referring primarily to the Islamic *umma*.[96] The *umam* in Amin's past 'Islamic nations' ('[kanat] al-umam al-islamiyya') were translated by Mugamiz as *akvam* (peoples, nations in the pre-nineteenth-century sense).[97] Moreover, whereas Asma'i regularly translated *umma* as *ümmet*, he did at times (albeit rarely) translate *umma* as *kavim*.[98] However, the Arabic *qawm* did not always get translated as *kavim*: in at least one instance, 'a people will say' (*sayaqulu qawm*) was rendered as *cema'at* by Asma'i. This term often, if not most commonly, referred to a religious community, that is, a *cema'at* of Muslims.[99] The same was rendered by the neutral term *bazıları* (some) by Mugamiz.[100] Asma'i's occasional shifts in the way he translated and used *umma* and *qawm* are not atypical of the period. Others, including the intellectual Mehmet Akif Ersöy, also used terms pertaining to peoples and nations erratically. As Hasan Kayali has argued:

> Terms that have come to be associated with explicit meanings after the 1920s, albeit with significant semantic variation from one Middle Eastern language to another, such as ırk (race), millet (nation), and kavim (tribe/ethnic group) were used interchangeably. Such variation cannot be explained by poetic licence alone; it points to the prevalent ambiguities about the definition of the group and the absence of a collective understanding of the objective bases of the community.[101]

There are no surprises in the way terms pertaining to civilisation (*tamaddun*) were translated – with words derived from the same root being used in Ottoman Turkish. The term for progress (*taqaddum*) was regularly translated as *tekaddüm ve terakki* in Asma'i[102] but with varied compounds by Mugamiz: *terakki ve i'tila* or *te'ali ve terakki*.[103] Change (*taghyir*) often became *tağyir ve tebdil* in Asma'i, and, more significantly, *inkılap* or *inkılap ve tahavvül* in Mugamiz. The Ottoman Turkish *inkılap* in the sense of radical change and revolution was obviously a key term after the

1908 Revolution. As we will see, Mugamiz went out of his way to inject the term whenever possible, even when there was no equivalent term used in the original Arabic.

Another related concept was 'decline', especially civilisational decline and the decline of the condition of women (both often noted in opposition to a historical rise and apogee). Thus, *inhitat* (decline) and its associated verb (*inhattat*) in the original were generally kept as *inhitat* in Mugamiz (as a verbal noun; as a verb he sometimes uses another verb, such as *sukuta düşmek*),[104] but usually avoided by Asma'i and translated as *tedenni* (decline)[105] or, for 'when [women in other nations] were ... in a cesspool or swamp of decline' (*yawma kanat fi khaid al-inhitat*) becomes 'the times when they were most backwards' (*en geride bulundukları zaman*).[106] On the rare occasion Asma'i used the term, it was in conjunction with another word, for instance, *te'ehhür ve inhitat*.[107] Asma'i's reluctance to use the term is somewhat perplexing, given that the term was used quite frequently in Ottoman Turkish in the late nineteenth century, with the meaning of decline.[108] Overall, the passages on decline and stillness/stagnation in Mugamiz's translation were lexically particularly close to the Arabic, and maintained the strong language of the original, whereas they were somewhat diluted in Asma'i.[109] Decline, of civilisation, morality or women's condition, was in Amin's text intimately connected to *fasad* (corruption) and that which corrupts morals (*yufsid akhlaqaha*). Here too, Mugamiz consistently kept *fesat*, sometimes doubling it with '*fesat ve seyyi'at*',[110] whereas Asma'i occasionally used plainer, more Turkish language.[111] Amin strongly linked decline and corruption to tyrannical governments and rulers. The term *istibdad* (absolutism; tyranny) was always maintained in translation, with a slight modification in the form for the adjective in the feminine or the plural.[112] Mugamiz often magnified the adjective *müstebidde* by adding another word to it (*müstebidde ve mutlaka*; *müstebidde ve mu'tesife*).[113] It is not clear how widespread the adjective *müstebidde* was in Ottoman Turkish, but the entries in Redhouse's dictionary of 1890 suggest neither *istibdad* nor *müstabidde* were very commonly used at that time, either because the term wasn't widespread then, or because it was censored. They do appear in Sami's Turkish dictionary around 1900, but again, it is not clear how commonly used they were in Ottoman Turkish by then, and by whom they were used.[114]

Some Arabic terms were consistently omitted in the translations and replaced by another word – because they either did not exist or were uncommon in Ottoman Turkish; there were other more dominant meanings associated to them; or they were too ambiguous, too strong, or had acquired an altogether different meaning in Ottoman Turkish.[115] Others were kept but almost invariably accompanied by an explanation for the term: such is the case for the term *hurra* (free) to indicate a non-slave woman, which was translated by Asma'i as *hürre*, with an added explanation: 'free, that is not a slave/captive' ('"hürre" yani "esire" olmayan bir kadın').[116]

Translating Sexuality and Desire

If the above-mentioned terms were generally translated in a consistent manner, less stable was the translation of terms pertaining to female sexuality, notably the term *'awra*, that is, the parts of a woman's body which should be covered, according to *shari'a*. 'Awra was translated by Asma'i as *'avret, 'ayıp yeri* or *utanacak yer* (the place to be ashamed of),[117] or with the explanation 'grass parts' (*ot yeri*),[118] and by Mugamiz either through neutral circumlocutions like 'the areas whose exposure is not allowed' (*açık kalması ca'iz olmayan yerler*) or 'parts whose covering is necessary' (*setri lazım gelen a'za*) or merely kept as *'avret*.[119] The Ottoman Turkish term *'avret* clearly carried different meanings and connotations, which might be why it was not consistently kept as such in translation. In the sixteenth and seventeenth centuries, *'avret* was the common term for an adult woman (at least in Istanbul and parts of Anatolia), and was the term used in court records to refer to a wife.[120] By the late nineteenth century, things had become more complicated. Some bilingual dictionaries claimed that while its first meaning was 'woman', it was no longer used as such and had acquired 'a negative connotation' and *karı* was the preferred term.[121] Others, such as the Turkish–English dictionary by Redhouse (1890 edition), provided as a first meaning

> the parts of the body which modesty requires to be concealed; in males, the body between the navel and the knees; in female slaves, the body from the waist to the knees, and the whole of the back; and in free women, the whole person, with the exception of the hands and the feet; the secret parts.

The fourth meaning was as a woman, and especially a wife – with an interesting twist in the pronunciation.[122] As for Şemsettin Sami's *Kamus-i Türki*, it defined *'avret* as

> the parts of the human body which are considered shameful to be seen or be shown, and being *haram* which should be covered in ritual prayer; there is a noble hadith that the leg (*bacak*) is considered *'avret*. 2. Colloquially pronounced *avrat*: woman (*karı, mer'e, zen*). 3. wife, spouse; eg. His wife died (*'avret i vefat etmiştir*).[123]

'*Awra* in the late nineteenth century could have different meanings in Arabic as well, including the parts of a human being's body that are covered out of prudeness, pride and shame, as well as referring euphemistically to a woman's sexual organs.[124] However, as used by Qasim Amin, it clearly refered to the parts of a woman's body that ought to be covered.

More generally, both translators were somewhat prude or reticent in translating the lexical field associated with pleasure and desire. Whether it was personal prudeness or having to pass the censor is a question which will have to remain unanswered. While Amin was quite explicitly referring to a husband's sexual enjoyment of marital rights and used the verb *yastamti'* (he enjoys), Asma'i erased any notion of enjoyment and replaced it by the more puritanical 'marital acts' (*ef'al-i zevciye*), and Mugamiz used the expression 'being in relations with women' (*kadınlar ile münasebatta bulunmaları*), the Ottoman circumlocution/euphemism referring to having a sexual relation.[125] The term *mata'*, which encompasses both pleasure and property ('and [God] has made the enjoyments of life (*mata' al-hayat*) common/shared between the two groups [men and women]') was turned by Mugamiz into 'the benefits of life' (*menafi'-i hayat*), and kept by Asma'i as 'the advantages/benefits of life' (*meta'-ı hayatı*).[126] And here, although Redhouse 1890 does not include the meaning of pleasure associated to *mata'/meta'* that is present in Amin's text, such a meaning would have been understandable for a readership familiar with the Qur'an, where the term and its derivatives appear multiple times – including in Surat al-Nisa', which is cited extensively in Amin's text.[127] Thus, not only did Mugamiz use a neutral term ('benefits') to refer to pleasure, including marital and sexual pleasure, but in this instance as well as others, he chose more secular terms, or at least terms without a specific Islamic connotation, whereas Asma'i kept the same terms as Amin.

Asma'i generally was more reticent in his translation of desire, attraction and debauchery. He provided a beautiful translation concerning the emotional facet of attraction, faithfully rendering Amin's 'she tended toward/was attracted to him with her heart' (*malat ilayhi bi qalbiha*) as 'she tended toward/was attracted to him from the soul of her heart' (*can-i gönülden meyl eder*), but omitted the much stronger *a'jabaha* (she was attracted to him/he causes her to be attracted to him). Differently, Mugamiz kept and translated the verb as 'her liking/being attracted to a man' (*bir adamı beğenerek*).[128] Elsewhere, Asma'i's urge to censor an explicit reference to debauchery made the translated sentence hard to understand and somewhat cryptic, since it translated 'debauched people' (*ahl al-khala'a*) as 'its people' (*erbabı*), and 'those who understand'.[129] Again, this was in stark contrast to Mugamiz, who was much more explicit and in fact amplified *ahl al-khala'a* into 'people of indecency and debauchery' (*erbab-ı fuhuş ve fücur*).[130] At the same time, Asma'i overstated the power of male desire and its deleterious effect on the intellect and morality. Amin employed fairly temperate formulations when arguing that those who supported the veiling of women 'from fear that men's desires may escape the control of their minds, and they may thus be tempted by any woman they see, however ugly or disfigured she be' were essentially arguing that women were stronger than men and more resistant to temptation, since handsome men were not asked to cover themselves. Asma'i rendered Amin's men 'losing the reins of their desire (*shahwa*) and being tempted by women' into the fear that man 'will have the reins of the passions of his carnal soul escape from the control of his intellect, and will straightaway descend into all kinds of corruption and sedition'.[131]

Overall, then, and outside of terms and expressions pertaining to sexuality, the terms for the basic conceptual blocks of *Tahrir al-mar'a* were overwhelmingly stable throughout the translations. At the same time, the two translations clearly differed in favouring certain terms or clearly avoiding others. It is hard to avoid the impression that Mugamiz opted for words that were strongly associated with the more secular part of the Young Turk revolution: he avoided *umma* and used *millet*; he used the term *inkılap* wherever he could, and he intensified the term *istibdad*, by adding an emphatic adjective to it. He also kept the term *inhitat*. In one instance, he even changed the original *mawt wa-ta'akhkhur* (death and backwardness) into *mevt ve inhitat* (death and decline), as part of his tendency to underline and 'dramatise' the level of stagnation and decline, and the need for movement, change and revolution. Asma'i, on the other hand, preferred to keep the term *umma*, and to use the Arabic echoes for terms such as *taghyir*. He seems to have refrained from using the term *inhitat* though it did appear a couple of times.[132]

At the same time, we do not wish to suggest that these choices were merely a reflection of ideological differences. After all, Asma'i was himself against Abdülhamid II's autocratic rule, was connected to publishing houses that were close to the Young Turks in Egypt, and seems to have rejoiced at the 1908 Revolution, or at least at the lifting of censorship that briefly accompanied it.[133] While we cannot offer any definite answers based on just two texts, one plausible hypothesis that additionally explains the difference in terms and expressions used by Asma'i and Mugamiz is that Cairene Ottoman Tukish differed from its Istanbuli counterpart, and that the Ottoman Turkish in the Arab provinces generally, and in Egypt specifically, was more 'Arabised', despite the fact that the language was becoming increasingly standardised throughout the Empire. Such regional variations most likely intersected and overlapped with the fluctuating and experimental nature of the language at a time when there was a strong drive among various intellectual groups to simplify the language in order to reach a much larger readership via periodicals and the printed text, as well as to Turkify it.

Thus, the translation of *Tahrir al-mar'a* shows how, when it came to the period under study – and probably well into the 1920s – much of the experimentation and many of the changes in Ottoman Turkish cannot simply be understood in terms of a binary between conservative, classical Ottoman Turkish on one hand, and Turkification, or even mere and linear simplification of the language, on the other. Indeed, Mugamiz's translation gives a taste of what sort of language was favoured by an editor and regular contributor to a number of Turkish periodicals that sought to reach a larger Turkish-reading audience, and someone who backed the Young Turks and referred his audiences to a great learned past among the scholars of 'Rum' (which by 1913, would have been understood to refer to Anatolia), in his preface to Amin's translated work. While his translation was more 'Turkish' and closer to modern Turkish than Asma'i's, Mugamiz also deployed recherché Arabic terms and expressions that were not in common use. And both Asma'i's and Mugamiz's translations strongly suggest that translation into Ottoman Turkish from Arabic texts played a crucial role in injecting or reinjecting specific Arabic words into Ottoman Turkish, and generally in experimenting with and expanding the Ottoman Turkish lexicon in this late Ottoman period.

Interventions into the Text: Mugamiz and the Injection of a Political Vocabulary

As alluded to earlier, Mugamiz's political colours began to show as early as the author's preface (*mukaddime*) where he intervened and modified Amin's first few lines. Such an intervention would have evidently not have been visible to unsuspecting regular readers who limited themselves to reading the translation. Mugamiz fleshed out Amin's preface by adding the term 'rights' (*hukuk*) after the word status or condition (*sha'n*) to Amin's sentence 'my goal is to draw attention to a subject that has been overlooked by many intellectuals, rather than to write a book that treats exhaustively the status of women and their place in human existence.'[134] More significantly perhaps, Mugamiz also inserted a sentence very early on: 'My purpose is merely to attract admonition and vigilance (*'ibret ve intibah*) about an important issue which has attracted the attention of very few men of reflection and discernment in our country.'[135] He also reordered some of the sentences, introducing Amin's argument about

Translating Qasim Amin's Tahrir al-mar'a into Ottoman Turkish

changing the nation earlier than in the original text, thus giving it a more prominent place.[136] He injected the term *inkılap* (revolution) as often as he could, translating the original *taghyir* (change) into *bir inkılab* (revolution), or *inkılap ve tahavvül* (revolution and transformation). In the conclusion of the author's preface, Mugamiz added revolutionary praxis to Amin's original reformist message, and to Amin's urging to 'a segment of the *umma*'s individuals that has a great influence on its society/totality (*majmu'iha*)' to partake in reforming our nation. Thus, in Mugamiz's invocation, the sentence becomes 'I request from the individuals with very great influence over the entire construct of the *millet* to extract the actual power of this revolution.'[137] In intervening in such a matter, Mugamiz thus invisibly trespassed into Amin's preface, and did so even more strikingly considering the brevity of his own preface, which de facto spilled into the author's, blurring the boundaries between author and translator.

Overall, Mugamiz seemed to take more liberties in translating Amin's preface, introduction, and conclusion than in the rest of the work – perhaps because Amin's authorial voice was strongest there, and the message more blatantly polemical and militant, whereas the rest of the work referred more to law and objective interpretations. Amin's scathing condemnation of the laziness and love of immobility or stillness of 'people like us', and the fact that 'we have neglected to use our minds to the point that they have become like a barren soil' was rendered even more strongly by Mugamiz, who magnified the criticism of 'our failures' and laziness by doubling key terms, some even more negative and critical than the original Arabic,[138] and emphasised the opposition to all good ideas, turning Amin's '[we show] opposition to all good thoughts/ideas' into 'we become enemies (*düşman kesiliyoruz*) to every good thought ... to every useful interpetation.'[139] One finds the same amplification of criticism, meant to rouse readers into action, in the conclusion, as Mugamiz translated Amin's original 'we have no excuse for holding on to them except ... that we were somnolent/neglectful (*innana ghafalna*) in our interests and putting order into our issues'[140] into the more potently critical 'this can not be ascribed to anything else but our own somnolence/ neglect and neglect' ('kendi gaflet ve ihmalimizden başka bir şeye haml olunamaz')[141] – whereas Asma'i toned it down, translating it into 'we have no excuse' (*ma'zur değiliz*) for 'embracing them with four hands'.[142] Mugamiz also transformed interests/benefits (*manafi'*) into national interests/benefits (*menafi'-i milliye*).[143] He also intervened in the passage where Amin defended himself against accusations of *bid'a* (innovation seen as unacceptable), adding a sentence which emphasised Amin's adherence to Islamic principles and values: 'this is not something contrary to the pure *shari'a*' ('şeri'at-i mutahhara-i islamiyeye muhalif bir şey değildir'), which he repeated in the following sentence as well ('this is not contrary to the *shari'a*'). Evidently, this is what Amin himself was arguing in this passage, but not as directly or insistently.[144] In other words, Mugamiz not only amplified the criticisms towards a national social class (Amin's 'people like us') – that is, an intellectual and social elite – for failing in its responsibility and task of protecting national interests; he also underlined once more that this critique was in line with the *shari'a*'s teachings. Thus, Mugamiz endorsed and magnified Amin's central message: namely, that the emancipation of women was an integral part of a larger reform project – political and economic – that was required from (Muslim) nations (in Amin's message, specifically Egypt), and where the major role had to be played by a specific educated class.

Jihad and its Different Uses

Mugamiz also intervened into the text and injected sentences into the author's introduction in ways that sought to rouse his readers even further in the name of protecting and developing the (Ottoman) nation and underlined even more boldly one of Amin's main premises – namely, that stasis equalled death. Amin, somewhat strikingly, evoked the Islamic concept of jihad quite a few times when referring to struggles taking place in Western countries. Perhaps controversially, he used a term that was simultaneously loaded with religious significance, but also more 'secularly' and neutrally used to mean 'struggle, effort', to describe the conditions of life and struggle in Western countries. He also kept the distinction between internal and external jihad (or what are conventionally considered the 'greater' and 'smaller' jihads). The original reads:

> The history of nations is full of disputes, arguments, and strife/brutality (*jilad*), and the wars that have erupted in order to establish the superiority of one idea or party/faction (*madhhab*) over another. During these encounters victory was sometimes for truth and other times for falsehood. And this was the situation in Islamic nations (*umam*) in the early days and the Middle Ages. This remains the case, and even more so, in Western countries, about which it is reasonable to state that life in it is a continuous jihad between truth and falsehood, between right and wrong: an internal jihad between the *umma*'s individuals in all branches of education the arts, and industries. And an external jihad among the various countries.[145]

Mugamiz kept all the references to jihad but modified them slightly. The first mention of a jihad, the continuous jihad (*mustamirr*) was amplified into a 'continual and perpetual jihad' (*cihat-i müstemir ve mustedim*).[146] He slightly modified the second, internal jihad (*dakhili*) into 'internally ... there is a jihad' (*dahilan ... bir cihat mevcuttur*), and translated the third jihad, *jihad khariji*, as 'externally as well nations in strife (*jihad*) with each other, it is as if they get at each other's throat' ('Haricen de milletler birbirleriyle cihatta 'adeta boğaz boğaza gelirler'). Might this suggest that concepts of *jihad dakhili* and *jihad khariji* and the distinction between them, were not (as) widespread or commonly used in Ottoman Turkish in the late nineteenth and early twentieth centuries? Perhaps.[147] Nonetheless, following Amin's model, Mugamiz did not feel the need to confine the use of the term jihad to Islamic societies, but also ascribed it to Western countries, and secularised it.[148] More so, Mugamiz's rendering of what the Arabic original simply described as 'an external *jihad* among the various countries' into 'it is as if they get at each other's throat' injects greater violence into the confrontation between various nations/countries. In fact, Mugamiz went even further in his intervention into the text here by adding a couple of sentences: 'Actually, the active life is always in a state of awareness and action. There is no state of stillness, no inertia of death' ('Zaten zinde hayat da'ima hal-i intibah ve fa'aliyette bulunur. Hal-i sükun, 'atalet-i mevt yoktur'). He also slightly expanded the passage of the various inventions which have increased speed and reduced distance, part of Amin's argument and the reference to jihad. After Amin's sentence 'these days those who wander around every side of the globe are counted in the thousands', Mugamiz interjected that 'in the present era this confrontation and struggle has taken a more steely, a more violent and active form' ('"asr–ı hazırda bu cidal ve cihat daha ahenin, daha şeddid ve zinde bir şekil almıştır'). Here, Mugamiz repeated the term *cihat* or *cidal ve cihat* a few times in a couple of sentences. As a consequence, the translated passage became even more forceful, more understandable in terms of its argumentation on the pervasive presence and multiple shapes of jihad.[149]

In contast, Asma'i clearly shied away from using the term jihad, and only did so in the context of an external jihad among the various countries. He omitted the first and second references to jihad, turning the sentence into some form of a quotation, with quotation marks and with a passive subject, and translating the internal jihad as 'an internal war is prevailing' (*bir harb-i dahili hükümfermadır*), and he only kept Amin's third reference to jihad, translating it faithfully (but doubling *umam* into *ümem ve akvam*). In other words, Asma'i refrained from using it more 'holistically' and secularly, and somewhat controversially perhaps, as Amin did, and applying it to western countries. This seems to be the only difference between Amin's text and Asma'i's translation of this passage. Otherwise, Asma'i faithfully translated what Amin was saying and did not add extra sentences.[150]

Mugamiz's decision to keep the term jihad, and even to expand on it, was symptomatic of a larger trend within Ottoman Turkish as well as Ottoman Arab society. As Mustafa Aksakal has argued, 'the concept of jihad occupied a quotidian place in the Ottoman cultural register, and its motley everyday presence.' It signified 'a generic call for marshalling all-out effort in the face of great challenges', and was not uncommonly used as such. More so, it was used in this larger sense by non-Muslims as well. Drawing from Ussama Makdisi's work, Aksakal reminds us that 'in the Ottoman world one did not even have to be Muslim to wage "jihad"' and that the same term was used by the Maronite patriarch in Mount Lebanon in the 1820s, who 'saw his church fighting a "struggle" [in the original: jihad] with all our power against those Biblemen [Protestant missionaries from the United States]'.[151] Jihad was thus a term that could be, and was, deployed beyond the confines of Islamic theology, and 'in the more secularized (but still religiously salient and resonant) sense'[152] that was gaining ground in the early twentieth century. That Asma'i generally shied away from using it indicates a more purist interpretation of the term, and a certain strictness regarding what he deemed to be the proper use of religious terms.

Accentuating Women's Deplorable State and Underlining the Inevitability of Change

Mugamiz also magnified Amin's critiques of current practices in passages describing women's seclusion and women's decline. Amin's sentence on how 'our inclination and proclivity' ('our inclination and weakness' in Mugamiz, *rağbet ve inhimakimiz*)[153] has led us to spoil 'the health of our women' and how 'we make them live at home between four walls, deprived of air, sun and any sort of physical or intellectual exercise', was upended, by Mugamiz, in a particularly harsh sentence: 'Indeed, we keep the poor wretches in a state of being buried all alive' ('Hatta biçareleri diri diri gömülmüş bir halde bulunduruyoruz').[154] He also rendered Amin's already provocative question 'what has the hijab (actually) done?' ('ma al-ladhi fa'ala al-hijab . . .?') – the answer being: not much, or nothing particularly good – into: 'And yet, what sort of benefits and goodness obtain from full covering and seclusion, one wonders?' ('Ma'mafih tesettürden 'acaba ne gibi *feva'it* ve muhsinat hasıl oluyor?'). He thereby rhetorically exaggerated the lack of positive consequences of *tesettür*.[155]

Translating Qasim Amin's Tahrir al-mar'a into Ottoman Turkish

In another passage, Mugamiz rendered Amin's 'strong decline' (*inhitat shadid*) of women today (Egyptian/Muslim women) into 'our women are in a deplorable and dreadful decline today' ('kadınlarımız elyevm elim ve müdhiş bir inhitat içinde').[156] As for Amin's earlier sentence, in which he scolded his readers by rhetorically asking them, 'have we done anything to improve the condition of women?', Mugamiz injected it with a more forceful, galvanising terminology, translating improvement (*tahsin*) as reform (*islah*),[157] and introducing a possessive so as to change Amin's 'women' into 'our' women (that is, 'the women of us, men', as well as 'the women of our nation').[158] Mugamiz also magnified Amin's argument that 'it is not easy (*la yashal*) nowadays for a husband to rule over his wife the way he would have forty years ago', by adding that such a thing was now 'unimaginable' ('bugün de o yolda mu'amele ve tahakkümde bulunmasına imkan tasavvur olunamaz').[159] He also described the men who resisted the lessening of heavy seclusion as declaring rebellion or mutiny (*'isyan*) against this inevitable situation – adopting the very loaded and negative term of *'isyan* that Amin did not use.[160] He thus further emphasised that change in the way wives should be treated was dramatic and necessary, and that a completely different worldview had set in, marking a profound rupture between past and present. This was also in line with Mugamiz's deep belief in the inevitability of progress and change, which appears in a number of interventions throughout the text – and which again is part of a specific worldview adopted by a number of Young Turks, especially those inspired by various Darwinian and social Darwinist theorists who viewed society as a biological system that has to change and evolve or else die.[161]

Finally, and most profoundly, Mugamiz shifted Amin's argument in the conclusion on the needs and necessities of the *umma* as far as women are concerned, to focusing on 'serving the elevation and progress of our women' (*kadınlarımızın te'ali ve terakkisine hadim olarak*).[162] Here as well, Mugamiz injected key concepts of the 1908 revolution: *te'ali* and *terakki*. But more revolutionary perhaps is that by doing so, Mugamiz seemed to suggest moving beyond Amin's functionalist argument (espoused by most other male writers of the period) that framed girls' education and women's emancipation as a necessary condition for strengthening the nation. This does not seem out of line with the little we know about Mugamiz. Indeed, almost twenty years earlier, a certain Zaki M. from Istanbul, who was almost certainly Zaki Mugamiz, had written an op-ed piece entitled 'Will Women Demand All Men's Rights?' to the Cairene periodical *al-Hilal* in which he argued that 'women have clearly demonstrated both their skills and intellectual abilities and therefore can demand "all the rights of men".'[163]

If Mugamiz tended to amplify Amin's criticisms of the current status quo and practices in Muslim societies (especially Egypt), Asma'i leaned toward watering down some of the author's forceful wordings and argumentation.[164] For instance, Asma'i excised Amin's sentence 'if our women are/were imprisoned, secluded/veiled' (*mahbusat mahjubat*), which suggests that he recoiled from the strength of 'imprisoned' (*mahpusat*) specifically.[165] He also omitted a sentence describing women making leaps and catching up with men in certain societies,[166] and excised Amin's half-sentence on 'the seclusion/imprisonment of women behind the hijab and locks/locked doors' (*qasr al-nisa' wara' al-hijab wa'l-aqfal*).[167] At times, Asma'i even demoted or slighted women and somewhat downgraded Amin's demands for them, in the passages where Amin advocated the good treatment and respect of women and/or deplored its lack: for example, the 'good treatment [of women] in the marital treatment of wives' (*husn al-mu'amala fi mu'asharat al-nisa'*), became merely 'the tending toward good marital treatment' (*hüsn-i mu'aşerete meyl*). Why would Asma'i omit the word *mu'amala* (treatment)? Perhaps because it could also mean sexual intercourse in Ottoman slang, according to Redhouse. Nonetheless, other equivalent terms could have been used.[168] Finally, in an instance where the Arabic original (interestingly and unusually) referred to 'their men' (that is, the women's men, *rijalihim*), Asma'i eliminated the possessive and simply translated it as 'men' (*erkekler*)[169] – in a telling reversal, given how often he translated Amin's 'women' into 'our women'.

Asma'i also seemed particularly concerned to tone down Amin's fierce attacks on what he viewed as the corruption of Islam. He made sure to name those in a position of authority when it came to Islamic knowledge, turning Amin's vague 'whoever knew it [Islam]' into ulama, the specific term for religious scholars.[170] In the same passage, he diluted Amin's strong condemnation of that which 'corrupts and disfigures/deforms it [Islam]' (*tufsiduhu wa-tamsakhuhu*), removing 'deforms' altogether and subtituting it by 'empties it into another mould' (*diğer bir kalıba ifrağ eyler*). Significantly, Mugamiz also toned down this harsh condemnation, opting to replace 'disfigurement' by the more neutral 'change' (*tağyir*).[171]

Footnotes as Paratext

If all these interventions were invisibly woven into Amin's text for the unsuspecting reader, a few others were clearly marked as the translator's addition onto the original text in the form of footnotes. On top of the few footnotes already present in Amin's text, which both translators kept and translated, Asma'i added fairly lengthy footnotes, and made sure to sign them as '*mütercim*', thus candidly inserting himself as a researcher, intellectual and author, not just as mere translator. Thus, in a footnote he inserted about Amin's reference to his rebuttal (*reddiye*) in French of a book by the Duke d'Harcourt, Asma'i explained that following his visit to Cairo, the Duc d'Harcourt had written a book in which he had ranted and raved (*atmış tutmuş*) about Muslim women, causing Amin to write a rebuttal, published in Cairo in 1894. Asma'i went out of his way to praise Amin's book for being 'seriously, carefully written and filled with clear evidence in defence of our customs'.[172] In another passage, Amin had noted that the contemporary practice of prohibiting women from coming out on the streets was on the decline, even within families who insisted on a full cover for their women, and that, in the past, women who needed to travel were transported at night so that no one would see them. Asma'i inserted a footnote 'updating' this information and reporting that 'in Cairo, until very recently, the bride was transported from her paternal house to the abode of her spouse at night, whereas the custom is still current among some families in Alexandria.'[173] Such an intervention suggests that Asma'i was keen to position himself as a good observer of contemporary Egyptian practices, and thus, again, as a reliable and authoritative witness and analyst of contemporary matters.

Elsewhere, a long footnote was added following Amin's passage describing women not being able to see or hear or learn much because of covering and veiling (*tesettür ve ihticap*), and their imprisonment in a small area with a curtain drawn between them and the world of life, thought, movement and action. Asma'i here seemingly quoted – in Ottoman Turkish and without quotation marks – from an Arabic book written in rebuttal of Amin, entitled *Tarbiyat al-mar'a wa'l-hijab* ('The education of women and covering/seclusion') which argued that the 'natural' duty of women was to bring up children and keep busy within the confines of their house, and severely restricting, even outright banning contact with men when on non-domestic duties.[174] All of this was for the protection of women's propriety and health (*muhafaza-i 'iffet ve sıhhati*). The quotation ended with a dire warning, entirely contrary to Amin's points: 'Women do not find freedom with the abandoning of covering and veiling and do not complete the education and learning they have already acquired.'[175] Although these sentences seem to summarise quite accurately the author Tal'at Harb's argument, they are not a direct quotation, or even a direct summary of Harb's sentences on page 122 (as specified in Asma'i's note). This suggests either that Asma'i was using another edition with different pagination, or that he rather translated and summarised the gist of Harb's critique of Amin's book, while possibly adding on top of this his own interpretation. It is unclear whether Asma'i agreed with Harb's critique, but the overall effect of these footnotes was indeed to challenge and somewhat undermine some of Amin's main arguments.

Again, at the end of the sections on *Tesettür ve İhticap* and *Kadın ve Ümmet* Asma'i felt the need to insert a very long footnote that picked up a point he had made in his own preface. He stated that these two sections were the target of the refutations. 'As the issue of *tesettür* and *ihticap* was considered to be a solely religious one,' Asma'i rather diplomatically wrote, 'it was defended in full force and with all available means, and there even were impetuous outburst which, in such a serious debate, opted for power rather than reason.' The objectors forcefully claimed that besides the *shari'a* requirements for veiling, women should be covered much more than was currently the norm even if the *shari'a* did not require it. Asma'i continued in a rather exasperated tone:

> Those who claim that the defence of honour and shame should be with shawl and overgarment much more so than with training and education (Muhafaza-yı 'ırz ve namusun ta'lim ve terbiyeden ziyade çarla çarşafla), grumble and snarl at the section on 'Women and the nation' [to the point where they are] as good as crossing it off with a pen (ceff el-kalem denecek bir surette dır etmişlerdir).

He then concluded his intervention by making it clear he felt obliged, as a dutiful translator, to express his views as he deplored the lack of dignity of the refutations, which should not have descended into impetuousness.[176] Finally, Asma'i added a rider footnote at the end of the chapter on polygyny and divorce, again stating that strong refutations concerning these topics had been published. Giving two titles of Arabic works, he claimed that he saw no need to say anything else as the matters were considered as 'solely religious' (*Bahis sırf dini i'tibar edildiği için*). He directed those 'wishing to investigate the issue' to read them themselves.[177]

By contrast, Mugamiz limited himself to translating the original footnotes, with two small exceptions. First, he added a footnote explaining how a specific expression got translated into Turkish: 'In Turkish, instead of these expressions (*ta'birat*), words like the following are used: "Your will is in your hand, I have released the binding on your leg, I have set you loose (*boşadım*)".'[178] Second, he very slightly expanded on an existing footnote by providing a bit more information on the nature of the source itself.[179] He thus sought to make himself as invisible as possible as a translator, while as we have seen, he in fact intervened in subtle but important ways in the text itself – perhaps more so that Asma'i.

Translations and Explanations of Qur'anic Verses

Finally, the last, and perhaps most important, difference between Asma'i's and Mugamiz's translations was in their handling of *Tahrir al-mar'a*'s Qur'anic passages. While both reproduced the Arabic original, Asma'i also provided a translation for all of them, whereas Mugamiz did not – with one exception.[180] This is quite striking, given that Mugamiz would (anonymously) publish a first fascicule of what was apparently a prepared full translation of the Qur'an the following year. One of the reasons – if not the main one – for not including any translations must have been Mugamiz's belonging to the Christian faith. It is understandable that he would therefore proceed with extreme caution when it came to the question of translating Qur'anic verses. Nonetheless, this might not have been the entire story. Indeed, as Brett Wilson's work has shown, the beginning of the twentieth century saw fierce debates between those advocating the translation of the Qur'an into Ottoman Turkish and their opponents. There were many circulating summaries of Qur'anic verses, in manuscript form as well as printed, and specific periodicals, especially *Sırat-i Müstakim*, had in fact started publishing excerpts of Qur'anic translation without labelling them as such.[181] The question of the untranslatability of the Qur'an, and the exclusive position that Arabic occupied within Islam, raged in the pages of periodicals such as *Sebilürreşad* and also in Rashid Rida's highly influential *al-Manar* (Cairo 1898–1935).[182] Thus, whether or not to translate the Qur'an – even, for some, mere verses of it – was a point of contention. And Mugamiz, knowing how controversial *Tahrir al-mar'a* had been and probably still was by the time he translated it, and knowing that he would be 'marked' for translating it (as well as feted, in certain circles), and the translation itself scrutinised, might have decided not to attract even greater attention to himself by translating the Qur'anic verses. Another, related hypothesis is that he did not want to leave any traces that might help identify him as the anonymous translator of the Qur'an in 1914.[183]

Asma'i, on the other hand, seems to have had no such anxieties (or qualms), since he translated all the Qur'anic passages, at times even inserting added explanations.[184] Overall, his rendition of the Qur'anic passage combined literal translation with derivatives of the same roots as the Arabic original with non-literal yet faithful renditions and outright explicatory periphrastic additions. It is clear that Asma'i was following a given *tafsir* tradition and this is what guided the explications. The source of *tafsir* (in at least one case, but most likely elsewhere) was most likely Bereketzade's, whom, as mentioned earlier, Asma'i had encouraged to pen *Ihticap* in response to *Tahrir al-mar'a*, which he himself subsequently translated from Ottoman Turkish into Arabic. Asma'i's translation into 'Turkish' (*Türkçesi*) of a fairly long verse from Surat al-Nur, on *tesettür*, interpreted in simple Turkish a whole set of detailed information on what was meant by ornamentation (*zina*), including the permissibility of a range of jewellery (the foot bracelet, *khilkhal*, seemed to have particularly preoccupied him). The translation also omitted lines that listed male relatives, but added an anthropological explanation regarding maternal uncles: 'For the Arabs, the maternal uncle is like a father.'[185] Here, Asma'i inserted, verbatim, Bereketzade's *tefsir* for parts of this sura.[186] Rather unfortunately for Asma'i, sticking to the original Arabic roots brought him into dangerous territory and probably caused him to commit a serious faux pas, as far as the use of the Arabic term *farj* was concerned, whose usage in Ottoman was on the whole restricted to the female private parts and the vulva in particular.[187]

Similarly, Asma'i clearly inserted a commentary in the verses from Surat al-Baqara 228: 'As their spouses have rights over them, those women have rights of chastity/propriety and protection (*'iffet ve siyanette*) over their spouses.'[188] More so, in translating the short excerpts from Surat al-Nisa', Asma'i again relied on a commentary and interpreted the verse: 'Treat your women with good manners and soft words' ('nisanızla hüsn-i hulk ve kavl-i leyin ile mu'aşeret ediniz'), and in al-Nisa' 21 likewise he explained the excerpt as 'in doing the required in the acceptance of the marriage contract that woman has made a strong pledge and guarantee with you', without echoing any of the Arabic roots.[189] In another section of Surat al-Nisa', he provided a small amplification. Where the Qur'an reads: 'But turn not altogether away (from one), leaving her as in suspense', Asma'i spelled out the meaning in colloquial style: 'Now, do not fully incline towards the one of your spouses for whom you have affection, and do not leave the one for whom you have no affection without any of the acts of marriage and without divorce.'[190] Interestingly, Asma'i's translation here contains not one but two minor trespasses of Turkish syntax of which even native speakers can be guilty at times.[191]

As for Mugamiz, he did not completely refrain from intervening in the passages containing Qur'anic verses, but did so more obliquely. For instance, when Amin adduced a verse from Qur'an 2.26 ('Thus He causes many to go astray just as He directs many to the Right Way')[192], Mugamiz first made the argument a little more polemical than in the original, rhetorically rephrasing Amin's argument with a slight addition: 'Fine, let us suppose that an aspect of science and knowledge may produce damage. Such a fear cannot serve as an obstacle to the acquisition and exchange of

Translating Qasim Amin's Tahrir al-mar'a *into Ottoman Turkish*

science and knowledge.' Then, after citing the Qur'anic verse in Arabic, he spelled out Amin's line of thinking and drew the startling conclusion that Amin and Asma'i with him had shied away from: 'If it happens that God humiliates the depraved sinners with His own Qur'an of exhalted fame, would it be right to consider the Qur'an as leading people astray?'[193]

Both translators, though, chose to translate the longer hadiths,[194] as well as the explanations/commentaries of the Hanafi jurist and mufti Ibn 'Abidin (AH 1198–1252/1783–1836 CE), which figured prominently in Amin's argumentation regarding marriage and divorce. Here as well, Asma'i's translations of the Ibn 'Abidin passages were infused with commentaries. For all that his style and diction became more colloquial and colourful with the examples he provided from *tafsir*, he remained faithful to the opaque and elliptical style of the original Arabic. In one particularly long passage by Ibn 'Abidin,[195] he fleshed out 'hanging hair' into 'curls, locks and the like', and shifted between echoing the Arabic roots (for instance, translating 'fear of sedition' into *fitne havfi*) and, at other times, resorting to the vernacular and clear Turkish.[196] For instance, after translating *'awra* into *'avret*, Asma'i added the explanation 'in other words, grass parts (*ot yeri*) whose discovery is not allowed' (*'avreti ya'ni keşfi ca'iz olmayan ot yeridir*). This is quite a colloquial and idiomatic expression, and Asma'i also exaggerated the point as his syntax is such that it sounds as if Ibn 'Abidin was claiming that the whole body of a woman is 'grass parts' (which was certainly not Ibn 'Abidin's argument). Most uncharacteristically, it must be stressed, he engaged in a rare (and unique?) serious misunderstanding as his omission of the voice (*savt*), within Ibn 'Abidin's discussion of what constituted *'awra* or did not, confused this entire point, thus making it virtually impossible to grasp.[197] It is most likely that he was innocently confused, probably because he missed out the reference to *savt*, rather than attempting to doctor the orginal text.[198] At times, Asma'i's use of Turkish verbs is a little problematic as well, making the text ambiguous or unclear.[199] That being said, it is not far-fetched to suggest that Asma'i might have committed a Freudian slip here, in the sense that his confusion, omission or 'misreading' (if this is what it was) not coincidentally pertains to women's sexuality and more generally desire – a topic which Asma'i especially seemed particularly uncomfortable translating.

In contrast to Asma'i's translation of parts of Ibn 'Abidin, which is sometimes difficult to follow or outright wrong for these passages (granted that parts of Ibn 'Abidin's writings are elliptical and not straightforward for the uninitiated), Mugamiz's translation made them crystal clear. One such passage which is particularly well translated reads as follows (in translation):

When a suspicion of lust/passion occurs it is not permitted to look at the face of either women or beardless youths.[200] If there is no suspicion of desire/passion then it is permitted (*müsa'ade*) to look at the face of a woman even if she might be beautiful.[201]

Nonetheless, Mugamiz also elided certain concepts: for instance, he avoided the loaded term for sedition (*fitne*) and modified it into 'attraction and fascination' (*incizap ve meftuniyet*), as he consistently did throughout the text.

Reception of the Two Translations

Having done a granular analysis of the translations themselves, let us now turn to the question of these translations' reception. Evidently, this is a question that may be more adequately addressed in future, when the large corpus of digitised Ottoman Turkish books and periodicals become fully searchable. At this point, though, it seems that direct references to the translations were scant. Asma'i's translation of *Tahrir al-mar'a* was mentioned in a 1909 article in *İçtihat*, but interestingly, the passages reproduced verbatim from Amin's book were clearly much more 'Turkish' than Asma'i's translation. And since the article also mentioned the Tatar translation, they were most likely taken from there. Nonetheless, Asma'i's translation was praised, and Asma'i himself was referred to as 'our dear friend'.[202]

At least one book in Ottoman Turkish did mention *Tahrir al-mar'a*, and even quoted directly from it. The influential intellectual Celal Nuri referred to *Tahrir al-mar'a* in his 1913 book *Kadınlarımız* ('Our women').[203] Evidently, he summarised some of the book's main arguments, and followed the sequence of authoritative religious references provided by Amin's work. However, here too, the translation does not match Asma'i's – and it most likely preceded Mugamiz's translation, since the author dated the completion of his book to Mart 1329 (March 1913). Nuri might have read Amin in Arabic and done his own translation; or, again, he might have relied on the Tatar Turkish translation of 1908. While there were references to the Turkish translations of *Tahrir al-mar'a* in the Arabic press, they did not comment on the quality of the translation.[204] We are yet to find references to Mugamiz's translation of *Tahrir al-mar'a* in the Ottoman Turkish press. Some of his other translations, of Zaydan's various works, and most especially of the Qur'an, gathered a great deal of attention and, in the latter case, attacks. But this is another matter.

Translating Qasim Amin's Tahrir al-mar'a *into Ottoman Turkish*

Finally, and perhaps most importantly, there was an order issued in 1910 banning *Tahrir al-mar'a* in Ottoman lands, because of 'its harmful contents' (*mündericat-ı muzırrasına bina'en*).²⁰⁵ The document did not specifically mention whether the ban applied to the Arabic version or a translated version. However, according to an essay by the Turco-Egyptian writer Wali al-Din Yakan, Asma'i's translation of *Tahrir al-mar'a* was banned in the Ottoman Empire at some point after the 1908 revolution. Yakan described Yusuf Semih Bey (that is, Asma'i) as

> one of the Free Ottomans who emigrated from his country ... and served [Egypt] loyally and it rewarded him sincerely. Thus, when the nation pulled out its liberty from the hands of its [robbers] and the people were [blessed with] a new age and a clear future, he decided to [endow] his friends of the Turkish race with a [precious] letter grouping the fragments of wisdom, that is the book *Tahrir al-mar'a* written by the free scholar, the late Qasim Bey Amin. He translated it into Turkish in the most beautiful style, but the Meclis-i Vukela in Istanbul issued a decree forbidding its entry to the Ottoman realm, and we learned that the government took this unjust measure to please the fanatic [group/party]. In other words, this is a ... pen, whose will/voice the free government wants to [break], and the constitution is subject to will, one day [deemed the object of divine inspiration], the other day being copied and abandoned, may God fight [whims].²⁰⁶

This might have been the main reason behind Mugamiz's translation: namely, after 1910, Asma'i's was no longer available, certainly not in Istanbul and the rest of the Ottoman provinces outside of Egypt. At some point, the ban on the original book must have been lifted, since Mugamiz managed to publish his translation. Why he (or whoever might have been behind the decision to translate and publish this work) decided to do so precisely in 1913 is a question that we cannot answer. Another mystery concerns Qasim Amin's other work, *al-Mar'a al-jadida*, which came out in 1900. Rather surprisingly, only a Tatar Turkish translation of it came out. Asma'i, in his preface, had stated that he had asked Amin for permission to translate both his works, and that Amin granted it to him. Perhaps he decided against translating *al-Mar'a al-jadida*, which was deemed to be even more controversial than *Tahrir al-mar'a*, after seeing the attacks (alluded to in Yakan's essay) on his translation? Or he might have translated it but it never got published, for similar reasons.

Another unanswered question is whether Mugamiz's rendering was a reworking of Asma'i's translation. While Mugamiz did not mention Asma'i's translation in his preface, a number of identical or near-identical turns of phrase make it likely that he had seen Asma'i's version. For instance, in at least one case, Mugamiz clearly reworded Asma'i's addition to the Arabic original.[207]

Yet Mugamiz was definitely not basing his translation on Asma'i's. This is made clear, for instance, in that he 'reclaimed' and translated a sentence that Asma'i had most probably unintentionally skipped.[208] After all, it is quite plausible that Mugamiz had gotten hold of a copy of Asma'i's translation, given his strong connection to Egypt. He had been the correspondent for two major Egyptian periodicals based in Istanbul, and he was close to a number of Egyptian intellectuals, including Zaydan. This is yet another question that awaits further investigation. If we could locate the private libraries and manuscripts of these two central, yet greatly understudied, translators and authors of the late Ottoman period, we would know more about what we can already see as the central role of translator intellectuals in the major issues of the time.

We wish to thank the editors and Francesca Orsini for their suggestions.

Notes

1. See, for instance, Muhammad 'Imara, who claims that the book was the most famous Arabic book of its time that triggered the first 'great intellectual battle that a book had caused since the beginning of the nahda'. Muhammad 'Imara, *Qasim Amin wa-tahrir al-mar'a* (Cairo: Dar al-Hilal, 1980), 136. See also Marilyn Booth, '*Woman in Islam*: Men and the "Women's Press" in Turn-of-the-century Egypt', *International Journal of Middle East Studies* 33: 2 (2001): 171–201.
2. Ibrahim Ramzi, 'Al-mar'a fi'l-Islam 1: Mas'alatuna al-hadira', *al Mar'a fi'l Islam* 1 (1901): 6, quoted and translated in Booth, 'Woman in Islam', 177.
3. Lisa Pollard, *Nurturing the Nation: The Family Politics of Modernizing, Colonizing and Liberating Egypt, 1805–1923* (Berkeley: University of California Press, 2005), 153.
4. For a good summary of Amin's book, see Albert Hourani, *Arabic Thought in the Liberal Age, 1798–1939* (Cambridge: Cambridge University Press, 1983), 164–7. For analysis and critiques of *Tahrir al-mar'a*, see Leila Ahmed, *Women and Gender in Islam: Historical Roots of a Modern Debate* (New Haven: Yale University Press, 1992); Marilyn Booth, 'Woman in Islam'; Lisa Pollard, *Nurturing the Nation*, esp. 152–65; Beth Baron, *The Women's Awakening in Egypt: Culture, Society, and the Press* (New Haven: Yale University Press, 1994). For an analysis of discourses that predated Amin's text, and that also tackled similar issues and commented on gender practices, see Marilyn Booth, 'Before Qasim Amin: Writing Women's History in 1890s Egypt', in Marilyn Booth and Anthony Gorman (eds), *The Long 1890s in Egypt: Colonial Quiescence, Subterranean Resistance* (Edinburgh: Edinburgh University Press, 2015), 365–98. Booth argues that

'in one way or another, by the mid-1890s, "women and the nation" already constituted a ramified discourse' (365).
5. Booth, *'Woman in Islam'*, 178.
6. According to Ahmed, 'The book is reckoned to have triggered the first major controversy in the Arabic press: more than thirty books and articles appeared in response to its publication. The majority were critical, though the book did please some readers, notably members of the British administration and pro-British factions,' Ahmed, *Women and Gender in Islam*, 162. See also Pollard, *Nurturing the Nation*, 153.
7. See Wali al-Din Yakan, *al-Tajarib* (Cairo: Mu'assasat Hindawi, 2012), 7.
8. The few exceptions include the work of Ceyhun Arslan, as well as the contributions to this volume.
9. Monica Katiboğlu, 'Specters and Circulation of Meaning: Edebiyat-ı Cedide on Modern Literary Language', *Comparative Studies of South Asia, Africa and the Middle East* 40: 2 (2020): 361–71; 362.
10. Beth Baron, 'The making of the Egyptian nation', in Ida Bloom, Karen Hagemann and Catherine Hall (eds), *Gendered Nations: Nationalisms and Gender Order in the Long Nineteenth Century* (London: Bloomsbury, 2000), 137–58; 137–8.
11. Booth, *'Woman in Islam'*, 174.
12. İlham Khuri-Makdisi, 'The Nahda, Translation Movements between Ottoman Turkish and Arabic, and Bilingualism, 1860–1914', unpublished paper delivered at the Middle East Studies Association Annual Conference, November 2019. This is part of an ongoing book project on translations between Arabic and Ottoman Turkish. It is also telling that three of the chapters in this edited volume deal with 'the woman question' in translation between Arabic and Ottoman Turkish.
13. İrvin Cemil Schick, 'Print Capitalism and Women's Sexual Agency in the Late Ottoman Empire', *Comparative Studies of South Asia, Africa and the Middle East*, 31: 1 (2011): 196–216; 207.
14. For instance, Fatma Aliye's work, the subject of Booth and Shissler's chapter.
15. See Maha AbdelMegeed and Ebru Akçasu's chapter in this volume on Muhammad Farid Wajdi's book.
16. To give a sense of how central 'the woman question' was, and how interconnected it was with translation, one of the first contributions of the prominent intellectual Mehmet Akif to the periodical *Sırat-ı Müstakim* was a translation of Muhammad Farid Wajdi's seventeen-part essay on women in Islam (*Müslüman Kadını* 1: 13–9 (November-December 1908). See Hasan Kayalı, 'Islam in the Thought and Politics of Two Late Ottoman Intellectuals: Mehmed Akif and Said Halim', *Archivum Ottomanicum* 19 (2001): 307–33 n. 17.
17. See also Abdullah Cemaleddin Bereketzade, *İhticap* (Cairo: Terakki Matba'ası, 1318/1901). Bereketzade wrote this short book, in Ottoman

Turkish, on the encouragement of none other than Asma'i, who then immediately translated it into Arabic the same year: Abdullah Cemaleddin Bereketzade, *al-Ihtijab* (trans. Asma'i) (Cairo: Matba'at al-taraqqi, 1318/1901).

18. C. Ceyhun Arslan, 'Entanglements between the Tanzimat and al-Nahdah: Jurji Zaydan between *Tarihkh adab al-lughah al-turkiyyah* and *Tarikh adab al-lughah al-'arabiyya*', *Journal of Arabic Literature* 50 (2019): 288–324.
19. We are borrowing Helen Pfeifer's felicitous expression to describe the engagement between sixteenth-century intellectual circles in Istanbul and the Arab provinces. Helen Pfeifer, 'Encounter after the Conquest: Scholarly Gatherings in 16th-century Ottoman Damascus', *International Journal of Middle East Studies* 47: 2 (2015): 219–39; 228.
20. Arslan, 'Entanglements between the Tanzimat and al-Nahdah', 303.
21. 1329, which refers to 1329 Rumi, which corresponds to 1913 CE While 'Rumi' was not specified on the cover of the work, the references to the translation in articles, such as on the pages of *al-Hilal* and other periodicals, make it clear that the book appeared in 1913 and not 1911 (which would have been AH 1329). Asma'i's translation has both the Hijri and the Justinian calendar date typed on the front page: 1908 [CE] and AH 1326.
22. According to Ekmeleddin İhsanoğlu, 'some state that he hailed from Adana and that his original name was Adanalı Yusuf Ziya Effendi, and he used also to sign his name Yusuf Samih'; Ekmeleddin Ihsanoğlu, *The Turks in Egypt and their Cultural Legacy* (Cairo: American University in Cairo Press, 2012), 236. A similar claim is made in Mehmet Tahir Bursalı, *Osmanlı Müellifleri 1299–1915* (Istanbul: Meral Yayınları, n.d. [1971]), 293.
23. İhsanoğlu, *Turks in Egypt*, 235.
24. İhsanoğlu, *Turks in Egypt*, 236.
25. See note 17 above. From *al-Ihtijab*'s introduction, it seems that Bereketzade had tasked Asma'i with doing so while he was ill. Bereketzade passed away in 1318 (1901), which is probably why Asma'i translated and/or published so many of his writings then.
26. İhsanoğlu, *Turks in Egypt*, 236.
27. Yakan (*al-Tajarib*, 7) referred to him c. 1910 as an attaché to the Ministry of War in Cairo.
28. 'Al-Hudud bayna Misr wa'l-Sham', *al-Hilal* 15 (1 December 1906): 173–6.
29. Johann Strauss, 'Who Read What in the Ottoman Empire (19th–20th Centuries)?', *Middle Eastern Literatures* 6: 1 (2003): 39–76; 73–4, n. 170.
30. Khayreddin al-Zirikli, *al-A'lam* (Beirut: Dar al-'ilm li'l-malayin, 1992), III, 48.
31. The first instalment was published in 1911/12; the translated volumes appeared 1912–14.
32. *Al-Hilal* 19 (1 October 1910), 60–1. Zaydan's *History of Islamic Civilization* had created quite a lot of commotion in the Arab and Ottoman worlds. It was criticised by influential Muslim thinkers for relying on and reproducing

Orientalist historiography, and following a periodisation of Islamic history set by Orientalist scholarship. Contemporary critics as well as modern ones have 'condemned [Zaydan's] reliance on Orientalist historical narratives that ultimately desacralize Islamic history and naturalize its figures'. Zeina Halabi, *The Unmaking of the Arab Intellectual: Prophecy, Exile and the Nation* (Edinburgh: Edinburgh University Press, 2017), 44. See also Anne-Laure Dupont's magisterial biography of Zaydan, *Gurgi Zaydan (1861–1914): Ecrivain réformiste et témoin de la Renaissance arabe* (Paris: IFPO 2006).

33. According to İhsanoğlu, 'Six of them were literary, three dealt with the political situation of the day, one was a medical dictionary, one was on sociology, one was on psychology, and the last was on the relationship between religion and science.' İhsanoğlu, *Turks in Egypt*, 351.
34. Kana'at Kitaphanesi was established in 1898 by Eliya Behar (1880–1945), a Jewish printer and publisher also known as İlyas Bayar, and continued long into the republican period; Johann Strauss, '"Kütüp ve Resail-i Mevkute": Printing and Publishing in a Multi-ethnic society', in Elizabeth Özdalga (ed.), *Late Ottoman Society: The Intellectual Legacy* (London: Routledge, 2005), 227–55; 235.
35. According to Strauss, 'The name chosen for his bookshop, "*Kitaphane-i İslam ve 'Askeri*", distinguished him from the surrounding Armenian booksellers of the *Bab-ı 'ali Caddesi* rather than denoting a specialization in religious or military works.' Strauss, 'Printing and Publishing in a Multi-ethnic Society', 236.
36. Strauss, 'Printing and Publishing in a Multi-ethnic Society', 238.
37. Gérard Genette, *Paratexts: Threshholds of Interpretation*, trans. Jane E. Levin (New York: Cambridge University Press, 1997), 1–2.
38. Ramzi, Al-Mar'a fi'l-Islam: Mas'alatuna al-hadira', 6 (quoted and translated in Booth, '*Woman in Islam*', 177; 197 n. 34).
39. Redhouse (1890 ed.) provides the following definition for *tahrir*: 'vn 1. A freeing from impurity, defect, ambiguity, or obscurity. 2. An emancipating a slave; manumission. 3. A writing, a setting down in writing. 4. An illuminating the pages of books. 5. A quavering the voice in reading or chanting.' As a compound verb (*tahrir etmek*) it did have the primary meaning of 'to free', but working the auxiliary into the title would have been too awkward.
40. For Yakan's reference on Asma'i's translation, see note 28 above. Ironically, Asma'i's translation was almost immediately banned from entering the Ottoman Empire, for reasons that remain unclear.
41. Asma'i, Preface, b: İslam kadınlarının hayat-ı mu'tadelerini daha muntazam bir hayata tebdil ve eski göreneklerini da'ire-yi vukufu dahilinde 'akl ve şer'a tevfikan tervice çalışmış bulunduğu için enzar-ı 'umumu kemal-i ehemmiyetle celp etmiş ve pek şiddetli bir mübahase-i kalemiyeye meydan açmış oldu.
42. Asma'i, Preface, b–c. We refer to Asma'i's translation of *Tahrir al-mar'a*

simply as Asmaʻi. Same for Mugamiz's translation, and Amin's original 1899 edition, where the name of the author/translator is provided, followed by the page number.
43. Asmaʻi, Preface, b–c.
44. It is important to note that Amin himself did not openly advocate co-education in primary schools, at least not in *Tahrir al-marʼa*. He did point out though that American girls and boys studied side by side in the same classroom, and that those familiar with American society believed that this did not affect the girls' morality, quite to the contrary. Amin, *Tahrir al-marʼa*, 94.
45. According to Redhouse's Turkish–English dictionary of 1890, '*ifrat ve tefrit*' as an expression appears under the fourth meaning under *ifrat*, as excess and deficiency in action. Of note is that Rashid Rida also used this classification in his Arabic periodical *al-Manar*, writing about '*al-Dallun fiʼl-ifrat waʼl-tafrit*' when discussing various interpretations within Islamic practices and beliefs. See Rida, 'Masʼalat al-qudr wa-fiʼl al-ʻabd bi-qudratihi', *al-Manar* 9 (26 March 1906), 81.
46. Asmaʻi, Preface, d.
47. Asmaʻi, Preface, d.
48. Asmaʻi, Preface, d–h.
49. Asmaʻi, Preface, w.
50. Asmaʻi, Preface, z.
51. Asmaʻi, Preface, z.
52. Asmaʻi, Preface, z.
53. Mugamiz, Preface, 4.
54. Mugamiz, 4.
55. Mugamiz, 4.
56. Reproduced in Ahmet Ali Gazel, 'Ikinci Meşrutiyet Döneminde Ittihat ve Terakki Fırkasi'ni Bölünme Noktasina Getiren Hizb-i Cedid Hareketi', *A.Ü. Türkiyat Araştırmaları Enstitüsü Dergisi*, Sayı 16 (Erzurum, 2001), 264.
57. Marilyn Booth, 'Girlhood translated? Fenelon's "Traité de l'Education des Filles"', in Marilyn Booth (ed.), *Migrating Texts: Circulating Translations around the Ottoman Medierranean* (Edinburgh: Edinburgh University Press, 2019), 266–99; 271.
58. See for instance, Asmaʻi's preface to *Abdullah Celaleddin Bereketzade's* Ihticap, which he translated into Arabic, as well as his preface to Mustafa Kamil's abridged version (introduction) of *al-Masʼala al-sharqiyya*. For instance, for the latter work, Asmaʻi simply wrote that this was an important work, and that he was doing his duty towards readers by translating it.
59. See Asmaʻi's translation into Arabic of Abdullah Cemaleddin Bereketzade, *Taʻrib al-siyasa al-sharʻiyya fi huquq al-raʻi wa saʻadat al-raʻiyya* (Cairo: Matbaʻat al-taraqqi, 1318).
60. Not surprisingly perhaps, Asmaʻi feels the need to provide an explana-

Translating Qasim Amin's Tahrir al-mar'a *into Ottoman Turkish*

tion about *burka*: 'A beehive veil which is used by women in Egypt and Arab lands to cover themselves'. Asma'i, 94. A fairly typical example of Mugamiz's approach is when he uses a simple Turkish word (*korku*) and amplifies the Arabic *khawf al-fitna* (fear of sedition) of the original; Mugamiz, 96).

61. Asma'i skips sentences on pages 10–11, 15 and 120.
62. This occurs in Asma'i after p. 68.
63. That being said, Asma'i's translation can at times be less alert, perhaps yielding to the temptation of the filler word 'şey', and misses the opportunity to use the same root, 'commodity' (*mata'*) when describing how men 'offer their women to their guests' employing the common word 'things' (*eşya*). Asma'i, 12. Mugamiz, on the other hand, provided a better translation: *En iyi meta'* (Mugamiz, 17).
64. The following sentence is fairly typical of Asma'i's style of translation: 'In that case, to not appreciate the power of love and affection and to overlook their progress and perfection is a repudiation of divine benefactions and a remissness in offering gratitude and thanks for them.' ('O halde 'aşk ve muhabbetin kadrini takdir etmemek ve bunun terakki ve tekemmülünden sarf-i nazar eylemek ni'em-i ilahiyeyi inkar ve hamd ve teşekküründe taksir olur.'). Asma'i, 68.
65. Asma'i's writing style in the translator's preface is no different from his language throughout the translated text itself. For instance, he writes in his own preface, on Amin's text, that 'this is why it had, in all seriousness attracted the attention of the public'; he uses the expression 'enzar-i 'umumu kemal-i ehemiyetle celp etmiş', displaying his command of good literary Ottoman.
66. For example, Amin, 8; Asma'i, 10 use the same vocabulary but sometimes with different forms of the root: Amin's *mudaraka* becomes Asma'i's *idrak*.
67. For example, in the long sentence where Qasim Amin decries the Westerners, who 'fancy ascribing everything good to their religion' (and become 'the Europeans' (*Avrupalılar*) in Asma'i), and their insistence that 'their religion helps the progress of their own women due to its proclivity for freedom', Asma'i sticks closely to the Arabic vocabulary, using a great number of the same words (*ümmetler, ahlak, eser*) and roots (*resm eylemiştir* for *yarsum* and *şekil almıştır* for *tushakkil*); Amin, 11; Asma'i, 14.
68. Asma'i, 50.
69. On one occasion, Asma'i (9) has the unidiomatic *bunların kendileri* as a word-for-word rendition of the Arabic *hal humm anfusuhum*. On another occasion, a word (*kadınların*) is repeated in a way that is contrary to rules of Turkish syntax but faithful to the original (Amin, 9; Asma'i, 11).
70. While this is generally the case, Asma'i is perfectly capable of introducing a couple of vernacular expressions and using short sentences all the while maintaining the formality of style. For instance, in a passage which decries the denigration of women through not allowing them a public life, Asma'i wrote of a 'curtain being drawn in front of all their occupations' ('Kadınlar

ile hayat-i 'umumiye ve zatlarına müte'alik bilcümle eşğalın arasına perde çekilmesi kadını tahkirdendir'), and of them 'not having a finger' in public works. Asma'i, 20. Mugamiz's translation of the same passage, whilst also being straightforward about the meaning ('they are prohibited from conducting business' and 'are not deemed to own a place and an influence in public works'), went for one long train of a sentence, nonetheless rendered palatable and easier to follow by the sequence of parallelisms created by his addition of no less than five synonyms for maximum rhetorical effect. Mugamiz, 25.

71. One feature of the colloquial style of Mugamiz is his tendency to use prescriptive optatives, which makes for vivid reading but borders on the inappropriately casual, especially next to Asma'i who tends to use a Turkish verbal suffix (*–mElI*), which conveys a stronger sense of moral compunction. For instance in a given passage Mugamiz (97) reads: 'A man who is afraid of being attracted and fascinated by women, when he chances upon women, let him turn his face away. Likewise women who are afraid that they might be fascinated by a man by seeing them, let them not turn and look at the faces of the men.' Whereas Asma'i (93), just like the original Arabic (*'ala man . . . 'an yaghudd basarahu*) is more austere: 'Just as the women who have the fear of sedition in their carnal soul will lower their eyes, likewise men who have a fear of sedition should not look at any other place except straight ahead from their eyes.'
72. For example, Mugamiz added '*meslek*' to the list of '*fikir* and *madhhab*', absent in the original. This made the translation more vernacular. Mugamiz, 11.
73. Mugamiz, 14.
74. Mugamiz, 12.
75. For instance, in the following sentence: 'Yahut her birinin kendi bar-i giran-i bed-bahtisini ila ahiri'l-'ömür çekmesinden başka bir şey olamaz' ('Otherwise it will be nothing short of everyone carrying their own inauspicious heavy load until the end of their life'). Mugamiz, 44.
76. For an example of a particularly beautifully translated sentence, see Mugamiz, 45. The Arabic original, which reads: 'and if the two [souls] met, each one of them would be seized by the tremor of pleasure', becomes *ra'şe-i şadmani ile titrerler*. The vocabulary for this entire section on the Platonic idea of souls is very close to that of the Arabic original.
77. As seen in his way of writing about women's strong decline (*inhitat shadid*), which becomes 'a deplorable and awful decline' (*elim ve müdhiş bir inhitat*). Mugamiz, 116.
78. See, for instance, his significant expansion of the Arabic original while translating the section of men losing their minds with the love of a woman. Mugamiz, 98.
79. See the following section on Ibn al-'Abidin.
80. For example, on page 11, where Mugamiz turned a statement into a rhetori-

cal question: 'Isn't it the case that if someone famous from the West writes a book it is translated to five–six languages even as it is still being printed?'; or page 97, 'Is it not strange/curious? (*'Garip değil mi?'*)'.

81. That said, Mugamiz's translation could at times lose some of the power of the original, either because a crucial word was omitted – for instance the term 'necessary' (*daruri*), which led to a softening of Amin's message regarding the necessity of reform – or because of Turkish syntax, which could lead to subject and verb being separated by a very long sentence (Mugamiz, 5). There is also at least one instance where Mugamiz kept Amin's long Arabic sentence, whereas Asma'i divided it up, thus making Asma'i easier to read. Asma'i 8; Mugamiz 12.
82. See Lawrence Venuti, *The Translator's Invisibility: A History of Translation* (London: Routledge, 1995).
83. Asma'i, 93; Mugamiz, 96.
84. Mugamiz, 97.
85. Mugamiz, 67 and elsewhere.
86. Amin, 8; Mugamiz 15.
87. Amin, 8; Mugamiz 14–15. *Huwa al-amr al-mashhur al-ladhi la rayba fihi*: both *mashhur* and *rayba* become two words: *meşhur ve müsellem*; *la rayba* becomes *şüphe ve tereddüt*.
88. For instance, *tarbiyat al-mar'a* (women's upbringing) becomes *terbiye-i nisvan* in Asma'i, and *kadınların terbiyesi* in Mugamiz.
89. A couple of exceptions though: Asma'i, 19, *kadınlar*, after a few *nisvan*.
90. Asma'i, 123.
91. Both as titles of subchapters and in the texts themselves.
92. Asma'i, 49.
93. Amin, 77; Asma'i, 93.
94. In fact, Amin used the term *hijab* to refer to a number of practices, not only covering and seclusion. As Pollard (*Nurturing the Nation*, 154) argued, 'Amin frequently used the term *hijab* to mean a kind of garment, especially when he discussed the different kinds of "veils" used in Egypt, distinguishing between such things as the *birqa'a* and the *habara*. He also used *hijab* to mean the segregation and seclusion of women from society, the treatment of women as property, the subjection of women to an uneducated state, and a determination to keep them ignorant of their legal rights. In other words, he appropriated the term hijab to transform the state of women and society.' (Pollard, *Nurturing the Nation*, 154.) But this might have been more the case for *al-Mar'a al-jadida*, or his article '*Asbab wa-nata'ij'*. It is not clear from Pollard's discussion whether this more capacious use of the term *hijab* applied to *Tahrir al-mar'a*, but it certainly seems to do so.
95. This is the chapter heading in Asma'i, 75, and Mugamiz, 81.
96. See for example the one sentence summary of the *madhal* (the author's *tamhid*), Asma'i, 5, used *ümmet*, whereas Mugamiz employed *millet*. A bit

later, *majmu' al-umma* in Arabic (Amin, 2), became in Mugamiz *milletin hey'et-i 'umumiyyesi*. Mugamiz, 6.
97. Mugamiz, 86.
98. Amin, 8; Asma'i, 11. In this same passage, though, Mugamiz stuck to *millet*. Mugamiz, 15.
99. See Şemsettin Sami, *Kamus-i Türki* (Istanbul: İkdam Matba'ası, 1900/1317), 480. The second meaning of *cema'at* is that of a religious community led by an imam during prayertime.
100. Mugamiz, 13.
101. Kayalı, 'Islam in the Thought and Politics of Two Late Ottoman Intellectuals', 322.
102. Asma'i, Preface, h, 11, 234, 239.
103. Mugamiz, 14, for first case; 229, 230, 239, for second case.
104. Here, the verb *inhattat* becomes '*sukuta düşer olmaz ise*' (Mugamiz, 15).
105. For instance, Asma'i, 11; Amin, 9.
106. Amin, 12; Asma'i, 14.
107. Amin, 13; Asma'i, 15. Thus, 'al-talazum bayna inhitat al-mar'a wa inhitat al-umma wa tawahhushiha' (Amin, 9) becomes 'kadınların te'ahhürü ümmetin tedenni' (here, he omits *tawahhush*). Asma'i, 11. Whereas Mugamiz keeps the same exact words as the original: 'kadının inhitat hali ile milletin hal-i inhitat ve vahşet'. Mugamiz, 16.
108. For instance, Ahmet Mithat classifed one of the ages of Ottoman history as *devr-i inhitat* (the Age of Decline) in 1881, and so did Mehmet Tevfik in 1885, for the period (1574–1789) (*devr-i tevakkuf ve inhitat*, for Mehmet Tevfik). Doğan Gürpınar, *Ottoman/Turkish Visions of the Nation, 1860–1950* (London: Palgrave, 2013), 184. See also Özdalga (ed.), *Late Ottoman Society*; Syrinx von Hees (ed.), *Inḥiṭāṭ – The Decline Paradigm: Its Influence and Persistence in the Writing of Arab Cultural History* (Würzburg: Ergon Verlag, 2017) on the notion of decline in Ottoman Turkish as well as Arabic.
109. *al-waqfa wa'l-jumud* in original (Amin, 7), are *hareketten kalmağı* in Asma'i, 9, and *tevakkuf ve cümudu* in Mugamiz, 13.
110. Mugamiz, 15.
111. The Arabic *yufsid akhlaqaha* thus became *ahlakı bozulacağı*, whereas Mugamiz retains the Arabic root: *ifsad etmesi*. Asma'i, 68; Mugamiz, 73; Amin, 57.
112. *Hukuma istibdadiyya* becomes *hükumat-ı müstebidde* in both Asma'i, 12 and Mugamiz, 16.
113. Mugamiz, 16 and 22.
114. Redhouse 1890 translates *istibdad* as 'a being or becoming alone, without a helper, sharer, or rival (in possessing or doing a thing); absolute, undivided possession and control', 89, and Şemsettin Sami defines it as 'ruling by oneself without following any order and without being subject to law' ('kendi başına ve hiçbir nizam ve kanuna tabi' olmaksızın hükm etme'); Sami, *Kamus-i Türki*, 96.

115. The term *sulta* for instance was never used. *Sulta* does not appear in Redhouse 1890 though it is there in the 'orange' *New Redhouse Turkish–English Dictionary* (1968). Instead, we find *salahiyet* (Mugamiz, 16) or *nufuz ve iktidar* (Asma'i). Other than this case, it is virtually always translated as *hükm* (for example, Amin, 11; Asma'i, 14). The reference to the sultan and his aides (*sultanuhum ve a'wanuhu*) in the Arabic is translated by Asma'i as heads of states (*ru'esa-i hükümetleri*), perhaps as a kind of censorship, since the passage in question is an attack on absolute authority (*sulta mutlaqa*). Amin, 12; Asma'i, 15. Similarly, the term *sunna/sunan* for law(s) – and Amin uses the term to refer to state legislations – was never translated as such (perhaps because of the completely different meaning of *sünnet* – namely, circumcision ceremony for boys, in Ottoman Turkish), but rather as *kanun, kavanin* or *takım kavanin*.
116. Asma'i, 85. Of note are the ways in which the translators translate slave and slavery (*raqq, halat al-raqiq*) either as *esir* (slave, prisoner, captive) or *kul* (slave, servant, but this has a very specific meaning in the Ottoman context), and their opposite term. Şemsettin Sami (*Kamus-i Türki*, 542) gives a similar definition under *hürr*: 'Köle ve esir olmayan, kendi nefsine malik ve istediği hareketi icrada muhayyir olan, azat'.
117. Asma'i, 84–5.
118. Asma'i, 84. According to Redhouse, *ot yeri* is 'any part of the body, from which superfluous hair is removed by a depilatory at the bath'; Redhouse, *Lexicon* (1890), 235.
119. Mugamiz, 88.
120. Leslie Peirce, 'Seniority, Sexuality and Social Order: The Vocabulary of Gender in Early Modern Ottoman Society', in Madeline Zilfi (ed.), *Women in the Ottoman Empire: Middle Eastern Women in the Early Modern Era* (Leiden: Brill, 1997), 169–96; 182.
121. Charles Barbier de Meynard, *Dictionnaire turc-français: supplément aux dictionnaires publiés jusqu' à ce jour*, vol. 2 (Paris: Ernest Leroux, 1886), 373–4. Meynard underlines that 'aujourd hui, ce mot est presque laissé de côté ou pris seulement en mauvaise part'. There were some notable exceptions, though, such as the Turkish translation of the Bible in the 1850s which used the term *'avret* to refer to wives, for instance in Paul's letter to the Corinthians (I). Türabi Efendi, *Kitab al-'ahd al-jadid: al-mansub ila rabbina 'İsa al-masih* (London: William Watts Matba'ası, 1857), 394.
122. Redhouse, *Lexicon* (1890), 1327: *'avret*: interestingly, pronounced slightly differently 'vulg', as *avrat* (instead of *avret*) and with the plural as *arwat* instead of *awrat*. The other meanings are '2. Any tie when people usually undress themselves. 2. Any thing usually kept concealed from public view'; and '5. A weak or unprotected place on a frontier'. This last meaning is of course the most interesting (and one which the Arabic term *'awra* also has), but is beyond the purview of this chapter. Suffice it to say that it connects

women with the nation in striking ways, in the sense that both need protection by men.
123. Şemsettin Sami, *Kamus-i Türki*, 955.
124. See Bustani's dictionary *Muhit al-Muhit* of 1869 (vol. 2), *'awr*, where he writes, *'wa'l-nisa' 'indahum 'awra'* ('and women have an *'awra'*), p. 1496.
125. Amin, 10; Asma'i, 12; Mugamiz, 16.
126. We are relying here on Redhouse (1890) for the translation of *meta'*.
127. *Bal ja'ala mata'* (pleasures) *al-hayat mushtaraka bayn al-sinifayn* (men and women): translated as 'bilakis bütün menafi'-i hayatı bila tefrik erkekler ile kadınların hakimiyyet-i müşterekesine tevdi' eylemiştir'. Mugamiz, 93.
128. Asma'i, 123; Mugamiz, 124.
129. Asma'i, 70; Amin, 60.
130. Mugamiz 76.
131. 'o erkek hemen zimam-ı heva-yı nefsi nüfuz-i aklından kaçacağı derhal fitne ve fesatlar içine düşeceği hafvından', Asma'i, 94.
132. Asma'i, 15, 115.
133. Yakan, *al-Tajarib* (2015), 7.
134. Mugamiz, 5. We are here relying on Peterson's English translation of *Tahrir al-mar'a* for this sentence, Samiha Sidhom Peterson (trans.), *The Liberation of Women and The New Woman, Qasim Amin: Two Documents in the History of Egyptian Feminism* (Cairo: The American University in Cairo Press, 2000), 1. Mugamiz's translation is: 'bundan gaye-i emelim kadınların hukuk ve mahiyetlerine, cem'iyyet-i beşeriyle içinde ha'iz oldukları mevki' ve ehemiyyete da'ir mufasal bir kitap yazmak değildir'.
135. 'Maksadım memleketimizde pek az erbab-i fikir ve iz'anın nazar-i dikkat ve itinasını celb eden mühim bir bahis hakkında nazar-i 'ibret ve intibahi celb eylemekten ibarettir.' Mugamiz, 5.
136. Mugamiz, 6.
137. Mugamiz, 8. Asma'i's translation of this section is faithful to Amin's work and doesn't indicate any major interventions, unlike Mugamiz's.
138. Mugamiz (11) beefed up the original (Amin, 6–7) *lam yarkun ila hubb al-sukun* as 'those who fall into the folly of loving tranquility and indolence' ('Sükun ve 'ataleti sevmek hamakatına düşenler'). See also Mugamiz, 12: 'The lazy ones and those worshippers of sluggishness particularly weak in debating' ('Tenbeller, münazarada pek za'if bulunan meskenet-perestler') (Amin, 7: *kathira la yaktafi al-kasul ...*). Also, Mugamiz in that same sentence amplified *batil* into *batıl ve buhtan*.
139. Amin, 6: 'wa hatta mala bina'l kasal ila mu'adat kull fikr salih ma ya'udduhu ahl al-waqt hadithan ghayr ma'luf sia'an kana min al-sunna al-saliha al-'ula aww qadat bihi al-masalih fi hadhihi'l azmina'; Mugamiz, 12: 'her iyi fikri ... her mufid-i mutala'aya düşman kesiliyoruz'.
140. 'lam yabqa lana 'udhr fi'l-tamassuk biha siwa ... annana ghafalna 'an masalihina wa tadbir shu'unina' (Amin, 188). Mugamiz adds the crucial *ihmal* (neglect), which is stronger than *ghafalna*.

141. Mugamiz, 233.
142. Asma'i, 236.
143. Mugamiz, 12. He repeats this expression in the section on divorce, whereas this expression is missing in the Arabic original. Mugamiz, 207–8.
144. Mugamiz, 13.
145. Amin, Tamhid, 5–6: 'fa inna tarikh al-umam mamlu' bi'l-munaqashat wa'l-jadal wa'l-jilad wa'l hurub al-lati qamat fi sabil isti'la' fikr 'ala fikr wa madhhab 'ala madhhab wa kanat al-ghalaba tarra li'l-haqq wa ukhra li'l-batil wa kanat al-umam al-islamiyya 'ala hadhihi'l-hal fi'l-qurun al-ula wa'l-wusta. Wa lam yazal al-amr 'ala dhalika aww yazid fi'l-bilad al-gharbiyya al-lati yasbah ann yuqal fiha anna hayataha jihad-un mustamirr bayn al-haqq wa'l-batil wa'l-khata' wa'l- sawab: jihad dakhili bayna afrad al-umma fi jami' furu' al-ma'arif wa'l-funun wa'l-sana'i'. Wa jihad khariji bayn al-umam ba'daha ma' ba'd.' As a note, Peterson, in her translation of this passage (1992: 4), uses 'ideology' for *madhhab* and 'continuous struggle' to translate *jihad mustamirr*.
146. Mugamiz, 11.
147. Mustafa Aksakal points out that the Young Turk government, when declaring the war against Britain, France and Russia in 1914, called it a 'greater jihad'. Rather than interpreting this as a sign of the Young Turks' ignorance of classical jihad doctrine, he convincingly suggests that this 'confusion' marked 'the erasure of the line between the individual's and the state's efforts in the age of anti-colonial mass movements and total war. The erasure between the personal and the official, the internal and the external, amounted to the "secularization of jihad".' Mustafa Aksakal, 'Holy War Made in Germany? Ottoman Origins of the 1914 Jihad', *War in History* 18: 2 (2011), 184–99; 188.
148. Mugamiz, 11. Again, here, we can note a more minor shift in the way *al-bilad al-gharbiyya* is translated: Mugamiz translated it as 'civilised western lands' ('*garp memalik-i mütemeddinesi*').
149. Mugamiz, 11.
150. Asma'i translated the first mention of jihad as 'as for the lands of Europe, where life, it might be said, is a permanent war and struggle between truth and falsehood, and even what is right, this aforementioned issue/situation continues to the same degree as in the past, if not even more accentuated' ('Hayatı hak ile batıl ve hata sevap arasında bir harp, ve niza'-i da'imiden 'ibarettir demeğe şayan olan Avrupa memalikinde'). Asma'i, 7.
151. Aksakal, 'Ottoman Origins of 1914 Jihad', 187, quoting from Ussama Makdisi, *Artillery of Heaven: American Missionaries and the Failed Conversion of the Middle East* (Ithaca: Cornell University Press, 2008), 131.
152. We are here borrowing and adapting Marilyn Booth's expression for the term '*Ijtihad*' in the 1890s. See Marilyn Booth, 'Before Qasim Amin', 397 n. 81.

153. Mugamiz, 116.
154. Mugamiz, 116.
155. Mugamiz, 124.
156. Mugamiz, 116.
157. Mugamiz, 71; Amin, 48.
158. Mugamiz also added the possessive on page 116. Asma'i also used it quite frequently.
159. Mugamiz, 130; Amin, 84.
160. Mugamiz, 130; Amin, 84.
161. In one passage, whereas Amin seemed to be arguing that everything had changed, and that Muslims should adapt to that change and be willing to regard customs as also changing, Mugamiz added to his translation: 'because even a Muslim is a human being' ('çünkü bir Muslim dahi bir insandır') – that is, even Muslims are subject to God's laws of constant change, without which there is death. Another example of Mugamiz's more powerful translation is the passage where Qasim Amin wrote about the inevitability of progress (*taqaddum*) and wrote that: 'This is a well-known matter ... about which there is no doubt' ('Huwa'l amr al-mashhur al-ladhi la rayba fihi') (Amin, 8). Mugamiz translated this as 'this is such a well-known and incontestable reality that does not allow any doubt or hesitation' ('Bu öyle meşhur ve müsellem bir hakikattır ki şüphe ve tereddüt götürmez'), translating *amr* with *hakikat* (truth, reality), which is stronger than the original Arabic; Mugamiz, 14–15.
162. Mugamiz, 229.
163. Zaki M[ugamiz], 'Hal li'l-nisa' ann yatlubna kull huquq al-rijal', *al-Hilal* 2: 10 (15 January 1894): 304–6, cited and analysed in Fruma Zachs and Sharon Halevi, 'From "Difa' al Nisa" to "Mas'alat al Nisa" in Greater Syria: Readers and Writers Debate Women and their Rights, 1858–1900', *International Journal of Middle East Studies* 41 (2009): 615–34; 625. According to Zachs and Halevi, 'Zaki's piece immediately drew numerous reader responses (including in other journals) in a drawn-out exchange', and 'when the debate showed no signs of abating after an entire year, the editors stepped in and terminated it' (625). See also Souad Abou-Rouss, '"al-Hilal", mawsu'a min al-nahda', in *A'mal mu'tamar: bi rifqat Jirji Zaydan – al-Nahda fi 'ahdat al-hadara, 15–17 Ayyar 2014* (n.p.: Publications of the University of Balamand, 2015), 77–8.
164. Amin, 11: *lakin hadha'l-i'tiqad batil* is rendered by Asma'i (14) as 'However, this belief is not right' (*Halbuki bu i'tikad doğru değildir*), whereby *batil* becomes *doğru değildir*, which is noticeably less strong. Or consider the example previously mentioned where talking of the time when women in other nations were in 'strong decline' (*fi khadid al-inhitat*); Asma'i spoke of the 'time when they were at the most backward state' (*en geride bulundukları zaman*), which is not as strong.
165. Asma'i, 120.

166. Asma'i, 10–1
167. Asma'i, 122.
168. Asma'i 127.
169. Asma'i, 128.
170. Amin, 9; Asma'i, 11: *wa-yunkiruhu kull man 'arafahu* becomes *ulama*.
171. Amin, 9; Asma'i, 11; Mugamiz, 16.
172. Asma'i, 75: 'Bu kitap hakikaten dikkatli yazılmış ve 'adatımızı müdafa'a babında pek mübeyyin delillerle doldurulmuştur.' (Mütercim)
173. Asma'i, 78: 'İşbu halin bakiye-i asarı olarak pek yakın zamanlara kadar Kahirede gelin, inası evinden zevcinin hanesine geceleyin götürülür idi. Hala da İskenderiye'de geceleyin götürmek 'adeti ba'z-ı 'a'ile arasında caridir. "Mütercim".'
174. The book in question is Muhammad Tal'at Harb, *Tarbiyat al-mar'a wa'l-hijab* (Cairo: Matba'at al-taraqqi, 1899). On this book, see Booth, '*Woman in Islam*'.
175. Asma'i, 110.
176. Asma'i, 168–9.
177. Asma'i, 231. Asma'i suggested reading two books: *Fasl al-khitab* – this is a reference to Mukhtar bin Ahmad Mua'yyid basha al-'Adhmi, *Fasl al-khitab, aww taflis iblis min tahrir al-mar'a wa raf' al-hijab* (Beirut: al-Matba'a al-adabiyya 1318 [1900]); and *Kitab Jalis al-anis*, a reference to Muhammad Ahmad Hasanayn al-Bulaqi's *al-Jalis al-anis fi al-tahdhir 'amma fi tahrir al-mar'a min al-talbis* (Cairo: Matba'at al-ma'arif al-ahliyya, 1899).
178. Mugamiz, 215, footnote: 'Türkçede bu gibi ta'birat yerine iraden elinde olsun, ayağının bağını çözdüm, boşadım gibi sözler kullanılır.'
179. Mugamiz, 223, footnote.
180. The one exception we found was for Surat al-Tahrim 66.6. In the instance of a short quotation from Surat al-Tahrim, Mugamiz provided a direct translation, preserving the keyword of Arabic, *nar* which is not in common use in Ottoman, but emphasising it with the addition of 'torment' ('*azab-ı nar*), whereas Asma'i used the more vernacular Persian *ateş*. Asma'i added the word 'children' in his translation of '*wa ahalihum*', thereby making the intended meaning of Qasim Amin's point clear, whereas Mugamiz added a *tafsir* explication: 'This verse implicitly contains the command "Make your children into gentlemen with an education that abhors evil and inclines to goodness"' ('Çocuklarınızı seyyiatten muteneffir, hasanata meyyal bir terbiye ile insan eyleyiniz emrini ihtiva eder'); Asma'i, 55; Mugamiz, 62.
181. Brett Wilson, *Translating the Qur'an in an Age of Nationalism: Print Culture and Modern Islam in Turkey* (Oxford and New York: Oxford University Press, 2014), 135.
182. Rida was opposed to the translation of the Qur'an into any language. Wilson, *Translating the Qur'an*, 118–20.

183. His identity was exposed later, when the translated Qur'an was (re?)published in 1926, and Mugamiz was violently attacked by quite a few authors for his translation; see Brett Wilson, 'The First Translations of the Qur'an in Modern Turkey (1924–38)', *International Journal of Middle East Studies* 41 (2009): 419–35; 422.
184. Elsewhere, remarkably, there is a typo in one of Asma'i's translation of a very short Qur'anic passage, all the more so because the small typo of a *mim* initial letter rather than a *sin* renders the work in question nonsensical and illegible. Ottoman texts are remarkable for their lack of such typestting mistakes, and to have one occur in a Qur'anic passage seems quite extradordinary, and is exactly the sort of thing that provided ammunition to those opposed to the idea of a 'Turkish Qur'an'.
185. Asma'i, 81–2.
186. Bereketzade, *İhticap*, 31.
187. Asma'i renders 'and they should protect their modesty' in a faithful way, employing the same roots as Arabic: 'let them protect their private parts' (*Ve ferclerin hıfz etsinler*). The Qur'an has the plural *furuc*, whereas Asma'i employs the Arabic singular, *ferc*, with the Turkish plural suffix (*fercler*). There can be no doubt that in Asma'i's rendition *ferc* is meant to refer to the private parts, obviously of both men and women, as it does in Arabic, but Ottoman usage would seem to bring Asma'i very close to a faux pas. Şemsettin Sami defines *ferc* as 'The reproductive organ of women and female animals' (*Kadının ve dişi hayvanın alet-i tenasülü*) with the note that 'In Arabic it is used for males as well' (*'arabide erkeğinkine de derler*). In none of the subsequent Turkish translations of the Qur'an is the word *ferc* used to translate *furuj*. Mugamiz in his 1926 translation has 'their shameful parts' (*utanacak yerleri*).
188. Asma'i, 177: 'ya'ni "zevclerinin onlara olan hukuku gibi ol nisvanın da zevclerinde 'iffet ve siyanette hukukları vardır" buyurulmuştur.'
189. Asma'i, 177–8, footnote: 'ya'ni "ol kadın 'akd-i nikahta olan icap ve kabulde sizinle muhkem 'ahd ve peyman eylemiştir" diye buyurmustur.'
190. Al-Nisa 3, 129. Asma'i, 191, footnote: 'İmdi onlardan muhabbetiniz olana fi'len külli meyl etmeyip ve muhabbetiniz olmayanı zevciyet mu'amelesiz ve talaksız onu terk etmeyesiniz.'
191. First, it employs a converb, which serves as a conjuct, and also uses the conjuctive '*ve*': (*meyl etmeyip ve ... onu terk etmeyesiniz*). And second, the main verb governs its direct object in the accusative (*muhabbetiniz olmayanı*) but there is also a resumptive pronoun (*onu*) which is redundant and throws the syntax off.
192. Surat al-Baqara (Q. 2.26). Translation from <http://islamicstudies.info/reference.php?sura=2&verse=26-27> (last accessed 16 January 2022).
193. Asma'i, 69; Mugamiz, 75.
194. Mugamiz kept the short, pithy hadith in their Arabic and without explanations. For an example of a short hadith, see Mugamiz, 206: 'innama'l a'mal

Translating Qasim Amin's Tahrir al-mar'a *into Ottoman Turkish*

bi'l niyyat hadis-i şerifinden istidlal olunduğu üzere . . .'. For a long one, see Mugamiz, 204.
195. Asma'i, 84; Mugamiz, 88–9.
196. As when he uses the Turkish verb 'to caress', *okşamak* for Arabic *ka-massihi*.
197. 'According to a preferred tradition which is less than preferable' ('Racihten akall bulunan mercuh rivayete göre'). Asma'i, 84.
198. 'However, the face, the hands and the feet are, according to a reliable opinion, parts of shame (*'ayıp yeri*) while accoding to a preferred (*mercuh*) opinion which is less than preponderant (*racih*), the arms too are parts of shame (*utanacak yeri*).'
199. In one instance, Asma'i used a compound verb, *şekk etmek*, which does not seem current in Ottoman and, if it were, would require a personal subject which is here not provided; it is not clear whether it refers to the woman or boy being stroked or the person doing the stroking. Asma'i, 85.
200. Asma'i avoided using the term *emred* and opted instead for the Turkish words for 'hairless boy' or 'beardless youth' (while Mugamiz kept the Arabic *amrad*) – a rather perplexing choice, as the term was fairly widely used and generally understandable to educated Ottomans. It might have been a form of censorship; perhaps *amrad* had a different meaning or possible inuendo also attached to it, something vulgar or obscene.
201. Mugamiz, 88–9: 'Şehvet şüphesi hasıl olduğu zaman gerek bir kadının, gerek bir emredin yüzlerine bakılmağa müsa'ade edilmez. Şehvet süphesi olmaz ise bir kadının yüzüne –velevki güzel olsa da- bakılmasına müsa'ade olunur.'
202. 'Kadının Kurtuluşu', *İçtihat*, 8, March 1909, reproduced in Faik Bulut, *İttihat ve Terakki'de milliyetçilik, din, ve kadın tartışmaları*, vol. 1 (Istanbul: Su Yayinevi, 1999), 154.
203. Celal Nuri [İleri], *Kadınlarımız* (Istanbul, Matba'a-yı İçtihat, 1331/1913).
204. For instance, '"Tahrir al-mar'a" tarjama turkiyya', *al-Manar* 13 (1910): 784.
205. Our thanks to Akın Sefer for finding the documents and providing copies of them. BBA BEO 3785 document '283843 (1328 B 20), p. 2: 'Mısırda tab' olunan Tahrir el-Mer'e nam kitabın mündericat-ı muzırrasına bina'en sa'ir memalik-i 'osmaniyeye men'-i duhulüne Matbu'at Kanununun otuzbeşinci ve Matba'alar Kanununun yedinci maddesi mücibince meclis-i mahsusu vükelaca karar ittihaz ve tebliğine müsa'ade-i 'aliye-i sedaret-penahileri sezavar buyurulmuş babında emr ü ferman hazret-i veli'ül-emrindir. Fi 18 receb sene <1>328 ve fi 12 temmuz sene 326. Dahiliye Nazırı namına. Müsteşar.'
206. Yakan, *al-Tajarib*, 7.
207. Amin writes that though some people would claim that the book he has published is an innovation/heresy (*bi'dat*) against Islam, his view is that is a *bid'at* aimed at the 'traditions and social dealings' (*'awa'id wa turuq al-mu'amala*) 'where demand for perfection is extolled' ((*al-lati yuhmad*

talab al-kamal fiha), Amin, 7; Peterson (trans.), 4). Asma'i (p. 8) speaks of 'traditions and social dealings concerning which the demand for perfection is considered praiseworthy and desired' (*kemale ermesinin talebi memduh ve mergup bulunan 'adat ve sevap*), adding the words 'praiseworthy and desired' (*memduh ve mergup*). Mugamiz (13) keeps these additional words, rewording them slightly into 'honour and virtue' (*şeref ve fazilet*): 'a number of traditions and ways of social dealing for which it is considered an honor and a virtue to work for their perfection and improvement' ('tekammül ve te'alisine çalışmak bir şeref ve fazilet 'add edilen bir takım 'adat ve turuk-ı mu'ameleyedir'). Clearly Mugamiz here is aware of Asma'i's version.
208. Asma'i, 10–1; Mugamiz 14–15.

Bibliography

Abou-Rouss, Souad, "'al-Hilal", mawsu'a min al-nahda', in *A'mal mu'tamar: bi-rifqat Jirji Zaydan – al-Nahda fi 'ahdat al-Hadara, 15–17 Ayyar 2014* (n.p.: Publications of the University of Balamand, 2015).

al-'Adhmi, Mukhtar bin Ahmad Mu'ayyid Basha, *Fasl al-khitab, aw taflis iblis min tahrir al-mar'a wa-raf' al-hijab* (Beirut: al-Matba'a al-adabiyya, 1318 [1900]).

Ahmed, Leila, *Women and Gender in Islam: Historical Roots of a Modern Debate* (New Haven: Yale University Press, 1992).

Aksakal, Mustafa, 'Holy War Made in Germany? Ottoman Origins of the 1914 Jihad', *War in History* 18: 2 (2011): 184–99.

Arslan, C. Ceyhun, 'Entanglements between the Tanzimat and al-Nahdah: Jurji Zaydan between *Tarikh adab al-lughah al-turkiyyah* and *Tarikh adab al-lughah al 'arabiyya*', *Journal of Arabic Literature* 50 (2019): 288–324.

Baron, Beth, *The Women's Awakening in Egypt: Culture, Society and the Press* (New Haven: Yale University Press, 1994).

Baron, Beth, 'The Making of the Egyptian Nation', in Ida Bloom, Karen Hagemann and Catherine Hall (eds), *Gendered Nations: Nationalisms and Gender Order in the Long Nineteenth Century* (Oxford and New York: Berg, 2000), 137–58.

Bereketzade, Abdullah Cemaleddin, *İhticap* (Cairo: Terakki Matba'ası, 1318/1901).

Bereketzade, Abdullah Cemaleddin, *al-Ihtijab*, trans. Asma'i (Cairo: Matba'at al-taraqqi, 1318/1901).

Bereketzade, Abdullah Cemaleddin, *Ta'rib al-siyasa al-shar'iyya fi huquq al-ra'i wa sa'adat al-ra'iyya*, trans. Asma'i (Cairo: Matba'at al-taraqqi, 1318/1901).

Booth, Marilyn, 'Before Qasim Amin: Writing Women's History in 1890s Egypt', in Marilyn Booth and Anthony Gorman (eds), *The Long 1890s in Egypt: Colonial Quiescence, Subterranean Resistance* (Edinburgh: Edinburgh University Press, 2015), 365–98.

Booth, Marilyn, '*Woman in Islam*: Men and the "Women's Press" in Turn-of-

Translating Qasim Amin's Tahrir al-mar'a *into Ottoman Turkish*

the-century Egypt', *International Journal of Middle East Studies* 33: 2 (2001): 171–201.

Booth, Marilyn, 'Girlhood Translated? Fénelon's "Traité de l'Education des Filles"', in Marilyn Booth (ed.), *Migrating Texts: Circulating Translations Around the Ottoman Mediterranean* (Edinburgh: Edinburgh University Press, 2019), 266–99.

al-Bulaqi, Muhammad Ahmad Hasanayn, *al-Jalis al-anis fi al-tahdhir 'amma fi tahrir al-mar'a min al-talbis* (Cairo: Matba'at al-ma'arif al-ahliyya, 1899).

Bulut, Faik, *İttihat ve Terakki'de milliyetçilik, din, ve kadın tartışmaları*, vol.1 (Istanbul: Su Yayınevi, 1999).

Bursalı, Mehmet Tahir, *Osmanlı Müellifleri 1299–1915* (Istanbul: Meral Yayınları, n.d. [1971]).

Dupont, Anne-Laure, *Gurgi Zaydan (1861–1914): Ecrivain réformiste et témoin de la Renaissance arabe* (Damascus: Institut français du Proche Orient, 2006).

Genette, Gérard, *Paratexts: Thresholds of Interpretation*, trans. Jane E. Levin (New York: Cambridge University Press, 1997).

Gürpınar, Doğan, *Ottoman/Turkish Visions of the Nation, 1860–1950* (London: Palgrave, 2013).

Halabi, Zeina, *The Unmaking of the Arab Intellectual: Prophecy, Exile and the Nation* (Edinburgh: Edinburgh University Press, 2017).

Harb, Muhammad Tal'at, *Tarbiyat al-mar'a wa'l-hijab* (Cairo: Matba'at al-taraqqi, 1899).

Hourani, Albert, *Arabic Thought in the Liberal Age, 1798–1939* (reissued, with a new preface) (Cambridge: Cambridge University Press, 1983).

İhsanoğlu, Ekmeleddin, *The Turks in Egypt and their Cultural Legacy* (Cairo: The American University in Cairo Press, 2012).

'Imara, Muhammad, *Qasim Amin wa-tahrir al-mar'a* (Cairo: Dar al-Hilal, 1980).

Kamil, Mustafa, *Mes'ele-yi şarkiyye* (trans. Asma 'i, and likely abridged by him as well) (Cairo: al-Adaab matba'asi, 1316/1898).

Katiboğlu, Monica, 'Specters and Circulation of Meaning: Edebiyat-ı Cedide on Modern Literary Language', *Comparative Studies of South Asia, Africa and the Middle East* 40: 2 (2020): 361–71.

Kayalı, Hasan, 'Islam in the Thought and Politics of Two Late Ottoman Intellectuals: Mehmed Akif and Said Halim', *Archivum Ottomanicum* 19 (2001): 307–33.

Khuri-Makdisi, İlham, 'The Nahda, Translation Movements between Ottoman Turkish and Arabic, and Bilingualism, 1860–1914', unpublished paper delivered at the Middle East Studies Association Annual Conference, November 2019.

Makdisi, Ussama, *Artillery of Heaven: American Missionaries and the Failed Conversion of the Middle East* (Ithaca: Cornell University Press, 2008).

Meynard, Charles Barbier de, *Dictionnaire turc–français: supplément aux dictionnaires publiés juqu' à ce jour*, 2 vols (Paris: Ernest Leroux, 1886).

M[ugamiz], Zaki, 'Hal li'l-nisa' an yatlubna kull huquq al-rijal', *al-Hilal* 2: 10

(15 January 1894): 304–6.
Mugamiz, Zaki, *Kur'an-i Kerim: Tercüme ve Tefsiri* (Istanbul: Kitaphane-i Islam, 1332/1914).
Mugamiz, Zaki, *Türkçe Kur'an-i Kerim Tercümesi* (Istanbul: Kitaphane-i İslam, 1344/1926).
New Redhouse Turkish–English Dictionary (Istanbul: Redhouse Yayınevi, 1968).
Nuri, Celal [İleri] *Kadınlarımız* (Istanbul: Matba'a-yı İçtihat, 1331/1913).
Özdalga, Elizabeth (ed.), *Late Ottoman Society: The Intellectual Legacy* (London: Routledge, 2005).
Peirce, Leslie, 'Seniority, Sexuality and Social Order: The Vocabulary of Gender in Early Modern Ottoman Society', in Madeline Zilfi (ed.), *Women in the Ottoman Empire: Middle Eastern Women in the Early Modern Era* (Leiden: Brill, 1997), 169–96.
Peterson, Samiha Sidhom (trans.), *The Liberation of Women and The New Woman, Qasim Amin: Two Documents in the History of Egyptian Feminism* (Cairo: The American University in Cairo Press, 2000).
Pfeifer, Helen, 'Encounter after the Conquest: Scholarly Gatherings in 16th-century Ottoman Damascus', *International Journal of Middle East Studies* 47: 2 (2015): 219–39.
Pollard, Lisa, *Nurturing the Nation: The Family Politics of Modernizing, Colonizing and Liberating Egypt, 1805–1923* (Berkeley: University of California Press, 2005).
Redhouse, James W., *A Turkish and English Lexicon, Shewing in English the Significations of the Turkish Terms* (Istanbul: Boyajiyan, 1890).
Sami, Şemsettin, *Kamus-i Türki* (Istanbul: İkdam Matba'ası, 1900/1317).
Schick, İrvin Cemil, 'Print Capitalism and Women's Sexual Agency in the Late Ottoman Empire', *Comparative Studies of South Asia, Africa and the Middle East* 31: 1 (2011): 196–216.
Strauss, Johann, 'Who Read What in the Ottoman Empire (19th–20th centuries)?', *Middle Eastern Literatures*, 6:1 (2003): 39–76.
Strauss, Johann, '"*Kütüp ve Resail-i Mevkute*": Printing and Publishing in a Multi-ethnic Society', in Elizabeth Özdalga (ed.), *Late Ottoman Society: The Intellectual Legacy* (London: Routledge, 2005), 227–55.
'"Tahrir al-mar'a" tarjama turkiyya', *al-Manar* 13 (1910).
Türabi Efendi, *Kitab al-'ahd al-jadid: al-mansub ila rabbina 'isa al-masih* (London: William Watts Matba'ası, 1857).
Venuti, Lawrence, *The Translator's Invisibility: A History of Translation* (London: Routledge, 1995).
von Hees, Syrinx (ed.), *Inḥiṭāṭ – The Decline Paradigm: Its Influence and Persistence in the Writing of Arab Cultural History* (Würzburg: Ergon Verlag, 2017).
Wilson, M. Brett, 'The First Translations of the Qur'an in Modern Turkey (1924–38)', *International Journal of Middle East Studies* 41 (2009): 419–35.
Wilson, M. Brett, *Translating the Qur'an in an Age of Nationalism: Print Culture*

Translating Qasim Amin's Tahrir al-mar'a *into Ottoman Turkish*

and Modern Islam in Turkey (Oxford and New York: Oxford University Press, 2014).
Yakan, Wali al-Din, *al-Tajarib* (Cairo: Mu'assasat Hindawi, 2015 [1913]).
Zachs, Fruma and Sharon Halevi, 'From "Difa' al Nisa" to "Mas'alat al Nisa"' in Greater Syria: Readers and Writers Debate Women and their Rights, 1858–1900', *International Journal of Middle East Studies* 41 (2009): 615–34.
al-Zirikli, Khayreddin, *al-A'lam* (Beirut: Dar al-'ilm li'l-malayin 1992).

Chapter 7

Muslim Woman: The Translation of a Patriarchal Order in Flux[1]

Maha AbdelMegeed and A. Ebru Akcasu

This obligation [of men to be responsible for feeding women] is analogous to the obligation that destines the working class of people to feed the thinking class so that the latter may be fully enabled to do its original task.[2]

Al-Mar'a al-muslima ('Muslim woman') was penned by the Cairo-based scholar Muhammad Farid Wajdi (1878–1954) in 1901. In the introduction, Wajdi clearly states that he wrote his book as a reaction to Qasim Amin's (1863–1908) *al-Mar'a al-jadida* ('New woman'), 1900. In fact, this may not have been Wajdi's first critical engagement with Amin's work; for he had purportedly written brief responses to Amin's earlier book, *Tahrir al-mar'a* ('Emancipation of women', 1899).[3] The publication of the latter book was a momentous event, resulting in an explosion of responses by the different cultural and intellectual stakeholders in Egypt. The wide-ranging debates reveal the relationship between the question of women and a number of other contentious issues. These range from attitudes towards science, positivism and materialism, to rethinking power and authority, passing through concerns with how to best draw the limit between the public and the private spheres. The accurate conceptualisation of human nature and of the civilisation that would be most harmonious with it are central to these debates. The controversy spurred by Amin's book was so intense that he decided to reply by writing another book: this is his *New Woman*. In it, he attempts to further clarify his argument.

Muslim Woman, then, is a response to a response since Amin's *New Woman* was framed as a reaction to the critics of *Emancipation of Women*. In this manner, Wajdi's book enfolds a series of articulated positions: Amin's initial polemic, the numerous responses to him, followed by Amin's response to those, and culminating in Wajdi's own reaction to all of that. In a few years, and specifically in 1908, *Muslim Woman* crosses

The Translation of a Patriarchal Order in Flux

over to the centre of the Ottoman Empire. The Istanbul-based writer and poet Mehmed Akif (1873–1936) began to publish a serialised Ottoman Turkish translation, *Müslüman Kadını*, of Wajdi's *Muslim Woman* in the newly established journal, *Sırat-ı Müstakim* ('Straight path', 1908–1925). To use Akif's words, *Muslim Woman* 'would occupy' space in several issues of the periodical,[4] the third through the ninth, from 10 September 1908 to 31 December 1908. In the process, the series of contentious debates enfolded within Wajdi's work are opened up against the 1908 Ottoman Turkish Constitutional Revolution as a moment of sociopolitical urgency. In other words, Akif's translation is not concerned with replicating the context of the debates in Cairo. Rather, it is invested in deploying the debates as an intervention in building the post-revolutionary society. Turning to Akif's translation, this chapter traces the encounter between 1908 on the one hand, and the series of debates on women conjoined in Wajdi's book on the other. We argue that because the translation does not replicate the chronology of the unfolding debates in Egypt, with its own investments and its own chronotope, it in fact clarifies their shared political stakes across the two distinct, though intimately interrelated, historically specific contexts: Cairo and Istanbul.

The chapter follows an arc that stretches from sketching out the patterns of the translations of Amin and Wajdi into Ottoman Turkish, to outlining the contexts of these translations, specifically 1908, before turning to a close textual examination of Akif's translation strategy. The overarching movement of the analysis reveals the role played by the question of women in re-envisioning patriarchy in the wake of the rising discursive hegemony of waged labour. The conclusion sketches the ways in which neo-patriarchy, waged labour and the question of women offer a new lens for seeing the debates, and intra-Ottoman links, between the groups often described as modernists, reformists and traditionalists in the Ottoman context.

Disjuncture: Patterns in a New Context

Despite Amin's ongoing canonical status in intellectual histories and Wajdi's relative marginality in comparison, the picture was strikingly different during their lifetimes. *Muslim Woman* was widely translated and circulated in the Ottoman Empire and beyond, with evidence of Bosnian and Urdu translations.[5] More importantly, the translations were not always invested in introducing their readers to the details of the debates surrounding these works and shaping them. Instead, they were motivated by an effort to mobilise these works as part of ongoing debates in their own contexts. The patterns of translating Amin and Wajdi interrupts the dialogic connection found between these two texts in their Arabic versions. Furthermore, Akif's framing of the translation disjoins *Muslim Woman* from Wajdi's corpus, belying the latter's explicitly articulated position about how the book was part of his wider project.

To reiterate, the echo of the context of these arguments' initial confrontation and entwinement in Egypt could sometimes be lost to readers of translated versions. This appears not entirely unintentional when one considers how these works were presented to respective audiences. For example, Akif's Ottoman Turkish translation of *Muslim Woman* was first serialised in 1908, in the *Sırat-ı Müstakim*, then published in a book edition the following year. While Akif links Amin and Wajdi in his brief introduction to both the serialised and book forms, the reader is nevertheless presented with a stand-alone piece that does not need to consult Amin's *New Woman*.[6] Indeed, *Sırat-ı Müstakim* never translated any of Amin's works and it is likely that the Ottoman-Turkish readership was more widely exposed to Wajdi, in Ottoman Turkish, before readers gained any familiarity with more than the general idea of what he was 'refuting'. While the first Turkic-language (Tatar) translation of *New Woman* was completed the same year as Akif's *Muslim Woman*'s serialisation, in 1908,[7] the former was not printed within the Ottoman dominions but rather in Kazan, within Russian territory. As such, the pattern of the Ottoman Turkish translations breaks with the chronology of the Arabic versions, placing Wajdi before Amin. More importantly, the translations seem to address two potentially distinct reading publics.

New Woman was translated by a Tatar subject of the tsar, Zakir Kadiri (1878–1954).[8] Kadiri saw the book to be an appropriate second instalment to be published for the 'Family Library', which was a series of translated works he had created, in part to 'show the way of knowledge and life to mothers who would serve hand in hand with men on life and civilisation's path and birth a nation of lions'.[9] The series was inaugurated with a translation of Amin's *Emancipation of Women*: Zakiri does not break with the chronology of the Arabic versions in the way the Ottoman Turkish translations do. The translator's introduction to *New Woman* claims the text to be relevant for all Muslims even though it had been produced in Egypt and was focused on Egypt's social organisation.[10] The foreword to Kadiri's translation included a reproduction of Amin's dedication to Sa'd Zaghlul, Egypt's minister of education by the time of the translation's publication, with the note that he wanted to give *New Woman* as a gift to the readers of the 'Family Library' just as Amin had given it as a gift to his closest friend, Zaghlul, in 1900.[11] Amin's first book was not translated until the following year; Kadiri published a Turkic-language version of Amin's *Emancipation of Women* the same year that Akif's serialisation was compiled as a book.[12] As such, the chronology of these books' publication in Arabic is fully reversed in Ottoman Turkish. Their publication setting was also subject to different bifurcations in comparison to those found in Egypt.

The issue of which translation appeared in which setting, and when, is particularly significant for thinking about how the 'question of women' was part of a constellation of debates on slavery, equality and language, as both the Russian and Ottoman empires experienced competing and coexisting forms of ethnic and civic nationalisms.[13] The first Turkic-language version of *New Woman* appeared in post-revolutionary Kazan, where Tatar Turco-Muslims of the Russian Empire (the envisioned primary audience) constituted a non-dominant group. Akif's *Muslim Woman* appeared in post-revolutionary Istanbul, where Turco-Muslims of the Ottoman Empire made up the core constituency. In such a setting, the latter would have wanted to protect their own interests by not only staking a claim to access to authority and power in a post-absolutist setting, but also by creating limits to such access.

It is thus noteworthy that when the Ottoman Turkish version of Amin's *Emancipation of Woman* was published within the imperial dominions, in 1911, it was penned by Zeki Mugamiz (1871–1932), a few years after the revolution.[14] As a Syrian Christian, Mugamiz was a member of the non-core constituency. He made his career in Istanbul as a journalist, translator and public figure. Mugamiz' translation appeared at a moment of existential questioning and severe disappointments – in Tripolitania and the Balkans, a moment when writers suggested that dystopia supplanted euphoria when freedom, equality, fraternity and justice were not being achieved for many among various members of the Ottoman core and non-core constituencies.[15] Even at this moment, it is evident that Mugamiz' task of delivering *Emancipation of Women* to open minds was challenging. His introduction explains how free societies debate all ideas, even controversial ones. As such, Mugamiz considered it his 'duty' to make sure that this book had a place in the 'Ottoman national library'.[16] Kadiri's foreword was much less apologetic. Engaging with Amin's main point, he wrote that it was necessary for Tatars and other Muslims to educate their women if they desired to become civilised.[17] Kadiri's use of 'civilised' was not imbued with negative (materialistic) connotations, as it was in Wajdi's *Muslim Woman*.

The power of a translator's foreword to suggest dominant positions in the intellectual and social climate of the readership, and by extension to reveal the addressed reading public, is also evident in Akif's *Muslim Woman*. Similar to Kadiri and very much unlike Mugamiz, Akif's introduction does not reveal any sense of weakness within the shared reading community of translator and hoped-for readers. In fact, he can be argued to be the strongest translator among the three, and as speaking to a relatively dominant audience socially, because he does not give any justification for rendering this translation. There is no attempt to prove alignment with constitutional slogans and collective aspirations of an Ottoman nation, such as 'freedom'. Quite the contrary, Akif's introduction suggests that the platform of *Muslim Woman*'s serialised publication, the *Sırat-ı Müstakim*, positioned itself at an opportune moment as an organ that took it upon itself to define the still-malleable definitions of revolutionary slogans and aspirations for a receptive audience. Consequently, the translation of *Muslim Woman* does not introduce the Egyptian context of the debates, but it opens the text up to the context of the Ottoman constitutional revolution in 1908. The following section turns to the encounter between 1908 and Akif's *Muslim Woman*, showing how the confrontation dissociated the book from Wajdi's broader project. Ironically, the rift allows us to better grasp Wajdi's project beyond its dominant reading through tropes of Islam and modernity or Islam and science.[18]

1908: Freedom/Gender/Equality

The Constitutional Revolution of 10 July 1324 (23/24 July 1908) is regarded as a watershed moment in Ottoman history.[19] Also called the Young Turk 'revolution', 'mutiny' or 'rebellion', the event lacked several elements of the 'spectacular', for example mass uprisings and a true regime change, and has therefore been evaluated as a 'curious revolution', perhaps not fully deserving of the title, as argued by Erik J. Zurcher.[20] Nevertheless, 1908 marked a juncture from which, going forward, the ability of a major world empire's monarchs to perpetuate their grip on the mandate of absolute power after half a millennium of the emergence of the Ottoman state was never recaptured. It thus remains consequential, not only in the histories of the Ottoman Empire, from the Balkans to the Middle East, and the wider Islamicate world, but also in global history.

Sultan Abdülhamid II became the last member of the House of Osman to exercise absolute authority over matters of empire. He was deposed on 27 April 1909, less than a year after the Ottoman parliament was reconvened and the constitution reinstated.[21] This date marked the official end of the '*istibdad*' (tyranny) era, though the sovereign's power had already been severely curtailed by this point. The July revolution that eventually relegated the Hamidian regime to the annals of history was ushered in and celebrated with chants of 'Liberty, Fraternity, Justice, Equality'. Given the multi-ethnic and multiconfessional nature of the Empire's polyglot constituency, revolutionary slogans have more frequently been recalled in reference to these obvious identity registers. *Muslim Woman* makes it amply evident that a couple of these aspirations, especially those of 'freedom' and 'equality' were additionally – and fiercely – debated with respect to gender and class.

It is against the backdrop of these events that would have a lasting impact in the public sphere that Akif invites his readers to consider his translation of Wajdi, which debuted in the pages of *Sırat-ı Müstakim* on 10 September 1908. Incidentally, this was around the time the Committee of Union and Progress (CUP) had taken it upon itself to send missions across the realms to 'explain the revolution' to the people.[22] The revolution did need explaining: many within the dominions were still unaware of it and there was not yet a consensus on what each of the revolutionary terms even meant. Due to the interests at stake in the potential applications of Freedom–Equality–Fraternity–Justice in the public sphere, it was inevitable there should be contestation over definitions. When the press joined the venture to explain such concepts, *Sırat-ı Müstakim* became one of the dominant voices in the contest over which significations should prevail.

Sırat-ı Müstakim's excitement about the revolution is clear. The founders joined countless others – with both similar and disparate ideological and political visions – in regarding 1908 as a moment of promise and release. To highlight this belief, the journal decided to declare, and commemorate, its birth as 11 July 1324, the day after the revolution. *Sırat-ı Müstakim* also benefited from links with the most credited harbingers of the constitutional revolution, the CUP.[23] The intersection of the religious, political and intellectual positions of the journal's founders is apparent in the timing of its debut, as well as much of its early content. The front page of its first issue had three pieces: (1) in Arabic, the first six verses of the Surat al-Fatiha, the opening to the Qur'an, ending one verse early, on the plea to be directed in the 'straight path', the inspiration for the journal's name, followed by an expressed dedication to the 'straight path' and a prayer to Muhammad, who is chosen as guide; (2) in Ottoman Turkish under the Arabic heading *al-Din al-nasiha* (true religion is perpetual self-alignment), an elaboration on the journal's sincere dedication to accepting the 'straight path', unambiguously in the service of Islam; (3) in Ottoman Turkish, 'Freedom – Equality', Musa Kazım's contribution on the slogans of the July Revolution.[24]

The *Sırat-ı Müstakim*'s intention of becoming a part of the debate and to actively participate in defining revolutionary slogans on its own terms is evident as early as the publication's release. Musa Kazım's contribution to the journal as soon-to-be Ottoman Şeyhülislam, the supreme Islamic religious authority, under the Unionist government was significant, as it lent legitimacy to the shared vision of the journal and religious authority, both constitutionalist and liberal within an Islamic framework, for the definitions of Freedom – Equality. Musa Kazım's piece on the front page of the very first issue stated that the collective was now released from slavery, and that the reinstated Ottoman constitution was a charter of freedom as well as a proof of equality.[25] He continued cautiously, however, expressing that he felt obliged to make some remarks on the notions of 'freedom' and 'equality' since the lack of advancements in the domains with respect to knowledge and education had sometimes resulted in shocking interpretations of what these meant.[26] By this means, the *Sırat-ı Müstakim* articulated its intention to also 'explain the revolution' to the constituency it so chided.

Sırat-ı Müstakim's content was active in tone and in engagement with concepts that could be read as being directly relevant to the sociopolitical climate of the Ottoman centre. Content was also ample since much had been 'prepared' for print prior to the journal's official debut.[27] *Muslim Woman*'s translator, in particular, had been especially prolific during the era he so frequently referred to as '*istibdad*':

> Poems Mehmed Akif composed during the Hamidian era and the works he had translated by authors like Muhammad 'Abduh (1849–1905) and Farid Wajdi but could not publish because he had not found the right platform, can be considered among these preparations.[28]

Indeed, Akif expressed as much in a foreword to one of his many translations of Wajdi, namely *Civilisation and Islam*, in 1911.[29] The foreword to the book version of *Muslim Woman* also mentioned that the work was translated in advance but waited for the age of 'freedom' to be published because there was no permission to print 'social' texts before.[30] Having produced so much during the Hamidian era and committing to the *Sırat-ı Müstakim* as a platform for his publications after, Akif was thus poised to become the most prolific contributor to the journal. Eventually, the texts he published there numbered 216, nearly half of which were translations, and a significant proportion of those translations were the works of Wajdi.[31] And the attention Akif placed on translation can be extended more broadly to the journal as a whole.

Sırat-ı Müstakim featured prominent 'Cairene' figures, although these were not necessarily Egyptians or based in Cairo at the time. The readership

The Translation of a Patriarchal Order in Flux

was presented with translated works of such individuals as the peripatetic reformist activist Jamal al-Din al-Afghani (1838–97) and Muhammad Ali's grandson and Ottoman politician Said Halim (1863–1921).[32] 'Abduh was the ninth most published author (forty-one entries) while Wajdi was the most translated author (eighty-eight titles).[33] Consequently, one could say that the *Sırat-ı Müstakim* and Akif had what Suat Mertoğlu has called an 'Egypt connection'.[34] This point is further supported by the paper's aspiration to have a similar impact on the transnational readership as Rashid Rida's (1865–1935) *al-Manar* (1898–1940).[35] Texts that came from or via the Egyptian 'channel'[36] (for example, Afghani, Rida) were therefore selected 'on the basis of the needs of the Ottoman people ... and overwhelmingly adapted to Istanbul's conditions'.[37] Authors whose works would be translated were chosen with considerations of ideological alignment, especially since they held the potential to sway the domestic readership's opinion on Ottoman-centric social and political concerns.

Neither were the choices of which Cairene authors would be translated for *Sırat-ı Müstakim* driven by more personal factors, such as promoting the works of friends and acquaintances over others. For all of Akif's numerous translations of Wajdi, for example, the two did not meet until Akif's 1914 trip to Egypt. The highlight of Akif's much anticipated meeting with Wajdi seems to have been the language of their communication, Turkish. His future son-in-law who had arranged the meeting recalls:

> The conversation between these two individuals who liked each other very much lasted quite long. And the three of us, in a dingy Arab neighbourhood of Cairo, spoke as if we were standing on a piece of [our] homeland (*vatan parçası*).[38]

Despite Wajdi and Akif's pleasant meeting, if the poet's letters to family and close friends from his Egyptian exile in the early republican era are any indication, it seems unlikely the relationship blossomed into a very close one.[39] Wajdi is absent in Akif's Egypt, as he presented it to those closest to him. In fact, these letters consistently impose a distance between him and the place where he sought refuge, making it evident that Akif is first and foremost an Istanbulite poet whose political orientation is fixed on the Ottoman centre. This may explain why Akif is not too concerned with introducing Wajdi when he frames *Muslim Woman* since the focus is on its post-revolutionary political utility.[40] This is evident from the manner of the translation's introduction to the readers of the *Sırat-ı Müstakim*.

The editorial board considered *Muslim Woman* significant and relevant enough to warrant it being spread out in instalments over sixteen issues of the journal's crucial first year of publications. The nature of this significance was quite particular, which is demonstrated in how the translator's introduction does not highlight Wajdi and *Muslim Woman*, but rather, signposts other concerns. The translator begins by raising awareness about 'recent' discussions on Muslim women, on their becoming more like Western women, living among men and leaving household confinement to participate in industry, and how, in recent weeks, Musa Kazım Efendi had provided a response to why such aspirations were not advisable.[41] Musa Kazım's comments, which Akif references, are to be found in the aforementioned 'Freedom – Equality' column. The framework under which Musa Kazım places 'the woman question', which is confirmed and reinforced by Akif, signals readers to interpret *Muslim Woman*'s relevance within the (political) confines of the Ottoman centre, distancing it both from Egypt and from Muslim women. In addressing his readers, Akif says Egypt, too, had discussions about 'covering' (*mesturiyet*)[42] in the past, thereby distinguishing this translation from the presumed first readers of the Arabic original: his readers are evidently not Egyptians. This method of distancing the text from its place of origin and explicitly linking it to Musa Kazım's elaboration on constitutional slogans engenders an original intention for Akif's *Muslim Woman*.

Musa Kazım articulates his thoughts on the condition of women in 'Freedom – Equality', his multi-instalment editorial contribution in *Sırat-ı Müstakim*.[43] By addressing 'the woman question' under the umbrella of this terminological duo, the future Şeyhülislam creates an opening to define the conceptual range of the social applications of constitutional slogans whose definitions had not yet been crystallised; this did not yet extend to gender difference, though it soon would. *Muslim Woman* was the perfect text to support the argument that the sexes were complementary, but not equal. This was a conclusion that could well be extended to society, at large. Ostensibly beginning the process of defining equality with a palatable debate on men and women and proposing a position with which many who held sway in public discourse would already be in agreement – that is equity not equality, and separate and complementary roles in place of the same rights – would prepare the ground. They would warm opinions to concerns that many authors, public figures and press organs, like Wajdi, Kazım and *Sırat-ı Müstakim*, saw as potential dangers in advocating wide sweeping social equality, amongst classes or in (men's) access to political power, for example. In the event that these arguments swerved away from the interests of these stakeholders, there would be the groundwork for reverting back to the questionable analogy of 'if everyone is equal and has an equal say, then are women also equal?' The intended audience of *Muslim Woman*, both Arabic-reading

The Translation of a Patriarchal Order in Flux

and Ottoman Turkish, would be inclined to answer this question in the negative.

The first and second issues of the *Sırat-ı Müstakim* set the stage for the intended manner of *Muslim Woman*'s reception by an Ottoman audience that was particularly Turco-Sunni, and arguably urban. The introduction and first instalment of *Muslim Woman* shared the 10 September 1908 issue with the third instalment of Musa Kazım's 'Freedom – Equality'.[44] By the time this issue hit the press, the *Sırat-ı Müstakim* had already established its values and defined its ideal readership. Wajdi's work, in general, and *Muslim Woman*, in particular, reinforced the journal's stance on social and ideological issues, which explains why Akif's introduction emphasised *Sırat-ı Müstakim* values rather than providing an intellectual profile of *Muslim Woman*'s author. In this unsigned introduction, Akif introduces Wajdi – with information on his current status as the head of a national society/assembly in Egypt,[45] in brackets – after he introduces Musa Kazım and Qasim Amin. Wajdi is nevertheless granted authority. Instead of reflecting on the topic of the book in his introduction, the translator found it suitable and, perhaps, more effective to instead immediately leave the authority to Wajdi, who he designated as knowledgeable, remarking that the 'individual' who had written *Muslim Woman* had analysed the matter from every angle.[46]

The book version of Akif's translation has a few additions to the serialised version's otherwise unchanged introduction, demonstrating *Muslim Woman* and its author's secondary importance even more firmly. Akif does not use the opportunity of the publication being bound in one volume to elaborate further on Wajdi or the work. Rather, the identification of Wajdi's occupation and status is removed without any other distinction taking its place. Both introductions, to the serialised and to the book versions, mention that *Muslim Woman* was translated considerably before the publication date. What is added to the latter is the reason why this was so: the aforementioned restrictions on the press during the previous, Hamidian, era. The book's introduction reads:

> Since the state of our press at that time did not allow for the publication of such a social (*ictimai*) piece, we waited for the coming of the age of freedom (*hürriyet*). Thank God that age has arrived, and *Muslim Woman* has sequentially been published and completed in the pages of the *Sırat-ı Müstakim*.[47]

Regarding the reason for going ahead and publishing an Ottoman Turkish book version of *Muslim Woman*, it is said to be in response to reader appreciation of the work's value and to having received repeated proposals to publish it as a book, with God's help.[48] Akif's introduction puts Egypt at a distance and emphasises local post-revolutionary changes, among which were a new intellectualisation of labour and freedom and the limits of equality. These are topics Wajdi addresses with less severe urgency than Musa Kazım, who is granted precedence in Akif's introduction to both the serialised and compiled translation. Let's return once again to Kazım's series of articles and the place women occupy in it.

Framing the Ottoman Muslim Woman

The question of women and their veils takes a prominent place in Kazım's editorialising on 'Freedom – Equality'. In dialogue with the reinstitution of the constitution, he introduces this topic in the journal's second issue, following his first instalment on freedom and equality, which establishes that complete equality is neither possible, nor practised, anywhere. Kazım begins his conversation on these revolutionary values by defining what freedom means according to the constitution, which is then juxtaposed alongside arguments for the necessity of the veil.[49] Thus, Musa bound these issues to one another by placing the conversation about freedom and the veil under the same heading. The line of argument supporting continued adherence to the veil is additionally bolstered by the reminder that the reinstitution of the constitution cannot signal the elimination of veils, as interpreted by some, he points out, especially since the fourth and eleventh articles of the constitution specify that the religion of the Ottoman state is Islam, and that its sultan is the caliph. Thus, he states, every Muslim under the sovereignty of the Sublime State is obliged to observe the rules of this religion.[50] Additional points made have to do with the division of duties among women (giving birth and educating children) and men – inside and outside of the home, respectively – and that an attempt at exchanging the realms in which the two conduct their labour would be against the laws of nature, as Kazım equates this with an effort to transform women into men and men into women.[51]

The concerns Kazım addressed in his third instalment of 'Freedom – Equality' shared with the first instalment of Akif's translation centred primarily on women's education, which is the topic of Amin's work, to which Wajdi's *Muslim Woman* responds. Kazım puts forth the view that women being covered does not entail their being deprived of civilisation's achievements.[52] Kazım promotes the education of women, but is opposed to their higher education (that is, at the Darülfünun) since their continuing 'like men and trying to graduate from there as engineers, architects, etc., would undoubtedly be tantamount to their abusing their natural necessary duties and thus betraying humanity'.[53] The opposition does not come from the fact that women are forbidden to learn the arts and sciences that are taught at higher education institutions, since religion puts no limits on the education that a Muslim can attain. Instead, Kazım's objection comes from the fact that the genders are designated to have different roles. Besides, he says, women not being provided higher education is implicit in the fact that not 'even' all of the country's men have access to such an education.[54] These arguments about women, in general, and women's education, in particular, demonstrate that Wajdi's *Muslim Woman* was very much in line with concerns the *Sırat-ı Müstakim* wished to address (and control the interpretative direction of) in the summer and autumn of 1908. Revolutionary slogans, and their interpretations, were intertwined with 'the woman question'. Judging by the order of 'Freedom – Equality' and *Muslim Woman*'s appearance in the periodical, however, it was Kazım's position that was dominant in formulating new definitions. Wajdi's *Muslim Woman* was the means of reinforcing it, and thus secondary.

While revolutionary slogans were chanted in the streets and sprinkled across the articles of the reinstituted constitution, as we have noted, definitions were clearly far from precise and up for debate. Women become a crucial node for negotiating the conversation on equality and freedom, not just as they relate to civilisation, in general, but to Ottoman constitutionalism, in particular. The intertwinement of women with questions concerning the naturalness of power are not just contextual. In fact, they can be better understood as we turn from the context and pattern of the translation to a closer analysis of Akif's translation. This move requires outlining the general structure of Wajdi's book. Akif's deceptively simple approach to translation reveals the importance of 'waged labour', as a source for social value, in the debates on women in Egypt as well as in the Ottoman centre.[55] In the next two sections, we look into specific translation strategies undertaken by Akif, revealing the epistemological and social stakes of the argument about women and its imbrication with both power and waged labour.

Translation as Intervention

Muslim Woman is comprised of thirteen chapters plus an introduction, conclusion and epilogue. With the exception of the introduction and the epilogue, each chapter revolves around one central question, which is articulated as the title of the chapter. To give a sense of the flow of the argument, one could divide the chapters into clusters. Chapters 1–4 grapple with the relationship between women's natural role and freedom. Chapters 5–7 contend with women's work outside the home.[56] Chapters

8–12 link the two previous clusters by conjoining arguments about the veil, true freedom and civilisation. Chapter 13, the final one, concerns the best mode of education for women now that their natural role, freedom, civilisation, and the connection between them, has been laid out. The issue of women's education is confined to the last chapter. Its connection to the rest of the argument is not integral and could be omitted. At its core, the book is concerned with adjoining women (and their veiling), freedom and civilisation in a manner that renders Amin's argument (and others like him) groundless. We turn to the specifics of the argument later. For now, we note that the veil was at the heart of a struggle for delimiting 'sex' versus 'gender', without necessarily having direct recourse to these categories. At stake were competing visions of the social and of the optimal division of power within it.

Muslim Woman presents a number of challenges for its translator. Wajdi's style is deceptively simple, almost minimalist. As mentioned earlier, each chapter revolves around the attempt to answer one question which is deemed central for understanding the connection between women, the veil and civilisation. In fact, the chapter titles are a sequence of questions, to which the author generally responds early in the chapter. He lays out his argument bluntly and succinctly, in brief and clear sentences with no sign of rhymed prose (*saj'*) or investment in poetic figuration. But his responses to his own questions are sometimes unconvincing, at least to us later readers, and riven with contradictions. Wajdi then rallies a wide range of references to support his point, with repeated recourse to long direct quotes from encyclopedias, statistics, historical narratives and European thinkers. Those featuring in *Muslim Woman* include Cesare Lombrosso (1835–1909), Enrico Ferri (1856–1929), Armand Trousseau (1801–67) and Auguste Comte (1798–1857). The latter is the most cited writer in the text. Wajdi often interjects these long quotes with explanations, elaborations or direct appeals to the reader to note a particular point. To a lesser extent, he evokes Qur'anic verses and prophetic sayings.[57] The references occupy the body of the chapter, culminating in a return to the initially posed question, now regarded as settled in the text's rhetorical stance, allowing the transition to the following chapter's central query.

It is at first sight tempting to read Akif's Ottoman Turkish translation of *Muslim Woman* as exemplifying the invisible translator: a case where the translator dissolves himself and completely disappears.[58] He reproduces the work's structure in his version of the text without shortening, merging or omitting chapters. The poet preserves the minute details of the argument in each and every chapter. He translates Wajdi's interventions but does not supplement them with his own. Yet, on at least two interrelated

The Translation of a Patriarchal Order in Flux

counts, the translator presents his readers with a text that is a departure from the original. For, *Muslim Woman*'s potentiality is simultaneously expanded and contracted with the release of its translation: Akif's readers inevitably consume a different text than Wajdi's because of the differences in both the content and contexts of the two *Muslim Woman*s. While both are intricately intertwined with the local and structural circumstances of their respective releases, the two versions are additionally embedded in different intellectual and sociopolitical contexts. Wajdi's *Muslim Woman* is, for example, presented in Arabic as an integral link within the chain of his broader intellectual project, for instance in an epilogue that Akif's translation omits. The second divergence, enmeshed in the first, concerns variances in the intentionality of how the work should be interpreted by the two respective audiences. The previous section has already shown how the initial serialisation of Akif's *Muslim Woman* places it in conversation with the revolutionary slogans of 1908. In this regard, despite Akif's apparent loyalty to Wajdi's work, the translator nevertheless subtly makes his presence and intentions emerge when the two versions of *Muslim Woman* are read together. Most significantly, he makes precise what Wajdi leaves ambiguous, by way of translatorial interjections.

Akif's translation does not include Wajdi's epilogue, which is fundamental in altering the text's potentialities. Furthermore, since Amin was not translated yet and his arguments were thus not as notorious within the Ottoman public sphere as they had been in Arabic, it becomes more challenging for the readers of the Ottoman version to see how Wajdi's introduction in *Muslim Woman* frames his response to Amin's *New Woman*. The epilogue, which does not appear in the translation, clarifies how Wajdi's text is, in fact, not a refutation of Amin's central thesis of the need to educate women to attain civilisational advancement but instead reveals itself to be most primarily concerned with the conceptual underpinnings of Amin's argument, that is, the question of a progression towards societal equality and a transformation of the labour market. This observation tallies with Wajdi's epilogue, where the author is at pains to make the point that *Muslim Woman* ought to be read as part of a larger body of work. It is here that Wajdi draws the reader's attention to the connection between *Muslim Woman* and some of his earlier publications, such as *Tatbiq al-diyana al-Islamiyya 'ala nawamis al-madaniyya* ('The application of the Islamic religion to the laws of civilisation', 1899), and *al-Hadiqa al-fikriyya fi 'ithbat Allah bil-barahin al-tabi'yya* ('The intellectual garden: the natural proofs for the existence of God', 1901).[59] In these texts, Wajdi explores different facets of his overarching goal. His disciples describe the aim as a relentless reconciliation between Islam and Science, and between Spirit and Matter. In fact, Wajdi is explicit in stating that he sees these works as interconnected. More recently, Marwa Elshakry has offered a sharper characterisation, which accounts for Wajdi's clear anti-positivism and anti-materialism, describing his corpus as striving to create an 'Islamic empiriospiritism'.[60] In other words, he is driven to deploy empiricism against positivism and materialism and in the service of proving the existence of spirit, spiritual truths, and by extension the divine. The issue explains his obsession with séance, and hypnosis – which was later described by some of his students as 'embarrassing'. Worried that the connection between *Muslim Woman* and his earlier texts might be lost on the reader, he informs his readers in that same epilogue that the book will be supplemented by a second volume where he would elaborate on what he means by civilisation in general and Islamic civilisation more specifically. The latter distinction is more apparent than real, for Islamic civilisation is revealed to be the *true* civilisation.

The Ottoman Turkish readership of the *Sırat-ı Müstakim* was not exposed to the facets of *Muslim Woman* that made it evident that Wajdi envisioned it as a prelude to his intervention in defining civilisation in the same way the audience of the book's Arabic version was – even if the second volume on (Islamic) civilisation alluded to in the epilogue seems to have never materialised.[61] This is not to say that Akif's *Muslim Woman* was not a discussion about civilisation; it was, just not one that was as intricately tied to Wajdi's personal intellectual musings and outputs. The debate on women had already become something of a civilisational benchmark in both intellectual centres, of Cairo and Istanbul – as a number of scholars have noted.[62] As such, 'the woman question' became imbricated with definitions of civilisation as a necessary precondition for formulating a stance in these debates.[63] Wajdi rendered the connection obvious by positioning *Muslim Woman* as an entryway into a broader discussion about civilisation. But the revolution of 1908 embedded the concern with civilisation within an explicit political question regarding the nature of power and its optimal mode of distribution in the body politic. This explicitness throws into sharp relief the specific political dimensions of the debate in Egypt, too. In the next two sections, we explore how Akif's translation strategy reveals competing visions of the social, shaped through the attempt to delimit access to power. This process entailed an attempt to envision a new patriarchal order in the wake of the arising discursive hegemony of waged labour.

Translation: Language and Keywords

Akif's linguistic mastery and ideological positionality become amply clear when the *Muslim Woman* in Arabic and in Ottoman Turkish are analysed side-by-side. Glances back and forth between the two versions make it apparent that Akif is equally capable of translating scientific neologisms and Qur'anic references into fluid and intuitive Ottoman Turkish. Furthermore, he devises nuanced strategies to evoke a parallel semantic range for crucial keywords deployed in the Arabic *Muslim Woman*.

Two pivotal strategies feature in this and the following section. The first is the systematic delineation of different terms in Ottoman Turkish to distinguish between layers of meaning inherent in the same keyword in Arabic. The most important example analysed here is that of the translation of *hijab*, the keyword around which these debates revolve.[64] The second, and seemingly antithetical, strategy is where Akif maintains Arabic words with the intention of interpreting them according to their meaning in Arabic even if that meaning does not exist in the life history of the word in Ottoman Turkish. Put simply, he broadens the meaning of Ottoman Turkish words, of Arabic origin, by insisting on introducing some of their other connotations in Arabic. Ironically, Akif's meticulousness and brilliant navigation of the semantic ranges between Arabic and Ottoman Turkish end up producing a distinctly different language register in his translation. Furthermore, the translation's seamlessness paradoxically highlights the contradictions in the vision of the social that is being worked out in this text – through both languages – in response to the challenges faced by the patriarchal order, socially and politically. As such, it sheds new light on the stakes and tensions in Wajdi's argument because it opens it up starkly to immediate questions about the building of a new society. The analysis of the translation of *hijab* (veil) demonstrates these points clearly.

Wajdi consistently uses the term *hijab* (veil) to refer (to): (1) the thin veil covering women's faces; (2) the practice of secluding women in designated private quarters within the home; (3) figuratively to the natural boundaries whose maintenance begets happiness and success while their trespass results in chaos. The third (figurative) meaning is crystallised in Chapter 11 entitled 'Can the veil be lifted?' where the analogy between women's veil as a physical manifestation of the natural boundaries between the sexes and the observance of natural limits that govern the organic functioning of society is explicitly expressed. Wajdi argues that the history of oppression experienced specifically by the West in the medieval period engendered an 'intense animosity towards everything even slightly suggestive of pressure or constraint. It directed its energy towards unlocking all bonds without bothering to assess either extreme against a principle of moderation.'[65] In responding to previous religious, intellectual, political and moral extremes – of censorship and control – the West produces another extreme: anarchy. Westerners, he says, have not demanded the reform of religion, but rather its disappearance; and the same pattern is purportedly repeated in each sphere. That is to say, in place of striving to reach a mean, they set out to dissolve the entire sphere, unleashing anarchy and chaos on the world.

Wajdi attributes impending anarchy to the vanishing of *veils* (here as boundaries or limits) which are necessary for human perfection, in the name of personal freedom and liberty.[66] As such, the veil is both an actual physical boundary that preserves the natural limit between the sexes as well as a metonymy; substituting part (women's veil) for whole (civilisation's natural boundaries) and combining the material (women's veil) and immaterial (civilisation's natural boundaries).[67] In this manner, the veil, as a keyword, enfolds the struggle over defining society and civilisation, offering itself as a symbol for competing visions of the social in the wake of perceived structural changes to the familiar patriarchal system.[68]

Akif amplifies this underlying value by employing an artillery of terms to render *hijab*. While Akif's tendency to opt for *tesettür* (being or becoming veiled, concealment) in place of *hijab* when referring to the piece of cloth women don was common enough in the day's translations from Arabic to Ottoman Turkish (see, for example, Booth and Shissler's contribution in this volume), the poet also utilised a host of other designators, such as *hijab* (barrier, veil), *peçe* (black face veil), *mestur* (a veil, a cover), *mesturiyet* (covering, covered-ness), *örtü* (cover) and *perde* (drape). Since the meaning conveyed by each encompasses that which is articulated by Wajdi's *hijab*, the terms could potentially be used interchangeably.[69] Yet, Akif's method is to reserve *hijab* to exclusively denote the figurative meaning of the veil – the above-mentioned point (3).

Hijab is the most used term in the Arabic version of the chapters Wajdi devotes to the veil, namely, Chapter 9, 'Is the Veil a Sign of Imprisonment or a Guarantee of Freedom?', Chapter 10, 'Is the Veil an Obstacle for the Attainment of Women's Perfection?', and Chapter 11, 'Can the Veil Disappear?' There is rare recourse to other forms of the same root, such as *ihtijab* (seclusion/veiling), *hajaba* (to seclude/veil), *muhajjaba* (secluded/veiled). The terms refer both to women's seclusion in private quarters and/or to putting on a physical cloth. The two acts comprise a continuum of women's seclusion rather than diametrically opposed or distinct practices. Akif does not invoke the same continuum in his translation. On the contrary, the manner in which Akif engages with the word '*hijab*' in these chapters provides one of the few instances in which the poet took the liberty to personally suggest, by patterned word choice, when Wajdi's words should be taken as literal or figurative, without ever altering equivalency among the meaning of the words that compose the original and translated text. In other words, Akif's strategy dissolved the multiple, and by extension ambiguous reference of the term in Arabic, choosing to distinguish between *hijab*'s literal and figurative meanings.

Though the meanings conveyed by Wajdi's *hijab* and Akif's various alternatives remained the same, the translator's method of patterned word choice would have created new associations and connotations for Akif's readers that Wajdi had not explicitly chosen for his text or readership. Akif overwhelmingly relies on alternative words for *hijab* when referring to the garment and maintains '*hijab*' when referring to social boundaries, thereby distinguishing between the layers of meaning deployed by Wajdi. The translator thus takes the liberty to eliminate the ambiguity and expansiveness of the arguably most significant word in the text, one that conveyed both abstract and immaterial boundaries and the specific material boundary of the cloth that was placed between women and the external world, by only employing it in the former instances. By this means, Akif spells out for his readers what Wajdi withholds in his original text.

In appealing to the physical veil, Akif most frequently opts for '*tesettür*', as suggested, a relatively unremarkable choice due to its common usage as a signifier for the veil in the Ottoman centre. The poet *substitutes* '*tesettür*' in each instance Wajdi uses '*hijab*' for the questions posed as titles for Chapters 9, 10 and 11. For the garment worn by Roman women, Akif uses both '*tesettür*' and '*peçe*'.[70] *Hijab* is left as is on two occasions in the ninth chapter. The first is in the context of a section on the fall of Rome, which Wajdi inextricably links to (previously veiled and subsequently revealed) women throwing themselves into the streets.[71] This is not the first instance Wajdi references un/veiling in a non-Muslim culture, a practice that has the effect of universalising the necessity of the veil for the readership. In this instance, Wajdi explains Rome's growth from a small and impoverished society to one that gave birth to all of Europe's civilisations alongside women's seclusion and veiling in the days of its rise. After Rome became illustrious and conquered the world, Wajdi explains, men – aggressive by nature – brought about its downfall by releasing women from seclusion. Akif retains Wajdi's *hijab* in his translation of this scene's details, that is the moment when men 'found the opportunity to ruin the morality of the helpless women, to soil their modest dresses and lift their *hijab*s, for the sake of their own carnal pleasures'.[72] This sentence blends the literal with the figurative to deliver visual imagery of the dire consequences following upon the lifting of veils. The second *hijab* of the translator's Chapter 9 is somewhat more informative, as it speaks exclusively about material and immaterial veils and alternates between '*rida*', '*tesettür*' and '*hijab*'. Wajdi explains here that the immaterial veil proposed by opponents of veiling (that is, self-guarding, preserving one's 'chastity') is infinitely heavier for women than the fabric they wear, which Akif translates as '*tesettür*' and the delicate material '*rida*', respectively.[73] because such individuals 'uphold the desire for this *hijab* to be strictly moral and immaterial, the type that precludes inclination for affection and carnal desire from this mortal world . . . they say women should be angels!'[74] In this instance, the immaterial veil seeks to extract women's humanity in a mortal world.

The tenth and eleventh chapters continue to consider the veil from material and immaterial perspectives. Chapter 10, on whether the veil is 'an obstacle for woman attaining freedom', discusses the veil as a material, sartorial, object and not as an immaterial barrier, social or otherwise; it does not use the word *hijab*.[75] In translating this chapter, Akif prefers *mestur*, *mesturiyet* and *tesettür*. This chapter presents a stark contrast between women who make men happy (the archetype, that is, '*Muslim Woman*') and those who do not (that is, those who are absent from their husband's side), and refutes arguments of veiling being harmful: namely, that the veil is bad for women's psychological health and deprives them of education, or that it prevents men from seeing women whom they might want to marry. It is Akif's translation of the eleventh chapter, 'Can the Veil be Lifted?', however, that fully demonstrates the poet's efforts to delegate *hijab* to the figurative realm and to associate the physical dimension, to which the material object of the veil belongs, with *tesettür*. This chapter draws dramatic conclusions about the fate of civilised and Eastern societies, linking the veil to societal boundaries and the anarchy that would ensue if the *hijab* were not maintained. Akif utilises *tesettür* three times (including the title question), *örtü* and *perde* twice, and *hijab* and *mesturiyet* each once. *Örtü* is the first substitution to appear. It is used twice in a row and is joined to the action of lifting. The first instance speaks to the cloth covering women's faces and the second to necessary cloths that have been lifted by materialistic civilisation (under the influence of its dishonest luster).[76] *Perde* (drape, or curtain) replaces other *hijab*s: 'The drape of modesty wrapped around the faces of our youth, and in fact, our elderly, has been pulled away,'[77] and the lack of social propriety, indecency and 'filth' that came with lifting drapes. *Tesettür* refers exclusively to the physical dimension of veiling. Akif is keen on not granting this term metaphorical connotations.

The poet keeps *hijab* in a single instance in his translation of the eleventh chapter. The sentence in which it is used is especially pertinent in the Ottoman context, as it likely resonated in a different, less amplified, manner with Wajdi's original audience than with Akif's, as many among the latter were no doubt anxious about the shape of the future in a post-revolutionary empire. The function of the use of *hijab* in this instance is telling, not least because it is in a sentence that unambiguously points to the abstract quality of *hijab* by exposing its plurality, which relegates *tesettür* to be one among many different kinds of *hijab*: 'Easterners have now wholly understood that many of those *hijabs* that have been lifted – destroyed – in the name and under the influence of "personal liberty" are necessary for humanity's perfection.'[78] Here, Akif signals his readers to interpret the word *hijab* as conceptual and severely consequential, more than a sartorial item, in a cautionary tone. The suggestion to limit the abolition of barriers in what could be forsaken for 'personal liberty' was dually significant in the Ottoman context at the time of the publication's release since personal liberty was a revolutionary value, protected by the ninth and tenth articles of the constitution that was reinstated in its aftermath.

Akif insists on showing his readers that there are two issues at stake. The first pertains to women themselves, and the other pertains to the natural limits necessary for social life. More accurately, the first issue (women) is an indication of the broader fate of social life. To think about the question of women in 1908 was to ask: what was this a revolution against and what did it hope to achieve? The clarity of the political stakes of the translation enables us to grapple anew with the contradictions in Wajdi's vision. He tried to posit a spiritual bond as an antidote to social conflict, taking women as the primary site for instilling this vision of spiritual social bonds. The contradiction takes on immediate class and political dimensions in Akif, allowing us to see how the question of women is coextensive with the burgeoning of waged labour as the source of social value, and the ensuing attempt to imagine a new patriarchal order in its wake.

Translation and the Political Faultlines

Amin's argument in *Emancipation of Women* – and, in a revised fashion, in his *New Woman* – hinges on the demonstration of an analogy between the family (microcosm) and the state (macrocosm). The arbitrary power granted to the man/father, as the head of the family, mimics and reproduces the arbitrary power held by the ruler, who is symbolically the father of the nation.[79] Within this schema, there is no clearer marker of such arbitrariness than the veil – an allegory for absolute power and tyranny, or '*istibdad*', incidentally (or not), the term used by opponents of the Hamidian regime, Akif included, to refer to the reign of the absolute monarch ousted by the revolution. Wajdi sets out to dissolve the grounds for this analogy, replacing it with a metonymy between the veil and natural necessary limits. The veil is not the materialisation of the arbitrary practice of power, but of the necessary limits without which civilisations would fall into anarchy and ruin, the preceding example of Rome being a case in point. As such, the comparison shifts its emphasis from family/state to society/nature.[80] We are no longer looking at how the veil manifests the arbitrary exercise of power by the head of the family, but at the veil as a materialisation of other abstract limits at the heart of the project of maintaining civilisation. Slightly diverging from Wajdi's method, Akif's grounding of the shift to society/nature through the exclusive allocation of a figurative connotation to *hijab* (as seen in the previous section) somewhat alters the manner of achieving this shift, for they still seem to appear as separate parallel realms.

Unlike Wajdi, Akif faces the challenge of the urgency of political questions raised by the 1908 revolution. In other words, the translator needs to specify the limits that need to be observed. He cannot simply present an intellectual abstract argument and stop there. Most crucially, what are the limits defining freedom and equality, and what are the limits of their extension to members of society? These are not merely theoretical questions for Akif, their practical political implications are immediate. This is obvious in minute, but key, interventions Akif makes in the translation.

Wajdi can quote a statement from Comte arguing for the incommensurability of state and family with no need for justification or elaboration. Consequently, Wajdi concludes that the comparison between ruler/ruled and men/women, which is central for Amin's argument, is unfounded.[81] In this manner, the explicit discussion of the political repercussions of the argument can be averted or at least sidelined since the question of women does not revolve on politics, according to Wajdi, but on the accurate adjudication of nature. While this clearly renders the discussions of nature and scientific knowledge political, the debate does not have to turn to issues pertaining to the state and its relation to society. But, in 1908, in the Ottoman centre, Akif cannot afford a similar luxury.

As mentioned above, the poet did not take many liberties as translator when transferring the contents and message of *Muslim Woman*. Yet, the articles in the the *Sırat-ı Müstakim* issues were methodically curated to

The Translation of a Patriarchal Order in Flux

highlight the political effects of the above argument, evidently shared by the editors, especially for the ongoing constitutional debates in the Ottoman context. The need to intervene directly in contemporary politics is not restricted to the simple placement of Akif's translation on the pages of *Sırat-ı Müstakim*. The manner in which the periodical's editors juxtaposed *Muslim Woman* with other contributions would have the effect of making its key points resonate with urgency in the public and political sphere. We have already mentioned how it is positioned alongside Musa Kazım Efendi's editorials that interpreted the critical concepts of freedom, equality and justice, in seven issues containing seven of the translation's sixteen instalments. An attempt to amplify the relevance *of Muslim Woman* is equally clear, in subtle ways, in Akif's actual translation. Chapter 11, 'Can the Veil be Lifted?' – discussed above – offers two seminal examples.

In unpacking the specificity of the Western historical trajectory, Wajdi claims that the ostensibly particularly Western understanding of intellectual freedom is an extreme reaction to Westerners' oppressive history. Akif inserts a subtle, but imperative, modification to Wajdi's description:

> In the era of absolutism, those in charge of the rational domain went overboard. They went so far as to forbid people the enjoyment of the benefits of thinking and the fruits of the mind. When civilisation arrived, it did not wish to stand with people at the point of equity. It sanctioned intellectual freedom to those who howl and yowl.

Akif supplements the above passage with short examples:

> Various constraints were imposed upon intellectuals in the times when despotism ruled; benefiting from the virtue of their intellect [and] the fruits of their minds was prohibited. Afterward, when it manifested itself, without wanting to fix people in parity, civilisation found intellectual freedom permissible for all **impoverished** people, perhaps up to the **firemen** and the ***vardacı***.[82]

The explicit evocation of lower social classes as ones to be barred from certain legally sanctioned political rights (here privileges) in order to avoid extremes is at once a logical culmination of the argument about women, and a contradiction that unsettles the society/nature continuum. Thus, it follows that barrier, namely *hijab*, ought to be maintained and that it is, for example, an error to universally grant intellectual freedom. Though both the Arabic original and Ottoman Turkish translation refer specifically to intellectual freedom, the implications are much broader and would, by implication, spill over into the social and political spheres.

Wajdi's edifice hinges on extricating the question of women from a wider debate on social stratification and the division of power towards the realm of nature as a stable system of harmony. The separation needs to simultaneously implicitly assume, yet aim at the replacement of, an atomic vision of society with an organicist one, as explained further in the next section.[83] It suffices here to note that for Wajdi's response to succeed in supplanting the family/state analogy, it must avoid making direct claims about the social division of power, at least until it has persuasively instilled an organicist view of society as indisputable in readers' minds. In a striking example, quoted at the start of this chapter, Wajdi compares men's duty towards women, or the patriarchal pact, to the pact between workers and thinkers; each is necessary for the other and cannot exchange their 'natural' duties. Nonetheless, he is careful not to discuss how this division of social labour between workers and intellectuals is supposed to happen, in order to maintain his focus upon the optimum functioning of society as a body, in which case the specialisation of organs should not be read as stratification. Akif's desire to immediately interfere in the ongoing political debates in 1908 renders it difficult for him to avoid direct social referentiality, the way Wajdi does. The liberty Akif takes of naming workers – the firemen and *vardacı* – surely has the effect of making the text more familiar for his readers, perhaps even prompting them to more vividly ponder the difference between the roles of labourer and intellectual, and whether the powers they are entitled to have, in order to exert an impact on social and political change, should also differ. At the same time, this interjection forces open the contradiction between stratification/specialisation in their vision of the social. Below, we focus on the linguistic mitigation of this contradiction before turning in the following section to their vision of the social in more detail.

Contradictions in the Language of a Spiritual Bond

Despite his intellectual and literary versatility, Akif was first and foremost a poet. Accordingly, Akif's form, language and style have undergone much analysis by scholars. Though currently one of the most studied figures in Turkey, works on Akif began to appear in his own lifetime, with publications on his oeuvre and personality by colleagues who were also friends, like Süleyman Nazif.[84] Midhat Cemal (Kuntay) was another individual to write a volume about Akif; his *Mehmed Akif: Hayatı, Seciyesi, Sanatı* ('Mehmed Akif: his life, character and art'), 1939, was among the early posthumous works. This biography is informative because it reflects on how the translator of Wajdi's *Muslim Woman* used language by a contemporary author, one who was nevertheless stylistically (and politically) more inclined to write in more colloquial language than Akif.

The Translation of a Patriarchal Order in Flux

Fellow poets, Midhat Cemal and Akif met in a sort of informal literary salon at the house of a common acquaintance late in the Hamidian era – a period often described by both as the age of '*istibdad*'. Slightly his junior, Midhat Cemal became curious about the quiet and elusive figure of Akif. Curiosity developed into admiration through acquaintance, which, in turn, developed into a lasting and close friendship. Midhat Cemal became a regular contributor to the *Sırat-ı Müstakim*, as well, which raised his literary profile by publishing the poem he and Akif had written together, '*Acem Şahı*' ('Iranian shah'), a poem that engaged with the most popular themes of the day, of justice, freedom and a call to end despotism.[85]

Speaking on Akif's poetry, Midhat Cemal emphasises its 'local' nature and argues that his use of language should be understood as Ottoman transformed into modern Turkish.[86] Nevertheless, he observes a feature of Akif's writing that not only complicates his initial remark but also speaks to the poet's *Muslim Woman*: Akif 'sometimes (but this 'sometimes' means very infrequently) neglected the Turkish use of Arabic words and would prefer their Arabic'.[87] Midhat Cemal offers a number of examples, for instance he points out that if '*kibar*' (Arabic for 'greatness') was to be used in an Ottoman Turkish compound construction, joined with the *izafe*, adopted into the language from Persian, it would only be found coupled with the word '*kelam*' (Arabic for 'word') but Akif wholly Arabised the word's function in his *Safahat* by employing it in the alternative, again, non-Turkish *izafe*, construction and delivered to his readers '*kibar-ı ümmet*' (great personage(s) of the *umma*).[88] Midhat Cemal scans *Safahat* for other examples of Akif's Arabic usages and points out words and usages that Turkish alternatives in wider circulation could have easily replaced, including *faka* (dire need, poverty), *mübin* (one that discerns good from bad), *belağ* (a message) and *reyb* (suspicion).[89] Thus, Akif tended to opt for Arabic uses of shared vocabulary in the event that the given term had a single Ottoman Turkish connotation or formulation. That is to say, Akif deployed Arabic to expand the meaning of particular words in Ottoman Turkish.

There is another example, also from Chapter 11 in *Muslim Woman*. Concluding the discussion about the Western civilisation of extremes, the Easterners' imitation is lamented: 'We are condemned to follow them in every aspect (*sha'n*) without criticism or deliberation.'[90] Akif chose to keep the word *sha'n* (here meaning aspect) although in Ottoman Turkish it was only used to refer to high social status: in fact, Redhouse's note for this word is that it is 'never used in Turkish with its Arabic pronunciation or meaning'.[91] Kuntay explained the tendency of such recourse to Arabic in two ways. First, Akif's approach to Arabic and Persian paralleled

European humanists' attitude towards Greek and Latin; they knew the languages but were not in need of using them for the purposes of showing off.[92] Second, the occasional resort to full-Arabic, Kuntay said, arises from Akif's assumption that because the book that he read the most, himself, was the Qur'an, he thought the same was true for his readers.[93] Put differently, Kuntay sees the 'rare Arabics' of Akif as derived from his central placement of the Qur'an as a mediator between him and his readers (who Kuntay assumes are primarily Turkish speaking Ottomans). Understood this way, the insight proves crucial for elucidating the contradictions in the vision of the social underlying *Muslim Woman*. For if the social is not formed out of individuals stratified into a material social structure and pitted against each other in constant competition, but is instead a whole harmonious body brought into existence through a spiritual bond, then in this specific context, Arabic and the Qur'an must be granted a prime position in bringing about and maintaining such a bond. At the same time, Akif's desire to intervene in a specific moment with a particular (mass) audience informs his linguistic choices. This tension between the need for preservation and amplification of Arabics and the imperative of addressing the audience in the Ottoman centre shapes Akif's language register, which is ironically even higher than the one deployed by Wajdi. The tension between mastery over language (Arabic) as a condition of power, rooted in a certain conception of the social, and language as a popular tool for acquiring ideological power is ultimately a question of class.

Waged Labour and Gender: Terms of Exchange

What we have argued above is suggestive for deepening our understanding of the cultural and political divisions between the divergent groups at the time: modernists, traditionalists, reformists and Islamists. While the question of women has often furnished a site for studying how the ideologies of these factions shaped their attitudes towards women, inverting the direction of the analysis might be more productive. That is to say, these divisions are the *effects* of the political questions underlying the debates on women, namely: what is the conception of society? What mode and division of power works best for society? The shift might aid in understanding the ostensible contradictions between the overly political positions and those regarding women within the same group. Hussein Omar argues, in the context of Egypt, that 'the notion that topical debates, such as those surrounding women's rights, could capture the essences of duelling visions of Islam – whether liberal, modernist and moderate, or radical, conservative and fanatical' have occluded the political stakes of

The Translation of a Patriarchal Order in Flux

these 'topical debates'.[94] To give an example from this paper: trying to understand Akif's position through appealing to his vision of Islam cannot account for his simultaneous enthusiasm for the constitutional revolution, delimiting the power of the caliph, and his approach to the question of women. In fact, the contradiction lies at the heart of the conceptualisation of the social itself. Akif inherits it from Wajdi, but in trying to stage a direct political intervention, these positions in tension become clearer.

To build on Elshakry's pithy characterisation of Wajdi's 'Islamic empiriospiritism': *Muslim Woman* attempts to contribute an empiriospiritual conception of the social capable of responding to the political and social pressures faced by patriarchy in a modern society structured around waged labour. The epigraph, in this chapter, already points in that direction. To enquire about the *natural* role and limit of women, then, is to engage in a wider political debate about the naturalness of any given division of power and the social order produced by it. In the process, patriarchy, science and social stratification are knitted together. These are the dimensions brought to light through tracing the Ottoman Turkish translation of *Muslim Woman*.

In focusing on Akif's translation strategies for *Muslim Woman*, our analysis bypasses the concern with categorisation along the familiar axis of modernists, traditionalists, reformists and Islamists, the importance of these categorisations notwithstanding. What is subtly revealed is the manner in which *Muslim Woman* aims to offer an epistemological foundation for delimiting political freedom through contributing a vision of the social that obliterates any sign of stratification or struggle. At stake is a 'new' patriarchal pact (socially and politically), capable of responding to the pressures owed to capitalist structural transformations. This is a patriarchy that does not assume the family economy model, but has to take into account generalised waged labour, and the family as a labour-free unit. Within this over-arching aim, the various positions and struggles of this transnational current of thought – amongst the factions belonging to it and against others – are formed. Below, we offer some brief remarks on how generalised waged labour is an undeclared premise in bringing together patriarchy, science and social stratification in *Muslim Woman*. The translation renders the relation between this vision and freedom more explicit, revealing it to be an epistemological foundation for a vision of freedom.

At the beginning of Chapter 5, 'Can Women Join Men in Working?', Wajdi claims that one of the ugliest manifestations of women's imprisonment is pushing them to work. He goes on to describe female labourers at European factories and the horrendous conditions of work and the dismal pay they get. He argues that 'this is the epitome of women's enslavement by men', yet: 'Our liberators of women, instead of considering this [that is, women's work] as a social ailment . . . would like to open the door for it since they think that we are following in the footstep of Europe.'[95] There are a number of variations on this idea. He explicitly states that: 'We do not believe that it is woman's immersion in the sciences and literature that makes men feel aversion towards her, but what makes her abominable and detestable, is her competition against him in outside work.'[96] The issue is repeated at every single tangent in the text. The striking aspect of Wajdi's argument, however, is that he projects what he terms as women's work outside the home into the future. It is a reality in Europe that the 'liberators of women' threaten to render as a reality of the East. The argument of a spiritual East in contradistinction to a material West is often replayed at the time, with persisting echoes until today. Yet, what is of concern, here, is the centrality of waged labour as part of what needs to be elided by this argument of a 'spiritual' bond.

Put differently, what Wajdi completely ignores is that it was also a reality of the East with women working in tobacco, textile and silk factories in the Ottoman Empire – not to mention women's traditional participation in agriculture.[97] In other words, some of these conditions of female workers in factories that Wajdi ascribes to what he calls the West were already an Ottoman and an Egyptian reality too – though he is keen on presenting it as a phenomenon characterised by a cultural divide between East and West – as belonging to two distinct types of society.[98] The first is tied together through spiritual bonds replicating the harmony of nature while the second chases after illusory ideas of stratification and struggle. There is another peculiar irony which brings forth the question of the female peasant, namely that the presence of the woman working in agriculture is actually acknowledged, but not construed as a form of 'outside' work.

Responding to an article published in *al-Muqattam* newspaper (Cairo), Wajdi argues that while it is true that female peasants and Bedouins do not observe the veil, they are living in the lowest echelons of social existence where their struggle is one of mere survival and as such they cannot be taken as a model.[99] Crucially, he does not wish to extend the prohibition on women's work to peasants and Bedouins. Their work falls under the banner of economic necessity and Wajdi has no interest in changing these economic realities. In an argument that may have sounded familiar to those debating women and labour in Egypt at the time, Wajdi projects their work as supplementary, in aid of family members, and as such as an element of the 'old' family economy. In refraining from arguing for rectifying the situation of peasant and Bedouin women, he is de facto revealing that he is not against women's work *in toto*. To phrase it more accurately, there are forms of women's work that are not discursively registered as labour even though they are widely recognised. What Wajdi reacts to are forms of labour that seemingly operate apart from traditional family constraints or needs. It is unclear, however, whether he would also object to blue-collar labour performed out of economic necessity. For it seems possible that women who work out of necessity, even outside the traditional bounds of family, can continue to do so, but their meagre existence should be pitied. It is the valorisation of female labour (here necessarily waged labour) and its transformation into a practice producing social value, that should be resisted. The concern is not primarily with halting the practice all together, but with hindering its transformation into a source of new conceptions of gender roles and relations. Wajdi is not alone in perceiving this threat in valorising waged labour, and it is precisely for this reason that we can read how an entire political and cultural current is shaped in the process of discursively eliding waged labour. The key, here, as shown with Wajdi, is not the eradication of women's work, but of contesting its discursive social value.

Amin's argument is premised, in part, upon the supposed disintegration of the patriarchal pact. His book belongs to a wide range of arguments that commented on the breakdown of the *nafaqa* system, at the heart of the Islamic legal framework of marriage whereby the husband is responsible for the material support of his wife and children. The idea that this system is collapsing belongs to a broader discourse elucidating the need to reform *shari'a* law and courts. Despite the disagreements amongst the diverse groups, their debates were underpinned by a shared perception that this system was falling apart. As a consequence, numerous women were forced to navigate the world without a male supporter (*'a'il*).

Per Amin's argument, women need to be educated so they may fill in the gaps whenever this system fails them (that is whenever there are no male relatives available, for whatever reason, to support them).[100] Much like Wajdi, he projects women's work as part of a future agenda. Evidently, however, neither of these writers is thinking about the existing massive participation of women in the family economy, primarily in agriculture, beyond the symbolic image of the female peasant as an unveiled local and traditional figure. Rather, they are engaged in rethinking gender relationships against the backdrop of family as a labour-free unit and labour as waged labour. In other words, they both assume, without much deliberation, a domestic sphere free from any form of labour (read waged labour). In this light, domestic labour (including slave labour) is invisible, but so are female peasants, who were summoned here as symbols, but not necessarily as participants in agriculture based on the family economy.[101] Nonetheless, these debates were not representative of a minority of elites; a classist argument mimicking a colonialist one as Leila Ahmed argued for example.[102] Rather, they are actively engaged in drawing the limits and defining the family versus the market, and a new patriarchal pact. In the process, the discursive hegemony of waged labour is sealed and the questions over what social values should govern gender and by extension politics, and who is responsible for their production are up for grabs. The year 1908 was central in bringing forth the double dimensions of the translation of the debates on the veil. On the one hand, rethinking gender relations on the level of the family in the wake of the normalisation of generalised wage labour, and on the other, pinning the epistemological foundations of political freedom rooted in a conception of a society whose patriarchy hinges on waged labour.

Conclusion

Analysing Wajdi's work in Akif's words – along with the timing and circumstances of the translation's release into circulation – allows the articulated social, political and patriarchal angles of the original *Muslim Woman* to come into sharper focus. Wajdi's *Muslim Woman* was an empiriospiritual reaction to forces that are perceived to threaten patriarchy, articulated through a treatise on women. Wajdi's argument on the need to maintain literal and figurative boundaries on women's visibility in public and their participation in formal waged labour was formulated and suggested as being transferrable to society at large, including men and across classes. Commencing this argument with biological sex has the effect of naturalising the division of power in the eyes of the readership. But this message was especially pertinent in the aftermath of the 1908 Constitutional Revolution that deposed Sultan Abdülhamid II. At a moment when boundaries had been dismantled to be reformulated – especially with respect to access to authority and power – Wajdi's implied need to impose limits and his insistence on the infeasibility of formal equality in society through a discourse on women was amplified to become a notch more explicit in Mehmed Akif's translation of *Muslim Woman*. Through the poet's methodic approach to word-choice in translating certain words he was able to create an association between a lack of figurative boundaries (always translated as *hijab*) and political and social anarchy. This intensified link between limits on women and limits in politics was further emphasised by the placement of Akif's translation alongside the *Sırat-ı Müstakim* issues that published Musa Kazım's pieces on 'Freedom – Equality', which were attempts to define these concepts at a time when their meanings had yet to be crystalised but were also frequently discussed through 'the woman question'.

Yet there is a further and deeper dimension shared between Wajdi's and Akif's platforms that allowed *Muslim Woman* to resonate with *Sırat-ı Müstakim* readers. We have briefly touched upon it by commenting on the tension between the appeal to a universal human body, anchored in science, and the patterns of circulation of the text that revolve around competing appeals to ethnic nationalisms within the Ottoman Empire, with their emphasis on cultural distinctiveness. *Muslim Woman*'s success in its translated form demonstrates several links between Wajdi, Akif, the *Sırat-ı Müstakim*, as well as other translators, platforms and audiences. We have already referred in passing to the centrality of anti-materialism as a shared and contentious epistemological thread. The latter is connected with holding up 'Easterners' as an empiriospiritual collective.

Besides their obvious shared identity facets as public intellectuals of the late Ottoman world, and members of the *umma*, Akif and Wajdi were also determined 'Easterners' – in Kayalı's words, identification with the East was an anti-imperialist stance that, 'from the point of view of Islamists, shielded Islam from recrimination. As the argument often goes, such identification replenished the hope for reform, particularly on the oft-cited example of Japan.'[103] Being of the East is a constant in *Muslim Woman*. It is a frequently and forcefully inferred commonality between writer and audience (and, translator and audience), especially for Akif. For example, Akif introduces *Muslim Woman* with a contrast between Westerners and Easterners and does not mention Islam or Muslims – though of course the predicate Muslim is already attached to women in the title. Furthermore, the poet is much more consistent in his translation of Easterners than of *umma*. Though *umma* may have frequently been translated as *millet* in Ottoman Turkish texts, Akif repeats his tactic of the patterned word choice for the community of believers, oscillating between *ümmet* and *millet* at a time when the latter was clearly undergoing debates for alternative – civic secular – meanings. How East/erners was/were imagined and translated, however, was consistent: *Şark/lılar*. Being an Easterner was a label of resistance and *Muslim Woman* was ultimately presented as a doctrine on social resuscitation and civilisational survival. This Wajdi, Akif and their respective readers could agree on as being crucial for their respective and collective societies.

There is a particular irony and tension at the heart of positing 'Easterner' as an umbrella for the transaction between writer 1 / writer 2 (translator) / readers. For the text clearly begins with the appeal to the Human and

Women as universal categories, knowledge of which can be attained via science. Revelation can support the points or can be argued to have asserted these points earlier, but the issue remains that science is the primary source for knowledge of these categories. Yet, universal knowledge is split between an Easterner and a Westerner identity (that is, natures), which sometimes seem to denote radical historical alterity that risks the coherence of the founding categories (human/women), and at other times is deployed to argue that Easterners are the product of better application of these universal laws (nature). Put differently, it seems possible that Easterners are the true manifestation of these universal categories while Westerners are illusory forces leading people away from their true nature.

Yet, it is unclear who are the referents of Easterners and if the latter in fact denotes a mobilisable political collectivity. It often seems as if Easterners are comprised of a multiplicity of collectives that are organised serially as all belonging to the East, but they do not seem to cohere as a single collectivity. Put differently, while each author on his own refers to his addressees, as Easterners, it does not seem like Easterners founded a political collective and project that could actually be realised as betrayed by Akif's own career. The question then becomes: how does the call to 'Easterners', as a seriality, negotiate and participate in the creation of political collectivities based on competing ethnic claims, if that is in fact what it was doing? In other words, what is the function of the call onto Easterners if the latter was not necessarily posited as a political collective, but as an empiriospirtual one, in the age of nation state formation? Tracing the network of circulation and connection between these authors, who converged on an anti-materialist stance, cannot be separated from elucidating who or what is the referent of their appeal to 'Easterners'. Together, these two threads bring us closer to understanding their political and epistemological intervention on an intra-Ottomanist scale, beyond mere categorisation along the axis of modernists, traditionalists, reformists, and Islamists.

Notes

1. This work was supported, in part, by a fellowship at EUME, Forum Transregionale Studien, and the European Regional Development Fund-Project 'Creativity and Adaptability as Conditions of the Success of Europe in an Interrelated World' (No. CZ.02.1.01/0.0/0.0/16_019/0000734).
2. All translations from Ottoman and Arabic are ours unless otherwise noted. The quote is attributed to Auguste Comte and translated by Wajdi and Akif in Muhammad Farid Wajdi, *al-Mar'a al-muslima* (Cairo: Matba'at

The Translation of a Patriarchal Order in Flux

al-taraqqi, 1901). The second edition was published by Matbaʻat Hindiyya in Cairo 1912. There are numerous modern reprints of the first edition. They are mostly produced by publishing houses specialised in 'Islamic' texts. All Arabic references here are to the first edition. Muhammed Farid Wajdi, 'Müslüman Kadını: Beşinci Fasıl: Kadın amal-i hariciyyede erkekle müşareket edebilir mi?', trans. Mehmed Akif, *Sırat-ı Müstakim* 8 (15 October 1908).

3. These responses are referred to in his biography. Muhammad al-Jarihi, *Muhammad Farid Wajdi: Hayatuh wa-atharuh* (his life and works) (Cairo: Maʻhad al-buhuth wa-al-dirasat al-adabiyya wa-al-lughawiyya, 1970), 70. They are based on a reference in Wajdi's encyclopedia, but Jarihi has not been able to retrieve these articles and neither have we.
4. Mehmed Akif, 'Lahika', *Sırat-ı Müstakim* 7 (8 October 1908).
5. We are grateful to Dženita Karić for pointing us to Bosnian translations of two works by Wajdi. Musa Cazim Catic (trans.), *Musilmanska Zena* (Muslim woman) (Sarajevo: Muslimanska Biblioteka, 1915). Ali Kadic (trans.), *Primjena Islama na principe Kulture* (the application of the Islamic religion to the laws of civilisation) (Sarajevo: Muslimanska Biblioteka, 1915). We are also thankful to Gregory Maxwell Bruce, for referring us to the Urdu translation of *Muslim Woman*, Abu al-Kalam Azad (trans.), *Musalman ʻAurat* (Lahore: Thana'ullah Khan, 1953).
6. 'Bir İki Söz [Müslüman Kadını]', *Sırat-ı Müstakim* 3 (10 September 1908).
7. There is slight uncertainty about the publication year for Zakiri's *New Woman* due to the lack of a date on the title page. The translator's note is dated 1908, the same year as the translator's note for the first book of the 'Family Library' series, Amin's *Tahrir al-mar'a yahud Kadınları Esaretten Azad itü*, which was published in 1909.
8. Qasim Amin, *al-Mar'a al-jadida yahud Yeni Kadın*, trans. Zakir Kadiri (Kazan: Örnek Matbaası, n.d.).
9. Qasim Amin, *Tahrir al-mar'a yahud Kadınları Esaretten Azad itü*, trans. Zakir Kadiri (Kazan: Örnek Matbaası, 1909), 6.
10. Amin, *al-Mar'a al-jadida yahud Yeni Kadın*, trans. Kadiri, 3.
11. Amin, *al-Mar'a al-jadida yahud Yeni Kadın*, trans. Kadiri, 4. Saad Zaghloul eventually became one of the leaders of the Egyptian nationalist movement and helped establish the political party 'al-Wafd' (the delegation).
12. Qasim Amin, *Tahrir al-mar'a yahud Kadınları Esaretten Azad itü*, trans. Zakir Kadiri.
13. Ehud R. Toledano, 'Late Ottoman Concepts of Slavery (1830–1880s)', *Poetics Today* 14: 3 (Autumn 1993): 477–506.
14. Qasim Amin, *Hürriyet-i Nisvan*, trans. Zeki Mugamiz (Dersaadet: Kitaphane-i İslam ve Askeri Sahibi İbrahim Hilmi, 1329).
15. By this point, censorship and authoritarianism had already made their way back into the political sphere. See Bedross der Matossian, *Shattered Dreams of Revolution: From Liberty to Violence in the Late Ottoman*

Empire (Stanford: Stanford University Press, 2014). Mugamiz experienced censorship first-hand, as he was also the unnamed translator of the first Ottoman Turkish Qur'an to be openly described as a translation (1914); it was confiscated. See M. Brett Wilson, 'The First Translations of the Qur'an in Modern Turkey, 1924–1938', *International Journal of Middle East Studies* 41: 3 (August 2009): 419–35; 422. Significantly, his translation of the Qur'an and of Amin were printed by the same publisher, Ibrahim Hilmi.

16. Amin, *Hürriyet-i Nisvan*, trans. Mugamiz, 3.
17. Amin, *al-Mar'a al-jadida yahud Yeni Kadın*, trans. Kadiri, 4.
18. His biographies offer the most sustained study of his works. In their titles, his name is placed next to Islam, describing him as a pioneer of uniting Islam with modern science. The book-length studies of Wajdi's work in Arabic seem to have almost exclusively taken the form of biographies. In addition to Jarihi's aforementioned biography; Anwar al-Jundi, *Muhammad Farid Wajdi: Ra'id al-tawfiq bayn al-'ilm wal din* (pioneer of reconciling science and religion) (Cairo: al-Hay'a al-misriyya al-'amma lil-kitab, 1974); Muhammad Rajab al-Bayyumi, *Muhammad Farid Wajdi: al-Katib al-islami wa-al-mufakkir al-mawsu'i* (Islamist writer and encyclopedic thinker) (Damascus: Dar al-qalam, 2003). He is mentioned in numerous encyclopedic dictionaries in both Arabic and English and makes an occasional appearance in scholarly books in English dealing with Islam, science and politics, and those dealing with the response to Amin. For example, see John W. Livingston, *In the Shadows of Glories Past: Jihad for Modern Science in Muslim Societies, 1850 to the Arab Spring* (New York: Routledge, 2018); Murad Idris, 'Colonial Hesitation, Appropriation, and Citation: Qāsim Amīn, Empire, and Saying "No"', in Burke A. Hendrix and Deborah Baumgold (eds.), *Colonial Exchanges: Political Theory and the Agency of the Colonized* (Manchester: Manchester University Press, 2017), 180–216.
19. For histories of the Young Turks and the revolution, see, among others, Noémi Lévy-Aksu and François Georgeon (eds), *The Young Turk Revolution and the Ottoman Empire: The Aftermath of 1908* (London: I. B. Tauris, 2017); Bedros der Matossian, *Shattered Dreams*; M. Şükrü Hanioğlu, *The Young Turks in Opposition* (New York: Oxford University Press, 1995); M. Şükrü Hanioğlu, *Preparation for a Revolution: The Young Turks, 1902–1908* (New York: Oxford University Press, 2001); Hasan Kayalı, *Arabs and Young Turks: Ottomanism, Arabism, and Islamism in the Ottoman Empire, 1908–1918* (Berkeley: University of California Press, 1997); Stefano Taglia, *Intellectuals and Reform in the Ottoman Empire: The Young Turks on the Challenges of Modernity* (London: Routledge, 2015); Eric J. Zurcher, *The Young Turk Legacy and Nation Building: From the Ottoman Empire to Atatürk's Turkey* (London: I. B. Tauris, 2010).
20. Zurcher, *The Young Turk Legacy*, 27.

The Translation of a Patriarchal Order in Flux

21. For a sketch of the Hamidian regime, see Benjamin Fortna, 'The Reign of Abdülhamid II', in Reşat Kasaba (ed.), *Cambridge History of Turkey: Turkey in the Modern World* (Cambridge: Cambridge University Press, 2008), 38–61.
22. Mustafa Kemal (Atatürk) was among those who were dispatched for such a mission; see Zurcher, *The Young Turk Legacy*, 126.
23. Al-Jarihi, 174, mentions a curious story about Wajdi and the Young Turks. Wajdi, who was a member of al-Hizb al-Watani (the National Party), a move that was partly responsible for losing the friendship of Rashid Rida, published a daily political journal titled *al-Dustur* ('The constitution') which was loosely affiliated with the party. In 1908 and due to numerous political clashes with the party, those loose ties were severed, and the paper lost many of its readers, who were predominantly young members/friends of the party. Purportedly, the Young Turks offered financial support in exchange for rendering the paper the Arabic organ for the movement, which Wajdi rejected. We have not been able to find non-anecdotal evidence to corroborate the story.
24. *Sırat-ı Müstakim* 1 (27 August 1908).
25. Musa Kazım, 'Hürriyet – Müsavat', *Sırat-ı Müstakim* 1 (27 August 1908).
26. Musa Kazım, 'Hürriyet – Müsavat', *Sırat-ı Müstakim* 1 (27 August 1908).
27. M. Suat Mertoğlu, ed. Mustafa Demiray, *Sırat-ı Müstakim Mecmuası: Açıklamalı Fihrist ve Dizin* (İstanbul: Klasik Yayınları, 2008), 11.
28. Mertoğlu, ed. Demiray, *Sırat-ı Müstakim Mecmuası*, 11.
29. Mehmed Akif, 'Bir İki Söz [Müslümanlıkta Medeniyet]', *Sırat-ı Müstakim* 125 (26 January 1911).
30. Wajdi, *Müslüman Kadını*, trans. Akif, 3.
31. Mertoğlu, ed. Demiray, *Sırat-ı Müstakim Mecmuası*, 15. Mertoğlu's volume provides a chart of the number of contributions per author. Akif's contributions number 216, 122 of which are translations. There is a wide margin between Akif and the second greatest contributor, Manastırlı İsmail Hakkı, whose contributions number 121, five of which are translations. It is important to note here that Akif was not the only one to translate Wajdi for the journal. In fact, it is not unusual to see the contributions of two translators, of two different Wajdi works, in the same *Sırat-ı Müstakim* issue, for example, Halil Nimetullah's *Felsefe-i Hakka* alongside Akif's *Müslüman Kadını* (1 October 1908).
32. Mertoğlu, ed. Demiray, *Sırat-ı Müstakim Mecmuası*, 11.
33. Mertoğlu, ed. Demiray, *Sırat-ı Müstakim Mecmuası*, 15.
34. Mertoğlu, ed. Demiray, *Sırat-ı Müstakim Mecmuası*, 19.
35. Mertoğlu, ed. Demiray, *Sırat-ı Müstakim Mecmuası*, 19.
36. Mertoğlu, ed. Demiray, *Sırat-ı Müstakim Mecmuası*, 19.
37. Mertoğlu, ed. Demiray, *Sırat-ı Müstakim Mecmuası*, 22.
38. Eşref Edip, ed. Fahrettin Gün, *Mehmed Akif: Hayatı Eserleri ve Yetmiş Muharririn Yazıları* (İstanbul: Beyan Yayınları, 2011), 432.

39. Yusuf Turan Günaydın (ed.), *Mehmet Akif Ersoy: Mektuplar* (Ankara: Atlas Kitap, 2016).
40. In the introduction of *Civilization and Islam*, Akif writes that Wajdi is one of the greatest and most industrious scholars – not only in Egypt, but in the Muslim world. Akif translated this work in the Hamidian Era and simplified the language for its serialisation in the *Sırat-ı Müstakim* in 1911. Other distinctions between this introduction and the one for *Muslim Woman* include the length, personal voice that is in defense of Islam, as well as the fact that Akif signs his name beneath it. Mehmed Akif, 'Bir İki Söz [Müslümanlıkta Medeniyet]', *Sırat-ı Müstakim* 125 (26 January 1911).
41. 'Bir İki Söz [Müslüman Kadını]', *Sırat-ı Müstakim* 3.
42. 'Bir İki Söz [Müslüman Kadını]', *Sırat-ı Müstakim* 3.
43. Musa Kazım, 'Hürriyet – Müsavat', *Sırat-ı Müstakim* 1–8 (27 August 1908 – 15 October 1908).
44. *Sırat-ı Müstakim* 3 (10 September 1908).
45. 'Bir İki Söz [Müslüman Kadını]', *Sırat-ı Müstakim* 3.
46. 'Bir İki Söz [Müslüman Kadını]', *Sırat-ı Müstakim* 3.
47. Wajdi, *Müslüman Kadını*, trans. Akif, 3.
48. Wajdi, *Müslüman Kadını*, trans. Akif, 3.
49. Musa Kazım, 'Hürriyet – Müsavat', *Sırat-ı Müstakim* 1 (27 August 1908).
50. Musa Kazım, 'Hürriyet – Müsavat', *Sırat-ı Müstakim* 2 (3 September 1908).
51. Musa Kazım, 'Hürriyet – Müsavat', *Sırat-ı Müstakim* 2.
52. Musa Kazım, 'Hürriyet – Müsavat', *Sırat-ı Müstakim* 3 (10 September 1908).
53. Musa Kazım, 'Hürriyet – Müsavat', *Sırat-ı Müstakim* 3.
54. Musa Kazım, 'Hürriyet – Müsavat', *Sırat-ı Müstakim* 3.
55. For an overview of the scholarship from this perspective see Hussein Omar, 'Arabic Thought in the Liberal Cage', in Faisal Devji and Zaheer Kazmi (eds), *Islam after Liberalism* (Oxford: Oxford University Press, 2017), 17–45.
56. Specifically, waged labour in contradistinction to the participation of women in family-economy agriculture which is not objected to.
57. For an example of Wajdi's reverence of Comte, 19, examples of Qur'anic verses can be found in 100 and 109, and samples of his interjections are on 129, 135–6.
58. The practice of translation in the nineteenth century is characterised by the fluidity of boundaries between translation, adaptation, rewriting and pseudo-translations. It would be intriguing to see whether that is the case in inter-Ottoman translations, or is the Wajdi–Akif case something of a norm in the latter cases, and whether that varied by genre (for example more liberties were taken in novels and history with a different approach to treatises or books of science).
59. The first book was later renamed as *al-Islam wa-al-madaniyya*. There is an English translation of an excerpt of it: Muhammad Farid Wajdi, 'Islam

and Civilization', in Mansoor Moaddel and Kamran Talattof (eds and trans.), *Contemporary Debates in Islam: An Anthology of Modernist and Fundamentalist Thought* (New York: Palgrave Macmillan, 2000), 135–44.
60. Marwa Elshakry, *Reading Darwin in Arabic, 1860–1950* (Chicago: University of Chicago Press, 2013), 282–4.
61. Jarihi, *Muhammad Farid Wajdi*, 77–9.
62. Marilyn Booth, *Classes of Ladies of Cloistered Spaces: Writing Feminist History through Biography in Fin-de-siècle Egypt* (Edinburgh: Edinburgh University Press, 2015), 4.
63. Omar, 'Arabic Thought in the Liberal Cage', 22.
64. We have opted for *hijab* to refer both to the Arabic and Ottoman Turkish word for simplification.
65. Wajdi, *al-Mar'a al-muslima*, 164; Wajdi, 'Müslüman Kadını, On Birinci Fasıl: Tesettür Kalkar mı?' trans. Akif, *Sırat-ı Müstakim* 15 (3 December 1908).
66. Wajdi, *al-Mar'a al-muslima*, 128; Wajdi, 'Müslüman Kadını, On Birinci Fasıl', trans. Akif, *Sırat-ı Müstakim* 15.
67. Earlier, Wajdi compares passingly between opponents of the veil, who describe it as a remnant of barbarism, to those who see all forms of government as dregs of primitiveness, 145–6. He returns to the comparison at the conclusion of Chapter Eleven, 166; Wajdi, 'Müslüman Kadını, On Birinci Fasıl', trans. Akif, *Sırat-ı Müstakim* 15.
68. Kenneth Cuno, *Modernizing Marriage: Family, Ideology, and Law in Nineteenth- and Early Twentieth-century Egypt* (New York: Syracuse University Press, 2018).
69. For comparison, refer to the translations of Fatma Aliye, studied by Marilyn Booth and Holly Shissler, and of Qasim Amin, studied by Yorgos Dedes and Illham Khuri-Makdisi, both in this volume. The exception among these is the word Akif replaces *hijab* with most frequently, *tesettür*, in that it is a verbal noun. It is understood, however, that the word *tesettür* had also come to be used as a noun.
70. Wajdi, 'Müslüman Kadını: Dokuzuncu Fasıl, Tesettür Kadınların Nişane-i Esareti midir, Yoksa Zamin-i Hürriyeti midir?', trans. Akif, *Sırat-ı Müstakim* 11 (5 October 1908).
71. Wajdi, 'Müslüman Kadını: Dokuzuncu Fasıl', trans. Akif, *Sırat-ı Müstakim* 11.
72. Wajdi, 'Müslüman Kadını: Dokuzuncu Fasıl', trans. Akif, *Sırat-ı Müstakim* 11.
73. Wajdi, 'Müslüman Kadını: Dokuzuncu Fasıl', trans. Akif, *Sırat-ı Müstakim* 11.
74. Wajdi, 'Müslüman Kadını: Dokuzuncu Fasıl', trans. Akif, *Sırat-ı Müstakim* 11.
75. Wajdi, 'Müslüman Kadını, Tesettür Kadınların İktisab-ı Kemal Etmelerine Manimidir?', trans. Akif, *Sırat-ı Müstakim* 13 (19 October 1908).

76. Wajdi, 'Müslüman Kadını, On Birinci Fasıl', trans. Akif, *Sırat-ı Müstakim* 15.
77. Wajdi, 'Müslüman Kadını, On Birinci Fasıl', trans. Akif, *Sırat-ı Müstakim* 15.
78. Wajdi, 'Müslüman Kadını, On Birinci Fasıl', trans. Akif, *Sırat-ı Müstakim* 15.
79. This analogy is not unique to Amin, it has a much wider history and relevance for the intersection between patriarchy, feminism and ideologies of power. Michael McKeon, 'Historicizing Patriarchy: The Emergence of Gender Difference in England, 1660–1760', *Eighteenth-century Studies* 28: 3 (1995): 295–322.
80. These categories are crucial and present for both authors. The distinction made above highlights the placing of the emphasis in how each author relates the categories to each other and is relevant for a broader conversation on conceptions of culture/nature at the time.
81. Wajdi, *al-Mar'a al-muslima*, 43; Wajdi, 'Müslüman Kadını, Dördüncü Fasılın Mabadi', trans. Akif, *Sırat-ı Müstakim* 7 (8 October 1908).
82. Wajdi, 'Müslüman Kadını, On Birinci Fasil', trans. Akif, *Sırat-ı Müstakim* 15. A *vardacı* is an individual who is employed to shout and notify those on the street that the tram is approaching.
83. Marwa Elshakry has analysed Wajdi's antagonistic position towards Darwinism (both as a scientific and a social theory). His organicist view of society may explain the latter position as well as his general opposition to what he describes as 'materialism'. He was invested in a particular vision of nature as a backdrop for his conception of the social. Said Halim, who was also translated by Akif, was equally adamant about arguing against materialism. For him, this included the insistence upon the inapplicability of class struggle and strife to 'Eastern' societies, which had a distinctly different nature. Syed Tanvir Wasti, 'Said Halim Pasha: Philosopher Prince', *Middle Eastern Studies* 44: 1 (January 2008): 85–104; 89. For a comparison of the social and political positions of Mehmed Akif and Said Halim, see Hasan Kayalı, 'Islam in the Thoughts of Two Late Ottoman Intellectuals: Mehmed Akif and Said Halim', *Archivum Ottomanicum* 19 (2001): 307–33.
84. Süleyman Nazif, *Mehmed Akif: Şairin Zatı ve Eseri Hakkında Bazı Malumat ve Tetkikat – Tarih-i Tahriri: 1919/1337* (Istanbul: Amadi Matbaası, 1924).
85. Mehmed Akif and Midhat Cemal, 'Acem Şahı', *Sırat-ı Müstakim* 11 (5 November 1908).
86. Mithat Cemal Kuntay, *Mehmed Akif: Hayatı – Seciyesi – Sanatı* (İstanbul: Timaş Yayınevi, 2010), 342.
87. Kuntay, *Mehmed Akif*, 335.
88. Kuntay, *Mehmed Akif*, 335.
89. Kuntay, *Mehmed Akif*, 335–6.

90. Wajdi, *al-Mar'a al-muslima*, 130; Wajdi, trans. Akif, 'Müslüman Kadını, On Birinci Fasıl', *Sırat-ı Müstakim* 15.
91. James W. Redhouse, *A Turkish and English Lexicon: Shewing in English the Significations of the Turkish Terms*, 4th Edition (Istanbul: Çagrı Yayınları, 2011), 1111.
92. Kuntay, *Mehmed Akif*, 342.
93. Kuntay, *Mehmed Akif*, 336.
94. Omar, 'Arabic Thought in the Liberal Cage', 22.
95. Wajdi, *al-Mar'a al-muslima*, 78.
96. Wajdi, *al-Mar'a al-muslima*, 63–4.
97. These studies offer an overview of the work undertaken by women (both waged, and domestic), how it becomes articulated with capitalism, and a broad overview of the scholarship. Akram Fouad Khater, '"House" to "Goddess of the House"': Gender, Class, and Silk in 19th-century Mount Lebanon', *International Journal of Middle East Studies* 28: 3 (August 1996): 325–48; Donald Quataert, 'Labor History and the Ottoman Empire, c. 1700–1922', *International Labor and Working-class History* 60 (Fall, 2001): 93–109; Donald Quataert, 'Machine Breaking and the Changing Carpet Industry of Western Anatolia', *Journal of Social History* 19: 3 (Spring 1986): 473–89; Fariba Zarinebaf-Shahr, 'The Role of Women in the Urban Economy of Istanbul, 1700–1850', *International Labor and Working-class History* 60 (Fall 2001): 141–52; James A. Reilly, 'Women in the Economic Life of Late-Ottoman Damascus', *Arabica* 42: 1 (March 1995): 79–106.
98. Ironically, for all of the insistence upon different trajectories, a university for women, Inas Dar'ül fünun, was established in 1914, not too long after these debates. Female students' protests ended the segregation in 1921 when women started attending classes with men and the Inas Dar'ül fünun was shut down. Yucel Gelişli, 'Education of Women from the Ottoman Empire to Modern Turkey', SEER *Journal of Labour and Social Affairs in Eastern Europe* 7: 4 (2004): 121–35. This is the same year women were allowed to study medicine, dentistry and pharmacy in Beirut at the American University of Beirut. The Egyptian University, founded in 1908, had a women's section from the start which was then closed in 1912 with the first group of women joining the university in co-ed classes in 1928.
99. *Al-Muqattam*, 8 February 1901, cited in Wajdi, *al-Mar'a al-muslima*, 137–8. There is a comparable argument, though with a different intention, in Qasim Amin, *Tahrir al-mar'a* (Cairo: Hindawi, 2012), 27.
100. Qasim Amin, *Tahrir al-mar'a*, 19–21, argues that the exemption of women from the duty of supporting themselves is first cause for the loss of women's rights. He makes a parallel argument in less direct terms in *al-Mar'a al-jadida* (Cairo: Hindawi, 2012), 47–8.
101. The discursive hegemony here of waged labour does not necessarily coincide with its total control over the actual sphere of production despite

subsumption into world capitalism. Khater, 'House', 327, refers to *mugharasa* where years of peasant labour were rewarded with land not wages.
102. Leila Ahmed, *Women and Gender in Islam: Historical Roots of a Modern Debate* (New Haven: Yale University Press, 1992), 162.
103. Kayalı, 'Islam in the Thought and Politics of two late Ottoman Intellectuals', 320.

Bibliography

Periodicals

Sırat-ı Müstakim, Istanbul

Books and Articles

Ahmed, Leila, *Women and Gender in Islam: Historical Roots of a Modern Debate* (New Haven: Yale University Press, 1992).
Amin, Qasim, *al-Mar'a al-jadida yahud Yeni Kadın*, trans. Zakir Kadiri (Kazan: Örnek Matbaası, n.d.).
Amin, Qasim, *Hürriyet-i Nisvan*, trans. Zeki Mugamiz (Dersaadet: Kitaphane-i İslam ve Askeri Sahibi İbrahim Hilmi, 1329).
Amin, Qasim, *Tahrir al-mar'a yahud Kadınları Esaretten Azad itü*, trans. Zakir Kadiri (Kazan: Örnek Matbaası, 1909).
Amin, Qasim, *al-Mar'a al-jadida* (Cairo: Hindawi, 2012).
Amin, Qasim, *Tahrir al-mar'a* (Cairo: Hindawi, 2012).
Azad, Abu al-Kalam (trans.), *Musalman 'Aurat* (Lahore: Thana'ullah Khan, 1953).
al-Bayyumi, Muhammad Rajab, *Muhammad Farid Wajdi: al-Katib al-islami wa-al-mufakkir al-mawsu'i* (Damascus: Dar al-qalam, 2003).
Booth, Marilyn, *Classes of Ladies of Cloistered Spaces: Writing Feminist History through Biography in Fin-de-siècle Egypt* (Edinburgh: Edinburgh University Press, 2015).
Catic, Musa Cazim (trans.), *Musilmanska Zena* (Sarajevo: Muslimanska Biblioteka, 1915).
Cuno, Kenneth, *Modernizing Marriage: Family, Ideology, and Law in Nineteenth- and Early Twentieth-century Egypt* (New York: Syracuse University Press, 2018).
Edip, Eşref, ed. Fahrettin Gün, *Mehmed Akif: Hayatı Eserleri ve Yetmiş Muharririn Yazıları* (İstanbul: Beyan Yayınları, 2011).
Elshakry, Marwa, *Reading Darwin in Arabic, 1860–1950* (Chicago: University of Chicago Press, 2013).
Fortna, Benjamin, 'The Reign of Abdülhamid II', in Reşat Kasaba (ed.), *Cambridge History of Turkey: Turkey in the Modern World* (Cambridge: Cambridge University Press, 2008), 38–61.

Gelişli, Yucel, 'Education of Women from the Ottoman Empire to Modern Turkey', SEER *Journal of Labour and Social Affairs in Eastern Europe* 7: 4 (2004): 121–35.
Günaydın, Yusuf Turan (ed.), *Mehmet Akif Ersoy: Mektuplar* (Ankara: Atlas Kitap, 2016).
Hanioğlu, Şükrü M., *The Young Turks in Opposition* (New York: Oxford University Press, 1995).
Hanioğlu, Şükrü M., *Preparation for a Revolution: The Young Turks, 1902–1908* (New York: Oxford University Press, 2001).
Idris, Murad, 'Colonial Hesitation, Appropriation, and Citation: Qāsim Amīn, Empire, and Saying "No", in Burke A. Hendrix and Deborah Baumgold (eds.), *Colonial Exchanges: Political Theory and the Agency of the Colonized* (Manchester: Manchester University Press, 2017), 180–216.
al-Jarihi, Muhammad, *Muhammad Farid Wajdi: Hayatuh wa-atharuh* (Cairo: Ma'had al-buhuth wa-al-dirasat al-adabiyya wa-al-lughawiyya, 1970).
al-Jundi, Anwar, *Muhammad Farid Wajdi: Ra'id al-tawfīq bayn al-'ilm wa-al-din* (Cairo: al-Hay'a al-misriyya al-'amma lil-kitab, 1974).
Kadic, Ali (trans.), *Primjena Islama na principe Kulture* (*The Application of the Islamic Religion to the Laws of Civilization*) (Sarajevo: Muslimanska Biblioteka, 1915).
Kayalı, Hasan, *Arabs and Young Turks: Ottomanism, Arabism, and Islamism in the Ottoman Empire, 1908–1918* (Berkeley: University of California Press, 1997).
Kayalı, Hasan, 'Islam in the Thoughts of Two Late Ottoman Intellectuals: Mehmed Akif and Said Halim', *Archivum Ottomanicum* 19 (2001): 307–33.
Khater, Akram Fouad, '"House" to "Goddess of the House": Gender, Class, and Silk in 19th-century Mount Lebanon', *International Journal of Middle East Studies* 28: 3 (1996): 325–48.
Kuntay, Mithat Cemal, *Mehmed Akif: Hayatı – Seciyesi – Sanatı* (İstanbul: Timaş Yayınevi, 2010).
Lévy-Aksu, Noémi and François Georgeon (eds), *The Young Turk Revolution and the Ottoman Empire: The Aftermath of 1908* (London: I. B. Tauris, 2017).
Livingston, John W., *In the Shadows of Glories Past: Jihad for Modern Science in Muslim Societies, 1850 to the Arab Spring* (New York: Routledge, 2018).
Matossian, Bedross der, *Shattered Dreams of Revolution: From Liberty to Violence in the Late Ottoman Empire* (Stanford, CA: Stanford University Press, 2014).
McKeon, Michael, 'Historicizing Patriarchy: The Emergence of Gender Difference in England, 1660–1760', *Eighteenth-century Studies*, 28: 3 (1995): 295–322.
Mertoğlu, Suat M., ed. Mustafa Demiray, *Sırat-ı Müstakim Mecmuası: Açıklamalı Fihrist ve Dizin* (İstanbul: Klasik Yayınları, 2008).
Nazif, Süleyman, *Mehmed Akif: Şairin Zatı ve Eseri Hakkında Bazı Malumat ve Tetkikat – Tarih-i Tahriri: 1919/1337* (Istanbul: Amadi Matbaası, 1924).

Omar, Hussein, 'Arabic Thought in the Liberal Cage', in Faisal Devji and Zaheer Kazmi (eds), *Islam after Liberalism* (Oxford: Oxford University Press, 2017), 17–45.

Quataert, Donald, 'Machine Breaking and the Changing Carpet Industry of Western Anatolia', *Journal of Social History* 19: 3 (Spring 1986): 473–89.

Quataert, Donald, 'Labor History and the Ottoman Empire, c. 1700–1922', *International Labor and Working-class History*, 60 (Fall 2001): 93–109.

Redhouse, James W., *A Turkish and English Lexicon: Shewing in English the Significations of the Turkish Terms*, 4th edn (Istanbul: Çagrı Yayınları, 2011).

Reilly, James A., 'Women in the Economic Life of Late-Ottoman Damascus', *Arabica* 42: 1 (March 1995): 79–106.

Taglia, Stefano, *Intellectuals and Reform in the Ottoman Empire: The Young Turks on the Challenges of Modernity* (London: Routledge, 2015).

Toledano, Ehud R., 'Late Ottoman Concepts of Slavery (1830–1880s)', *Poetics Today* 14: 3 (Autumn 1993): 477–506.

Wajdi, Muhammad Farid, 'Islam and Civilization', in Mansoor Moaddel and Kamran Talattof (eds and trans.), *Contemporary Debates in Islam: An Anthology of Modernist and Fundamentalist Thought* (New York: Palgrave Macmillan, 2000), 135–44.

Wajdi, Muhammad Farid, *al-Mar'a al-muslima* (Cairo: Matba'at al-taraqqi, 1901).

Wasti, Syed Tanvir, 'Said Halim Pasha: Philosopher Prince', *Middle Eastern Studies* 44: 1 (January 2008): 85–104.

Wilson, Brett M., 'The First Translations of the Qur'an in Modern Turkey, 1924–1938', *International Journal of Middle East Studies* 41: 3 (August 2009): 419–35.

Zarinebaf-Shahr, Fariba, 'The Role of Women in the Urban Economy of Istanbul, 1700–1850', *International Labor and Working-class History* 60 (Fall 2001): 141–52.

Zurcher, Eric J., *The Young Turk Legacy and Nation Building: From the Ottoman Empire to Atatürk's Turkey* (London: I. B. Tauris, 2010).

Chapter 8

Fatma Aliye's *Nisvan-ı İslam*: Istanbul, Beirut, Cairo, Paris, 1891–6

Marilyn Booth and A. Holly Shissler

In October 1891, the Istanbul-based Ottoman Turkish-language newspaper *Tercüman-ı Hakikat* began serial publication of a work presented as three conversations among women of the Ottoman elite and well-heeled French and English female tourists in Istanbul. Echoing a subgenre circulating in Europe and North America – travel books narrating 'harem visits' – *Nisvan-ı İslam* ('Women of Islam') was penned by Fatma Aliye (1862–1936). It was not a work of 'travel literature', but Fatma Aliye's work did travel to new languages and other places: Arabic and Beirut, and then Cairo; French and Paris; Chicago but probably not in English. Our chapter maps the linguistic and geographical journeys of *Nisvan-ı İslam* in the 1890s (for its boundary-crossing was almost immediate). It was a work in which cultural translation was a central theme and organisational principle. How did its textuality re-sound and proliferate in other languages? And for whom?

Fatma Aliye began her writing career anonymously but became a celebrated Ottoman Turkish writer and advocate for women. Born into an elite family, she was the daughter of Adviye Rabia Hanım (dates unknown) and the renowned Ottoman statesman, legal scholar and historian Ahmet Cevdet Paşa (1822–95). From a young age, Fatma Aliye's home-based education occurred in several venues, for her father was posted as provincial governor to Aleppo (c. 1866–8) and Damascus (c. 1878). She learned French, Arabic and Persian. At the age of seventeen, in 1879, she was married to military officer Mehmet Faik Bey (d. 1928), an aide-de-camp to Sultan Abdülhamid II (r. 1876–1909). They would have four daughters. Similar to the experience of her older contemporary 'A'isha Taymur (1840–1902) in Egypt, Fatma Aliye may have had a husband who did not condone at least some literary pursuits: he is said to have disapproved of her reading novels in foreign languages (a practice frowned on by many). But she had an encouraging mentor in the novelist and newspaper publisher Ahmet Midhat Efendi (1844–1912), who supported her publicly and produced a biography of her incorporating extracts from her letters describing her childhood and young life, as well as co-authoring an early novel (*Hayal ve Hakikat*, 1891).[1] Fatma Aliye published other works of fiction and non-fiction and was a regular columnist for the women's journal *Hanımlara Mahsus Gazete*, 1895–1908, where her sister Emine Semiye (1864–1944), an early feminist, was on the editorial board.

Fatma Aliye's first publication was a translation from the French (of Georges Ohnet's novel *Volonté*, 1888), appearing anonymously ('by a woman', *bir kadın*) in 1889, with the consent of her father, husband and brother. By the time she published her first of five 'solo' novels, *Muhazarat* (1892), under her own name, she had already published *Nisvan-ı İslam*. In Ahmet Midhat Efendi's daily newspaper *Tercüman-ı Hakikat*, it appeared in thirty instalments, from no. 3968 (6 October 1891) to no. 4004 (17 November 1891).[2]

The work became an internationally circulating work almost instantly and was published in book form soon after.[3] Only weeks after its serialisation in *Tercüman-ı Hakikat*, it began appearing in Arabic translation in the Beirut newspaper *Thamarat al-funun* and was announced as a book.[4] Before long, it was available to readers of French. In 1894, a translation appeared in Paris under the name Nazime Roukié, its referent still uncertain.[5] In 1896, a second French translation appeared, this one explicitly supported by the Ottoman state and rendered by Ol'ga Lebedeva (1852 or 1854–1933?).[6] 'Gülnar Hanım' – an 'Ottoman' moniker that she adopted – was a transnational figure who spent time in Egypt and the Ottoman Empire, and translated from and into Russian, Ottoman, Arabic and French. There was said to be an English translation of *Nisvan-ı İslam* made in North America, which Fatma Aliye mentioned in her correspondence, but never herself saw. We have been unable to locate any trace of this.[7]

The Arabic translation reappeared in Lebanese-Egyptian writer Zaynab Fawwaz's (c. 1850–1914) biographical dictionary of women, *al-Durr al-manthur fi tabaqat rabbat al-khudur* (1893–6), as a mammoth 'appendix' to a one and a half-page biography of Fatma Aliye. Indeed, her biography becomes the paratext introducing the translation.[8] Three excerpts appeared in the Islamic-reformist Arabic journal *al-Manar* from December 1901 to February 1902. These were framed by summaries, and the editor criticised the 'weak' translation of the existing Arabic version, calling its own abbreviated and slightly different version 'sounder'.[9] A shortened version of Fatma Aliye's introduction, with somewhat different wording, appeared in the early women's magazine *Fatat al-sharq* (est. 1906), as part two of a biographical profile of Fatma Aliye, in the magazine's 'famous women' feature for March 1907; the next month, it would profile 'Gülnar Hanım'.[10] In a graphic illustration of cultural circulation, an Ottoman-language biographical sketch of Fatma Aliye appeared in 1900 in *Hanımlara Mahsus Gazete* – a translation from Arabic of Fawwaz's profile of this by-now celebrated Ottoman female intellectual![11]

The whole text reappeared in Arabic in book form in Cairo as *Kitab nisa' al-islam*, with some emendations and editorial additions, published at the expense of publisher Ibrahim Faris.[12] This text is undated but the paper quality, typeface and prefatorial references suggest an early twentieth-century publication, c. 1909.[13] Much later, a version of this text was issued by an Islamic publishing house in Cairo (1989), edited by Muhammad Ibrahim Salim with consistent and major unacknowledged changes and deletions made to the text and framing, including dropping the entire third dialogue as 'unimportant' due to its focus on dress.[14] Finally, the original Ottoman Turkish text was transliterated into modern Turkish script by Mübeccel Kızıltan in 1993 and 'translated' into modern Turkish by Ayhan and Amine Pekin as *İslam kadınları* in 2009 and again by Orhan Sakın in 2012 as *Osmanlı'da kadın: Cariyelik, çokeşlilik, ve moda* ('Woman in the Ottoman [Empire]: female slavery, polygamy and fashion').[15]

Comparing the Ottoman Turkish original to the earliest Arabic and both French renderings, taking into account paratextual apparatuses and publication venues, we trace this work's remaking for its different audiences. We link these acts of rewriting to the themes and format of the original Ottoman work, gesturing to its participation in the era's intensive debates on women's rights, gender and space, and notions of civilisational hierarchy prevalent in Istanbul, Beirut, Cairo and Paris.

Fatma Aliye gained an international reputation for her publications as well as her high level of education and her worldly acumen: she was given the responsibility of receiving foreign women guests at the sultan's palace. *Nisvan-ı İslam* contributed to this image. She was widely enough known to be invited to submit her work to the 1893 World Columbian Exposition in Chicago, specifically for display in the Exposition's heralded yet controversial Women's Library. Arabophone and Turkophone women (including Zaynab Fawwaz) were seeking textual representation there, a site wherein 'the status of women' trans-locally was embedded in a rising (and contested) racialised discourse of (white) American superiority.[16] Fatma Aliye received a letter confirming receipt of her contributions, which had generated considerable interest, it said. Possibly, *Nisvan-ı İslam* was among them; in the printed hand-list of books sent to the Women's Library we find only: 'Fathma Alié, three books in Turkish, not examined'.[17] If Fatma Aliye did intend *Nisvan-ı İslam* to be a corrective to the imperially shaped 'civilisational' views that women visiting Chicago might have had – views which could only have been corroborated by the 'Ottoman' and 'Egyptian' 'Streets' on the Midway, built for the Exposition and scandalous worldwide for their 'belly-dance' exhibitions – it is ironic that for those who catalogued arriving books, hers was unread – and unreadable.

Part I: Text as Translation

Fatma Aliye began her publishing career with a translation from the French. *Nisvan-ı İslam*, appearing very soon thereafter, was also in a sense a 'translation'. For, even before it appeared in translation, *Nisvan-ı İslam* was a translational text, thematically and through its staging of language politics. That is, translation as an act of communication and a mode of understanding organised the text. Whether in the form of characters dialoguing through translation, or comparative discussion of sacred texts, in translations and in their originals, or material culture as both marking out differences and creating bridges between civilisations, translation inhabits this work from start to finish. Furthermore, the work staged what European women were allegedly saying about Ottoman and Muslim women – what they had learned of Ottoman society 'in translation'. The work 'translated' these European views for the benefit of Ottoman and Muslim readers, paralleling the way Fatma Aliye's mentor, Ahmet Midhat, challenged European Orientalists on their understandings of Ottoman and Muslim societies, including their expressed beliefs about Muslim women.[18]

A 'Multilingual' Text

A first-person narrator (and author-figure) 'transcribes' three dialogues with European women, held in French, as well as interleaved conversations with other Ottoman women. Inside the text, the narrator translates for these conversing interlocutors. All are referred to by their first initials.[19] The narrator tells readers that these were based on conversations with Europeans who visited her and family members in their home, in other words, in that popular tourist stop for European and American elite female visitors known as 'the harem visit'. The book's introduction discusses difficulties European visitors have in meeting families where the women are educated and speak French (since the visitors generally do not know Ottoman), and yet live in observant Muslim fashion. It highlights the misconceptions that arise from this lack of access.

Fatma Aliye's Nisvan-ı İslam

Ostensibly, then, the book is an explication of Muslim women's experiences and outlooks for the European interlocutors in the text. Thus, it is easily taken as aimed at an external audience of Europeans, parallel to the 'audience' inside the text.[20] Yet, it was written in Ottoman Turkish and published in the Ottoman press. We regard it as a canny work that turned the tables on European Orientalist representations of 'Eastern women'. It did so through its representation of highly articulate, knowledgeable, cosmopolitan, fashion-conscious and devout Istanbul women, likely for purposes of self-modelling to Ottoman female peers as its foremost target audience. (Of course, Fatma Aliye may have also had translation, and European audiences, in mind when she wrote.) It speaks to a strong sense of being misunderstood by 'Westerners' that was prevalent among Ottoman elites, especially with regard to 'the Woman Question', and their sense that it was both their own responsibility and within their means to project more accurate images of themselves. As Fatma Aliye herself put it: 'What is the source of [the Europeans'] mistaken ideas? . . . We must first of all look for the shortcoming in ourselves.'[21] That it circulated immediately in Arabic suggests its relevance to literate women across and beyond the Ottoman Empire, including in Egypt (officially an Ottoman province, semi-autonomous from the Ottoman State and occupied by Britain since 1882).

Notions of cultural and linguistic translation permeate the Ottoman Turkish text (and are closely translated into the Arabic version). First, the introductory text prefacing the dialogues critiques the channels of information – and associated urban spaces – whereby foreign (read: European) visitors were acquiring 'knowledge' of Ottoman society, Islamic institutions and Muslims' practices, and the implications of all of this for (elite) women. Such information, observed the narrator, came in written form but also through the local tourist industry. Foreigners tended to go straight to the hotels of Pera/Beyoğlu (henceforth, Beyoğlu), where they 'resort to the *tercüman*s [interpreter-guides] who don't know anything about anything outside the Beyoğlu world . . . They have to answer the foreigners' questions, whether they know anything or not, and so their words cast our reality/conditions (*ahval*) in the form of improbable tales.'[22] These cultural-linguistic 'mediators', the narrator suggests, are one-way information charlatans.

Hovering behind these mediator-figures critiqued in the preface was a long history of European writings on Ottoman society and Islamic history, doctrine and practice that framed Fatma Aliye's very decision to write, as the narrator set it up rhetorically. Even as information transfer had sped up, she said, it had fed erroneous information to an ever-larger audience.

> It became clear to me, as these dialogues took place between me and some eminent female European tourists, that Europeans' views of us are wrong, illusions in a representation that truly compels wonder. Thus it was that when I heard these false tales (*ihbar-ı kazıbe*) from them, I was as astonished as they had been alienated by the corrupt and confused tales they had heard [about us]. I suspected [at first] that they must have been reading about some other community.[23]

The text engages in genre criticism: such material appeared in 'travel books', not works of scholarship, and the contents were fanciful, a point Fatma Aliye made in comparing these 'tales' – Orientalist travel writing – to popular lore and the more recent novel.

> The things I heard from these guests (Arabic: female tourists, *sa'ihat*) were published in written European works by way of travel accounts. But in that case, the mentioned travel accounts were not books that provided information about true/real conditions; the majority of their contents resembled imaginary tales (Ottoman *hikayat-i muhayyile*; Arabic *hikayat khayaliyya*) written in novel form.[24]

The reference to *tercüman*s in Beyoğlu follows shortly thereafter. If there existed a body of literature propagating false information, Fatma Aliye suggested this was partly the fault of local actors (who were often Ottoman subjects of minority linguistic-confessional groups).

But Fatma Aliye also intimated local culpability on the part of the Ottoman elite. As the preface assessed prevalent sites of information exchange between differently placed individuals in Istanbul, it evaluated local attitudes as complicit in the circulation of erroneous information. It channelled this partly through a critique of girls' education. It was impossible to learn a culture, Fatma Aliye observed, by 'circling round the souq' and 'seeing famous sites'; one must meet the locals (in context, she did not mean *tercüman*s). Since women were confined to domestic spaces and generally gender-segregated (Ottoman *mestur*; Arabic *mutahajjabat*)[25] – and the implied referent is elite women – only female tourists could meet with them. But without a common language, no mutual education could occur. There was a bigger problem, said Fatma Aliye; most Ottoman Turkish women conversant in French 'have been raised in *alafranga* (Arabic *ifranji*, 'Frank') style with a European nanny, known as *institutrice*', and their French was learned 'not to gain knowledge but from a desire to be out-and-out foreigners. They are ignorant of the precepts of right religious practice (*ahkam-ı şeriye*) and have outwardly erased their native (*milli*) habits ... encountering them is like conversing with European families living in Beyoğlu', the fashionable area wherein the tourist interpreter-guides worked.²⁶ French and Frenchness invaded the text, as Fatma Aliye transcribed the French word *institutrice* to name these girls' foreign governesses, thereby characterising this group of Ottomans as foreignised.

Across the Ottoman Empire, including Egypt, criticism of European-style educations that were said to alienate young women (especially) from their own cultures, leading them to disdain their families and milieus, was ubiquitous in the era's discourse on women, men and modernity. Some commentators deployed 'European education' as a scare-term to attack the very notion of educating girls, by discrediting the alleged results. Others used that loaded trope to call on the state and local elite to found 'national' or 'Islamic' schools in lieu of relying on Euro/American missionary education projects.²⁷ This was not Fatma Aliye's approach. What concerned her (like her contemporary in Egypt, Zaynab Fawwaz) was ill-informed interlocutors who would 'claim that customs are taken from *shariʻa*', confusing certain popular practices (a constant target of reformers) with sanctioned religious practice: *shariʻa* as the 'religious Way', the body of practices and guidance derived from Qur'an and Sunna. On the other hand, noted the preface in strong language:

> There is a group among the observant Muslim families (*ehl-i İslam familyalar*) who cannot cram into their fanaticism even training in Turkish for women, beyond what is necessary for getting by, much less learning French, as though acquiring learning and knowledge (*tahsil-i ulum ve maarif*) were a sin.²⁸

These people were unaware of 'the pure wives and pious daughters, and the many learned and cultured women in the first era of Islam who possessed high degrees of knowledge and excellence'.²⁹ Fatma Aliye would present these in her collection of biographies of early Muslim women (*Ünlü İslam Kadınları*, 1895), as did Fawwaz, in the same volume where she reproduced Fatma Aliye's work. Such willed ignorance led to cultural confusion:

> Although uncovering women's faces is not prohibited by the *shar'*, while covering one's hair is obligatory, we see some of our women covering their faces ... and uncovering their hair. In effect, we have no middle ground. It is as if we are bewildered³⁰ no matter which way we go. Yet, in all things excess and exaggeration are bad.³¹

In this long and careful preface, Fatma Aliye returned to the question of intercultural understanding. Visitors who wanted to understand Ottoman society 'must meet and talk with families who know French and live according to the fundaments of Islam, preserving its religious guidelines and ideas and its communal habits'. She referred again to the perpetuation of erroneous notions and implied the centrality of gender – or rather, of 'woman' – to Orientalist constructions:

> As all humankind knows, the Europeans have nothing to say when it comes to the tenets of our religion which are in accord with wisdom/reason; it is only that they think the women of Islam are oppressed and wronged, and in this matter they are violent in their criticisms.[32]

An oft-heard complaint, Fatma Aliye made it work as an argument for girls' thorough education, including knowledge of a European language. Women must take responsibility as cultural mediators, particularly since so many false understandings clustered precisely around women's status and experience.[33] This was an adept recasting of the European Enlightenment notion that women's status was a key indicator of a society's rung on the 'civilisational' ladder, and of feminists' uses of it to place women and girls at the centre of social-political work in the name of 'progress' (however that was defined). If it was a notion used 'liberally' by imperialists, it could be and was appropriated by imperialism's objects for their own agendas.[34]

Thus, *Woman in Islam*'s preface embedded the ensuing text in the narrator's own coming-to-awareness and her sense of social-intellectual responsibility as an educated Muslim believer, a role that governs the dialogues. The concern about misinformation – mistranslation – is so central to this work that the preface's framing of it is reiterated in the first dialogue, when the visitor echoes the narrator's earlier reflection that the views she had heard from foreigners sounded as if they applied to an entirely different society than her own. The visitor exclaims:

> But according to the information I have gotten from you, I [could] imagine that I am not come to the Turkey that I have heard and learned about, but by mistake to some other country.[35]

> [The narrator speaks:[36]] The reason for this is that the Europeans, upon arriving in Dersaadet [Constantinople], descend directly to the Beyoğlu hotels. They stay only among Beyoğlu folk, and get their information up to a certain point based on their [Beyoğlu folks'] situation. They merely pass through the streets and quays of Istanbul, Uskudar and along the shores of the Bosphorus. The manner of living, ways and customs of these [other areas] do not admit of any comparison to Beyoğlu.[37] As an indication, the translator-guides whom they keep by their side don't even know anything other than the world of Beyoğlu, and so they just make something up and say whatever comes into their heads, because they have to give explanations for questions that are posed. The travellers, believing the things they have heard from them are true, add them to their travel accounts. And when we read some of these travel accounts, we think some country unknown to us is being discussed.[38]

Fatma Aliye's Nisvan-ı İslam

Ending her preface, Fatma Aliye gestured to a double audience in the context of the false-news economy she so carefully traced. It was the motivation for this act of writing.

> In my conversations with some esteemed ladies among these travellers, I learned about the oh-so-mistaken suppositions the Europeans had about us (*o kadar yanlış zehablar/fasad dhununihim*), such that I was unable to conceal the astonishment in my heart on this matter and I was forced to commit three of these conversations and dialogues to writing, as will now follow.[39]

In sum, the preface's framing discourse on knowledge production and modes of education marks the entire text structurally, thematically and linguistically. For in contrast to the *tercüman*s of Beyoğlu, the narrator *in situ* is a cultural mediator who moves knowledgeably between French and Turkish, and between culture-bound understandings. This strategy is borne out when the visitor at the end of the second dialogue – assiduous in recording new Ottoman lexica – remarks that she has spent considerable time and money trying to learn about Turkish society, but has learned more in these few hours than everything she had learned before. The narrator responds that she, too, has learned: the exchange models a true sharing of knowledge and generates an emotional connection.[40]

TRANSLATING IN THE TEXT: FROM LANGUAGE TO CULTURE

The first two dialogues and part of the third – as readers are reminded frequently – took place in French. The author-figure/narrator is the interpreter between the European and Ottoman women present in the scene of verbal exchange and hospitality. The Ottoman home is the locus of cultural translation, a 'semi-private'/'semi-public' gendered space that complicates preconceptions about the 'proper' place for political discussion.[41]

Therefore, already in its Ottoman textuality, the 'transcription' that is said to yield this text is a translation, or at least a fictional *mise en scène* of translation, on multiple levels. First, in the process of composition – in other words, in the movement from its (staged?) oral to its written existence – the work has been translated by the author-narrator from bilingual French–Turkish conversation into written Ottoman Turkish. Second, the didactic construction of these dialogues, and their smooth and often subtle transitions from one topic to another, suggest a carefully thought-out composition, likely a product of multiple conversations reworked into text rather than a transcription: a 'translation-adaptation' of myriad oral exchanges (or partly imagined conversations) into a reordered text. Even so, it enacts oral exchange beautifully, with humour and repartee, capturing a remarkably warm and lively set of interactions. Third, as we elaborate further, the encounters narrated in the work repeatedly produce 'translations' of local practice (in Europe, in the Ottoman Empire) into comparative explications that interlocutors in the text can find legible.

Thus *Nisvan-ı İslam* assumes an activist stance on behalf of intercultural understanding. The act of translation as such is foregrounded in the work and is also a metaphor for what stands at its heart: a notion of careful, contextually rich cultural translation. This, in its Ottoman form, is what the text is all about. As already suggested, we see it as first and foremost a primer for *Ottoman* women on how to take control of knowledge creation and communication, educating them on the Orientalist errors shaping European travellers' preconceptions as the latter sought to enter the fabled 'Ottoman harem'. But this was also a gender translation: Ottoman men were a second, implicit audience for Fatma Aliye's enactment of educated-and-authentic Ottoman womanhood and her explication of doctrine, belief and practice modulated to elite women's lives. It is no wonder, then, that a series of encounters, discussed further below, confront hosts and guests repeatedly with *mistranslations*: these are often funny moments (amusing to the participants as well as for readers), told with relish, staged in lively conversations, in a women's world where women take control of the discourse. When the text migrates to Arabic and French (now becoming translations of a staged translation), of course it hails new audiences, which we shall imagine in and through the translation practices of each new rendering, each new context of publication and reception.

How does language itself emerge in the text? At the start of the first dialogue – which took place 'in the noble month of Ramadan last year',[42] 'we learned that a European matron called Madame F and a nun of ascetic practices wished to come to our home (*hâne/manzil*) to observe the Ramadan *iftar*.' Describing the scene of encounter, the text immediately marks interlinguality:

> After half an hour, upon being informed that they were coming inside, and since the responsibility (*vazife*) of acting as translator for our *hâne* was the duty of my inadequate self (*uhde-i acizanemde*), taking a couple of *cariye* (enslaved female attendants) by my side to receive the ladies' coats and umbrellas, we went to the garden door to meet them. Saying a formal 'welcome' in French as the ladies entered, we shook hands.[43]

Because the narrator is the translator, she takes a predominant role in the ensuing conversations. Female family members (including, pointedly, the *cariyeler* (Arabic *jawari*; sing., *jariya*)) and friends are an internal audience, posing questions or giving answers mediated by the narrator-author.

For instance, as the narrator and Madame F discuss the treatment and legal status of former slaves in elite households, an Abyssinian *cariye* well endowed with jewellery enters. To a query on her status the narrator explains that the *cariye* had grown up from early childhood in the household. When the time came for her to be freed, she refused the offer, and so the household provided her with a document allowing self-manumission at a time of her choice. 'Madame called over the aforementioned Abyssinian and got her to sit close by, and asked her through me why she refused manumission and freedom. I gave [lit. told] the Abyssinian's response below to the Madame, translating it into French.'[44]

Other 'translational moments' emphasise parallel practices and understandings, rather than difference, as when they hear the cannon announcing the end of the day's fast, whereupon they enter the dining room. They find a platter of food on the table, described as *iftar tepsi* in Ottoman and as *saniyat al-iftar* (the *iftar* platter) in Arabic. The visitor, studying it, remarks that 'among us, too, a variety of things of the appetiser/tidbit sort are put on the table before the main meal. They are called hors d'oeuvres. So, this is also customary among you.'[45] Both the Ottoman Turkish and the Arabic transcribe the French 'hors-d'oeuvres'. The narrator agrees as to its customary nature, but then explains its specificity to Islamic practice, as 'akin to the table that was lowered to Hazret-i İsa (Arabic *hadrat* 'Isa; Jesus), peace be upon him, and it is a custom particular to the month of Ramazan'.[46] This generates another response. 'Upon hearing this, the nun, who until that moment had not engaged in [our] talk and perhaps not giving any importance to the conversation, had remained silent, [said]: What is this table of Jesus that you imitate?'[47]

The narrator explains that this incident, related in the Qur'an (5.112–15), concerned Jesus's disciples requesting a miracle, 'a table spread with food'. This miracle serves as inspirational guide – explains the narrator – to those foods customarily consumed to break the fast before the main meal is brought out.

> According to those who saw it, there were various comestibles. There are a variety of reports as to what sorts of things these comestibles were. But a famous report says that on that table were bread, fish, some vegetables, oil, honey, piyaz [a bean and onion dish] and pastirma.[48]

Discussion of Turkish food and the meaning of the fast ensues, as a matter for cultural comparison. This displays the narrator's detailed grasp of Christian practices and yields a moment of cross-cultural agreement. The narrator protests at the visitor's remark that fasting is 'difficult', for the hardship is nothing compared to the divine grace it accrues. She adds that surely Christian ascetics who fasted felt the same. Asked for her view, the nun acknowledges that 'whatever arises from worship in thanks for God's grace and charity is easy'. At this point, a new theme is introduced: the proximity – quoting the Qur'an – of Muslims and Christians, along with a distancing of Jews and polytheists. Fatma Aliye quotes the Qur'an as saying: 'You will find that the ones who say "we are Christians (*nasara*)" are the closest to the believers from the point of view of affection.' The proximity is elaborated through internal translation-cum-elaboration: 'That is because among the Christians there are priests and monks, and these exalt Him and do not refuse to accept Him.' Here 'priests' is given as *kasisler/qasisin* but glossed parenthetically as *alemler/'ulama'* (the term for Muslim religious scholars), while monks are *rahipler/rahban*, glossed as *zahitler/zuhad*, ascetics.[49]

Finishing *iftar*, the women move to the salon to take coffee, 'and I began to translate between the two visitors and the lady of the household [the narrator's mother, *sahibe-i hane/sahibat al-manzil*] and family members.'[50] The visitors are shown into other rooms, accompanied by the narrator-translator. In one, they find a woman reading or reciting from a book. Because her head is covered and she is 'reading with utter respect', the nun asks whether she is reading the Qur'an. She is told it is a *tafsir* (commentary on the Qur'an), in Ottoman Turkish, of – explains the Qur'an reader – Surat 'Imran.[51] 'After I explained her answer to the nun in French', the nun asked who was meant by 'Imran. The narrator explains that there are two 'Imrans; this one refers to Mary's father. The scene is a reminder of Ottoman Turkish women's learning, displaying the narrator's comparative knowledge. At the nun's request, the reading woman recites verses from Surat Maryam (the Chapter of Mary). 'As for me, I began translating this into French.' If her implied aim is to instruct visiting Europeans, the narrator's summary is also for the benefit of her Ottoman readers. It yields another doctrinal discussion, this time about the Christian concept of the virgin birth, via discussion of the Greek term *paraclete*.[52]

The narrator happens to have to hand Albert de Biberstein-Kazimirski's (1808–87) popular 1841 French translation of the Qur'an, nicely evoking the multilingual library of an elite Ottoman home. She reads out loud the translator's note on this word; the French appears, in Latin characters, in the Ottoman Turkish work.[53] As the narrator remarks that the Prophet Muhammad 'caused his *umma* to know the earlier prophets', the call to prayer sounds, and most women leave the room. The narrator, 'delegated to perform hostessing', does not. When the visitors ask to observe the prayers, the narrator ushers them into the women's prayer space, translates

Fatma Aliye's Nisvan-ı İslam

for them, and continues to answer their questions on Qur'an texts, again acting implicitly as a pedagogue for readers outside the text.

Thus, the first dialogue comprises a multifaceted 'translation' of Qur'an references, Muslims' beliefs and comparative religion, arising from the parallel-in-difference initiated by *iftar tepsi/hors d'oeuvres* to yield a far-reaching discussion of similarities and differences in belief, a primer for Ottoman Muslim readers on how to mediate the issue of different beliefs in conversation with European Christian visitors. Translation as act and as metaphor is explicitly part of it, a substantive element, moving between Turkish and French, Bible and Qur'an, Madame F and the *cariyeler*.

But as we have suggested, translational transactions may be equally about 'mistranslation', from the utterances of the Beyoğlu *tercüman*s to the perceptions of visiting Europeans, represented not only through words but also gestures: translation as about much more than language or even text. The question of cultural mis/translation hovers over the first dialogue from its start. At the beginning, when the two visitors approach the residence and the narrator emerges with the *cariye*s, one visitor tries to shake a *cariye*'s outstretched hand rather than handing her a coat and umbrella as expected.[54] When the visitors ask to see 'a Turkish room', they are startled and disappointed to find rooms that, to a European eye, appear too ordinary. Too familiar.

INTERPRETATION *INTER PARES*

In the second dialogue, with an Englishwoman 'who spoke French almost like a Parisian' (this recognition suggesting the narrator's precise and cosmopolitan familiarity with that language), translation as an explicit motif recedes. Yet cultural translation is ever-present. This dialogue focuses on marriage and gender-segregation practices. The theme's proximity to women's lives seems mirrored in the growing intimacy between the female characters. As the evening draws to a close in the garden, with narrator and visitor engaged in one-on-one conversation, the night sky and trees generate the visitor's monologue on matters astronomical and biological. Through the narrator's description of the guest and her own self-description (mediated/translated by the narrator), this guest is more fully described than were the earlier ones: an exemplar of a modest, learned, enthusiastically scientific woman who also takes care of her appearance and is sensitive to social mores and her husband's needs. Her narrated speech even offers an 'auto-critique' of European expectations for elite women's behaviour, a different sort of cultural translation, *for* the narrator's benefit, a different inscription of 'custom' as a critical aesthetic.

> I go around, I go to balls and soirees. I don't like to depart from custom. But I don't go in for finery/showing off my toilette or making myself attractive [Arabic: exposing myself to people's gaze] as most women do. I don't wear the heaviest silks [Arabic: expensive silk garments] to give myself airs [lit., to sell my greatness; Arabic, to signal greatness and self-pride]. I wear them to listen to the sweet sound of their rippling in the breeze. In this way I put into practice the lessons in wisdom that I have received.[55]

The visitor implicitly criticises a range of related social practices and underlying behaviours in the 'West', notably hypocrisy and excessive status consciousness in public social relations. Fatma Aliye's text is a meditation on social participation through sensitivity to custom, and yet also, judicially critical understanding of it and of one's own intellectual and social needs as an individual. That this is voiced by the visitor makes the point that this is a cross-societal concern. The narrator truly meets her counterpart in this shared and egalitarian discussion. Here, it is the visitor who provides a guide for Ottoman readers on self-comportment, echoing critiques in the Turkish and Arabic press on local elite women's alleged propensity for budget-busting finery.

The dialogue culminates in an intensely personal exchange, almost erasing the cultural-linguistic distinctions between host and visitor. The evening conversation in the garden transcends language. The visitor's excursus on hypocrisy leads her to speak of the veracity inherent, she says, in the language of the eyes.

> At this point, Madame R stopped talking and was silent, placing her elbow on the windowsill of the pavilion[56] and resting her head in her hands.[57] Though her voice had fallen silent, I was still listening, as though she were yet speaking. Or, more accurately, I was astonished, struck by admiration at that wise and erudite (*edebane*) discourse so that, like one who does not want a beautiful vision (*hayal*) to vanish from his sight, my ears yet wanted to be occupied with the vision-echo/imaginary echo (*aks-i hayal*) of her words.[58]

FEMININE FASHION AND ITS TRANSLATIONS: HOW TO DEBATE MODERNITY AND CIVILISATION

The third dialogue of *Nisvan-ı İslam* is a reflection on fashion, understood in broad terms to include not only clothing, but hair styles, accessories, and indeed other cultural fashions such as the use of the piano. Mixed in with this is a conversation about marriage and women's right to divorce. Modern readers not infrequently find this part of the essay out of place; they focus on the discussion of marriage and divorce and tend to pass over that on fashion and music. (As mentioned earlier, in the latest

Fatma Aliye's Nisvan-ı İslam

Arabic edition, the third dialogue is not even included.) Yet, sartorial matters were of great importance in the Ottoman Empire, involving profound issues of modernity, authenticity, correctness, thrift and economic nationalism. Significantly, the first half of this third section takes place entirely among upper-class Ottoman women, before any foreign guests arrive. This first portion allows Ottoman readers to reconsider their own categories, which are then revisited form a different angle in the 'cross-cultural' portion of the dialogue. Both sections are constituted by cultural translation.

The scene is set in the garden of the narrator's home. It is May and Fatma Aliye – as narrator and as character – is conversing casually with two friends over breakfast and coffee. None of the three have yet donned formal attire for the day. Having had an English governess, S. Hanım's English is much better than her French. In fact, her written English is better than her written Turkish, it is said. She loves adornment and is addicted to fashion. Keeping up to the minute with the latest European styles is an obsession; being caught out is a constant worry. The other companion, N. Hanım, reads and writes quite well in Turkish. She professes herself uninterested in fashion and normally dresses in what is characterised as *alaturka* style. In this dialogue, language is aligned with personal style.

Initially, conversation dwells on a problem S. Hanım is having. In anticipation of attending a wedding, she had ordered an expensive custom-made gown in the latest Europeanised fashion. But the event was postponed and now – only months later – the gown is out of fashion. It upsets her to let such a gown go to waste. N. Hanım explains that her approach to formal dress is a traditional gown (*entari*) made of the best fabric. This she dresses up with belts crafted from precious materials. Thus, her outfits are not subject to the vagaries of passing fashion. The belts can be sold for the value of their metals, and new ones commissioned with no financial loss. The narrator represents a third way. Sometimes she adopts one style and sometimes another, she explains.

> S. Hanım's heart desires ordering something *alafranga*. She will have it made so. You [N. Hanım] enjoy *alaturka* [style]. You will have [your outfits] made *alaturka*. I, as I find neither style unattractive, will have [my outfits] made *alaturka* when I want and *alafranga* when I want. As I already said a moment ago, since none of us is going beyond what is customary *for her*, we won't be ridiculed. And there is also this: if we are going to dress as French women do, let's dress in the latest fashion so that we will not make ourselves the butt of humour for those who are *alafranga*. *It is anyway a blessing that we have this degree of independence in attiring ourselves.*[59]

This seems a simple enough staking out of middle ground. But her discussion also engages with the economics of fashion. A major factor in the high cost of ordering *alafranga* dresses is the imported fabric. But local silks are just as good, if not better. Local artisans must be encouraged to adopt greater innovation in their patterns, and then, Ottoman customers will come. Failure to do so, it is implied, is both wasteful and a form of thoughtless imitation. The synthesis proposed here – modern or *alafranga* dresses executed with Ottoman fabrics and offering new and innovative patterns – suggests a vision of a local modernity and challenges the idea that what is seen as 'tradition' is or must be static. Again, the text enacts a cultural translation that emphasises negotiation: a 'translation' is never either wholly the same or wholly different, and 'borrowing' is also creation. This theme of tradition as not static is reiterated when an older woman enters the room and the narrator's friends ask her about the fashions of earlier generations. They are shocked to discover that women of her generation wore low-cut gowns, and also had fashion differences vis-à-vis their parents! The episode ponders the tide of times: the realisation that there is no 'authentic' past or present. It also slyly foreshadows the European visitors about to appear, who will long to see an 'authentic' local past based on expectations formed by Orientalist imagery.

Towards the end of this Ottoman-only part of the dialogue, conversation moves to their mutual friend F. Hanım, whom they miss. Her difficult husband makes it hard for her to leave the house. She is unhappy and wants a divorce, but her husband won't give her one. The women discuss the unfairness of divorce in their Muslim-majority society: easy for men and extremely difficult for women. The narrator describes a supposed custom in Antakya. There, she relates, women write it into their marriage contracts that anytime they don a blue outer robe (*ferace*), this conveys that they are fed up with their husbands and divorce shall be immediate. The friends are fascinated. S. Hanım wishes out loud that Ottoman women had some similar arrangement. The narrator expands on her story by observing that these women simply want a man able to provide for them. Polygyny does not necessarily bother them, as a co-wife reduces the burden of physical labour for other individuals in the household. By implication, divorce is rare. The group continues to ponder issues of marriage and divorce. It is acknowledged that, though there are exceptions, men are typically better managers than women, and this is why European women do not control their own finances. But S. Hanım states forcefully that she would never turn the management of her own money over to a husband.

At last the guests arrive. Three upper-class French ladies have come to call: two young women who are sisters, the elder already married, and an older, unmarried lady, their aunt. They are well dressed, attractive and well educated.

The guests are escorted to the sitting room where the narrator, always in control of the narrative and the simultaneous translation, meets them, in the company of her friends and family. Immediately, the French women express distress: they had sent word ahead expressly to request that their hostesses meet them wearing traditional Ottoman clothing, but the narrator and companions seem not to have done so. What, the Ottoman women ask themselves, might the European ladies mean by traditional Ottoman costume? It's a brilliant moment of cultural mistranslation. The narrator resorts to showing them images in an album, asking whether this was what they had in mind. When they reply in the affirmative, it is revealed that these are pictures bought in the local market. The photographs are fakes in the sense that the women in the photographs are professional (non-Muslim) actresses, the pictures were produced for the tourist trade, and the costumes are a kind of fantasy or pastiche that never existed in any real Ottoman context. The text deftly turns on its head the Orientalist paradigm of knowledge production and knowledge ownership. The Ottoman women are the worldly ones, the sophisticated and critical knowers. The French women, believing that there must be an authentic, traditional Ottoman lady and lifestyle, are shown as naive victims of a marketing ploy. It is this moment that echoes the earlier moment in the third dialogue when the narrator and her friends are made aware by her elderly relative that the question of modern fashion is nothing new. As they have learned from their elder, now the French women learn from them that neither 'modern' nor 'traditional' are immutable categories. Rather, adaptation to changing times and mores is an ongoing process. There is no 'old time' nor 'traditional' in any static sense, just as there is no definitively correct answer to the problem of the 'properly' modern. As in the case of the envisioned 'modern' garb crafted in Ottoman silk by Ottoman professionals, everything is endlessly hybrid.

From fashion and national costume, the women move to the marriage institution. Marriage as such is not questioned as a 'good' for women. The focus is on aspects of marriage, including a woman's autonomy in terms of spatial movement or handling her own affairs, and the 'problem' of spinsterhood. At the time, these were much-discussed issues in the Arabic and Ottoman presses.

The French women are quick to articulate a European trope of Muslim women as 'slaves' of their husbands who lack rights to move about freely and are required to ask permission for everything. They do concede that they have seen Muslim women moving freely in the public spaces of the city. Their Ottoman hosts respond by pointing out that Muslim women control their own wealth and Muslim men have the absolute obligation to support their wives: maintenance of herself or of the household is never a wife's duty. This leads to discussion of the older French woman's unmarried status. Because her father went bankrupt, she explains, she lacked a dowry. She had one serious suitor, an energetic and successful 'self-made' man, but she was forced to reject his suit because he was born outside of wedlock. The Ottoman ladies make the point that in Muslim society, all young women, whether rich or poor, whether considered beautiful or not, will find spouses. For them, this emerges from the societal value placed on family life and on flexibility in dower.

Lurking just behind this conversation about men's obligation to support wives is a discourse on polygyny and bastardy. Earlier in *Nisvan-ı İslam* the point was made that polygyny, if undesirable, had redeeming features. It eliminated the need for the European custom of keeping mistresses and the attendant curse of bastardy laid on offspring. As with discussion of clothing styles, the interaction between these Ottoman and French women revisits topics that the Ottoman women, alone, had already covered, and this is significant. Who translates whom? Their unfortunate friend F. Hanım and the difficulty of her securing a divorce resonates. The Ottoman women acknowledge – and emotions of friendship and sadness are unmistakable in the text – that their friend's demanding husband hardly lets her out of the house, and they find this unjust. Fatma Aliye was not the only published woman saying these things. Women were speaking up on the pain caused to women by the difficulty of obtaining a divorce.[60] What this text brilliantly accomplishes is the co-translation of equivalent situations. Once both groups of women are present, cultural comparison and translation are not only possible but inevitable. The easy divorce available to men in Islam is a problem, but so is indissoluble marriage among Christians. Muslim women have more freedom of movement than Europeans imagine, including the freedom to stay at home; Muslim women control their own property and wealth and thus overall have better marriage prospects. Women's situation is acknowledged as much less than perfect in either context, but conversation among the Ottoman women first (importantly), and then between them and the French women, elucidates strengths, weaknesses, and – yes – similarities in both systems, even as they subtly emphasise the superiority of the Ottoman/Muslim system in terms of social morality. The French women ask: is what they have heard true? Is it an Ottoman custom that if a man sees slippers outside his wife's bedroom door, he knows that he is welcome, but if there are no slippers, he must return to his own room? The Ottoman women burst into laughter;

they compare it to the story of the blue *ferace*s of Antakya. When their laughter is explained, the French women join in. What appears foreign has been revealed to be an issue held in common. The women of both cultures immediately recognise that the ability of a married woman either to limit her husband's sexual access to her or to secure a divorce easily and according to her own desire, is so far beyond the realm of the conceivable that the mere idea must elicit hilarity. The shared laughter – in a text with many moments of humour across assumed cultural divides – gives a sense of the two groups of women as peers and accomplices in the project of modern womanhood.

The final pages of the third dialogue are devoted to music. One of the French ladies notices a piano in the room and asks if the Ottoman women play. There follows a disquisition on what it might mean to 'play'. All the women agree that real mastery requires more than ten years of study and is embodied in the ability to play even the most complicated pieces by sight without error or hesitation. The narrator says she realised at a certain point that she would never attain this and so she gave up any real pretension of learning to 'play'. Yet, as it turns out, she and her Ottoman friends can produce music on a piano very well, while the French women are also proficient. When the European lady opens the piano, she notices that it is from Paris and expresses surprise that in Istanbul she has not seen any pianos of Turkish manufacture. Our narrator informs her that Turkish industry is not yet advanced enough to produce them. Whereas once pianos went from East to West, she remarks, now the reverse is true. She claims that the piano must be derived from an organ that Harun al-Rashid sent as a gift to Charlemagne. Then the ladies proceed to entertain each other with music. All the women, French and Turkish, play well. First the French women play European pieces, and then the Ottomans play Turkish airs on the piano, then with oud, keman and kanun. Next, the French women ask to hear European music on Turkish instruments, and the Ottoman ladies oblige. Finally, the Ottoman ladies play European cantos, using the piano and the keman in combination. The music offers a perfect metaphor for Fatma Aliye's message in *Nisvan-ı İslam*. Recognising cultural difference, it challenges the notion of a fixed authenticity and instead emphasises cosmopolitanism and adaptation. Translation, in fact. She presents the concept of civilisation in circulation, where elements are remade as they travel from place to place, appearing in different places at different (or the same) times. Civilisation 'goes on tour' and belongs to all it touches, to all who touch it. All that is required is a willingness to put time into developing the knowledge and skills to participate thoughtfully: to have translational conversations.

Marilyn Booth and A. Holly Shissler

Part II: Text in Translation

FATMA ALIYE IN ARABIC

On 13 Jumada I 1309 (14/15 December 1891) readers of the weekly Beirut newspaper *Thamarat al-funun* found this announcement on page three:

> Women of the Muslims, by *al-fadila* Fatma Aliye
> We read in the *Tercüman-ı Hakikat* newspaper under this title a short piece (*nabdha*) from the pen of the aforementioned woman of excellence amongst the secluded,[61] the daughter of a house anciently rooted in virtue and glory. And so we elected to translate it, for the true words it contains, and to publish it in our newspaper sequentially beginning with this issue.[62]

Thamarat al-funun's editor, 'Abd al-Qadir al-Qabbani (1849–1935), was amongst the Beirut-based literati who had benefited from new types of schooling while remaining firmly grounded in Arabic letters' longer legacy, and who were propagating reformist ideas. He had studied at Butrus al-Bustani's (1819–83) non-sectarian Madrasa Wataniyya (National School, est. 1860) and was one founder of a philanthropic society that started schools for Muslim girls and boys, Jam'iyyat al-maqasid al-khayriyya.[63] Another society, Jam'iyyat al-funun, established *Thamarat al-funun* in 1875 as a collectively held enterprise which soon passed to the proprietorship of al-Qabbani. It became a leading weekly with a particularly large Muslim readership.[64] Its columns paid close attention to events in Istanbul, and drew material from periodicals there, including items on politics and society in Europe.

Fatma Aliye's preface fit well in this communications context. As we have seen, it began with contemporary history, a spatial sketching of the information age, the old and new technologies that made intercontinental and regional communication and news transmission possible, as configurations of market and empire made them necessary. But, the framing argument went, these processes could foster the circulation of Orientalist stereotypes by local translator-guides, profiting from an expanding tourist trade.[65] On the other hand, *Thamarat al-funun*'s own preface to Fatma Aliye's text underlined the speedy material and discursive circulation of sources between Turkish and Arabic amongst cities of the Ottoman Empire. Al-Qabbani had read the text in *Tercüman-ı Hakikat*; the forty instalments in Arabic were possibly translated by al-Qabbani himself.[66] The series ended on 1 November 1892, and as early as 6 February 1893, readers were told they could purchase the translation in book form.[67] Thus, *Nisvan-ı İslam* was beginning to appear in Arabic only one month after

Fatma Aliye's Nisvan-ı İslam

its final instalment appeared in Ottoman Turkish – in both cases, in major urban newspapers, the era's discursive vehicle of choice.[68]

In their study of discourses on gender in late Ottoman Syria, Zachs and Halevi distinguish *Thamarat al-funun*'s intervention in the 1890s 'debate on women' from other Arabic periodicals' contributions. They do so on the basis of its being 'embedded in a larger general debate on the family, and the modern Muslim family in particular'.[69] Family was a key focus of other newspapers, too, such as Cairo's nationalist daily *al-Mu'ayyad* and Beirut's *Lisan al-hal*. But Zachs and Halevi perceive a particular approach in *Thamarat al-funun*. Rather than articles focused on 'women's education, rights and activities', it carried features 'on breastfeeding, nannies and women's fashions, within which were inserted views and comments about women and their social roles', as well as features on marriage in Europe. Those who wrote in it 'did not conceive of women (or men for that matter) as individuals distinct from their instrumental, relational and sexually discrete social roles'.[70] Whether or not one agrees that its approach was distinct, *Nisvan-ı İslam*'s presence in *Thamarat al-funun* over so many issues challenges this characterisation. It was a different kind of intervention in a different kind of voice, as our analysis of themes and the construction of character suggests. That the narrating voice was feminine, and the conversations occurred entirely among women, contrasts with the male-editorial and 'mostly unidentified' writers that Zachs and Halevi find predominating in this journal's articles 'on women'. At the same time, Fatma Aliye's focus on Islamic beliefs and practices in a comparative framework was consonant with *Thamarat al-funun*'s outlook, though it shared 'civilisational' themes with many other outlets as well.[71]

The work's appearance in a leading newspaper reminds us of the variety of genres, often translated, that newspaper editors saw as appropriate. In announcements-cum-ads for the upcoming book version, *Thamarat al-funun* characterised Fatma Aliye's work as *riwaya* – 'narrative', but increasingly signifying imaginative prose: a novel, short story or play. Less than two weeks after the final instalment of this 'novelistic' text appeared, in the same slot there began appearing an Arabic translation of Tolstoy's novella *Family Happiness* (1859) – translated from the Ottoman Turkish translation rendered from the Russian by 'Madame Gülnar', whose translation of *Nisvan-ı İslam* into French would appear in 1896.[72] As the newspaper placed and defined it, *Nisvan-ı İslam* was akin to the serialised novels appearing in many Arabic newspapers and magazines.

That Fatma Aliye's text was labelled a *riwaya* leads one to ponder the readerly effect of a text that appeared in almost every weekly issue of the newspaper for ten and a half months, to be followed by Tolstoy's text. To advertise or position it as a *riwaya* might seem rather ironic. After all, its author posed its content and raison d'être in opposition to the 'fictional tales' on which European tourist literature about the Ottoman Empire, she opined, was based. But its didactic-dialogic structure bore affinities with the era's prose fiction and plays; in both Turkish and Arabic, these were often pointedly didactic and framed in sternly directive prefaces about morality, appropriate behaviours and East/West difference. Moreover, as didactic as Fatma Aliye's text is, the characters were vivid. They were not simply didactic mouthpieces – even if they did stand in for 'types'. They were rounded characters with histories, networks, desires and anxieties. The prevalence of dialogue, the memorable characters and the descriptive scene-setting likely led *Thamarat al-funun* to call it a *riwaya*, and perhaps led readers to receive it as imaginative writing.

FROM BEIRUT TO CAIRO

Fatma Aliye's contemporary Zaynab Fawwaz (c. 1850–1914) was a forthright, uncompromising commentator on women's expanded rights in nineteenth-century Egypt. That her entry on Fatma Aliye (including the entire text of *Nisvan-ı İslam*) took up fully one-tenth of her enormous (554-page, large-folio) biographical dictionary of world women suggests she believed this was an important text. (The only longer entry was the 'Epic/Life of Josephine', taken from the journal *al-Lata'if*).[73] Fawwaz highlighted Fatma Aliye's education as spearheaded by a supportive, hands-on father:

> When her father assumed the governorship of Aleppo in 1282 [1865/6], she was three years old. With signs of her intelligence clearly evident, her father had grown to love her intensely. He took her with him. She stayed throughout his governorship: for two years she remained under his watchful eye and supervision.[74]

Back in Istanbul, he hired 'male and female' instructors to teach her at home.

While there is no doubt that Fatma Aliye had a strong education from tutors at home, or that Cevdet Paşa supported his daughters' education, this biography implies a closer involvement than was likely. Ahmet Midhat's biography noted that her father took a direct interest in her education and was pleased by her early progress, but a telling anecdote also suggested his involvement was less close and constant than Fawwaz described. When Fatma Aliye was six years old, her mother held up a book, telling her father that Fatma Aliye could read it. Surprised, he opened it at random

Fatma Aliye's Nisvan-ı İslam

and asked her to read. She did so, to his slightly astonished pleasure.[75] Fawwaz, on the other hand, implied that from the age of three the girl showed unusual intelligence that galvanised her father's immediate interest and intensified his affection. Fathers' engagement in educating their daughters comprised a repeated thematic emphasis in nineteenth-century Arabic biographies of 'famous women' (including those in Fawwaz's biographical dictionary), as one pillar in the girls'-education agenda that advocates for female betterment called for.

We do not know the source for Fawwaz's biography of Fatma Aliye, which went into detail on the breadth of her studies, modelling a comprehensive, intellectually strong, feminine education. One might think, remarked Fawwaz – voicing a common emphasis in the era's biographies of women – 'upon seeing her devotion to these sciences, that she neglected the most important obligations of secluded women': care of home and family. Yet, Fawwaz insisted, this was not the case. But Fawwaz's narrative suggested that these duties indeed hampered a woman's intellectual ambitions. Though Fatma Aliye developed 'her own style in composition, she was not able to devote herself fully to publishing her works, given that she was busy first and foremost with the matters naturally acquired by women such as home management and child raising'.[76] (Here and elsewhere, Fawwaz's vocabulary subtly resisted the widespread notion that female education ought to consist only of training girls in 'domestic arts': such, she insisted or implied at some points, was unnecessary.)

For Fawwaz, *Nisvan-ı İslam* exemplified contemporary Muslim women's contributions to society as educated individuals, and so she wanted her readers not only to know of it but to read it. Fawwaz explained that *Thamarat al-funun* had translated the work, and gave her reasoning for including it in her own compendium:

> This turned out as the very finest treatise composed by a wearer of the veil, with its skilled rhetoric and literariness. I decided to reproduce it below this biography, despite its length, due to its usefulness and as the fine sign and legacy of this excellent woman.

Fatma Aliye, said Fawwaz in conclusion, was

> amongst those secluded women who are sources of pride for us within Islam, unmatched by any woman of East or West. She lives in Istanbul; may God increase her likes and through her, expand scholarship and knowledge among our female sex.[77]

By incorporating the text into her own compilation, Fawwaz was playing a parallel role to that of Fatma Aliye. She was seeking to expand women's reading and learning, in her case partly by circulating the writings of other women, in an act of participatory feminism. There are more specific ways in which this work buttressed Fawwaz's emphases both in her biographical dictionary and in the essays she published in Cairo and Beirut beginning in 1892. Both women focused on Islamic practices and criticised erroneous understandings amongst 'Westerners' and locally. Both demonstrated concern with encouraging women themselves to learn the fundamentals of their religion and its history, to hone their self-understanding, allow them to defend themselves against spurious arguments that men used to deny their rights, and equip themselves to debate these topics. This was to be one outcome, ideally, of the formal education for females that both women supported vocally. Both used early Muslim women as exemplars and anecdotes about them as proof-texts for right practices lost through centuries of masculinist interpretations of the Qur'an and Sunna. And, as writers in public, both played with pseudonyms as survival skills for female writers; yet their identities were not fully veiled by such monikers. Recall that Fatma Aliye first signed herself modestly as *'bir kadın'* (a woman), and then as 'translator of' the work where she had signed herself thusly. Fawwaz – not so modestly – used pseudonyms such as 'Shajarat al-Durr' (the name of a famous Fatimid ruler) and 'Hamilat Liwa' al-'Adl' (Bearer of the Banner of Justice), but it is likely that readers knew her identity, especially as both of these appeared subsequent to her public use of her own name. Within Fatma Aliye's text, the use of first initials conferred autobiographical referentiality on the text and yet withheld it, much as the use of pseudonyms could do. Finally, both women engaged in *munazara* (disputation, debate) in print with their male mentors; and indeed, these mentors engaged briefly with each other in a Turkish–Arabic *munazara* published partially in *Tercüman-ı Hakikat* in Istanbul and *al-Mu'ayyad* in Cairo.[78]

FROM ARABIC TO ARABIC

Textual variances between *Thamarat al-funun*'s columns and Fawwaz's republication are mostly minor and insignificant: a few inserted conjunctions, and variant spellings that illustrate distinct typographical practices in Beirut presses versus those in Cairo.[79] There are occasional typographical errors (dropped words, misspellings) in one or the other version. When *al-Durr al-manthur* clearly has the correct version, perhaps we see an editing process at work. We do not know whether Fawwaz got her text from the newspaper columns or from the ensuing published book, which we have been unable to consult. Corrections may have been made in the latter that then appeared in *al-Durr al-manthur*.

The two venues exhibit a few lexical differences that suggest divergent cultures of production and reception – and of familiarity with European language use. Transcribing the French *institutrice*, *Thamarat al-funun* is more accurate than *al-Durr al-manthur* (*instītūtrīs* versus *al-stīnūtrīs*, which substitutes the Arabic definite article for the first syllable of the French).⁸⁰ *Al-Durr al-manthur*'s odd transliteration is not surprising. Fawwaz was monolingual, and the correctors/typesetters at the government press in Bulaq, where her volume was printed, likely did not know this word. To our knowledge, it was not commonly used in Egypt. The same divergence in apparent familiarity with foreign lexica is suggested in other transliterations: 'Kazimirski': *kāzimīrskī* versus *fārmīrskī*, where the letters *qaf* and *za'* appear as the very similar *fa'* and *ra'* (in each case, the difference is a dot).⁸¹ *Thamarat* shows more propensity for European vocabulary, reflecting linguistic practice amongst the Beiruti elite: *al-madamatayn* (the two Madames) where *al-Durr* uses *al-za'iratayn* (the two female visitors).⁸² Yet, reproducing in Arabic a footnote from Kazimirski, *Thamarat* localises but *al-Durr* does not: only the former adds the conventional phrase following mentions of the Prophet Muhammad, '(*salla 'alayh wa-sallim*)'.⁸³ Although Fawwaz's version omits one or two other phrases, there are infrequent intra-Arabic vocabulary changes: introducing the visitor, *nabila* (the distinguished woman) in *Thamarat* versus *'aqila* (Mrs, madame, a word then coming into vogue),⁸⁴ or *sanadiq* versus *khaza'in* for chests, *Thamarat*'s choice possibly a tad more modern.⁸⁵

Differences in format signal the coexistence of differing, changing and genre-specific practices of textuality in a transitional era. *Thamarat al-funun* followed its introduction (translated above) with a section title ('al-Muqaddima') while *al-Durr*'s version gave no heading and introduced the work simply: 'Here is the promised treatise (*al-risala al-maw'ud bi-idrajiha*); she said: . . .'.⁸⁶ But, since *al-Durr*'s republication of the work was not immediate, to the Ottoman and *Thamarat*'s introductory 'in the noble month of Ramadan last year' *al-Durr* adds, 'that is, in the *hijri* year 1308', a dating followed by later Arabic versions.⁸⁷

Thamarat's format would have appeared more modern, while *al-Durr*'s befitted the premodern biographical dictionary genre. Fawwaz used *qalat/qultu* (she said/I said) to introduce every speech, placing it at the end of the paragraph before the reported speech. *Thamarat* generally eschewed this, in favour of a dash to signal dialogue, and started a new paragraph with every new speech act. This followed the practice then becoming standard amongst Ottoman Syrian novelists in reproducing direct speech, which gives this text as reproduced in the newspaper a more 'novelistic' feel. Perhaps in keeping with this, occasionally *Thamarat*'s text appears slightly less formal (if only because an element may be omitted erroneously!): *sarrahi* (explain: fem. sing. imper.) for *fa-sarrahi* (thus explain).[88] Whether this less formal tenor was deliberate or not, it was enhanced by a greater tendency to use French words, injecting a note of colloquialism or bilingual orality. Later Arabic versions would make more consequential changes, without signalling their editorial interventions.[89]

FROM OTTOMAN TO ARABIC

Do divergences between these Arabic renderings correspond to distinctions between the Ottoman Turkish text and the first Arabic versions? In fact, there are very few divergences (we have signalled some in quotations above, but in general, they are not semantically significant). However, one consistent difference is the presentation of French-language texts within the text, and this is interesting as an index of assumed readership. In the Turkish, most such texts were left in French, and reproduced in Latin letters, for example a lullaby sung to baby boys in France – which the Arabic omitted altogether.[90] Discussing a Qur'an passage, which the narrator reads to her listeners in French from a published translation, the Ottoman reproduced an explanatory note from the translator, Kazimirski, in French, in Latin letters.[91] Both Arabic versions gave the note's contents, but only translated into Arabic. Fawwaz followed the wording of the Ottoman but added an explanation. The translation, following the original closely: 'I indicated the marginal note of the translator (Farmirski [*sic*]) concerning that, and here I give it word for word.' The Arabic added: 'and she gave it word for word, and its Arabisation is as follows.'[92] *Thamarat* had omitted the first-person explanation and introduced the note thus, with a more accurate transliteration of the commentator's name: 'She mentioned what was quoted word for word in French, and we Arabise it as follows.'[93]

Divergent practices in reproducing French may reflect typographical capabilities in each venue. But they are more likely a product of different senses of audience. Fatma Aliye was writing for a local audience many of whom, she could assume, read French, but that was not the case for *Thamarat al-funun* or Fawwaz. Differing levels of familiarity with French surface elsewhere. When Fawwaz's text reproduced *institutrice* (*al-stinutris*), unlike in the Ottoman, it explained the meaning: 'European child-raisers known by the name *institutrice*'.[94] Where the Ottoman used the term *alafranga* to signify 'European-style' education (and attire), the Arabic read: *tarbiya ifranjiyya sarfa* (wholly European training/upbringing). The Arabic explained venues in Istanbul: 'Bayughlu [Beyoğlu], an

Fatma Aliye's Nisvan-ı İslam

area in Dar al-Sa'ada where the *afranj* live'.[95] The Arabic sometimes eschewed Turkish terms, such as that for the senior female slave/administrator in the household (Ottoman: 'the woman who was at my side, in the role of *baş kalfa* of our household'; Arabic: 'the *jariya* who undertook to serve as head of the servants (*ra'isat al-khadam*) in our household'). These nuances suggest an intended focus on local Arabic audiences who might not know Ottoman Turkish or Istanbul society.

Other divergences might suggest attention to slightly different religious sensibilities and expectations for print, though we do not want to make much of this. In the Arabic, in the second dialogue when Madame R refers to *nabikum* (your prophet), this is followed by the customary utterance of respect *salla 'alayh wa-sallam* (God's prayers on him) which, in the context, was presumably meant as a narratorial/translatorial addition rather than something that the European Christian Madame R would say. In the original Ottoman text, Madame R says simply, 'your prophet' (*peygamberiniz*).[96]

THE FRENCH TRANSLATIONS

The two translations into French, both under feminine translator signatures, appeared in 1894 and 1896 in Paris, the second of them by a figure already well known in Istanbul and Cairo, 'Mme Olga de Labedeff [*sic*], connue sous le pseudonyme de Gulnar-Hanoum', as the title page announced.[97] Their brief prefaces are our first clue to translation strategy or at least attitude. The first one introduced the author as 'Alihe Hanoum' and altered the work's title to 'Contemporary Muslim women: Three conversations'. The second preserved the original's title and translated it as 'Muslim women' (rather than 'Women of Islam').[98]

The earlier translation, signed by 'Nazimé-Roukié', carried a brief 'Avis' that praised Aliye as renowned for her intelligence and mentioned her father's high position – one reason, it said, that the work had 'created a sensation in high Ottoman circles'.[99] The translator(s) praised its elegant style and fine use of detail, and called it 'picturesque'. 'The translator has tried to remain as faithful to the text as possible, to preserve its sense of originality and its Asiatic savour' (*cachet d'originalité, saveur asiatique*). Perhaps this was intended also to signal the translator(s)' close cultural relationship to the original's site of production. If this translation displayed a 'foreignising' strategy, retaining Ottoman usages – as we shall suggest – this was partly to maintain the 'Asiatic' flavour. But, the introduction noted, it had added a few 'differences' to conform to French style.

The Lebedeva translation's slightly longer preface, in the voice of the publisher, framed the French-language rendering in the politics of East and West, presenting Fatma Aliye as both an agent of attitudinal change and an 'Orientalist' exhibit: as both 'painter' and 'model', to satisfy but also to challenge the curious gaze of the Western consumer. At the same time, it played with the notion of 'exhibit', Ottoman women as object of the gaze, subject of the (European Orientalist) painter, a European heritage no doubt well known to many potential readers of the French translation. In this case, the object was also the subject-creator.

> This work we are publishing will be read with all of the eagerness stemming from a very natural curiosity. In effect, it has the great merit of being an original painting, drawn by the model herself: it is written by a Turkish woman. Already we see smiles of incredulity, because in the West, where no one takes the trouble to study modern Turkey, it is generally accepted that the Turkish woman's education consists of learning the art of making herself beautiful, and that her daily routine varies between consuming sweet preserves, coffee, and the nonchalance of doing nothing [FAR NIENTE].
>
> Turkish women are never represented with a pen or brush in hand.
>
> Thus, this book ... will come as a revelation, proving how much change has occurred among young Muslim women. These are no longer the pretty dolls that one imagines, hidden behind walls, but rather young women educated in History, Geography, the Sciences, and Belles-lettres.[100]

Although published in Paris, this was in a sense a 'local' production, for it was printed at the press of a newspaper funded by Sultan Abdülhamid II.[101] The preface praised him as 'author' of the 'transformation' in lives of the young through the founding and funding of educational institutions. The book proved, said the preface, that the author – of the book – and 'the women, her companions, are not at all victims of ignorance, [a notion that] certain people – who have seen nothing of Turkish life except the walls – have propagated in Europe.'[102] Thus, this preface framed the translation in a declarative sense of mission towards a European audience, echoing the author's own sense of mission toward ill-informed European visitors to the Ottoman capital. With its official overcast, the preface also reminds us of the crucial role of directive state institutions in propagating Ottoman culture to eager readers in Western Europe. Translation prefaces can play strong roles in shaping readers' expectations and orientating their reception of a translation: this one is suggestive of how that might be. Through prefaces and also within the translation itself, the 'translator's voice' is much more explicit in these French renderings than it is in the first Arabic rendering.[103]

If this sense of mission foregrounded an important theme in the work itself, it also spoke to the views and activism of the translator. That the book was published by a press associated with the sultan might attest to the translator's strong connections in Istanbul. Ol'ga Lebedeva was a transcultural figure who fascinates. Russian by birth and family, she spent part of her adulthood in Kazan and studied languages there, developing a career as an Orientalist and translator. After meeting Ahmet Midhat Efendi in Stockholm, she travelled to Istanbul where she spent much time in the 1890s, and came to know Fatma Aliye personally. In fact, it was through Ahmet Midhat's mediation that she made her own obligatory 'harem visit' to Fatma Aliye's home. She later spent time in Cairo, acquainting herself with intellectual women there. She translated from Russian into Ottoman, and from Ottoman and Arabic into French. She was a strong advocate for Ottoman women as well as for Islamicate culture and history, playing a leading role in Russian Orientalist academe.[104]

The publication by a regime-supported press also speaks to Fatma Aliye's position as Cevdet Paşa's daughter (the great statesman held many important offices during the reign of Abdülhamid II). An invited guest at the palace, she clearly drew approval and respect: she was asked subsequently, based on her learning and her excellent French, to receive foreign female guests to the palace. She was, then, an interpreter not only in the pages of her own book, staged at home, but also at the heart of the Ottoman system. Her representation of articulate, worldly Muslim Ottoman women must have seemed a perfect public-relations artifact to those in the regime concerned with European public opinion.

LOCATIONS OF FRENCH, LOCUTIONS OF PROXIMITY

Notwithstanding Lebedeva's familiarity with Ottoman Islamic culture and her ties to the 'well connected' like Ahmet Midhat Efendi, Nazimé-Roukié's translation often appears closer to the Ottoman/Arabic in language and understanding, more comprehensively attuned to Ottoman Muslim practices. One striking indicator of the translator(s) embeddedness in the Ottoman scene is that the text reveals signs of knowledge, beyond the original text itself, of who was present for the conversations that serve as the basis for *Nisvan-ı İslam*.[105]

In different ways, both translations distance the text from its own immediacy, its context of production. At least in the introduction, where the Turkish and the Arabic display the deictics of locality and first person, the French creates distance by omitting the first-person plural. Thus, where the Turkish and Arabic say 'Because among us women are segregated/veiled',[106] both French texts lose 'among us'. Lebedeva's reads simply 'since the Turkish woman must remain veiled', while Nazimé-Roukié opts for a longer explanation incorporating 'veiling' and 'seclusion/segregation' as two aspects of one institution or practice: 'The custom established in the East, for Muslim women, to hide from view concerning the masculine sex and to only show oneself veiled.'[107] Note a distinction that will remain consistent: Nazimé-Roukié refers to 'Muslim women' whereas Lebedeva references 'Turkish women'. We wonder if this was because Lebedeva, coming from a different Muslim region and society, wanted to emphasise the Turkish specificity of the book's descriptions, while for Nazimé-Roukié, likely an Ottoman subject, or two (Turkish-ethnic or not, at least by choice of pen name suggesting the former[108]) this distinction is not immediately relevant, and preference goes to highlighting the Muslimness of the community described.

Is the translator's proximity to or embeddedness in the culture of the original text the reason why Nazimé-Roukié 'foreignises' the work in certain ways, in lexica remaining closer to the original while reshaping these lexica to a new linguistic environment? This translation preserves certain Ottoman terms, adding explanatory text, generally set off by parentheses, as they are introduced. This strategy implies that some things are not really translatable but must be seen as part of a different cultural complex: they can be explained but not translated. This rendering preserves everyday usages such as '*konak*', '*selamlık*', '*cariye*', '*kalfa*' and '*hanım*', which are presented in the French text with Gaulicised spellings like '*calfa*' and '*hanoum*'.

Hanım/hanoum provides an interesting example of the effects that the translators' different strategies can have. Nazimé-Roukié glosses *hanoum*s, at first use, as '*dames*', but uses *hanoum* frequently thereafter, while Lebedeva generally uses *dames*.[109] But '*hanım*' in Turkish is not merely a word denoting 'lady' or 'woman'; it is also an honorific. Like Fatma Aliye herself, Nazimé-Roukié generally uses *hanım* when talking about or addressing upper-class Ottoman women. (Fatma Aliye used *hanım* for Ottoman ladies and referred to the European women in the text as *madam* and *madamlar*, as did the Arabic, though in Fawwaz's volume, they are also referred to by Arabic descriptives). One important effect of this is to afford upper-class Ottoman ladies in the text their status and dignity. They are, for example, 'Melek Hanoum', not merely 'Melek'. This establishes them as the equals of the European visitors, who are always described and addressed as 'Madame R', 'Madame F', and so forth, and yet as distinct from both the European *dames* and the Ottoman *cariyes*. Lebedeva more often drops the Ottoman honorific, thus diluting these social distinctions.

Where the Ottoman uses the French word *institutrices*, noted earlier, and the Arabic reproduces it with a gloss, Nazimé-Roukié follows the

Fatma Aliye's Nisvan-ı İslam

Ottoman – 'foreignising' precisely *by* retaining a French word from the original – while Lebedeva uses *gouvernantes françaises*.[110] A further example of Nazimé-Roukié's foreignising tactics is her insertion of Ottoman terms that were *not* part of the original text into the translation. Thus, in the third dialogue, she describes Sabire Hanım as 'une bonne amie, notre missaphir', and then parenthetically glosses *misafir* as 'hôte; mot turc très usité à Constantinople dans toutes les langues'. The word *misafir* does not appear in the Ottoman text at this juncture.[111]

Nazimé-Roukié uses *şerî* (from the Arabic *shari'a*) as in the original, though changing the spelling (Chéri), and explaining the term, while Lebedeva simply uses *connaissances religieuses* though she uses *Le Cher'y* elsewhere.[112] Both choose the European term Pera to refer to Beyoğlu, the neighbourhood frequented by Europeans, as Nazimé-Roukié explains but Lebedeva (who lived there) does not.[113] Where the Ottoman articulates an Arabic maxim, offering it both in Ottoman Turkish and in Arabic – *khayr al-umur awsatuha*, the best matters are the moderate/middle ones – Nazimé-Roukié gives a Frenched transliteration of the original, along with a translation: 'according to the Arabic maxim, *Haïr-ul-umur essadouha*'.[114] Lebedeva simply says, 'moderation is necessary in everything', without localising the phrase.[115] The reader may remember that the Ottoman passage reads: 'In short, we have no middle [ground]. It is as if we are bewildered as to which direction we should go. Yet, in all things excess and deficiency are bad. In every matter, moderation is required (*her hususta itidal gerektir*)', followed by the Arabic aphorism in parentheses.[116]

At times, though, Lebedeva translates literally, and the results might not always have been explicable to French readers not versed in Islamic locutions. For example, she refers precisely as Fatma Aliye did to the wives and daughters of the Prophet, using a familiar Arabic/Ottoman phrase for these female paragons: 'les chastes épouses et les filles pures'. Nazimé-Roukié gives the more straightforwardly descriptive 'daughters and wives of the Prophet'. Their slightly different renderings of the next phrase correspond to the Ottoman in different ways. The entire passage in Ottoman reads (and the Arabic is near-identical): 'They [the Europeans] for their part do not know to what a degree of perfection in knowledge and virtue the pure wives and undefiled daughters [of the prophet] and countless other accomplished scholars and writers of earliest times attained.'[117] Nazimé-Roukié follows the Ottoman and Arabic closely: 'et tant d'autres qui se sont distinguées aux premières années de l'islamisme comme femmes auteurs et poètes'. Lebedeva expands this slightly, perhaps echoing an agenda signalled in her translation's preface: to get readers to recognise

Muslim women's high degree of learning, even if in that preface the focus was on contemporary, young women. Her expansion reads:

> et les autres femmes de nos pays, étaient très instruites. Postérieurement à elles, bien d'autres femmes de la première époque de l'islamisme étaient célèbres par leurs connaissances littéraires et scientifiques, aussi bien que par la supériorité de leur esprit et de leurs vertus.[118]

Beginning the first 'dialogue', we notice divergences. Lebedeva does not explain or define 'Ramadan'. Nazimé-Roukié gives quite a long explanation; here (on the first page of the translation itself) readers are informed that all explanations added by the translator are set off by parentheses. The gloss refers to Ottomans/Muslims as 'they'; these explanatory interventions are not put into the mouth of the author-narrator of the original text. Having explained the meaning, Nazimé-Roukié then retains the Ottoman/Islamic/Arabic term *iftar* (*l'iftar*). Lebedeva amplifies by explaining the original within the translation, as if in the words of the speaker: 'the dinner which we customarily make to break the fast after sunset'.[119] This is not set off, and use of the term 'we' thus suggests to readers of the translation that this explanation is given by the narrator, for her listeners in the text, rather than added by the translator for an audience *hors-texte*. With such tactics, Lebedeva's text moves *Nisvan-ı İslam* towards being a descriptive text written for Europeans rather than primarily an inter-Ottoman one, for Ottoman women: a shift of audience, of translator's focus, that the translator's preface, with its reference to European stereotypes, signalled. Nazimé-Roukié's text, on the other hand, preserves the Ottoman-directed character of the text by maintaining a clear separation between translation and narrator's glosses.

Lebedeva's attention to European stereotypes is manifested in other ways. In the third dialogue, for example, after the European and Ottoman ladies have all shared the humour of the imagined custom of the slippers outside the bedroom door, the original text goes on to remark that the more distant one is from something, the more likely it is that mistaken notions will creep in – significant to the narrator's stated sense of mission at the start. At this juncture, Lebedeva inserts an anecdote directed at racial stereotypes. In her version, the narrator (ostensibly Fatma Aliye) recounts that once when young she was on a ship from Beirut to Istanbul on which there was also an American family. While strolling on the deck with other women of her family, heads covered, the American women approached her group, staring, and at last asked whether they were from Constantinople. Receiving an affirmative answer, the Americans exclaimed that, based on their blue eyes, they must be Greek. When Fatma Aliye answered that they were Turks, the Americans expressed surprise and disbelief, leaving the young girl flustered.[120] Thus we see that in various ways, Lebedeva domesticates the text into becoming French, in terms of usages, narrator's perspective and implied audience. For readers of Nazimé-Roukié, the text remains an Ottoman text, the translator an externalised commentator (and thus, visible mediator), the vocabulary heavily Ottoman/Arabic and the French reader an onlooker rather than a direct addressee.[121]

EUROPEAN HISTORIES IN THE TEXT?

As in the preface, Nazimé-Roukié continues to retain Ottoman terms consistently, for instance, *cariye* (*djarié*; Arabic *jariya*), giving *esclave* in parentheses at first use, while Lebedeva simply uses the French word (*esclave*), glossing *bach-calfa* (her transliteration for the Ottoman *baş kalfa*) as 'senior slave'.[122] But this figure illustrates how Nazimé-Roukié does domesticate to some extent, although generally in the parenthetical notes, the translation's 'asides' to French readers, assimilating Ottoman understandings to European ones but setting them off from the text. Explaining this head female administrator (the *baş kalfa*, or in Nazimé-Roukié's usage, *calfa*), the translation calls her 'a sort of *demoiselle d'honneur ou suivante*'. Further on, the term *novice* is used to refer to the junior *cariyeler* or *çırak*s, the result sounding rather Catholic. (Lebedeva uses 'inexperienced'.)[123] The Ottoman terms '*kalfa*' and '*çırak*' describe a hierarchy among the *cariye*s of the household, with the youngest children at the bottom, then the more adept adolescents ready to be married off (*çırak*s), then the *baş kalfa*. These Ottoman terms are borrowed from the world of the guilds and might be given as 'apprentice' and 'master'.

While in French, '*novice*' is a synonym for '*apprendi*', the text nevertheless emphasises the 'family-like' nature of the relationships, as well as the fact that the *baş kalfa* is answerable for the behaviour and wellbeing of those beneath her. Thus, we may ask whether Nazimé-Roukié's word choice here is canny, giving the text a new resonance and giving French readers a familiar image – particularly in light of a French nun's presence in this scene. Upper-class Ottoman girls did attend convent schools; there may be a cross-cultural gesture here, the *baş kalfa* as a kind of Mother Superior with her novitiates, explained in the hearing of a French nun. Do Nazimé-Roukié's occasionally oddly target-culture-bound equivalents bespeak a relative lack of knowledge of French society, or to the contrary, do they suggest such a level of familiarity or intimacy that the translator dares to make the occasional imaginative translational leap? To domesticate 'Women of Islam' into a French Catholic setting, even as, in other ways, the translation reads as an Ottoman text? The convent, with its language of sisters and mothers, offers fictive kinship within a framework of un-freeness/discipline and authority, partly mirroring the fictive kinship among *cariyeler*, *baş kalfa* and free wives and daughters in the elite Ottoman household. There is a whiff of the 'peculiar institution' in the Ottoman original and in Nazimé-Roukié's translation, with the familial aspects emphasised in ways that obscure the true nature of the relationship, which is a master–slave relationship.[124] At the same time, the usage *suivante*, gesturing to hierarchical relations within the Ottoman household, might say something about relations of dependence between economic classes in Europe as much as it speaks about the world of the text translated. What was the status of servants in European households, readers might be prompted to ponder. Were they so different to the Ottoman *ceriyeler*? The original text invited readers to consider these questions, and Nazimé-Roukié's rendering magnified them, if anything.

The discussion of slaves versus servants displays nuanced divergences between the Ottoman and the Arabic, on the one hand, and both French translations, on the other. Having explained practices of manumission, the narrator argues that in Ottoman society, slaves and ex-slaves are considered part of a family, whereas servants 'when no longer useful' (Ottoman) or 'needed' (Arabic) are dismissed.[125] Both French translations give a different, more negative, impression: 'when she displeases us' (Lebedeva) or 'as soon as we are discontented with them' (Nazimé-Roukié).[126] Where the Ottoman reads: 'It is just as if they are members of the family', the Arabic diverges slightly: '*Jawari* are considered members of the family completely' (*akhissa' al-'a'ila tammaman*). The French translations emphasise the 'as if' rather than the 'completely': Lebedeva adds *presque* (almost), while Nazimé-Roukié says: 'Master and slave are considered, to put it this way, like members of the same family', the interjected phrase and simile creating a distance.[127] Thus, amongst all the versions, the Arabic most strongly insists on slaves' incorporation in families (and not just 'households'), the Ottoman and Nazimé-Roukié slightly less so, and Lebedeva the least. We may follow Ehud Toledano here in noticing the often-made apologetic argument, amongst Ottoman reformists, that Ottoman slavery, particularly household or *kul/harem* slavery, was 'mild' in nature.[128] The French translations' handling of this might suggest sensitivity to histories of enslavement and movements for emancipation in European contexts.

In the second dialogue, Nazimé Roukié uses the term *bas-bleu* (Bluestocking) to describe the learned English visitor, a term with specific historical associations in the French context, and which would not have been a term of approbation in France – or in Britain.[129] The term translates *feylesof* in the original and in the Arabic (philosopher; Arabic *faylusufa*), rendered by Lebedeva as 'la femme philosophe'.[130] Appropriate to this semantic or contextual shift, for Nazimé-Roukié this woman 'professes a certain scorn for fashion' whereas in the Ottoman and Arabic, she is portrayed more as indifferent to it; as wanting to be correct, tasteful and conforming to social norms, but eschewing vanity and display. Yet, Nazimé-Roukié's domesticating translation (*bas-bleu*) has probably got it right. In the Ottoman, the longer passage expresses the preconception of the intellectual woman as dowdy (which *bas-bleu* could connote to turn-of-the-century French readers), and then rejects this prejudice, implicitly setting up the intellectual as an appropriate role model, balancing intellectual enthusiasm and care for appearance but without ostentation as this character turns out to do. The French interlocutor had given the narrator the impression that Madame R could be termed a *feylesof*, a term in Ottoman that carries a valence of dowdiness. In translation from the Ottoman:

> [The author of the letter of introduction] informed me that Madame R, whom she was commending to me, although English, managed several languages, and knew French as well as her own language, such that we would have no trouble in communicating. She concluded her letter – by way of giving more detailed information on Madame R – by adding that she did not refrain from saying that she [Madame R] could be considered a *feylesof*....
>
> Although I expected an aged 'feylesof madame' to appear before me, based on what I had learned from the letter writer, I rather saw a quite attractive madame of about thirty. Madame R, after removing a *manto* (overcoat) of a quite elegant and heavy fabric [that is, of good quality], was [seen to be] dressed in a manner suitable to the latest fashion and proper for a formal (*ağır*) call (*vizite*). When she took off her hat, it was revealed that her hair had been combed and arranged by a skilled *femme de chambre*.[131]
>
> According to what the Parisian madame had written, shouldn't the woman I was going to see have been dressed in a very plain manner, as though she didn't give any importance to ornaments, adornments, and fashion?[132]

The Arabic differs slightly, adding twice that the narrator expected the visitor to be 'of an advanced age', perhaps a slightly different reading of *faylusufa*. The Arabic does not connote 'dowdy' so much as 'pedantically intellectual': perhaps when feminised, this term has tended to assume something about a female's appearance.[133]

Thus, European usages and expectations are introduced into the text through culturally specific lexica that highlight possibilities and limitations of cross-cultural comparison. At a few points, though, distance rather than domesticating equivalence is most striking. In these cases, rendering a 'local' artefact or usage, Nazimé-Roukié resorts to an orientalising mode. Notably, at the very start to the first dialogue (quoted earlier) and elsewhere, the translation uses the terms *harem* and *selamlık*.[134] The Ottoman simply says that the European visitors were coming inside (*içeri*), and the guests are conducted to the 'salon'. The Arabic uses *manzil* (residence) or *al-dukhul ila fana' al-dar* (entry to the residence's courtyard; in the Ottoman the first round of guests are met at the garden gate, *bahçe kapısı*).[135] Lebedeva phrases it differently, and does not use '*harem*'.[136] Only in the third dialogue, when the guests, who are accompanied by a man, bypass the door to the women's quarters, does the Ottoman use *selamlık*.[137]

FROM DIALOGUE TO TREATISE?

In the passage from Ottoman/Arabic to French, a shift in tone and register is discernible. The language of the Ottoman and the Arabic texts, while formal, includes conversational features, and at times the text is even playful, bantering. This feature is often lost in the French versions.[138] In French, the work becomes more a treatise, less an enactment of dialogue.[139] The conversational structure and tone of the original convey real personal equality among its various participants, and this is much less vivid in the drier essayistic tone of the French. Such modulations for a new audience seem particularly evident in Lebedeva's rendering, which at times mutes the localness of the work, leaves out details, and dilutes the force of the language.

Lebedeva particularly, but also Nazimé-Roukié, omit certain verbal practices, notably the use of *hadrat/hazret* before the names of prophets and utterance of the phrase 'upon him/her/they be peace' following their names (which the Ottoman text uses in narrative situations and whenever an Ottoman woman is speaking, though not when a European is speaking. The Arabic uses them at certain points if not always).[140] These customary usages also enhance the oral quality of the Ottoman and Arabic. At times, both French translations abbreviate discussions of other customary practices or Islamic norms and guidelines. When, at the request of the visitor, the Abyssinian slave[141] who had refused manumission sets out her goals for a good marriage – her expectations as to food, clothing, shelter and required work – these details suggest she knows the *shari'a* stipulations on what a wife is due from her husband. In Lebedeva's rendering, not only are the slave's words put in third-person indirect reported discourse rather than in first-person speech, but also, her reply is only that 'she wanted a husband who would support her as well as her master had done' and would

Fatma Aliye's Nisvan-ı İslam

give her 'a tranquil existence'. While Nazimé-Roukié retains the direct speech, she translates this as: 'A husband who can give me what I enjoy here, without demanding in exchange more work; otherwise, I prefer not to marry.'[142] Both French translators apparently saw this rendering of legal stipulations in the speech of the slave as unnecessary (or implausible?) for European readers.

At other times, they chose to offer their own glosses on Islamic ritual practice. Lebedeva's text inserts a long explanation of the prayer ritual, which does not appear in the Ottoman or Arabic, certainly signalling a difference in audience, but again, implied to be the narrator's own speech for the benefit of foreigners. Nazimé-Roukié sets off a briefer explanation in parentheses, thus marked as a translator's note.[143] Both texts use the European derivation 'Mahomet' and Mahometan', despite the fact that these terms had acquired negative connotations through centuries of hostile usage, not to mention the misunderstanding of Islamic belief connoted by the label 'Mahometan'.

Another gesture to a Francophone audience emerges in apparent editorial decisions Lebedeva took, showing sensitivity to European readers. This translation edits out the Ottoman text's less complimentary comments on European visitors and on Christian beliefs (which are by no means the prevailing attitude to European society or Christian doctrine in the text). When the text reprises European tourists' gullibility to ignorant 'guides' plying the streets of Pera/Beyoğlu (quoted earlier), which the narrator emphasises as the source of distorted information, Lebedeva omits most of this, while Nazimé-Roukié remains close to the original.[144] When the narrator reads out Kazimirski's gloss on 'Paraclete', the final clause refers to 'the weak beliefs of Christians', which Nazimé-Roukié preserves but Lebedeva omits.[145] Is it also for reasons of audience that Lebedeva compresses the description of the second dialogue's visitor? As already suggested, this English *feylosof* models the diligent, self-motivated intellectual woman who does not neglect her looks but does not attend to them overly: a role model, perhaps for the Ottoman audience. Lebedeva, writing for a French audience, is less interested in the *European* women who appear in Fatma Aliye's text, and their circumstances.[146] Nazimé-Roukié follows the Ottoman/Arabic; again, this translation appears as more 'Ottoman' in its investments and interests, surfacing in its translation strategies, despite occasional resort to western-Europeanist stereotypes (the harem), as in discussions of language, so significant to this Ottoman work. The Ottoman text (followed closely by the Arabic) describes the Englishwoman's French, and pronunciation of Ottoman lexica, admiringly.

Although Mme R had not spent above one week in Darsaadet, she had assigned one hour of her day to learning Turkish and had memorised a large number of words. As I was translating the words of our lady guests, she sometimes responded herself with *evet* or *hayır* (yes, no; Arabic *na'm, la*), while this incapable self translated the rest. The Turkish words she had learned by heart in a week were written in her notebook, and the number was surprising. She said that when she returned to her country, she would not give up but would complete [or perfect] her study of Turkish. When she said some words she had learned, we realised her pronunciation was good. This was due to her natural aptitude, because [also], despite being English, she spoke French like a Parisian lady.[147]

Nazimé-Roukié lends more drama to this scene by turning much of this into the Englishwoman's direct reported speech. She describes her notebook directly; it is her pronunciation in reading her word list that stirs admiration amongst the listeners, while not only her responses but her facial expression indicate she understands some of the Turkish conversation. She tells those assembled that she has already acquired dictionaries and other learning tools and is studying the alphabet – none of this is in the Ottoman/Arabic. Nazimé-Roukié expands emphasis on her linguistic abilities and in the process, complements Ottomans of the capital, as the original does not.

> Despite her English origin, Mme F [*sic*] had a very pure accent in French; it would be difficult to distinguish her from a Parisian; and from some Ottoman words she pronounced, it was evident that she would speak our language like a true Constantinople hanoum. (The Ottomans of Constantinople are reputed to have the most pleasant accent.)

Lebedeva follows the Ottoman fairly closely, making a rather pointed interpretative addition to the passage's final line: 'she spoke French like a Parisian, which is very rare for an Englishwoman.'[148]

FEMINISM IN TRANSLATION

Occasionally, Nazimé-Roukié editorialises in an overtly feminist mode, especially noticeable because not only does the translation diverge from the original, but also it is distinct from the Lebedeva rendering published two years later. For instance, the Ottoman and Arabic complete their description of the English visitor as follows:

> As for her clothing: if as I have already described, it was good quality and the latest fashion, yet it was utterly simple and was not decorated with flowers or similar kinds of ostentatious ornmentation (Ottoman *cicili bicili*, ornaments; Arabic *al-bahraja*), and indicated her dignity.

Lebedeva says: 'Other than her pretty gown (*robe*), fashioned simply and charmingly, she carried no *colifichet*; her entire *toilette* was simple and distinguished.' But Nazimé-Roukié says: 'Although her *toilette* was very rich, she lacked those ridiculous ornaments and thousand *colifichets* that give men the right to consider women unable to attain any intellectual merit, and good only as dolls.'[149] Significantly, this is not composed in relation to Ottoman men, but to men in general.

Another instance is interesting for its possible feminist slant yet also, its addition of a typical European generalisation about Muslim marriages. Nazimé-Roukié's rendering of the long discussion of polygyny intensifies the theme of misery and oppressiveness for women, and omits a section where the narrator states (rather simplistically, it must be said, though not entirely inaccurately) that a woman has the right to leave and remarry should her husband take a co-wife. This translation does include the narrator's explanation of the stringent conditions for equal treatment of co-spouses, a leitmotif in late nineteenth-century Ottoman and Arabic reformist discussions on marriage. Defensive about European women's payment of dowries (which the narrator has contrasted with Muslim practice), the visitor says: 'In reality, even if we do pay money, the men desire and like us totally.' In Lebedeva: 'In effect, we bring them money sometimes, but also we enjoy great esteem from them.' But Nazimé-Roukié expands, perhaps in line with what she thought a French audience might believe: 'Yes, women among us do bring a dowry to their husbands, but they [masc.] respect us and have regard for us. They do not treat us as inferior beings, as Mahometans treat their women/wives.'[150]

Are these the translator's own views, or is this text aiming to make the European interlocutor look more judgemental and more ignorant than she appears in the Ottoman and Arabic? Or is the translator playing to a presumed audience's prejudices? It is certainly possible that translator and anticipated audience shared this point of view. Nazimé-Roukié's rendering may well be an Ottoman example of interventionist feminist translation, if an implicit and only intermittent one, not altering the text so much as explicitising its latent potential for a feminist reading.[151]

A Conclusion, and an Epilogue

The two translations, made by subjects close in different ways to the original's context of production, render readings that diverge in emphasis. The earlier translation, by Nazimé-Roukié, remains much closer to the original. Though it self-consciously addresses a European audience, it still retains more of the original character. One might say that it displays an interest in introducing European readers to Ottoman female society *on its own terms*. While less lively and more heavy-handedly didactic than the original or the Arabic, it generally makes efforts to dispel Western stereotypes and to convey something of the fabric of life for an Ottoman lady who is not part of the 'Pera scene'. The Lebedeva version, also hewing fairly closely to the original, focuses more on exploding myths, and on apologetics, than on what might be seen as broader feminist questions (on conditions of women of both continents and religions) or how to carry off an 'authentic modernity'. Lebedeva was interested, as her preface makes clear, in convincing European readers that Ottoman womanhood was not benighted and backward as readers might imagine; in this, her mission dovetailed nicely with the goals of the authoritarian regime that sponsored the translation's publication. Socially conservative, yet supremely interested in modern developments such as public image and popular legitimation, and therefore in presenting a 'civilised' face to the outside world, Abdülhamid II doubtless saw in Fatma Aliye and her work a golden opportunity to make his case to European and American audiences: hence the inclusion of her works as part of the Ottoman entry at the Columbian World's Exposition. The vehicle of a translation executed by an informed, trusted and widely recognised European woman like Lebedeva must have been especially welcome.

The French translations' existence reveals most clearly the original's 'straw-man' premise. That is, though the Ottoman Turkish (and Arabic) versions *seem* to be directed at misinformed Europeans, they are aimed at Ottoman audiences: after all, the original publication appeared in Ottoman Turkish. The aim is instruction of upper-class Ottoman women simultaneously on how to respond to misapprehensions and Orientalist stereotypes of their visitors, and how to be themselves models of modern womanhood. In other words, *Nisvan-ı İslam* is a reflection on what constitutes a viable path to authentic and dignified self-realisation in a changing world. This is as true for the contemporaneous Arabic publications of the text as for the Ottoman Turkish. The period translations are close to the original in style, tone and language. The inclusion of the entire work within the entry 'Fatma Aliye' in Fawwaz's biographical dictionary of women could hardly make this clearer. Fawwaz was concerned with how to be a modern and forthrightly Muslim woman, in terms of women's work towards creation of a modern society/nation, and the uplift of women themselves, including crucially the creation of feminine self-identities shaped by knowledge and dignity, to be met with respect. Like Fatma Aliye and other (if not most) female activists of the period, she saw these facets as inseparably entwined. These Ottoman (Turkish and Arabic) editions are concerned

Fatma Aliye's Nisvan-ı İslam

with how women can strike the proper balance: how can they be authentic and worldly? How can they be modern and locate themselves articulately within the tenets of their religion? These are questions both local and universal. What level of autonomy vis-à-vis men can a woman anywhere aspire to? To what extent can she control her wealth? Dissolve an unhappy marriage? Find marriage or live unmarried? Control her body whether with regard to sexual access or sartorial choices?

The structure of the original reveals this entwined dual mission and carries it forward in a way that builds from one dialogue to the next. The introduction reveals the new global mobility, and rampant misunderstandings that attend it. The first dialogue focuses on two prominent Western concerns vis-à-vis the Ottoman 'East': harem slavery and Islam in relation to Christianity. This dialogue appears almost exclusively concerned with correcting (Western) foreigners' views. It provides an apologia for the institution of the *cariye* and a comparative approach to Islamic and Christian scriptures, highlighting their similarities and the respect shown to both Jesus and the Christian scriptures in Islam. The guests, Madame F and the nun, are pleasant and respectable but neither especially cultured nor especially *sympathique*. The second dialogue also addresses issues commonly discussed in the West as negative features of Muslim society and religion, especially polygyny and the veiling/segregation of women. But these are handled so as to constitute more than a mere apologia for Muslim practice or a simple corrective to European imaginings. Madame R is presented as the perfect modern woman, the European alter-ego of Fatma Aliye as narrator. She is married and highly educated, with an intellect that has remained lively and outward-looking long beyond her 'schoolgirl' years. She arrives with an open mind and having already made efforts to learn some Ottoman. The dialogue proceeds as an occasion for exchange of knowledge and ideas among true equals. Various rationalist arguments for polygyny are advanced, and a long discussion of scriptural versus customary strictures around veiling and segregation ensues, incorporating the difficult issue of arranged marriages.

While correcting misinformation, *Nisvan-ı İslam* is proposing a modernist approach to religion, making a call *to Ottoman women* to reject certain customs as not religiously mandated. All present – Ottoman and European – agree that all things being equal, monogamy is desirable, but they also recognise that all things are not always equal. The Ottoman ladies, asked how they would react if their husbands took a second wife, give a variety of answers related to their different life situations. There is a comparative discussion about the relative strengths and weaknesses of the Christian and Muslim marital systems, with the problems of dowry, mistresses and bastardy in Europe laid out side-by-side with the question of polygyny. Madame R's reflection on her own moral and intellectual approach to European high society (she values diamonds for their refraction of light, not because they are precious; she wears heavy silks for their beautiful rustling, not to impress; she goes to the gaming rooms and dance floors to observe human nature, not to envy or triumph over others' successes and failures) offers not only a pattern of right-minded behaviour for enlightened upper-class women, but also a thinly veiled critique of the free ways of European society. The dialogue ends with an exchange of astronomical information and mutual, and affectively full, assurances as to the value of the day's exchange.

Finally, the third dialogue offers a purely 'Ottoman women among Ottoman women' reflection on education, relations between the sexes, women's personal freedom and its limits, self-presentation, authenticity balanced between the 'traditional' and the 'modern', and the very nature of 'traditional' and 'authentic'. The arrival of a new group of European women allows the text to revisit and explode European tropes about the subordination and seclusion of Muslim women as well as about the 'authentic harem costume' through which they are represented and reduced. Readers are implicitly invited to compare the Ottoman ladies' discussion of the trials of their friend F. Hanım, caught in an unhappy marriage, with the sad story of the visiting European aunt, denied marriage because she lacked a dowry and could not be allowed to disgrace the family by marrying a man who, though true-hearted and successful, was born out of wedlock. Finally, all the women present arrive, through the medium of humour, at the recognition of their shared lack of perfect autonomy as women. And, as we have noted, this final dialogue's discussion of music is an extended metaphor on the universality of civilisation in its multifarious local incarnations. The project of *Nisvan-ı İslam* in its Middle Eastern incarnations is, then, as much about the becoming of women – Muslim women but also European women – in conditions of modernity as it is about disabusing foreigners of their mistaken notions.

While these themes inhabit the French translations, their pitch to new audiences necessarily dilutes the intra-Ottoman focus. Even more does the later history of this text in Arabic reveal that focus, ironically through its radical reorientation of the original, which we have not been able to discuss in great detail. This reorientation is signalled and reinforced in its framing of the text through preface and footnotes, use of subtitles and bold font, and most of all in its dismissive exclusion of the third dialogue.[152] Its Islamist interpreters, children of a different era, are interested only in aspects that emphasise Muslim identity: that is, sections that engage in

Fatma Aliye's Nisvan-ı İslam

discussion of Qur'an and hadith, explicate and defend Muslim practice, and disclose the comparative weaknesses and failings of European and Christian customs. (This interest is evident in the edition's subtitle: 'dialogue between a Muslim Turkish writer, a French nun, and an English philosophe on principles of humanity and the Islamic creed'.) The final dialogue, by contrast, is viewed as frivolous and as detachable from the rest precisely because it engages most forthrightly with the questions of creating a new tradition, of locating commonalities in feminine experience and grounds for solidarities, and of the self-modelling of new women at home and abroad. For the later publishers, these questions fall outside what they take to be the work's scope and purpose. Indeed, for them, these questions are superfluous, excessive, exhibiting a kind of feminine weakness and frivolity erupting at the end of the text, embarrassingly, in an otherwise remarkably 'serious' – and masculinised – work. Thankfully, we can return to the original, and to its translator-interlocutors in that era.

Notes

1. The biography appeared in book form as Ahmet Midhat, *Fatma Aliye Hanım yahut bir Muharrire-i Osmaniyenin Neşeti* (Istanbul: Kırk Anbar Matbaası, 1893). On Ahmet Midhat's fiction, see A. Holly Shissler, 'The Harem as the Seat of Middle-class Industry and Morality: The Fiction of Ahmet Midhat Efendi', in Marilyn Booth (ed.), *Harem Histories: Envisioning Places and Living Spaces* (Durham, NC: Duke University Press, 2010), 319–41; A. Holly Shissler, 'Haunting Ottoman Middle-class Sensibility: Ahmet Midhat's Gothic', in Marilyn Booth (ed.), *Migrating Texts: Circulating Translations around the Ottoman Mediterranean* (Edinburgh: Edinburgh University Press, 2019), 193–209; on his role in translation, see Marilyn Booth, 'Introduction: Translation as Lateral Cosmopolitanism in the Ottoman Universe', in Marilyn Booth (ed.), *Migrating Texts: Circulating Translations around the Ottoman Mediterranean* (Edinburgh: Edinburgh University Press, 2019), 1–54; 26–8, 33–4. All translations in this chapter, from Ottoman, Arabic and French are our own unless otherwise noted. If we mention only an Ottoman transliterated term in a quotation (in brackets), we do not give the language; if both Ottoman and Arabic, we do.
2. We wish to acknowledge the ground-breaking work of Mübeccel Kızıltan on Fatma Aliye. Her careful transliteration of *Nisvan-ı İslam* into modern Turkish script, with its accompanying introductory discussion of Fatma Aliye's life and works, analysis of *Nisvan-ı İslam*, and bibliography of Fatma Aliye's works, are foundational. Her catalogue of documents relating to Fatma Aliye held at the Atatürk Kitaplığı is an essential research tool for anyone interested in Fatma Aliye. See Fatma Aliye, *Fatma Aliye Hanım: Yaşamı, sanatı yapıtları ve Nisvanı İslam*, edited by Mübeccel Kızıltan

(Istanbul: Mutlu yayıncılık, 1993); Mübeccel Kızıltan and Tülay Gençtük (eds), *Atatürk Kitaplığı Fatma Aliye Hanım evrakı kataloğu* (Istanbul: İstanbul Büyük Şehir Belediyesi Kültür İşleri, Daire Başkanlığı Kütüphane ve Müzeler Müdürlüğü, 1993).

3. The book was published in Istanbul, giving a publication date of 1309. It is not specified whether this is 1309 Hijri or 1309 Rumi. If Hijri, that would be 1891/2 – this seems the most likely; if Rumi, 1893/4. The secondary literature we have seen is not clear on this, though the Hijri date seems to be generally favoured. Both dating systems were commonly used in late Ottoman times.

4. On *Thamarat al-funun*, see below. The Arabic book is referenced in the preface to the 1993 transliterated edition of Kızıltan (p. 60) as *Ta'rib-i* [sic] *Nisa' al-muslimin* (Beirut: Matba'at Jam'iyyat al-funun, 1309 [1891/2]). We have not seen this. The c. 1989 Arabic 'edition' reproduces four pages in facsimile, calling this 'the book'; this follows the Beirut orthography, and reproduces *Thamarat al-funun*'s preface. (See note 14 below.)

5. In an undated draft letter – probably c. 1895/6 because it mentions her grief at her father's death – Fatma Aliye writes to an unnamed person who is almost surely Ol'ga Lebedeva. In it, she mentions that she has received partial proofs of the book version of the French translation of *Nisvan-ı İslam* that the *Orient Gazette* was publishing, and she has seen her addressee's name on it, that is, Ol'ga Lebedeva. She goes on to say that she has also seen another French translation, about which she had no previous knowledge, which is being published as a book in Paris. She relates that the translators are two Ottoman Orthodox Christian (*Rum*) mademoiselles who are members of the Christoforides family (*Chrisroforideszadeleri olup*). She gives no additional specific information about who they are, but adds that they have used a Muslim name as a pseudonym. She goes on to say the the translation is not bad (*fena değil*) and that they have not distorted the work. Kızıltan and Gençtük, *Atatürk Kitaplığı Fatma Aliye Hanım evrakı kataloğu*, 29. Fatih Altuğ, who has studied Fatma Aliye, believes the Greek women were sisters, daughters of Christoforides, a senior jurist and associate of Ahmet Midhat and Ahmet Cevdet Paşa (email from Fatih Altuğ to M. Booth, 29 August 2020). He may well be the same Christoforides who presided over the trial of Ahmet Midhat Paşa. We thank Fatih Altuğ for sharing his information and Johann Strauss for putting us in contact.

6. She often signed as de Lébédeff. The possible death date is thanks to Carina Hamilton and colleagues of hers working in Russian archives.

7. Fatma Aliye mentions in a personal letter (1913) that there exists an English translation, but she has never seen it. Kızıltan and Gençtük, *Atatürk Kitaplığı Fatma Aliye Hanım evrakı kataloğu*, 27. The existence of an English translation was mentioned, along with the Arabic and French translations, by Mahmud Zeki in a piece published in *Hanımlara Mahsus Gazete* about Fatma Aliye Hanım (1900). After appearing in *Tercüman-ı Hakikat*,

Fatma Aliye's Nisvan-ı İslam

he says, the work was translated and published in Arabic by Beirut journal *Thamarat al-Funun* and subsequently translated into French and English, garnering the author even greater fame. Mahmud Zeki, 'Meşahir-i Nisvan-ı Osmaniye hakkında Yazılan Arabi al-İbare Makalatın Birincisi: İsmetlu Fatma Aliye Hanım Efendi Hazretleri', *Hanımlara Mahsus Gazete*, no. 256–54 (5 Zilhicce 1317/23 Mart 1316), 3. The title implies this piece was one in a series of entries originally in Arabic, on famous Ottoman women. It turns out to be based on the entry in Zaynab Fawwaz's biographical dictionary (see note 8), which mentions the English translation (370).

8. Zaynab bt. 'Ali b. Husayn b. 'Ubaydallah b. Hasan b. Ibrahim b. Muhammad b. Yusuf Fawwaz al-'Amili, *Kitab al-Durr al-manthur fi tabaqat rabbat al-khudur* (Bulaq/Misr: al-Matba'a al-kubra al-amiriyya, 1312), 368–426; text, 370–426. Hereafter, DM.

9. 'Nisa' al-muslimin', *al-Manar* 4: 19 (12 December 1901): 752–6; 4: 21 (26 January 1902): 832–6; 4: 23 (24 February 1902): 913–15. These are drawn from the first dialogue. No further excerpts appeared in vols 4–5.

10. The biography: 'Shahirat al-nisa': Fatima 'Aliya', *Fatat al-sharq* 1: 5 (15 February 1907): 129–31. The introduction: 'Shahirat al-nisa': Fatima 'Aliya', *Fatat al-sharq* 1: 6 (15 March 1907): 161–3. 'Shahirat al-nisa': Jullanar [Gulnar] Hanım', *Fatat al-sharq* 1: 7 (15 April 1907): 193–201. The biography follows Fawwaz's text closely, though it 'updates' the language somewhat, and expands on the exemplarity motif that ends it. Marilyn Booth, *May Her Likes Be Multiplied: Biography and Gender Politics in Egypt* (Berkeley: University of California Press, 2001), 28, 94.

11. See note 7.

12. He was proprietor of al-Maktaba al-sharqiyya; but printing information is: (Cairo: Matba'at 'Ayn Shams (n.d.)).

13. *Kitab nisa' al-islam, bi-qalam al-katiba al-dha'i'at al-sit Fatima 'Aliya Hanim, karimat al-'allama al-shahir Jawdat Pasha* (n.p.: Matba'at 'Ayn shams, n.d.). In his preface, Faris announces this as second in a series of republished 'valuable, beneficial Arabic-language books for the two sexes'; first was 'the late Qasim Amin's book [*Tahrir al-mar'a*, 1899], which Faris lauds as causing an 'intellectual revolution'. It is interesting that Fatma Aliye's work appears in the same series. This means Amin's book must have appeared after 23 April 1908, Amin's death date, and Fatma Aliye's after that. Ibrahim Faris, 'Bismillahi, khayr al-asma'', *Kitab nisa' al-islam, bi-qalam al-katiba al-dha'i'at al-sit Fatima 'Aliya Hanim, karimat al-'allama al-shahir Jawdat Pasha* (n.p.: Matba'at 'Ayn shams, n.d.), unpaginated. 'Ayda Nusayr's bibliography of books published in Egypt 1900–25 lists the 'third printing' of Amin's book as by al-Maktaba al-sharqiyya, 1908 but lists nothing by Fatma Aliye. 'Ayda Ibrahim Nusayr, *al-Kutub al-'arabiyya alati nushirat fi Misr 1900–1925* (Cairo: American University in Cairo Press, 1980), 179.

14. Fatima 'Aliya Hanim, *Nisa' al-muslimin: Hiwar bayan katiba turkiyya*

muslima wa-rahiba faransiyya wa-faylusufa ingiliziyya hawla al-mabadi' al-insaniyya wa-al-'aqida al-islamiyya, edited and with commentary by Muhammad Ibrahim Salim (Cairo: Maktabat al-Qur'an, n.d. [c. 1989–90]).

15. Fatma Aliye, *Fatma Aliye Hanım: Yaşamı, sanatı, yapıtları ve Nisvanı İslam*; Fatma Aliye, *İslam kadınları*, edited by Ayhan Pekin and Amine Pekin (Istanbul: İnkılab, 2009) – hereafter PP; Fatma Aliye, *Osmanlı'da kadın: Cariyelik, çokeşlilik, ve moda*, edited by Orhan Sakın (Istanbul: Ekim, 2012). Pekin and Pekin render the text in modern Turkish, but attempt to remain close to the original. The sentence structures remain longer and more complex; only words not commonly used today are translated. They provide subtitles for the dialogues, such as 'cariyelik üzerine' (on female slavery (cariyedom)). Sakın's modernisation is more radical. The text is rendered in very simplified modern Turkish with the long periods broken up into short sentences. He divides the three dialogues into subsections with headings like *'Harem hayati ve cariyeler'* (Harem life and cariyes) or *'Ramazan ve oruç'* (Ramadan and fasting).

16. On the Exposition as a focus of Arabic discourse on gender and imperialism, see Marilyn Booth, *Classes of Ladies of Cloistered Spaces: Writing Feminist History through Biography in Fin-de-siècle Egypt* (Edinburgh: Edinburgh University Press, 2015), chap. 7; as a location for Ottoman self-presentation and discourse on gender, and the role of Fatma Aliye's work, see Öyku Potuoğlu-Cook, 'Night Shifts: Moral, Economic, and Cultural Politics of Turkish Belly Dance Across the Fin-de-Siècle', PhD dissertation, Northwestern University, 2008), especially chaps 1–2.

17. On the invitation to send her work and confirmation of its receipt, Mücebbel Kızıltan, 'Öncü bir kadın yazar: Fatma Aliye Hanım', *Journal of Turkish Studies* 14 (1990): 283–322; 293–94. For the list of works received by the Women's Library, see Booth, *Classes*, 293. The source is Board of Lady Managers of the World's Columbian Commission created by Act of Congress USA organised 1890, *List of the Books in the Library of the Woman's Building, World's Columbian Exposition, Chicago, 1893*, compiled by Edith Clarke. Available at <http://digital.library.upenn.edu/women/clarke/library/library.html> (last accessed 25 October 2005).

18. At the 1889 Congress of Orientalists in Stockholm, where Ahmet Midhat and Olga Lebedeva met, Ahmet Midhat introduced the book on 'women's rights in Islam' written for the Congress by Egyptian delegate Hamza Fathallah (1849–1918). He gave a short speech challenging prevailing European views on 'Muslim women' in French to those listening in Stockholm, reproduced in Fathallah's book, and mentioned in the travel narrative by the son of another Egyptian delegate, accompanying his father, and by Ahmet Midhat. On the Arabic work and speech, see Marilyn Booth, 'Before Qasim Amin: Writing Women's History in 1890s Egypt', in Marilyn Booth and Anthony Gorman (eds), *The Long 1890s in Egypt: Colonial Quiescence, Subterranean Resistance* (Edinburgh: Edinburgh

University Press, 2014), 365–98; 387–91. Also Carter Vaughn Findley, 'An Ottoman Occidentalist in Europe: Ahmed Midhat Meets Madame Gülnar, 1889', *American Historical Review* 103: 1 (February 1998): 15–49. The travelogue: Muhammad Amin Fikri Bek, *Irshad al-alibba' ila mahasin Urubba* (Cairo: Matba'at al-Muqtataf, 1892), 658–62, on Fathallah's speech and a poem, but not mentioning Ahmet Midhat's speech.
19. In the Nazime-Roukié translation, the Ottoman ladies of the third conversation are named, unlike in the original and Lebedeva translation.
20. The work is described as a response to 'Western misapprehensions' or stereotypes (though the audience is not defined) by Cimen Günay-Erkol and Senem Timuroğlu Bozkurt, 'Dreams beyond Control: Women and Writing in the Ottoman Empire since Asiye Hatun's Diary', *Journal of Research in Gender Studies* 4: 1 (2014): 364–75; 371–2; Elif Ekin Akşit, 'Harem Education and Heterotopic Imagination', *Gender and Education* 23: 3 (May 2011): 299–311; 306.
21. Cevdet Paşazade Fatma Aliye, *Nisvan-ı İslam: Bazı adat-ı İslamiye hakkında üç mühavereyi havidir* (Istanbul: Maarif Nezaret-i Celilesinin rahsatile *Tercüman-ı Hakikat Gazetesine* derc edildikten sonra ilk defa olarak ayrıca risale şeklinde dahi tab olunmuştur, 1309 (1891/2 if AH or 1893/4 if Rumi), 6; hereafter, Nİ. Readers are informed: 'Having been included in *Tercüman-ı Hakikat Gazetesi*, with permission of the illustrious Ministry of Education, it is also [now] published separately in treatise (*risale*) form for the first time.' The implication is that Tercüman-ı Hakikat Press issued it, but nowhere is this said explicitly.
22. Nİ, 11; DM, 372. For the Arabic, we rely on DM; on divergences between it and *Thamarat al-funun*'s text, see below.
23. Nİ, 4–5; DM, 370.
24. Nİ, 5; DM, 371. Arabic: 'in the form[s] of stories, that is, the novel (*'ala tarz/turuz al-qisas (al-ruman)*).
25. Nİ, 6; DM, 371.
26. Nİ, 7; DM, 371.
27. On early discourses on female education in Arabic (mostly in Egypt), Beth Baron, *The Women's Awakening in Egypt: Culture, Society, and the Press* (New Haven, CT: Yale University Press, 1994); Margot Badran, *Feminists, Islam and Nation: Gender and the Making of Modern Egypt* (Princeton: Princeton University Press, 1995); Booth, *May*; Booth, *Classes*, 58, 70–80, 225–8; Mona L. Russell, *Creating the New Egyptian Woman: Consumerism, Education, and National Identity, 1863–1922* (New York: Palgrave Macmillan, 2004); Hoda A. Yousef, *Composing Egypt: Reading, Writing, and the Emergence of a Modern Nation, 1870–1930* (Stanford: Stanford University Press, 2016), chap. 2. On women's education, and the interrelated topics of the women's movement and women's publications in late Ottoman society: Serpil Çakır, *Osmanlı Kadın Hareketi* (IIstanbul: Metis Yayınları, 1993); Serpil Çakır, 'Feminism and Feminist

History-writing in Turkey: The Discovery of Ottoman Feminism', *Aspasia: International Yearbook of Central, Eastern, and Southeastern European Women's and Gender History* (2007): 61–83; Fanny Davis, *The Ottoman Lady: A Social History from 1718 to 1918* (New York: Greenwood Press, 1986); Aynur Demirdirek, *Osmanlı Kadınlarının Hayat Hakkı Arayışının Bir Hikayesi* (Ankara: İmge Kitabevi, 1993); Elizabeth Frierson, 'Unimagined Communities: State, Press, and Gender in the Hamidian Era', PhD dissertation, Princeton University, 1996; Şefika Kurnaz, *İkinci Meşrutiyet Döneminde Türk Kadını* (IIstanbul: Milli Eğitim Bakanlığı, 1996); Çiğdem Oğuz, '"The Homeland Will Not be Saved Merely by Chastity": Women's Agency, Nationalism, and Morality in the Late Ottoman Empire', *Journal of the Ottoman and Turkish Studies Association* 6: 2 (Fall 2019): 91–111; Barbara Reeves-Ellington, 'Embracing Domesticity: Women, Mission, and Nation Building in Ottoman Europe, 1832–1872', in Barbara Reeves-Ellington, Kathryn Kish Sklar and Connie A. Shemo (eds), *Competing Kingdoms: Women, Mission, Nation, and the American Protestant Empire, 1812–1960* (Durham, NC: Duke University Press, 2010); S. A. Somel, 'Osmanlı modernleşme döneminde kız eğitimi', *Kebikeç* 10 (2000), 223–38; Hülya Yıldız, 'Rethinking the Political: Ottoman Women as Feminist Subjects', *Journal of Gender Studies* (2016): 1–15; Ayşe Zeren-Enis, *Everyday Lives of Ottoman Muslim Women: Hanımlara Mahsûs Gazete (1895–1908)* (Istanbul: Libra Kitapçılık ve Yayıncılık, 2013).
28. Nİ, 7; DM, 371. The phrase *taassuplarına sığdıramıyorlar* is rather strong: more or less, 'get it into their [tiny,] bigoted/zealotic minds'. The Arabic uses the verb that yields this Turkish verbal noun: *ta'assaba*, 'to be extreme about'. The Arabic phrasing differs slightly: 'There exists a set of Islamic families whose members reckon that teaching women knowledge is a sin, to the extent that they not only have extreme views about teaching them the French language but are also extreme about teaching them any more of the Turkish language than is minimally necessary.'
29. Nİ, 9–10; DM, 371–2.
30. This could also mean 'surprised' or that one has lost one's way.
31. Nİ, 10; DM, 372.
32. Nİ, 11. The Arabic follows closely, although: 'They imagine that the women of the Muslims are oppressed and wronged, and so they let loose their tongues in censure, expressing themselves violently [or intensely] in this regard' (DM, 372).
33. The second dialogue's exchange on polygyny enacts this situation; see below.
34. Booth, *Classes*, 3–5, and chaps 5–6; Marilyn Booth, 'Peripheral Visions: Translational Polemics and Feminist Arguments in Colonial Egypt', in Anna Ball and Karim Mattar (eds), *Edinburgh Companion to the Postcolonial Middle East* (Edinburgh: Edinburgh University Press, 2018), 183–212; Margrit Pernau, Helge Jordheim et al. (eds), *Civilizing Emotions: Concepts*

in Nineteenth-century Asia and Europe (Oxford: Oxford University Press, 2015).
35. Arabic: 'I will not hide from you that the clarifications I've heard from you, in comparison to what I had heard and was aware of previously, have caused me to fancy that I have not come to Turkey but rather have arrived by mistake in another country' (DM, 379).
36. In Arabic, this is made explicit: 'I said'.
37. Arabic: 'I will not hide from you that the scenes of life over there, the principles by which people live and their customs, have no similarity to those in Beyoğlu, indeed there is no analogy whatsoever.'
38. Nİ, 42–3; DM, 379; Fatima 'Aliya, 'Nisa' al-muslimin', *Thamarat al-funun* 18: 869 (25 Jumada II 1309/25 January 1892): 3 [instalment #7].
39. Nİ, 11–12; DM, 372. The Ottoman book oddly says 'conceal it *from* my heart'. The rendition to modern Turkish script and to modern Turkish language says 'in', suggesting the editors thought it an error in the original text. We wonder; but it does not substantively change the meaning, as far as we can tell.
40. Nİ, 168–9; DM, 404–5.
41. Akşit argues that Fatma Aliye's fictional writings highlight 'interlinks between the public and private spheres and challenge the association of the family with the private sphere and religion with the public sphere'. Elif Ekin Akşit, 'Fatma Aliye's Stories: Ottoman Marriages beyond the Harem', *Journal of Family History* 35: 3 (2010): 207–18; 208. One could think of this as questioning the 'public/private' dichotomy altogether, at least in the context of elite Ottoman households – but was that division even meaningful to Ottoman subjects? *Nisvan-ı İslam* suggests intellectual mobility on the part of educated elite women. Inviting European interlocutors into the home, they are ready to range knowledgeably across institutions and topics associated stereotypically with 'the public sphere', and 'women contribute actively to a moral philosophy that derives from Islam' (Akşit, 'Fatma Aliye's Stories', 210). Zaynab Fawwaz's fiction suggested that public–political success (that is, integrity) was inseparable from transparent and egalitarian behaviour in the 'private' sphere. Marilyn Booth, *The Career and Communities of Zaynab Fawwaz: Feminist Thinking in Fin-de-siècle Egypt* (Oxford: Oxford University Press, 2021), chap. 9.
42. Nİ, 12; DM, 372. Fatima 'Aliya, 'Nisa' al-muslimin', 18: 864 (20 Jumada I 1309/21 December 1891): 3–4; 3 [#2].
43. Nİ, 12–13; DM, 372.
44. Nİ, 44–46; DM, 379; Fatima 'Aliya, 'Nisa' al-muslimin', 18: 869 (25 Jumada II 1309/25 January 1892): 3 [#7].
45. Nİ, 46. Arabic: 'We too have the habit of putting on the table a variety of foods, customarily called preliminary food, or that taken with drinks (hors d'oeuvres) (*muqaddamat al-ta'am aw al-naqul (hurdur)*)' (DM, 379). *Naqul* may be a version of what Kazimirski mentions under *tanaqqala* as

being served food eaten 'alternately' with drinks, usually wine; he gives this as 'dessert' but presumably it could refer to appetisers. A. de Biberstein Kazimirski, *Dictionnaire arabe-français*, edited by Ibed Gallab, 4 vols (Cairo/Bulaq: Imprimerie V. R. égyptienne, 1875), 4: 613.

46. Nİ, 46; DM, 379.
47. Nİ, 46–7; DM, 380.
48. The Arabic differs slightly: instead of oil, *samn* (clarified butter); and then 'honey, cheese and strips of dried meat' (*muqaddadat*, equivalent to *pastirma*). (DM, 380).
49. Nİ, 51 and a translation of Qur'an 5:82.
50. Nİ, 51; DM, 381.
51. But *tafsir* could also describe a translation of the Qur'an, since God's Word cannot really be translated, only interpreted or approximated.
52. Nİ, 50–1; DM, 381.
53. M. Kasimirski [Albin de Biberstein Kazimirski], *Le Koran, traduction nouvelle faite sur le texte arabe* (Paris: Charpentier, 1840, 1841, 1844).
54. DM, 372.
55. Nİ, 138–9; DM, 398. Differences between the Ottoman and the Arabic are noted here, for illustration. In most cases we only highlight differences we find highly significant. In Ottoman, *balo, soiree* (in Ottoman script); the Arabic does not use European terms but rather: 'al-maraqis wa-layali al-farah wa-al-musammarat'. Ottoman: making myself attractive; Arabic: exposing myself to people's gaze. Ottoman: heaviest silks; Arabic: expensive silk garments. To give myself airs: Ottoman, lit., to sell my greatness; Arabic: to signal greatness and self-pride.
56. *köşk*, a structure that can be either a mansion or a garden pavilion. The latter are generally the size of a salon and normally glassed in, but when the glass is removed (as it was that evening seemingly) it is like a summer house. An Ottoman köşk can be a very substantial and elaborate structure.
57. The Arabic adds: 'as if she was communing with the spirits'.
58. Nİ, 143; DM, 399.
59. Nİ, 192 (emphases ours).
60. For example, Zaynab Fawwaz. Booth, *Career*, chap. 5.
61. *Min rabbat al-khidr*, 'women of the private chamber', signifying a 'respectably' secluded woman; this signifies a certain class belonging.
62. 'Nisa' al-muslimin, bi-qalam al-fadila Fatima 'Aliya', *Thamarat al-funun* 18: 863 (13 Jumada I 1309/14 December 1891): 3. The final instalment appears in 19: 902 (10 Rabi' II 1310/1 November 1892).
63. Filib di Tarrazi, *Tarikh al-sihafa al-'arabiyya*, Pts 1–3 (Beirut: al-Matba'a al-adabiyya, 1913–14), Pt 4 (Beirut: al-Matba'a al-amrikaniyya, 1933), 2: 100.
64. On the newspaper, see Tarrazi, *Tarikh*, 2: 25–7; on its editor, 2: 99–101. Ottoman Arabophone Muslims, this source observes, had great confidence in this newspaper as representing their interests (25–6). Fruma Zachs and

Fatma Aliye's Nisvan-ı İslam

Sharon Halevi, *Gendering Culture in Greater Syria: Intellectuals and Ideology in the Late Ottoman Period* (London: I. B. Taurus, 2015), 36.
65. Fatima 'Aliya, 'Nisa' al-muslimin', *Thamarat al-funun* 18: 863, 3 [#1]; DM, 370.
66. This is implied in the bio-bibliographic introduction to the early twentieth-century Arabic printing effected by Ibrahim Faris, though it could mean that al-Qabbani had it translated. Faris' foreword largely echoes Fawwaz's, though he does not acknowledge it as a source or mention her publication of the work; and he claims that after al-Qabbani's publication, the text 'languished'. He does not mention an earlier book version. The biography may have appeared elsewhere, and he may not have sourced it from Fawwaz. [Ibrahim Faris], 'Man hiya al-mu'allifa', *Kitab nisa' al-islam, bi-qalam al-katiba al-dha'i'at al-sit Fatima 'Aliya Hanim, karimat al-'allama al-shahir Jawdat Pasha* (n.p.: Matba'at 'Ayn shams, n.d.), 1–4; 4.
67. *Thamarat al-funun* 18: 916 (19 Rajab 1310/6 February 1893): 1. Here it is referred to as a *riwaya*.
68. Recall that it appeared in Ottoman from 6 October 1891 to 17 November 1891.
69. Zachs and Halevi, *Gendering*, 37.
70. Zachs and Halevi, *Gendering*, 37.
71. It is very interesting that this appeared at a time when the Ottoman censor in Beirut was discouraging publication of female authors by other newspapers there; Booth, *Career*, chap. 5. Surely this had to do with its 'Islamic' focus and the status and ethno-linguistic identity of the author's family.
72. 'Sa'adat al-'a'ila', *Thamarat al-funun* 18: 904 (24 Rabi' II 1310/14 November 1891), continuing in subsequent issues, skipping some.
73. On Fawwaz's writings and outlook, Booth, *Career*. On this biography of Joséphine de Beauharnais, see the Introduction to Pt 3. On her biographical dictionary, Booth, *Classes*; on Fatma Aliye's biography in greater detail, 114–20.
74. DM, 368.
75. Both citations, Ahmet Midhat, *Fatma Aliye*, 33.
76. DM, 369.
77. DM, 370.
78. Booth, *Career*, chap. 2.
79. Conjunctions: for instance, DM drops a *lakin* appearing in *Thamarat al-funun* (DM, 370; 'Aliya, 'Nisa' al-muslimin, *Thamarat al-funun* 18: 863, 3 [#1]). A few examples of variant spellings are: *al-faransawiyya* in *Thamarat al-funun* and *al-faransāwiyya* in DM; *haqayiq* in *Thamarat al-funun* (18: 864, 3 [#2] versus *haqa'iq* (DM, 372); *al-sharakisa* in *Thamarat al-funun* 18: 869, 3 [#7] versus *al-jarakisa*, DM, 379.
80. Fatima 'Aliya, 'Nisa' al-muslimin', *Thamarat al-funun* (18: 864, 3 [#2]; DM, 371).
81. DM, 382; Fatima 'Aliya, 'Nisa' al-muslimin', *Thamarat al-funun* 18: 872

(17 Rajab 1309/15 February 1892): 4 [#10]. Similar inaccuracies are found in transliterations of non-Arabic/Ottoman lexica in Fawwaz's biography of Fatma Aliye: the title of the novel she translated, *Volonté*, is transliterated as *dūlāntah*, it's author's name (Ohnet) as Adnāh (DM, 369).

82. DM, 381; Fatima 'Aliya, 'Nisa' al-muslimin', *Thamarat al-funun* 18: 871 (10 Rajab 1309/8 February 1892): 4 [#9].
83. DM, 382; Fatima 'Aliya, 'Nisa' al-muslimin', *Thamarat al-funun* 18: 872, 4 [#10].
84. DM, 372; Fatima 'Aliya, 'Nisa' al-muslimin', *Thamarat al-funun* 18: 864, 3 [#2].
85. DM, 375; Fatima 'Aliya, 'Nisa' al-muslimin', *Thamarat al-funun* 18: 866 (4 Jumada II 1309/4 January 1892): 2–3; 3 [#4].
86. DM, 370.
87. DM, 372. The Ottoman book version says: 'One day last year in the noble month of Ramazan'. The AH dates for publication in *Tercüman-ı Hakikat* are 2 Rebiü'l-Evvel 1309 to 15 Rebiü'l Ahır 1309, so Ramazan 1308 would make sense.
88. DM, 377; Fatima 'Aliya, 'Nisa' al-muslimin', *Thamarat al-funun* 18: 867 (11 Jumada II 1309/11 January 1892): 3 [#5].
89. Later versions do make changes. Ibrahim Faris's early twentieth-century volume adds subtitles, such as 'Between me and two French ladies' (*bayni wa bayna sayyidatayn faransawiyyatayn*, 12); 'The virtues of fasting' (*fada'il al-sawm*, 36); 'a religious discussion' (*bahth dini*, 39), and so forth. It inserts full names where the earlier translations – like the Turkish – had only first initials (NR uses names in the third dialogue). It replaces French *madame* with an Arabic usage that had come into vogue and is sometimes used in the earlier Arabic versions. Madame F becomes *al-'aqila Firdiynand* (Mme Ferdinand) (DM, 372; Faris, 12). The Ottoman women in the third dialogue are referred to in Faris as Safiya Hanım, Najiya Hanım and al-Sayyida Qadin Hanım, with no indication of the source for these (Faris, 119, 120, 143). This is particularly odd in that Faris includes the exchange between the narrator and 'Safiya Hanım' about permission to reproduce the conversation – and one reason Safiya Hanım gives for happily doing so is that 'you will conceal my name' (Faris, 120); only one time, the name is given as Safiya . . . signifying that her family name is withheld (121).

Occasionally, Faris omits phrases where Fawwaz did not. Thus, in the following translation of the text as it appears in Fawwaz, underlined words are omitted in Faris: 'Most of our group [gathered in the garden] were smoking <u>the cigarettes that are smoked after the *iftar* with especial enjoyment, and the sparks from</u> the cigarettes glowed and flashed through the flowers and trees' (DM, 396; Faris, 89–90).

The 1989 version makes more radical changes (for example, omitting the cigarette-smoking scene altogether, p. 134). It omits the third dialogue altogether: saying that since it discusses how similar Turkish fashion has

Fatma Aliye's Nisvan-ı İslam

become to European fashion, and how skilled Turkish women are at the piano, the editor observes that 'he sees no need to publish it' – missing the point of the dialogue entirely, and perhaps deliberately, as otherwise this version tends to emphasise *differences*. There are changes to vocabulary and word order; the reproduction of four pages of a manuscript in Arabic said to be at the Egyptian National Library (Dar al-kutub) indicates that the changes are (unmarked) editorial decisions since they do not follow that manuscript. A heavy paratextual apparatus includes footnotes (especially on Qur'an, hadith and *fiqh*, often privileging a certain reading of the text over other possible readings), bolded phrases, punctuation (especially exclamation points) and headers that do not appear in *Thamarat* or Fawwaz. (The first header is, perhaps coincidentally, also in Faris but others are not.) It is beyond this chapter's temporal scope to go into further detail, but the unmarked differences in a 'republication' in 1989 for a new audience are an element in the 'repackaging' of *al-nahda* at the end of the twentieth century; see our conclusion.

90. DM, 376; Faris edn, 23–4; Fatima 'Aliya, 'Nisa' al-muslimin', *Thamarat al-funun* 18: 866, 3 [#4]; Nİ, 29.
91. Nİ, 60–1. The narrator says: 'I got the French translation of the Exalted Qur'an (Qur'an-i Kerim) from the library and I read [aloud] ayet 6 of Süre-i Saf and I pointed out the explanatory note of the translator, Kazimirski, pertaining to it, which is reproduced exactly below.' This is followed by a longish passage – the relevant note – in the original French in Latin script.
92. DM, 382.
93. Fatima 'Aliya, 'Nisa' al-muslimin', *Thamarat al-funun* 18: 872, 4 [#10].
94. DM, 371. *Thamarat al-funun* does the same but again, with a more correct transliteration: Fatima 'Aliya, 'Nisa' al-muslimin', *Thamarat al-funun* (18: 864), 3 [#2].
95. DM, 371; Fatima 'Aliya, 'Nisa' al-muslimin', *Thamarat al-funun* (18: 864), 3 [#2].
96. Nİ, 155–6; DM, 391; Fatima 'Aliya, 'Nisa' al-muslimin', *Thamarat al-funun* 18: 877 (22 Sha'ban 1309/21 March 1892): 3–4; 4 [#15]. In the Ottoman text, the customary '*aleyhisselam*' or '*Hazret*' is used when Fatma Aliye is speaking of any prophet (such as Noah or Adam). Occasionally she uses them together, but usually it is one or the other: thus, in the same passage at one juncture she refers to '*Nuh aleyhisselam*'; later in the same passage she says '*Hazret-i Nuh*'.

Both Arabic versions generally include believers' respect utterances; *Thamarat al-funun* slightly more so. On DM, 382 (Fatima 'Aliya, 'Nisa' al-muslimin', *Thamarat al-funun* 18: 872, 4 [#10]), only the latter follows the name Muhammad with the phrase; but in the following section, both use it (DM, 383–93; Fatima 'Aliya, 'Nisa' al-muslimin', *Thamarat al-funun* 18: 872, 4 [#10] – Fatima 'Aliya, 'Nisa' al-muslimin', *Thamarat al-funun* 18: 877 (29 Sha'ban 1309/28 March 1892): 3–4; 3, 4 [#16].

97. Fathma-Alié, *Nisvan-i-Islam, 'Les femmes musulmanes'*, trans. Mme Olga de Labedeff [*sic*], connue sous le pseudonyme de Gulnar-Hanoum [*sic*: no umlaut] (Paris: Le Journal 'L'Orient', n.d. [1896]). We think this translation was almost complete by January 1894, however; in a letter to Aliye dated 8 January 1894, Ahmet Midhat complains that Lebedeva has turned it over to a less-than-competent editor. Letter cited in Findley, 'An Ottoman Occidentalist', 33 n. 79. Elsewhere, the translator's name appears in various spellings: Lebedeva, Lebedef, Lebedeff, the latter two sometimes with accents over one or two e's. We have elected to use the Russian spelling, since the spelling on this translation is not among common spellings of the name. On the name 'Madame Gülnar', see Findley, 'An Ottoman Occidentalist', 28, 31 n. 70; Johann Strauss, 'Ol'ga Lebedeva (*Gülnâr Hanım*) and Her Works in Ottoman Turkish', *Arts, Women and Scholars: Studies in Ottoman Society and Culture (Festschrift Hans Georg Majer)*, ed. Sabine Prätor and Christoph K. Neumann (Istanbul: Simurg, 2002), 287–314.
98. Alihe Hanoum, *Les musulmanes contemporaines: trois conférences, traduites de la langue turque par Nazimé-Roukié* (Paris: Alphonse Lemerre, Éditeur, 1894). The Arabic versions carried different titles: *Thamarat al-funun* changed it to *Nisa' al-muslimin*, 'The women of the [male-'inclusive'] Muslims', turning women into a possessed subcategory, while Fawwaz referred to it as 'Nisa' al-Islam' (DM, 370) as did the Faris edition. The 1989 reworking reverted to *Thamarat al-funun*'s title. One can speculate on reasons for these variant choices.
99. 'Avis', in Alihe Hanoum, *Les musulmanes contemporaines*, 10–11. The translated text is paginated in Roman numerals for the preface (v–xii) and then in Arabic numerals. This work is henceforth cited as NR.
100. 'Avant-propos', Fathma-Alié, *Nisvan-i-Islam, 'Les femmes musulmanes'*, trans. Mme Olga de Labedeff, 5–6; 5. This work is henceforth cited as OL. 'Far niente' does appear in capital letters in the original.
101. Strauss, 'Ol'ga Lebedeva', 295.
102. 'Avant-propos', OL, 6.
103. There is much work on paratextual framing in translation, while the *locus classicus* on paratexts in general, relevant to translation, is Gerard Genette, *Paratexts: Thresholds of Interpretation*, trans. Jane E. Lewin (Cambridge: Cambridge University Press, 1997/2001). Mona Baker's work on translation framing as politically resonant is important; for instance, Mona Baker, 'Reframing Conflict in Translation', in Mona Baker (ed.), *Critical Readings in Translation Studies* (Abingdon: Routledge, 2010): 113–29. For an excellent recent example of prefaces' importance, in a highly sensitive translation situation, see Nora S. Eggen, 'On the Periphery: Translations of the Qur'an in Sweden, Denmark and Norway', in Sameh Hanna, Hanem El-Farahaty and Abdel-Wahab Khalifa (eds), *The Routledge Handbook of Arabic Translation* (Abingdon: Routledge, 2020), 65–80. On the 'transla-

Fatma Aliye's Nisvan-ı İslam

     tor's voice' and paratext, see Theo Hermans, 'The Translator's Voice in Translated Narrative', in Mona Baker (ed.), *Critical Readings in Translation Studies* (Abingdon: Routledge, 2010): 193–212 (first published 1996).
104. Strauss, 'Ol'ga Lebedeva'; Findley, 'An Ottoman Occidentalist'. Further research on her is being carried out by Carina Hamilton, whose help we gratefully acknowledge.
105. Whereas in the original Ottoman text and the Lebedeva translation the English visitor in the second dialogue is Madame R, in the Nazimé-Roukié translation she is Madame P. In the third dialogue, Fatma Aliye's close Turkish friends are given in the original as S. Hanım and N. Hanım; their absent friend who is suffering at the hands of a tyrannical husband is F. Hanım, and this is also true of the Lebedeva translation. Nazimé-Roukié, however, gives full names for these personages: Sabire Hanım, Melek Hanım, Fatma Hanım. When one considers that the appearance of the name of a respectable woman in print was the subject of some dispute in polite Ottoman society of the day (Fatma Aliye herself first published as 'A Lady/bir Hanım' for this reason) and that the opening of the third dialogue contains an interchange between Fatma Aliye and S. Hanım in which Fatma Aliye asks for permission, with some reticence, to reproduce their conversation, this choice on the part of Nazimé-Roukié seems remarkable. It may reflect familiarity with Fatma Aliye herself and, perhaps, the other subjects of the text. Of course, these may be fictional names, but still, it is a bold gesture.
106. Ottoman: *mestur*, veiled/hidden; Arabic: *mutahajjabat*, 'hijabed', with a similar connected dual meaning 'veiled' and 'behind a separation barrier'.
107. Nİ, 6–7; DM, 371; NR, viii; OL, 9.
108. Though we think it likely that this was a collaborative translation by two individuals, we treat the translator here as a single entity.
109. NR, ix; OL, 9 and later. Lebedeva does use '*hanoum*' occasionally, especially in the third dialogue where two close friends of Fatma Aliye are present, and where the first half of the dialogue takes place entirely among the three Ottoman ladies. But this is exceptional and sporadic in her text.
110. Nİ, 175; DM, 405; OL, 91; NR, 123. At a later point, Lebedeva uses *institutrice*, as does Nazimé-Roukié, to refer to the English governess of an Ottoman Turkish woman. They use this French word where the Ottoman original uses *mürebbiye* and the Arabic, *murabbiyya*, 'female child-minder' or 'teacher/governess'.
111. NR, 123.
112. Nİ, 8 'Ahkâm-i şeriye'; NR, ix (and see below); OL, 9; 'Le Cher'y', OL, 10. Both are nominalising the Ottoman adjective, Şeri; the noun form would be Şeriat.
113. NR, ix; OL, 9. The Arabic uses and glosses Beyoğlu, as noted earlier (DM, 371).
114. NR, xi.

115. OL, 11.
116. NR, xi; OL, 11; DM, 372; Nİ, 10. The Arabic for this passage is slightly more metaphorically phrased: 'As a result, we've lost the middle way; waves of confusion pitch us this way and that in billows, the way lost.' It follows with the proverb, unmarked as such: 'Excess and falling short in everything are harmful and blameworthy, and moderation (*al-i'tidal*) is praiseworthy in all cases, for *khayr al-umur awsatuha*.'
117. OL, 10; NR, x. Ottoman: 'Bunlar da ezvac-ı mutaharrat ve benat-i zakiyatın ve sadr-ı evvelde gelen nice alimat ve edebiyatın ilm ve fazılda ne âli derecelere varmış olduklarını yine bilmeyenlerdir' (Nİ, 9–10). Arabic: 'al-azwaj al-mutahhirat wa-al-banat al-zakiyyat wa-kathir min al-'alimat al-adibat alati kunna fi sadr al-Islam min rafi' al-darajat fi al-'ilm wa-al-fadl' (DM, 371–2).
118. NR, x; OL, 10–11.
119. NR, 4; OL, 13.
120. OL, 129–30.
121. Occasionally, Nazimé-Roukié adds cultural translations directly (not as a set-off translator's addition), as when the narrator offers a visitor her arm 'since we have no men in our gathering' (Nİ, 79; DM, 386), and the translation adds 'because we Muslim women are not permitted to take men's arms' (NR, 51). The Turkish word employed for 'gathering' here, *cemiyet*, can also mean 'society'. The 2009 Pekin and Pekin rendition into modern Turkish translates this passage as 'since in our homes men and women cannot be in the same space, let me introduce myself to you on my own, I said, and I introduced myself' (PP, 37). This is quite different in meaning and vocabulary from the original. The Arabic translation, which generally follows the Ottoman closely, better reveals the intent. In the same scene, where Lebedeva omits details of the coffee's provenance found in the Ottoman and the Arabic, Nazimé-Roukié expands their description (NR, 52; OL, 45; Nİ, 80–1; DM, 386), one of several moments wherein this translation exhibits a sense of local knowledge as Lebedeva's does not; another is in the rendering of a *hadith*, where Lebedeva translates closely Aliye's phrasing, whereas Nazimé-Roukié uses a longer version of the *hadith* than that in the original (Nİ, 103; DM, 391; OL, 56; NR, 68).
122. NR, 4; OL, 13.
123. NR, 4–5; NR, 6, OL, 15.
124. Madeline Zilfi provides a fascinating discussion of the Ottoman tendency to gloss over the true nature of slavery, especially kul-harem slavery. She highlights the particular way that slave labour in the Ottoman Empire (especially that of women) constituted part of a labour continuum that included enslaved, free, and many gradations in between, in all cases strongly affected by class. Madeline C. Zilfi, 'Servants, Slaves, and the Domestic Order in the Ottoman Middle East', *Hawwa* 2: 1 (2004): 1–33; Madeline C. Zilfi, 'Thoughts on Women and Slavery in the Ottoman Era and Historical

Sources', in Amira Al-Azhary Sobol (ed.), *Beyond the Exotic: Women's Histories in Islamic Societies* (Syracuse: Syracuse University Press, 2005), 131–8.
125. Nİ, 29; DM, 375.
126. OL, 19; NR, 12.
127. Nİ, 29; DM, 375; OL, 20; NR, 13.
128. Ehud Toledano, *As If Silent and Absent: Bonds of Enslavement in the Islamic Middle East* (New Haven, CT: Yale University Press, 2007), 15–17; Ehud Toledano, 'Late Ottoman Concepts of Slavery (1830s–1880s)', *Poetics Today* 14: 3 (Autumn 1993): 477–506; 492ff.
129. On 'bluestocking' as a pejorative term, Alexis Easley, *First-person Anonymous: Women Writers and Victorian Print Media, 1830–70* (Abingdon: Ashgate, 2004), 21, 37, citing the work of Sylvia Myers. For a somewhat different view, Benjamin Dabby, *Women as Public Moralists in Britain: From the Bluestockings to Virginia Woolf* (London: Royal Historical Society/The Boydell Press, 2017), 4–8, 24, 44–5, 52–4.
130. NR, 48; Nİ, 74–5; AR, 385; OL, 42. On Fatma Aliye's take on the *bas-bleu*, see Elizabeth Frierson, 'Unimagined Communities: Women and Education in the Late Ottoman Empire, 1876–1909', *Critical Matrix* 9: 2 (31 December 1995): 55–90; 73–5.
131. In the Ottoman, these terms are transliterated from French, in Ottoman characters.
132. Nİ, 74–5.
133. Arabic: 'A *jariya* came in to our presence and said, I have been informed from outside that the madame has arrived and is about to enter the courtyard of the house.

'Hardly had she completed her sentence than I rose quickly to welcome the aforementioned guest. What I gleaned from the letter writer's narrative gave me to suspect that I would be receiving a *faylusufa* advanced in age (*ta'ina fi al-sinn*), yet here I was, viewing a pretty young woman no older than thirty. This madame wore very fine clothing, over her shoulders a winter *kiswa* in accord with the latest fashion and appropriate to visits of the most consequential kind. As I came up to her, she raised her hat (*qub'a*). It was easily visible to all that her hair had been knotted by the most skilful of hairdressers. It was gathered on top of her head in a way that would draw the eye.

'Without a doubt, the aforementioned letter writer's words had led me to believe that the *faylusufa* I would see in the Abode of Felicity must be one of the elderly ladies (*al-nisa' al-musinnat*) who are not concerned with adornment and do not care about clothes.

'But after I was able to get to know Madame R . . . I learned that she is not one of the ignorant women (*al-jahilat*)' (DM, 385). The Arabic does not transliterate *visite* or *femme de chambre*, using Arabic terms and phrasing: *a'zam al-ziyarat, amhar al-mawashit*.

134. NR, 4, 47, 51; *selamlık*, 47.
135. Nİ, 12; DM, 372, 385.
136. Nİ, 12, 74.
137. Nİ, 225.
138. For example, where the Ottoman suggests 'I might almost think' (Nİ, 42), and the Arabic reads 'I will not hide from you that' (DM, 379), NR omits these conversational tactics (22–3); in OL (27) they appear slightly less coy though not absent.
139. Also the case, at least in Nazimé-Roukié, with discussion of polygyny; that translation reduces the repartee element (Nİ, 88; DM, 388; NR, 57–8; OL, 48).
140. Nİ, 46 ff. DM, 381–3; OL, 32–4; NR, 31–3. Lebedeva first translates '*Isa aleyhusselam*' in the mouth of the narrator as 'N. S. Jésus-Christ' (Our Lord Jesus Christ) though afterwards she uses his name without any honorific (OL, 29). In the second dialogue, when the visitor refers to 'your prophet', the Arabic follows this with the usual phrase of respect – presumably not something the visitor would have said (DM, 391). This does not appear in the Ottoman, nor in the translations (Nİ, 155–56; NR, 68; OL, 56). See note 96.
141. Nazimé-Roukié translates Abyssinian as 'negress'.
142. Nİ, 45–6; DM, 379; OL, 28–9; NR, 25.
143. Nİ, 63–4; OL, 37; DM, 383; NR, 36–7.
144. Nİ, 42–3; OL, 27–8; NR, 23.
145. Nİ, 61; DM, 382; NR, 35; OL, 36.
146. Nİ, 75–9; DM, 386; OL, 43–4.
147. Nİ, 83–4; DM, 387.
148. Nİ, 84; NR, 54–5; OL, 46.
149. Nİ, 79; DM, 368; OL, 44; NR, 51.
150. Nİ, 100; DM, 390; OL, 54; NR, 65.
151. See Luise von Flotow, *Translation and Gender: Translating in the Era of Feminism* (Manchester: St Jerome; Ottawa: University of Ottawa Press, 1997). Von Flotow and others have developed these insights further since, but this study remains extremely useful to thinking about strategies in and approaches to a feminist translational practice.
152. The editor's preface comments: 'As for the third dialogue, it took place between the author and three Turkish friends, joined by three French women who did not have those interests which came to the surface in the first two dialogues.

'It is dominated by a feminine stamp, following the latest fashions and comparing eastern and western dress, and the extent of Turkish women's interest in music and the "piano" especially, such that there is no point, and no use in republishing it . . . with our concern to highlight the Islamic aspects that must be a focus of interest, understanding and awareness, so that our creed is not shaken by the ideas of missionaries and agents in various locales, and so that whimsical passions do not stir us.' Muhammad Ibrahim Salim, "'Ard li-ma tadminuhu al-kitab', in Fatima 'Aliya Hanım, *Nisa' al-muslimin*, 21–5; 24. This is part of a more complicated paratext (11–27) that presents a quote from Aliye's preface (in translation) as the 'secret' behind her writing ('I was privy to the fancies of the Europeans and the corruptness of their suspicions concerning us', 13). The editor's footnotes, bold-faced text, added subheads and punctuation, and omissions constitute paratextual elements, as does linking this text to a later history of 'Muslim–Christian dialogue' which highlights 'the religious' as the context of enunciation (6–7).

Bibliography

Periodicals

Fatat al-sharq, Cairo
Hanımlara Mahsus Gazete, Istanbul
al-Manar, Cairo
Tercüman-ı Hakikat, Istanbul
Thamarat al-funun, Beirut

Books and Articles

Ahmet Midhat, *Fatma Aliye Hanım yahut bir Muharrire-i Osmaniyenin Neşeti* (Istanbul: Kırk Anbar Matbaası, 1893).

Akşit, Elif Ekin, 'Fatma Aliye's Stories: Ottoman Marriages beyond the Harem', *Journal of Family History* 35: 3 (2010): 207–18.

Akşit, Elif Ekin, 'Harem Education and Heterotopic Imagination', *Gender and Education* 23: 3 (May 2011): 299–311.

Baker, Mona, 'Reframing Conflict in Translation', in Mona Baker (ed.), *Critical Readings in Translation Studies* (Abingdon: Routledge, 2010): 113–29.

Board of Lady Managers of the World's Columbian Commission created by Act of Congress USA organised 1890, *List of the Books in the Library of the Woman's Building, World's Columbian Exposition, Chicago, 1893*, compiled by Edith Clarke, <http://digital.library.upenn.edu/women/clarke/library/library.html> (accessed 25 October 2005).

Booth, Marilyn, *May Her Likes Be Multiplied: Biography and Gender Politics in Egypt* (Berkeley: University of California Press, 2001).

Booth, Marilyn, 'Before Qasim Amin: Writing Women's History in 1890s Egypt', in Marilyn Booth and Anthony Gorman (eds), *The Long 1890s in Egypt: Colonial Quiescence, Subterranean Resistance* (Edinburgh: Edinburgh University Press, 2014), 365–98.

Booth, Marilyn, *Classes of Ladies of Cloistered Spaces: Writing Feminist History through Biography in Fin-de-siècle Egypt* (Edinburgh: Edinburgh University Press, 2015).

Booth, Marilyn, 'Peripheral Visions: Translational Polemics and Feminist Arguments in Colonial Egypt', in Anna Ball and Karim Mattar (eds), *Edinburgh Companion to the Postcolonial Middle East* (Edinburgh: Edinburgh University Press, 2018), 183–212.
Booth, Marilyn, 'Introduction: Translation as Lateral Cosmopolitanism in the Ottoman Universe', in Marilyn Booth (ed.), *Migrating Texts: Circulating Translations around the Ottoman Mediterranean* (Edinburgh: Edinburgh University Press, 2019), 1–54.
Booth, Marilyn, *The Career and Communities of Zaynab Fawwaz: Feminist Thinking in Fin-de-siècle Egypt* (Oxford: Oxford University Press, 2021).
Dabby, Benjamin, *Women as Public Moralists in Britain: From the Bluestockings to Virginia Woolf* (London: Royal Historical Society/The Boydell Press, 2017).
Easley, Alexis, *First-person Anonymous: Women Writers and Victorian Print Media, 1830–70* (Abingdon: Ashgate, 2004).
Faris, Ibrahim, 'Bismillahi, khayr al-asma'', *Kitab nisa' al-islam, bi-qalam al-katiba al-dha'i'at al-sit Fatima 'Aliya Hanim, karimat al-'allama al-shahir Jawdat Pasha* (n.p.: Matba'at 'Ayn shams, n.d.), unpaginated.
[Faris, Ibrahim], 'Man hiya al-mu'allifa', *Kitab nisa' al-islam, bi-qalam al-katiba al-dha'i'at al-sit Fatima 'Aliya Hanim, karimat al-'allama al-shahir Jawdat Pasha* (n.p.: Matba'at 'Ayn shams, n.d.), 1–4.
Fatma Aliye, *Fatma Aliye Hanım: Yaşamı, sanat,ı yapıtları ve Nisvanı İslam*, edited by Mübeccel Kızıltan (Istanbul: Mutlu yayıncılık, 1993).
Fatma Aliye, *İslam kadınları*, edited by Ayhan Pekin and Amine Pekin (Istanbul: İnkılab, 2009).
Fatma Aliye, *Osmanlı'da kadın: Cariyelik, çokeşlilik, ve moda*, edited by Orhan Sakın (Istanbul: Ekim, 2012).
[Fatma Aliye], Cevdet Paşazade Fatma Aliye, *Nisvan-ı İslam: Bazı adat-ı İslamiye hakkında üç mühavereyi havidir* (Istanbul: Maarif Nezaret-i Celilesinin rahsatile *Tercüman-ı Hakikat Gazetesine* derc edildikten sonra ilk defa olarak ayrica risale şeklinde dahi tab olunmuştur, 1309 (1891/2 if AH or 1893/4 if Rumi).
[Fatma Aliye], Mübeccel Kızıltan and Tülay Gençtük (eds), *Atatürk Kitaplığı Fatma Aliye Hanım evrakı kataloğu* (Istanbul: İstanbul Büyük Şehir Belediyesi Kültür İşleri, Daire Başkanlığı Kütüphane ve Müzeler Müdürlüğü, 1993).
[Fatma Aliye] Mahmud Zeki, 'Meşahir-i Nisvan-ı Osmaniye hakkında Yazılan Arabi al-İbare Makalatın Birincisi: İsmetlu Fatma Aliye Hanım Efendi Hazretleri', *Hanımlara Mahsus Gazete*, no. 256–54 (5 Zilhicce 1317/23 Mart 1316), 3.
[Fatma Aliye] Fatima 'Aliya, *Kitab nisa' al-islam, bi-qalam al-katiba al-dha'i'at al-sit Fatima 'Aliya Hanim, karimat al-'allama al-shahir Jawdat Pasha* (n.p.: Matba'at 'Ayn shams, n.d.).
[Fatma Aliye], Fatima 'Aliya Hanim, *Nisa' al-muslimin: Hiwar bayan katiba turkiyya muslima wa-rahiba faransiyya wa-faylusufa ingiliziyya hawla al-mabadi' al-insaniyya wa-al-'aqida al-islamiyya*, edited by Muhammad Ibrahim Salim (Cairo: Maktabat al-Qur'an, n.d. [c. 1989–90]).

Fatma Aliye's Nisvan-ı İslam

[Fatma Aliye], Fathma-Alié, *Nisvan-i-Islam, 'Les femmes musulmanes'*, trans. Mme Olga de Labedeff [*sic*], connue sous le pseudonyme de Gulnar-Hanoum [*sic*: no umlaut] (Paris: Le Journal 'L'Orient', n.d. [1896]).

[Fatma Aliye] Alihe Hanoum, *Les musulmanes contemporaines: trois conférences, traduites de la langue turque par Nazimé-Roukié* (Paris: Alphonse Lemerre, Éditeur, 1894).

Fawwaz al-'Amili, Zaynab bt. 'Ali b. Husayn b. 'Ubaydallah b. Hasan b. Ibrahim b. Muhammad b. Yusuf, *Kitab al-Durr al-manthur fi tabaqat rabbat al-khudur* (Bulaq/Misr: al-Matba'a al-kubra al-amiriyya, 1312).

Fikri Bek, Muhammad Amin, *Irshad al-alibba' ila mahasin Urubba* (Cairo: Matba'at al-Muqtataf, 1892).

Findley, Carter Vaughn, 'An Ottoman Occidentalist in Europe: Ahmed Midhat Meets Madame Gülnar, 1889', *American Historical Review* 103: 1 (February 1998): 15–49.

Frierson, Elizabeth, 'Unimagined Communities: Women and Education in the Late Ottoman Empire, 1876–1909', *Critical Matrix* 9: 2 (31 December 1995): 55–90.

Geneology of the Imperial Ottoman Family (Paris: n.pub., 2004).

Genette, Gerard, *Paratexts: Thresholds of Interpretation*, trans. Jane E. Lewin (Cambridge: Cambridge University Press, 1997/2001).

Günay-Erkol, Cimen and Senem Timuroğlu Bozkurt, 'Dreams beyond Control: Women and Writing in the Ottoman Empire since Asiye Hatun's Diary', *Journal of Research in Gender Studies* 4: 1 (2014): 364–75.

Hermans, Theo, 'The Translator's Voice in Translated Narrative', in Mona Baker (ed.), *Critical Readings in Translation Studies* (Abingdon: Routledge, 2010): 193–212 (first published 1996).

Kasimirski, M. [Albin de Biberstein Kazimirski], *Le Koran, traduction nouvelle faite sur le texte arabe* (Paris: Charpentier, 1840, 1841, 1844).

Kazimirski, A. de Biberstein, *Dictionnaire arabe-français*, edited by Ibed Gallab (Cairo/Bulaq: Imprimerie V. R. égyptienne, 1875 [1860]).

Kızıltan, Mücebbel, 'Öncü bir kadın yazar: Fatma Aliye Hanım,' *Journal of Turkish Studies* 14 (1990): 283–322.

Nusayr, 'Ayda Ibrahim, *al-Kutub al-'arabiyya alati nushirat fi Misr 1900–1925* (Cairo: American University in Cairo Press, 1980).

Pernau, Margrit, Helge Jordheim, Emmanuella Saada, Christian Bailey, Einar Wigen, Orit Bashkin, Mana Kia, Mohinder Singh, Rochona Majumdar, Angelika C. Messner, Oleg Benesch, Myoungkyu Park and Jan Ifversen (eds), *Civilizing Emotions: Concepts in Nineteenth-century Asia and Europe* (Oxford: Oxford University Press, 2015).

Potuoğlu-Cook, Öyku, 'Night Shifts: Moral, Economic, and Cultural Politics of Turkish Belly Dance Across the Fin-de-Siècle', PhD dissertation, Northwestern University, 2008.

Salim, Muhammad Ibrahim, '"Ard li-ma tadminuhu al-kitab', in Fatima 'Aliya Hanim, *Nisa' al-muslimin: Hiwar bayan katiba turkiyya mulima wa-rahiba farnasiyya wa-faylusufa ingiliziyya hawla al-mabadi' al-inasniyya wa-al-'aqida al-islamiyya*, edited by Muhammad Ibrahim Salim (Cairo: Maktabat al-Qur'an, n.d. [c. 1989–90]), 21–5.

Shissler, A. Holly, 'The Harem as the Seat of Middle-class Industry and Morality: The Fiction of Ahmet Midhat Efendi', in Marilyn Booth (ed.), *Harem Histories: Envisioning Places and Living Spaces* (Durham, NC: Duke University Press, 2010), 319–41.

Shissler, A. Holly, 'Haunting Ottoman Middle-class Sensibility: Ahmet Midhat's Gothic', in Marilyn Booth (ed.), *Migrating Texts: Circulating Translations around the Ottoman Mediterranean* (Edinburgh: Edinburgh University Press, 2019), 193–209.

Strauss, Johann, 'Ol'ga Lebedeva (*Gülnâr Hanim*) and Her Works in Ottoman Turkish', in Sabine Prätor and Christoph K. Neumann (eds), *Arts, Women and Scholars: Studies in Ottoman Society and Culture (Festschrift Hans Georg Majer)* (Istanbul: Simurg, 2002), 287–314.

Tarrazi, Filib di, *Tarikh al-sihafa al-'arabiyya*, Pts 1–3 (Beirut: al-Matba'a al-adabiyya, 1913–14), Pt 4 (Beirut: al-Matba'a al-amrikaniyya, 1933).

Toledano, Ehud, 'Late Ottoman Concepts of Slavery (1830s–1880s)', *Poetics Today* 14: 3 (Autumn 1993): 477–506.

Toledano, Ehud, *As If Silent and Absent: Bonds of Enslavement in the Islamic Middle East* (New Haven: Yale University Press, 2007).

von Flotow, Luise, *Translation and Gender: Translating in the Era of Feminism* (Manchester: St Jerome; Ottawa: University of Ottawa Press, 1997).

Zachs, Fruma, and Sharon Halevi, *Gendering Culture in Greater Syria: Intellectuals and Ideology in the Late Ottoman Period* (London: I. B. Tauris, 2015).

Zilfi, Madeline C., 'Servants, Slaves, and the Domestic Order in the Ottoman Middle East', *Hawwa* 2: 1 (2004): 1–33.

Zilfi, Madeline C., "Thoughts on Women and Slavery in the Ottoman Era and Historical Sources', in Amira Al-Azhary Sobol (ed.), *Beyond the Exotic: Women's Histories in Islamic Societies* (Syracuse: Syracuse University Press, 2005), 131–8.

Index

Note on Indexing Conventions

This Index incorporates language- and era-specific conventions on how names are alphabetised. Thus, Ottoman-era individual who would be indexed in Arabic as Aghayev (Ajayif), Ahmad, would be indexed as Ahmet Ağaoğlu according to Ottoman usage. We have indexed by balancing the following: contributor preferences, our assessment of how subjects are most commonly identified, and the primary context in which the subject appears in this volume, usually her or his primary language of writing. Thus, we find Fawwaz, Zaynab (following Arabic conventions), but Fatma Aliye (Ottoman).We acknowledge that balancing these considerations yields a measure of inconsistency, for which the volume editor who compiled the index (M. Booth) takes full responsibility. Moreover, many of our Ottoman-era subjects moved across linguistic and political boundaries, and not all are cross-referenced, so it is best to check all possibilities! We do not give post-Ottoman surnames unless they are used in the body of the text.

While we index 'translation from or into' individual languages, we do not index this for Ottoman Turkish, as it is nearly ubiquitous through the volume. Terms that occur in both Arabic and Ottoman are indexed under the Arabic form, generally with cross-references. Although contributors were free to choose their transliteration practices, we have opted for minimal Arabic transliteration in the Index. We hope the outcome's usefulness outweighs its possible idiosyncracy.

AbdelMegid, Maha, 18, 20, 230
'Abdu, Ṭanyus, 74–5
'Abduh, Muhammad, 292, 293
Abdülaziz, Ottoman Sultan, 69, 123, 128
Abdülhak Hamit Tarhan, 16–17,
   190–200, 202, 205, 206, 207–8,
   209–10, 213
   Tarik, 190–2, 194–213
Abdülhamid II, Ottoman Sultan, 70, 124,
   141, 192, 195, 199, 251, 290–2,
   314, 327, 354–5, 366; Hamidian era,
   291–2, 295, 306, 309

Abdurrahman (Süreyya; Mirduhizade),
   141, 142, 172
Abu Hamid Muhammad, 141
adab, *ādāb*, 32, 81, 145, 146, 167–8, 171
   edebiyat, 168, 171
Adviye Rabia Hanım, 327, 348–9
al-Afghani, Jamal al-Din, 291
Afghanistan, 200–2, 211
Aghayev (Ajayif), Ahmad (Ahmet
   Ağaoğlu), 1–4, 8, 21n4, 194
Ahmad I, Bey of Tunis, 128
Ahmadi, Wali, 201

Index

Ahmed, Leila, 31
Ahmedani, Usman, 4, 16–17, 20
Ahmet Ağaoğlu *see* Aghayev, Ahmad
Ahmet Midhat Efendi, 23n26, 106, 328, 330, 348–9, 355, 372–3n18
'a'ile see family; *see also* marriage; polygyny
Akcasu, A. Ebru, 18, 20, 230
Aksakal, Mustafa, 256
Alexandria, 101, 232, 259
Algeria, 88, 121, 130, 131, 136n57
allegory, 14, 29, 35, 48, 306; *see also* Pilgrim's Progress
Altuğ, Fatih, 370n5
Amin, Qasim, 3, 4, 20, 161, 211, 227–31, 233, 235–44, 247–8, 250–60, 262–6, 286–9, 295, 298–9, 305–6, 313, 371n13
  Tahrir al-mar'a, 10, 12, 17–18, 227–30, 232–4, 235–6, 239, 240–2, 251–2, 261–2, 264–6: titles of, in Ottoman translation: *Tahrir al-Mar'a, yahut Hürriyet-i Nisvan*, 232, 235; *Hürriyet-i Nisvan*, 232, 235
  al-Mar'a al-jadida, 18, 227, 235, 265
anarchy, 302–6, 314
Anatoli, 106–9, 114, 115
Anatolia, 104, 108–9, 241, 249, 252
Andalusia, 16–17, 190–1, 192–4, 205, 210, 213
Arabic, 30, 32
  Khayr al-Din al-Tunisi's work in, 121–31
  translation from or into, 1–5, 10, 11, 12, 13–17, 29, 32, 70–81, 86–90, 140–72, 190, 198, 199, 200, 205–6, 208, 211–13, 228–66, 287–91, 295, 297–310, 314–16, 328–9, 331, 336, 341, 346–53, 360, 362, 368–9
Arabic literary production, premodern, 2, 30, 81, 143, 147, 193, 351; *see also* biographies of women
Arabness, as identity, 82–9, 203–4
Armenian, translation from or into, 4, 71, 77
Arslan, Ceyhun, 193, 231
al-Asma'i, Yusuf (or Yusef) Semih, 17–18, 232–3, 235–53, 255–6, 258–66
atf-ı tefsir(î), 146, 147, 161, 164, 172, 245
Aubert, Francis, 129
audiences *see* readerships, audiences, and reception
Avicenna, 143
'awra/'avret, 249–50, 263, 275–6
Aydın, Cemil, 207
Azerbaijan, 1
Azhari (Moyal), Esther, 12–13

Badran, 'Abd al-Rahman ('Abdurrahman), 149
Baille, Frédéric, 129, 136 n50
Balkan Wars, 204, 207, 208, 210
Baron, Beth, 229
Basiret, 141
Bayram V, Muhammad, 126
Beirut, 9, 11, 19, 32, 128, 149, 323n98, 327, 328, 346–7, 350–1, 358
Bengal, 1–2, 30, 34, 42
Bengali, translation from or into, 5, 13–14, 30, 34, 36–9, 40, 42, 55–7
Bereketzade, Abdallah Cemaleddin, 232, 236, 245, 261–2, 267–8, 270, 280
Bereketzade, İsmail Hakkı, 141
Beyoğlu (Pera), 104, 106–7, 110, 114n16, 331–2, 334, 339, 352–3, 357, 363, 366
bhajan (musical form), 40–1
Bible, 31, 35–6, 39, 56
biographies of women, 2, 4, 328, 329, 333, 348–9
Bismarck, Otto von, 129
Blackburn, Stuart, 33
Booth, Marilyn, 11, 12, 18–19, 20, 209, 228, 229–30, 234, 242, 246, 266–7n4, 277n152, 302
Bosnian, translation from or into, 5, 16–17, 190, 198–9, 204, 205–9, 211–13, 287
Bowley, Reverend William, 34, 42–3
Boym, Svetlana, 193
Britain, 2, 29, 61n55, 70, 73, 113n10, 131, 277n147, 331, 360–1; *see also* Egypt; imperialisms, European; India; missionaries; tourists

Index

Brown, C., 142, 172
Brown, Sylvia, 47–8
Buhajib, Salim, 126, 132n3
Bulaq Press, 144, 351
Bunyan, John, 6, 13–14, 29–30, 36–8, 40–1, 50–5
  The Pilgrim's Progress: translations of: into Arabic, 32; into Bengali, 34–5, 36–9; into Hindi, 40–1; into Oriya, 41–2; into Tamil, 33–4; into Urdu, 42–5, 48–55
al-Bustani, Butrus, 32, 193, 346
Buyers, Rev. William, 34, 42

Çağlar, Behçet Kemal, 198
Cahun, Léon, 128
Cairo, 1, 7, 9, 14, 17, 69, 70, 74–7, 86, 88, 101, 144, 230, 232, 259, 286, 287, 292–3, 300, 327, 329, 347, 350, 353, 355
capitalism, 122, 130–1, 311; *see also* labour, waged
Carey, Felix, 34, 36–8
caupaī (poetic metre), 36
Celal Nuri, 264
censorship and regulation of publications, 8, 18, 74, 86, 125, 173n3, 208, 228, 236, 251, 265, 281n200, 302, 317–18n15, 377n71
Ceride-i askeriyye, 141, 142
Cevdet Pasha, 141, 143, 145, 148, 327, 348–50, 353, 355, 370n5
  Belâgat-i osmaniyye, 141
Charrière, Etienne, 11, 20
Christianity
  compared to Islam, 47–8, 54–5, 194, 197, 204–8, 238, 337–8, 367–8, 385
  doctrines, beliefs and rituals in, 14, 39–41, 44, 47, 50, 54, 56, 337–9, 359–60, 363, 367
  see also allegory; Bible; Bunyan, John; missionaries
Christian communities, historical and in literature, 17, 31, 40–4, 45, 47, 54, 86, 108–9, 156, 191, 193, 194, 197, 204–8, 233, 261, 289, 339, 353, 370n5
Christoforides family, 370n5

citizenship, concepts of, 47, 50, 54, 72, 82–5, 161, 205, 208
civilisation (*tamaddun*)
  concept of, 45–6, 50, 108–9, 130, 160–1, 204, 247–8, 286, 296–300, 302, 306–7, 309, 315, 345, 347, 368
  hierarchies of, 19, 87, 108, 130, 329–30, 334
Clancy-Smith, Julia, 125
class and social stratification, 10, 52, 54, 87, 103, 112n7, 130, 131, 166, 254, 286, 291, 294, 305, 307–8, 310–14, 322n83, 341, 356, 360, 366, 376n61, 382n124
Clift, Jack, 13–14, 20
colloquial language *see* vernaculars and vernacularisation
colonialism *see* imperialism and colonialism; Egypt; India
Columbian Exposition (Chicago, 1893), 329–30, 366, 372–3n18
Comte, Auguste, 298, 306
Constitutional Revolution (1908), 12, 18, 196, 208, 228, 230, 235–6, 241–2, 248, 251, 257, 265, 287, 289–92, 300, 305–6, 311, 314
  slogans in, 290–2, 294, 297, 299
  see also Young Turks
Constitution, Ottoman (1876), 124, 128, 131, 151, 171; *see also* Young Ottomans
Constitution, Tunisian *see qanun al-dawla*
Conti (secretary/translator), 127
Cox, Jeffrey, 31–2
Crimean War, 208, 210
'customs', commentary on and critique of, 49, 104, 195, 197, 237–8, 251, 259, 278n161, 333–4, 339–41, 344–5, 358, 362, 369; *see also* hijab; marriage; polygyny; veiling

al-Dahdah, Rushayd, 129
Damascus, 179n93, 201, 327
Darwinism, 257
de Certeau, Michel, 105–6
'decline', 165, 190, 192, 194, 207, 240, 248, 251, 256, 257, 259, 274n108, 278n164

Index

Dedes, Yorgos, 10, 12, 17–18, 20, 161
Desfossés, Edouard, 129
de Lesseps, Jules, 128
Deringil, Selim, 84
desire
 pleasure and, 12, 250, 304
 sexuality and, 249, 263–4, 365
Deuchar, Hannah Scott, 14–15, 20
dictionaries, 156, 180n12, 185n190, 248–9, 269n33, 364
 biographical, 2, 19, 24n39, 328, 348–50, 351, 366, 370–1n7
divorce, 260, 262, 263, 277n143, 340, 342, 344–5
dohā (poetic metre), 36
Doyle, Laura, 82
dress, 19, 36–7, 196, 197, 329, 331, 340–3, 347, 363, 364–5, 368, 378–9n89, 384–5n152; *see also* hijab; *tesettür*; veiling
Ducis, Jean-François, 15, 72–5, 77–8, 83–5
Dumas, Alexandre (père), 72, 74, 76, 100, 102
dustur/düstur, 151

East India Company, 33, 45, 158
economic conditions, 6, 11, 23n24, 109, 254, 312–13, 341–2; *see also* class; labour, waged
edebiyat see *adab/ādāb*
Edip, Halide, 193, 196, 198, 211
education, 39, 47, 50, 60n49, 140, 143, 190, 195, 238, 240, 254, 279n180, 292, 296, 327, 329, 335, 346
 female, 12, 17, 191, 210–11, 213, 227, 237–9, 242, 257, 259–60, 270n44, 289, 296–9, 304, 313, 330, 332–4, 336, 339, 343, 347, 348–50, 352, 354, 359–60, 367–8
 languages and, 46, 72, 73, 75, 104, 108–9, 126, 140, 149, 173n8, 281n200, 332, 334
Egypt, 3, 4, 74–6, 102, 144, 198, 208–9, 227–8, 230, 232, 236, 254, 258–9, 265, 266, 286–90, 292–7, 300, 310, 312 328, 348
 British occupation and administration

of, 24n37, 70, 73–4, 82, 86–7, 90, 232, 267n6, 331
 language in, 79–80, 245, 251, 351
 see also Alexandria; Cairo; nationalisms
Elsadda, Hoda, 191
Elshakry, Marwa, 300, 311
English, 1–2, 31, 46, 57, 69, 72, 73, 327, 341
 translation from or into, 2, 9, 10–11, 13–15, 19, 29, 32, 34, 40, 41–2, 69–71, 72–6, 78–83, 86–90, 126, 128, 142, 172, 195, 203, 208, 320–1n59, 328–9
equality, 166, 207, 289, 290–2, 294–9, 306–7, 314–15, 362
epithets *see* names and naming practices
Ertürk, Nergis, 78–9
European languages, translations from, generally, 4, 5–6, 9, 13–14, 17, 46, 70–3, 76, 79, 87, 100, 144, 195, 201, 228, 231; *see also* individual languages
Europeans in the Ottoman Empire, 332–3, 381n110; *see also* tourists

Fahmy, Ziad, 79–80
familia see family
family, 108, 109, 199, 227, 229, 237–9, 246, 266, 305–6, 308, 311–14, 330, 333, 343–4, 347, 349, 359–60; *see also* marriage
'Family Library', 288
Faris, Ibrahim, 329, 377n66, 378–9n89
Faris, Salim, 128, 129
fashion *see* dress
Fatat al-sharq, 329
Fathallah, Hamza, 372–3n18
Fatma Aliye, 2, 4, 11, 18–19, 20, 246, 267n14, 327–31, 333, 341, 344, 346, 349–50, 353–4, 358, 366, 367, 381n85
 Nisvan-ı Islam, 2, 9, 11, 18–19, 20, 327–69
Fawwaz, Zaynab, 2, 4, 9, 19, 328–9, 333, 348–52, 356, 366, 370n7, 370n10, 375n41, 377n66
femininity, 190, 191, 196–7, 199, 204–5,

Index

209–13; *see also* dress; education; 'woman question', the
feminism, 10, 219n89, 322n79, 328, 334, 350, 364–7
Féval, Paul, 101–2
food, 337, 339
France, 73, 74, 101, 103, 128, 131, 185n194, 195, 277n147, 352, 361; *see also* imperialisms, European; Paris
French, 4, 72, 74–5, 160, 165, 169, 171, 196, 200, 327, 330, 332–3, 335, 339, 361–3
   Khayr al-Din al-Tunisi's work in, 121–31
   translation from or into, 2, 5, 9, 10–11, 14, 16, 18–19, 72–8, 82–7, 89–90, 99–104, 203, 228, 328, 330, 335–7, 351, 353–65

Gaspiralı, İsmail, 194
gender *see* education, female; femininity; feminism; *hijab*; masculinity; 'Nature'; 'woman question', the; veiling
gender segregation, 237, 332, 335, 343–4, 355–6, 367; *see also* hijab
Genette, Gérard, 234
German, translation from or into, 1, 69, 181n28, 198, 204, 208
ghazal (poetic form), 40
Gibb, E. J. W., 195
Gill, Bridget, 14–15, 20
Gökalp, Ziya, 156, 177n57
Goussopoulos, Konstantinos, 102
Granara, William, 193
Greek, translation from or into, 4, 5, 15, 29, 32, 99, 100–4, 107, 110, 156, 157, 168, 182n133, 310, 338, 363
Guizot, François, 131
Gülnar Hanım *see* Lebedeva, Ol'ga

hadith(s), 3, 53, 249, 263, 369, 379, 382n121
Hagopian, V. H., 147
Hakikat, 141
Halevi, Sharon, 347
hamd (poetic form), 48
Hamilton, Carina, 20n3, 370n6, 384n104

Hanımlara Mahsus Gazete, 328, 370–1n7
Hannun, Marya, 211
Harb, Muhammad Tal'at, 259–60, 279n174
Hari, John, 34, 43–4
Hartmann, Martin, 148
Hasan Bedreddin, 72
Hayreddin Pasha *see* Khayr al-Din al-Tunisi
Hebrew, translation from or into, 4
hendiadys, 146, 147
hijab (system of gender separation/face covering), 246–7, 256, 258–9, 273n94, 279, 301–7, 314, 381n106; *see also* gender segregation; *tesettür*; veiling
Hill, Peter, 16, 20, 32
Hilmi, İbrahim, 234, 317–18n15
Hindi, 31, 39, 46, 49
   translation from or into, 5, 13–14, 19, 29, 30, 34–6, 39–42, 45–6, 55, 203
Hirschkind, Charles, 192
Hofmeyr, Isabel, 29, 35
Hourani, Albert, 129
Howell, Yvonne, 12
Hugo, Victor, 75, 77, 86, 92n26, 93n52
Husayn, General, 126, 128

Ibn 'Abidin, 263, 272
Ibn Abi Diyaf, 126, 128
Ibn Battuta, 2, 143
Ibn Khaldun, 2, 143, 145, 161, 183n158
İbrahim Efendi, Hacı, 141
idafa, 144
Ihsanoğlu, Ekmeleddin, 232
imperialism and colonialism, European, 5, 6, 14, 30–1, 35, 45, 48, 50, 69–71, 73, 76, 79, 82, 89–90, 131, 136n50, 155, 193, 195, 201, 204, 207, 240, 277n147, 314, 334; *see also* colonialism, resistance to; Egypt; India; Orientalist representations; tourists; missionaries
imperialism, Ottoman, 84, 191–3
India, 3, 6, 29–57, 196, 198, 210
   British colonialism in, 30, 31, 33, 45–6, 49–50, 55, 56, 195, 199, 202
   Islam in, 194, 207, 208

Index

India (*cont.*)
  see also Bengal
inşa, 146, 147
Ioannidis, Petros, 102
Iran, 1, 2, 3, 21n4, 49, 195, 309; *see also* Qajar Empire
Irmak, Sadi, 198
'Isa'i, Sharafuddin, 44–5, 46, 47, 48–55
Islam
  as belief system and outlook, 1, 16–17, 19, 53, 55, 86, 129–30, 190, 193, 203–13, 237–8, 247, 253–4, 290–2, 296–7, 299–300, 310–11, 313, 315, 320n40, 331, 333–4, 347, 350, 368–9, 384–5n152
  and Christianity, 47, 131, 196–7, 337–9, 344–5, 367–9
  reformism in, 16, 63n95, 123–5, 130–1, 310, 328
  ritual practices in, 337–9, 363, 367–8
  see also hadith(s); *hijab*; *jihad*; Qur'an; *shari'a*; ulama; veiling; 'woman question', the
Islamic history, 157, 161, 193–4, 196, 207, 210, 233, 268–9n32, 333; *see also* Andalusia
Islamiyet, 149, 206, 240
Istanbul, 7, 9, 14, 15, 16, 17, 18–19, 69, 70, 73–6, 77, 99, 101, 102, 104–6, 109, 110, 115n24–5, 123, 124, 126, 129, 141–2, 149, 169, 195, 201, 208, 230, 232–4, 249, 257, 265, 266, 287, 289, 293, 300, 327, 329, 331, 332, 334, 335, 346, 348, 349, 353, 355; *see also* Beyoğlu
istibdad, 142, 238, 248, 251, 290, 292, 306–7, 309
İstikbal, 141
Italian language and translation, 15, 69, 72, 73, 75, 76, 89, 157, 158, 184n179
izafet (terkib-i izafî), 144, 155

Japan, 315
al-Jawa'ib, 126, 128, 141, 151, 173n6
Jesus, 40, 41, 43, 63n87, 337, 367, 384n140
Jews and Judaism, 75, 99, 114n18, 192, 338

jihad, 207, 211, 254–6, 277n147, 277n150

Kamil, Mustafa, 193, 232, 270n58
Kana'at Kitaphanesi, 234, 269
Karamanli (Turcophone Orthodox Christians), 107–9, 112, 114, 116, 118
Karamanlidika (Greek-scripted Ottoman Turkish), 4, 15, 99–100, 107–10, 114–18
Karić, Dženita, 4, 16–17, 20
Katiboğlu, Monica, 229
kavim see qawm
Kayali, Hasan, 247, 315
Kazan, 20n3, 230, 288, 289, 355
Kazimirski, Albert de Biberstein-, 338–9, 351, 352, 363
Khayr al-Din al-Tunisi
  life and career, 16, 123–5
  Muqaddima, 16, 20, 121–89: *taqariz* (blurbs) of, 133–4n19; English translation of, 126
  Réformes nécessaires, 16, 121–40
Khaznadar, Mustafa, 123–5, 129, 131
Khérédine *see* Khayr al-Din al-Tunisi
al-Khuri, Khalil, 128, 129
Khuri-Makdisi, Ilham, 10, 12, 17–18, 20, 161
Kia, Mana, 194
Kitaphane-i İslam ve 'Askeri, 234
Kızıltan, Mübeccel, 329, 369–70n2
Knight, Stephen, 105
Kyriakides, Epaminondas, 15, 99, 104–6

labour, translation as/and, 8, 14, 20, 56
labour, waged, 18, 287, 297, 300, 305, 310–14
Ladino, translation from or into, 4, 112n3
language reform, 11, 16, 20, 71–2, 78–80, 82, 90, 94n58, 141, 146, 154–7, 160, 162, 170–2; *see also* lexicon
Latin, 142, 156, 157, 310
Lebedeva, Ol'ga, 19, 328, 347, 353–66, 370n5
lexicon
  shifts in through translation, 16, 17, 144–72, 228, 245–6, 252, 335, 351,

Index

356; *see also* individual terms; translation, strategies in liberalism, 130, 131, 137n60, 292, 310
Litvin, Margaret, 20n2, 71, 74, 77
Lymberiou, Demosthenes, 102

Makdisi, Ussama, 84, 256
Makki, Mahmud 'Ali, 193
Malta, 13, 32
al-Manar, 260, 328
Manastırlı Mehmet Rifat Paşa, 72
marriage, 12, 191, 197, 205–6, 209–10, 246, 262–3, 313, 327–8, 339, 340, 342–5, 347, 362–3, 367–8
Mary, Jules, 101
masculinity, 190–2, 194, 205–13, 229–30
materialism, 286, 289, 300, 304, 315–16
Megamiz, Zeki *see* Mugamiz, Zaki
Mehmed (or Mehmet) Akif, 18, 247, 267n16, 286–326
 Safahat, 309
Mehmed Ali (or Muhammad Ali) Pasha, ruler of Egypt, 144, 174n27, 293
Mehmet Faik Bey, 327
Mertoğlu, Suat, 293
Mestyan, Adam, 75–6, 79–80, 88
metaphor, 13, 20, 146, 148, 172, 191, 305, 336, 339, 345, 368, 382n116
microhistory, translation as, 8
Middleton, Anne, 11
Midhat Cemal (Kuntay), 308–10
Midhat Pasha, 128
Mill, John Stuart, 131
millet and millet system, 111, 162–3, 171, 191, 207, 240, 247, 251, 315
Minawi, Mustafa, 84
Misailidis, Evangelinos, 15, 100, 106–11
missionaries, Christian, 13–14, 29–33, 35–6, 39, 41, 44–7, 256, 333, 384–5n15
Montépin, Xavier de, 100–1
Morsy, Magali, 125, 126, 127, 136 n54
Mugamiz, Zaki (or Zeki), 17–18, 24n39, 232–6, 239–58, 260–6, 289–90
Mughal Empire, 30, 121
Muhammad, prophet of Islam, 2, 132n3, 190, 291, 338, 351, 353, 357, 379n96, 384n140

Muir, Sir William, 45–50
multilinguality, 1, 4–6, 9–10, 20, 30–3, 73, 77, 79, 99–100, 111, 229–31, 338
Munday, Jeremy, 8
Murad V, Ottoman Sultan, 70, 141
Musa Kazım, 291–7, 307, 314
music and musical performance, 15, 31, 36, 74, 76–7, 81, 340, 345, 365, 368, 378–9n89
 in north Indian, 39–42
 see also opera
Muslims, 19, 47, 106, 191–2, 197, 210, 213, 237–8, 240–1, 247, 315; *see also* Islam, *umma*
Mustafa Fazil Pasha, 128–9
Mustafa Kemal (Atatürk), 201, 319n22

Nahda, Arab, 7–8, 12, 22n17, 125, 193, 230–1, 378–9n89
Najmabadi, Afsaneh, 208
names and naming practices, 39, 49, 53, 54, 63n87, 72, 74–5, 85–8, 124, 147–8, 160, 163, 258, 350, 373n19, 378n89, 381n105, 384n140
 of places, 107, 115n24, 155, 160
names, translators' and authors', used or elided, 4, 74, 232, 234, 268n22, 269–70n42, 317–18n15, 320n40, 328, 350, 356, 370n5, 380n97, 380n105
Namık Kemal, 85, 193, 195, 196, 199, 207–8, 209, 210, 235
nationalisms and proto-nationalisms, 1, 9, 16–17, 22n17, 70, 75, 78–80, 82, 85–6, 89, 124, 131, 156, 190, 191, 193, 197–8, 207–9, 289, 315, 341, 347
'Nature', as basis for human society and gender difference, 18, 87, 211, 238, 259, 286, 291, 293, 296–8, 302–8, 309, 311–12, 316, 322n83, 349
Nazim Hikmet, 196
'Nazimé Roukié', 19, 328, 353–66, 370n5
Newman, Daniel, 126
Nigar, 203
Nigar Hanım, 203, 234

Index

novels and novel reading, 7, 15–16, 30, 42, 79, 99–111, 128, 193, 194, 233, 320n58, 327–8, 332, 347, 351, 373n24, 375n41

Ohnet, Georges, 328
Omar, Hussein, 310–11
opera, 72–6, 79, 88
Orientalist representation(s), 19, 74, 83–4, 86, 128, 190, 191, 192, 195, 204, 268–9n32, 330–2, 334–6, 342, 343, 354, 362, 363, 365–8; *see also* missionaries
Oriya, translation from or into, 41–2
Orsini, Francesca, 9
Osmanlı kütüphane-i milliye ('Ottoman national library'), 241, 289
Osmanlı Matba'ası, 232–3
Ottoman *see* Turkish, Ottoman
'Ottoman Arabic', 148, 149, 154, 171
Ottoman Constitution *see* Constitution, Ottoman
Ottoman Empire, 1, 3, 4, 9, 14, 19, 69–71, 73, 79, 82, 84–5, 100–2, 108, 121, 122, 123–4, 129–30, 158, 166, 171, 172, 191–2, 193, 195, 201, 205, 207, 210, 228, 232, 265, 287, 289, 290, 296, 312, 315, 328, 333, 348; *see also* Constitution, Ottoman; imperialism, Ottoman; Istanbul; Young Turks; Young Ottomans
Oz, Abraham, 71, 74, 77
Ozoğlu, Müge, 191

Palaiologos, Grigorios, 106
paratexts, 2–4, 7, 15, 17, 20, 48–50, 72, 190, 197, 228, 234, 236, 239, 243, 258, 269, 328 358, 368–9, 377n66, 378–9n89
  translators' footnotes 2, 34, 127, 234, 239, 258–60, 351, 358, 368, 378–9n89
  translators' prefaces, 3, 38–9, 43–4, 48, 73, 82–3, 198–203, 204, 232, 236, 239–40, 242–3, 260, 271n65, 288, 289–90, 292, 293–6, 353–4, 368, 384–5n152
Paris, 1, 77–8, 103, 110, 124, 125, 128, 129, 160, 195, 327, 328, 339, 345, 353, 354, 361, 364, 370n5; *see also* Sue, Eugène
Parsons, John, 34, 35, 39–42
Partovi, Parvaz, 71, 74, 77
Pashto, 201
patriarchy and patriarchalism, 246, 286–7, 300–2, 305, 308, 311, 313–14
patriotism, 79, 86, 140, 191, 207, 208, 209, 213; *see also* nationalisms; *vatan*
patronage, 8, 44–8, 114n16, 328, 354–5, 366
peasants, 124
  female peasants, 312–14
Pekin, Amine, 329
Pekin, Ayhan, 329
pen names *see* pseudonyms
Pera *see* Beyoğlu
periodicals and translation, 10–11, 12–13, 15, 18, 19, 77, 82, 199, 202, 203, 230, 252, 261, 264, 288, 290–4, 328–9, 346–7; *see also* serial publication; titles of individual periodicals
Persian, 2, 4, 30–1, 40, 44, 46, 50, 76, 104, 141, 144, 146–7, 151, 155, 156, 157, 175n30, 175–6n40, 176n42, 176n54, 179n89, 183n166, 196, 199, 201, 202, 229, 243–4, 247, 279n180, 309, 327
  translation from or into, 4, 5, 17, 19, 31, 32, 71, 126, 199
Persian, Dari, translation into, 190, 195, 198, 200–2, 204, 205–6, 208, 211–13
Petro, 'Isa, 32
Pharaon, Florian, 135n43
Pirizade Mehmed Sahib, 143
poetry and verse forms, 31, 38, 39, 41, 44, 49, 74, 77, 78, 81, 89–90, 145, 167, 195, 197, 199, 208, 298, 309
poets, 2, 13, 18, 30, 169, 190, 194, 196, 199–200, 202, 203, 212, 234, 287, 293, 308, 309, 357
Pollard, Lisa, 227
polygyny, 197, 202, 209–10, 246, 260, 329, 342, 344, 365, 367–8
Ponson du Terrail, Pierre-Alexis, 101
Powell, Avril, 31, 45–6
pseudonyms, 202, 350, 353, 356, 370n5, 378–9n89, 381n105

396

Index

pseudo-translation, 70–71
public/private dichotomy, 210–11, 212, 271–2n70, 286, 314, 335, 343–4, 375n41; *see also* family; *hijab*; 'woman question', the

Qabadu, Mahmud, 128
al-Qabbani, 'Abd al-Qadir, 346
Qajar Empire, 121, 208
qanun (law), 130
al-qanun al-asasi (basic law), 151
qanun al-dawla (Tunisian 'law of state'), 123, 124
qawm, 162, 247
 kavim, 162, 238, 247
Qub'ayn, Salim, 1–4, 8
Qur'an, 53, 206, 231, 250, 291, 298, 310, 333, 350, 369, 381–1n103
 terminology of, 12, 63n87
 translatability of, 228, 279
 translation into French, 338–9, 352
 translation into Russian, 1
 translation into Turkish, 233–4, 264, 280n184, 317–18n15
 translation of verses from, 3, 261–4, 280n184, 280n187, 301, 337–9, 352
 untranslatability of, 20–1n3, 261, 279n182

Rac, Katalin, 204
race and racialist discourses, 14–15, 20, 70, 72, 75, 83, 86, 87, 89, 196, 329, 358–9
al-Ra'id al-Tunisi, 129
Ramzi, Ibrahim, 227, 234–5, 242
Rastegar, Kamran, 76
readerships, audiences, and reception, 7, 8, 9, 10–12, 14, 16, 19–20, 29–31, 33–4, 43–4, 54–5, 122–3, 127–9, 199, 203, 227–8, 235, 240–2, 245–6, 252, 287–8, 294–5, 330–1, 336, 338–9, 360, 362–6
Reynolds, Matthew, 12
Richebourg, Emile, 101
Rickardsdottir, Sif, 11
Rida, Muhammad Rashid, 260, 293
rights, 19, 84, 166, 206, 234, 241, 250, 252, 257, 262, 273n94, 294, 307, 310,
 323n100, 329, 340, 343, 347, 348, 350, 365, 372–3n18
Robb, Megan, 210
Rocca, Nonce, 128, 131–2n1
Russian Empire, 1, 85, 208, 209, 288, 289
Russian language and translation, 1, 3, 4, 10, 12, 19, 203, 328, 347, 355
Rustum, General, 126, 128

Sabri, Ibrahim 198, 200
Said Bey, Kemalpaşazade, 156
saj', seci (rhymed prose), 79, 81, 93n53, 146, 147, 298
Sajjad Hyder Yildirim, 198, 202, 203, 210
Salih Bakamović, 198–200
Salim, Muhammad Ibrahim, 329, 378–9n89
Samartzidis, Christophoros, 106
Sanskrit, 30, 38, 46, 55–6
al-Sanusi, Muhammad, 126
Schick, Irvin, 230
scripts, 14, 31, 34, 40, 42–3, 111, 329; *see also* Karamanlidika; Turkish, modern
Şemseddin (or Şemsettin) Sami, 168, 180n108, 180n112, 185n190, 192, 248–9, 274n114, 275n116, 280n187
seci see *saj'*
serial publication, 9, 11, 15, 18, 99, 101, 102, 106–7, 108, 115n21, 126, 128, 141, 142, 199, 202, 203, 233, 287–9, 290, 295–6, 299, 320n40, 327, 328, 346–8
şeriye see *shari'a*
sexuality, 12, 197, 249–51, 263–4, 275, 304, 344–5, 367
 and race, 83, 87
Shakespeare, William, 6, 13, 14–15, 69–90
 Hamlet, 13, 74, 75
 Othello, 14–15, 20, 72–90
Sharafuddin see 'Isa'i
shari'a(t), şeriye, 53–5, 122, 125, 130, 152, 206, 227, 231, 237, 249, 254, 260, 313, 332, 333, 357, 362–3
al-Shidyaq, Ahmad Faris, 128
Shissler, A. Holly, 11, 18–19, 20, 246, 302
Şimşek, Şehnaz Şişmanoğlu, 11, 20
Singh, Yunis, 34, 43–4

Index

Sırat-ı Müstakim, 287–97, 300, 306–7, 309, 314–15
siyasa (state justice), *siyasa/siyasiyya* (politics/political), 130, 150, 154, 158, 159
slavery and slaves, 20, 74, 83, 84, 85, 92n22, 123, 229, 235, 249, 275n116, 289, 311–12, 313, 329, 336–7, 339, 353, 359–60, 362–3, 367
Smith, Wilfred Cantwell, 204
Spain *see* Andalusia
Stoler, Anne Laura, 82
Strauss, Johann, 16, 20, 73, 129, 232–3, 370n5
Sudan, 70, 87
Sue, Eugène, 6, 13, 15, 99–104, 107, 110
 Mystères de Paris, Les, 99, 100, 102, 113, 116
Suez Canal, 128
Süleyman Nazif, 308
Sultan Ahmad Khan, 198, 200–3
Sunna, 275n115, 333, 350; *see also* Islam; hadith(s); Qur'an; *shari'a*

al-Tahtawi, Rifa'a, 93n44, 128, 144, 155, 157, 175n28
tamaddun see civilisation
Tanzimat era and reforms, 73, 108, 123, 124, 125, 127, 130, 131, 143, 146, 150, 154, 156, 158, 163, 166, 171, 176n41
tanzimat, linguistic usage of, 150–1, 154, 196
Tatar and Tatars, 194, 230, 264, 265, 288–9
Taymur, 'A'isha, 2, 327
Tercüman-i Hakikat, 23n26, 232, 327, 328, 346, 350
tesettür, 240, 247, 256, 259–60, 262, 302–5; *see also* hijab; veiling
Thamarat al-funun, 328, 346–8, 350–2
theatre, 194, 195–6, 202, 208
 and translation, 13, 14–15, 16–17, 76, 77, 79, 80, 81, 85, 86, 88, 168
titles of works, in translation, 15, 69, 74, 102, 106, 107, 122, 141, 178n68, 182n139, 232, 233, 234–6, 240, 246, 315, 353, 368–9, 380n98

Toledano, Ehud, 360
Tolstoy, Leo, 1, 3, 347
tourists, European, 19, 327, 329–42, 363
translation
 domestication in, 12, 15, 29, 55–6, 99, 359–62
 intellectual history and, 7–8, 10, 20
 prismatic, 7, 11, 12
 secondary or relay, 10–11, 29, 32, 36–7, 42–3, 70, 71, 72–5, 142, 201, 203
 strategies in, 2–3, 11–12, 36, 55–7, 82, 83, 86, 141, 157–70, 228, 242, 246–52, 287, 297–9, 301, 311, 335, 353, 356–65
 as theme in original text, 330–2, 335–7; *see also* translator-guides
 see also individual languages and terms; lexicon; pseudo-translation; titles; names and naming practices
translation criticism, 12–13
Translation Studies, 5–6, 12, 70, 99
translator-guides (*tercüman*) as characters, 331–4, 339, 363
translator in/visibility, 8, 14, 228, 273; *see also* labour, translation as/and
travel literature, 327, 332–3, 372–3n3; *see also* al-Tahtawi
al-Twati, Muhammad al-Bashir, 126
Tunis, 16, 123, 124, 125, 126, 128, 131
al-Tunisi, Khayr al-Din *see* Khayr al-Din al-Tunisi
Tunisia, 122, 124, 154, 172, 185n197, 192
Turkey, Republic of, 17, 196, 200–1
Turkish, modern, 172, 204, 329, 369n2, 375n39
Turkish, Ottoman, usage of, 5, 70–2, 144–72, 245–8, 251–2, 293, 333, 335, 341, 362–3, 367; *see also* language reform

ulama, 124, 126, 127, 129, 130, 134n33, 143, 147, 172, 173n6, 241, 258, 279n170, 338
Ülken, Hilmi Ziya 143
umma, 130, 150, 152, 155, 156, 161, 162–3, 165, 171, 206, 247, 251, 253–4, 257, 309, 315, 338

Index

ümmet, 162, 237–8, 247, 260, 273–4n96, 315
urban mysteries, as genre, 100, 102, 103, 104, 110, 113
Urdu, 31, 46
   translation from or into, 4, 5, 13–14, 19, 29–30, 34–5, 42–5, 48–57, 190, 198, 201–3, 205, 208–9, 211–13, 287

van Krieken, G. S., 129
vatan see *watan*
veiling, 18, 109, 238, 240, 242, 246, 251, 258–60, 270–1n60, 273n94, 296, 298, 301–7, 312–14, 321n67, 333, 349, 355–6, 367; *see also hijab*; *tesettür*
Venuti, Lawrence, 70
vernaculars and vernacularisation, 30–1, 38, 41, 46, 79–81, 229, 243–4, 262, 263, 272n72, 308, 352
Viardot, Louis, 192
Villet, Victor, 128, 129
Voltaire, 1, 13, 167
Vréto, Marino, 128

Wajdi, Muhammad Farid, 18, 211, 230, 267, 286–326; *Muslim Woman*, 286–326
watan, 85, 126, 152, 163, 208
   vatan 84–5, 89–90, 152, 190, 207–10, 293

Wien, Peter, 193
Williams, Richard David, 13–14, 20
'woman question', the, 1, 3–4, 10, 17–19, 20, 227, 229–30, 236, 246, 267n16, 291, 294, 298, 310–14, 329, 331, 334, 347, 366–9; *see also* education; femininity; feminism; *hijab*; gender segregation; masculinity; 'Nature'; patriarchy; veiling
women as translators, 19, 328–30; *see also* feminism; Lebedeva, Ol'ga; Nazimé-Roukiyé

Young Ottomans, 128–9, 130, 195, 199
Young Turks, 128, 199, 201, 202, 251–2, 257, 277n147, 290; *see also* Constitutional Revolution (1908)
Yusuf Semih *see* al-Asma'i, Yusuf Semih

Zachs, Fruma, 191, 347
Zaghlul, Sa'd, 288
Zakir Kadiri, 288–90
Zarruq, Larbi, 126, 132n6
Zaydan, Jurji (or Jirji), 161, 193, 233, 264, 266, 268–9
Zervos, Ioannis, 102
Zervos, Sokrates, 102
Ziya Pasha, 199
Zurcher, Eric, 290

EU representative:
Easy Access System Europe
Mustamäe tee 50, 10621 Tallinn, Estonia
Gpsr.requests@easproject.com

www.ingramcontent.com/pod-product-compliance
Lightning Source LLC
Chambersburg PA
CBHW061704300426
44115CB00014B/2552